T0373507

THE

PUBLICATIONS

OF THE

SURTEES SOCIETY

VOL. CXLII.

THE

PUBLICATIONS

of the

SURTEES SOCIETY

ESTABLISHED IN THE YEAR

M.DCCC.XXXIV.

VOL. CXLII.

FOR THE YEAR M.CM.XXIX.

PREFACE.

THIS volume comprises abstracts of some of the wills and inventories in the Durham probate registry belonging to the period James I.—Charles I.

The editor acknowledges with gratitude the help of Mr. J. J. Howe, who made copies of the original documents in the registry, and of Mr. A. F. Radcliffe, M.A., who read the proofs and gave other assistance and advice.

WILLS

AND

INVENTORIES

FROM THE

REGISTRY AT DURHAM

PART IV.

Published for the Society by

ANDREWS & Co., SADLER STREET, DURHAM:
AND BERNARD QUARITCH, 11, GRAFTON STREET,
NEW BOND STREET, LONDON, W.
1929

Reprinted 1968 for
Wm. DAWSON & SONS LTD., LONDON
with the permission of
THE SURTEES SOCIETY

At a Meeting of the SURTEES SOCIETY, held in Durham Castle, on Tuesday, March 3rd, 1925, the DEAN OF DURHAM in the chair.

It was resolved :—

" That a volume of Durham Wills and Inventories should be edited for the Society by Mr. Herbert Maxwell Wood, B.A., F.S.A."

A. HAMILTON THOMPSON,
Secretary

ORIGINALLY PRINTED IN GREAT BRITAIN

PRINTED IN GREAT BRITAIN
BY PHOTOLITHOGRAPHY
UNWIN BROTHERS LIMITED
WOKING AND LONDON

DURHAM
WILLS AND INVENTORIES.

MARGRET LYDDELL.[1]

Feb. 21 [1603-4]. In the name of God, Amen, I, Margret
Lyddell, late wife of Mr. Thomas Lyddell, of the towne of Newcastle upon Tyne, merchant and alderman. To be buried in the
quere of St. Nicholas Church in Newcastle, where the bodye of
my late husband doth lie entombed. I give and bequeath unto
my sonne, Francis, all that my house in the head of the Side,
wherein he at this psent doth dwell, together with the Carres
Milnes and also my shopp on the bridge where he at psent doth
occupie with so much of the loft above it as doth directly upward
answer to the same, and also a seller in the close which he now
occupieth with the wast belonging unto it, to him and his heires
for ever, and for default of such his heires all the premises to
come to my neighest heires. I give and bequeath unto my sonne,
Thomas, my house in the Cloth Market, wherein his sonne Thomas
now doth dwell, with my shop in the bridge which he at this
psent doth occupie, together with so much of the loft above it as
doth directly upwards answer to the same, as also my place called
the freires with the appurtenances, wherein he now dwelleth, to
him and to his heires for ever, and in default of such his heires
all the premises to come unto my neighest heires. I bequeath with
the shopp on the bridge, which he now doth occupie, with as much
of the loft above it and doth directlie upwards answere to the same,
together also my close in Gateside, to him and his heires for
ever, and for default of such his heires all the premises to come
unto my neighest heires. I give and bequeath unto my sonne
Robarte a signet of gold, together with the third parte of all my

---

[1] The first mention of Thomas Liddell is his apprenticeship, Feb. 18,
1539/40, to Robert Lamb, mercer; he was admitted 1544/5. Having
made his will, May 8, 1577, he was bur. the following day at St.
Nicholas, Newcastle. His widow, who proved his will, was bur. at
the same place, Oct. 31, 1604. Her eldest son Thomas' will is printed
in this Vol., as also is that of her son Francis.

plate. I give and bequeath unto Isabell Dawsonne my best gowne
and chamblet kirtell. I give and bequeath unto my maiden, Janet
Foster, a whoole year's wadges at the heure of my death, togither
with the mattres and bedclothes she lyeth upon. I give and
bequeath unto Barbary Liddell a sillver tablet guilt. The rest of
my goods moveable and unmoveable, my legacies and funerall
expences discharged, I give unto my sonns Thomas and Francis,
whom I constitute and make my full Executors of this my last Will
and Testament. Witnesses, George Liddell, Willyam Sherwood,
Gawen Suffeild, David Johnson. Proved, 1605.

WILLIAM REED.[1]

June 2, 1604. Reed William, Sir of Fenham, in the parish
of Holie Island, Knight. My bodie shall be buried at the discretion
of my executors. I give and bequeath unto Thomas Swinhoe of
Goswick, gentleman, and to William Swinhoe, his sone, and to
their heirs for ever All that lande in the Holie Iland which I have
of 'the said Thomas Swinhoe in mortgage of 110l., which should
have been paid unto me or my assigns at Michaelmas in 1601. I
give unto William Towers, Francis Towers, George Towers and
Bartholomew Towers four of my wife's children, each 20l. to be
paid by my executors to their tutors or governors for their use.
I give unto Chartie Bell, alias Reede, my base begotten daughter,
50l., and I desire the Right Worl Myres Mathew, the wife of the
Right Reverend father in God, dcor Mathew Bishop of Durham,
to take the tuition of her with her portion during her minortie.
I give unto William Reynnarde, alias Reed, my sone, now com-
monly known by the title of Capt. Reed, all my whole right of
inheritance title and estate of whatsoever within the towne of
Berwick and his heirs for ever. I give unto my said sone, William
Reed, the remaynder of my leases and tithes whatsoever, either by
Letters Patent from Our late Sovereign, Lady Elizabeth, of
famous memorie, under the great seal of England, and also the
Leases from the Dean and Chapter of Durham, or by any other
leases, conveyances, which I assigned and set over to Capt. Robert
Carvell and Mr. John Crayne for the use of the ladie Elizabeth,
my wife, as by Indenture dated the 10th day of Aug. last. My
wife also to have the tithes of the several townes of Holie Iland,
Skrymerson, Fenwick and Lowlin, and also parcell of the Rectorie
or psonage of Holie Iland. All the rest, my goods moveable and

---

[1] June 6, 1604. Sr Willm. Reede, Knight, bur. *Holy Island
Registers.* His tombstone near the reading desk bears the following
inscription :—" Contra vim mortis non est medicamen in hortis." He
had three wives, all of whom were bur. at Holy Island : his first
Elizabeth, Dec. 24, 1585; his second Mary, Oct. 24, 1595; and his third
Elizabeth, widow of Charles Towers (bur. July 3, 1600), July 30, 1612.

unmoveable, I give to my said sone, Capt. William Reede, and the ladie Elizabeth, my wife, and appoint them Executors.

This will was redd to Sir William at his own appointment on Satterdaie morneing, being the second daie of June, 1604, in the presence of my Ladie Elizabeth Reede. Witnesses, Henry Jones, Ralph Parkin, Thomas Cuthbert, Richard Barton. INVENTORY amounted to 447*l*. 16*s*. 4*d*.

ISABELLA CHARLTON.

Jan. 20, 1604. Isabella Charlton, daughter of James Charlton of Bellingham. To be buried in Bellingham church. I give to James Charlton of barnardstead, two kyne. To the said James's daughter a reade quiqe styrke. To Barbara Charlton a black kowe. To Christopher Charlton of Greatsteade, foure poundes English money, which Marke Charlton of Harytethe is owen me. To the said Christopher Charlton a branded kowe, which is with Walter Charlton of Hasrop. I give the residue of my estate to the said Christopher Charlton and appoint him sole Executor. Witnesses, Trestie Charltone of Greasteade, John Charlton of the same. Probate, 1604.

ELIZABETH JENYSON.[1]

Jan. 19, 1604. In the name of God, Amen, I Elizabeth Jenyson of Walworth, in the countie Palatine of Duresme, widow, doe make this my last Will in manner and forme following. My bodie to be buried in the Chaanncell of the Church, where it shall please God to call me to his mercye. At my buriall I will not have any black to be bestowed, but onlie will that my bodie be caried to the ground in decent and formlie manner, on which daie of my buriall also I will that 5*l*. in money be bestowed upon the poore. I give unto the Schole at Heighington a great newe English bible with a chaine to fasten to a deske, and also the Dictionary of Thomas Thomas. I doe give to my sone in lawe, Sir George Frevile, Knight, 10*l*. to buye him a gelding, one of my litle barrells or vessells of irish aquavite and my Tie that standes at my bed side. I bequeath to the wief, the lady Eliz Frevile, my daughter, the bed whereon I lie, with the bedsteed, Testerne and curtaines, a new mattrass marked with my name, a blewe rugg,

---

[1] She was the daughter of Edward Birch, of Sandon, Co. Beds, groom porter to Henry VIII., bur. at Heighington, April 7, 1605, mar. Thomas Jenison of Walworth, auditor of Ireland, who died Nov. 17, 1586. There is a pedigree of Jenison of Walworth in Surtees' *History of Durham*, iii., pp. 290-2.

a white rugg, a paier of pillowes and pillowbers, the sheete that I lie on, as also a paier of fine sheets of my owne making marked with the lres. E.F., my spice box, my black cheste with drawinge tills, both my french hoodes, my bone grace, my little painted cofer, my little greene chaire, my martin skynns, and twenty poundes in money. I give to my sonne, Willm. Jenyson, the younger, my lease of the tythe corne of Walworth Lordshipp, two ruggs thone checkquered blewe and yellowe, the other a faire white shagee rugg which lie in the new presse over the milke house chamber, my gray stagg stoned coming forth with two geares, the short table in the hall with one longe forme to it, eight long ioynes stooles, my blewe mantle, and fourtie poundes in money. I give to Elizabeth Jenyson, daughter of the said Willm. Jenyson, the younger, 10*l.* in money, one Jewel which the lady Freville, my daughter, hath, after her decease, if she die without issue. And if it happen the said Elizabeth Jenyson to die before my said daughter, the lady Frevile, that then it shallbe in my said daughter's disposcion, and I give the said Eliz. Jenyson my little blacke chest. I give and bequeath Two ruggs thone chequered russett and redd, thother a white rugg which lie in the new presse over the milkhouse, my baye fole under the . . . baye meare, and fortye poundes in money. And to my said sone, Thomas, his wief, all my hempe. And to their sonne, George Jenyson, for his educacon and bringing upp at schole the first yeare, tenn poundes, and one rugge that lies upon the Lady Frevile's bedd, chequered redd russett and blewe. And to theer Daughter, Margarett Jenyson, 10*l.* I doe further give and bequeathe to my said sonns, Willm. Jenyson, the younger, and Thomas Jenyson, all my lynnen in my two chests standing in my chamber (whereof one a wanscoate chest standing at my bedd's feete). To my said sonne, Willm., the younger, thother standing under the west window. I give to my sonne, Thomas, the said lynnen to be equally divided between them, saving the lynnen in the said two chests contained before given and bequeathed. I give to the lady Frevile, my daughter, my sonns, William Jenyson, the younger, and Thomas Jenyson, my booke of Marters to be in use amongst them. And whereas my sonns that are contrary in religion, Doe not deserve to have any thinge, yet notwithstanding, in regard of naturall affecon which parents must needs beare to their children, I doe give and bequithe to them as hereafter followeth. To William Jenyson, the elder, my first sonne, I give and bequeth twenty poundes in money and six ordinary quishions, and to his sonne, Robert Jenyson, 10*l.* I give to my sonne, John Jenyson, partlie in consideraeon that he had noe benefitt of my house at London, partlie in regard that he shall suffer my executors quietlie and peaceblie to execute my will, the moietie and half of my cropp of corne which shallbe standing and ground upon the ground at Walworth at the time of my death, and all the

bordes which shallbe then unlaied and unnailed, provided
alwaies that if he, my said sonne, doe any way molest or hinder
my executors in executing of my will, or will not allow them
convenient time to be sett down by four men indifferentlie chosen
by him and them for carying awaie of such goodes and cattell as
I shall leave behind me in the house or upon the ground at
Walworth, That then the said John Jenyson, my sonne, shall
reape noe benefitt by my said Will. I further give unto my said
sonne, John, seaven table clothes of hempon cloth, whereof three
for the long table in the hall, two long ones for the table in the
parlor, the leaves being drawne forthe, and the . . . , two other
for the side table and six dozen of napkins all of hempen clothe.
I will that for my said sone, John, there be as much broad grene
clothe bought as will make a carpett for the table standing in
the little parlor. And I doe further give to him as much white
cloth as shall make curtanes for the bed in the lowe courte chamber,
which my said sone must gett died redd. I give and bequethe to
my said sone, John Jenyson, the new great bedstead standing in
the chamber over myne owne chamber, the new great presse over
the milkhouse chamber, the newpresse in the buttery, and the
long new table in the hall with fower newe formes belonging to
the same, to remaine as heirlomes to the house of Walworth. I
doe further will that my executors pay to my said sone, John
Jenyson, all such things as he cann demand as due to him by an
Inventory made betwixt me and him, which he hath not received
alreadie. I doe give to my sone, John Jenyson's eldest sonne,
named John Jenyson, a sute of Diaper of eight yardes long and
my husband's black Armour as heirloomes to the house. And all
the residue of my Armor which is unbestowed (except the common
Armor) I doe give to my son, John Jenyson. I further give to
my sonne John Jenyson's other children, viz., to Thomas, Michaell,
Richard, Mary and Martha Jenyson, 20*l*. equally amongst them.
I give unto my sonne, Michael Jenyson, 20*l*. and a guilt Jugg
with barrs, and aboute half a garnishe of pewter vessell marked
with the lres M. and J. I further give to my daughter, the lady
Eliz. Frevile, 20*l*. freelie in money, in consideracon if she will
please to take the educacon and bringing upp Elizabeth Jenyson,
daughter to my son, Willm. Jenyson, the younger, provided
alwaies that her father finde her apparell and all other necessaries.
I bequeth to my L. Bishop of Durham nowe being, for a small
remembrance, one double soveraigne, and to Mrs. Matthewe one
Spurroyall. I give to Mrs. Bowes, of Aske, one Spurroyall. I
give to Richard Frevile one Spurroyall, and to his wief one
Spurroyall, and to their children to each of them 10*s*. I give to
my cosen, Driscibla Cowlton, my plaine guilt Jugg. To my
cosen, Ann Horsley, my furred gowne guarded with vellatt, and
my black grogeran kirtle fringed. I give to my neece, Dorothy
Birch, 20*l*., my beste stuffe gowne, my silke grogeran kirtle and

best petticoate belonging thereto, my cloake and safegard, my presse standing in the brusshing chamber, my great testament, and fifty two shillings which I owe her. I give to mv cosen Girlington's wief my best hatt. I will that Ann Newbie shall have 10*l*., to my sister Clifton's use to keep her with, and that her owne children amongst them shall find her meate, drink and apparell during her lief, and further that after mv sister's decease, Ann Newby shall have the said 10*l*. freelie to her self. I give to my said sister my night gowne. I give to Mr. Gifford, of Darnton, a booke, being a conference betwixt Doctor Whitguifte and Mr. Cartwright, and 40*s*. and to his wief six silver spoones with apostles' hedds. And to his brother, Simon Gyfford, 40*s*. I give to Mr. Throckmorton 10*s*., and to his wief 10*s*. To Mr. Garthewayte 10*s*. I give to John Gadge one Spurrogall. To Richard Dighton 40*s*., and to his wief as much silke grogeran as will make her a doublett. I give to Hercules Brabant 10*s*., to Gilbert Frevile 10*s*., to Nicholas Petefer 10*s*., to George Parkins 10*s*. I give to my servants as followeth : To Francis Newby 10*l*. in money and a peece of purple clothe to make him a cloake, and to his wief my plaine clothe gowne of french russett, my redd frisadoe petticote with an upper bodye of Crymson cholmelett. I give to Nicholas Flynn 20*l*., or 40*s*. by yeare during his naturall lief, whether he shall like of. To Robt. Wren 40*s*. To John Drye 40*s*. I give to Ann Robinson my old grogeran gowne. and 5*s*. in money. To Eleanor Earle my old greene gowne, my old red petticotte and old clothe kirtle. All the rest of my servantes, both men and women, I give one quarter's wages. I give to John Newbie, servant to my sone, William Jenyson, the younger, 10*s*. To Edward Johnson 10*s*., and to Merill Wilkison 2*s*. 6*d*., servante to my sone, Thomas Jenyson. To the Church of Heighington for ever a carpett for the communion table, a pulpytt clothe, and quishions all of greene velvett ready to be furnished and made upp with lyninges and fringe. I give to Francis Newbie's two children, George and Elizabeth Newbie, 6*s*. 8*d*. each to buye them two gimmer hoggs. To William Garth, son to George Garthe, one ewe and a lamb. To Mr. Throckmorton . . . 6*s*. 8*d*. to buy him a gimmer hogg. I will that my executors, after the hour of my death after twelve months, to satisfye and pay my legacies and debts. I give to my cosen Wyngate's wief, as a token of remembrance, a guishenett and a purse wrought with needle work. I nominate and appoint my sonns, William Jenyson, the younger, and Thomas Jenyson, Executors of this my Will, and my sone-in-law, Sir George Frevile, Knight, Overseer. Witnesses, Robert Harrison, Francis Newbye, Thomas Wilkenson, Edward Johnson, Henry Lewen, John Newbye. Proved, 1605.

MATTHEW CHAPMAN.[1]

Feb. 19, 1604. In the name of God, Amen, I, Matthew Chapman, of the town of Newcastle upon Tyne, in the county of the same towne, Merchant. To be buried in the parish church of St. Nicholas in the towne of Newcastle upon Tyne aforesaid, where I am a psonier in the place, or as neare to my father where he lieth buried as convenentlie maybe by the discretion of my executor under-named. And as to touching my worldly goods, chattels and possessions, I give and bequeath the same in manner following, that is to say : I give and bequeath to my sonne, Matthew Chapman, the sume of two hundred pounds of lawful money of England, and to my daughter Marie Bonner I give and bequeath the sum of one hundred pound of like money. I give and bequeath unto the foure children of my said daughter Marie. That is to say, Henry, Matthew, William and Agnes Bonner, every of them 20l. a peece of lawful money of England, amounting to all to the sume of four score pounds to be paid within two yeares next after my death. And whereas I am seized for terms of the natural life of my sone-in-law, William Bonner, of one messuage or tenement with appurtenances thereof, situate and being in the street called the Syde, in the parish aforesaid, and in the said towne of Newcastle, late in the occupation of the same William Bonner, I give and bequeath the same and all my estate, right, title, claime and demand, in and to the same, to my daughter, Elizabeth Kirkley, To have and to hold the same messuage or tent with appurtenances, and all the same estate, right, title, claime and demand of me the said Matthew, to the said Elizabeth, my daughter, and her assigns for the said life time of my said sonne, William Bonner. And I doe further give and bequeath to the same Elizabeth Kirtley, my daughter, the sum of 200l. of lawful money of England. I give and bequeath to my daughter, Agnes Chapman, 200l. of like lawful money of England. And to the poore I give and bequeath fyve markes, to be distributed at and by the discretion of my Executor under named.

[1] For the wills of his parents, Oswald and Marion (dau. of Henry Anderson), see 38 Surtees Soc., p. 73 and 73N. His first wife, Elizabeth, was bur. at St. Nicholas', May 14, 1587 [he mar. secondly Anne or Agnes Shafto, widow of John Greenwell, Nov. 18, 1600]. His second wife, Anne, was bur. Oct. 13, 1604, at St. Nicholas'. His son, Henry, mar. Jane Greenwell, Jan. 28, 1604/5, was Sheriff of Newcastle 1613/14, and Mayor 1620/1 (probably) and 1627/8, and was bur. Feb. 18, 1631/2; his daughter, Elizabeth, bapt. April 21, 1583, mar. Michael Kirkley, Jan. 17, 1602/3; his daughter, Mary, mar. William Bonner, May 2, 1597; his daughter, Agnes, appears as Ann Eden in the will of her uncle, Henry Chapman, Sept. 17, 1620 (*Welford's Newcastle*, iii, 250); she was probably wife of Henry Eden (see baptisms at St. Nicholas' Church, Aug. 8, 1609, Jan. 8, 1610/11, Sept. 5, 1616, April 6, 1623). The testator was bur. at St. Nicholas', Nov. 3, 1606.

I give and bequeath to my loveing Brother, Mr. Henry Chapman, Alderman, one portugue of golde, and to my ever good friend, Mr. Francis Anderson, Alderman, two Angells in tokens of my good will, ordeyning them the supvisors of this my last Will and Testament. And all the residue of my money, substance, goods, and chattells and possessions, whatsoever of my propertie, kind or qualitie soever the same be, my debts and legacies aforesaid being paid, with my funerall, I whollie give to my sonne, Henry Chapman, whom of this my present last Will and Testament I constitute and appointe to be my full and sole Executor, giving also and bequeathing to the same Henrie, my sonne, and his heires, all and singular, my lands, tents and hereditaments whatsoever. And I doe by these presents renounce and foresake all former Wills, legacies and bequests whatsoever by me, in wise heretofore made, given or bequeathed, desiring and entreating hereby my said loving brother, and my said friend, Mr. Francis Anderson, to extend their endeavours to see this my last Will and Testament executed according to my true meaning and the tenor of these presents above expressed, as my trust is in them. Memorandum : that my will and mynd is, and I ordaine by these presents, that all the said legacies of money with all bequests above limitted and bequeathed to my said sone, Matthew Chapman, Marie Bonner, my daughter, and Elizabeth Kirkley and Agnes Chapman shall be in full payment and satisfaction of their child's parts or porcons of all my goods and chattells, and not otherwise. This Codicill was made by the said testator 29 October, 1606. Witnesses, H. Chapman, Fran. Anderson, Willm. Bonner, Mich. Kirkley.   Proved, 1606.

ALISON SHERATON.

May, 1605.   In the name of God, Amen, I, Alison Sheraton, late wife of Willm. Sheraton, of Elwick, deceased, in the parish of Harte.   To be buried within the pish church of Harte aforesaid, with my mortrary dewe and accustomed according to the Lawes of this Realm.   I do gyve and bequeth to my youngest sonne, James Sheraton, the one half of all my goods movable and unmovable, my Iron band whealer, my fether bedd, and my coffer without clothes.   I give and bequeath to my sonne, Robt. Sheraton, the table in the forehowse and one Read Cowe, and to his wyfe my next best cote.   I give to my eldest sonne, Willm. Sheraton, one oxe called bowehorne, And to his wyfe my newe furr chist.   I give to John Done, son of Jerrard Done my son-in-ley, one cawell and one counter in the forehowse.   And to Katheryne, my daughter, the said Jerrard Done, his wife, my best black cote, and the worste my two Read petticots, together with all my lynen clothes.   To Richard Pension's children, every

one of them, a sheep hogge. The residue of all my goods I give unto my sonns, Christopher Sheraton and James Sheraton, whom I make executors. Witnesses, James Watson, Edward ——.
INVENTORY, 79*l*. 19*s*. 8*d*. Proved, 1605.

THOMAS HODGSON.[1]

June 7, 1605. In the name of God, Amen, I, Thomas Hodgson, of Coldhirst, within the Countie of Durham yeoman. To be buried in the parish churchyard of Hamsterley. I give unto my brother, Willm. Hodgson, three swarmes of bees and my whipp . . . to be delivered at the feast of St. Michael next coming, if it shall please God to call me to his mercye. I do owe unto Thomas Hodgson, my brother William Hodgson his sonne, one sword, one rucke of haye, one coffer, which was my mother's, with the lynen clothes therein. I give unto Christopher Stevenson one stacke of haye. I do give unto my unckell, John Stephenson, one litle rucke of hay. I do give unto the daughter of Christopher Stevenson my presser and a red petticote that was my mother's. I geve to Leonard Wind 3*s*. 4*d*. The rest of all my goods, both movable and unmoveable, I doe give to my brother, Christopher Hodgson, my debts and funnerall expences discharged, whom I doe make my executor. Witness, Peter Hodgson. Proved, 1605, 2 November.

RICHARD LIDDELL.[2]

July 13, 1605. In the name of God, I, Richard Liddell, of the townshipp of Westmerrington, within the pish of St. Andrew, Awckland, husbandman. To be buryed within the pish Church of St. Andrew, Awckland. I give to Elizabeth, my wife, the third part of my farmhold in West merrington, and the other two parts of my farmeholde to my Brother, Anthonie Liddell, for better bringing up of my foure children during the yeares that is to come and unexpired in my lease thereof, and my will is that before the lease be runn, if my eldest sonne Francis, be livinge, that he shall renew the said Lease in his owne name. And if he be not livinge, then that my younger sonne, Charles, shall renew it in his owne name. My Will is that if my wife be liveing at the renewing of the aforesaid lease, that she shall paie the third part

[1] 1605, July 12, Thoms Hodgson of Coldhirst, bur. *Hamsterley Regs*, 1612, April 5, Christopher Hodgson, clearke, bur., *ibid*.

[2] The testator was bur. at St. Andrew's, Auckland, 27 Aug., 1605, his son Charles bapt. there 6 May, 1602 (godparents, Mr. Charles Wren, Thomas Lever, and Mrs. Ety Wren), was apprenticed with the Drapers Company, London, 17 October, 1617. The testator's widow was also bur. there, 12 July, 1614.

of the fine due to the lord for the renewing of the same lease,
and then thereafter enioy the moitie and full halfe parte of the
said whole farme during hir life naturall, paying yearly half the
rent due therefor. To my sonn, Francis, one Cubbord, one
Cawell, one Arke, one flanders chist, and one presser, and I also
give him one fillye that is a yeare old and all my plous geare and
waine gear for his legacie; And my will is that my wife and my
brother, Anthonie Liddell, shall have the use of the said plowe
and wayne geare during my lease of the farme unexpired. To
my younger sonn, Charles, a colt fole that is of my gray meare.
I give to my wife all my Bees. To my two daughters, Elizabeth
and Jane, all my gimmer hoggs. All the rest of my goods whatsoever, after all legacies and funerall expences, to my wife,
Elizabeth, my sonne, Charles, and my two daughters, Elizabeth
and Jane. I make my brother, Anthonie Liddell, and my two
sonns, Francis and Charles, sole Executors of my will. I make
supervisors hereof Mris. Elizabeth Wren and my brother, William
Liddell, giveing unto eyther of them 10s., and I doe appoint and
ordeyne Mris. Elizabeth Wren and my brother, Anthonie Liddell,
to be tutors and guardians to and of my foure children untill
they come to competent aidge. To my two servants, Ralph
Paverell, and Gracie. mv maid, I give 12d. each. To Richard
Johnson 6d. and Janet Whitfeild 6d. To every child I xpenned
12d. apeece. Witnesses, John Lax, Anthony Lax, Anthony Liddell,
Ralph Lexon.

FRANCIS SAIRE.

Aug. 12, 1605. In the name of Gode, Amen, I, Francis Saire,
of Bernardcastell, in the Bishoprick of Durham, Mercer. To be
buried in the churche of Bernardcastell so neare my former wife
as conveniently may be, nothing doubting, but according to the
Article of my faithe at the great day of generall Resurrection,
when we shall appeare before the Judgement seate of Christ, I
shall receive againe the same by the mightie panes of Christ,
whereby he is able to subdue all things to him selfe, not a corruptible, mortall, weake and vile body as now it is, but an In-
corruptible, Imortall, strong and pfect bodye, lik to the glorious
body of my saviour Christ. I give to Mr. Barker, if he be
living when I dye, or som other godlye preacher for my funerall
sermon, if God so pmitt, Tenn shillings. I give towards the
reparacion of the Church of Barnardcastell 10s. I give to the
poore people of Barnardcastell 3l. 6s. 8d., and to the poore people
of Startforthe 20s. As touching Margarett, mv wife, with whom
I have joyned my selfe in honorable matrimonye. I doe frelv give
unto her the whole and full third parte forthe of all my land and

goodes chattels and debts according to the lawe in that behalf.
And I will that all such som and somes of money as my father
in lawe, George Hutton, her father, is oweing me, shall be accepted
and taken of her, in part of satisfaction and payment of the
premises whereunto she hath given her consentt, And I give to
her for remembrance of my good will, Three gold rings and six
silver spoones, upon condicon that all the said premises before
to her bequeathed shallbe to her a full payment and satisfaction
of all her part, porcon and purpart, as well of all my said landes,
chattells, goods and debts; as also of all the lands and tenements
by me heretofore sold to any pson or psons, whereunto she hath
also given me her full consentt. I give and bequeathe unto my
sonne, George Sayre, All my landes, tenements and hereditaments
within the Territories of Lartington, in the Countye of York,
with all and singular their appurtences. And also all the lands,
with theer appurtenances, which I purchased of Thomas Allen,
and also one close of ground which I purchased of William Wilson
as it liethe in Galgate, and also one burgage with appurtenances
which I purchased of Launcelot Shepherd, and also that most
Northmost of those two houses, with the appurtces, which were
given to me and my brother, Ralph Saire, joyntlie by the last
Will and Testament of my Kinsman, John Glenton,[1] for which I
gave to my brother, Ralphe Saire, five markes in exchange, he
yielding and paying yearly forth of the same according as is
mentioned in his said last Will and Testament, All which said
last recited premises are situate, lieing and being in the territories
of Barnard Castle aforesaid. To have and to hould All the said
landes, tenements and hereditaments in Lartington and Barnardcastle aforesaid, with their appurtenances, unto my said sonne,
George Saire, and the heires of his body lawfully begotton : And in
default of such heires, Then I give and bequeath all the said lands,
tents and hereditaments unto my sonne, John Saire, and his heirs
lawfully begotten, And in defaut of such heires Then I give and
bequeath all my said lands and appurtenances unto my sonne,
Samuel Saire, and his heirs lawfully begotten. And in defult
of such heires, Then I give my said lands and hereditaments unto
my daughter, Phillis Saire, and the heirs of her body lawfully
begotten. And in defalt of such heires, Then I give my said
lands and tenements to my daughter, Elizabeth Saire, and the
heires of her body lawfullv begotten. I give and bequeath unto
my said sonne George. All my estate, title and tenant right of
and in all that Burgage or messuage wherein I dwell, and one
messuage in Briggate. in Barnardcastle aforesaid, both of which
I hold of the King's Majestye in right of his crowne, and also one
house in Galgate, which I hould of his Majestye for terme of

[1] John Glenton's will dated 3 Dec., 1578, proved, 28 Jan., 1578/9, is
printed in this Society's publications, vol. 112, pp. 80-2.

yeares. I give to my said sonne, George Saire, all that my
standing bedstocke and Teaster, with all furniture thereto standing in my long great chamber in my now dwellinghouse, and
also one long table in the same chamber with the frame and
Buffett stooles thereto belonging, withall the sealings and bedds
standing within, and as pcell of the said sealings, in and
through every chamber of the said house, And also my great
Iron Chimney. And my will is that the said premises shall
remayne as heireloomes in the said house to my right heyres
successwelye. And I give unto him also my Warlike furniture,
as my steele cote, my peece and halbert, also my books and silver
peece gilt and my lute. And my will is that my lands and
premises so to my said sonne, George Saire, bequeathed shallbe
unto him a perfect and full contentacon of all his filiall and child's
porcon, part and purport of all my lands, goodes, chattells and
debts. I give and bequeath to my sonne, John Saire, all that
close of ground somtime devided into two closes called Brigg End
Close, and two houses belonging to the same, with their appurtenances, and being in the Territories of Startforth, in the County
of York to have and to hould all the said close called Briggend
Close, houses and premises before mentioned, to my said sonne,
John, and the heires of his body lawfully to be begotten. And in
default of such heires, Then I give and bequeath the said lands
and premises unto my said sonne, George Saire, and the heirs of
his body lawfully begotten. And in default of such heires, then
to my said sonne, Samuel Sayre, and his heirs of his body; and
in defalt of such heires, then I bequeath the said lands and
premises to my daughter, Phillis Saire, and the heirs lawfully
begotten of her; and failing heirs, I bequeath the same to my
daughter, Elizabeth Saire, and the heirs of her body lawfully
begotten. I give unto my said sonne, John Saire, a hundred
markes of lawful money of England. I give unto my said sonne,
Samuel Saire, and his heirs for ever all that close of grounde in
the parish of Startforth, which I purchased of Robert Taylor.
And I will that the said Robert Taylor shall make Deeds and
assurances thereof to such feofees in trust, to his use, as by the
supervisors of this my Will to him shallbe nominated and
appointed. I also give to the said Samuel Saire six score pounds.
I give and bequeath unto my said daughter, Phillis Saire, all
those closes of ground in the Lordship of Starforth commonly
called or known by the name of Dobbye closes, and also the close
of ground and appurtenances adjoining the said Dobby closes
commonly called freholdes, and also another close in the said Lordshipp called Gillbeck close, and also that burgage in Bernardcastell which I purchased of Mr. Forest, and the heires lawfully
begotten of her; and failing issue to my daughter, Elizabeth Saire,
and her heires lawfully begotten. I give unto my said daughter,
Phillis Saire, more 120l. and a silver salt pcell gilt, six silver

spoones, a silver Bottell, and a gold Ring. I give also to the said Phillis all such lymber, trees, boordes and sawne wood as I have in Barnardcastle and Marwood. I give unto my said daughter, Elizabeth Saire, my tenementt with appurtenances at Egeseburne, which I bought of Henry Richardson, and also the sum of 20*l.* I give unto my brother, Ralph Saire, 3*l.* 6*s.* 8*d.*, and also my best gowne, my satin dublet and my velvett hose. I give to Phillis Atkinson, the daughter of my said brother, Ralph, 40*s.* I give unto Jane, my sister, the wife of William Whorton, 20*s.* I give to Frances Whorton, 10*s.* I give unto my late servant, Gabriel Whorton, 3*l.* 6*s.* 8*d.*, and my next sute of apparell. I give to my sister, Agnes, the wife of John Perkin, 40*s.* I give to my brother in lawe, the said John Perkin, 10*s.* I give to Mr. Melott, 10*s.* I give to my sister, Helayne, the wife of Roger Bainbrigg, 20*s.*, and to her daughter 6*s.* I give Gosseppe Isabell, the wife of William Barnes, 6*s.* I give to Phillis Hodgson, of Hullerbush, 10*s.* To Robert Appleby, my servant, 6*s.* To Thomas Allanson 10*s.* To Jane Sanderson, my maide, 20*s.* The residue of all my goods, chattells and creditts whatsoever I give unto my said children, John Saire, Samuel Saire, Phillis Saire, and Elizabeth Saire, and make them joint executors, and that my brother in lawe, Roger Bainbridge, shall have the tuition and upbringing of my said daughter, Phillis Saire, until she come to the age of one and twenty yeares. And my will is that my brother, Ralph Sayre, my brethren in law, George Hutton and John Perkin, and my nephews, Francis Whorton and Gabriel Worton, shall have the tuycon and government of my lands and filiall porcons of my said children, George Saire, John Saire, Samuell Saire and Elizabeth Saire, during their minority. And my will is also that Margaret, my wife shall have the tuicon of my said four children, so long as she remayneth sole and unmarried, she bringing them up vertouslye and in godly learninge at the good like of my supervisors, and that my said wife shall have yearly allowed for their education during the tyme of their continuance with her, such sufficient allowance forth of their several porcons by Tutors, as shall be thought feet and convenient by my Supervisors. I ordeyne and appoint my trustye and loveing friends, Mr. William Barker, preacher of the Word, my said Brother Roger Bainbrigg, Thomas Bainbrigg, of Brigg house, my father in law, George Hutton, my brother in law, William Whorton, and my said Gosseppe Michael Walker to be Supervisors of this my Will. Witnesses, Michael Walker, Ralph Sayre, Francis Whorton, Gabriell Whorton and Francis Atkinson.

INVENTORY, 1,401*l.* 5*s.* 3*d.*, which included debts oweing to him, appearing by his debt bookes 546*l.* 18*s.* 9*d.* Severall leases prased at 354*l.* 4*s.* 8*d.* Bonds and Bills prased at 362*l.* 11*s.* 5*d.* Debts owing by testator, 249*l.* 1*s.* 5*d.*

ISABELL TEMPLE.[1]

May 30, 1606. In the name of God, Amen, I, Isabell Temple, of the parish of All Saints' within the towne of Newcastle upon Tyne, Widow. To be buried in the said parish church of All Saints' soe neare my late husband, Henry Temple, as maie be. I give and bequeath unto my sonne, Bartram Simpson, all that my house or tenemt, with all and singular, the appurts whatsoever thereto belonging, lying and being in Pilgrim Streete within the aforesaid town of Newcastle on Tyne, now in the occupation of William Beadnell. To have and to hold unto my said sonne, Bartram Simpson, for and during his life natural, and after his decease to his sonne, Thomas Simpson, for and during his life naturall, and after his decease to the heires male of his body lawfully begotten; and for default of such issue, unto George Simpson, son of the said Bartram Simpson, for and during his lyfe natural, and after his decease to the heirs male of his body lawfully begotten; and for default of issue unto William Simpson, son of the said Bartram Simpson, for and during his life naturall, and after his decease to the heirs male of his body lawfully begotten; and for default of such issue, then to come to the right heires of me, the said Isabell Temple, for ever. I give and bequeath unto Ellen Simpson, daughter of George Simpson, late deceased, an oversea coveringe. I give and bequeath to Margaret Simpson a cubbord in the hall howse, wherein I now dwell a pewter platter, a candlesticke, and a danske pewter pott. I give unto Elizabeth Simpson a table and a forme in the said hall howse, a pewter dubler, a candlesticke, and a Danske pewter pott. I give and bequeath unto Isabella Simpson, daughter of the said Bartram Simpson, a great danske chiste, a fether bed and all such other clothes as belongs thereto, two paire of lynen sheets, a paire of hardner sheets, twoe pillowberes, two feather cods, an Iron chimney in the said hall howse, my best gowne, my best petticoate and frocke. I give and bequeath unto Henry Dodshon, a marriner, an iron chimney and a bedstead, a presser standing in his, the said Henrie Dodgson, own howse, a paire of lynen sheets, and a paire of strakin sheets. I give and bequeath unto the said Thomas Simpson a flanders bedstead standing in the said Henrie Dodgson's howse, three silver spoons and Iron chimney, now being in the custodie of one Elizabeth Bewick. I give and bequeath to George Simpson afore named three silver spoons. I give and bequeath to my daughter, Emette Simpson, a greete brass pott and a flower candlestick as a token. I give and bequeath to Margaret Simpson and Isabella Simpson, daughters of the said Bartram Simpson, three panns, a yetlinge, a little possnett, seven

---

[1] 1606, June 5, Isbell, wif was to **Henry Temple**, mr., bur., *All Sts.* *Newcastle, Regs.*

porringers, and four dublers that goes about them equally to
be divided between them. I give and bequeath to the same
Margaret other two pewter patters. I give and bequeath unto
Elizabeth Dickson a long table, a new table clothe, fower table
napkins, a caldron and a mashing tubb. I give to my maid,
Jane More, a prosser and an iron chimney. I give and bequeath
to Jane Errington the bedstead wherein I now lye. I give and
bequeath Ralph Simpson 20s., to be paid him out of the above
mentioned howse or tenement, by me bequeathed, within two yeares
next after my death. I give and bequeath to William Simpson,
John Simpson and Edward Simpson, children of my son, Edward
Simpson, ten shillings a peece for token, and to everie of his
daughters 10s. apeece for tokens. I give and bequeathe to their
father, Edward Simpson, one angel for a token. All the rest of
my goods, moveable and not moveable, my debts paid and funerall
expences deducted, I give and bequeath to my said sonne, Bartram
Simpson, whom I make sole executor of this my laste Will. Richard
Rey, Isabell Readhead, Isabell Motion and William Vincent.
Proved, 8 July, 1606.

WILLIAM MADDISON.

July 28, 1606. In the name of God, Amen, I, William
Maddison, of East Murton. To be buryed decentlie in Christian
burial. Item, I give and bequith to my three brethren three
yewes equally to be devided. I do give 3s. 4d. to be distributed
among the poor of this parish. My will is that my wife and my
two sonns, William Maddison and Jhon. Maddison, shall be my
executors, and shall give all my goodes and chattels, moveable and
unmoveable (my debts discharged), equally to be divided amongst
them, and I do nominate and intreat Mr. Marmaduke Blaxton to
see the true government of this my last Will and Testament. In
witness hereof I have hereunto subscribed my name the 28 of July,
1606. Jhon. Barker, John Follansbye, John Maddison.

A true Inventorie of the goods and chattels, moveable and
unmoveable, which was William Maddeson's, late of East Murton,
deceased, praised by Anthony Robson, Dennes Corner, William
Wrenn and William Richeson the 9 day of September, 1607,
Inprimis : 8 Kyen, 18l. 13s. 4d. Item, three whyes, 3l. 10s. Five
calves, 40s. One meare, 3l. One younge fillye, 26s. 8d. Six
yows, 4l. 15s. Thirteen lambs, 40s. Three potts, one kettle, one
little pann and eight little pewther dishes, 13s. 4d. One cupboarde, one little chist, with other wood implements, 10s. Suma,
36l. 8s. 4d. Proved, 1607.

WILLIAM CRAWFOOT.[1]

Oct. 27, 1606. In the name of Gode, Amen, I, William Crawfoot, of the towne of Newcastle upon Tyne, Mariner. To be buried
in the south side within the parish church of All Sts. as near
my mother as convenientlie as may be. Touching my worldly
goods, lands and possessions, I give and bequeth in manner and
forme following, that is to say, I give and bequeath unto my
sister, Ursula Crawfoot, her executors and assigns, All my estate
and interest, terme of yeares and demand in, and to these two
tenements in Pilgrim Street, within the saide towne of Newcastle
upon Tyne, which I holde by severall leases, the one from one
Robert Stobbes, the other frome Robert Archbold, or otherwise,
now in the severall occupations of William Harrison and the other
in the occupation of . . . Whitfield. To have and hold the same
for all the years in the severall leases as conteyned. I give and
bequeath unto my loving friend, Nicholas Atkinson, marriner,
my silver wissell and chayne. And to my loving cosen, Thomas
Wimphrey, two angells for a token. I give and bequeath to
George Robinson, my wieffe, Margaret, her daughter's sonne, one
hundred poundes of lawful money of England, to be paid at the
decease of the same, my wieff, Margaret. And to Margaret Carr,
daughter of Nicholas Carr, 10*l*., to be paid at the decease of the
same, my wieff, Margaret. I give and bequeath to my said loving
wieff, Margaret, all those my four tenements lying behind All
hallows Church, in the said towne of Newcastle upon Tyne, to have
and hold the same to her and her heires and assigns for ever. I
give and bequeath to my said wieffe, Margaret, all that burgage or
tenement, with the appurts, in Pilgrime Street, now in the
occupation of Nicholas Byncks for terme of her natural liefe, and
the reversion and remainder thereof I give and bequeath to the
said George Robinson, my wief's daughter's sonne and the heirs
of his body lawfully begotten; and for lack of such issue, to
Mathew, his brother, and the heirs of his body lawfully to be
begotten; and for lack of such issue, to John Robinson, another
of the brethren of the said George, and the heirs of his bodye
lawfully to be begotten; and for lack of such issue to Thomas
Robinson, another of his brethren, and the heirs of his body
lawfully begotten; and for lack of such issue to the heires of the
said George Robinson for ever. All the residue of my goods and
chattels not by these presents given or bequeathed (my debts being
paid and my funeralls discharged), I whooly give and bequeath
to my said wief, Margaret, whome of this my last Will and
Testament I make and ordeyne my full and sole executor, and
my loving friends, the said Thomas Wimphrey and Nicholas
Atkinson, supervisors, Renouncing and for saking all former Wills

---

[1] 1610, June 27, Willm. Crawforth, mariner, bur., *All Sts., Newcastle, Regs.* 1608, May 25, Urseley Crawforth, bur., *ibid.*

and legacies by me in any wise heretofore made and bequeath. Witnesses, Nicholas Atkinson, Jane Commyn, Henry Anthony, Thomas Humphreye.

INVENTORY, 247*l*. 6*s*. 6*d*.

Debts oweing by the testator : To George Robinson for his child's part and porcon of his father's and mother's goods, 12*l*. And to Mathew, John and Thomas Robinson, his brethren, and to every one of them, for their like porcons, or 12*l*., which is in all 36*l*. To Elynor and Katheren Robinson, their sisters, to either of them, for their like porcon, or 12*l*., which is in all 24*l*. The funeral expences of the testator, 10*l*. The mortuary for the testator, 10s. Proved, 12 March, 1610.

WILLIAM SUTHACK.[1]

Nov. 20, 1606. In the name of God, Amen, I, William Suthack, Clarke. To be buried in the Chancel of Mugglesworth, I give unto the church of Mugglesworth one ewe, or 5*s*., to be paid at Whitsuntide next ensuing. Also I give unto Christopher Eagleston, my brother-in-law, three gimmers. Also I give unto Rowland Dawson's two children, Willm. Dawson and Jane Dawson, either one lamb. Also I give to everie widdow in Mugglesworth parish and within Mugglesworth lordship, 2*d*. Also in most humble and reverend wies, I give unto the Right Reverend Father in gode, Willm., by god's divine providence Lord Bishop of Durham, my sonne, Thomas Suthack, as also one pcel of ground called the Calfe Hall, lying and being within Mugglesworth parke and belonging to the Right Worshipful Mr. Francis Buney. All the rest of my goods and chattels, moveable and unmoveable, debts and legacies discharged, I give unto my wife, Alse Suthack, whom I make my full executrix, and she to bring up my two daughters, Jane and Rebecca, as hir ableness will afford. Witnesses, Rowland Harrison, Nicholas Laborne. Proved, 1607.

THOMAS DOBSON.[2]

March 30, 1607. In the name of God, Amen, I, Thomas Dobson, of the towne of Newcastle upon Tyne, Feltmaker, of the parish of St. Johne's, within the said Towne. To be buryed within the parish churchyard of St. Nicholas, within the said towne of Newcastle upon Tyne, near the litle church dore there. I give unto the poore of this pish of St. John's, to be distributed

[1] Appointed Perpetual Curate of Muggleswick, 1586, which he held until his death in 1607.

[2] 1607, June 23, Thomas Dobson, Feltemaker, bur., *St. Nich., Newcastle, Regs.*

The testators brother, Anthony, who was married at St. Nicholas, Newcastle, 10 Oct., 1579, was the father (with others) of Anthony Dobson who heads the Visitation pedigree; he mar. Grace (bapt. 8 Nov., 1573, at Jarrow), dau. of [Robert] Layburn of Follonsby, 8 Jan., 1603/4, at St. Nicholas, widow of William Milbanks, he was bur. there 12 Feb., 1620/1 and she, 27 Oct., 1654.

at the discrecon of my well beloved wife, the sum of ten shillings.
I give and bequeath unto my brother, John Dobson, of Benwell,
one sute of appell, viz., one dublett, one jerkin, one paire of
britches, and my rideing cloke, and also twenty shillings in money
for a token. I give and bequeath unto my cosen, Christopher
Dobson, my Rapeare and also twenty shillings for a token. I give
unto Anthony Dobson, the elder, my brother, and to my cozen,
Anthony Dobson, his sonne, my best cloake and my best jerkin,
and my brother, Anthony to take his choice whether of them he
will have. I give and bequeath to my cozen, Valentine Dobson, my
best doublett and britches, and also my ridinge sword. I give and
bequeath to my cozen, George Dobson, twenty shillings as a token.
I give and bequeath to my cozen, Margaret Dobson, a debt of
26s. 8d., wich one . . . Felpe, of Usworth, is owing me, being
the remaynder of a debt which he oweth me for a maire I sould
him, and I will that my executors under named shall make
authoretie unto her father, Anthony Dobson, for the calling for
security thereof when it shall growe due, if neads require for his
daughter's use. I give unto my cozens, John Dobson and Suzan
Dobson, my Cozen Anthony his children, to either of them
twenty shillings for a token. I give and bequeath unto my sister.
Margaret Tailor, widow, 26s. 8d. for a token. I give and
bequeath sone of John Collingwood 20s. for a token. I give and
bequeath to Elizabeth Boothbye, daughter of . . . Boothbye, late
of Usworth Yeoman, deceased, 20s. for a token. I give and
bequeath unto Mark Smith, my god sone, a french crown for a
token. And all the rest of my goods, chattells and debts, moveable
and unmovable, my debtes, legacies and funerall expences payd
and discharged, I give and bequeath unto my said beloved wife,
Susan Dobson, whom I make and ordeyne my full and sole
Executrix of this my Will. Provided alwayes that my full mynd
and pleasure is, that if my said Brethern, Anthony Dobson and
John Dobson, and my sister, Margaret Tailor, or anye of them,
do make any further challenge or clame unto any of my goods
or cattell any manner of waye other then above said, That then
the same legacy or legacys or tokens gyven them, the said Anthony,
John and Margaret, or any of them, or there children above
mentioned, to be clearly voyd and noe waie to be challenged.
Witnesses, William Pearson, Francis Leighton.

GILBERT SPENCE.[1]

April 16, 1607. In the name of God, Amen, I, Gilbert Spence,
of the Cittie of Durham, Clerk, Notary Public. To be buried
in the Church or churchyard, where it shall please god to take
me out of this miserable lyfe. I give and bequeth to the aged

[1] In his will he is described as " Clerk, Notary Public," there can
be no doubt that he is the man who in Foster's *Alumini Oxonienses* is
described as of Yorks., pleb. of St. Edmund Hall, matric., 3 April, 1584,

and impotent poors people and fatherless children of the pish of
Tynnmouth 5*l*., to be carefully and warylie distributed by my
executors or their assigns at the direction and careful considerations of my supervisors of this my last Will and Testament hereafter named, and the discreet Ministers of the churches of Durham
and Tynnmouth at their remayning and dwellinghowses, alwaies
regarding that no part thereof be given to needless lewde and
idol persons, nor to drunkards, swearers or any infamous persons
notoriouslie detected of any vice or wicked crime. I give and
bequeth to Allice Spence, my wife, two milke kyne for her help and
relief with milknes. I give to my sonne, Cuthbert Spence, one
cowe that is young and branded. I give to George and Katherine,
my first wive's youngest children, viz., to either of them 3*l*. 6*s*. 8*d*.
for their advancement, for whose upbringing I have heartofore
given and disbursed 16*l*., which 3*l*. 6*s*. 8*d*. apiece I give to either
of them in lew consideracon and full satisfacon of all things that
they may or can claime or demand of my goods, and by
name of filiall portions or otherwise then of my free gifte
upon their dew desert and good behaviour. And if they or either
of them pretend or make any clame or demand of or to any part
of my goods other then such as I give them by legacies, Then
my will is that all my aforesaid bequests and legacies to them
made and given, viz., to such of them as shall pretend or make
any such challenge or demand, shallbe utterlie voyed and as not
given. And therefore, I will that their legacies shall not be given
to them nor to any to their uses untill they come to twenty and
one yeares of age, either and both of them, and doe give to my
executors general release acquaitance and discharges not to
make any challenge or demand of or to any parte of my goods
other than is to them hereafter bequeathed in this my last Will
and Testament. My will is that the wood furniture in the hall,
howse or rooms of my dwellinghouse in the North Bayley of the
Cittie of Durham that are to be removed as wainscott and
panelled work, cupbords, long table with frame chayres, Buffett
stooles there, nor any of the standing bedds, also stand bedd
steads or stocks that are placed in any part of the said howse,
nor the furniture belonging to the said bedds, nor the brass
vessells and pewther vessells in the Kytching and butterie, nor any

aged 32; Vicar of Tynemouth, Northumberland, 1588 (subscribes
'notarius publicus') to his death, 1607. He married, firstly, Margaret
Knighton, 25 May, 1574, at St. Mary-le-Bow, she was bur. at St.
Oswald's, 2 Feb., 1592/3; by her he had Thomas, bapt., 14 Oct., 1576, at
St. Mary-le-Bow, bur., 28 Feb., 1576/7, at St. Mary the less: Cuthbert,
bapt., 12 Jan., 1577/8, at St. Mary the less (mar. Jane Longstaff,
30 July, 1605, at St. Oswald's, who was bur. there, 25 Apl., 1619); and
two daurs., Susanna, bapt, 7 May, 1580, at St. Mary the less, mar. John
Walker, 14 Jan., 1603/4, at St. Oswald's; and Anne bapt., 24 July, 1583.
He mar., secondly, Alice Smith, 15 May, 1598, at St. Mary-le-Bow,
where she was bur., 5 August, 1623; he was also bur. there, 13 May, 1607.

vessell placed in the cupbord heads in the hall howse (saving
the stand bedd or stocks in the litle parlour nighe the . . .
which I give to my wyfe), and the long table with frame and
long setle in the great low plour of the same howse shall not be
removed, but there in their places to remain to such pson or
psons as shall, by vertew of this my Testament and last Will and
my bequests herein made, have and enjoy my said dwellinghowse
in the said North Bayley, nor any of the furniture placed or
remayning in the chambers, on the wall or Roomes under the
same, they according to their times of occupation, and enjoying
the same according to my limitation hereafter made, paying and
allowing for the same furniture and household stuff towards the
payment of my legacies and other dewtes to be paid, as they
shallbe apprised and valewed unto. I give and bequeath to my
aged servant 3s. 4d. I give and bequeth to my well beloved wyfe,
Alice Spence, during her lyfe naturall (if she so long contynew my
widow after my death) the whole use, occupacon and commodytie
of my dwellinghowse, garden and other howses thereto belonging
situate and being in the North bayley att the Cittie of Durham
aforesaid, being parcell of the possessions of the disolved monas-
teries of Blanchland, and also the whole use, occupacon and
commodties of my chamber howses of the blessed virgin Mary
nigh St. Oswald's Churche, of the suberbes of the said Cittie of
Durham, commolie called the Aucreage, of my meadow close
thereto adjoining called the Ladie close, of meadow ground in the
meadow field called the Bellasses, nigh the said Cittie of Durham,
together with the use, proffitts and commodytes of all the gardens,
orchards, pastures, commons and common of pastures, and other
the appurtenances, to the premises belonging for and in consideration and full satisfacon of her thirds Dowrie and widow
right of my goods and chattells and not otherwise. And that if
it shall fall out that my said wife shall not think or hold herself
well contented with these things to her bequeathed in lew and full
considerons and satisfacon of her said widow right, dowrie and
thirds of my said goods and chattells, then I will that all these
things to her by me in this last Will and Testament given and
bequeathed shallbe voyed and become utterlie frustrate, of none
effect and as not at all given and bequeathed to her, and that
she shall not have any part of the aforesaid things to her so
bequeathed, but that the same shall and may presentlie upon her
refusal come to such psons and uses as I have here also in this
my last Will and testament given, bequeathed and lymited the
same, and she upon the same refusall shall have her thirds dowrie
and wydow right of the other of my goods and chattells as that
shall chance unto her in the valuacon and division of the same.
And further, my will is that if my wyfe stand contented and
satisfied with the said legacies given her in manner aforesaid, yet
she shall not borrow, lett, alyenate nor sell the said tenemts,

howses, gardens, garthes, grasing meadows nor any there appertaining aforesaid to her bequeathed, nor any implements of
household stuff before mentioned, nor any part thereof to any
person or persons (saving that she may place tenents in the howses
that she need not use from yeare to yeare, as heretofore I have
usually done, and that she may sell her hay been mowen and
gathered and her foggages in any year or years she shall not
need to use it her self) but that if she shall endeavour as about
or at anytime offer to let, sell or alyeate the said tenemts, howses,
gardens, garths, grounds, meadows or any other there said
appurtenances, or any other howsehold stuff mentconed in this my
last will and testament, to her in manner aforesaid given and
bequeathed, or any part or piece thereof to any pson or psons
whomsoever, otherwise then is either before limitted or shall
marrie and take to husband any man after my death, or commit
any forfeiture for nonpayment of rent or other dewtes.   That
then and presentlie thereupon this my guift and bequest of all and
singular the said tentts, howses, gardens, garths, grounds,
meadows and their appurtances and premises with the said household stuff to her bequeathed and given in manner aforesaid, or of
so much thereof as she shall go about, endeavour or offer, Taverne,
sell or alyenate or suffer to be forfeited and in danger thereof,
shall so cease and be utterlie void and of non effect, anything as
is aforesaid given or bequeathed to the contrary notwithstanding.
And further, my will is that my said wyfe shall have for that
which is termed her coffer all such things as belong her for her
apparell and her bedstead before to her bequeathed, sufficient and
reasonablie furnished with to her bedd, mattrass, bolster and
other competent bed clothes for one bedd, but not the best bed
covering, best fether bedd, nor best sheets, And also if so be she
doe not lay in to my execatorgood assurance for the redelivery of the
said howsehold stuffe in as good state as she shall receive the
same, or the true value thereof as the same shall be priced, with
assurance for the said deliverie of the said howse stuff or the
valew aforesaid, and shall bind both herself, her executors, administrators or assigns to deliver the same as is aforesaid to my
executors at her death or marriage or other her departure from
the said legacies then I give, assign, legate and bequeathe, after
my wyfe's said refusall of her said legacies, if any such shallbe
and from and after any other her departure from the same
legacies, and after her death or mariage to an other husband as
is aforesaid, my lease of my said dwellinghowses and gardens in
the North Baily of the said Cittie of Durham, and all my tearms
of years then to come of and in the same howses and gardens
with their appurtenances whatsoever to me in my said lease
granted, and all my right, title, interest and claime of in and to
the premises and every parcel thereof to Katherine Spence, my
daughter, after my wive's death, mariage or refusall aforesaid,

Also I give and bequeath my lease of the Chambrie of the blessed virgin Mary nigh St. Oswald's Church aforesaid, of the meadow ground and close called the Ladie close, and of my acre and a half of meadow ground in the Bellases aforesaid, and all my terms of yeares then to come of and in the said lease, howses, tents, garths, grounds and other the premises, with their appurtenances, whatsoever to me in the said leases granted (Except the howse in Kirkgate, which I give to my sonne, Cuthbert Spence, immediately after my death), and all my right, title, interest and claime of in and to the premises and every part and parcels thereof to John Spence, sonne of my sone, Cuthbert Spence, of the Cittie of Durham, after my wive's death, refusall or marriage or forfeiture. And if the said John Spence dye within the age of one and twentie yeares, or before he can lawfully come to the occupacon of the premises, Then I bequeath all the premises to him given to the rest of the said Cuthbert Spence his lawfully begotten children. Provided that if the said children of the said Cuthbert shall dye or already sell or put away the aforesaid bequests to them, Then my will is that George Spence, my nephew, and his children shall have the title and interest thereof, and hereunto in as ample manner as the aforesaid John Spence, or the lawfull begotten children of the said Cuthbert Spence, have or ought to have the same by virtew of this my last Will and Testament. And that these my purposes bequests may the better be effected, and that my wyfe and children or other my legators doe not harrie one another I most humbly request my Wor. Mr. Dean and the Chapter of Durham to take the said custodie of my said leases into there howse of Records as a place most indefferent for all my legataries and executors. And all be it, John Walker, who maryed my daughter, Susanna, hath made a generall acquittance and entred bond never to challenge any of my goods, yet in way of gifts and considerations I give unto them my second round cloake, a jacket and a payre of pritches and a hatt, and to my sone, Cuthbert, my best round cloake, a dubblett and a hatt. The residue of all my goods, moveable and unmoveable, my debts, legacies and funeral expences paid and discharged, I give, legate and bequeath the moietie in one halfe thereof to my wyfe, Alice Spence, to have, occupy and enjoy during her naturall lyfe, and after her life to come, or the price thereof, to Katherine Spence and to my sonne, George Spence; and the other halfe thereof I give and bequeath to the said Katherine Spence and my sonne, Cuthbert Spence, his children. But my will is that if any to whom I have given anything in this my Testament and last Will shall offer, goe about, or actually defraude or doe any iniure to the other having interest to any thing in this my last Will and Testament he shall thereupon and by reason of that evil and wrongfull dealing loose, fall from and foregoe all the benyfitts, tytle and interest that otherwise such deserver and fraudulent dealer might or should have in and by this my last Will and Testament, or any things therein conteyned. And that this my last Will and Testament may be dewley executed, I doe ordaine, constitute and make my said daughter, Katherine Spence, my trew and lawfull executor of this my aforesaid last Will and Testament. And I humbly desire the ordinarie who it shall please god to approve this my last Will and Testament to take order by strong bonds that they that have interest in and by this my last Will and Testament doe not wrong one to another. And that this my last Will and Testament be dewlie executed.. I will that these my bequests, devises and purposes conteyned in this my last Will and Testament be not expounded, conserned, freed or wrased from my words and my plaine and trew meaning by any collorable, superficall or synister argument or sence otherwise then the plane words will beare and afford. And I will that whosoever shall be quarrelous, contencous or troublesome herein shall loose and forgoe his or their whole interest and benefit of this my Will and Testament and of whatsoever is therein mentioned. And finallie I ordeyne and make my trustie and well beloved friend, Mr. John Richardson, of Durham, my Kinsman, Mr. Richard Jackson, Mr. Christopher Boa . . . and Mr. Henry Barker, Supervisors of this my last Will and Testament, and I hereby desire them to see and procure that this my last Will and Testament be proved and putt into execution. Witnesses, Hen. Barker, Richard Jackson. Proved, 1607.

ISABELLA ROBSON.[1]

July 11, 1607. In the name of God, Amen, I, Isabella Robson, of the towne of Newcastle upon Tyne, in the parish of All Saints', widow. To be buried in the parish church of All Saints' soe neare my late husband as convenientlie maybe. I give and bequeath to my brother, George Readheade, locksmith, a full twoe thirde partes in three equall partes being devided of all my householde stuffe. I give unto him over and besides a whole bedding of clothes. I give and bequeath unto Robt. Smale, Keilman, his wife, a round cubbord now being in my howse, a great damske chist in the loft, a sane yard and a kirtle. I give and bequeath to John Readhead, sone of Richard Readhead, shipwright, a danskpott, pewterpott and 2 platters of pewter. I give to Isabell Readhead, the said Richard's wife, my silver gowne crooks. I give to Mallie Wilkinson my gown taicke. I give to Thomas Readhead, marriner, another full thirde parte of all my household stuff, and to his wife my worsted apron and a paire of

[1] The Testatrix was bur. at All Saints, Newcastle, 18 July, 1607.

crookes to it. I give and bequeath unto Thomas Readhead, sone
of the said Thomas, a .pewter pottle pott. I give unto Mally
Errington, wife of Gilbert Errington, a fether bed. Whereas the
said Robert Smale is oweing me 8s. I doe freely forgive it him.
I give unto my sister, Eppie Brown, 2 pewter platters. My mind
and will is that all such legacies and gifts as I have heare in this,
my will,. given and bequeathed, shall be delivered and taken out
of all my goodes, and then my brother, George Readhead, and
Thomas Readhead, to have their partes according as before. I
have given and bequeathed them all the rest of my goods moveable
and unmovable, my debts being paid and funeral expences discharged, I give and bequeath unto my said brother, George
Readhead, and my cozen, the said Thomas Readhead, whom I do
make executors jointly of this my psent will. Witnesses, Gilbert
Errington, Robt. Smale, Mallie Wilkinson, Isabella Readhead and
William Vincent.

WILLIAM SCURFIELD.[1]

July 25, 1607. In the name of God, Amen, I, William
Scurfield, of Grindon, in the county of Durham, Yeoman. To be
buried in the church or churchyard of Bishopwarmouth. First
I give and bequeath unto the poore of the parish which are most
needful at the day of my death or buriall 20s. I give and
bequeath unto my sone in law, James Farrowe, and to Alice, his
wife, my daughter, and their children, the sum of 5l. over and
above their porcons which I have alreadie paid to the said James
and Alice, of which 5l. James Farrowe is oweing me 30s. I am
contented to forgive him 10s. thereof, so my will is he allow that
20s. which he is oweing me and I will that the other 4l. be paid to
them or either of them that shallbe living at a years end after my
death. Whereas my son-in-law, John Thompson, is oweing me
fiftie shillings, I forgive him 10s. thereof and I give to him and his
wife, Ellen, and their children, the sum of five pounds, namely

---

[1] William Scurfield was bur. at Bishopwearmouth, 30 Sept., 1609, at
which place his wife had been bur. 26 Aug., 1597; she bore him four
children, Rowland, bapt., 25 June, 1577, bur. 28 May, 1620, mar. Alice
Jervice, 26 Mch., 1607 (by whom he had four sons, Robert, bapt.,
17 Jan., 1607/8, John, bapt., 8 July, 1610, William, bapt., 4 Oct., 1612,
and Barnard, bapt., 18 May, 1615); Robert, bapt., 4 Mch., 1574/5, mar.
Isabel Merriman, 1 May, 1598 (by whom he had three sons and four
daurs, William, bapt., 2 Mch., 1599/1600, bur. 25 Sept., 1600, Peter,
bapt., 27 Jan., 1604/5, John, bapt., 13 Oct., 1608, bur., 26 Oct., the same
year, Alice, bapt., 11 Sept., 1602, Joan, bapt., 25 Mch., bur., 26 Apl.,
1607, Elizabeth, bapt., 22 Apl., 1610, Margaret, bapt., 3 May, 1618);
Alice, bapt., 1 May, 1569, said in the will to have mar. James Farrow,
and Ellen who mar. John Thompson, 27 April, 1596.

40*s.* which he is oweing, and 3*l.* more to be paid to him or his wife or children two yeares after my death. I give and bequeath unto my sone, Rowland Scurfield, 5*l.*, to be paid three years after my death. I give and bequeath unto the late children of John Dixson, that is to say, Elizabeth, Mary, Jane and Isabella to every one of them, 20*s.* apiece. All the rest of my goods, my debts, legacies and funeral expences discharged, I give unto my sone, Robert Scurfield, whom I make my full and sole Executor of this my last Will and Testament. Witnesses, Peter Dentone, Thomas Markland, Wm. Cooke. Proved, December 2, 1609.

NICHOLAS LAYBORNE.

Sept. 1, 1607. In the name of God, Amen, I, Nicholas Layborne, the Elder of Durwancoate. To be buried within the quere of Meddomsley, my pish church. I give and bequith the full half of my farmhold and tenement, which I dy now possessed of, unto my wife, Jane Layborne, for the yeares unexpired to bring up my small children. I give and bequith unto my daughter, Margery Layborne, three score poundes for her filiall, [portion] And if that my goods will not amount and extend to that sum, then I will that shee shall have that which remayneth or shall . . . made oute of my half tenement : Provided always that my said dowghter Margery doe follow and obey her mother's advice and advices of the supervisor of this my Will and Testament in her matching, it please Gode ; otherwise that she will not have her porcon, but be at her mother's discretion. And I will that my wife shall give to the rest of all my children, viz., John Layborne, Peter Layborne, Arthor Layborne and William Layborne, their portions at her discretion as she shall think good, with the advices of the supervisors of this my Will and testament. And also that if the haff shall come to my wife's use, I will that she shall geive unto Henry Halsall 40*s.* and to Ambrose Halsell 26*s.* 8*d.*, my dowghter's children. Also I doe take that upon my conscience at this present before you all here, That if halfe should come by [and] in wright to the use of me or my successors fower yeares before the end and expiration of Mr. Headlye's lease . . . And I make my wife, Jane Layborne, my sole and full and lawfull executrix of this my last Will and Testament. And I also make my brother, Anthony Swinborne, and my nephew, John Stephenson, Supervisors of this my last Will and Testament, to see that it be fully accomplished and fullfilled according to the true meaning (as my trust is in them). Witnesses, John Rogersonn, Anthony Swinburne, John Stephenson, Geo. Wrightson.

INVENTORIE, 158*l.* 17*s.* Proved, 1607.

THOMAS COMYN.[1]

Sept. 15, 1607. In the name of God, Amen, I, Thomas Comyn, of Croisgait, in the pish of St. Margaret's. To be buried in the pish church of St. Margaret's aforesaid. I doe give unto my sister, Dorothie Richardson, one french crowne in gold for a token. I doe give unto my sister, Jane Sympson, ten shillinges in money for a token. I doe give unto my Brother in lawe, William Sympson, my black meare. I doe give my father, John Comyne, my clooke lined with baise. I doe give to my brother, John Comyn, my best clooke. I doe give to my brother, George Comyn my green suite of apparell I doe give unto my brother Nicholas Comyn, my best dublett. I doe give unto my man, George Ullocke, one olde dublett and a paire of britches and paire of white stockings. I doe give unto my sonne, James Comyn, thirtie pounds, and my wife to have the tuision and government of my said sonne, James Comyn, and of the aforesaid some of thirty pounds for and during hir widowhood and att the daye of hir marriage I give the tuison and government of my said sone, James Comyn, and the said some of Thirtie pounds to my brother, John Comyne, of Newcastle upon Tyne, Merchant, and all the rest of his porcon due unto him the said James Comyn att the day of my death, and dew unto hym fourth of all my goodes and chattels moveable and unmoveable. I doe give the said Thirtie pounds, the which I have geven unto my sone, James Comyn, by legacy, unto John Comyn, George Comyn and Nicholas Comyn, my three brethern, equally to be devided amongst them, if thatt my said sone, James Comyne, do fortune to dye and departe fourthe of this wicked worlde before he come to the filiall age of one and twentie yeares. I doe give unto the poore twentie shillings. All resydue of my goods and chattells moveable and unmoveable, my debts, legacies and funerall paid and discharged, I doe give and

---

[1] John Commyn, the father of the testator, was bur. at Redmarshall (from which registers all dates are taken unless otherwise mentioned), 1 Oct., 1613, " an anncient inhabitant." The testator, bapt., 18 June, 1581, mar. Margaret Bayles, 8 July, 1606, at St. Margaret's, Durham, where his only child James was bapt., 30 July, 1607 (his marriage is also recorded in the registers of Redmarshall, " Thomas, son of John Cummin of Redmarshall, to Bales, his daughter, of Durham "); His brother John was apprenticed, 24 June, 1601, as son of John of Cleemar Hall, co. Durham, yeo. (bapt., 20 Feb., 1583). He mar. at St. Nich., Newcastle, 1 July, 1611, Elizabeth, dau. of Ralph Cock, in whose will (dated 29 Aug., 1611, *Arch. Ael.*, 3 Ser., xiii., 38) he and Elizabeth are mentioned. He was bur. at St. Nich., 12 Aug., 1616. (His master, Alexander Davison, had mar. Agnes, dau. of the same Ralph Cock). His brother George was bapt., 24 July, 1586, and his brother Nicholas, 8 July, 1589; he also was apprenticed in Newcastle. His sister Dorothy, bapt., 1 Sept., 1572, mar. Thomas Richardson, 19 Sept., 1595. His sister Janet, bapt., 21 Nov., 1574, mar. William Simpson, 27 Apl., 1593. The testator although expressing a wish in his will to be bur. at St. Margaret's, Durham, was bur. at Redmarshall, 16 Oct., 1607.

bequeth unto my wyfe, Margare Comyn, and my sonne, James Comyn, whom I make my full executors of this my last Will and Testament. Also I doe make my Brother-in-law, Thomas Richerdson, and my brother, John Comyne, survisors of this my last Will and Testament, desiring them, as my trust is in them, to see all things pformed according to the trew meaninge hereof. Proved, 28 November, 1607.

WILLM. BLAXTON.[1]

Feb. 5, 1607. I, Willm. Blaxton, of Gibside, in the Countie of Durham, Esquire. My bodie to be buryed in my pish church of Whickham in decent order at the discretion of my executors and supervisors, wthout anie vaine pompe, as neare unto the place where my lait wife was buryed as convenientlie may be. And whereas I have alwayes had, and still have, a great care for the pferment and advancement of my welbeloved nephew, Ralph Blaxton, eldest sonne to my nephew, William Blaxtonn, of Hedley, in the Countie of Durham, hoping that he, will feare God and seek the advancement of his house and posteritie. I give unto my said Nephew, Ralph Blaxton, all that my messuage or tenement called Netherfreerside, with all lands, tenements thereunto belonging lying and beinge in the parish of Tanfield, in the Countie of Durham, to him and his heirs for ever, in as large and ample manner as they are granted to me from my Brother, Sir Nicholas Tempest, of Stelley, in the Countie of Durham, Knight. Also to my said nephew, Ralph Blaxton, one Rent charge of Three score pounds to be issuing and going forth of the lands, tenements in the County of Durham, to be paid to the said Ralph and his heires for ever at the feasts of Penticost and St. Martin's the

---

[1] I. Roger Blakiston of Gibside, will dated, 12 Nov., 1569 (the Inventory is printed in this series, 112, p. 49) by his wife, Eleanor, dau. of . . . . Millot of Whithill, had, with other issue—
II. William of Gibside, bur. at Whickham, 18 Feb., 1607/8, mar. Joan, dau. of Robert Lambton of Lambton, bur. at Whickham, 14 Mch., 1604/5, died without issue.
III. George of Hedley Hall, mar. Eleanor, dau. of John Thaine of Swaffham, co. Norfolk, had, with other issue,
IV. Sir William of Gibside, knt., aged 38 at his uncle William's *Inq. p.m.* taken 17 Mch., 1607/8, at Durham, bur., 18 Oct., 1641, at Whickham, mar. Jane, dau. of Robert Lambton of Lambton (sister to the wife of his uncle William), bur. 11 Nov., 1648, and had, with other issue.
V. Sir Ralph of Gibside, aged 26, 1615, created a Baronet 30 July, 1642, bur., 20 Jan., 1650/1 having mar., firstly, Frances, dau. of Sir Charles Wren of Binchester (bapt., 1 Sept., 1598, at St. Andrew's, Auckland, and died without issue); and, secondly, Margaret, dau. of Sir William Fenwick of Wallington, Northumberland, by whom he had five sons and two daughters.

Bishop in Winter, and such yearly rent to be paide att or within
the Manor house or Capitall messuage of Gibside aforesaid. I give
and bequeath unto my nephew, William Blaxton, of Hedley, these
parcells of plate and household stuffe hearafter followinge—that is
to say—Three gobletts with one cover, six white bowells, three
bigger and three lesser, two white silver peeces, one gilded saltt,
one white salt, and one white trencher salt, three dozen and fower
silver spoons, two London bedsteads, the one in the great chamber,
the other in the new hie chamber, with two trunkle bedds to them
belonging, three tables, two in the hall and one new London table
in the great chamber, with a court cupbord belonging to the
same, One great presse in the old parlour, The brewing lead
withall vessells thereunto belonginge. Nevertheless, my Will and
pleasure is absolutelie that my said nephew, William Blaxtonn,
shall not during his life alyenate or sell anie of the said plait,
implements of householde before mentioned, but shall suffer them
to remayne and to be in the said house at Gibside as heirelooms
to the said house, and shall either by his last Will or by some
Deed executed in his lifetyme, soe dispose of the said plait and
implements of household aforenamed as the same shall come to his
sone, Ralph Blaxtonn, after the death of him, the said William
Blaxtonne, or to such heires as shall happen to be heire unto the
said William Blaxton. My will and pleasure is that my nephew,
Henry Blaxton, shall have my colemynes in the Snipe, as well
opened or not opened, and do hereby give unto my said nephew,
Henrie Blaxton, all lands and grounds within the Snipe to sink
pitts and to wynn and work the said pitts for his use and benefit
from and after the death of me the said William Blaxton, for and
during the term of 21 years from thence next insuing, which said
coalmynes and libertie of Egress and Regress . . . . I give to my
nephew, Ralph Blaxton, my two golde chymes. I give and
bequeath to my sisters, Grace Shaftoe, Marie Hardcastle and
Ellinor Bennett, to everie of them, 6l. 13s. 4d., and to my sister,
Barbara Blaxton, 20l., And to my sister, Dorothie, 5l. I do give
unto my nephew, Christopher Hedworth, of Pockerley, his children,
10l. I give unto my nephew, Henry Blaxton, three score pounds.
I give unto my two neeces, Johann Morrell and Alice Hix, each
6l. 13s. 4d. I give and bequeath unto my nephew, William
Blaxton, my best horse. I give unto my neece, Jane, wife of my
nephew William Blaxton, all my lait wiffe's apparell. To my
nephew, Nicholas Blaxton, second son of my nephew, William
Blaxton, 200l. to pay one annuity or yearly rent charge for the
natural life of the said Nicholas Blaxton. I give and bequeath
unto my nephew, William, his other seven children, that is to say,
John Blaxton, Roger Blaxton, Lyonel Blaxton, William Blaxton,
Dorothie Blaxton, Jane Blaxton, and Barbara Blaxton, each 20l.
My will is that, if it please God, my neece, Jane Blaxton, be
saiflie delivered of one livinge child or more, that then the said

child or children borne alive shall have the like somme of 20*l.* a peece of lawful English money. I give and bequeath unto my wellebeloved brother-in-law, Sir Nicholas Tempest, of Stelley, Knight, one graye gelding now in the custodie of my nephew, William Blaxton. I give unto my wellbeloved sister in law, the ladie Isabell Tempest, wife of the said Sir Nicholas Tempest, one olde Ryall, and to every one of the children of the said Nicholas, that is to say, Thomas Tempest, William Tempest, Henrie Tempest, the ladie Isabella Bulmr, Mrs. Jane Chaitor and Margaret Tempest, each one olde Angell. I give unto my well-beloved friend and cozen, Thomas Riddell, of Gateshead, Esquire, fower old angells. To everie of my household servants, 5*s.* apeece. To the poor prisoners in the goale of Durham from the tyme of my death for and dureing the tearm of twentie yeais, the sume of 20*s.* yearly issueing out of all my lands in this my Will not bequeathed, and the like sume of 20*s.* yearly for the tearme afore-said unto the poore people of the pish of Whickham. And my will is that the 20*s.* to be payed to the prisoners in Durham goall shall be paid yearly unto the Maior of Durham for the time being, to be distributed amongst the said prisoners according to the meaning of this my Will. And the 20*s.* to be payd unto the poore of the pish of Whickham shall be paid unto the churchwardens of the said parish. I give unto my nephew, Ralph Blaxton, the full moytie and one halfe part of all my goods and chattels in this my Will not formerlie bequeathed, and I doe hereby appoint my said welbeloved Nephew, Raph Blaxtonn, sole Executor of this my last Will and Testament. I give the residue of my goods and chattels, moveable and unmoveable, unto my said nephew, Ralph Blaxtonne. I do intreat and require my wellbeloved brother-in-law, Sir Nicholas Tempest, Knight, and my loving friend and Cozen, Thomas Riddell, Esquire, to see this my last Will pformed and executed, and also appoint them supersrs. Witnesses. Nicholas Tempest, Tho. Riddell, John Johnson, Roger Colsonn, Robert Forster.

Feb 24, 1607. INVENTORY of all the goods and chattels of William Blakiston, late of Gibside, in the parish of Whickham, Esquire, deceased, praised by these fower honest men, vizt., William Porter, James Shaftoe, Anthony Meaburne and John Blarton.

In the Kitchinge : Fower brass potts, three old mellen potts, two iron potts, one posnett, three yetlinges on morter and a pestell, six panns, three candlesticks, one dripping pann, one baster, with all other furniture as Iron and pewter vessel in the Kitchinge = 5*l.* 16*s.* 3*d.* In the Maid's Chamber : Two borded bedsteads with clothes to them, 6*s.* In the Hall, wch are heire-looms : One table with a frame and a cupboarde table, one other cupboarde and a side table, 42*s.* 6*d.* In the Butterie : Eight puter dublers, two basons and ewers, fower candlesticks, five

chamberpotts, two dozen trenchers, three canns, three potts, 30s.
In the Celler : Five hogsheads, two barralls, five halfe barrells,
13s. 4d. In the olde'Parlor in heirloome : a pressor, 13s. 4d.,
one stand bedd, one hurle bedd, one square cupboarde, one hie
cupboard, one long settle, six pistolls, one pair of virginalls,
two Joyne stolls, one lowe stoll, one little chair, 2l. 19s. All the
plaite which is an heyrlome, 40l., also three gobletts with a
coveringe, six bowells, two cupps, one nest of tunnes, one gilt
salt, one white salt, and one trencher salt, three dozen and fower
spoones. Item, twentie howle puter dishes, 14 sawcers, 12 jellie
dishes, 12 trencher plates, 6 slaife dishes, 2 pie plates, 4 candlesticks with 3 nossells, one warming pann, one pfume pann, one
featherbedd, one bolsterr, one mattrice, a pair of blanketts, 2
happings, one coveringe, 3 Read curtaine with vallance and
frindge, 3 old cuishions, 6l. 16s. 6d.; lynninge and napperie,
10l. In the new Porlour : 1 table, 2 forms, 2 chairs, 8 joyne
stools, 6 Turkie cuishions, one lyvorie cupboard, one litle firr
cheste and 2 carpetts of blew and grene, 4l. In the middle
Chamber, wch are heirloms : One standbedd and a truckle bedd,
one table and a leverie cupbord, 6l. 10s. Other furniture in the
same chamber as beddinge, one carpett, 14 joyne stooles and two
chares, with two lowe stooles, 8l. 10s. In the Hie Chamber, wch
are heirloms : One standbedd, 50s. Other furniture there, as
beddinge, a lyvorie cupbord, 2 chaires, 4 litle chistes, 2 trunks
and an Iron chimney, 5l. 10s. In the Scholehouse Chamber : A
borded bedsteade, with furniture and a litle cupborde, 10s. In
the White Chamber : One standbedd and a truckle bedd, with
furniture for the hie bedd, one trunck banded with iron, one
Court cupboarde, and an olde cuishion, 5l. In the Yellow
Chamber : One standbedd and a hurle bedd, with beddinge and
one chaire, 4l. In the painted Chamber : Two stand bedds, one
boarded bedstead, with their furniture, and 2 chistes, 4l., his owne
apparell, 20l., his two cheynes, 36l., his laite wife's apparell, 40l.
In the brewhouse, which are heyreloms : A brew lead with all
brewinge vessells, 40s. In the milk house : A kettle with other
wood vessell. Att Gibside : Ten draught oxen, 35l. Twelve
stotts, 24l. Twenty one Kyne, 40l. Two whies, 3l. Twelve
calfes, 6l. 10s. Rie, forty threaves, 6l. Six score ewes, 27l.
Oats, three score threaves, 5l. Fifteene bowells oat malt, 3l. One
graie stoned horse, 8l. One graie geldinge, 12l. One other
graie geldinge, 6l. Two maires and one nagge at grasse, 7l.
In corne on the grounde att Marley hill and Gibside, 7l. Att
Marley hill : Twelve draught oxen, 42l. Four kyne and calfes,
8l. Ten whies, 15l. Rie, thirtie threaves, 3l. 15s. Oats, twenty
foure threaves, 36s. Att fenhouse : Twentie winter stotts and
whies with three bull stirkes, 20l. One cowe and a calfe, 2l.
Eleven score weathers, 49l. 10s. Nine score ewes, 36l. Seventy
seven gimmers, 13l. 6s. 8d. Forty dinmoths, 8l. **Forty olde**

tupps, 6l. Twenty eight young tupps, 3l. 13s. 4d. Six score hogges, 18l. Eighteen hogge sheepe, 3l. 12s. Debts owinge to the testatore: Anthonie Layborne, 5l. Ralph Hardinge, 10l. Nicholas Arnolde, 2l. Henry Laiborne, Richard Dobsone and John Hunter, 4l. In readie money, 469l. Debts which the testator oweth: To William Marley, 3l. 6s. 8d. To John Cook, 2l. 1s. Funerall expences, 50l. Servants' wages, 3l. 11s. 6d.

BRIAN BELLASSES.[1]

July 15, 1608. In the name of God, Amen, in the yeres of the raigne of or sovereign lord James, by the grace of Gode, King of England, Scotland, France and Irelande, Defender of the faithe, etc., That is to saie, of England, France, and Ireland the sixte, and of Scotland by one and fortity. I, Brian Bellasses, of Morton, in the County of Durham, gent, Esquire. To be buried where and in such maner as my friends and executors shall thinke fitt. And for the disposicon of such lands, goods and chattells as it hath please gode to bless me withall my mynd and will is to dispose of them as hereafter followeth. First I give and bequeathe my lease of Morton, in the parish of Houghton, and my lease of my landes in Great Haswell, in the parish of Easington, unto Sir Thomas Metham, of Metham, in the County of York, Knight, and Thomas Swinburne, of Captheton, in the County of Northumberland, Esquire, and during the terme of

[1] He was the 4th son of Sir William Bellasis of Newbrough, co. York, born there, 19 July, 1559, bur. at Houghton-le-Spring, 18 July, 1608; he mar. Margaret, dau. of William Lee of Brandon, by Elizabeth, dau. of Thomas Lawson of Usworth; she re-mar. Charles Hedworth of Harraton. His brother James (died, Oct., 1640), mentioned in the will, bapt. at St. Andrew's, Auckland, 3 Dec., 1562, mar., firstly, Mary, dau. of Thomas Tunstall of Scargill, and, secondly, Isabel, dau. of Thomas Chaytor of Butterby. His eldest son, Sir William Bellasis, aged 15 at the *Inq. p.m.* of his father, taken 10 Sept., 1608, at Durham, of Morton house, Durham, bur. at Houghton-le-Spring, 6 Dec., 1641, mar. Margaret, eldest dau. of Sir George Selby of Whitehouse, 15 Jan., 1610/11, at Ryton, bur. at Houghton-le-Spring, 29 Nov., 1671; his 2nd son Timothy, bapt. 29 Dec., 1594, at St. Andrew's, Auckland, his 3rd son Richard, bapt. at St. Andrew's, Auckland, 7 May, 1598, bur. at Houghton-le-Spring, 2 June, 1624, his 4th son Henry, bapt. at St. Andrew's, Auckland, 17 May, 1599, bur. at Brancepeth, 28 May, 1603; his fifth son Charles, bapt. at Houghton-le-Spring, 14 Nov., 1603, bur. at Brancepeth, 27 July, 1606, his daus. were Mary, bapt., 10 Aug., 1601, at Houghton-le-Spring, mar. Gerard Salvin of Croxdale, bur., 19 Nov., 1678, at St. Oswald's, Durham; Joan, mar. John Vasey of Newlands, 26 Oct., 1620, at Houghton-le-Spring; Timothea, bur. at Houghton-le-Spring, 7 Feb., 1601/2; Elizabeth, also bur. there, 3 Dec., 1602; Katherine, bur. at Brancepeth, 22 July, 1606, Margaret, bur., St. Oswald's, Durham, 23 Nov., 1622; and Anne.

six yeares to the use, benifit and behoof of Richard Bellasses, my second sone, and of Mary, Joane and Margarett, my three daughters, whome my. will is shall have the benefitt and pfit of the said termes, and after the said sixe yeares, then my will is that the residue of my termes in Morton and Haswell aforesaide shall come to Willm. Bellasses, my eldest sonne, for and during the residue of my termes then therein to come and un-expired, provided alwaies and upon condicon that my said sonne, Willm. Bellasses, shall within two yeares after he shall accomplish his full age of one and twenty yeares make a good and sufficient estate in the lawe, unto Richard Bellasses, my second sonne, of soe much lande as shallbe worth in yearly value the some of 50l. of lawful money of England in the Judgmt of Sir Thomas Metham aforesaide, Knight, and Thomas Swynburne aforesaid, Esquire, and William Thursbie, Thomas Wilkinson and Robert Rutter, my trustie friends, or soe many of them as shallbe then livinge To have and to hold the said estate for and during the life naturall of the said Richard Bellasses, my second sonne, and to such wief as he, the saide Richard Bellasses, shall marry, and to the longer liver of them. And my will further is, that if my saide sonne William shall not within the said terme of two yeares after he shall accomplish his full age, make and assure so much lande and in such maner as in this my will is formerlie mentioned and sett downe unto my said sonne, Richard. That then my said sonne, Richard, shall from and after the expircon of the said two yeares enter unto my said leases of Morton and Haswell aforesaid, and then shall enjoye and the pfitts thereof, and to take unto his owne use and behoof until such time as my said sonne, Willm., shall assure and convey soe much lande as shall be worthe the yearlie value of 50l. in manner and forme as is aforesaid expressed. I give and bequeath to my said sonne, Willm., all my implements and howsehold stuff at Morton aforesaid Provided that my sonne, Willm., shall pay to my said three daughters in considercon of the said household stuffe the sum of 300l. of lawful money of England That is to saie, to each of them 100l. to be paid to them as they shall accomplish their age of one and twenty yeares or at the day of their marriage which of them shall first happen. Nevertheless my will is That Margarett, nowe my wife, shall have the use and occupacon of my howsehold stuff at Morton aforesaid, and of my howse at Morton with courtlege, orchards and gardens thereunto belonginge untill such tyme as my said sonne, Willm., shall accomplish his full age of one and twenty yeares. I give and bequeath to Margaret, my said wief, my howses in Durham during her naturall life, and also all my howsehold stuffe nowe remayning in Durham, and also my howshold stuff remayning in Newcastle provided for my saide howses at Durham, she my said wief paying unto my three daughters aforesaide the sume of 200*l.* of lawfull money of England, to be paid unto my said three daughters equallie to be divided amongst them att the day of their marriage or to when they accomplish the full age of one and twenty yeares of which of them shall first happen. Provided that if my saide wief shall not paye the said sum of 200*l.* as is afore limitted, that then this my bequest of my saide household stuff be voyde and the said household stuffe to be divided amongst my said three daughters. My will and pleasure is that if any of my said daughters shall die before they shall accomplish their full age of one and twenty yeares, or be married, that then the said sum of 300*l.* to be payd by my said sonne, Willm., for my said howsehold stuff at Morton, as the saide 200*l.* shallbe paide by my saide wief, Margaret, for the howsehold stuff at Durham, shall goe unto the survivor or survivors of my said three daughters. For the disposition of my plaite, my will is that my said sone, Willm., shall have my great bason, one ewer of silver, one great gilded salte which was my uncle's, one white silver cowle with a cover. I give and bequeath unto Margaret, my said wife, my little bason and ewer of silver, one salt dooble gilded with cover, one half dosen of gilded spoons, one great standing Cupp double gilded with cover. I give and bequeath to Willm., my sonne, my lease of Ivesley, in the parish of Brancepeth, during all the yeares therein to come and unexpired. I give unto my servante, John Fenwicke, 5*l.* of lawful money of England over and beside his wages which is due and oweing unto him. I give unto Thomas Williamson 5*l.* of lawful money of England over and above his wages due and oweing unto him. I give and bequeath unto Robert, my cooke, 10s., and to every of my woemen servants 5*s.* over and above their due wages. I give and bequeath unto my servants, Willm. Thursbie, Robert Hutton and John Rickerbie and to each of them, 3*l.* 6*s.* 8*d.* I give unto the poore the sume of 50*l.* of lawful money of England, to be given and distributed at the discretion of my well beloved wief, Margaret, Thomas Swinburne, of Captheton aforesaid, Esquire, and William Thursbie, my trustie friends, 20*l.* where of my will is it shall be distributed the daye of my buriall. I give and bequeathe unto Charles Hedworth, Esquire, my father-in-lawe, one twenty shilling peece of golde, unto my mother-in-law, his wife, two twenty shilling peeces of golde, and unto my brother in lawe, Lancelot Hodgson, and Marie, his wife, to each of them spurriall. I give to Thomas Swinburne, of Captheton aforesaid, Esquire, and to John, his sonne, to each of them one spoorriall. I give to Sir Thomas Metham, Knight, one graye mare, unridden, and unto my brother, James Bellasses, one black mare, and unto Sir Thomas Bellasses, Knight, one sparrioll. The residue of all my goods and chattells I give unto Richard, my sone, and three daughters aforesaid, whom together with Sir Thomas Metham I make my full executors of this my last

Will and Testament. Nevertheless, my will is that the said Sir Thomas Metham shall not take any interest or benefitt of my goodes by his executorshipp. For the disposition of my lands, I give and bequeath two full parts of all my lands in three parts, to be divided unto my well beloved friends, Sir Thomas Metham aforesaid, Knight, and Thomas Swinburne aforesaid, Esquire, for and during the nonage of William, my sone, for the use of Richard, my second sonne, and my afore named three daughters for their porcons. Witnesses, Tho. Swinburne, John Swinburne, Thos. Riddell, Willm. Thursbye. Proved, 11 September, 1608.

CUTHBERT COLLINGWOOD.[1]

Aug. 12, 1608. In the name of God, Amen, in the yeare of our lord after the computacon of the Church of England, 1608, and the sixth year of the raigne of or sovergn Lord James, by the grace of gode King of England, france and Ireland, defender of the faith, and of Scotland, the XLjjth, I Cuthber Collingwood, of Branton, in the County of Northumberland, Gent. To be buried in the pish churche of Eglingham as nere my ancestors as convenyentlie may be. I will and gyve to my second sonne, Thomas Collingwood, for his liefe tyme, All those two farmeholds, with lands and appurtenances thereof, in Branton aforesaid, nowe in the occupacon of the same Thomas, and his assigns, and another farmholde, with lands and appurtenances thereof, now in the occupation of Robt. Harrigate, when it falleth, he paying the accustomed rents. And I will and bequeathe to Barbara, his wyfe, halfe of the same three farmholds during her widowhood if she survive the said, Thomas, my sonne. And I will and bequeath from and after the decease of the saide Thomas, my sonne, the other halfe of the said thre farmeholds during the said widowhood of the said Barbara to the children of the same Thomas Collingwood, my sonne, and after she shall marrye, the whole thre farmholds, paying the rents accustomed for and during the terme of twenty one yeares to be accomplished

---

[1] The testator's son Daniel was his son and heir, whose noncupative will is dated, 17 June, 1618 and in whose *Inq. p.m.* 16 Jas. I., it is stated he died 18 June, 1618; he (Daniel) mar. Eleanor, dau. of Robert Mitford of Mitford; his son John was apprenticed, 13 Feb., 1611/12, to Francis Parkinson of Newcastle; his son Ephraim was not apprenticed in Newcastle.

from the decease of the same my sonne, Thomas. I gyve and bequeath to Dorothie Collingwood, my daughter, the some of Two hundreth poundes of lawful English money to be payd as followethe, that is to say, at the age of nineteene yeres fiftie poundes, and yearlie after fyftie pounds till the same some of Two hundred pounds be paid. And also I will and bequeath to the same Dorothie, towards her mayntenance till the said two hundred poundes be fullie paid, the sum of Eight pounds, saving I will and my mynd is that as every fiftie poundes shallbe paid, there shallbe fortie shillinges abated out of the said eight poundes yearlie. Provided alwaynes and upon this condition, I gyve the said some of Two hundred poundes and eight poundes yearlie to the said Dorothie, my Daughter, that she doe bestowe her self in mariage with the liking and consent of my loving frendes, Mr. Thomas Swynoe, Mr. George Muschampe and George Collingwood, Esq., otherwise she be left one hundred poundes pcell of the said legacy of two hundred poundes. I gyve and bequeath to my sonne, John Collingwood, whome I will shallbe bounde to some good occupacon or trade, the some of One hundred pounds, part whereof shallbe paid at his entrance in his apprenticehood and the other parte and residue thereof to be paid him when he shall come forth of apprenticehood or shall come to his lawful age of twenty one yeares, which shall first happen. I gyve and bequeth to my sone, Ephraime Collingwoode, the some of one hundred poundes, whom I will also shallbe bound to some good occupacon or trade, of which some I will parte thereof shall be payd at his entrance in his apprenticehood and the residue thereof as before I have lymited to my said sonne, John Collingwood. I gyve and bequeath to my sister, Jane Collingwood, one anuitie of three pounds, six shillings and eightpence during the naturall lief of the same Jane, in full payment and satisfacon of her porcon to be payd yearlie at the feasts of Pentecost and St. Mtyns the Bishop in Winter by even payments. I give and bequeath to every of my children, Thomas, Dorothie, John and Ephraime, each of them, two whyes, and to my brother's sone, George, one whie. All the residue of my goods and chattells, my debts and funerall charges being discharged, I wholy give and bequeath to my loving sonne, Daniel Collingwood, whome of this my psent testament I make and ordaine the full executor Renouncing and forsaking all former Wills and gyfts, legacies and bequests by me in any wise heretofore made or given, willed and bequeathed. And I require and intreat my loving friends, Mr. George Muschampe, Mr. Thomas Swynhoe and Cuthbert Collingwood of this my last Will to be the overseers and to se the same performed in what in them lieth, as my trust is in them. Witnesses, Geo. Collingwood, Cutht. Cheeseman, Henry Anthony, Not. Pub. Proved, 1618.

CHRISTOPHER CONYERS.[1]

Sept. 12, 1608. In the name of God, Amen, I, Christopher Conyers, of Horden, in the County of Durham, Esquire. To be buried under the blew marble stone before the church porch dore at Easington. I give unto my sone, John Conyers, one guilded salt with the cover and my signet. I give unto my daughter, Frances Conyers, wife of the saide John, one silver peece having the madens hand graven on it, and one pair of virginalls. I give unto Marie Conyers, my youngest dawghter, one winde Milne near Easinton commonly called Easinton Mille, with the lease and all other my claime, interest and tithe thereto belonging. I give unto my Brother, John Hedworth, his wife, one angell in golde. I give unto my brother, John Catherike, his wife, one angel in golde. All the rest of my goods, moveable and unmoveable, my debts, legacies and funerall expences discharged, I give unto my three daughters, Anne, Isabell and Marie Conyers, whom I make executors of this my Will and Testament, whereof I do appoint my brother, John Catherike, and Cuthbert Conyers, gentleman, supervisors, and desiring them [to see] the same faithfully executed, and to either of them I give 10s., provided I give unto my said youngest daughter, Marie Conyers, the said Wynd Milne in consideration of ten pounds given unto her by her grandmother's will, which I received to despose of to her use. Witnesses, Abraham Robinson, the Elder, John Dixon. Proved, 8 Oct., 1608.

---

[1] He mar., firstly, Elizabeth, dau. of Cuthbert Conyers of Layton, she died without issue; he mar., secondly, Anne, dau. of John Hedworth of Harraton, 14 Nov., 1586, at Chester-le-Street, she was bur. at Easington, 19 Jan., 1597/8. With other issue they had John, bapt. at Easington, 8 July, 1593, created a Baronet, 14 July, 1628, bur. 6 Dec., 1664, at Easington, whose marriage is entered in the Easington registers as follows :—" 1608, John Conyers and Francis Graves, did acknowledge that (wth theire owne most willinge consent, as alsoe wth the consent of their parents Expofer Conyers, Esq., John Hedworth, gent., and An, his wife) the sayde John and Francis were solemnly married att Yorke about towe years before the registringe hereof. In the prsence of us, witnesses of this acknowledgment as alsoe of the givinge and recevige of one peece of gould for the further confirminge of this acknowlegmit, test. Thomas Bambridge, Cuthbert Conyers, Expofer Bainbridge, John Dixon. Abraham Robinson, Clric—" John Hedworth had mar. Ann, widow of Thomas Graves, alderman of York, the mother of Frances, at Skelton, 1606, Frances was bur. at Easington, 24 Jan., 1634/5. The testator's daus Isabel, mar. Charles Hall, 19 Dec., 1610, at Easington, and Marie, bapt., 18 Sept., 1597, mar. 14 July, 1624, Samuel Hessell, also at Easington, where the testator was bur. 23 Sept., 1608. His *Inq. p.m.* was taken at Durham, 12 Jan., 1608/9; his son John, aged 15, is his son and next heir.

37

JOHN RICHARDSON.[1]

Jan. 10, 1608. In the name of Gode, Amen, I, John Richardson, of Bp Auckland. I give unto my wyfe, Magdalen, my nowe dwellinghouse unto such tyme as my eldest sonne, Richard, shall come to the full age of 21 yeares, and if it please gode that my wyfe doe live longer and doe not marrye, I geve unto her duringe hir lyfe the house which Richard Slater now dwelleth in. I give unto my sonne, John, my tenement in L. Hunwick, if it may stand good with the favour of the Deane and Chapter; if it may not stand good my will is that whether soever of my executors it shall lawfullie come unto, that they paye unto my sayd sone, John, the sume of foure score poundes within one whole yeare after my decease. Also I gyve unto my said sonne, John, all that my free house and lands in Barnard castle to him and his heires for ever. I give unto my sonne, Ambrose, my burgage that Martyn Todd dwelleth in and all my land which I bought of Bryan Downes to him and his heires for ever, and 20*l.* in money. I give unto my daughter, Anne Richardson, and to her heirs for ever my two burgages in Newgate which John Willson and Robt. Crokelt dwelleth in, and 30*l.* in money. To my daughter, Susanna, and her heires my burgage which Willm. Frissell dwelleth in, and 30*l.* in monie. I give to my daughter, Cicely, the sum of 5*l.* I give to my daughter, Phillis Richardson, three score pounds. To my daughter, Margaret, three score pounds To every child which I did christen, 5*s.* a piece. To the stock of the parish of St. Andrew's, Auckland, for the poore, 40*s.* I give to my mother in law, 40*s.* To my Brother, Bartholomew Mason, 40*s.* To Christopher Martyndale, 6*l.* 13*s.* 4*d.* To my base sonne, Symon Richardson, 6*l.* 13*s.* 4*d.* To my sister-in-law, Margaret Trinkle, 40*s.* To Mr. Fell, the Curat, 40*s.* To the children of my cosen, Hugh Hyendall, 20*s.*, to be equally devided amongst them. I give to my brother, Gawen Ratclife, 5*s.* To the mending of the high wayes, 10*s.* To the three youngest of Henry Bayles' children 5*s.*, to be equally divided. The residue of all my goodes, moveable and unmoveable, I give to Magdalene, my wief, and Richard Richardson, whom I make executors of this my Will and Testament. Lastlye, I make supervisors of this my testament Henry Bayles and Roger Bradley, desiring them to see it fulfilled and kept accordinge to my true intent and

[1] The testator was bur. in the Church of St. Andrew, Auckland, 12 Jan., 1608/9; his widow, Magdalen remar., 27 Nov., 1610, Emanuel Grice, also at St. Andrew's, from which registers the following dates are taken. His son Richard, bapt., 28 Oct., 1595, mar. Joan Wright, 6 Jan., 1617/18; John, bapt., 11 Mch., 1598/9; Ambrose, bapt., 10 Apl., 1603, bur., Mch., 1609. " of the plague "; Cicely, bapt., 15 Feb., 1600/1, bur., 29 Sept., 1619; Anne, bapt., 6 Oct., 1605; Susanna, bapt., 20 Mch., 1607/8. In the *Inq. per br. de mand.* taken at Durham, 9 Mch., 1610/11, his son Richard, aged 13, is his next heir.

38

meaning. And I give unto eith of them 5s. for their paynes. In witness whereof I have sett my hand this 10 day of January, 1608, in the presence of John Fell, minister, Henry Bayles, Bartholomew Mason, Christopher Martindale. Proved, 18 January, 1608.

THOMAS OTWAIE.[1]

Feb. 26, 1608. In the name of God, Amen, I, Thomas Otwaie, of Preston, of the pish of Tynmouth. To be buried in the parish Church of Tynmouth aforesaid. I give to my wife, Jane Otwaie, all my houses and free land in Tynmouth during her life naturall. I give to my said wife one cottage house in Preston next adjoining unto the nowe dwelling-house of Robert Speerman on the east side and all my free land in Preston during her life naturall. I give to my said wife three kyne, one baye fillie and thirteene sheepe. I give to my sonne, Thomas Otwaie, eight oxen and foure horses, with all my husbandry geare, also foure kie and thirteen sheepe. I give to my daughter, Katheren Otway, foure kyne, twenty sheepe, one black meare and the three score pounds which Richard Hodgson, of Whitley, is bound to pay unto me if his sonne and my said daughter do not agree to proceed in marriage according to the covenants agreed upon betwixt him and me. I give to my said daughter Two oxen and fower stotts. I will that my executors shall give to my said daughter her wedding clothes and a bridwaine according to the custom of the country. I give to my said daughter two howses and two garthes in the west end of Tymouth in the South Rowe, and an other howse and a garthe situate and next adjoining unto the now dwellinghouse of John Pearson on the west side, and one howse and a garth in the back Rowe next adjoining unto the ladies howse on the east side and the free land belonginge to that howse. After the decease of my wief, my will is that my wife shall have (dureinge her widowhood) my farme at Backworth, with the corne on the grounde. And my sonne, Thomas, to have my farme in Prestone, with the corne on the grounde. I give to Robert Otwaie, of Preston, one boule of malt and a boule of wheate. I give to Robert Otwaie, of Tynmouth, seven shillings. I give to my sister, Elizabeth

[1] Thomas Otway was bur. at Tynemouth, 28 Feb., 1608/9. His son Thomas, mar., 18 Nov., 1610, Elizabeth Mills, and making his will, 17 Nov., 1634, was bur. at Tynemouth, 6 Dec., 1634; Katherine does not seem to have mar. Richard Hodgson as their marriage has not been found, but we do find a man of this name marrying, 24 May, 1612, Margaret Errington, and also on the 27 Oct., in the same year, a Katherine Otway marries Roger Morton; there is a pedigree of this second Thomas in the *New County History of Northumberland*, viii., 346.

Hyndmers, of Tynmouth, nine Bowle of wheate, to be delivered at Mychellmass next, and to her youngest daughter seven shillings. My will is that my executors shall give twenty shillinges to the poore of the parish. And all the rest of my goods I give to my wife, Jane, and my sonne, Thomas, whom I make joint executors of this my last Will and Testament. Witnesses, John Hyndmers, Robert Spearman, Tho. Bell, Robert Potts. INVENTORY, 145*l.* 11*s.* 4*d.* Proved, 1609.

RALPH TROLOP.[1]

April 11, 1609. In the name of God, Amen, I, Ralph Trolop, of Elvitt, within the suburbs of the Cittye of Durham, Gentleman. To be buryed in the parish churchyarde of St. Oswald's in Durham. I give and bequeath unto my sone, John Trolop, 10*l.* for his child's porson. I give and bequeath to my daughter, Jayne Trolop, 10*l.* for her child's purson. I do give to my daughter, Elizabeth Trolop, 10*l.* for her child's porshon. I give unto my wief, Margaret Trolop, 5*l.* All the rest of my goods, moveable and unmovable, my debts and funeral expences, to be discharged, I doe give it to my wief, Margarett Trolop, whom I doe make my executor of this my Will. For my now dwelling-house I doe give it to my wief, Margarett Trolop, during her life, and then for to come to my daughter, Elizabeth Trolop, and defer back to my sone, John Trolop and his heirs, and for lack of issue to come to my daughter, Jane Trolop, and her heires. Witnesses, Robert Pearson, Thos. Atkinson. Proved, 15 December, 1609.

WILLIAM SANDERSON.[2]

Sept. 7, 1609. In the name of God, Amen, I, William Sanderson, of Barnard Castle, in the Bishoprick of Durham. To be buried in the Church of Barnard Castle in or near my stalle where my wife lieth, the dueties thereto accustomed, contented and paid. I give to the poore of Barnard castle tenn shillings. Whereas my nephew, Charles Sanderson, by a bill under his hand acknowledged, is owing to my daughter, Elizabeth, the sume of seven pounds, six shillings and fourpence,

[1] Ralph Trollop was bur. at St. Oswald's, Durham, 13 Apl., 1609, and his widow Margaret at the same place, 3 Nov. 1612, where their children were bapt., viz.:—John, 10 Apl., 1603, Thomas, 28 July, 1606, and Elizabeth, 17 Jan. 1607/8.

[2] The diary of Christopher Sanderson is printed in this Society's publications, vol. 118, pp. 35-42, and William Sanderson's will amplifies the pedigree printed in that vol. on page 36.

which formerly I did give and grant to her to be set forward to
her use; over and beside the said sume, I give to her soe much
more money to be taken forth of my goods as will make the same
tenne pounds, and I give to her beside all such implements of
householde as are conteyned in one Schedull in the custody of
Michael Walker, and also my second cloke to make her a cote,
and my best hatt and my best band, and my will is that the
premises to her given and bequeathed as aforesaid shallbe unto
her a full satisfaction contenacon and paymentt of all her filiall
and child's pporcon of goods. Whereas I have formerly given
to my son, Christopher Sanderson, the sum of tenn pounds which
is imployed to his use over and above the same. I give to him
my best cloke, two fuschian dubletts, three paire of breeches,
and my new Deune, third stockings, my shirts, and the rest of
my shert bands, and my seate in the south porch of the Church.
And my will is that the said legacies and premises shallbe to him
a full contentacon and paymentt of all his filiall and child's
porcon of goods. I give to my Brother, Thomas Sanderson, my
best Jackett; and to his sonne my second hatt, and to Bartholo-
mewe, his second sonne, twelve pence. And whereas I have been
at great charges in education of my sonne, George Sanderson,
in respect whereof he of his good will hath given me his consentt
that whatsoever was his right by me, I should bestowe the same
on his Brother, Ralphe, yet my will is that my said sonne, Ralph,
in respect thereof and as a remembrance to confirm his former
consentt shall give my sonne, George, foure angells of gold,
which I hertily pray my said sonne, George, to accept in good
part in respect to the premises. I give to my sone in lawe,
Gabriel Wharton, the fogging and wintering of one cowe, from
St. Michaell's day next to the third day of May then next after.
And I give to his thre children, each of them, 6s. 8d. I give
to my said nephew, Charles Sanderson, my best dublett. I give
to Isabell Sanderson, his sister, two shillings to buy her a Lynnen
aprone. I give to my sister in lawe, Mary Thorpe, and my
daughter in law, Phillis Thorpe, a french crowne as a token of
rembrance between them. I give to the youngest children of my
brother Bartholomew Sanderson, Robert, Reynold and Arthur,
each of them, two shillings. I give to my said sonne, Ralph Sandersone, the seate in the Church in the stall with Ralph Rowland-
son. And I give to my said sone-in-law, Gabriell Wharton, my seat
in that stall in the Middle of the Church beside the Middle pillare.
In respect of some household implements not given to my daughter,
Elizabeth, which my will is shall remayne to my sonne, Ralphe,
that is to say, all the sealed work in my house, one stand bedd in
the chamber, one arke, a presser, one iron chimney, my gowne,
one table in the Hall house with a forme theire to belonginge,
I will that if my said daughter do marry, my said sone, Ralphe,
shall give my said daughter 6s. 8d. The rest of all my goods,

chattells and cattell whatsoever not before bequeathed, my debts, legacies being paid, and my funerall expences honestly discharged by my said sone, Ralphe, I give and bequeath the same to him, I order and make him my full executor. Witnesses, Charles Sanderson, Gabriell Wharton and Michael Walker. Proved, 7 October, 1609.

THOMAS SALVEN.[1]

Oct. 15, 1609. In the name of God, Amen, I, Thomas Salven, of Thorneton, in the County of Durham, gent. To be buried, if it shall please almightie gode to call me to his mercy, within the Bishoprick of Durham, to be buryed within the Quere at St. Oswold's, in the suborbs of Durham, so nye as maie be to my first wife, my brother, and nephew Salvin, givinge the daie of my funerall to every poore bodie that shall come to demande the sume, a peny, and five pounds within the said pish to be distributed by my executors or friends putt in trust for the same to the poore sorte within the said pish at their discretions, and to the poore prisoners there at their discretion. I give to my loving wife, Rebecca Salven, the coch and horses with all furniture for the same And all the bedds and bedding in the Chamber called the gallerie chamber att Thornton Also two silver boules, one of the greater sorte, the other of the lesser, A dosen of silver spoones with round ends, half a dosen of throwen work stooles, and two chares, one of velvet, other of greene, as she liketh best, also a gylt boule, a gilt salte which was hers A good horse for a servinge man neather best or worse. I give and bequeath to my daughter, Mary Salven, 500l., and to each of my other children 400l. apece, to be yearley taken and had of the rents of my lease of Thorneton under Rysebrough, the rent for the first halfe yeare after my decease to be paid to my daughter, Mary, the second halfe yeare to my sonne, Robert, and for every halfe yeare after to others of my children as they are in aige, and when everie of them have had 100l., then the next to Mary and soe to the rest till they have received the said severall sums, and to be maynteined with 10l. a peece till they have received each of them 100l. And as each of them shall receive 100l., then to have after but 5l. a peece till 200l. for each of them respectively shall have been

[1] Thomas Salvin, son of Gerard Salvin of Croxdale, by his wife Eleanor, dau. of William Wren of Billyhall, was bur. at St. Oswald's, Durham, 15 Oct., 1609, where his first wife Jane was also bur., 9 Aug., 1592, his second wife, Rebecca, 7th dau. of Sir Cuthbert Collingwood of Dalden and Eslington, being also bur. at St. Oswald's, 10 Jan., 1655/6, "aged." In the *Inq. per br. de mand.* taken at Durham, 22 June, 1610, John, aged 13, is his son and next heir.

received 200*l*. apeece, and after not to have any allowance for
and in lew and full satisfaction of there filiall and child's
porcons of all my goods and chattells whatsoever The said summes
of monie as they shall arise to my said children I most hartely
intreat my loveing and kind friendes, William Wicliffe, of
Wicliffe, Esq., my nephew, Jarrard Salvin, Esquier, and my
brother, Robt. Collingwood, gent, to take speciall caire of the
disposcinge thereof for the good of my said children. And if
anie of my daughters be not ruled in there marriage by consent
and advice of there mother if she be livinge, or if deceased, by
the advice of the other three or the survivors of them, then
she that shall marrye in other sorte to lose halfe hir porcon,
to be divided equally amongst these that shall marrye with
consent and allowance aforesaid. I doe give unto my eldest
sonne, John Salvin, all my plate not before bequeathed to my
wife, or that were not given to my other children as godbarne
gifts, which my wife knoweth in particular. I give to Edward
Wright, sone of Richard Wright, 20*l*., if I doe not in my life
tyme disburse the same to him or for his use. I give and
bequeath to my servant, George Man, all the interest I have in
the walke mill close, and to his wife a 20*s*. peice in gould, and
to his sonne, Thomas Man, 6*l*. 13*s*. 4*d*. I give unto Christopher
Bulman 3*l*. 6*s*. 8*d*. by yeare dureing his life, to be paid halfe
yearly by equal porcons. I doe moreover given unto George Man
and Christopher Bulman, to each of them, a suite of apparell,
reserveing the best to my eldest sone, vizt., to each of them,
dublett, hose and Gyrkin. I give to Henry Davis, my man,
6*l*. and a dublett and hose. To all my other servantes I give and
bequeath a quarter's wages over and besides there dew wages.
I give unto the poore of Coniscliffe parish, 40*s*. And to the
poore of Ayckliffe pish, 3*l*. 6*s*. 8*d*. To Mr. Thomas Chaytor five
pounds in twenty shillings peices if I die before him; if he dye
before me I am to have the like of him. I give to my neice,
Ellenore Salven, to whom I helped to given Christendome, 5*l*.
I give to my niece, Anne Salven, widow, one old angell which
hir husband did give to me. Lastly I make, constitute and
ordaine my loveing sonne, John Salvin, my sole executor, and
until he come of age I desire my said trusty and well beloved
friends, William Wicliffe, Jerrard Salvin and Robt. Collingwood, to have, receyve and take the disposition of all things
during the minoritie of my said sonne. And for that my said
wife is not capable of dower thirdes or jointure, being not
obedient to the lawes, yet my heartie desire to my said friends
is dureing the minority of my said sonne she be found with all
things necessarie for her and in as good sorte as she haith
been maynteyned in my time, and after my sonne shall come
of aidge, I bequeath him to doe the like, as in all dewtye and
nature he is bounde. And I doubte nothing but he will. I

give to each of my said friendes, Willm. Wicliffe, Jerrard Salven and Robt. Collingwood, 5*l.* a piece in gold for a remembrance of me and myne, desiring them in this my last request to have care of the education of my children and disposing of that which [is] to befall them. In witness whereof to this my psent will, revoking all former Wills, I have putt my hand and seale the 15th of October, 1609. Sealed and delivered in the psence of us, William Blakeston, Richard Salven, Henry Davis.

Memorandum. That my mynde is that Thomas Man shall have 20 markes to bind him apprentice againe, and that his father, when his lease ends of the Walke Milne, shall have 40*s.* every duringe his naturall life, and that my executors shall paie the same and my sonne when he comes of yeares. My minde is if my Cooke be in my service at my deathe then my mind is that my Cooke shall have a yeares wages and a dublett and a piece of hose.

THOMAS WAYLES.[1]

Nov. 3, 1609. In the name of God, Amen, I, Thomas Wayles, of Sandgate, nighe unto the towne of Newcastle upon Tyne, shippe carpenter. To be buryed after my departure from this lieffe in the Church of All Sts. in the towne of Newcastle aforesaid nighe unto my father and other my children there already buryed. Secondly, I give and bequeath to the poore of All Sts. tenne shillings. I give and bequeath unto my sonne, Robt. Wayles, my great celler and howse wherein Jenkyne Pottes now dwelleth. I give and bequeath to Thomas Collyer and his wiffe, Barbarie, and their eldest sonne, John, and to the longer liver of them, three of my howses wherein they nowe dwell, they and the longer lyver of them paying yearly to my sone and his heyres or assigns three pence lying money at the feaste of St. Martyn the Bishopp in winter, and after the decease of the longer liver thereof of them three, then I will that the sayd howses shall retorne to the possession of my sonne, Robt., and his heires, and for wante thereof to his next of kindred. I give and bequeath to my daughter, Jane Wayles, the head howse where now Peter Bowton dwelleth, and after her decease to the heyres of her body lawfully begotten, and in want of such her heyres, I will that the sayd howse shall retorne to the possession of my aforesayd sonne, Robt., and his heyres or next of kindred in want of him and his heyres. And I will that my daughter,

[1] The testator was bur. at All Saints', Newcastle, 5 Nov., 1609, his widow being also bur. there, 16 Feb., 1635/6. Their son Robert, bapt., 13 Mch, 1602/3, mar. Barbary Crawforth. 13 Oct, 1625, she being bur. at All Sts., 27 Dec., 1628.

Jayne, and her heyres, so long as they enjoye that house, shall yearly payre to my sonne, Robt., or his heyres three pence at the feaste of St. Martyne the bishoppe in winter as a knowledge pennye. I give and bequeath to my daughter, Margaret Wayles, and her heyres of her bodye lawfullie begotten, the howse wherein wydowe Chamber now dwelleth, my said daughter Margaret Wayles, and her heyres yelding and paying yearlie to my sonne, Robt., and his heyres three pence yearlye at the feaste abovesayd as a knowledge penny, and after her decease or wante of such heyres, then I will that the sayde howse shall retorne to the possession of my sonne, Robt., and his heyres or next of kindred. I give and bequeath to my daughter, Elizabeth Wayles, and the heyres of her bodye lawfully begotten the howse adjoining to thee howse wherein Thomas Richardson, Keylman, now dwelleth, she and her heyres aforesaid paying at the feaste of St. Martyne aforesaid to my sonne, Robt., and his heyres three pence as a knowledge penny, and after her decease and want of heyre of her bodye lawfully begotten, I will that the said house shall returne to the possession of my sonne, Robt., and the heyres of his bodye lawfully begotten or next of kynred. I give and bequeath to my wyffe, Margery Wayles, my now in dwellinge and the other two howses adjoininge to my daughter Jane her house adjoining during hir lyffe naturall, my said wyfe paying all outrents belonging to the said howses, and after the decease of my said wyffe, then I will the possession of the aforesaid howses to retorne to my sonne, Robt., and his heyres and he to pay all outrents. I give and bequeath to my sonne, Robt., the new howse yett to builde and the outrente which are dewe unto me and myne, viz., out of the lands and tenements of Burtromes howses, 6s. 4d.; out of the howse of Henry Brantingham, 5s.; out of Thomas Reedes house, 9s. 4d.; and out of John Sotheranns howse, 7s. And for as much as I have alreedye endowed and payd to Ann Moulde, my daughter, and wyffe to John Mould, according to my promise, 20l., and her husband craveth 20l. morre I think that in money and household stuff at dyvers tymes geven (as is not unknowen to my wiffe) I have fullv satisfied the same and done more to my sayd daughter then I can do to any other of my daughters yett to marrye, yet I give and bequeath to every childe that she now haith one angel apiece and to her selfe thirteen shillinges and four pence as tokens. I give and bequeath to Thomas Collyer his three children, to either of them, one angel. I give and bequeathe to my man, Richard Ellezone, a newe siute of apparell, one axe and a theecke and a sea chyste. The rest of my goods, moveable and unmoveable, my debts, legacies, children's porcons yet unmarried, and funeral expences dyscharged, I will they be ordered at the discretion of my wyffe, as my speciall trust is in her, and of my sone, Robt., when he cometh to discretion. And I will that

my sayd wyffe shall have the tuition and education of my sayd
sonne and his other sisters yett unmarried. And I constitute,
ordeyne and make my sone, Robert Wayles, sole Executor of this
my last Will and Testament. Witnesses, John Wood, Curate,
Mary Wilkinson, wydowe, Thomas Collyare, Barbary Collyor,
with others. Proved, 1609.

RAPHE FETHERSTONHAUGH.

Nov. 27, 1609. Will of Raphe Fetherstonhaugh, of the par
of Stanhope, County of Durham. To be buried within the church
of Stanhope. To the poor people of Stanhope, 20s. To Cuthbert
Emmerson, son of my sister, Joan Emmerson, £4. To Esabell
and Ann Emmerson, my said sister's daughters, either of them,
£3, and to every one of her other children, 50s. I give to Elizabeth Todd, my aunt, 20s., to be paid unto her in fower yeares
next after my death, and if it please God to take her out of
this life before she be fullye paid, etc. To Thomas Emmerson,
my servant, one yow. To Janet Robynson, my maide, one lambe.
My will is that my wife shall withal convenient speed that may be,
renew the lease of my tenement of the Newpark in my daughter
Phillisse' name, if it please my Lord of Durham so to grant it,
and if my said daughter happen to marry, then my will is that
ther be so much of my tenement bestowed on her as to the
discretion of John Featherstonhaugh, Esquire, my kind friend,
Mr. Ralph Featherstonehaugh, Mr. Anthony Pagge, George
Emmerson of Ludwell, and William Stobbes. I give to John
Featherstonhaugh, one young mare. I give to George Hall,
Curate of Stanhope, 10s. I give to John Fetherstonhaugh, parish
clerk, one yow. The rest of all my goods, movable and unmovable,
I give to Elizabeth Featherstonhaugh, my wife, and to Philisse,
my daughter, whom I make executrixes of this my will. Will
proved 11th Jan., 1609, by Elizabeth Featherstonhaugh, Widow,
the Relict for her use and also that of her daughter, Philisse
Featherstonhaugh (now a minor), the other executrix. *Sum totalis*,
£527 10s. 11d. Proved, 1609.

ROGER WAILES.

Dec. 15, 1609. In the name of God, Amen, I, Roger Wailes,
of Throckley, within the parish of Newburn. To be buried within
the parish church of Newburne, willing my executor to discharge
all dewties and dewes thereto belonging. I bequeath and give
to my daughter, Jane Wailes, foure oxen and two kye with calfe
of the best. I have and withall one stote and one qui and ten
sheepe, five ewes and five hoggs. And also I bequeath and give
to my daughter, Jane Wales, the third of all my household stuff

thereto belonging to her. I bequeth and give to Elynor, my wife, two kye and the other halfe of my household stuff to my wife, and likewise I bequeath and give to Elynore Wailes, my wiffe, the third of all my corne during the yeares that is betwen Gawen Taylor and me. I bequeath and give to my sonne, Mathew Wailes, two oxen, the best that I have, and two other oxen. I bequeath and give to my sonne, Mathew Wales, one horse to discharge my funeral. I give and bequeath to Mathew Wales, my sonne, two parts of my corne during the yeares between Gawen Taylor and me. And I give and bequeath to my said sonne, a long waine, short waine, plow and plow irons, sommes, yokes, and all things else belonging to husbandry, Whome I make my whole executor of this my last Will and Testament by these presents or witnesses. Witnesses, John Wilson, Edward Swinburne, Richard Carnabye, John Mylburne, Edward Richardson, Roger Breckley, with others.

INVENTORY, 23*l*. 10*s*. 10*d*. Proved, 18 December, 1610.

ELIZABETH MADDESON.[1]

Feb. 16, 1609. I, Elizabeth Maddeson, of the pish of Chester, in the County of Durham, widow. To be buryed wthin my pish Church of Chester in hoop of a joyful resurrection to everlastinge life. Item, I give tenn shillings to the poor to be distributed by my executors. I give to Isabel Maddeson, eldest daughter to Richard Maddeson, one gowded white stirke and an ould Armorie. I give to Margaret Maddeson one blacke guye calfe and one chist. I give to Margaret Pounshon, dowghter to Edward Pounshon, one close Cawle, one new chist in the chamber. And to Elspeth Pounshon, younger daughter of the said Edward, one cowle. I give to Richard Maddeson, my sone, my plough, plough geare, waen and waen geare, and all the tyrement thereto belonginge. I give one branded stott of two yeares old to Richard Maddeson. The resydue of all my goods and chattels, moveable and unmoveable, unbequeathed I give to Richard Maddeson and Margaret Punshon, my two children. And I do constitute, ordaine and make the said Richard Maddeson and Margaret Poushon, executorix of this my last Will and Testament. Witnesses, Thomas Liddell, minister, Robert Marley and Leonarde Summersyde.

An INVENTORIE conteninge a true note of all the goods and chattells, moveable and unmoveable, that Elizabeth Maddeson, late of Pelton, died possessed of at the houre of her death truly prised by foure honest men, viz., Robert Marley, Leonard Summercide, William Maddeson and John Laying, the 30th of Julie, 1611.

[1] She was bur. at Chester-le-Street, 21 July, 1612; her dau. Margaret mar. Edward Punshon, 25 May, 1588.

Impris : Two oxen and one oxe stirke, 6*l*. Four kie, 30*s*. a peece, amounting to 6*l*. One gowded stirke, 15*s*. One black guye calfe, 4*s*. One branded stott, 16*s*. Two acres sowen of hard corne, 40*s*. Two acres sowen of other corne, 6*s*. 8*d*. Plough and plough geare, waen and waen geere, prised to 30*s*. One meate table with formes to the same, 3*s*. 4*d*. One Iron chymney, with implements, 3*s*. 4*d*. One leden tub and one oulde Amorie, 3*s*. 4*d*. One ould brocken chist, 6*d*. One close cawell, 5*s*. One other chiste, 12*d*. Her apperall, 10*s*. Summe, 19*l*. 13*s*. 2*d*. Proved, 1612.

ROBERT LAWSON.

July 26, 1610. Robert Lawson, of Longhirst, in the parish of Bothall, Yeoman. To be buried in the parish of Bothall. To the poor of the parish, 10*l*. To the Churchwardens of the said parish, 10*s*., towards repaireing of the church. I give unto my eldest sone, Robert Lawson, and his heirs male lawfully begotten my tenement or farmhold wherein I dwell at this instant, with all buildings, cotages and hereditaments thereon with all my crops. Also two large chists, one great brass pott and potts which are heirlooms. I give unto my second sone, William Lawson, and the heirs male of his body lawfully begotten, all that my tenement or farmhold lying and being in Longhirst, now in the tenore and occupation of my said sone, William Lawsone. I give unto my two youngest sons, Thomas Lawson and Henrie Lawson, all my insight and outside goods whatsoever being the residue of my estate. I make and ordaine Thomas Ogle of Eslenton, Esq., Supervisor, and appoint my sons, Thomas and Henry Lawson, Executors. I give as a token unto my wife's sister daughter, Ann Graye, one black whye. I give to Isabella Lawson, daughter unto Robert Lawson, my sone, another whye. Witnesses, Robert Clough, Thomas Brown, Thomas Lawson.

INVENTORIE amounted to 73*l*. 10*s*. 0*d*. Probate, 10 June, 1611.

MARGARET GOODCHILD.[1]

Sept. 19, 1610. In the name of God, Amen, I, Margaret Goodchild, of Ryhope, in the pish of Bishope Warmouth. To be buryed within the Church of my pish, Bishop Warmouth. I gyve and bequeathe to my brother, Robert Goodchild, 20*l*. of

[1] The testatrix was bapt. at Bishopwearmouth (from which registers the other dates are taken from), 29 Feb., 1585/6, dau. of John Goodchild of Ryhope by his wife, Mary More (mar. 4 July, 1581); her father was bur. 17 May, 1587, her mother re-mar. George Shipperdson of Ryhope, 29 July, 1588 (he was bur. 8 Oct., 1611, and she, 26 June, 1635). Her

lawful money, to be payd to him forth of my goods that of right belongeth to me for filiall and childe's portion. I give to my sister, Agnas Gybson, twenty markes of English money, to be likewise payd forth to her of my goods yt of right belongeth to me. I give and bequeath to my sister, Jane Huntlye, twenty markes of lawful English money, to be payd to her forth of my goods and portion that belongeth to me. I gyve and bequeathe to my sister, Joane Sheperson, twentie marks of lawful Englishe moneye, to be payd to her out of my goods and portion that belongeth to me. I give to be distrybuted and geven to the poore three pounds, six shillings and eightpence, to be in like force paid forth of my goods. The rest and resydue of all and singular my goods that of right belongeth to me for my portion of my father, John Goodchild's, goods, deceased, I do wholly gyve and bequethe to my father and mother, George Sheperson and Mary Sheperson, and do also make my father and mother, George Sheperson and Marye Sheperson, Executors of this my last Will and Testament. Witnesses, Anthony Watson, Wyllym Burdon and George Sheperson, with others.

JAMES WALLIS.[1]

Jan. 3, 1610. James Wallis, of Coupland. My bodye to be buried in the porche commonly called the Walleses Porch in the Church of Newtone. I give unto my wyfe, Jane Walles, six whyes, fourtie ewes and fourtie lambes, and wille that she shall remaine and dwell in my hall howse in Coupland during her widowhood. I give to Ellyoner Wallis, the Daughter of my sone, Gilbert Wallis, six whyes. I give unto my sone, William Wallis, twenty marks. To my sone, Robert Wallis, twenty marks. To my son, Michael Wallis, twenty marks, and unto my sons, James Wallis and Richard Wallis, twenty marks each. To my daughters, Jane Wallis and Cecilia Wallis, each twenty marks. To my daughter, Dorothie Wylson, twenty markes. I appoint my sone, Roger Wallis, sole Executor. I do make Supervisors of this my Will, Thomas Burrell, Fergus Storye, John Wallis and Christopher Pearsone, Clerke. Witnesses, Ralph Carre, John Andersone and Walter Grame.

INVENTORY, 160*l*. 17*s*. 0*d*. Probate, 1612.

brother Robert of Pallion, bapt., 24 Mch., 1582/3, mar. Frances (bapt. 20 June, 1587), dau. of Adam Holme, 22 Nov., 1608, he bur., 22 Nov., 1622, she bur., 26 Aug., 1626. Her sisters were Joan, wife of William Shipperdson of Murton, Agnes, wife . . . . Gibson, and Jane (bur. 21 Dec., 1614), wife of Richard Huntley.

[1] This will adds to the information given of the Wallis descent in the *New County History of Northumberland*, vol. xi., pp. 222, 235.

LANCELOT STROTHER.[1]

July 30, 1611. Lancelot Strother, of Kirknewton, in the
Countie of Northumberland, Esquire. My bodie to be interred
in the quier of the Church of Newton. I give unto Elinor, my
wife, my household stuff both at Newton and Fowberrie. I also
give her out of my whole goods and chattels 200*l*., and I further
give unto my wife, Elinor, my tithe of corne and graine in
Langton, and I also give her my tithe of corne and grain of
West Newton. For the preferment of my younger sonns now
unborn, and of such sone as my said wife is now with (if it
happen to be a sone), I give unto William Strother, my second
sone, all my tithe of corne and graine in Akefield. To Lancelot
Strother, my third sone, my tithe of Millfield, and my water corn
Mill, lately in the occupation of Thomas Strother. Whereas my
said wife is now with childe, my will is, that if she be delivered
of a Sone, that then he shall have during his naturall life all
my tithe of corne and graine at Crookhouse. Whereas I, the
said Lancelot Strother, have by my deed indented, bearing the
date of this my Will, and made between me, the said Lancelot
Strother, of the one part and Sir William Selbye, of Tynemouth
Castle, Knight, Thomas Riddell, of Gateshead, Esquire, Clement
Strother, of Langton, Gent, and Lyonell Strother, of Berwick
upon Tweed, of the other part, doth demise, grant and form
letten unto Sir William Selbye, Thomas Riddell, Clement Strother

[1] Some notes on the Strother pedigree which appears in the *New
County History of Northumberland* (vol. xi., pp. 132-4) may not be out
of place here. (1) The William Strother there represented to be grandfather of this testator does not appear in the visitation pedigree of 1615
(ed. Foster, p. 115), and should almost certainly be deleted. It was
probably the testator's father who (in childhood) was contracted, 26
Nov., 1535, to marry Agnes, dau. of Thomas Grey then of Adderstone
(where with his wife Dorothy, widow of Sir Thomas Forster, he was
residing; on the death, 6 Jan., 1542/3, of his father, Sir Roger Grey;
he succeeded to Horton, and was knighted, 23 Sept., 1545). The contract was not fulfilled. Agnes, who was born about 1533 (according to
the findings at her father's *Inq. p.m.*, 9 Apr., 1571), was mar. not later
than 1556 to Robert Clavering of Callaly (who died 30 Nov., 1528), was
living in Nov., 1586, and was probably, bur. at St. Nich., Newcastle,
2 Oct., 1616. (2) William Strother, this testator's father, cannot have
made a will on 8 May, 1612, for Sir William Selby, by will dated 19
May, 1610 (P.C.C. 18 Fenner), gives a ring to Lancelot Strother, "sonne
of my late Brother in lawe, William Strother, deceased." (3) The
testator died, ult. Aug., 1611, as per *Inq. p.m.* taken 27 Sept, 1613; he
mar. Eleanor, dau. of John Conyers of Sockburn, marriage settlement,
dated 10 Nov., 1589 (she mar., secondly, Sir Ephraim Widdrington, 7
Aug., 1615, at Gateshead). He had a dau. Elizabeth, bapt., 5, bur., 7
Oct., 1592, at Sockburn. (4) John, his son and heir, died 2 Feb., 1630
(*Inq. p.m.*, 3 Sept., 1631). (5) Mary, dau. of the testator's grandson,
Col. William Strother, bapt., 25 Sept., 1656, at St. John's, Newcastle,
was bur. at St. Nich., Newcastle, 31 March, 1657. The dau. Mary who
mar. (about 1694), Thomas Orde of Felkington, was bur. at Norham,
4 Jan., 1736/7, having died (according to an inscription on the back
of her portrait at Nunnykirk), 1 Jan., aged 65.

and Lyonnell Strother, all my Manors, Lordships, lands and hereditaments, Rectories, parsonages, tithes and other things in the
said Indenture mentioned, for the term of eight yeares, to such uses
and purposes only as mentioned in My last Will and Testament.
My mind and will is touching the implements of my said lands
and tenements in the said Indenture mentioned. I give yearly
to my eldest son and heir apparent, John Strother, the sum of
50*l*. To my eldest daughter, Agnes, 500*l*. To Elizabeth, my
second daughter, 400*l*. To Jane, my third daughter, 300*l*.
To Ellinor, my fourth daughter, 300*l*. And to Katherine, my
fifth daughter, 200*l*., and three score poundes unto Mary, my
sixth daughter, and also 240*l*. to the child that my wife is now
with. The residue to my eldest sone. Probate, 1612.

WILLIAM BRIGGS.[1]

Anno dommi, 1611. In the name of God, Amen, I, William
Briggs, of Harum, in the pish of Brancepeth. To be buryed in
the pish Church of Brancepeth. Also I give and bequeathe to
Michaell Briggs, his three children, 6*l*., everye one of them 2*l*.,
to be paid at Whitsuntide next, and to be putt into the handes
of Richard Wrenn, my son in law, and to goe forward for the
use, and the said Richard Wrenn to lay in bonde to Robert
Pemberton, of Eshe, gentleman, and Nicholas Briggs, of Harum,
Yeoman, for the payment of the said money as the children shall
come of age. Also I give to Elizabeth Wrenn the feather bedd
which I now lye on. I give to Margarett Wrenn a stone of
lynte, and to the two young twinnes, tow younge hoggs. I give
Elizabeth Wrenn, my daughter, my mare. To my sonne in law,
Richard Wrenne, a paire of white britches, a white dubblett and
a payre of white stockins and a sherte. To Ralph Walker, my
work day britches, a doublett and a cap. Also my will is that
Christopher Badminson shall have payd at Penthecost, 1613, that
he shall have payd 20*s*. Also I give to the poore in Brancepeth
pish, 13*s*. 4*d*., and to the poore of Lanchester and Eshe parish,
10*s*., to be distributed as Mr. Cockey and Nicholas Briggs thinks
good. Also my Will is that my sonne, Nicholas Briggs, shall see
that I be honestlye brought forth, as other of my neighbors
have bene in time past, with my owne goodes, and all other my
goodes and chattles, moveable and unmoveable, my debts, legacies
and funerall expences discharged, I give to Jane Briggs, my
wife, whom I make my sole Executor. Witnesses, Nicholas
Briggs, John Forster, Thomas Rodde, Nicholas Briant.

[1] The testator was bur. at Brancepeth, 24 Jan, 1611/12. His son,
Nicholas, mar., at Esh, 13 Dec., 1631, Katherine, widow of John
Lampton, draper of the City of Durham (whom she mar. 26 Aug., 1623,
at St. Oswald's, Durham, as " Mrs. Katherine Kirbie "); she was bur.
at Durham Catherdal, 1 Sept., 1641. His dau. Elizabeth mar. Richard
Wren at Brancepeth, 22 July, 1600, and was bur. there, 1 Dec., 1657.

ROBERT LAWSON.[1]

Jan. 13, 1611. Robert Lawson, of Cramlingtone, in the Countie of Northumberland, Esquire. My bodye to be buried in the quear and chappell of Cramlington. I give to my well beloved wife, Elizabeth Lawson, thee thirds of my lands and goods, moveable, unmoveable, with leases and other goods, my debts to be first deducted. I give to my well beloved friends, Sir Ralphe Lawson, Knight, Roger Lawson, Esq., William Fenwick, gent, and Thomas Cramlington, gent my eldest sone Thomas Lawson, the two parts of my lands and goods to see my other children's portions paid as hereafter followeth : To my sons, George, Robert, Ralph, Michaell and William, 100*l*. each. I give to my daughters, Mary and Dorothy, 100*l*. each. Witnesses, Roger Lawson, Esq., Thomas Cramlington, gent, and Lyonell Fenwick, gent.

Debts oweing by Robert Lawson : Unto Margaret Read, 30*l*. To Richard Swane, 10*l*. To George Wallis, 10*l*. To George Huntlye, 10*l*. To James Claveringe, 15*l*. 14*s*. 0*d*. To John Stobes, 1*l*. 9*s*. 5*d*. To Mke Hudcheson, 2*l*.

INVENTORIE amounted to 919*l*. 9*s*. 2*d*. Probate, 12th June, 1612. Tuition of Michael Lawson and Dorothy Lawson (minors) granted to their brother, Thomas Lawson, of Cramlington.

PHILLIP HAGTHROPPE.[2]

Jan. 20, 1611. In the name of God, Amen, I, Phillip Hagthroppe, of Daringe Crooke, within the County of Durhame, gen. I bequiethe my bodye beweridd in Chester Church as near unto the place wher my lovinge mother lies, because she was the wonne that brought me forthe as a clote of day to wander in this wicket wordle. I charge my sonne, Phillipp Hagthorpe,

---

[1] The testator, 2nd son of Thomas Lawson (who died, 24 Dec., 1547, *Inq. p.m. Chanc.*, Ser. ii., 87/40) by Edith his wife, succeeded to Cramlington on the death, 16 Nov., 1574, of his elder brother William, being then aged 30 and more (*Inq. p.m. Chanc.*, Ser. ii., 172/405). He died at Cramlington, 19 Jan., 1611/12 (*Inq. p.m. Chanc.*, Ser. ii., 330/58). The testator's wife, Elizabeth, dau. of Lionel Fenwick of Blagdon, died a fortnight before Candlemas, 1615/16 (Raine's *Prob. and Admon.*, i., 235). His son and heir, Thomas, aged 30, at his father's death (Inv. dated 17 Dec., 1618), mar. Adeline, dau. of George Brabant of Brancepeth east Park, 29 July, 1612, at Brancepeth; she mar., secondly, Roger Anderson of Newcastle, and, thirdly, James Chomley of Brancepeth.

[2] He was son of John Hagthorpe of Nettlesworth by his wife Isabel (bur., 31 Jan., 1597/8, at Chester-le-Street), dau. of John Vavasour of Weston, co. York. The testator was bur. there, 5 Feb., 1611/12, his first wife Anne having been also bur. there, 30 Nov., 1607; his second wife Margaret Hedworth, widow, was married to him, 21 Nov., 1609, at Chester-le-Street. Philip, the son by the first marriage, was buried beside his father, 17 May, 1619.

as he will answer me before god, that whereas it is a fasshon and a greit vainingly to bestowe a greit dinner and other charges vainly on men when thay are goin, my will is that ther shall bee no such thing, but that he, the said Phillipp, shall deliver 5*l.* in monye oute within three monthes after my deathe in the hands of the fower Churche wardens, to remain for the use of the power of Chester parish, by thos fower Churchwerdens and ther yerly sucksesers, shall be lent unto the first power and needful laste marryed cupple, thay beinge bound for the same, and to pay 2*s.* for that yeire, and so from one to one in god's name for ever, and that thay pay 2*s.* at the pound is my meanninge. If I dye at Darin Crooke, then I geve unto the power of that parishe, 6*s.* 8*d.*, and 2*s.* to the Ringers of the bells. I give unto my neace, Mary Silliman, 20*l.*, to be paid forthe of my goodes within one yeir after my death. I give the said Mary halfe of the howshold stofe that shall fall to my Exsecutors' part. I give unto my sister, Dorithye Silliman, 5*l.* in mony, to be paid within two monthes after my death, forder I do charge my said sone that he do upon his owen charges find my sister, Dorrithe Silliman, one convenient house to sit in so long as she shall lyve. I geve unto Phillipp Daveson, 40*s.* in mony, to be paid within three monthes after my death, and that the same 40*s.* shall be put forthe for his use to the most commeddetye for him only. Forther, my will is that if the said Phillipp Daveson do dye before he come to one and twenty yeirs, that then that said 40*s.* and the intrest shall go Margery Daveson, his sister. I give to avary one of my sarvants 5*s.*, to be paid tham forthe with upon my death besydes other wages. I geve unto my aforesaid sone, Phillipp, my best horse or gelding, or coilt or at chose, to travell upon abut his bissines. Also I geve and a lowe the said Phillipp, wherever he be when I die, to take his young graye filly which my wiffe did bestowe on him, and to maker for his use. If the said Marey Silliman aforesaid dowe chance to dye before she be married, then that gifte be void and reteirn to the aforesaid Phillipp, my aforesaid sone, and then the said Phillipp shall geve unto Phillipp Silliman, hir brother, 5*l.* in mony within three monthes after my death or his death, if she dye unmarryed, or else to stand good to hir. I geve all my implements and toills belonginge to my howse to my said sone, Phillipp Hagthropp. I give unto Mr. Harry Hilton, my best grewe Dogg or Doggs; even so, I geve unto Mrs. Hilton, his bedfellow, my ould peacock and his hen or hens. I make my aforesaid sonne, Phillipp, my only soille executore of all my right, and in the right of him self alwaies, provided the said Phillipp shall see all my detts paid and discharged, and if my sone dowe chance to dye or to refuse this my Will, then I make Phillipp Silliman and James Lodge, my sisters' sones executores. I make this little book protesting this to be donn with my very conscience to as good a meining

as though it wer in the best forme before any Curiet at my very
death, and this I dowe because I am sickly and sometimes wake,
and my saviore may call sudenly. I have made this my last
Will and the Rather because if this come before the ordinary,
I trust he will see my said sone to have his rights by
this my only gifte by this my Will, if I dowe no waye reforme
it at any time heirafter. Witnesses, Thomas Morland, Thomas
Burrell and others. Proved, 1613.

JOHN HUTTON.[1]

Feb. 20, 1611. I, John Hutton, pson of Gatesheade. To be
buried in the pish of Gateshead at the will and pleasure of my
Executors. I give unto my wife, Florence (which she gave me
for a token), 5*l.* in gould as a token. I give unto her two
gownes, two kirtles, two petticots and a velvet hat (which I
bought for my wife, Elizabeth) for a legacie. I give unto her,
for a legacie, the syde saidle which I bought last at London, with
all the furniture that belongs to it. I give to my sister, Margaret
Blackburne, one little peece of East Countrey plate for a token,
in full satisfaction that is dew to her out of my goodes. To my
sonne, Henry Farniside, 3*l.* 6*s.* 8*d.* To James Farniside, a New
Mr of Artshood and 40*s.* I give to Edward Miller, my sister's
daughter's sonne, 10*l.* To Jacob Farniside, Edwyne Nicholson,
Willm. Cooke, my wive's children, and to every one of their
wyves, a french crowne apeece for a token. Unto everie of my
servants, their waige and 5*s.* apeece more. I give to Thomas
Cuthbert, notarie public, a french crowne for a token. The
residue of all my goodes, moveable and unmoveable, my debts,
legacies and funerall expenses (saving the tenn poundes given by
me to Edward Miller), I give and bequeath unto my said wife,
Florence, and James Cole, of Newcastle, yeoman, to be equally
divided among them, the said James Cole paying out of his part

---

[1] He matriculated from Jesus College, Cambridge, Michs., 1565,
B.A., 1569/70, M A., 1573, Fellow, 1571-5, ordained deacon and priest,
8 June, 1584, Rector of Gateshead, 1595-1612. Preb. of Southwell,
1601-12, bur. at Gateshead, 10 March. 1611/12. He mar., firstly,
Elizabeth, dau. of Laurence Dodsworth, rector of Gateshead, and widow
of William Blythman (will dated 1603, proved 1606), 14 Nov., 1609, at
Gateshead, and bur. there, 27 Jan., 1610/11. He mar., secondly,
Florence (bur., 10 June, 1633, at St. Nich., Newcastle), widow of James
Farnisyde. Rector of Whickham (bur., 10 Dec., 1610). His stepchildren
James Farnisyde, bapt., 12 Aug., 1589, at Whickham, B.A., from St.
John's College, Cambridge, 1611/12, Vicar of Long Benton, 1621, until
his death in 1628; Henry Farnisyde, bapt., 29 June, 1591, at Whickham;
Mary, mar. at Whickham, 19 Nov., 1609, Edwin Nicholson; Jane, bapt.,
24 Aug., 1583, mar. at Whickham, 2 Nov., 1607, William Cooke; Jacob
Farnisyde, mar. Isabel, dau. of John Gray, draper, 24 Jan., 1608/9, at
St. Nich., Newcastle, and was bur. there, 22 April, 1623

of my goods the sume of 10*l*., which I have given to Edward
Miller, and do require the said James Cole to take the tuicon
and keeping of the said Edward Miller with the said sum of
10*l*. into his handes, and until he come to be bounde a prentice
or otherwise. And I doe make my wife, Florence, and James
Cole, executors. I doe give unto Janie Cole, the wife of Nicholas
Cole, and Elizabeth Rand, the wife of Willm. Rand, either of
them, a booke thone called, learne to lyve, and the other, learne
to dye, for a token. Witnesses, Jacob Ferneside, Edwin Nicholson, Thomas Cuthbert, Mergerie Lamb. Proved, 28th March, 1612.

ROBERT SMÝTH.[1]

April 1, 1612. In the name of God, Amen, I, Robert Smyth,
of the towne of Newcastle upon Tyne, in the County of the same
towne, Tallow Chandler. To be buried in the parish church of
St. John's in Newcastle at the discretion of my executors hereafter
named, and to the poor of the said parish I doe give and bequeathe 10*s*. to be distributed at the discretion of the Churchwardens. And as touching the ordering, setling and disposing of
my lands and goods wherewith the Lord in this life hath blessed and
endued me, I doe give and bequeath as following : Whereas heretofore I, the said Robert Smyth, by my Deed indented, dated the
third daie of June, in the 44th yeare of the reign of our lawful
sovereign, Lady Queen Elizabeth, confirmed unto John Cliborne,
late of Newcastle aforesaid, Scryvener, deceased, and Thomas
Marley, of the same towne of Newcastle upon Tyne, Feltmaker,
their heires and assigns for ever All those two burgages or
tenements, with there appurtenances, then late in the several
tenures or occupations of me, the said Robert and John Swyn-
borne, gentleman, lying and being in a street in Newcastle aforesaid, called the Iron Markett, to have and to hold the said two
burgages or tenements, with their appurtes, unto the said
John Cliborne and Thomas Marley, and their heires for ever, to
the uses and behoofe in the said Deed limitted My will and
mind is that the said two burgages or tenements, with their
appurtenes, in the said Deed specified, shall remayne continuous,
and be unto the use and behoofe in the said deed limitted, and to
no other use, intent or purpose. Whereas also I, the said Robert
Smyth, by another Poll Deed or writinge of assignment, bearing
date the 21 day of September, 1610, I have given, granted and
assigned and sett over to Ann and Dorithye Smith, my daughters,
all my right, estate by the terme of yeares to come, claime and

---

[1] The testator mar. for his second wife, Christobell Thompson, 25
Nov., 1595, at St. John's, Newcastle, where he was bur. 19 April, 1612,
and his son Rowland was mar. 14 Feb., 1612/13, to Alice Shafto.

demand whatsoever, which I, the said Robert Smith, have everie
right, or ought to have, of and in or to all the tythe corne and
the clayme and other tythes within the fields and tenements of
Litle Thrickleby, in the County of York. Wherefore, the yearly
rent of twenty markes is to me due, or to be paid out of or for
the said tythe, my will and mynd also is, and the said yearlie
rent of twenty markes, and other rents dew for the said tythes
as aforesaid, shall contynue, and be unto the use of the said Ann
and Dorrithie, my daughters, according to the said assignment.
And further, my Will and mynd is that my sonne, Rowland
Smyth, shall be paid by my executors hereafter named the sume
of 100l. by 10l. a yeare out of my goods and chattells, according
to the lymitacon of one Deed by me heretofore made to the said
Rowland, bearinge date the 20 daie of September, 1610, in full
discharge of his, the said Rowland's, filliall pt and porcon of
all and singuler my lands, tenements, woods and chattells whatsoever. And whereas heretofore I have purchased to me and
myne heires for ever, certain lands in Firley, in the pish of
Bedall, within the County of Yorke, of Thomas Jackson, of
Baulke, in the said County of York, gentleman, my will and
mynd is also that the same lands and the issues and profitts
thereof shall remayne, contynew, according to the same are
lymitted in one Deed or writing, which Deed is nowe in the
custodie of Cuthbert Harrison, my brother-in-law. I give and
bequeath unto my unckle, John Smyth, of Chester, for a legacy,
3l. I give to my Aunt, Elizabeth Smith, 20s. I give to my
sister, Sibill, wife of John Browne, in Gateside, 20s. I give
to my sister, Elizabeth, wife of Robert Ranson, of Whickham,
20s. I give to my sister, Margaret, wife of John Wheldon, 20s.
I give to my brother-in-law, Edward Harrison, of the City of
Durham, clarke, my best gray horse, now going at Plawsworth.
I give to my brother-in-law, Cuthbert Harrison, 20s. I give
unto my brother-in-law, George Harrison, 20s. I give unto my
brother in lawe, Richard Harrison, of Durham, 20s. I give and
bequeath to my daughter, Dorothie Smith, her heirs and assignes
for ever my house in Westgate, in Newcastle aforesaid, which I
purchased of Mr. Harden, of Hollinsyde. And if it shall happen
the said Dorothie to dye before she come to the age of sixteene
yeares, or be married, then my will and mynd is that the said
house and appurtenances shall remaine and come to my daughter,
Anne Smyth, hir heires and assigns for ever. I give the rent
to me dew and payable out of the burgage or tenement now in
the occupation of Thomas Ewbank, haberdasher, unto my said
daughter, Ann. I give to my said daughter, Ann, my Bay Mare.
I give for a remembrance to my frend, Thomas Ewbank, 10s.,
and to his wife, other 10s. I give and bequeath unto Elizabeth
Thompson, daughter unto Christobell Thompson, some tymes my
wife, 22l., to be paid to the said Elsabeth, her executors or

assigns, at Pentecost next coming, within three monthes next
after my decease, upon condicon that upon receipt thereof that
she, the said Elsabeth, her executor or assigns, shall sealle and
deliver unto me the said Robert for my Executor, one generall
acquittance or release of all her filiall pt or porcon of the goods
and chattells of Bartram Thompson, her father, deceased, and
Christobell, her mother. And my will and mynd is that Anne
my now wife, shall receive and take for the use of my said
daughters, Dorothie and Ann, the said yearlie rent of twenty
markes a yeare, issuing out of and for the said tythes of litle
Thrickby aforesaid, until they, the said Dorothie and Anne, be
of lawfull yeares or otherwise be lawfully married. The residue
of all my Goodes and Chattells whatsoever, my debts, legacies
and funerall expences being first paid and discharged, I give and
bequeath unto my said wife, Ann, and to my said two daughters,
Dorothie and Ann, whom I herebye ordeyne, constitute, make
and appoint them my joint executors of this my last Will and
Testament, revoking all former Wills, gifts and legacies whatsoever heretofore by me made, and doe publish and declare this
my psent writing to be my last Will and Testament, and none
other. Witnesses, George Fenwyck, Edward French, Tho.
Arrowsmyth. Proved, 9 June, 1612.

ROBERT WAWGHE.

April 24, 1612. I, Robert Wawghe, of Chester-ley-Street,
within the Countie of Durham, Yeoman. To be buryed within
the pish Church of Chester aforesaid in ioyful hope of a glorious
resserection. I doe give sixe shillings and eightpence yearely for
ever, out of my freehold land called and knowne by the name
of Rogerfield, as it is situate, lyeing and being within the limitts
and towne of Chester, to be distributed to the poore of the Towne
and pish of Chester by the hands of the Churchwardens of Chester
aforesaid, for their time or times succesively being for ever at the
two fesvall feasts, that is to say, Whitsontyde and Martymas, by
even and equal porcons. I give unto Robert Frysell, my eldest
daughter's sonne save one, 20s. in moneye. I give to Marmaduke
Hirde, 20s. Unto Robert Hird, 20s., if he should outlive
me. To Frances Smyth, of Hexam, my sister, 20s. in money
To Robert Welch, eldest son of William Welch, 30s. in money,
and to William Welch, younger sone of William Welch, the elder,
30s. I give unto William Waughe, my grandchild, 20s. To my
trew and faithfull servante, Elsbeth Godskirk, 40s., to be paid
unto her by my executors fore under named, one loade of malte,
also or fourteen shillings in money. And also my Will is that
she shall have that howse of myne in Chester, lying and beinge
between the house of William Wels on the west, and the howse

wherein I dwell. I give unto the worshipfull, and my most true
and faithfull friend in this transtorie world, Thomas Chaytor,
of Butterbie, Esquire, 3*l.*, for a token and remembrance of my
hartie love and good will towards him. To Elsbeth Godskirk, my
servant, a paire of stand bedsteads, together with the bed clothes
and furniture to the same belonginge. I give to Robert
Hallyman my best jackett, and to William Welch, my best black
britches. To the poore, to be distributed to them at my buryall,
20*s.* To Robt. Hallyman, that Cloake which was his owne father's
cloake in his life tyme. To Isabel Drews, ten groats. To Alice
Thompson, ten grotts. I doe give sixe pounds in money, to be
bestowed in a dynner to make my honest good neighbors welcome
for my laste faire well to them out of this synfull worlde. I
doe give unto Sir Thomas Lyddall, curate of Chester, 2*s.* for a
remembrance, and I give my worke day clothes to Robt. Hirde.
And I doe constitute and ordayne Margaret Wawghe, wedow,
Margarett Hallyman and Margaret Welch, executors of this my
Will. Witnesses, Martyn Hallyman, Thomas Liddall, minister
of God. Whereas James Wilson, and Margarie Wilson, his wife,
are owne me 20*s.* that they borrowed. I doe forgive them the
same, and doe by this my last give to her, the said Margarie
Wilson, other 20*s.*

ROBERT WAUGHE.[1]

September 7, 1613. I, the aforesaid Robert Waughe, doe give
unto Robert Welch, younger, 4*l.*, to be paid out of my pcell of
ground called Turnar Mares, at or within twelve months of my
depture. I also give unto William Welch, younger, 4*l.*, to be
paid out of Turnar Mares at the end of two yeares next ensewing
after my said depture of this transtorie worlde. To John Welch,
sonne of William Welch, elder, 4*l.* out of the said Turnar Mares
at the end of three yeares next ensewing after my departure
out of this mortal lyfe. To Robt. Hird, 40*s.* in money, to be
paid within three months after my decease. I give to Janet
Smith, wife to Thomas Smith, of Hexam, my sister, 20*s.* To
Isabell Lyddall, 20*s.* To Margarett Wawghe, 20*s.*, and to
William Wawghe, 20*s.*, and to Robert Wawghe, younger, 20*s.*
Witnesses of this, Thomas Lyddall, Minister, John Clayton, John
Bird.

[1] He was bur. at Chester-le-Street, 1 Sept., 1613; his wife Margery
was also bur. there, 17 Feb., 1594/5. His dau.. Elizabeth. mar. Robert
Frisell, 1 Aug., 1583, and their son Robert was bapt. 27 Oct.. 1588.
His *Inq. per br. de Mand.*, taken at Durham, 23 Oct., 1613. Robert,
aged 22, is his grandson, and next heir, viz. :—son of John, son of the
said testator. By deed dated 14 Apl., 1612, he granted an annuity to
Margaret Waughe, the mother of the said grandson. By a deed three
days later he settled land for his own use for life, with remainder to
William, son of his son John.

HERCULES BRABBANT.[1]

April 27, 1612. In the name of God, Amen. I, Hercules Brabbant, of Redworth, in the parish of Heighington. To be buryed in the parish church of Staindrop in or neare to the grave of Ralphe Brabant and his brothers. I give and devise to my wife, Marye Brabant, all my freehold lands and tenements lyeing within the townshipp of Redworth and Heighington, in the Countye of Durham, for and during her naturall lyfe. I give to my wyfe, Marye Brabant, my lease of Midderidge Grainge, and where the lease of the tythe corne of Readworth is renewed by my consente, in the name of George Brabant, of the East Park Lodge, of Brancepeth, my will is that my wife doe enioye the said tythe wholy for foure yeares next ensuing the daie of the date thereof, and afterwards she to have the moietie of it during the said tearme, if she live so longe, according to an agreement betwixt the said George Brabant and me, my said wife paieing the whole rent for the said tythes to the dean and chapter of Durham for the said first foure yeares, and the halfe rente after during her life. Where the lease of the demeanes of Heighington is latelie renewed in the name of the saide George Brabant for three lives, my will and meaning is that my wife have and receive the profitts of the said demeanes to her owne use during her life, she paieing yearly the said rente and all other dewtyes and services for the same, and after her decease, my mynd and will is that Adalyne Brabant, daughter of the said George Brabant, shall have the said demeanes, the whole interest of the said leases, to her owne use, accordinge to the truste I have reposed in the said George Brabant. Also, for the furthere sellinge and disposing of all my said freehold lands, withall and singular the appurtenances lyeing and being in Redworth and Heighington aforesaid. I doe by this my laste Will and Testament give, grant and devise the same, after the deathe and decease of me and Mary, my said wife, to the said George Brabant for and duringe his naturall lyfe, and after his decease, the same to remayne to John Brabant, sonne and heire apparent

[1] Hercules Brabant was bur., not at Staindrop as desired in his will, but at Heighington, 13 June, 1612. His *Inq. p.m.* taken at Durham, 30 Oct., 1612, and printed in the *Deputy Keeper's Report*, vol. 44, p. 340, says that he died without an heir. He mar. Mary Robinson at Heighington, 22 Dec., 1589, their only son Hercules being bur. there, 9 Aug., 1590, unbapt.; she mar., secondly, Gilbert Freville, 9 Feb., 1612/13, at Heighington, and was bur. there, 25 Aug., 1616.

George Brabant, mar. Anne, dau. of Ralph Whitfield of Whitfield, and was bur. at Brancepeth, 30 Apl., 1642, where his widow was also bur., 6 Apl., 1646; his brother, Charles Brabant, was also bur. there. 20 Apl., 1631; John, s. of George Brabant, mar. Jane Johnston of Piercebridge. His *Inq. p.m.*, taken at Durham 17 Sept., 1625, is printed in the *Deputy Keeper's Report*, vol. 44, p. 344.

unto the said George Brabant, and to the heires of his bodie to be begotten for. And for default of such issue, the same to remayne to the said Adaline Brabant, daughter of the said George Brabant, and to their heires of her bodie for ever. And for default of such issue, the same to remaine to Charles Brabant, brother of the said George Brabant, and to their heires of his bodye lawfully begotten. And for defaulte of such issue, the same to remaine to Raiphe Maddeson, second sone of Mr. Henry Maddeson, of Newcastle, and to the heires of his bodie for ever. And for default of such issue, to Thomas Todd, of Redworth, and to the heirs of his bodye lawful begotten for ever. And for default of such issue, the same to remaine to George Heighington, sonne of Richard Heighington, of Graystones, and the heires of his bodie lawfully begotten. And the said land and every part and parcel thereof to descend to the partye next in remainder and mentioned as aforesaid. I give and bequeathe 20s. rent charge yearly for ever, to issue out of my said freehould lands, to be paid upon great Mondaie after Penthecost and great Mondaie after Martinmas imediately after the decease of my said wife, by equall porcons, to the handes of the Vicar and Churchwardens of the pish church of Heighington for the tyme being and their successors, to be by them, with the consent, oversight and advice of Mr. Anthony Byerlay, George Gryser, gent, Thomas Todd, and Christopher Raine, distributed and bestowed in the Church porch there upon twentye of the most aged and impotent poore people of that parish. In like manner, I doe give 20s. rent out of my said landes to be payed yearlie for ever as aforesaid to the parson, Rector and Churchwardens of the parish Church of Brancepeth for the tyme being and their successors, to be payd at the tymes to be by them distributed, with the consent, advice and oversight of George Brabant, Richard Dighton and Thomas Hull, upon twentie of the most aged and impotent poore people of that parish. In like manner, I doe give the like yearlye rent of 20s. out of my said landes to · be payd yearly for ever as aforesaid to the Vicar and Churchwardens of Staindropp, to be distributed as aforesaid, with the advice and oversight of John Dowthwaite, of Newsham, and Bernard, his Brother, and olde Charles Brabant and Robert Brabant, upon the most aged and impotent poor people of that pish. And also my will is that George Brabant and his heires shall for ever hereafter have one speciall voyce in nominating or electinge of the poor people of the three severall pishes to whom I have given this yearlye benevolence. And likewise my will is when any of the aforesaid psons appointed to have oversight and consent in distributing the said rents fortune to dye, then the other survivors shall have power to elect and choose some substantiall man or men well devoted in religion for the distribution of the said money according to this my Will. Also

I charge my land with the paymente of three score pounds of lawful English money, which I give unto Adaline Brabant, to be paid unto hir by George Brabant, hir father, or John Brabant, his heires or assigns, within one year next ensuinge the death of Mary, my now wife, and in default of non payment of the three score pounds, it shallbe lawful for the said Adalyne Brabant to enter into the said landes, and the same quietly and peacefully to have, hould and enioy for the terme of five yeares then next following, and after the said yeares to be complete I give and bequeathe to the Worsll my Mr. Sir George Freevile, Knight, 20*l.* for a token. To my Worll good Mris, the Lade Frevile, 20*l.* To Mr. Thomas Jenison, of Irchester, 6*l.* 13*s.* 4*d.* I give to the said George Brabant one gray colt, and to Mris Anne Brabant, his wife, 5*l.* To there sonne, John Brabant, one other graie colt, which colt goeth now in the olde close, and I also give to the said John Brabant one newe table, now standinge in the hall, and one cupbord, now standinge in the plor, pannelled with lattine, for heire loumes. I give more to Adalyne Brabant, 20*l.* To Mr. George Frevile, for a token, 10*s.* To Gilbert Frevile, 53*s.* 4*d.* To Robt. Bellas, 6*s.* To Richard Dighton, 10*s.* To Mr. John Sage, 5*s.* To his wife, 5*s.* To Mris Dighton, 5*s.* To Nicholas Fynn, 6*s.* To Robt. Layburne, 11*s.* To George Graie, 6*s.* To Thomas Dowthwaite, 2*s.* 6*d.* To Samuell Sir George Frevile's man, 2*s.* 6*d.* To Nycholas Hodgson, 2*s.* To Ralphe Newbye, 2*s.* To Ralph Emmerson, 2*s.* To George Parkin, 2*s.* To Nicholas Pettifer, 2*s.* I give to Charles Brabant, brother to George Brabant, 6*l.* 13*s.* 4*d.*, and a bay mare which was some time his owne. To Richard Heighington, 10*s.* To his sone, George, 10*s.* To his sone, John, 5*s.*, and to his daughter, Marie, 5*s.* To Mr. Siles Garthwaite, clerk, 5*s.* To his wife, 5*s.* To Mr. Croser, 5*s.* To his wife, 2*s.* 6*d.*, and to his daughter, Smithson, 5*s.* I give to Thomas Todd, 10*s.*, and to his wife, 10*s.*, and to his daughter, Elinore, whom I christened, 20*s.*, and to every other child he haith, 2*s.* 6*d.* I give to Willm. Greene, 10*s.*, and to his daughter whom I xpenned, 20*s.*, and to every other childe he haith by his late wife, Elizabeth, deceased, 2*s.* I give to Thomas Hull, 2*s.*, for a token. To Thomas Robinson, 5*s.* To Samuell Moberlaye, 2*s.* To George Young, 2*s.* To his wife, 2*s.* I give to Charles Brabant, the elder, 10*s.*, and to Robt. Brabant, 10*s.* To Christopher Rayne, 10*s.*, and to his wife, 10*s.* To Robert Robinson and his wife, either of them, 10*s.* To Christopher Hodgson, 10*s.*, and to Hercules Robinson, 20*s.* To Robert Bell, 5*s.* To Edward Wilfoot, 5*s.* To John Richinson's wife, 5*s.* To William Peverell, 3*s.* 4*d.* To An Cockson, 6*s.* 8*d.* To William Dawson, if he remaine my servant till my death 3*l.*; if he doe not, 20*s.* To John Emerson, if he contynew my servant till my death, 16*s.* 8*d.*; if not, 10*s.* To Hercules Rayne, in considercon of a litle whie I had with him, 3*l.* To

John Wilfoot, if he contynewe my servante, 26s. 8d; if not, 10s.
To Isable Rawlinge, 20s. To Anne White, 10s. To Margarett
Adamson, 3s. 4d. To every child I helped to xpenned, 2s. To
Mr. John Hutton, preacher of God's worde, a Angell of gold.
I give to Mr. Anthony Byerley, to Mr. Henry Maddison, and to
his wife, each of them an angell of golde for a token. To George
Trotter, 5s. To his wife, 2s. 6d. And for all the rest of my
goods, moveable and unmoveable, my legacies paid and funerall
expences discharged, I doe given and bequeath unto Marie
Brabant, my wife, whom I doe make sole Executor of this my
last Will, giving and limitinge unto my said Executrix the
space of three yeares next after my decease for the payment of
all my legacies above given. And for the due execution of my
Will, I doe make any Maister Sir Henry Frevile, Knight, Mr.
Thomas Jenyson, of Irchester, Mr. Anthonye Byerlay, of Pickhall,
and Mr. Henrye Maddeson, of Newcastle, Supervisors hereof.
In witness whereof I have hereunto set my hande and seale the
daie and yeare first above written. Witnesses, Thomas Hull,
George Trotter, Richard Dighton, Thomas Robinson.

DANIELL GALLON.[1]

May 22, 1612. In the name of Gode, Amen, I, Daniell
Gallon, of Shilbottle, in the Countie of Northumberland, Gentleman. My bodie to the earth to be interred at the discretion of
my friends. As for my land in Shilbottle, I bequeath to my
wife, Isabell, for and during her life natural, and after her
decease, the same to come and descend to my daughter, Ellinor
Gallon, and to the heires of her bodye lawfully begotten for
ever, and for default of such issue, to come and remaine to my
brother, George Gallon, and to the heirs male of his bodye
lawfully begotten for ever, and for default of such issue male in
him, to come and be devolved to my brother, John Gallon, and
the heires of his bodie lawfully begotten. I give unto my
daughter above said the whole tythe, corne, yearly renewing in
and upon the fower several tenements, with the appurtenances,
in the west end of Shilbottle aforesaid, and to the heires of her
bodie lawfully begotten for ever, and if by god's pleasure she
die without issue, and my wife survive her, that then it shall
come and remaine to my wife for her life naturall, and after
her decease to George Gallon, my brother, and his heirs male
lawfully begotten, and for default of such issue male in him, to

---

[1] There is a pedigree of the Gallons of Alnwick printed in the *New
County History of Northumberland,* vol. ii., pp. 486/8. The administration of the goods of George Gallon, the father of the testator was
granted, 27 July, 1620, to Edward Delaval of Alnwick, his brother John
and his sisters, Alice and Jane, being mentioned.

my brother, John Gallon, and the heires of his body lawfully
begotten. Also my will is that my wife bring upp my daughter
vertuoslie in the feare of gode, at her booke, needle and such
other commendable qualities as will best enable her for the service
of god, and her maintenance and preferment in this worlde.
And if it please gode my wife marrie againe, that then my
father, George Gallon, and Edmond Finch, of Warkworth, in
case they dislike the education and usage of my daughter under
her mother, shall take her into one of their tuitions, or at their
discretions during her non age see her well and vertuostlie
brought upp, and the profitts of the tythes of those fower severall
tenements, and employed to that use and end. I give to my
daughter, Eleanor, above said all my whole estate, right, title,
interest of the whole burgage or tenement, with the appurtenances, situate, lying and being in Barwick on Tweed, and which
of right doth descend unto me by the right of my late grandfather, Robert Lowther, and to the heires of her body lawfully
begotten for ever; and for default of her and such issue lawfully
begotten, I give my whole right therein to my wife, Isabella
aforesaid, and to her heires for ever. I give to my daughter
above said two kyne and two calves, to be marked at the hour
of my death for her use. I give unto her moreover, the one half
of all my household stuffe and implements, to be given to her
when she shall come to lawful full yeares, and the other halfe of
all my goods and chattells, moveable and immoveable, whatsoever,
with the corne alreadie sowen and hereafter in that season to
be sowen, I leave and give to my wife, Isabella, aforesaide. And
I make and ordeine my wife, Isabella, and daughter, Eleanor,
abovesaid, joint Executors of this my last Will and Testament,
requesting my well beloved father, George Gallon, of Calledg-
Pk, and my especiall good friends, Fargus Storie, of Yea . . .
ing, and Edmond Finch, of Warkworth, to be supervisors for the
ordering and assisting them in their rights. Witnesses, Richard
Garrett, Charles Atkinson, John Harte. Proved, 11 March, 1612.

THOMAS NEWTON.[1]

Aug. 20, 1612. Thomas Newton, of Hawkwell, in the parish
of Stamfordham, in the countie of Northumberland, yeoman. To
be buried in the South Porch of the parish church of Stamfordham.
I comit my sone Arthur unto William Ray, whom I make and
appoint his tutor to bring him up in a godly and christian

---

[1] There is an account of the Newtons in the descent of the Hawkwell
property in the *New County History of Northumberland*, vol. xii., pp.
360-1. The testator's son Arthur was bur. in the church porch of
Stamfordham, 19 May, 1663.

manner, for which I do give unto the said William Ray the one-
half of my land and messuages in Hawkwell during my sonn's
minortie. I give unto my wife, Agnes Newton, fower kine, tenne
ewes and tenne sheepe hoggs. I give to my sister, Jane Newton,
my land in Hawkwell if it shall please god to call away my sone,
Arthur, by death, before he comes of age, to enable him to dispose
of the same, conditionally that shee marry with a Newton to keep
it in the name. To John Bell, of Dewly House, one loade of rye
and one loade of oatts, being Newcastle measure. To Jane Newton.
my sister, 13s. 4d. To Isabell Stawper, my sister, two ewes. To
John Bell, my uncle's sone, one browne whye. To Mr. Mathew
Newtone, of Stockfield Halle, one black hawked oxe. To Thomas
Thompson, my godesone, two ewe hoggs. To either of my men
servants, one ewe hogge. To young William Ray, one black nagge.
To Pervicall Dicksone, one bay fillie. If my wife prove to be with
childe to mee, then I do give the one halfe of my goods not bequeathed unto the said child. I make my said sone, Arthur, my
sole Executor, and William Dixsone, my brother-in-law, Supervisor of this my Will.

INVENTORY, amounted to 50l. 12s. 6d.

RAILPH WATSON.[1]

Sept. 22, 1612. I, Railph Watson, of Thorpthewles, in the
parish of Grindon, in the Countie of Durham, yeoman. To be
buryed within my said pishe church of Grindon. I give to the
poore people and neadie of my said pish of Grindon, 20s. I give
unto every godchild that I xpenned, 7d. a peece. I give unto my
wellbeloved wyfe, Ann Watson, an acre of winter corne and an
other of waire corne yearly during hir life, which said acres are
to be appointed by two indefferent men to be chosen for that purpose by my said wife and my sonne William, one of my executors,
and continually from time [to time] duringe all the life of my said
wife shall be plowed, manured, harrowed, and repeied by my said
sonne William, or his assigns for the use, benefitt, comodotye and
pfitt of my said wife, of his owne proper costs and charges in and
after the best manner of husbandrie according to the use and
custome of the towne and countrie, she only findinge and preparing
seede for the sowinge of those acrees at all tymes when they are to
be sowen and laying it upon the groundes, and my will is that my
said sonne or his assignes in tyme of harvest when hir corne shall
be ready and at all tymes during hir lyfe shall take lead and
carrye home at hir appointmente unto the staggarthes or barne,
now upon my farme, where it maie be in saftye, all such corne

[1] He was bur. at Grindon, 23 Oct., 1612, his widow being bur. beside
him, 27 Mch., 1615.

and Grayne as shall grow and increase upon the same acrees, and
shall also allowe unto hir sufficiente barne roome for the threstinge
of the same in dewe and convenieyent tyme and season. I give
unto my said wyfe my wheat racke standinge a litle above the
back barne and two bushles of Rie. I doe give unto my wife foure
of my best milke kyne to go and depasture from time to time
during hir lifetime upon the best pastures in somer belonging my
farme, and in winter to goe to the best winter groundes belonging
the same to be foothered and fedd. My will is that my sonne,
William, shall, during hir lyfe, deliver or cause to be delivered
one foother or wagneload of Cooles, she paieing for it at the pitt,
and one foother or wagneload of whinnes. I give unto my
dawghter, Margaret Watson, three score of good tenn poundes
and god's blessing on myne. Unto the said Annie Watson, my
wife, and Margaret Watson, my dowghter, all my household stuff
and implements of husbandry. I give unto John Burdon, my
sonne-in-law, 10s. I give to my daughter Katherine's two
children, Rowland Burdon and Robt. Burdon, three ewes and their
lambes. I give unto my daughter Elizabeth's children, Tobias
and George Readheed, either of them a cowe. I give the rest of
my goods to my sons, William Watson and John Watson.
Witnesses, Francis Green, William Bambrough.

THOMAS APPLEBYE.[1]

Nov. 4, 1612.. I, Thomas Applebye of East Rainton. To be
buryed in the Church or Churchyarde where it shall please god to
call me. I give to James Jackson, sonne of Thomas Jackson, my
land and rent thereof in Northumberland lyeing in Thornton. I
give unto Elizabeth Ranson my black why. To every one of my
sisters' three children a yow and a lambe. I give to Mergery
Applebye, in Newcastle, 30s. I give to Robt. Atkinson, 4l. To
Railph Atkinson, 4l. I give to Robt. Jackson, 3l. 6s. 8d. To
James Atkinsone, 3l. 6s. 8d. I give to the poore of Houghton
parish, 40s. To Thomas Jackson, 10s. To Jane Jackson, his
daughter, 5s. (My debts that I owe.) I owe unto Anthony Surrell,
of Newbottle, 15l. 8s. Unto John Chilton, shoemaker, of Durham,
6l. To William Ingledew, 13l. 6s. 8d. To Edward Nickson,
shoemaker, for fower payre of shooes. To James Atkinson, upon
a bond, 5l. (Debts owen to me.) Mr. John Heeth, of Ramside,
doth owe me 60l. Edward of Weston doth owe to me 10l. 5s.
Thomas Pearesonn, of Hart, doth owe to me 11l. Mrs. . . . .
Forser, of Harbress, 11l. Robt. Wheateley, of Chester, 8l. 13s. 4d.
Bernard Arkle, of West Herington, 10l. 13s., and what els that

[1] The testator was bur. at Houghton-le-Spring, 6 Nov., 1612, and
his widow, Jane, 25 May, 1626.

will appeare by specialtye in writinge. Anthony Cotes, of
Pensher, 5s. Mr. Henry Whitheade, 10s. Mris Barbary Middleton
for a load of oats, 6s. William Storie, of Washington, 10s.
Mr. Robt. Davill oweth me 10s. I doe make and ordaine my
wife, Jane Applebye, and James Jackson, sonne of Thomas Jacksone, joynt executors of this my will and Testament, whom I give
and bequeath all the rest of my goods and chattalls, except such
as is specifyed in this my will. I give to John Jackson a yowe.
To Anthonye Airay, for writing this, my last Will, 3s. 4d.
Witnesses, Anthony Ayray, Curate, Thomas Jackson.

JOHN HETHE.[1]

Nov. 24, 1612. Will of me, John Hethe, the elder, of Kepeyere,
in the County of Durham, Esquire. I doe give and bequeth to all
my household servants as well men as women which have served
me a yere before my deathe, and then shall be alyve and in service,
to every one of them one whole yeres wages over and above the
wages then due to them. Also I give and bequeth to John Booth,
who was my servante, 10s. And to Elysabeth Booth, his wife,
10s., in remembrance of my good will. Also I doe give to
Christopher Aireson, my Bailyfe, 10s., and to Alice, his wife,
10s. Also I doe give to Thomas Pryorman and Awdeley, his wife,
to eyther of them, 5s. Also I give and bequeathe to my brother,
Mr. Nicholas Hethe, fower Angells, to by him a ringe for a
remembrance in token of my good will. Also I bequeathe unto
my nephewe, John Heathe, of Ramside, my godsone, fyve marks
for a remembrance of my good will. Also I give and bequeath
unto my brother-in-law, Mr. John Kinge, 10s., and to my sister,
An, his wife, 10s., in remembrance of my good will. Also I give
to Thomas Billingham, sone to Richard Billingham, of Durham,
Marchant, 10s. Also I doe and bequeth and forgive my daughter,
Dorothy Heth, wife of my sone, John Hethe, the sume of three
and fyfty shillings and fower pence, which I payd for hir to
John Widdowes. Also I give to my said daughter, Dorothy Heth,

[1] The testator, eldest son of John Heath of London after of Kepyer,
was bur., 28 Jan., 1617/18, at St. Giles', Durham; he mar. Elizabeth
dau. of John Parker of Norwich; she was bur., 21 Oct., 1612, at St.
Giles. His brother Nicholas mar. Anne, dau. of John Topp of Shalling-
ford, co. Berks., and was bur. at St. Giles, 16 July, 1627. His son John,
born 1568, bur., 7 Jan., 1639/40, aged 71, at St. Giles, mar. Dorothy,
dau. of John Blakiston of Blakiston (she was bur. at St. Giles, 19 Oct.,
1631, aged 70), his son Thomas mar. Dorothy, dau. of Richard Bunny of
Newlands, she was buried at St. Giles, 17 May, 1642. their son John of
Gray's Inn, bapt., 30 Sept., 1604, at Pittington, bur. 7 Mch., 1664/5, at
St. Giles, mar. Margaret, dau. of William Smith of Durham, 27 Oct.,
1623, St. Mary-le-Bow (bur., 9 July, 1670, at St. Oswald's). His dau.
Thomasine (bur. 28 Sept., 1654, at St. Oswald's) mar. Thomas Lever,
9 Nov., 1590, at St. Giles.

wyfe of my said sone, John Hethe, tenn Angells, for a remembrance of my good will. Also I give and bequeth to my daughter, Dorothy Heth, wife of my sone, Thomas Heth, tenn Angells. Also I give and bequethe to John Heth, eldest sone of my sonne, Thomas Heth, which is my godsonne, fower Angells. Also I give to my sonne-in-law, Mr. Thomas Lever, six Angells, to make him a ringe. Also I give and forgive to my said sonne-in-law, Mr. Thomas Lever, the hundreth pounds which he doeth owe to me which I lent to him as by his Bill will appeare. Also I give and bequeath to John Lever, eldest sonne of my said sonne-in-law, Mr. Thomas Lever, my godson, fower Angells. Also I give and bequeath to Elizabeth Lever, daughter to my said sone-in-lawe, Mr. Thomas Lever, two Angells. Also I bequeath to my cosin, George Martin, two Angells, in remembrance of my good will, and to his wyfe, my cosin, Thomazin Martin, two Angells. Also I give and bequethe to Hethe Lever, daughter to my said son-in-law, Mr. Thomas Lever, one Angell. Also I doe give and bequethe to my daughter, Thomasin Lever, wyfe to Mr. Thomas Lever, these things followeinge, viz. : All the plate which is att Little Lever in her owne possession, and all such household stuffe, linnen, pewter, brasse, beddinge, and whatsoever is myne, and is now at Little Lever which I lent to hir husband, Mr. Thomas Lever, to occupye and use as by a note of his hand subscribed by him will appeare. And whereas I have and am seazed in fee of the reversion of two closes or peels of ground, the one called Beadwell and the other Goodrigg Close, lyinge and being within the terrytoryes of Newton, nigh Durham, expectent upon a lease for fower thousand yeares, heretofore made by me to George Middleton upon which lease was reserved and is yet payable to me, my heirs and assignes during the said terme the yearly rent of 20l., upon the tenth daye next after the feast day of Pentecost, and the tenth day next after the feast day of St. Martin, the Byshopp, in winter by equall porcyons at or in the house or great gaites of the house of Keepyere, betwixt the hours of one and three, in the after noone of the same tenth daye with a condicon that if the said rent be not payd accordinglye that then the saide lease be voide as by the saide lease bearing date the tenth day of December, in the three and thirtyth yere of the Reign of the late Queen Elizabeth, may appeare, Now I doe by this last Will devise and give the said resercon and rent of 20l. to my daughter, Thomazin Lever, wife of Thomas Lever, of Lettle Lever, in the Countye of Lancaster, Esquire, and hir assignes, for and during her naturall life, and doe also immediately after my decease give and devise the same rent and revercon to the executors and administrators of the said Thomazin Lever for the terme of two yeares after hir death, and after the death of the said Thomazin and the said two yeares notice being left att the great gate of Keepyere, or have given unto the said Thomas Blakiston, or his heirs, of the tyme, the same

rent and resercon to remaine to Thomas Blackiston, of Newton,
aforesaid, and his heirs for ever, which Thomas Blackiston hath
alreadie the interest of the said longe terme and is now tenant in
possession of the said closes and is to pay the said rent. Provided
alwaines and upon condicon that if the said Thomas Blackiston
his heirs, executors or administrators shall not well and truly
pay the said rent of 20*l*. yearly to my saide daughter, Thomazin
Lever, or hir assigns, during hir lyfe, and shall not and doe not
likewise within two yeares after hir death pay or cause to be
payed the sum of 240*l*. unto such of the children of the saide
Thomazin or to others, to and for their uses as the saide Thomazin
shall by hir last Will and Testament nominate and appointe and
if she dye, [intestate], or make any appointment, howe to whome
the said 240*l*. shall be payed, Then if the said Thomas Blakiston
and his heirs do not within the said two yeares pay or cause to be
payed the said sume of 240*l*. to the right heires of me, the said
John Heth to and for the use of the said Thomazin Lever, which
shall be unpayed at the time of hir death equally to be divided
amongst them, I doe will and devise and appoint that upon
faile of payment of the said 240*l*. and the 20*l*. rent by the said
Thomas Blackiston or any part thereof, that then my right heires
shall sell the inheritance of the said closes and grounds at the best
price and rate can be gotten for the same, and the money and
price thereof to devide, give and distribute to such of my said
Daughter's children equally amongst them as were to have had
the saide 240*l*. Also I doe give and bequeathe to my sonne,
Thomas Heth, a lease I have of Edmond lese, or otherwise called
Edmund leses, made by Mr. William Tempest for certain yeares
yet to come if the said William Tempest shall lyve so longe as by
the lease will appeare my sonne, Thomas Heth, paying the rent
and observinge the covenants couteyned in the lease which I
should doe, And the 40*l*. which I lent him I doe forgive him.
Also I doe give unto my said sonne, Thomas Heth, my gould ringe
with my seale of Armes graven in it in cristall. And I give unto
my said sonne All mv household stuffe at the East Grange, called
Powlton Grange, where he now dwelleth, which to me belongeth.
Also I doe give to my said sonne all these things hereafter
mentioned, wheresoever they be whether att Keepyere or the
Grange where Dame Morland dwelt, or at the east grange, aforesaide, viz. : One deepe bowle for beere of silver, one silver bowle
gilt for wine, a silver salt Double gilt, without a cover being the
best salt sellar except one, twelve spoones parcell gilt, one silver
birker with a cover, a silver cupp chalice fashion. Also I give
in plate more which he hath in his own custodye that I lent him,
viz. : A silver tunne for beere and a little silver tunne for wine.
Also in linninge fower pare of large linnin sheetes, apare of
fustion blanketts, two paire more of linning sheets. Also two pare
of new linning sheets, two pare of large linninge sheets, three

pare of other linning sheets, one pare of strakinge sheets, two
pare of harden sheets, three pare of courser harden sheetes. Two
dozen of Dyaper napkins, one dozen of fyne linning napkins, ten
ling napkins sewed with blewe, two dozen of other linn napkins,
one dozen of course linn napkins, fower linn table clothes two of
the best and two next best, one fyne linn table cloth, the best
dyaper table clothe, one long linn table cloth which was for the
hall at Keepyere, three course table clothes of linn, two table clothes
of straken, the best dyaper towell, one fyne longe dyper towell,
one large linn towell, two linn towells shorter, three course linn
towells for servants, six short straken towells, two dyaper cupboard
clothes the best of all and the best but two, one fyne linn cupbord
cloth, one lared cupbord cloth of linn, one plaine cupbord cloth
of linn, one pare of fine pillowbers, fower pare of courser pillowbers, two pare of them better and two pare wórse. Also the best
beefe pott but one, one lesser brass pott, one other lesser brass
pot, one yetlinge pan, one latten pan, one brass pott for beefe,
two little pans a greater and a lesse, one great fish pann with an
iron bowl which was bought of my cosinge, John Heth, of Ramside,
one possnett, two best spetts, the best kettle of all and the best
but one, the best dripping pann, the brass laddle with the handle
of brass, a chaiser, the best frying pann, a candle case, one great
voider of pewther, foure large platters of pewter, fower lesser
platters of pewter, three large deepe dishes of pewter, three lesser
deepe dishes of pewter, two lesser deepe dishes of pewter, three
shallow dishes of pewter, two lesse sallot dishes, three lesse deepe
dishes of pewter, two other sallot dishes, two dishes for butter of
pewter, two lesser dishes of pewter than they, one dozen of the
best plates of pewter, six lesser plates of pewter, two large pye
plates one lesser pye plate of pewter, the best hand bason, one
deepe pece bason, one little bason to soitt in all of pewter, two
chamber potts, two flower potts of pewter, two large sawcers,
five lesser sawcers of pewter, one dozen of pottendishes, three large
dishes of pewter, one large fishplate sanded, two lesse sanded dishes,
two little deepe sanded dishes, fower of the best sanded dishes
of all, all of pewter, two high candlesticks, two lower candlesticks,
one great beer pott, one quart pott, one pyntt potte, one gill pott
all of pewter, one searcher, one broylinge iron. I doe give and
bequieth to my sonne, John Hethe, if he be lyving at the tyme
of my decease, all these things following in manner and forme as
they are expressed, viz. : One spout potte of silver, the best salt
seller of silver dowble gilt with a cover, one little trencher salt of
silver gilt with a cover, to use during his natural life, and after
his decease to come to my sonn, Thomas Hethe, and his heirs, and
so to remaine as heirelomes to the house for ever, one silver bowl
for beer, one silver bowl for wine, one gilt silver boole for wine,
sixe silver slippt spoons, two silver tunnes and six other silver
slippt spoons, which I lent him, and he hath in his owne keepinge.

Also I give and bequieth to my said sonne, John Heth, all my
househould stuff at Keepeyere, unbequeathed in this will, and also
excepting all such chists, boxes, writtings and other things in my
studdye there, which I will my executour shall have. Also I doe
give to my said sonne, John Heth, all such househould at the
Grange where Dame Morland did dwell, unbequethed before in
this Will, and also excepting all maner of cattle, horses, swyne and
all other quick goodes whatsoever, and also excepting all corne in
the barne in on the groundes, hay in the stack garth in all the
feilds or aboute the house, also all waines and waine geare,
ploughes and plough geare with all things thereunto belonging
whatsoever. Also I doe give and bequiethe to my said sonne, John
Hethe, all such debts and summs of monney as Mr. Robert Bowes,
some tymes Treasurer of Barwick, and his sonne, Mr. Railph
Bowes, did owe to my father, and is dewe to me, his executour,
amountinge to the sum 107l. 15s. 10d., as by his bills and reckings
will appeare. Also whereas I have lente to my said sonne, John
Heth, at dyvers tymes, so muche moneye as doth amount to the
sume of 454l. as by dyvers bills will appeare, vizt., by one bille of
200l., bearing date 1 April, 1599, And by another bill of the sum
of 100l. date the 29 March, 1602, as also by another bill of the
sume of 100l. bearing date the 2 April, 1602, now my will and
meaninge is that if my said sonne, John Heth, not make any wast
in destroyeinge the woods that are upon any of my groundes, but
shall have power only to take convenient hedgeboote, ploughboote
and houseboote to uphold the houses, neyther shall digge any
cooles or colemines therein, but shall only take the annuall and
yerely increase of the premises. Also my will is that yt he doe
not molest nor trouble my sonne, Thomas Hethe, nor suffer him to
be troubled by his meanes or procurement, but suffer him quietly
to enioye all whatsoever either landes or goods which I have given,
granted, bequiethed or conveyed unto him by my manner or meanes
whom I doe make my sole Executour, then my will and meaninge
is that my said sonne, Thomas, shall keep the said bills in his hand
and putt them in suite att all, but yt my said sonne, John Heth,
shall doe contrary to this my will in felling or makeing wast of the
woods belonging to the premises or diggings of any mynes for coles
or any other matters, or doe not sufficyentlye repaire and keepe
upp all the houses in his possession and yf he doe molest my said
sonne, Thomas Heth, by anv meanes or procurement of his behalfe
in any of the premises which I have given, granted, bequeithed or
conveyed unto my said sonne, Thomas Heth, then my Will is that
my said sonne, Thomas Heth, shall sewe, putt in suite, and recover
the benefitt of the said bills before rehearsed to his own use and
behoof. And I doe make and ordayne my sonne, Thomas Heth,
sole Executour of this my last Will, whom I will to pay and pforme
all such things as shallbe by me left undone att my decease,
which I promsed my wyfe to do in hir lyfe tyme as by a note of

hir owne hand will appeare, whome I also trust will see my bodye decentlye brought to the grave, and after my funnerall discharged, my father's debts and mine payd and my fathers and my legacies pformed, and all my wyve's requests and desires performed as by hir aforesaid note of hir hand shall appeare. And I doe give to mv said Executour, Thomas Heth, all such debts which are due to me, goods and household stuffe, plate, cattle, Chattells and whatsoever goods properly appertayneth to me, John Heth. And also I make and ordeyne my wellbeloved brother, Nicholas Heth, overseer of this my Will and Testament. And here I make an end of this my last Will, and I doe revoke and disannull all and every other former Wills by me in anywise before this tyme made or done. Witnesses, John King, John Watson, Robt. Hudspeth, Stephen Hegg, Mark Forster, Wilm. Murray, Christopher Ayrson. Sma totalis, 298*l*. 4*s*. Proved, 1617.

EDWARD CHARLTON.

Dec. 28, 1612. Edward Charlton of Bellingham. My bodie to be buried in Bellingham Church or quier. I give to my wife and my daughter all my whole lands, tenements, houses, corn and oatts goods and whatsoever I have, and my brother John to be onely tuter to my daughter. And if my wife chance to marrye agayne that then she shall remove from all my lands and houses, and that my brother John shall use the same. And that if my Brother John chance to have a man childe hereafter lawfullie begotten, that then he have my lands. I make my wyfe sole Executor. Witnesses, John Charlton of Readsmouth, Edward Charlton of Auton hill, John Douglass of Woodespinles, James Aynsley of Bellingham. Probate, 13th November, 1615, to Jane Charlton, Widow (formerly the wife of John Dodd), Isabella Charlton, the Daughter.

RALPH DENNIS.

Feb. 27, 1612. In the name of God, Amen, I Ralph Dennis of Scremerston, of the pish of Ancroft within the liberties of Norham pcell of the Countie Pallatine of Durham. To be buryed at the discretion of my friends. I make Helene, my wife, and Michaell Ewart, my sone-in-law, my sole and full Executors to execute this my Will. I request my loveing friend, Thomas Wrey of Ancroft, aforesaid, to be supervisore of the same. I bequeath to Isabell Ewart, my daughter, fortie shillings to be pd at suche tyme or tymes as my said wife may best paye the same. I hereby requeste Michaell Ewart, the husband of my said daughter, to have a speciall care that my sonne Edmund being now an Infant, be not wronged so farr as he may be able to procure help for him. I bequeath unto my daughter Margaret, 30*s*., to be pd in mannr above written.

Debts oweing by the Testator. Oweing to Thomas Cooke of
Durham the sume of 5*l.* The said Thomas received of me an over
Sea Cloth for the whie Edward Sur . . . my brother-in-law an
oxe worth 46*s.* 8*d.*, George Wray of Scremerston payd me lease for
the said oxe wherefore I think that the said Thomas should be well
content to abate 40*s.* for the same. Owing to Harry Smith of
Haggerston for an oxe, 50*s.* I ow to Isabell Selbye 20*s.*, to be pd
at the annunciation of the Virgin Mary, comonly called Lady day
in Lent. Owing to Ralph Wray of Scremston for a nagg 3*l.* 10*s.*,
to be paid at candelmas next. I ow to Thomas Dennes there for
an young oxe 33*s.* 4*d.*, to be pd at Candelmas as is above written.
I ow to Mr. Thomas Swynhoe of Goswick for two boles of pease
26*s.* 8*d.*, whereof the one boll is to be paid this yeare and the
other at Candlemas. I ow to Richard Wilsone of Scremerston,
40s. I ow to John Bell of Beale, 8*s.* 6*d.* I ow to my mavde, Jane
York, 10*s.* To Mrs. Haggerston for cheese, 3*s.* 4*d.* Owing to my
cosin, Thomas Dennes, 4*s.* Owing to my other mayde, 2*s.* 6*d.*
Item. These my debts, legases and funerall Dewes be dyscharged.
I bequeath to my wyfe the third of all the rest. And in case if
either god shall call upon hir out of this lyfe or that she . . . . to
the worlde againe, and that hir future husband will not be content
that she Kepe my said sone with her, in consideration thereof
I bequeath the tuition of my sonne to Michaell Ewarte above
written, and his wife, my daughter, together with all that I shall
dye possessed off, my debts above written, funerall dues, legacies,
and my wyve's thirds being first payde. I bequeath unto my sonne
Edmunde, my bed, my boorde and my chaire which was my
father's, together with my ryding geare, viz., my Jack, my steale
cap, and my sworde, and all my work hames. This to be my last
Will and Testament hereby by me made. Witnesses, Thomas Wray,
William Dennis. Edward Cook, and Adam Batie. Clerk. Proved.
25 Feb., 1613.

ANTHONY RICHESON.[1]

The last Will and Testament of Anthony Richeson of Kirklay,
in the Countie of Northumberland, yeoman, deceased the 12th day
of March, 1612. In the name of God, Amen, I Anthony Richeson.
To be buried in Ponteland Church. I give unto my brother Cuthbert, my eldest sonne, William Richeson, all my four noble farme,
with all my plue geare thereto belonging. And to my frend,
John Lowyreson, my youngest sonne, John Richeson, and a marke
farme with a house thereto belonging, and to my brother, Micheall
Richesonn, my daughter Elizabeth, an armorary, a beink and a
poott, and all the inseed except twoo bedding of clothes for my twoo

[1] The testator was bur. at Ponteland, 14 March, 1611/12 (*sic*); his
son John was bapt. there, 27 Jan., 1607/8.

sonns, and for all the reste of my goods and catle for to be equallie devided, and parted in three equal porrions for the use of my twoo sonns and my daughter, except one branded whye, which I give unto my sister Maly Pyes sonne which I christened, and to every one of the rest of hir children a bushill of oates, and to a sonne of Heugh Willye which I christened, a yowe lamb, and more to my Brother Michael's wife a bushill of harde corne every yeare during three yeare, and unto my Brother Cuthbert twoo nages, a graye and a blacke, for the payment of debt in New-castell, I mor give unto my Brother Cuthbert a browne kowe for to buy him corne for to find his house untill Whitsonday next ensu-ing the dat hereof. Given to Allis Lightfoot a branded whye, and to Mark Ogle, the younger, Gentleman, a bay maire (1612). Witnesses, Henry Thompson, John Twissell, Anthony Twyssell. Proved, 13 Oct., 1612.

JAMES HALL.[1]

1613. In the name of God, Amen, I, James Hall, of Bishop Middleham, in the County of Durham, yeoman. I give to my eldest sonne, Christopher Hall, in consideration of his fyliall por-con, 50*l*. To my second sonne, John Hall, 50*l*. To my daughter, Ann Hall, three score pounds in consideration of her filiall porcon, and the whole of my houshold stuffe. To my daughter, Jane Hall, three score pounds and the moyte of my household stuffe. To my youngest sonne, James Hall, three score pounds. I give to the poore of Bishop Middleham pish, 5*s*. . To my well beloved Mother Margaret Hall, 5*s*. for a token of remembrance. To Dorothye Hall, my wive's browne coate and a paire of my hose and shewes, which were my wive's. To my servante, Elizabeth Litster, a browne wastcoate. To Anne Widdifield a peece of silver of 5*s*. I will that my mother have some parte of my wive's apparell at the discretion of my executors. I give to Christian Hutcheson a peece of gold of 5*s*. 6*d*. If any thing remaines, that my two eldest sonns shall be made equally with my sonne, James. I doe make and ordayne my well beloved friende, John Lee, of Fishburne, gentleman, my sole Executore. And I doe make Edward Blaxton, of Chilton, John Warde, of Middleham, and my Brother, Francis Hall, of Worsall, Supervisors of this my Will. Witness, Edward Blaxton, John Warde, and Richard Middleton.

Memn that the above named John Lee being at the time the probacon of the said testament, demannded to whose use he was made executor of the said testament, he answered and confessed that he was made executor only in trust to and for the use of the said testator's children only. Sic : subscript, John Lee.

[1] The testator's wife, Mary, was bur. at Bishop Middleham, 17 Oct., 1613, and he on 13 Nov., in the same year.

RAULPH PRESTON.

April 14, 1613. Raulph Preston, of Cowpen, in the Countye of Northumberland. My body to be buried in the church of Horton. I give unto my sister, Gilyan Preston, 9*l*. 10*s*., the which I remaine indebted unto her, 6*l*. whereof is in my brother, John Preston's hand, and 3*l*. 10*s*. in George Watson's hand, dwelling att Kempley Carre, due to be paid unto me. I give and bequeathe unto my three brethern, John Preston, William Preston, Gawin Preston, and my two Sisters, Elizabeth Watson and Gilyan Preston, and to my cosin, George Askeham, the third part of my shipp called the gods grace of Sunderland and the fourth part of a shipp called the gods help of Sunderland, and likewise 16*l*. which one Rychard Moores of London doth owe unto me, as by his bond—Witnesses, Thos. Handley, Thomas Haigh. Probate, 6th July, 1613.

ROBERT HORSLEY.

April 20, 1613. Robert Horsley of Alneham. My body to be buried within the church or chancell where it is most convenient to be done by my friendes and wife. I bequeath to my mother when the corne comes of the ground, one bushell of wheate or rye, one bushell of oatts, one bushel of pes. I also bequeath to my brother Thomas Horsley's two children, either of them, one guye stirke. The residue of my goods to my sone, John Horsley and my wife. I also leave my sone, John Horsley, to Mr. Charles Horsley my verie goud friende, and be a father unto him to be brought up in the feir of god, kept at the schoole, after put to an apprentice. Witnesses, Thomas Ollenex, Richard Herron, Edward Robson, Robert Horsley and Thos. Horsley. Witnesses to Inventory, Robert Horsley in Ailenham, Thomas Horsley of Scranewood, and Robert Chatter in Ailneham. Probate, 23 Feb., 1613.

ELIZABETH WRENN.[1]

June, 1613. In the name of Gode, Amen, I, Elizabeth Wrenn, of Bushop Awcklande, widow, late wife of Anthonie Wren of Binchester, in the County of Durham, Esq. To be buried in the

[1] Daughter of Christopher Wandisforde of Aldwark, co. York; she was bur., 22 Dec., 1613, at St. Andrew's, Auckland. She mar. Anthony Wren who was bur. at Auckland, 11 Nov., 1595. Charles, the eldest son, was bapt., 26 June, 1564, at Auckland (from whence the other dates are taken); Francis, bapt., 10 Mch., 1565/6, mar. Elizabeth Spenceley, 30 July, 1594, at Egglescliffe, and bur. 5 Nov., 1630; Mary, bapt., 2 Feb., 1561/2, mar. Sir John Claxton of Nettlesworth (bapt. 25 Oct., 1560, bur. at Chester-le-Street, 3 Jan. 1637/8, son of Robert Claxton); Jane, bapt., 5 May, 1569, bur., 12 Feb., 1605/6, mar. at Escomb, 3 July, 1592, Sir Henry Frankland. There will be found a pedigree of the Wren family in this Society's publications, vol. 124, pp. 205-8.

Quire of my pish church of St. Andrew, Awckland. As for my
wordly goods my mind and will is as followethe. I give to my
revert Lord, the Lord Bp. of Durham, a 30 shillings peece of gold
as a poore token, my thankfulnes for all his hond favoures and
goodness to me and myne. I give to his sonns, Mr. Timothie and
Mr. Francis James, to eyther of them, an halfe ryall of gould as
a token. I give and bequeathe to my grandchilde, John Claxton,
sonne of Sir John Claxton, Knight, 20*l*. of the 50*l*. his father dothe
owe unto me as a remembrance of my love unto him. I give to
his mother, the Ladie Mary Claxton, my daughter, my crosse of
gould. I give to my grandchilde, Anthonye Frankland, sonne
of Sir Henry Frankeland, Knight, 50*l*. out of that two hundred
and thirtee pounds which my sonne, Francis Wren, oweth unto
me, to be paid unto him when he shall accomplishe the age of
twenty one years. The residue of the said sume I give and bequeath
amongst my grandchildren, the daughter of my sonne, Francis
Wren, accordinge to an order an agrement maid by the right
reverd father, the Lo. Bp. of Durham, that now is, and Michaell
Pemberton and Robt. Pemberton, gent., which said order and agreement if my said sonne, Francis Wren, refuse to pforme of his
parte, then my mynde and will is that the said sume of two hundred and thirtie pounds shall stande and remayne as a dew debt
unto my executors, and that they do paie the said sum of 50*l*.
formerly bequeathed to my grandchilde Anthonie Frankland,
when he shall accomplish the full age of 21 yeares. I give to
Lyndley Wren my grandchild my wedding ringe my best dozen
of sylver spoones and the cupp which was my brother Wandisfords.
To my grandchild Charles Wren, 40*l*. towards his maintenance
at the Univsities. I give to Henry Wren, my grandchild, 20*l*.
to be paid out of my houses in Awckland. To the Ladie Wren, my
daughter-in-lawe, my gold ringe with the turcasse stone. To my
grandchild, Francis Wren, one of my white cupps of sylver. To
my worll friende, Mr. Doctor Colmore, one angell of gold, and to
his daughter, Mrs. Fulthorp, my best kyrtle, and to my good sone,
Mr. Clement Colmore a band and paire of Cuffs. I give to my
kind cozen, Thomas Chaytor, an angell of gould. To my cozen,
Mr. Edward Hutton, and to my niece, his wife, to eyther of
them a 20*s*. peece of gould. To my nephew, Mr. Christopher
Lassells, an angell of gold. I give to my sister, Downes, and to
my cozen, George Downes, to either of them, an angell of gould.
To my cozen, Mr. Roger Lazenbie, 4*l*. whereof he oweth me 40*s*.
To my cozen, William Blackett, 40*s*. To my kind friend, Martyn
Jackson, a 20*s*. peece of gould. To my kind friendes, Robt.
Armstrong and Willm. Brasse, to eyther of them, an old ryall.
To John Martindale, Robt. Tompson, Chrisfer Wrene, and John
Clarke, to every of them, an angell of gould, and to my godsoon,
Charles Martindale a french crowne. To my cozen, Mr. Clement
Lambert, 5*s*. and to my kind neighbor, John Wilson, 5*s*. To my

worll and kind friende, Mr. Morecrooft, parson of Stanhope, a 20s. peece of gould, requestinge him to preach at my funerall and to burye me. I give to the stocke of the poore of St. Andrew, Auckland parish, 5l. and 5l. to be distributed amongst the poore householders and neadie people of the said pish, at the discretion of my executors. The residue of all my goodes and chattells, I give and bequeathe unto my loveing sonne, Sir Charles Wren, Knight, whom I make sole executor. Witnesses hereof, Ferdinand Moorecrooft, Robt. Armstrong, George Lazenbye, William Blackett.

HENRY STEVENSON.[1]

June 23, 1613. In the name of God, Amen, I, Henry Stevenson, of Clapurth, in the Cittie of Durham, cordiner. To be buried in St. Nicholas Church in the cittie of Durham. I give to the poore of St.Nicholas pish, tenn shillinges in money, to be bestowed amongst them in bread and cheese, the morrow next after my buryall. I bequeathe to, Margaret Stevenson, my wife, the house with the appurtenances wherein I now dwell so long as she is my wife. I also give her the burgage lying nigh the yarde yaits, wherein Ralphe Waide now dwells, and after her decease, that the said burgage shall come wholly and clearly to my sonne, Henry Stevenson, and his heires for ever. I will that the burgage and appurtences wherein I now dwell, after the death of my said wife, or immediately after her marriage, shall come fullv to my sonne, Christopher Stevenson, with all the right and title thereof for and with my Stall Roome in the Church. I give to my wife all my household stuff and gear, and also my malt stocke, and my wife to pay unto John Ayre, of Wolsingham, three poundes in money, which I owe unto him. I give unto my foure sonns, 20s. apeece. Witnesses, Edward Taylor, George Craggs, John Inglebye, John Lyttle.

WILLIAM DALTON.[2]

July 19, 1613. In the name of God, Amen, I, William Dalton, the elder, of the towne of Newcastle upon Tyne, in the County of the same towne, gentleman. To be buryed in the pish

[1] The testator was bur., 29 June, 1613, at St. Nicholas, Durham, where he mar. his wife, Margaret, 27 Oct., 1588, and where she was bur., 19 Apl., 1622; by her he had Henry, who mar. Elizabeth Hudson, widow, 11 Sept., 1621, and was bur., 8 Aug., 1641; Christopher, bapt., 20 Apl., 1589, bur., 31 Mch., 1628, mar. Margaret Harrison, 13 June, 1613, at St. Mary-le-Bow; Ralph, bapt., 22 July, 1591, bur. 25 May, 1653, mar. Mirriel, 20 June, 1614; Thomas, bapt., 22 May., 1595, bur., 28 Nov., 1681 (all dates from St. Nich., Durham).

[2] He was bur. at St. Andrew's, Newcastle, 23 July, 1613; his son William's wife, Barbary, was bur., 12 May, 1646; his son, Lionel, was bur., 5 Aug., 1620.

church of St. Andrews, within the towne of Newcastle upon Tyne aforesaid, where I am a pshioner, where my ancestors lye, or as nigh thereunto as convenientlie as may be. And touching my lands, tenements, goods, chattells, and possessions, which by god's pmission I have and possess, I give and bequeath them in manr and forme followinge, that is to say, first whereas I have advanced and estated my eldest sonne, William Dalton, of certain of my lands and tenements in the County 'of Northumberland, I will he and his heires male of his bodye lawfully begotten, shall have hold and enjoy the same duringe their naturall lives, and for want of such issue male my will is that the said lands shall pass unto the heires male of the next of kin of the Daltons for ever. And touching the tenements and farmhold situate in Northwetsled, in the same County of Northumberland, now in the occupation of Ralph Walker and John Walker, I give and bequeath the same to the heires male of my said sonne William, of his heirs lawfully begotton of his body, and for want of such issue male my will is that the said lands shall pass unto the heires male of the next of kindred of the Daltons for ever. I will give and bequeath those two tenements, with their appurtenances, situate and being in Pilgrim Street, within the said towne of Newcastle, the one in the occupation of me the said William Dalton, and the other in the occupation of Richard Browne, baker and brewer, as followeth, that is to say, to my sonne, Lionell Dalton, and the heirs male of his body lawfully begotten, and for default of such issue to William Dalton, sonne of the said William Dalton, and the heires male of his bodye lawfully begotten, and for default of such issue to the next heires male of me the said William Dalton for ever. I will give and bequeath all those my sixteene butts or riggs of land called tempest Lyezes, situate lying, and being in the territories of Elswicke, in the County of Northd., late in the occupation of Bertram Anderson Marchant, deceased, to my aforesaid sonne, Lyonell Dalton, and the heires male of his bodye lawfully begotten; and for default of such issue to the said William Dalton, sonne of my said sonne William, and the heires male of his body lawfully to be begotton; and for lack of such issue to my next heire male for ever in manner and forme as before is lymitted for the said tenements in Pilgrim Street, Touching two tenements situate in the Midle street, within the said towne of Newcastle, now in the several tenours or occupation of John Atkinson and John Selbye, I give the same tenements to my sonne Lyonell to have one of the said howses to the heires of his bodye lawfully begotten. I give one howse wherein John Selbye nowe dwelleth standing in the said Midle Street unto my daughter Elizabeth, during her naturall lyffe, and after her natural lyfe, to my said sonne Lyonell, and the heires male of his bodye lawfully begotten as aforesaid. And where I have one covenante without Pilgrim Street gates and a certain pcell of land thereunto belonginge nowe to the severall tenours or occupations of Robert Anderson Marchant and one Ralph Hall which I heretofore bought and purchased in the name of my said sone Lyonell, I will and devise that the same tenement and land in part of satisfaction of my said sonne Lyonell, his child's part and portion of my goods and chatteles shall remaine to him and his heire as aforesaid for ever. I give and bequeath to Robert Dalton, sonne of William Dalton, my out rents going out of the tenements hereunder mentioned to him and his heires for ever, that is to say, the outrents going out of a tenement now in the occupation of John Malaber, glover, the sum of 3s. 4d. situate near the heade of All Hallow bancks within the said towne of Newcastle, and 3s. going out of a tenement thereunto next adjoining now in the occupation of Robert C. . . . Sadller, and 12d., yearly going out of cellar at the topp of the painter heugh a cellar there now in the occupation of Robert Gibson Marchant, or his assigns, and 12d. going out of a howse next adjoining to the . . . mose howses in the prior chaire now in the occupation of John Stobbs. I give and bequeath to my daughter, Elizabeth Dalton, the sum of 40l. of lawful money of England for full payment and discharge of her filiall and child's part of my goods, chattells, rights and debts, the same sume to be paid hir within thre years next after my decease. I give to my sister Grace, 40s., and to Robert Dalton of Newcastle, Baker, 6s. 8d. for a token. Whereas I have given to my said sonne, Lionell Dalton, reversion of the tenements in Pilgrim Street aforesaid, and of the said tenements and lands without Pilgrim Street Gates, all which I estimate to be worth 5l. in the yere the same shall be to him in part satisfaction of his filiall and child's part of all and singular my goods, chattels, rights and debts. And further I doe give unto him in full payment and satisfaction of his said child's part and porcon the howse which Thomas, the Millenner, doth dwell in without Pilgrim Street gates, and one little howse above which Ralph Hall dwells in with the rest above named. I give to Robert Dalton, sonne and heire to my son William Dalton of Wetsled, one yellow oxe for a remembrance. . . . . I doe give unto the said Robert Dalton of Wetsled to give unto his sister, Poley Dalton, the sume of 20l. I give unto Barbarie Dalton, my sone William Dalton, his wife, one brown oxe which my sonne William hath in his occupation. I doe give her as a remembrance. I give unto Barbarie Dalton, Alison Dalton, and Jelyon Dalton, two oxen which were bought at Whitmonday laste paste, to be divided equally amongst them or every of the said children to have the sume of 20s. a piece. I doe give unto my sone William, the sume of 20s. which he did borrow of me, I doe freely give it him. I doe give unto William Dalton, sone unto my sonne William, one black quye. I give unto Dorothie one Black quye which I bought of Andrew Brocket. I give unto my daughter, Elizabeth Dalton, all my goods which

I have at Northwetsled. I have tenne heads of Cattle unbequeathed which I doe give unto hir in parte of hir child's porcon, and twenty yewes and fourteene lames, all which I give unto hir as aforesaid. I give unto Margarie Smith, my sister Daughter, the sum of 6s. 8d. I doe give unto my sone, Lionell Dalton, seven head of cattell which are going twoo of them at Seghell, one at Burowton, and two at Killingworth and two at Newcastle, with one browne naige all which several Cattell I do give unto my sonne Lionell to pay such legacies as I have hereto set downe. I doe give unto Marie Dent, my servant and kinswoman, the sum of 10s. I give unto Michael Baites for a remembrance, 5s. I doe give unto Thomas Claphamson for a remembrance, 3s. I give unto Philipe Dalton the sum of 6s. 8d. I doe give unto James Dalton, 6s. 8d. I give unto Thomas Dalton of Southwetsled the sume of 6s. 8d. I give unto William Dalton of the same towne the sume of 6s. 8d. I doe give unto Geane Dunfere, widow, the sum of ten shillings. I give unto William Dente, Sailor, for a token the sum of 3s. 4d. I give unto Thomas Dente for a token the sum of 3s. 4d. I give unto my mother in law, Elizabeth Railstone, for a remembrance the sume of 6s. 8d. I give unto William Graye of Northwetsled the sume of 5s. for a token. All the residue of my goods, chattels, rights, and debts oweing unto me, my debts and funerall charges being payd and discharged. I wholly give and bequeath to my said sone, Lionell Dalton, in full satisfacon of his porcon, further I ordeyne that he the said Lyonell Dalton, my sone, shall pay all the aforesaid legacies above mentioned and everie part and pcon of the same. And I doe hereby ordeyne and make of this my last Will and Testament my full and sole executor my sonne, Lyonel Dalton, and Elizabeth Dalton, my daughter, to pforme all things herein contained according to my good meaning of this my last Will and Testament. I have given unto Lancelot Hall, my son in law, the sum of 50s. in hand paide moreover. I doe give unto William Hall, my daughter's sone, the sum of 8l., to be paid unto him when it shall please god that he shall come unto the age of 21 yeares, to be paid unto him, by my sone Lyonell out of the porcon which I have given him. I give unto the aforesaid William Hall, one spanged quye, and the said William Hall is to enter upon the profitts of hir presentlye upon my departure, and my sonne William shall keepe hir to the use of the said William Hall. My will is that all the household stuff I have in my howse I will that it shallbe equally devided between my sonne, Lyonell Dalton, and Elizabeth, my daughter. Witnesses, Wm. Readhed, Thomas Pearson, Cuthbert Readheed, Thomas Claphearson, John Pigge, Thomas Myers.

INVENTORY, 62l. 16s. Proved, 1613.

CHRISTOPHER MYTFORD.[1]

Sept. 11, 1613, Christopher Mytford, of the towne of Newcastle upon Tyne, merchante. And my bodie to be buried in the pish church of St. Nicholas within the towne of Newcastle. I give and bequeathe unto Bartram Mytforth, my sonne, all such evidences and writeings which are in my counting house, and all my estate, right, title, interest, and clayme which I nowe have or hereafter to have of and in the messuage lands and tenements, leases, rents whatsoever, except one lease of the house upon the Sande hille now in the tenure of John Milbanke, which he, the said John, is to hold during the said lease, and after the expiration of such lease, to my said sonne, Bartram Mytforth. I give to my said sone, Bartram, and Mrs. Jane Burrell, my daughter, all that my title and interest in a lease of a coale myne in Whitbie more within the lordship of Kenton equallie between them. To my said sone, Bartram Mitforth, one fourth part of a small fishen barke called the Elsabeth. To my son-in-law, Mr. Francis Burrell, and my said daughter, his wife, two several peaces of gold of 22s. the peace. To Peter Burrell, Elinor Burrell and Marie Burrell, to each of them a peace of gold of 22s. the piece. The rest and residue of my goods to my sone, Bartram Mytforth, whom I make sole Executor. I doe appoint Mr. James Claveringe, of the said towne of Newcastle, Alderman and George Fenwick of the said Town Merchant Supervisors of this my Will. Witnesses, James Claveringe, Isabell Mitforth, George Dobsone, William Wandsworth.

INVENTORY, 285l. 15s. 4d. Probate, 1613.

[1] Son of John Mitford by his second wife, Magdalen, dau. of John Fenwick of Kenton, he was probably bapt. at St. Nich., Newcastle (from the registers of which the following dates are taken), 7 Feb., 1561/2. He mar. Elinor Nicholson, 15 Sept., 1590. She was bur., 6 July, 1610, he, 21 Sept., 1613. They had five children, viz. :—Jane, bapt., 10 Sept. 1592 (she mar., first, 2 Feb., 1607/8, Francis Burrell, who was bur., 15 May, 1624, at All' Saints, second, 22 Aug., 1626, Ralph Carnaby of Halton); Roger, bapt., 23 Sept., 1593, bur. 31 May, 1596; Bertram, bapt., 27 July, 1595, mentioned, 29 Sept., 1623, in the will of his cousin John Mitford of Newcastle; Christopher, bapt., 28 May, 1597, bur., 22 Oct, 1599; Timothy, bapt., 18 May, bur., 29 Sept., 1606. Roger Nicholson in his will, 2 Dec., 1590 (38 Surt. Soc., p. 186) mentions his dau., Ellinor Mitford, and his son-in-law, Christopher Mitford. Sponsors at the above-mentioned baptisms include many relations of Elinor, dau. of Roger, viz. :—Henry Chapman, uncle, Mrs. Jane Mitford, great aunt, Matthew Chapman, uncle, Daniel Heckstetter, second husband of her sister Jane, Francis Anderson's wife (Barbara) her sister, James Clavering husband of her sister Grace, the wife of her uncle Henry Chapman, and Francis Anderson, brother-in-law. (The notes in 38 Surt. Soc., p. 187, on Roger Nicholson's sons-in-law, Bertram Anderson and Christopher Mitford, require revision.)

WILLIAM YOUNGE.[1]

Sept., 1613. I, William Younge, of the towne of Sedgefield, in the Bishoprick of Durham. To be buried in the churchyard of Sedgefield and touching the goods which gode hath given unto—thus dispose of them as followeth : I bequeath unto my sonne, Ralph Young, if he returne to Sedgefield anytime within the space and tyme of seven yeares, all my goods whatsoever within and without. I give unto him my two kyne and two calves and tenn sheepe with all my other goods, but if my sonne come not within the time aforesaid that then all my goods whatsoever shall be given and distributed unto four equall parts, the three parts thereof to be given to the poore of Sedgefield towne, the fourthe to rest to the poor within the parish. And this distribution to be made within the term of three yeares next following the expiration of the said seven yeares, and these my goods all of them in the méantime I committ unto the trust and putt into the hands of my nephew, Robt. Younge, of Sedgefield, the elder, to be disposed of by him as aforesaid, and this doe I acknowledge by this my Will—George Wood, curate, Ralph Ellison, Robt. Younge the younger, John Pattison. The testator died, the 9th of September, 1613.

JOHN GAGE.[2]

May 20, 1614. In the name of God, Amen, I, John Gage, of Sedgefield, in the County of Durham, Gent. To be buried in the church or churchyarde of Sedgefield as shall bee appointed. And touching my goods I thus dispose of them, first, I bequeath unto the poore of Sedgefield towne, 3l. I give and bequeath unto my brother, George Gage, 10l. I bequeath to John Gage, sone of my said brother, 10l. I bequeath to Christian Hutchinson, the wife of Robert Hutchinson, of Byshop Midlehan, my sister's daughter, 10l. I bequeath to John Hutchinson. my godsonne, the sonne of the said Robert and Christian Hutchinson, 5l. I give to my wives kinswoman, Jaine Fishburne, wife of Robert Fishburne, of Sedgefield, 40s. I give to John Valyan, of Bradbury, 40s. I bequeath to John Gibson, my servant, 10s. To each of my other servantes, 2s. 6d. I bequeath to each of my godsonns, Christopher Hickson, William Bellarby, Henry Johnson, John Lynne,. John Johnson, the sone of Samuell Johnson, and to everie one of these one lambe. I bequeath to John Valyan, the sone of John Valyan, of Bradbury, one lambe. I bequeath to each one of Robert Fishburne's children

<hr/>

[1] He was bur. at Sedgefield, 12 Sept., 1613, his wife Jane having been bur. there on the 15 August in that year.

[2] He mar. at Sedgefield, *Agnes* Barnes, 2 Dec., 1600, and was bur. there, 29 May, 1614. Christian Hutchinson was bur. at Bishop Middleham, 17 June, 1618. There is a pedigree of Hutchinson in *Arch. Ael.*, 3rd Ser., vol. xiii., pp. 184-5.

to every one of them one lamb a peece. I give and bequeath to my
wife the lease of the messuage and two oxgangs of land in Sedgefield during her naturall life, and after her life ended. I give
and bequeath the said lease to my kinsman, William Tunbridge,
who in that regard shall give at the time of his entrance there
upon the sume of 5*l.* to his brother, Ingraime Tunbridge. I give
unto Mr. George Wood, 22*s.* in gould. I give and bequeath to
Sir George Freville and my ladie, his wife, to each of them, 10*s.*
in gould. My will is that my kinsman, William Tunbridge,
continue in his service to my wyfe dilengently, faithfully and
dutifully, shewing therein all good and kind respect that she may
in which regard he shall have as wages 53*s.* 4*d.* by the yeare with
meate and drinke. I give to all my god daughters to each of them
a lambe, only to my god daughter, Frances Welles, at Merington.
I give and bequeath one young quye to make her a cowe. To every
one of my godsonns, not before named, I give to each of them
one lambe. I signifye by this writinge for the greater security of
my wife that all bills, bonds and other writings and accounts
whatsoever between Sir George Freville and my selfe are discharged and reckoned for, only whereas he layd out about 23*l.*
for that land in great Steynton, he received of me in lieu thereof
one stoned colt, one gelding and one nagg. And lastly all my other
goods moveable and unmovable, my debts, legacies and the charges
of my funerall discharged I give and bequeath to my wife, Anne
Gage, whom by this writinge I doe ordeyne and appoint sole executrix of this my Will, praying Sir George Freville and my Ladie
to see that none doe or offer any wrothe unto my wife. Witnesses,
George Wood, curate.

INVENTORY, 203*l.* 19*s.* 4*d.*

ROGER HEARON.

June 30, 1614. Roger Hearon, of Riplington, in the Countie
of Northumberland, Gentleman. My bodie to be buried in my
parish church of Walton. I give and bequeath all my lands of
Riplington to Sir William Selby, of Shortflat, Knight, and to
Mr. Roger Widdrington, of Cartington, gentleman, to them and
their heirs for ever. I mean as well all my houses and edifices,
buildings, barns, byers, with all lands, pastures of comon to me
belonging. Providing allways that the said Sir William Selby,
Knight, and Mr. Roger Widdrington, gentleman, shall minister
sufficient maintenance unto my selfe during my life, natural, out
of my said lands at Riplington. I give to Jane Pott and her
heirs for ever, 20*s.* a yeare out of my lands aforesaid. I give to
my daughter, Margarett Hearon, and her heirs for ever, yearly,
the sum of 20*s.* and also to Roger Barton and his heirs for ever,
yearly, 30*s.* out of my said lands. I give unto the said Sir
William Selby, Knight, and Mr. Roger Widdrington, all my

lands in Walton. I give to Jane Pott and hir sonne, Ralph Pott, all that my cottage in Thornton, now in the occupation of Ralph Nicholson, to them and their heirs. To Robert the sonne of Elizabeth Sheapford, 10s. To the poore of Walton, 20s. I give to my daughter, Isabell Errington, 20s. Residue of my goods whatsoever to Sir William Selby whom I make sole Executor. I ordaine Roger Pott and Roger Barton, Supervisors. To Mary Robson, one cowe. Probate, 26 August, 1614.

THOMAS CHAITOR.[1]

July 6, 1614. In the name of God, Amen, I, Thomas Chaitor, of Buterbie, in the Countie of Durham, Esquire. To be buried in St. Oswald's Church in Durham, as near unto my beloved parents as convenientlie maie be if I dept this lyff near there unto or els where it shall please my executors here undernamed. And now concerning my worldlie goods wherewth it hath pleased god to blesse me, I give and bequeth as followeth. I give and bequeth all that my mannor or capitall message of Buterbie sotheron closes with all and singular ther appurtences unto my dearlie beloved wiffe, Jane Chaitor, for and during her liffe, naturall, praeing her and pswadinge my selfe she will be kind and loveing to my sone, Henrie. I give and bequeth to my sonne, Henrie, to be and remaine as heire loomes all my brewing vessel, my clock in the Hall, my base viall, my watch that was Sir Henrie Lindlies, and the imbroided waste coate, my ring with the Turcas, my ringe with the bload stone: and I reserve it to my wyfe and executors what houshold stuffe he shall have more then I express, and I give him all glass windows and wainscott. I give him my house and houses in Durham with the appurtences. I give unto

---

[1] The testator was son of Christopher Chaytor of Butterby by his wife, Elizabeth, dau. of William Clervaux of Croft, co. York. He mar., firstly, Eleanor, dau. of . . . . Thornell of East Newton, co. York, who died without issue and was bur. at St. Oswald's (from which registers the following dates are taken), 22 July, 1603; he mar., secondly, Jane, dau. of Sir Nicholas Tempest, bart., of Stella, by his wife, Isabella Lambton; she was bur., 1 Sept., 1666, leaving issue, Henry, who was aged 11, at the *Inq. p.m.* of his father taken at Durham, 3 Apl., 1619, bur., 1 May, 1629, aged 20; Thomas, bur., 27 June, 1631; Nicholas, bapt., 6 Dec., 1608, died, 10 Feb.,1665/6, mar. Ann, dau. of Wm. Lambton of Great Stainton, 19 Jan., 1635/6, at Haughton-le-Skerne, where she was bur., 2 Aug., 1664; Jeronima, bapt., 1 Sept., 1605, mar. Thomas Swinburn of Barmston; Elizabeth, bur., 31 May, 1610; Isabel, bapt. at Ryton, 13 Oct., 1606, mar. James Belasys of Owston; Mary, bur., 8 Sept, 1631; Trothe, bur., 27 Feb., 1631/2; Margaret, mar. Ralph Bates of Halliwell, she was bur. at Earsdon, 24 Feb., 1685/6, he was bapt. at Earsdon, 29 Aug., 1613, and bur. there, 11 Mch., 1690/1. The testator's burial entry reads as follows: "1618, July 20. The right worshipfull Mr. Thomas Chaytor of Buterbie Esquire, a most wordy houskeper both for riche and poore, he beinge of the age of lxiiii yeares, unto whome God send a joyfull resurrectione."

my sonne, Nicholas, my lease of the tiethes of corne and sheeves of Towen Kelloe and Cassop. I give him my lande in Huton Henrie in the tenore and possession of John Lambe or his assignes, and this my bequeste to be to him in full satisfacon of his child's part and porcon of my goods. I give to my sister Whitfeild, 40s. and to my sister Tanckard I give an angell in gold for a token. I give to everie one of my clerks that shalbe my servantes att my death, one angell of gold for a token. I give to Robt. Denninge, my servant, twenty nobles, to be paid him within one quarter of a yeare after my death. I bequeth to the poore of Saint Oswald's in Durham parish, 40s., and to everie pish in Durham except the two balies, 10s. a peece, to be distributed amongst the poore and neede there, and to the two pishes of north and south balie, 6s. 8d., to be equallie devided amongst the poore of them, and I give to be devided amongest the poore prisoners in Durham Gaole att my death, 10s. I bequeth to the poore in Saint Andrew, Awkland, 20s. To the poore of Cassop and the pish where I have tithes att it and Towen Kelloe, 6s. 8d. I constitute and ordeyne my beloved father, Sir Nicholas Tempest, Knight, and my brother, Thomas Tempest, Esquire, myne executors of this my last will and Testament. I give unto my father in law the best nagg I leave att his choice, att my death, and to my said brother one angell of gold a peece for a simple token. All the rest of my goods not bequethed I give and bequeth unto my daughters to be devided amongst them except my daughter Jeromina and Isobell, to whom I bequeth twenty pounds a peece over and above ther part in that division, and I praie my wife to bestow such of her jewells as she shall think fitt on Jeromina when it shall please god she shall happen to be maried or come of full age, and likewise what of her jewels that were mine she shall think fitt att her pleasure to bestow on my sonne Henrie, when he shall accomplish the age of one and twenty years. I give and bequeth to my sonns, Henrie and Nicholas, all my books to be equallie devided betwixt them when they shall come to lawfull age, and I frelie give god's blessing and myne to all my children beseeching god to blesse preserve and prosper them in all there waies, words, works and thoughts to god's glorie and there salvacon in and by Christ Jesus. Amen, Amen, Amen.

NUNCUPATIVE WILL OF THOMAS CHAITOR.[1]

Memorandum, That Thomas Chaitor, of Butterbe, in the County of Durham, Esquire, did divers and sundrye tymes in his life tyme, long before his death (who died the 19 July, 1618), saye, declare and make known to his wife and others that it was alwaies

---

[1] It will be noticed his former will is not attested. It has been thought advisable to print his nuncupative will next to his first one.

his intendment, will, purpose and meaninge, that his sonne and heire, Henrye Chaitor, should have his moitie which he had of the tieth corne of the prebend of Awkland and Binchester, and willed them to bear witness thereof, if it please god, he should dye and not declare itt acordinglie in his will. And having afterwards solde his said intereste, of his said tiethes, to Sir Charles Wrenn, Knight, and havinge receyved the monies he sold the same for, which was 300*l*., on or aboute the 23 day of June, 1617, he, the said deceased, did divers and several tymes shortlye then after (being of sound and perfect health and memorye) signifie and declare to his wife and some of his servantes (whom he called upon purposelye to heare him) that as he always intended that his said sonne and heire should have the said tythes if he kept them unsola so it was his full will and meaning that he should have the said 300*l*. which he had solde the same for, and did absolutely give the same unto him and willed and required his said wife, Mrs. Jane Chaitor, and Anthonye Thompson, Thomas Bullock, and otheres, his servants (to whom he declared the premises), to beare witnesse thereof accordinglie. And furthermore the said deceased (accordinge to and in confirmation of his former speaches) havinge a care that the same should take effectt, Did himself negotiate the said monies to and for the use and benefitt of his said sonne and heire, and did on or about the said 23 daie of June, 1617, aforesaid, lend forth the same monies to Roger Tockett of Alnaby, Esqr., to be repaid on or about Whitson tuesday and then next after and now last past, and to that end and purpose did take the bonde thereon in the name of Thomas Tempest, of Stelley, Esquire, his brother in law, wherewith (as also with the recited premises) he shortlye then after acquainted his said brother and requested him to see the same effectted accordinglie. And having receyved 200*l*. of the said 300*l*. of the saide Mr. Tockett at or about the tyme that the same was and became due as aforesaide, he, the said deceased, did lend the same shortlye after to Robert Brandlinge, of Fellinge. Esqr., and tooke the bond in his owne name, yet very shortlie after, he (espyinge and repentinge his over sight in taking the bonde in his own name, whereas formalye he had used his brother's name) tolde his said brother and wife and others thereof and withall told them, that albeitt he had unadvisedly taken that bond in his own name, yet he intended itt to lend for the use of the said Henry Chaitor, his saide sonne and heire, as thoe he had taken itt in the said Mr. Tempest's name. And the other 100*l*. parcell of the said 300*l*. is yett in the said Mr. Tocket's hands upon the bond taken in the said Mr. Tempest's name as aforesaid. Witnesses to the premises, Jane Chaytor, Tho. Tempest. Proved, 1618.

Sept. 29, 1618. An Inventory of all the goodes and chattells, moveable and unmoveable, and credits thatt lately were and did belonge unto Thomas Chaitor, of Butterbye in the Countye of Durham, Esquire, deceased, at the tyme of his decease valewed, seene and praised by Cutht. Maltbye, John Farrowe, John Kirkley, and Ralph Younger, yeomen, as followeth. In the Hall: a short table, a long table with their frames, and a lenyen cupbord, 13*s*. 4*d*., the carpett, clothes to them belonginge, 6*s*. 8*d*., three longe settles, two formes, two chares, a childes chare, three lowe chares, 13*s*. 4*d*., a palk, a little low cupboard, 3*s*. 4*d*., apaire of tonges and a fire shovell, 18*d*. In the Parlor : a longe table with two drawe leaves, 20*s*., a square table in the windowe and a rounde table, 13*s*. 4*d*., a lenyen cupbord, 5*s*., a little lowe cupbord, 3*s*. 4*d*., and embroydered chare, 3*s*. 4*d*., two lower chares, 3*s*. 4*d*., a dozen and an halfe of buffett stooles and a shorte forme, 16*s*., the carpett clothes upon and belonginge to the saide three tables and lenyen cupbords, 10*s*., two desks, 8*s*., and a dozen of cushiones, 6*s*. 8*d*., pare of virginals, 20*s*., an iron chimley, a parr of tonges, and a fire shovell, 5*s*. In the Inner Parlor : a lenyon cupbord and a chare, 6*s*. 8*d*., a bedsteade with a teaster of firr, 10*s*., the clothes upon it, a mattress, a featherbedde, a bolster, two pillowes, a pare of blanketts, a coverlett and a white rugg with the courtinge rodds, courtinges and vallances, and a longe cushon upon the Lenyon cupbord, 40*s*. In the Chamber over the Parlor : a little square table in the window, 2*s*. 6*d*., a presser, 8*s*. 4*d*., a lenan cupboard, 5*s*., a little wainscott chist, 5*s*., a truckle bedd for children for the clothes upon itt, 6*s*. 8*d*., three old truncks and a wanded chare, 5*s*., two carpett clothes for the leyon cupbord and little table and a long cushion, 3*s*. 4*d*., an iron chimney, a pare of tonges and a fire shovell, 2*s*. 6*d*. In the green Chamber : a bedstead with a canopye and courtings, 6*s*. 8*d*., and the clothes upon a feather bedd, a bolster, a parre of blankets, two fustion pillowes, two coverletts, 20*s*., a litle chare, table, an old charre, 4*s*., a long cushon, 2*s*. 6*d*., two old trunks, 18*d*., a litle carpett clothe, 12*d*., the hanggings about the chamber being old, 10*s*. In the Chamber over the Hall : a standing bedstead with the curtings, courtinge rodds, and vallances, 40*s*., the clothes upon itt, to witt, a mattrass, a featherbed, a bolster, two fustion pillowes, a pare of blankets, a coverlett, a green rugg, 40*s*., a palliett pece, a feather bedd, a bolster, a pare of pillowes, a paire of blanketts, a coverlett and a rugg, 20*s*., a leyeon cupbord, 4*s*., two longe embrowdered cushions, 8*s*., a chare embrowdered, a lowe chare covered with needle worke, 6*s*., foure lowe stoolles, two embrodered and two covered with silke, 4*s*., a longe chist of firr, 2*s*. 6*d*., the iron barrs, a paire of tonges and a fire shovell, 3*s*. 4*d*., the hanggings about the chamber, 13*s*. 4*d*. In the little Chamber att the Starehead : a standing bedstead with a teaster, 10*s*., the clothes upon itt, to witt, an old featherbedd, a bolster, two pillowes, a pare of blanketts, a coverlett, 13*s*. 4*d*., an olde chare and a longe old chist, 2*s*. In the Nurserye : two bedsteads for children and servantes with the clothes upon them, 20*s*., a counter table and a longe chist, 4*s*., a pare of iron barrs with tonges and fire shovells,

2*s*. 6*d*., two stills for stilling waters, 8*s*. Item, the lynnen of all sorts estimated altogether to 13*l*. 6*s*. 8*d*. Item, all the pewter aboute the house of all sorts, 5*l*. Item, the plate (besides a Dooble salte, guilt, a great guilt bowle with a cover, a brode guilt wine bowle, a lave goblett, called Lockwood's cupp, and a dozen apostle spoones) given to the heire, valewed to 18*l*. Item, his apparall with two grogoran crownes and a cloke lyned through with velvett, 20*l*. In the Kitchinge : a great iron chimney, a pare of fire shovells, a pare of tonges, a pare of iron casks, seven spitts, a dripping pann, two fryeinge panns, crooks and other . . . utensills, 40*s*., the brasse, viz., six potts, three kettles, two yetlings, fower greater panns and three lesser, a preservinge pann, three brasse laddles, a baister, a brasse morter and the pestle and a grate, 5*l*. 5*s*. In the brewe, vessells in the brewhouse, to witt, brew lead, mash fatt, gile fatt and cooler with tubbs and other things for that purpose therein, 5*l*., in the milk house skeeles, kitts, bowles, chirnes and other wood vessells, 10*s*., in the buttrye, a litle table, a cupbord, a binge for bread, hoggsheads, gantrees and other things, 23*s*. 4*d*. Item, in the Gatehouse, a bedstead, with a canopie, and clothed on itt, viz., featherbedd, a bolster, two pillowes, a pare of blancketts, and two coverlets, 25*s*. Item, in the chamber over the milkhouse and kitching, three old bedsteads, with a little old counter table, 10*s*. Item, in the stable, saddles, bridles and other furniture, 13*s*. 4*d*., five horses and mares, 16*l*., three kine, 6*l*. 13*s*. 4*d*., waine and waine gear, ploughes and plough gear, with some wood upon the greene, and work geare, with other implements, 5*l*. In the House at Durham : Item, a square table with two drawe leaves, 6*s*. 8*d*., a wainscott chare, 2*s*. 6*d*., a long table, a frame, a linen cupboard of firr, 3*s*. 4*d*., a skreene and pewter vessell, two long settles, 13*s*. 4*d*., an iron chimney, a fire shovell and tonges, 3*s*. 4*d*., a pare of virginalls, 13*s*. 4*d*., cushions and a carpett cloth, 5*s*. In the Kitchinge : an iron chimney with crooks, a table with a frame, 4*s*., two brass potts, two possnetts, foure panns a little kettle two brass candlesticks, a brass morter, a pestle, a little brasse morter and a brasse pestle with other smail geare, 30*s*. In the chamber over the Hall : a standing beddstead with a teaster, 5*s*., the clothes on itt, vizt., a featherbedd, a bolster, two pillowes, a pare of blanketts, a coverlett and rugg with courtings and vallances, 5*s*., a palliet there, viz., two old feather bedds, two pillowes, a codd, a pare of blanketts and a rugg, 30*s*., a shorte table with a frame, 4*s*., a lennin cupbord of firr, 3*s*. 4*d*., a chare of wainscott and . . . . . , 4*s*., a long chiste and three truncks, 13*s*. 4*d*., apare of iron barrs with tonges, 2*s*. In the Nursery : a standing bedstead, 7*s*., an olde featherbedd and a bolster upon itt, 10*s*., an old chiste and long settle bedd, 5*s*., a pare of iron barrs, 2*s*. In the litle Garner : a tubb for beaf, a bord and other things, 5*s*. 4*d*. Item, in the little chamber at the Hall, a standing bedstead, 5*s*., two truncks,

10s., apare of litle barrs, 18d., a litle square table . . . . . Item, in the white chamber, two standinge beddsteads, 20s., a lennon cupbord, 5s., a litle table with a frame, 3s. 4d., a pare of iron barrs, 2s., a press, 13s. 4d., a trunck, 5s. Item, in the brewe house, one brewe lead with tubbs and other brewing vessells, 4l. Item, in money, in his clerks hands, viz., in Thomas Bullock's, 7l., and in Anth. Thompson's, 12l. 12s. 2d. Item, in readye monye and gould 900l. Item, in debts owne unto him upon specialties, 500l. 17s. Item, John Lyons is indebttered and owes to the said deceased 100l. which he paid for him for his Matie. Some totall of the goods ready monie and debts aforesaid besides the said John Lyons debt which is despute is 1579l. 19s. 0d. Debts owen by the said deceased for malt, 9l., to Richard Sarr, a gardener, for seaven daies work, 7s., to a labourer, 10d., to the wallers for making up the wall in his orchard att Durham, 10s. 10d., to Raph Younge for butter, 14s., to George Rackett for coles, 14s., for goods bought shortly before his death, 30s., to Mr. John Lampton, draper, for clothe, 4l. 16s. 6d., to Tho. Cook, mercer, for wares bought of him, 4l. 11s. 6d., to George Martyn, for rent of a certaine peece of ground which the deceased did take to farme of him, 8l. 10s., to the Mr. and brethren of Shereburn hospittall for the half year's rent of the tieth corne of Cassop and towne Kelloe, 3l. 16s. 8d., for the half year's rent of the house in Elvett, 6l. 5s., for servants' wages, 6l., paide for pcuring of a quietus upon the payment of the 100l. for Lyons, 5l. 5s., for the funerall, vizt., for mourninge gownes to his wife, children and his two sisters, and black clokes for the servants, 20l., the funeral charges and church dues whereof for a hearse and scutchions, 48s., and give to the poore att the churche att the buriall, 3l. 4s. 6d., to Mr. Hudspeth for wine, 35s. Suma Debitor et expenses pd 81l. 18s. 8d.

CHRISTOPHER ILE.[1]

Oct. 30, 1614. In the name of Gode, Amen, I, Christopher Ile, of the pish of St. Nicholas, within the towne of Newcastle upon Tyne, Apothecary. To be buryed within the pish church of St. Nicholas, aforesaid, within the said towne. I give and bequeath

[1] No record of his burial has been found in the registers of St. Nich., Newcastle (from which the following dates are taken), or elsewhere. He mar., 10 Dec., 1593, Alice Carr, who was bur., 23 May, 1632. They had one son Robert, bapt., 30 March, 1595, bur., 16 Jan., 1599/1600, and six daus., viz. :—Jane, bapt., 20 June, 1596, bur., 23 March, 1618/19. wife of Cuthbert Ellison (bapt., 31 Jan., 1579/80, bur., 5 Jan., 1626/7); Barbara, bapt., 25 Apl., 1598, bur., 10 Aug:, 1637, mar. Anthony Errington, 19 June, 1615; Eleanor, bapt., 6 Sept., 1599, bur., 25 Aug., 1627, mar. Charles Kellio (who was bur. at St. John's, Newcastle, 15 Oct., 1638, having re-mar. before 2 Oct., 1630, Jane, dau. of Sir Ralph Delaval); Alice, bapt., 14 Apl., 1601, bur., 28 July, 1629, mar. 4 Feb., 1618/19, Henry Shadforth, who was bur. 8 Sept., 1633; Elizabeth, bapt.,

unto Alice, my wife, my now dwellinghouse wth the appurtenances, within the said towne, in a street there called the Side, and
a garden lying and being in the Hy Castle thare adjoining upon
the mute hall theare for and during her natural life, and after her
decease to remaine and come unto Cuthbert Ellison, Merchant, and
Jane, his wife, my daughter, and their heires, according to a Deed
formerly made unto them at or before their marriage. I give and
bequeath unto Barbara Ile, my daughter, and the heires of her
body, one burgage or tenement with the appurtences lying and
being at the head of the Side within the said Towne, now in the
tenour and occupation of Eleanor Turpin, widow, together with
such implements and untensils therein as do belong to me, and also
two little tenements and one brew house lying and being in St.
Nicholas church yard near and adjoining upon the said burgage
or tenament, and if the said Barbara happen to dye without issue
of her Body then my will and mynde is that the same lands so
formerly bequeathed unto her shall remayne and come unto
Eleanor, Alice and Elizabeth Ile, my three daughters, and the
survivor of them and their heires for ever equally to be
divided amongst theme.   I give and bequeath unto Eleanor,
my daughter, and the heires of her body, one burgage or tenements
with the appurtenances nowe in the tennor or occupation of John
Forster, saidler situate and being in the said towne at the foote of
the Side there near the Pannt, before and neare against Mr.
Barker's howse there, and if the said Elynor happen to dye withoute
heires of her bodye then my will and mynd is that the same landes
so formerly bequeathed unto her shall remayne and come unto the
said Barbara, Alice and Elizabeth, my daughters, and the survivors of them and their heires for ever equally to be divided
amongst them.   I give and bequeath unto Alice Ile, my daughter,
and the heirs of her body, one burgage or tenement with the
appurtenances now in the several tenuers or occupacons of Mark
Hutchinson, tailor, and Thomas Ewbank, feltmaker, situate and
being wthin the said towne of Newcastle upon Tyne, in the Iron
Markett theare adjoyning upon the said tenement nowe in the
occupation of the said John Forster, and if the said Alice happen to

6 July, 1603, mar., 14 Feb., 1620/1, William Anderson; Mary, bapt.,
21 Apl., 1605, bur., 10 March, 1605/6. The testator's wife was not (as
suggested in Longstaffe's, *Darlington*, p. lxxxvii.) Alice, bapt., 5 Feb.,
1575/6, dau. of Oswald Carr (for she was bur., 28 Apl., 1594), but
probably Alice, dau. of William Carr, alderman, still under age at the
death of her mother Joan (dau. of John Trollope), Sept., 1587 (see
Raine's M.S. *Prob. and Admon.*, i., 115), godmother, 12 Apr., 1588, to
her nephew John, posthumous son of John Carr, and 5 Aug., 1593, to a
child of Robert Eden, who mar. her eldest sister Isabel. This would
explain the testator's "kinship" to Robert Shafto, who mar. Jane,
second of the fifteen children of Robert and Isabel Eden. For the
descendants of his brother Robert Ile, see *Northumberland Visitation
Pedigrees* (ed. Foster, p. 70), and Longstaffe's *Darlington, loc. cit.*

dye without heires of her body then my will and mynd is that the
same lands so formerly bequeathed unto her shall remayne and
come unto the said Barbara, Elynor, and Elizabeth, my three
daughters, and the survivors of them and their heires for ever
equally to be divided amongst them. I give and bequeath to Elizabeth Ile, my daughter, and the heires of her body, one moiety or
halfe part of one burgage tenement with the appurtenances now in
the tenoure or occupation of Thomas Hodgson, yeoman, situate and
being within the said towne of Newcastle upon Tyne in a street
there called Shodefryer Chaire, and also the moiety or half pt of
a tenement with the appurtenances now in the tenure or occupation
of . . . . , situate and being within the said towne near Newgate
there which I purchased of Mr. Robert Eden, together also with
the moytie or halfe pte of a meadow close and nowe in the tenure
or occupacon of Thomas Cole, cordyner, situate and being in Gateside, in the County of Durham, neare Bustye borne theare, which
I lately purchased of William Eden, Appothecary and grocer, and
if the said Elizabeth happen to dye without heires of her bodye
then my will and mynd is that the same lands so bequeathed unto
her shall remayne and come unto the said Barbara, Eleanor and
Alice Ile, my three daughters, and the survivors of them and their
heires for ever equally · to be divided amongst them. Provided
alwaies and my mynd and will is that Alice, my wife, shall have
and enjoy all the said landes, tenements and hereditaments so by
me formerly bequeathed unto my foure dawghters, Barbara,
Elynor, Alice and Elizabeth, to her owne use, profitts and comidy
until they and every of them shall respectively come unto the age of
one and twenty yeares or be married which shall first happen
or come. I give and bequeath unto my daughter Jane, six silver
spoones with knopper gildes and to either of her two sonnes an
unyon peece of golde. I give and bequeath to everie of my foure
daughters, Barbara, Elynore, Alice and Elizabeth, fifty poundes
a piece for a porcon of my goods, chattells and debts to be paid
unto them and every of them, when they shall respectively accomplish the age of one and twenty yeares or be maryed when then
shall first happen or come, and if they said Barbara, Eleynor, Alice
and Elizabeth, or any of them happen to dye before they shall
accomplish the age of one and twentye yeares or be marryed, then
my will and mynd is that the porcon of them so deceasing shall
remayne and come to the survivors of them, equallie to be divided
amongst them surviving, hoping if they do prove dutifull children
to my said wife, that my said loveing wife will augment my said
children's porcons. All the reste of my goods and chattells, and
cattells and debts whatsoever my debts, legacies and funerall
expences being payd and discharged. I give and bequeath unto my
loveing wife, Alice Ile, whom I make and ordayne full and sole
executrix of this my last Will and Testament. I make and ordayne
my well beloved frends and kinsmen, Mr. Peter Riddell and Mr.

Robert Shaftoe, supervisors of this my Will and Testament, and I give and bequeath to either of them one angell for a token. I give and bequeath unto my brother, Robert Ile, twenty shillings for a token. I give and bequeath unto my cozene, Clement Ile, forty shillings for a token. I give and bequeath unto my Aunte Suerties, wife to Mr. Robert Suerties, of Durham, tenn shillings for a token. I give and bequeathe unto Bowmer Ile, tene shillings for a token. I give and bequeath unto my two servantes, Ralph Pattison and Henry Watson, either of them tenn shillings for a token, and unto my servante, Mary Mills, ten shillings for a token, and to either of my two other servantes, Anne Wright and Eleynor Powell, five shillings for a token. Witnesses, Peter Riddell, Robt. Shaftoe, Ric. Baker, Francis Leighton. Proved, 1614.

ROBERT ANDERSON.[1]

Jan. 9, 1614/15. In the name of God, Amen, in the twelfth yeare of the reign of our sovereign, Lord James, by the grace of god, King of England, France and Ireland, Defender of the faithe and of Scotland. I, Robert Anderson, of the towne of Newcastell upon Tyne, Marchant and alderman. To be buried in the parish church of St. Nicholas in Newcastell aforesaid. I give to the pore people of the same towne, to be geven them at my buriall, the some of five poundes. I give to Robert Anderson, sone to Isack Anderson, who is nowe in howse with me, the sum of fiftie poundes, at his age of twenty one yeres, if he live to the said age, otherwise this bequest to be voyd, and I will he shallbe brought upp by my sonne Robert till he be fitt to be bound as apprentise and then to be disposed of my said sonne and by his care ordered as shallbe fittinge. I give to my eldest servant and kinsman, Anthony Metcalf, the sume of forty shillings yearly,

[1] Uncertainty haunts any attempt to classify Andersons of Newcastle, and the following note should be accepted with that reservation. *Registers of St. Nich., Newcastle. Robert Anderson, father of the testator, was a son of Robert Anderson of Alnwick (*Visn.* pedigrees, ed. Foster, p. 5), was apprenticed to George Selby, 17 Apl., 1530, mar. a dau. of .... Lambe of Newcastle, was sheriff, 1559-60, and mayor 1567/8, joined Richard Hodgson and "Mr." Selby in a purchase of Winlaton Manor about 1573 (Welford's *Newcastle*, ii., 459), was brother and (with his son Robert and many others) devisee, 27 Aug., 1577. of Simon Anderson of Newcastle, clerk, and was bur., 5 June, 1593.* The testator mar., 16 Nov., 1585,* Agnes Anderson, was sheriff, 1600/1, and was bur., 13 Jan., 1614/15.* His wife Agnes (or Anne) was a dau., born later than 1560/1 (122 *Surt. Soc.*, p. 171), of Henry Anderson (bur., 5 Feb., 1602/3,* known as "the elder" to distinguish him from his nephew, Alderman Henry Anderson, son of Bertram) by Dorothy (bur. 5 Oct., 1597*) dau. of Giles Wood of Pickering; she was a godmother, 28 Aug., 1582,* as was her sister Dorothy (also born after 1560/1), 5 July, 1579,* 12 May, 1580,* 7 Oct., 1582.* Among her brothers was Francis, almost certainly the ancestor (who was sheriff, 1595-6) of

to be paid to him during his natural life, issuing owte of my
Manor of Wynlington, in the County of Durham, and owt of all
my landes, tenements and hereditaments in Wynlington payable
at the feasts of Pentecost and St. Martines the Bishope in Wynter
by equal porcons, and if the same shall be behinde by the space of
tenn dayes after any of the said feastes, that then it shall be lawfull
for the said Anthony and his assigns into the sayd Mannors and
certified premises to enter and destraine, and the same distress
to holde and kepe till of the sayd yerely rent with the arreaarages,
if any, be fully satisfied. I give to my howshold servants
the some of fiftie shillings to be distributed amongst them at the
discretion of Robt. my sonne, and Anne my wife. I geve unto
the said Anne, my wellbeloved wiffe, in liewe and full satisfacon
of her dowre which she may challenge or demand owt of all or
any my lands, tenements and hereditaments, and in liew and full
satisfacon of her reasonable pt or porcon which she maye in any
way challenge or demand owt of all or any my goodes, chattells,
creditts and debts whatsoever, all my lands, tenements and hereditaments in Wyngate, in the Countye of Durham, and all the
coales and profitts from time to time arising owt of my pt of
colliery in Whickham, in the same Countye comonly called the
rounde lease colliery, and all the profitts and coles from time to
time arising owt of my pte of the colliery at Ravensworth, in the
same countye to have and to hold the said lands, tenements and
hereditaments in Wyngate, and to pserve, take and have the sayd
coles and profitts from tyme to tyme arising owt of my saide
collierye of Whickham and Ravensworth unto the said Anne and
her assignes during her naturall lyffe, and I give unto her all
my coles of the same Colleryes of Whickham and Ravensworth
being alreddy wrought and which said coles remane either at pitts
or stathes, and I give unto her the moytie or halfe of all my plate
and utensills of howhold to her owne use absolutely, except bed-

the Andersons of Bradley (" Mr. Francis Anderson, shirefe, and *his
mother*, Mrs. Dorothy Anderson," appear as sponsors, 15 Aug., 1596*).
The testator's " worshipful kinsman," Sir George Selby, was son of
William Selby, who was son of George Selby by Margaret, dau. of . . . .
Anderson. Simon Anderson gave by will his half-quarter of " Winlington " to his nephew William Selby. It would seem that Margaret was
sister of Simon. The testator and his wife had two children, viz. :—
Robert, bapt., 26 Oct., 1592 (sureties, Robert Mitford, Robert Ellison.
merchants, and the grandmother, wife of Mr. Henrie Anderson, elder),*
and Dorothy, bapt., 12 Dec., 1594 (sureties, Dorothy Anderson grandmother, the wife of Robert Tempest and Isaac Anderson),* and probably
bur., 27 Feb., 1594/5.* Robert, the son, mar. at St. Andrew's, Newcastle, 24 Apl., 1615, Jane (who probably survived him), dau. of Thomas
Liddell, alderman, was sheriff, 1619-20, and mayor, 1630-1 died 9 and
was bur., 12 May, 1640.* By his will dated 6 May, 1640 (111 *Surt. Soc.*,
p. 103n.) he named as executor and residuary legatee his " cousin "
Francis (afterwards Sir Francis) Anderson, son of Roger, son of the
above-mentioned Francis.

steds, tables and chymnies of iron. Provided alwaies that she shall neither demand any dower owt of my lands nor any reasonable or other pt. owt of any of my goods, chattells, credits and debts as aforesaid. All the residue of my goods, chattells, creditts and debts not hereby already bequeathed, I give to Robt. Anderson, my sonne, whom I make sole Executor of this my last Will and Testament, and I make my worshipful kinsman, Sir George Selbye, Knight, Francis Anderson, Alderman of Newcastle, and Robt. Ellison, mv Supervisors of the same. Witnesses, F. Anderson, Robert Ellison, William Selbye. Proved, 1614.

CONAND STEVENSON.[1]

Sept. 28, 1615. In the name of God, Amen. I, Conand Stevenson, of the parish of St. Andrew's, in Newcastle upon Tyne. To be buried in the pish church of St. Andrew's aforesaid, I give then unto my wiffe, Elizabeth Stevenson, a brewe copper and the furniture belonging to it. I give unto my wife the houses I bought during her lifetime, and after hir life they to come to my two daughters, joyntlie, severallie, and to her heires after them (fayling her heires to come to the next of kinne of me the said Conande). I give to my wife sixe bouls of malte. I give to my two daughters either of them, 40s. The pewter dishes, dublers and also potts and pans, candlesticks and all other such implements to be devided betwixt my wife and my said two daughters by equall porcons, that is to say, to my wife a part, to Hellenor Pile a parte, and to my daughter, Agnes Stevenson, a part, and as aforesaid. I give and bequeath unto my wife all the brewing vessells, and other vessells, and other utensills, and woode, excepting to my daughters either of them, two drink stands. I give unto my two daughters, ether of them, a paire of sheets and a paire of pillowbears. I give to Hellenor a new happin, and to Agnes a coverlet and a happine of twenty four yeards of linen. I give the full halfe to my wife and the rest to be delivered betwixt my two daughters. I give to my wife two featherbedds with the appurtenances to them. I give to my wife the best Ambrie and the best cheste, and I give to my daughters ether of them a cheste. Also I give unto my daughter, Agnes, an ambrie that next to the best. I give to my wife the table in the hall and forme belonging to it and to either of my daughters a stoole. I give to Helenor Pile the table in the low howse and the forme belonging to it. I give to Willm. Pickering my haulbert staffe and my steal cape. I give

[1] He was bur. at St. Andrew's, Newcastle, 7 Oct., 1615, where his two sons were bapt., viz. :—Francis, 24 June, 1599 (bur., 21 Dec., 1600), and Robert, 13 Sept., 1601; his wife Isabel was bur. there, 27 May, 1600; he re-mar., 30 Nov., 1600, Dorothy Pickering at St. Nich., Newcastle.

to my wife the iron chimney also the bedstead in the hall, and I give to Hellenor that bedstead at the Maudlines, and to my daughter, Agnes, the bedstead in the lofte. I give to my two daughters a browne cowe to be solde and the money equallie to be divided betwixt my two Daughters, I give to my wife the white cowe. I give of the sixe swine unto my wife and she to pay to my two children at Easter next coming to ether of them, 10s. I give to my wife my cloke and best stockings. I give to George Pile a browne jerkine and a paire of briches, allso all the rest of my clothes (except my greenin jerkin). I give to George Pile also my old hate. I give to my wife a longsetle bedstead and all the rest of my goods movable and unmoveable, and also I make my wife full executor of this my last Will and Testament. A note of the debts oweing to Conande Stevenson. Willm. Haddock is oweing to me 12s. Randell Milburne is oweing to me 19s. William Robson is oweing me 19s. Robt. Wetherup, of Elswick, is owing me 15s. Mr. James Cole is oweing to me 1l. 3s. 3d. Wm. Wallis is owinge 1l. 4s. 6d. Proved, 1615.

JOHN ALDER.[1]

Oct. 28, 1615. Will of John Alder, of Alnwicke, Merchant. To be buryed at the parish church of St. Michaell's Archangell, here at Alnwicke, at the descretion of my frends. I give to Robert, Richard, Thomas, Luke and Edwarde, my sones, 40s. each. To my daughter, Barbara Clarke, my goulden ringe or signett. I leave my shop goods and chattels and leases to pay my debts withall. To John Alder, my sone, 20s. I leave to my daughter, Isabell Forster, for her poron, £10. I give to Geo. Forster, 50s. I give to my sone, George Alder, £4 a yere duringe the space of three yeres next ensuinge, beginninge to pay 20s. a quarter at Martinmasse next after the date hereof, which was agreed upon before George Gallon and William Hunter, Arbitrators, betwixt us. I leave Jane, my wife, my full executrix of all my leases, goods and chattels. I leave to Geo. Alder, my sone, 3 bowels of rye to be payed unto him a bowel yearly for the space of 3 yeares next ensuinge. My will is that Mathew Clarke and Nicholas Forster doe sue Jo. Buller for an over sea cloathe wrought with nedle worke for the behalfe of Barbara and Isabella, my daughters, and their wifes. Francis Alder, Rob. Fenwicke, Jo. Harbottell and Henry Smith, Supervisors. Witnesses to will, Robt. Stevenson, clarke, Francis Alder, John Herbottell, Edward Stanniers. Proved, 9 Dec., 1615.

[1] Son of Richard Alder, see *Arch. Ael.*, 3rd series, v., 38.

JOHN SWAYNSTON.[1]

Dec. 27, 1615. The Inventorie of all the goods and chattels, moveable and not moveable, of John Swaynston of Gainforthe, deceased, prsed by Cuthbert Burrell, Georg Garthe, John Garthe and Henry Swainston.

Imprimis : His purse and apparell, 2*l*. Fower oxen, 16*l*. 10*s*. Sixe kyne, 12*l*. One other cowe, 1*l*. 13*s*. Fower yong beast, 9*l*. Five yonger beaste, 5*l*. Fower calves, 2*l*. 30 old sheepe 10*l*. 10*s*. One and twentie hoggs, 3*l*. 10*s*. One horse and a mare, 3*l*. In hay aboute the house, 2*l*. Three swyne, 18*s*. All the corne in the barne, hard corne otes, 10*l*. Thirteen acres of corne in the field, 17*l*. 10*s*. Corne in the house, 1*l*. 6*s*. 8*d*. One cupbord and a cawell, 1*l*. 16*s*. 4*d*. Two old cupbords and a cawell 10*s*. Fyve potts of brass, 1*l*. 10*s*. Thre kettells and 4 pans, 1*l*. 4*s*. Eighteene pece of puther, 12*s*. Fower candlesticks, two salts, and a litle bottle, 3*s*. Thre stande bedds, 1*l*. Two fether bedds and two mattrasses, 2*l*. 13*s*. 4*d*. Fyve pair of lynen sheits and fyve pair of harden, 2*l*. Coverletts and happins, 1*l*. 16*s*. 8*d*. Codds and blanketts, 6*s*. 8*d*. Pillowes, napkins, one table clothe and other napperie, 6*s*. 8*d*. Table formes and stooles, 9*s*. 6*d*. Chestes, 6*s*. Two arkes, 13*s*. 4*d*. Tubbs and skeales and kytts, 5*s*. Halfe a stone woole, 4*s*. Windowing clothes, sacks, pokes, bushell, peck and other suche stuffe, 12*s*. In fleshe, butter and chease, 26*s*. 8*d*. Pullen aboute the howse, 4*s*. Thre ducks, 12*d*. Bowels, dishes, chese fatts, spoones, trenchers and cans, 4*s*. Tongs, reckon, crooke, axes, spete and racks, 6*s*. Two stone trowes, 12*d*. Wayn, wayn gear, ploughe, ploughe geare and all wood about house, 6*l*. 10*s*. Spades, shovells, dung forkes, iron forke, shafts and all other implements about the house, 3*s*. 4*d*. Suma : 112*l*. 2*s*. 2*d*. Debts oweing the testator : John Hutchinson, for a yoke of oxen, 6*l*. 13*s*. 4*d*. John Lockson, 16*s*. Debts which the testator ought : To Jo. Hutchinson, 2*l*. Wm. Appleby, 2*l*. John Hood, 8*l*. 10*s*. To old Cramforth's wyfe, 50*s*. The King's Maties rent, 22*s*. For other rent, 2*l*. 9*s*. 5*d*. To Mr. Jervaux Kuype, 14*s*. Charges of funerall and mortuarye, 2*l*. 2*s*.

WILLIAM SADLER.[2]

Jan. 4, 1615. In the name of God, Amen, I, William Sadler, of the towne of Newcastle upon Tyne. To be buried in the Churchyard of All Saints near to my children deceased. The rest of my funeral discharged, the debts that are oweing to me are these that follow : A Note of the debts oweing in record to me, William

---

[1] The testator was bur. at Gainford, 16 Dec., 1615.

[2] He was bur. at All Saints, Newcastle, 5 Jan., 1615/16, there is a marriage there of a William Sadler and Isabella Pearson, 23 Dec., 1609.

Sadler, as followeth. Edward Wright is oweing me 5*l*. of the which sume to be paid the next Saterday. Edward Sadler of the Ould Moore is owing to me, William Sadler, 2*s*. Gerard Walker of the Ould Moore is oweing to me 12*s*. Anthonie Pottes, of Paysworth, is oweing to me 12*s*. James Sadler, my Brother, is oweing to me 1*l*. Cuthbert Awbon and Christopher Awbon is oweing to me 2*l*. 6*s*. 8*d*. Cuthbert Awbon, for a stone and three quarters of linte, coming to 10*s*., which he is oweing for to me. James Rowell is oweing to me 8*s*. David Man is oweing to me 1*l*., the which if I dept this lyfe I give to David's childe, John Man. Edward Hall, of Sandgate, is oweing me, for coales, 1*l*. 4*s*. I have a cowe greate with calfe with Cuthbert Awbon and a stott and a whie that Cuthbert Awbon did deliver prazed at 3*l*. Item: I give to my brother, James Sadler, 1*l*. I give to John Mann, the son of David Man, 1*l*. I give to Cuthbert Awbon for his two children, 1*l*. I give to Randall Awbot, a whie. All the rest of my goods, moveable and unmoveable, I give to my well beloved wife, Isabella, whom I make full Executor of this my last Will and Testament. Memor dum: That William Sadler is not owing any thing of vallew but such small things as he referreth to his wife to paye. Witnesses, John Rosdon, James Man, Jane Browne and others. Proved, 24 Feb., 1615.

ALICE SELBYE.[1]

Jan. 15, 1615. In the name of God, Amen, I, Alice Selbye, of the towne and countie of Newcastle upon Tyne, Widow. To be buried within the parish church of St Nicholas as near unto my late husband, George Selbye deceased, as possible may be; if no place there can be had neare hand him then I will that it be laide as neare my former husband, Robert Carre, in the same church of St. Nicholas. I give to Margarett Clibborne, widow, my bed, in which I lye, with curtens, featherbed and all furniture belonging to it. I give to pore widows that are decayed householders, 30*s*., at the discretion of my executors. I give to Agnes Coates in money, 10*s*. and one paire of corse sheets. I give to Margaret Adamson, 10*s*. in money, and a paire of corse sheets. I give to Elizabeth Brameling, widow, 6*s*. in money and a round curtell. I give to Jane Baits, daughter of Thomas Baits, my silke apron. I give to Isabella Readhead, of Sandgate, a gold ring for a token. I give to Cuthbert Baites, sone of Thomas Baites, 10*s*. for a token.

[1] Her second husband George Selby was bur. at St. Nich., Newcastle, 13 June, 1613, having made his will 8 June, in that year, he mentions his wife Alice, dau. Elizabeth Moysere (she mar. Christopher Moyses, merchant, 16 Nov., 1596, at St. Nich.), dau. Jane Charteris, dau. Margaret Banne, dau. Ursula Lace—also Sir George Selby, knt. The burial entry of the testatrix in St. Nich., Newcastle, runs as follows, 1615/16, Jan. 30, oulde Mrs. Selby, bur.

The residue of all my goods and chattells, moveable and unmoveable, I give and bequeath unto William Powre, Robert Selbye, Thomas Baits and Margaret Clibborne, whom I make and ordaine my sole Executors of this my last Will and Testament. Witnesses: John Taylor, Nicholas Harll. Proved, 1615.

ROBERT GOFTON.[1]

Jan. 17, 1615. In the name of God, Amen I, Robert Gofton, of the towne of Newcastle upon Tyne, Cordiner. To be buryed within St. Nicholas Church garth, within the towne of Newcastle aforesaid. I give and bequeath unto my wife, Agnes Gofton, and to my daughter, Agnes Gofton, my house, in the Flesh Market, as it standeth, and to the longer liver of them and their heires for ever. I give unto my daughter Jane Milburne, wife unto Peter Milburne, my howse in the Meddle Street, adjoining upon a tenement of Peter Tompson, Merchant, for his wife, Jane Milburne, lyfe tyme, and then to come to my wife, Agnes Gofton. I give unto my brother, Edward Gofton, of hie Callerton, yeoman, 10*l*. I give and bequeath unto my brother's sonne, Robt. Gofton, a black whie. I give unto my daughter's sonne, John Milburne, 20*l*. I doe give and bequeathe unto to my daughter Jane Milburne, 10*l*. I give and bequeath unto Richard Gofton, my cosinge, a twenty two shillinge peece of gold called a Jacobus. I doe give and bequeath unto my cozen, Hugh Gofton, of Byrkley, yeoman, a peece of gold of twenty two shillings price called a Jacobus. I doe give and bequeath unto Heugh Gofton, of Elland Hall, the younger, yeoman, a peece of golde of twenty two shillings price called a Jacobus. I give and bequeath unto my cozen, Richard Brykus, cordiner, a peece of gold of twentie two shillings price called a Jacobus. I doe give and bequeathe unto my sister, Allie Simpson, 6*s*. 8*d*. yearlie, so long as my wife, Agnes Gofton, livethe. And I doe make my wife, Agnes Gofton, and my daughter, Agnes Gofton, my whole executors of this my last Will and Testament, to whom I give and bequeath all the rest of my goods, moveable and unmoveable, my debts, legacies and funerall expences discharged. And I make Richard Byrkus, of the towne of Newcastle upon Tyne, Cordn., and Richard Gofton of Elland Hall, yeoman, Supervisors of this my last Will and Testament. Witnesses, Edward Gofton, Richard Byrkus and Richard Gofton. Proved, 1615.

[1] The testator was bur. at St. Nich., Newcastle, 19 Jan., 1615/16, and his widow, Agnes, was bur. there, 17 Feb., 1624/5. There is a pedigree of the family of Gofton of Eland Hall in the *New County History of Northumberland,* vol. xii., pp. 468-9.

WILLIAM REED.[1]

Mar. 3, 1615. Sir William Reed, of Fenham, in the County of Northumberland, Knight. To be buried at the discretion of my executors and friends. I give and bequeath to Dame Margaret, my wife, and unto Susan Reed, Ephraim Reed and John Reed, all my tithes of corne, graine, groweing and renewing within the townes and fields of Fenwick, in the Countie palatine of Durham, during the terms of years unexpired in the letters patent made from Her late Soveryn, Lady Queen Elizabeth, unto William Kinnord, alias Reed, father of me, the said Sir William Reed, Knight, bearing date att Westminster the 30th day of May in the 21st yeare of Her Heighness' late reigne. I give unto William Reed, my eldest sone, my mannor house of Fenham with the appurtenances and the closes thereunto adjoining with all the tithes, And also the tithe of corne and graine in Beele for and during the residue of the said terme ' of the said recited Letters patent, he, the said William Reed, paying yearly thereto the sum of 40*l*. to Mary, the wife of Robert Coniers, Dorothy Reed, Philadelphia Reed, Margaret Reed, Lancelot and Robert Reed, Elizabeth Reed, Lucie Reed and Jane Reed, my children, for and towards their maintenance and education, in like manner and forme as the same ought to be paid by Sir William Selbie, of Shortflatt, Knight, Henry Jones and William Steward, gentlemen, if they should possess and enjoy the said tithes by virtue of an assisment to them made. I give unto Francis Reed, my sone, 10*l*. To Marie, the wife of Robert Coniers, 50*l*. I give unto Dorothie, Philadelphia, Margaret, Lancelott, Robert, Elizabeth, Lucie and Jane Reed, my children, 40*l*. a piece. I will that my burgage house in Berwick and all my household stuff, plate, goods and chattels, whatsoever, shall be sold for payment of my debts. I appoint my sone, William Reed, sole Executor, and I do heartily request my right well beloved friendes, Sir William Selbye, of Shortflatt Knight, Henrie Jones and William Steward, Supervisors of this my Will. Probate, 1618.

---

[1] The will of the testator's father William is printed in this volume. The testator was bur. at Holy Island, 16 Mch., 1616/17; his widow, Margaret, having made her will, 9 Dec., 1618, was bur. at Berwick, 14 Dec., following; their children were William, bapt., 23 July, 1592, at Holy Island; Lancelot, bapt. at Berwick, 10 May, 1603; Robert, bapt. at Kyloe, — Aug., 1606; Mary, bapt., 3 Aug., 1595, at Holy Island, mar. Robert Conyers of Hoppen; Margaret, bapt. at Berwick, 9 Oct., 1601; Jane, bapt. at Holy Island, 2 July, 1611, bur. there, 5 Oct., 1621. The baptisms of Francis, Dorothy, Philadelphia, Elizabeth and Lucy have not been found.

98

JOHN CLAXTON.[1]

March 18, 1615. In the name of God, Amen, I, John Claxton, of Chester in-the-street, within in the Countie of Durham, gent. To be buried in the pish churche of Chester. I give and bequeathe unto Arthur Blande, my sister's sonne, the sum of 10*l*. I give to the dowghter of George Waynewright, of the City of Rye, the sum of 10*l*. I give unto my cosen, Sir John Claxton of Nettlesworth, Knight, one, two and twentie shillings piece of golde. To Robt. Catchesyde, of Birtley, one old angell. I give to my cosen, Jane Marshall, in service with Mr. Conyers of Layton, 40*s*. To John Claxton, of Darlington, 20*s*. I give to the poore of Chester pish yearlie, 6*s*., to be paid out of thre Pounde stocke which wydowe Wayles hath in possession and use. I give to the poore at my deathe, 10*s*. To my brother, Sir George Claxton, mynister at Cawodd, in Yorkeshire, as a token of my good will, 20*l*. And my further will is that, if it please God, my said brother dye before me that the 20*l*. aforesaide shall goe to his nowe wife if she be liveinge, and if they be both dead before me, then to returne to my executors. All the residue of my goods and chattels not formerly bequeathed, my debts and my legacies discharged, and funerall expences deducted, I give and bequeathe to younge Thomas Scott, of Allerton, the sonne of Thomas Scott, thelder, whom I doe ordaine and make sole Executor. Witnesses, Leonard Somersyde, Cuthbert Browne.

Memn. Thomas Scott of Alnerton, Sadler, in the Countie of York, father unto younge Thomas Scott, executor in the last Will and Testament of John Claxton, of Chester in the street, gent., late deceased, did voluntarlie and of his owne mind and consent freelie appoint, ordeyne and constitute Cutht. Browne of Gaitsed, Tailor, brother in law unto the said Thomas Scott, to be in full power to deal and doe for him the said young Thomas Scott, being uncle unto him, and to crave and obtayne of the Right Worshipful Mr. Doctor Colmore, Chancellor of Durham, the tuicon and gardianshipp of the said young Thomas being of the age of 20 years, and to bring forth the said last Will and Testament of the said John Claxton to be proved by the testimonie of witnesses in that behalf before the said Right Worl. Mr. Doctor Colmore, ecclestical judge. In witness whereof the said Thomas Scott, father of the said young Thomas, hath hereunto sett his hand and seal the 7th day of April, 1616.

[1] The testator was bur. at Chester-le-Street, 5 April, 1616. His brother George may perhaps be identified with the George Claxton who matric pens. from St. John's College, Cambridge, Michs., 1555, ordained at York, 24 Apl., 1574. His cousin, Sir John Claxton, bapt. at St. Andrew's, Auckland, 25 Oct., 1560, mar. Mary, bapt., 2 Feb., 1561/2, at St. Andrew, Auckland, dau. of Anthony Wren, he was bur. at Chester-le-Street, 3 Jan., 1637/8.

HENRIE ATKINSON.[1]

May 27, 1616. In the name of Gode, Amen, I Henrie Atkinson, of the towne of Newcastle upon Tyne, in the countye of the same towne, Cordwr. To be buried in the parish Church of St. Andrew's, and concerning my worldlie landes, goods and chattells, wherewith it hath pleased god to indew me, I give and bequeath the same as followeth. First I give and bequeath unto my sonne, William Atkinson, all that burgage or tenement with the appurtenances wherein Robert Winter, my father in lawe, dwelleth, situate and being in the noult Markett in Newcastle upon Tyne aforesaid, To have and to hold the said messuage or tenement with the appurtenances unto the said William Atkinson and to the heires of his bodye lawfully to be begotten for ever, and for default of such issue then to remaine and come to my sonne, Henry Atkinson, and to the heires of his body lawfully to be begotten for ever, and for default of such issue then to remaine and come to my daughter, Margaret Atkinson, and to the heires of her bodie lawfully begotten for ever, and for default of such issue then to remaine and come to the right heires of me, the saide Henry Atkinson, for ever. I give and bequeath unto my said sonne, William Atkinson, all that my close lying and being at Pandon Cawsey head with the appurtenances which I purchased of Mr. Anthonie Swinborne and his wife, and the little house without the neare gate in Sidgate and the garth on the back side thereof now in the occupation of Andrew Dowr. To have and to holde the said close att Pandon Cawsey head the said little house and garthe in Sidgate aforesaid unto the said William Atkinson and the heires of his bodye lawfully to be begotten for ever, and for default of such issue then to remaine and come to my said sonne, Henry Atkinson, and the heires of his bodie lawfullie to be begotten for ever, and for default of such issue then to remaine and come to the said Margaret Atkinson and to the heires of her bodie lawfully to be begotten for ever ; and for default of such issue then to remaine and come to the right heires of me, the said Henrie Atkinson, for ever. I give and bequeath unto my said sonne, Henrie Atkinson, all that my burgage or tenement with the appurtenances wherein I now dwell, situate and being in Pilgrim street, in Newcastle upon Tyne, aforesaid. To have and to holde the said burgage or tenement with the appurtenances unto the said Henrie Atkinson, my sonne, and to the heires of his body lawfully to be begotten for ever, and for default of such issue then to remaine and come unto the said William Atkinson, his brother, and to the heires of his bodye lawfully to be begotten for ever, and for default of such

[1] He was bur. at St. Andrew's, Newcastle, 24 May, 1616, his widow being bur there, 7 April, 1617; his son William was apprenticed to Robert Bowes, 24 Jan., 1622, enrolled, 27 Sept., 1621 (sic).

issue then to remaine apd come to the said Margaret Atkinson and to the heires of her bodie lawfully to be begotton for ever, and in default of such issue then to remaine and come to the right heires of me, the said Henrie Atkinson, for ever. I give to my said daughter, Margaret Atkinson, one hundred markes in money, I give to my father-in-law, Robert Winter, twenty shillings, to my mother, his wife, twenty shillings. To my brother, John Atkinson, 20s. and to Isabella his wife, 10s. To John Joplyn and his wife, 10s. To George Newton and his wife, 10s. To Eleanor Goodwin, 5s. To Gilbert Newton, 5s. To Margaret Lynn, 5s. To Heugh Maison, 5s. To Henrie Whitfield, 5s. To Lawrence Carr, 5s. To Thomas Watson, 5s. I give to George Best and Margaret Best the rent of the house that Raph Scurfield dwelleth in during the lyfe tyme of my mother equally amongst them, and the residue of all my goods and chattells unbequeathed I give and bequeath to my wife, Marie Atkinson, whom I make ordeyne sole Executrix of this my last Will and Testament, and I also will that the said Marie shall give to my sonns Willm. and Henrie Atkinson 10l. a peece to bind them prentices and 40s. to Henry Atkinson my brother's sonne. Witnesses, Robert Winter, George Newton. John Atkinson, Heugh Maison, Lawrence Carr, Thomas Watson. Proved, 13 November, 1616.

RICHARD THOMPSON.[1]

June 24, 1616. In the name of God, Amen, I, Richard Thompson, of the pish of All Saintes, within the Town of Newcastle upon Tyne, Barber Churgion and Tallow Chandler. To be buryed (if Gode so permitt) within the pish churche of Sainte Andrewes within the said Towne, And for my worldly goods, landes and tenements, I give and bequeath the same as followeth, viz., I gyve and bequeathe unto Margarett Thompson, my loveing wief, all that my messuage, burgage or tentt with the appurtenances nowe in myne occupation situate within the said towne of Newcastle, in a Streete there called the Keyside, also one tenement with the appurtenances thearunto adjoyning and belonging, nowe in the tenere or occupation of Roberte Armery, mariner, and also one Howse mylne and mylne Howse thereunto belonging and likewise adjoining now in the tenure or occupation of James Thompson, Mylner, for and duringe her naturall life : and after her decease then I give and bequeathe same premises unto the heires of our two bodyes lawfully begotten and to be begotten for ever and after the decease of us two and the heires of our two bodies then to descend and come to right heires of me, the saide Richard Thompson, for ever according to the tennre and purport of a Deed of feoffment thereof formerly made to the uses and intents

---

[1] He was bur. at St. Andrew's, Newcastle, 6 July, 1616, where his sister Alice was mar. to Ralph Thompson, blacksmith, 27 Nov.. 1603.

aforesaid dated the 22 daye of December, in the tenthe yeare of the nowe Kings Majties reigne and by the same, whereunto reference be hadd, more at large appears. My will and mynd is that my sonne, John Thompson shall within twelve months after he shall enter or maie lawfully enter into the possession of the said messuage or tenemt the said tenement and howse, mylne and mylne howse, with their appurtenances or any of them after the death of his said mother, Margaret Thompson, shall content and paie and cause to be paid unto his brother, Robert Thompsone, out of the said tenemt, howse milne, and milne howse the sume of twenty pounds of lawful money of England, which I do not doubt but he will pforme accordingly, I give and bequeath unto my sister, Alice, wife to Ralph Thompson, Blacksmith, ten shillinges for a token. I gyve and bequeath unto Francis Gray, sone of my uncle, Robt. Gray, twenty shillings in money and my suite of apparelle. All the rest of my goods, cattells and debts, my debts and funerall expences being payd and discharged, I give and bequeathe unto the said Margaret, my loveing wife, and the said John and Robert Thompson, my two sonnes, whom I make and ordayne full executors of this my last Will and Testament, revoking and foresaking all wills whatsoever by one formerly made. Witnesses, Henry Gray, Robert Gray, Francis Leighton. Proved, 13 November, 1616.

THOMAS LYDDELL.[1]

July 27, 1616. In the name of God, Amen. I, Thomas Lyddell, of the towne of Newcastle on Tyne, merchant and alderman. To be buried in the parish church of Saint Nicholas, within the queare of the same, where my two wives lieth. Inprimis : I give and bequeath to my eldest sonne, Thomas Lyddell, my mannor of Ravensworth with the appurtences thereto belonginge, and my house in Newcastle, called the ffryars, with the grounds and appurtenances thereto also belonginge he paying therefore yearlie out of the said Mannor the some of twenty markes unto my servante, Emme Foster, during her life. Item, my will is that my sonne, Henry

---

[1] The testator's mother's will is the first printed in this volume. He was bur., 19 Aug., 1619, at St. Nich , Newcastle, from which registers all dates are taken except where otherwise mentioned. By his first wife, Margaret, mar.. 9 Sept.. 1576. bur., 21 Apl., 1586. dau. of John Watson of Newcastle, he had issue. Thomas, bapt., 14 Apl., 1578, created a Baronet. 1642, will dated 7 Jan., 1650. mar. Isabel (bapt., 3 Aug., 1582), dau. of Henry Anderson. 23 Feb., 1595/6, at St. John's, Newcastle. bur.. 27 June, 1632, at Lamesley; John, bur.. 7 July. 1584; Elizabeth, bapt., 28 July. 1579, mar., 19 Feb.. 1598/9, William Sherwood at St Andrew's, Newcastle, as his second wife (his first wife, Eleanor Jackson, having been bur.. 12 Dec., 1598), she was bur.. 11 Mch., 1638/9, and he, 15 April, 1640; Agnes, bapt., 6 Sept., 1580, bur., 12 Oct., same year; Eleanor, bapt., 14 Oct., 1581. mar., 10 Oct., 1602, at St. Andrew's. Timothy Draper as his second wife (his first wife, Dorothy, widow of Roger Rowe, whom he mar., 9 Oct., 1598, bur., 1 Jan., 1601/2), he bur.

Lydell, shall have my Mannor of farneacres with the appurtances according to ann Indendure formerly by me passed of the same to the said Henry Lyddell together with all the household stuff wherewith the Mannor house of ffarnacres is now furnished (excepting one farme in Woollsingham, parcell of the said Mannor of ffarnacres which by this will I doe give to my servante, Emme Foster, during her naturall life). Item, my will is that my sonne, Roger Lyddell, shall have all those my severall lands, tenements and hereditaments as, namely, Darwen Crooke, a messuage in Grindon chaire, sometimes the inheritance of Sir Ralphe Lawson, the house wherein John Commen dwelleth, my shope upon the bridge end, my house and closes in Sidgate, The Croft, the Collier close with the colemynes, Patton Close and Milne, Sandewardson Close, Skabmaister leazes, with all my estate and interest in my lease of Archdeacon Newton, with all and singular their appurtences to the said premises and everie of them belonginge according to the meaning heretofore expressed in an Indenture which I have lately past or intended to have past to the use of the said Roger Liddell. Item, my will is that my daughter, Elizabeth Sherewood, shall have 200*l.* in full discharge of her filiall porcon. Item, I give to my said daughter, Elizabeth Sherewood, my house in the flesh markat, now in the occupation of William Sherwood, during her life naturall and after her decease to Thomas Sherwood, her sonne, and his heirs. Item, my will is that my daughter, Alice Saffield, shall have in full discharge of her filiall porcon, 50*l.*, my further will is that the children which my said daughter, Alice Saffeild, now hath shall have 150*l.* equally amongst them which shall be disposed of by my sonne, Thomas Lyddell, for their best profit until they shall come to lawful yeares or be married. Item, my will is that my daughter, Barbara Sanderson, shall have 150*l.*, for a legacy and further give to my said daughter's sonne, Thomas Sanderson, 50*l.*, as a token. I give unto my daughter, Jane Anderson, 200*l.*, for a legacy in full discharge of her filiall porcon except those legacies hereafter bequeathed unto her with her sister,

13 Feb., 1622/3, she bur., 4 Sept., 1603; Alice, bapt., 14 Nov., 1582, mar. Gawen Salkeld. The testator mar., secondly, 13 Jan., 1586/7, Jane, dau. of Henry Mitford, bur., 12 July, 1602; by her he had Henry, bapt., 20 Aug., 1590, bur. at Whickham, 22 Jan., 1641/2, mar. at Grindon, 26 Feb., 1608/9, Elizabeth (bur. at Whickham, 31 July, 1675), dau. of William Jenison; Roger, bapt., 22 Oct., 1592, mar., firstly, 3 May, 1614, Grace, dau. of James Clavering of Axwell (bapt., 30 Nov., 1592, bur., 16 Aug., 1642, at Lamesley), mar., secondly, 6 Dec., 1642, Mrs. Elizabeth Thorpe; George, bapt., 2 Apl., 1594, bur., 26 Jan., 1595/6; Barbara, bapt., 4 Dec., 1595, bur. at Lanchester, 17 Aug., 1672, mar. Samuel Sanderson of Brancepeth and Hedley Hope (died, July, 1650, M.I. Lanchester), 18 Dec., 1610, at Brancepeth; Jane, bapt., 26 Jan., 1597/8, mar. Robert Anderson, 24 Apl., 1615, at St. Andrew's, Newcastle. His *Inq. p.m.* was taken at Durham, 12 April, 1620, see also the *Inq. p.m.* taken at Durham, 1629, of his grandson, Thomas, son of his son, Thomas Liddell.

Barbara. I give unto my brother, Francis, 20*l.* as a token. I give to William Lyddell, of London, Merchant Talor, 50*l.*, as a legacy. I give to Thomas Lyddell, sone of my sonne, Thomas Lyddell, all that my parte of the colemynes of Blackburne, in the parish of Lamesly, in the County of Durham. To my servant, Emme Foster, 100*l.* and a bed full furnished, for a legacy. To my grandchild, Mary Draper, 50*l.*, as a legacy. I give to my daughters, Barbara Sanderson and Jane Anderson, my two best carpets and one dozen and a half of quissons of the best tapstrie, work with my best bedstead, silk curtaynes and bedding thereto, belonging equally betwixt them, To my cozen, Thomas Car, 10*l.* To my cozen, Elizabeth Crome, for the use of her first husband's children, 10l. I give to my three sonns, Thomas, Henry and Roger, thre gold rings, Thomas to have the best, Henry the next and Roger the worst. Item, my will is that my lynnen shallbe equallie divided between my daughters, Barbara Sanderson and Jane Anderson. The rest of my houshold stuff to be equallie divided between my two sonns, Thomas and Roger. To my servant, Gawen Adon, 10*l.* To my servant, Railph Fowler, 5*l.* To everie one of the residue of my household servants, 20*s.* a peece. To Nicholas Punder, 40*s.* To Theodor Wright, 40*s.* I give to Mr. William Jenison, Alderman, one vuyon peece, for a token. To my cozen, Francis Burrell, an old angell, for a token. I will that my brother, Robart Lyddell, have 150*l.*, which I owe him, and my further will is that the poore shallbe liberallie rewarded at the tyme of my funeral as shallbe seeminge fitting to my executors. All the rest of my goods and chattels, my funeral debts and legacies discharged, I give to my thre sonns, Thomas, Henry and Roger, whom I do constitute and appointe my full and joint executors. And lastly I desire that my good friends shall be supervisors of this my Will to see the same executed, that is to say, Sir Henry Anderson, Knight, Mr. James Clavering, Alderman, Mr. Timothy Draper, gentleman, and my Brother, Francys Lyddell, and I give to each of them an vuyon, for a token. Witnesses to will, James Clavering, L. . . . Burrell, Ralph Fewler, William Baynes, Gawen Adon. Proved, 1619.

LANCELOT EWBANKE.[1]

July 29, 1616. In the name of God, Amen, I, Lancelot Ewbanke, of Drerige, in the Countye of Northumberland. Gentleman. To be buried within the chappell of Wooddrington paying my accustomed fees. I bequeath unto my sonne, Thomas Ewbank,

[1] The following entries taken from the registers of Woodhorn may relate to the testators family, 1625/6, Feb. 5, Isabel, dau. of John Ewbank, bapt.; 1630, July 20, " Lancelot, s. of Thomas Ewbank," bapt.; 1635, June 13, Henry, s. of Thomas Ewbank, bapt.; 1623, May 20, Thomas Ewbank and Elizabeth Hardburn, mar.; 1636, Apl. 2, Thomas Ewbank, bur,

thre Jacobusses. I bequeath unto my daughter, Margery
Ewbank, foure Jacobusses. I bequeath unto my sonne, Henry
Ewbanke, one Jacobus. I give and bequeath unto my Maister's
sonne, Mr. William Woodrington, my puppy coult now going in
Woodrington Parke. I bequeath unto my sister, Annas, a quye
and a calfe. I will that my wife and my children shall have my
goods equally devided amongst them, and that my wife shall have
20*l.* more then any of my children, and if she will not stand to
this, in liew of her thirds, then she shall have nothing but that·the
Law will give hir. And that my wife and my sonne, John, shall
keepe house together and bring up my younger children according
as my Maister, Sir Henry Woodrington, shall thinke most fittinge,
and if they cannot agree together that then my Maister shall see
where the fault is and cause it to be reformed by him, and then
that part of demayne Drerige which I now dwell, one shallbe
equally devided betwixt them. And the farme and the cotage
which I have in Woodhorne shall goe to the bringinge upp of my
younger children, untill my maister thinke good to bestowe it
one my sone, John. I make and ordayne my wife and my sone,
John Ewbank, my sole Executors of this my last Will and Testament. And my Mr. Sir Henry Woodrington my Supervisore
before these witnesses. Witnesses, Robert Woodrington, Thomas
Sakeld, Andrew Clennell, Ambos Lowraunce.

INVENTORYE of all the goods of Lancelot Ewbank, Gentleman,
of Drerige, late deceased, praised by Edward Dodsworth, Gentleman, Henry Kirton, Gentleman, Martin Barde and William
Crastor the 26th of September, 1616.

Imprimis : 20 oxen, 53*l.* 6*s.* 8*d.* 20 kyne and calves, 40*l.*
4 quyes, two which have calves, and two geld, 6*l.* 6 geld kyne,
10*l.* One bull, 40*s.* 3 marte oxen, 6*l.* 3 mayres, 5*l.* One stond
horse, 8*l.* 10 yewes, 40*s.* 4 score of hogges, 9*l.* A eleven score
thraives of wheat, estimated to *l.* boules, 30*l.* 8 score threives of
oates, estimated to 40 boules, 8*l.* 10*s.* Twenty nine threives of
Reare, estimated to 8 boules, 4*l.* Six score threives of peese and
beanes, estimated to 20 boules, 8*l.* Three longe waynes, 3 coupe
waynes with their furniture, 4*l.* 2 plowes, 2 Iron harrowes with
other harrowes, 16*s.* A fraime of a butterye, a cubbert and a
cawell Armarie, 13*s.* 4*d.* 6 brass potts, more or less, 24*s.* One
caldron and spanns, 26*s.* 8*d.* Twenty one peace of puter vessell,
7 candlesticks, 2 quarte potts of putter, and 4 salts, 42*s.* One
putter chamber pott, 12*d.* Six chists with corne chestes, 35*s.*
A presser, five bedsteads and a featherbedd, 18*s.* 4*d.* Twenty four
paire of lynning and coarser sheats. 2*l.* Six paire of blankets
and six coverlets, 32*s.* Fourteene boulsters and codds, 8*s.* One
Iron Cheamney, 2 Spitts, 2 Iron poors, a paire of tonnges and 2
Iron Crookes, 5*s.* 10*d.* One table, 2 Chaires and 2 formes, 3*s.* 6*d.*
Brewing vessell, 10*s.* Eleven Swyne, elder and younger, 22*s.* A
turkey cock, a turkey henn, 3*s.* Twenty other pulline, 6*s.* 8*d.*

Twenty geese, 10s. His wearing apperill with his other furniture, 40s. Eighteen stone of wool, 8l. Goods goeing in the Hye Lands : Two oxen and 8 stotts, 21l. 13s. 4d. Twelve stots and quies of the age of two yeares ould and the vantage, 16l. Sixteen year oulds, 10l. 13s. 4d. Three fylles of two yeares ould and the vantage, 7l. One ould mayre and hir foale, 40s. Three-score yewes and seven, 14l. 10s. 4d. Six score demmonds and semmers, 30l. Thirteen Jacobusses, 14l. 6s. Twenty three stone cheese, 2l. 8s. Thirteen stone of butter, 40s. of money, 3l. John Browne and Henry Armerye, of East Chevington, is indebted for a score of yowes and lambes, 9l. Henry Anderson, of Newcastle, is indebted 13l. Staven Bell is owinge 18s. Debts that the Testator Owethe :—oweinge to my Maister, Sir Henrye Woodrington, in rent for half of the demayne of Drerig, due to be paid at Martinmass next Comminge, 22l. 10s. Proved, 18 November, 1616.

JOHN RICHARDSON.[1]

Sept. 28, 1616. In the name of God, Amen, I, John Richardson of Trimdon, in the Countye of Durham, Yeoman. To be buried in Kelloe Churchyarde. I give to the poore of Trymdon, 20s. for a stock and the use thereof to be distributed yearly unto 12 of the poorest of them upon St. Thomas' day before Christenmas by William Richardson, my sonne, his heirs and assyns for ever and a note of the names of them to be given to the Minister and churchwardens, and the same to be expressed in their book of account yearly and for the better execution and discharge of the same, presentment to be made yearlie of the payment or non-payment of the same according to the Artickle to that end constituted. I give to the poore of Kelloe, 2s. 6d., whereof widow Colson to have 6d. I give and bequeath unto my nephew, Ralph Smith of Pittington, 6l., all my whole apparell whatsoever ; every year two pecks of wheate, alwayes at Christenmas, so long as the lease doth last that I have of William Brasse, except the said land be sowen with oates or any other graine : then the said Ralphe to have a bushell of that graine during those yeares, and also a black heffer with a white rigge upon the back. I give unto my nephew, Christopher Smith, three pounds. I give unto Margaret Smith, my neece, one heffer, the bed steed in the upper chamber with the materesse, one happing, one coverlett, the third part of the pewder, and one of the brass pottes. I give unto my wife, Margaret, the great cupboarde which standes at the table ende, in my now dwellinghouse. I give unto my neece, Elsabeth, the wife of William Burton of Gilligate, in Durham, three poundes. I give unto my nephew, William Burton, Four poundes. I give unto my nephew, Robert

---

[1] A William Richardson of Trimdon has an *Inq. per br. de mand.* taken at Durham, 28 Mch., 1629, in which it is stated John, aged 3, is his son and next heir.

Burton, foure poundes. I give unto Mary Burton, my neece, two
pounds. I give unto my sister, Kathrine, two pounds. I give
to my sister Kathrine sonn which dwelleth with . . . . Heiton,
four pounds. I give to my sister Katherine other sonne, thirty
shillings. I give unto Christopher Robinson of Ferry-hill, five
shillings. I give unto my son, William's wife, one ewe and a lamb.
I give and bequeath unto John Richardson, being my grandchild,
which I christoned at my cottage. I give unto Robert Roper's
daughter, which I christoned, one ewe and a lamb. I give unto
the saide John Richardson, my grandchild, one close which I
bought being 15 akers, upon these condicions followinge, First,
that my wife, Margret, shall have them for her life time, 2ndly,
that my sonne, William, shall pay to his two daughters, Elsabeth
and Frances, the sum of 60*l*. within three yeares next after Proba-
tion of this my Will, by equal porcons, 3rdly, that the said cottage
and close with the appurtenances shall returne unto Elsabeth and
Frances Richardson, daughters of my sone William, and to the
lawful heires coming of them for want and defalt of lawful issue
of the said John, theire brother, or his heires. My will is that
my said cottage and close with the appurtenances shall come to the
next of my kinn after the death of the said John, Elsabeth and
Frances Richardson, and their heires, for defalt of heirs lawfully
issuing from them, any of them, or their heires. I give and bequith to Frances Richardson, daughter of my sonn William, 10*l*.
I give to John Richardson, my godson, foure pounds. I give to
Margarett Spurner, my servant, 3*s*. 4*d*. I give unto my sonne,
William Richardson, all my husbandrye geare who had had of me
a large porcon alreadye. The rest of my goods, moveable and unmoveable, my debts, legacies and funerall expences first payed and
discharged, I give unto Margaret Richardson, my wife, Elabeth
and Frances Richardson, daughters of my son William Richardson whom I doe make my executors of this my last Will and Testament. I make my said sonne, William, and James Shadforth of
Trymdon, Supervisors of this my Will. Witnesses, Robert Ward.
William Fisher, William Richardson. Proved, 21 June, 1617.

ANTHONY ROBINSON.[1]

Nov. 22, 1616. In the name of God, Amen, I, Anthony Robinson, of West Herrington, in the Countye of Durham, Yeoman.
To be buried in the parish church of Houghton. I give to the
poore of the parish of Houghton, to be distributed at my buriall,
and the remainder thereof (if any thing be left) to be delivered
to the collectors for the poore to the use of the poor, 20*s*. To
my sister Margaret's children I bequeath to every of them, 10*s*.
To my uncle, Robert Harrison, I give the corne groweing upon the

[1] The testator was bur. at Houghton-le-Spring, 27 Nov., 1616.

rigg that lyeth westward next to the rigg sowen for his use and more I give to him in money, 20s. I bequeathe to Margaret Collyer, my wives sister's daughter, the two cupbords standing in the fore-house, all my pewter, all the wearing apparell that belonged to my wife, all the bedding belonging to the bedd steed in the fore house, and more I give unto her in money, 10l. All the rest of my goods and chattells, moveable and unmoveable (my debts legacies and funerall excepted and discharged), I leave and bequeath to William Collyer and Robert Collyer, my wives sisters sonns, whom I make ioynt executors. Debts that I doe owe unto others : To George Shawdforth, 5l. To William Chilton of Newbottle, 4l. 8s. To John Chilton of Houghton, 3l. 6s. To Ralph Wilson of Cassop, 8s. To Robt. Collyer of Pensher, 10s. To Robt. Maland, 30s. To Matthew Smith of Newbottle, 6l. To the wife of Henry Dobson of Offerton, 20s. To Thomas Mathew of bishop-wearmouth, 7l. To Thomas Mathews wives mother, 20s. To Robt. Stevenson of Newbottle, 4s. 2d. To Mark Hawk upon a bond, 44s. To Roger Haswell of Chester, of wheate one bowle, of oats six bowles, of bigg foure bowels and one bushell and in money upon one reckings, 30s., and upon another recking, 23s. 9d., amounting to 53s. 9d. Debts owen to me by whose names are underwritten : William Cooke of West Herrington, 7s. Anthony Passmore of West Herrington, 6s. 2d. Edward Gillerie of West Herr., 12s. I doe entreat William Todd, of West Herrington, and Pearcivall Barkus, of Houghton in-the-Spring, to be supervisors of this last Will and Testament, and I bequeath to either of them, 10s. Witnesses Robt. Stevenson, Mathew Smith, William Todd, Peivall Barkas.

ROBERT TEMPESTE.[1]

Dec. 4, 1616. Memorandum, Robert Tempeste, of the towne of Newcastell upon Tyne, Marchant, Adventurer, being sicke in bodye but pfect in mynd and memory, Did make his last Will and Testament noncupatively and by words of mouth as followeth, Imprimis he did give and bequeath unto his Brother, Charles Tempest, his lease of the Butlerige of Mynes, he did give to his wife a thowsand poundes in full satissfacon of the reasonable part of his goods, he did give to his doughter, Jane Tempest, for her

[1] Bur. at St. Nich., Newcastle, 9 Dec., 1616, son of Nicholas Tempest of Thornley, he mar. Anne, dau. of Robert Shafto of Newcastle; she re-mar. John Clavering of Axwell, 8 Sept., 1618, at St. Nich., Newcastle, her second husband was bur. there, 6 May, 1648, she, 18 Nov., 1673. She had a dau., Jane, by her first husband, bapt. at St. Nich., 10 Nov., 1616. His brother, William Tempest, mar. Marion, dau. of William Aynsley of Shafto, and was bur. at Ryton, 27 July, 1652. His brother, Charles Tempest, bur. at St. Nich., Newcastle, 17 Dec., 1642; mar., 29 June, 1619, at St. Nich., Newcastle, Elizabeth, dau. of Thomas Surtees of Newcastle.

filiall porcon, five hundred poundes, which he said would be faire
porcons for them, and he said further that if his said Doughter
should happen to dye before she came to full age, then he gave the
one halfe of the said 500*l.* to his said wife, and the other halfe
to his Brother, William Tempeste. And all the rest of his goods
he gave to his said Brother, William Tempest, whom he made sole
executor, to performe and execute that his mynd and will as
aforesaid, in the psence and witnesse of thes whose names are
under written, My Ladie Margaret Selbie, Mr. Robert Shaftoe,
Mr. Willm. Lyeley, Nicholas Tempest. Proved, 1617.

STEPHEN WARDE.

Dec. 28, 1616. In the name of God, Amen, I, Stephen Warde,
of Blackwell, in the Countie of Durham, Yeoman. To be buried
at the South porch door of the parish church of Darlington, as
near unto my lait deceased parents as convenientlie be devised.
I give to the poor of the parish of Darlington, to be distributed of
John Midletonn and Thomas Emerson, 50*s.* I give to my godchild,
Stephen Potter, sone of Thomas Potter, six and twenty shillings
and eight pence, to be paid him by my executors or their guardians
or tutors at his accomplishment of one and twenty yeares upon his
acquittance of the same. The rest of all and singular my goods
and chattells not given nor bequeathed, my debts, legacies and
funeral expences deducted and discharged. I give and bequeath
unto my five youngest children, That is to say, Ralph Ward,
Christopher Ward, John Ward, Stephen Ward and the young
infant now newlie born, as yet not baptised, whom I make Joint
Executors of this my last Will and Testament humbly intreating
Thomas Emerson and John Midleton the younger, of Gilling, to be
supervisors of this my said Will, and to se the execution performed
according to the true intent and meaninge of the same. Witnesses,
John Midleton, Senr., Thomas Emerson, John Midleton, Junr.,
Richard Pickering and Leonard Emerson.

INVENTORY, 271*l.* 19*s.* 10*d.*, as Debts oweing to the Testator.
Suma Totalis 438*l.* 0*s.* 4*d.* Will Proved, 11 April, 1617.

FRANCIS BUNNY.[1]

Jan. 20, 1616. I, Francis Bunny of Ryton in the County of
Durham, clerk. To be buried in the Quyer of the parish church
of Ryton at the west end of my sone Franciss grave. And that I
may be better to dispose of my land at Newsham, I have given,
granted and confirmed, and do by these presents give, grant and

[1] He was the 3rd son of Richard Bunny of Newlands, by his wife,
Bridget, dau. of Edward Restwould of the Vache, in the parish of
Chalfont St. Giles, co. Bucks.; he was born, as is stated, on a brass in
Ryton Church. 8 May, 1543, entered as demy at Magdalen College,
Oxford 1559/61, fellow 1561-72, B.A. 10 July, 1562, M.A. 9 July, 1567,

confirm to my worshipful good cozin, John Calverley, of Little-
Burn, in the County of Durham, Esquire, to my wor : good brother
in law, Timothy Draper, of the town of Newcastle upon Tyne,
Esquire, and to my loveing brother in law, John Horsfal, of
Studeley, in the County of York, Yeoman, and to their heirs and
assigns, my said lands at Newsham lying and being in the County
Palatine of Durham, with all howses, buildings and appurtenances
whatsoever to all such uses, limitations, provisions and purposes
as in my last Will and Testament in writing, publish, limit and
declare, as by two deeds of Feoffment under my hand and seale
with libertie and seizine thereupon by me executed (both which
Deeds beare date the sixth day of September, 1616) may now
plainly appear. Now therefore my will is that my forenamed
feofferers their heirs and assigns and every of them stand and be
seized of and in all that my manor of Newsham and all the
appurtenances thereto belonging, to the use first of Jane Bunny,
my wife, for the term of her natural life, and until the third day
of May next after her decease, to dispose thereof as she shall
think good. And after the said estate made to my wife in the
premises ended and determined. I do hereby will advise and
appoint that all the said lands and grounds of Newsham shall
remaine unto the above named John Calverley, Timothy Draper
and John Horsfal, their executors and assigns, for and during the
term of forty years next ensuing after the estate made to my wife,
to the uses, purposes and trusts hereafter limitted and declared.
And after the said term of forty years the said tenements and
premises wholy to remain to my nephew, George Bunny, and his
heirs male of his body lawfully begotten, and in default of
such issue to remaine to Richard Bunny now eldest son of my
nephew, Francis Bunny, and the heirs male of his body and
in default of issue to remain to the second sone of my nephew,
Francis Bunny, and in default of issue to remain to the
third sone of my nephew, Francis, and in default of
issue to every of the other sons of my nephew, Francis. And
whereas I have before limited by this my Will in estate for forty
yeares of and in the said premises unto my said trusty friends,
John Calverly, Timothy Draper and John Horsfal, my meaning and
intent is that if my said nephew, George Bunny, his executors,
administrators, and assigns shall not withstanding after the estate

licensed to preach 26 Feb., 1583/4, Canon of Carlisle 1572, Archdeacon
of Northumberland 20 Oct., 1573, and rector of Ryton 11 Sept., 1578,
until his death there, 16 April, 1617. He mar. Jane, dau. of Henry
Priestly, and by her he had issue, John, born, 11 July, 1583, bur.,
15 Oct., 1585; Francis, born, 9 Nov., 1584, died, 23 Feb. 1610/11, M.I.
Ryton, mar. Mary, dau. of John Wortley of Unthank, 17 Nov., 1606, at
Jarrow, and Elizabeth, mar., 27 Sept., 1596, at Ryton, William Finney
of Finney, near Almondbury, co York, she died, 25 Feb., 1608. Timothy
Draper mar. as his third wife, Frances, dau. of Christopher Consett of
Newcastle, and widow of . . . . Priestly, 3 Nov., 1606, at Ryton.

made to my wife is determined, enter into and possess and take
the whole pfit of the premises to his and their owne use, so alwaies
that he pay the sum of six hundred and three score pounds of lawful money in manner and form followinge that is to say to pay
such sume to myne Executrix if I in my lifetime do not give and
deliver the same, that is to say, to the University of Oxford wherein I reaped whatsoever enabled me to be any way pfitable to the
church or Comon wealth, one hundred marks towards the finish-
ing or furnishing of their buyldings, or to dispose to any good
use. I give and bequeath to Magdalen Colledge in Oxford my
kynd nurse, from whose breasts I sucked that milk of knowledge
which god hath voutchsafed to bestow upon me (the lord call mee
not to account for my negligent use thereof) 33l. 13s. 4d. I give
also to the Cathedral Church of Durham, 30l. towards the making
of a librarie in the vestrie, if Mr. Dean and the chapter approve
that course, or else to furnish with books (to that value) that which
is now the librarie. To the Citty of Durham, as a token of mv
good will, I give 20l. by the discretion of the Maior or other chief
officer and two or three of his brethren to be lent to some poor
men decayed, not by unthrifty causes but by other casualties,
though they have taken paines to live in some honest calling. And
to the parish of Ryton wher I have laboured for forty years I
give 50l. to be bestowed (if not by myne own hands) not by my
executrix, as by the gentlemen and other discreet men of the
parish shallbe thought most beneficiall, provided that if the 20l.
bequeathed to the City of Durham, or this 50l. to Ryton parish
be not disposed of to some good use within two yeares after, these
sums be delivered to them, then I give power to my executrix or
my cozin George Bunny to receive the same for their own use.
To my wife's niece, Mary Priestley, for her good and painful service now more then 16 yeares I give and bequeath 100l., and if she
die before the said legacy be paid to her, then I bequeath
50l. thereof to my niece Priscilla Bunny and the other 50l. I give
to Joseph Priestly her brother, somewhat to make amend for the
great loss that the said Joseph had and susteined by the hard and
unconscionable dealing of one who because he pfesseth christianity
should not so unchristianly have cirmvented a better christian then
himself and for some respects of kyndness which reason would
him to have showed more to him then to some other, he
should not have tainted himself with a scorn of inhumanity. I
give to my nephew Henry Bunny 100 marks. To my neece Wortley 100 marks. To my neece Priscilla 100 marks. To my neece
Heth (for whom god hath already well pvided) I give for a token
40l., and to her Daughter Tomason Heth my god-daughter I give
10l. I give to the parish of Winston wherein Newsham is situated
10l. to be employed in such sort as the 20l. which I bequeathed
to the City of Durham. I give to my cozine, George Wortley, the
best horse or mayer young or old that I have at the tyme of my

death. To the parish of Ryton I bequeath the two livery cans
which I bought and used only to bring wine to the communion
table. To my cozin, John Piggot, of Ovingham one piece of gold
of 22*s*. To George Pickering, 40*s*., and to every of my men
servants who have served me one yeare besydes their wages, 40*s*.
The maid servants I leave to the consideration of my wife, Jane
Bunny, whom I make sole Executrix. Proved, 1617.

NOTE.—Rector of Ryton and Prebend of Durham Cathedral.

MATTHEW NOBLE.[1]

Feb. 20, 1616. In the name of God, Amen, I, Matthew Noble of
Elvitt, within the suburbes of the City of Durham, Myller. To
be buryed within my parish church of St. Oswald's, as near my
wiffe may be. I doe give unto the poore of St. Oswald's pish, 10*s*.
I doe give the lease of Shincliffe Milne, the rent of the said Myill
to be equally devided among all my children during the terme of
six yeares, I give all my reversion of years after the term of six
yeares be expired with all my interest, right and title, with the
lease of Shincliffe Myll. I doe give it unto my sone, Henry Noble,
as freely as ever I had the same. I give unto my sone-in-law,
John Kitchin, and unto my daughter, Jayne, his wiffe, my own
dwellinghouse in Elvitt with all and singular the appurtenances
with brew lead, malt kiln and loftes belonging to the said house
during the terme of ten yeares after my decease. I doe make my
son in law, John Kitchin, and Jane, his wife, for to be tutors and
governors of my two youngest daughters, Esabell Noble, and
Margarett Noble, during the terme of Ten yeares after my death,
and after the expiration of the sad ten yeares. I do give my said
house withall and singular the appurtenances with malt loftes
unto my son, Henry Noble, and to his heeres lawfully begotten
for ever. I doe give unto Matthew Noble, being my son James
Noble sone, the sume of 10*l*. of good and lawful money to be paid
unto the said Matthew Noble by my sone, Henry Noble, and after
the term of ten yeares after my death, and that the saide 10*l*. shall
be payd forth of my said now dwellinghouse unto the said Matthew
Noble towards his porchon, and in full lew and consideracon of
his porchen and for a legacye. And for lacke of issue

[1] The testator was bur. at St. Oswald's, Durham, 21 March, 1616/17,
he is called in the registers " a mylner and a veric grave man of yeares; "
he mar., firstly, Margaret Rutter, 6 Aug., 1581, at St. Oswald's. There
are two Margaret Nobles bur. there, one on 18 Apl., 1585, and the other
12 July, 1590. His son Henry mar., at Gateshead, 2 Nov., 1619, Eleanor
Graime; his son James, bapt. 11 Nov., 1582, bur. 23 Aug., 1616, had a
son James, bapt., 13 Feb., 1613/14; his dau. Jane, bapt., 1 July, 1599,
mar. John Kitchen of old Durham 14 Jan., 1616/17, she was bur., 14
Jan., 1621/2, " a verie honest nighbore " leaving a dau. Barbara, bapt.,
17 Mch., 1618/19; Margaret, bapt., 2 Sept., 1602, bur., 1 May, 1636;
Elizabeth, mar., John Barton, taylor, 3 Oct., 1619.

if my sone, Henry Noble, have no children, then I do
give my said house with the appurtenances unto my
daughter, Jane Kitchin, and to her heires for ever and
for lack of issue if my said daughter, Jane Kitchin, have no
children, then I do give my said house with the appurtenances
unto my daughter, Elizabeth Noble, and to hir children of hir
bodye lawfully begotten, and for lack of issue of my daughter,
Elizabeth Noble, if she have no children, then I give my said house
with the appurtenances unto my daughter, Esbell Noble, and to
hir heirs lawfully begotten, and if she have no children then I give
my said house with the appurtenances unto my daughter, Margaret
Noble, and to hir heirs lawfully begotten for ever. I do give unto
my daughter, Elizabeth Noble, my lease withall my interest, right,
and title of three houses wth the appurtenances in the terratorie
of Elvitt, which said three houses, with the appurtenances, I do
hold by lease of the Church of St. Oswald. I do give unto my
daughter, Margaret Noble, forty shillings, for a legacie. I also
give unto my daughter, Esabell Noble, forty shillings, for a
legacie. All the rest of my goods, moveable and unmoveable, my
debts, legacies and funeral expences to be first payd and discharged, all the rest of my goods to be equally divided among my
children, viz., Henry Noble, Jayne Kitchin, Elizabeth Noble,
Elsbell Noble, and Margaret Noble, and, further, I doe make my
son-in-law, John Kitchin, and Jayne, his wife, my full executors
of this my Will. Witnesses, John Ridley, Chris. Hucheson, Th.
Atkinson. Proved, 1617.

THOMAS WOODRINGTON.[1]

April 2, 1617. In the name God, Amen, I, Thomas
Woodrington, of the towne of Newcastle upon Tyne, Gent., a
pensioner of his Majtes towne of Barwick on Tweed. To be buryed
at the discretion of my executors hereafter named, and as for the
worldly goods which the lorde hath indewed me withall, I give
and bequeath as followeth :—I give and bequeath unto my Ladie
Woodrington, wife of Sir Henry Woodrington, Knight, five pounds
of lawful English money. I give unto my Cozens, Roger, Ralph,
Benjamine, and Lewes Woodrington, and to everie one of them,
five aingells in goulde. I give and bequeath unto my Cozen, Sir
Ephraham Woodrington, Knight, nine poundes of that debt he
is oweing me, and the remainder of this debt being five poundes,
I give the same to his eldest sone, Henry Woodrington. I give
unto my Cozen, Elizabeth Horsley, late wife to Launcelot Horsley,
late of Brenckhaugh, foure poundes. I give unto Claudeus
Woodrington, my cozen, whome I did helpe to Christin, three

[1] Bur. at All Saints, Newcastle, 18 April, 1617. There is a pedigree
of this branch of the Widdringtons in the *New County History of Northumberland*, vol. v., pp. 304-5.

poundes sixe shillings and eightpence. I give and bequeath unto
my neece, Isabell Bewicke, wife to Christopher Bewicke of Newcastle-on-Tyne, Marryner, forty pounds in money, and all such
implements and furniture as is nowe within my chamber. I give
unto Elizabeth Bewicke, daughter, unto the said Christopher
Bewicke, twenty poundes in money, and if it shall please gode to
gyve unto my said neece, Isabell, any other children of her owne
bodie begotten, then I will the said twenty poundes shall bee
equally divided amongst them, and fayling of her said children, to
come absolutelye to my saide neece her selfe. I gyve to my neece,
Agnes Potts, wife to Mark Potts of Harton, twenty poundes, and
to the fyve children of my said neece, Agnes Potts, and to every
of them, five poundes. And if any one or more of the said five
children doe chainge this mortall life before they come to the age
of eighteen yeares, then I will that his or her portion so dying
shall come to the rest of the said children, to be equally divided
amongst them. I give to my cozen, Katherin Airdale, forty
shillinges. I give unto Thomas Neill, sonne of Robert Neil, of
Mounkseaton, three poundes. I give unto Ellinor Swinborne,
wife of John Swinborne of Newcastle, Baker and Bearbrewer,
Three poundes. I give unto the man child of my sister, Ellenore,
five poundes, and to the woman child of my said sister, Eleanor,
ten poundes. I give unto Katheron Woodrington, wife of Lewes
Woodrington of Cheseborngrange, one, two and twenty shillings
peece of golde. I give unto Thomas Woodrington, sone to the
saide Lewes Woodrington, tene pounds. I give unto Henry Woodrington, sonne of the said Lewes, five poundes. I give to my cozen,
Mr. Robert Woodrington of Chibborne, my best cloake. I give to
the said Christopher Bewick, five poundes. I give unto William
Hall, servante to the said Robert Woodrington, 40s. I give to
Isabell Doods, daughter to Matthew Doods, tailor, 40s. I give
unto the poore, six poundes thirteen shillings and eightpence, to
be distributed at the discretion of my executors. I give unto
Mr. William Alder, preacher of god's word, forty shillings. I
give and bequeathe unto Marie Alder, wife of Richard Alder of
Alnwick, fyve poundes. Whereas it is intended that a gallerie
shallbe builded and erected for the placing of Scollers within the
pish church of All Saints, within the towne of Newcastle, I give
and bequeath towards the erecting and buylding of the said
Gallerie the sume of six poundes thirteen shillings and four pence,
to be paid by my executors when the same shallbe gone about
to bee buylt. And I doe appoint and make executors of this my
last Will and Testament, my well beloved cozens and friends, Sir
Henry Woodrington, Knight, to whom I give my best gould ring
for a token or remembrance, the said Robert Woodrington and
Lewes Woodrington, Gentleman, Isabell Bewick, wife of the said
Christopher Bewicke, and Agnes Potts, wife of the said Mark
Potts, requiring my said executors to paie all my debts, legacies

and bequests, whatsoever shall appeare to stand justly indebted
within one monthe after my decease, except that which I have
appointed and lymitted to be paid at the severall tymes above
mentioned. Witnesses, Matthew Dodes, Nicholas Forster, Anthony
Norman. Proved, 1617.

JOHN BURRELL.[1]

April 24, 1617. Ane Inventorye of the goods and chattells of
John Burrell of Howtell what he died seazed of in the yeare of
the King's reign 1616.

Item, one browne meare, priced to 4*l*. Seven booles of oatts,
priced to 28*s*. Three bushells of Rye, priced to 18*s*. Six old
puther dishes, priced to 2*s*. Two candellsticks, priced to 1*s*.
One old pot, one pan, two washers, priced at 5*s*. 6*d*. One bedsted,
one board, priced at 3*s*. One old fether bed, one paire of sheetes,
two hapens, one bolster, one pillow, priced to 8*s*. 6*d*. Prased by
John Armestronge and Robt. Thompson of Killim, being sworne
men.

JOHN TONSTALL.[2]

June 28, 1617. In the name of God, Amen, and in the
fifteenth yeare of the reigne of or Sovaigne lord king James of
England, France and Ireland, Defender of the faithe, etc., and of
Scotland the fifteth. I, John Tonstall, of the Towne and County of
Newcastle upon Tyne, yeoman, pish clerk of All Hallowes within
the same towne. To be buried in the churchyard of All Hallowes
near unto my former wife and children. And as touching such of
my tenements and goods as it hath pleased the lord to bless and
endow me withall, I do dispose of them as followeth. First I do
give and bequeath unto my well beloved wyfe Barbary Tonstall
for and during her naturall lyfe all that my nowe dwellinghouse
with the rowmes and appurtenances thereof now being in my own
occupation and the garden now in the occupation of Suzan Selby
in full satisfacon and contentment of and for all her title, interest
and clayme of thirdes jointers and dower in and to all and any
my howses, burgages and tenements, she paying yearly during
that tyme five shillings to the lord of the see at the usual termes.

[1] He was probably the John Burrell who mar. Elizabeth, dau. of
Oswald Collingwood of Etal, see the *Visitation of Northumberland* (ed.
Foster, 21) and *New County History of Northumberland*, vol. xi., pp.
199, 200.

[2] His first wife, Anne, was bur. at All Saints, Newcastle, 27 Oct.,
1604; where also his children were bapt. and bur., William, bapt., 24
June, 1603, Mary, bur., 9 Oct., 1604, Barbara, bapt., 7 May, 1609,
Nicholas, bapt., 30 Sept., 1610, Thomas, bapt., 29 June, 1614, Ann, mar.
Edward Robinson, 21 July, 1631. The testator was bur. there, 7 July,
1617. His widow re-mar. William Cape, 4 June, 1620, at All Saints.

And after the decease of my said wife, then I give and bequeath the same tenements now in my occupation and the garden aforesaid, unto my eldest sone, Henry Tonstall, he paying the same outrent and to his heirs for ever. I give and bequeath unto my sonne, John Tonstall, to him and his heires for ever all those upper rowms or lofts opening to the fore strete, called Silver street wherein one Anne Mallabar, widow, now dwelleth together, with that yard or yards joining to the backside of the said howse or rowmes, paying yearly thre shillings to the lord of the see at the said termes. And also I do give unto my saide sonne John, two suites of apparell of the best I have. I give and bequeath unto my sonne William Tonstall and to his heires for ever, all those my two low rowmes situate under the said upper rowmes or lofts which two low rowmes are now in the seuerall tenures or occupacons of my tenants, William Morrison and William Marke. And also all that my garden which is now in the tenure or occupation of Edwin Nicholson of Newcastle, aforesaid, merchant, with fre liberty ingress regresse in and from the same, he paying yearly three shillings to the said lorde. I give and bequeath to my daughter, Anne Tonstall and her heirs for ever all my right, title, interest, clayme, and possession of and in, to, one howse Burgage or tenement in Manwells Chaire, near the Keyside in Newcastle, aforesaid, which by deed or writinge is morgaged to me by John Marshell, Taylor upon condicon for paymt of a certaine sume of money, and I also give unto her and her heires, all somes of money in the same writinge conteyned, if the premises shall be redeemed, which I give to her as a legacy only. I give and bequeath unto my said eldest sonne, Henry Tonstall, and his heires for ever, all that right, title, interest and clayme which I now or oughte to have of, on, or to the now dwellinghouse and two mylnes within pandon yate, now in the occupation of George Reasley, cordiner, together with all profitts and comodities to me dew or to be dewe by reason of a writinge of morgage to be made by the same George, and the same writeinge and all sums of money therein conteyned and the obligacon made for pformance thereof, wherein the said George Reasley and Thomas Reasley, Mylner stand bound to me in a certaine penaltye which I give to him as a legacy only. I give and bequeath to my said sone Henry, his executors and assigns as a legacy only one obligacon wherein Thomas Watson and John Marshall stand bound to me for the payment of twelve poundes at several dayes by paste of which twelve poundes I have only received three poundes. And also I gyve unto him my best cloake. I give to my daughter, Anne Tonstall, for a token, one silver spoone with a guilded Knopp at the end and other two plaine silver spoones more, I gyve unto her three paire of Lynnen sheetes, fyve pillowbeares, five table clothes and two dozen and a halfe of table napkins. I give unto my daughter Barbary, one peece of gold at the value of twenty two shillings, for a token. I give to my sonne

Thomas one peece of golde of the like value of twenty two shillinges, for a token. I gyve unto my sonne Nicholas one peece of gold, of the value of twenty two shillings, for a token. I give to my servante, Margaret Stowte, 2s. 6d. Provided alwayes and my will is that if any of my said sonnes shall go about to sell or putt away any of my said howses to them bequeathed, situate in or near Silver Street, aforesaid, that then his estate herein to be voyd and the same to remayne and come to his next heire at the common lawe. The residue of all my goods, moveable and unmoveable, my detts, if any be dewe, being paide and my funerall expences and childrens porcons discharged, I give unto my said loveing wife and leave them to her disposing, whom I make sole executrix of this my last Will hopeing that she will prove a kind and faithfull mother to all my children. And I intreate my loveing friendes, William Potter, and Thomas Arrowsmith of Gateside, to be supervisors of the same. Witnesses, William Potter, Tho. Arrowsmith, Andrew Ainsley. Proved, 30 August, 1617.

THOMAS GREENWELL.

July 10, 1617. Thomas Greenwell of Thorneley, in the parish of Wolsingham, Yeoman. I will that my body shall be buried, if God permitt me life till I come home, in the church or churchyard of Woolsingham, where I have bene this long time a parishioner, referringe the charge of my funerall to the discretion of my executors hereafter named, and concerninge the disposing of all and singular my goodes and chattels and other things whatsoever which God hath given me, I wholly give and bequeathe in manner and forme followinge :—First, I give and bequeathe to the poor people inhabitants in the parish of Wolsingham, 10s. I give to my sonne, Rowland Greenwell, the sum of 8l. To my sone, Thomas Greenwell, 5l. To my sonne, Michail Greenwell, 5l. To my sonne, William Greenwell, 5l. To my sonne, John Greenwell, 8l. To my sonne, Samuel Greenwell, 6l. To my daughter, Ann Hodgson, now the wife of John Hodgson, 3l. To Elizabeth Younge, the Daughter of my daughter, Margaret Younge, the late wife of Henry Younge, Cittzen of London, 3l. The rest of my goods and chatels, my debts beinge paid, I give to my sonne, William Greenwell, whom I make full and sole Executor, and I nominate and appoint my loveinge friendes, William Rawe and Cuthbert Hartley, Overseers of the same. Witnesses, Hen. Medhope, William Yorke, Tho. Kirklawe.

INVENTORY, 90l. 18s. 0d., consisting of purse, wearing apparell, stock, crop and household utensils. Debts oweing by the testator : To his sonne, Rowland Grinwell, 6l. 9s. 0d. To his sonne, Samuele Grinwell, 4l. 9s. 4d. To his sonne, William Grinwell, 9l. 8s. 0d. To his sonns, Jo. and Samuel, 1l. 15s. 0d. To his sonne, John, 1l. Funeral expences, 3l. 18s. 0d. His mortuarie,

10s. We are informed at the making of the Inventorie by John Greenwell, son of the deceased, that his uncle, Mr. William Greenwell of London, doth chalenge a debt of 31*l*., and is due to himselfe by his brother, deceased, which we referr to your worshipfull, Clement Colmore, Vicar General for consideration. And likewise a debt challenged by Michael Greenwell, son of the said deceased, due by himslfe as he saithe the sum of 5*l*. As also another debt challenged by William Greenwell of Greenwell Hill, for the sum of 12*s*. 6*d*. And likewise a debt challenged by John Hodgson, son-in-law of the said deceased, due to himselfe as he saith the sume of 8*l*. 6*s*. 8*d*. All which we refer to your Worshipfull's consideration. Probate, 29th November, 1617.

GEORGE SHAWDFORTH.[1]

July 31, 1617. In the name of Gode, Amen, I, George Shawdforth of Tonstall, within the parish of Bushopp Weremouth, in the County of Durham, Yeoman. To be buried in the parish church att Dalton. My will is that my well beloved wife shall labour by all means possible to pcure the wardshipp of my eldest sonne. I give to my second sone, Anthonie Shawdforth, my lease and all intereste of Tunstall for all the yeares therein unknown and yett to come, in full contentacon of his filiall porcon, and all other bequests whatsoever thereof maid by my well beloved Uncle, John Shawdforth, to the said Anthonie, I give all the rents and profits whatsoever arising out of my moiety of Warden Lawe unto my onely daughter . . . . Shawdforth, for the tearme of ten yeares, for the raising upp of five hundred pounds which I give her in full satisfacon of hir filiall porcon. I give to every of my sister Isabell, hir children, 40*s*. apeece. I give to every of the children of John Shawdfourth of Warden, 20*s*. apeece. I give to Mary Bell, twenty markes. All the rest of my goods and debts due to me, I doe give to my well beloved wife, Isabella Shawdforth, for the true payment of all such debts as I am oweing to any person, and for the payment of my legacies in this my Will conteyned. And I doe make my said wife sole Executor of this my last Will and Testament. And I make George Collingwood of Eppledon, Esq., and John King of the Citty of Durham, Supervisors, of this my Will, and I give to either of them 20*s*. for a token. Witnesses, Geo. Collingwood, John King.

INVENTORY, 543*l*. 3*s*. 4*d*. Proved, 1617.

[1] He was the son of Anthony Shadforth. His son, Thomas, aged 12, in 1617, bur. at St. Margaret's, Durham, 23 Mch., 1671/2, mar. Elizabeth, dau. of Marmaduke Blakiston, rector of Sedgefield, 28 Nov., 1631, at St. Margaret's, Durham, she was bur. there, 24 Sept., 1695 (according to the registers of St. Nich., Durham); Anthony bur., 14 Aug., 1650, at Dalton-le-dale (according to the registers of Bishopwearmouth), mar. Mary (dau. of Edward Lee of Monkwearmouth), 26 Nov., 1633, at St. Giles', Durham, bur., 14 June, 1683, at Dalton-le-dale.

NICHOLAS HOPPER.[1]

Aug. 25, 1617. In the name of Gode, Amen. I, Nicholas Hopper of Black Hedley in the Countye of Northumberland in the parish of Shotley, Yeoman. To be buryed in the Chappell of Shotley, at the discretion of my friends, I give and leave my houses and tenements with the appurtenances thereof belonginge unto my eldest sonne, Cuthbert Hopper, and my wife, his mother during her life naturall, equallie to be devided betwixt them, and my said sonne to enter to the moietie or one halfe at the day of the invention of the Cross commonlie St. Helene daye next cominge immediately, and after the decease of my wife to come fullye unto my abovesaid sonne. I give and bequeath unto my aforesaid sonne, all my plough geare with long wayne, short wayne yoakes, bowes, and somes with all my other implements belonging to husbandrie, I leave him one nagg or else 3*l*. 6*s*. 8*d*. to buy him one. I leave unto him the halfe crop now growing upon the ground which is to be sowen this next yeare to come. I give my daughter, Jane Hopper, foure oxen, two stots, sixe kyne and two quyes. I give her three score old shepe and twentye lambes, and I give her 10*l*. of money. I leave all my inseight goods to my wife, to be att her disposing. I give and bequeath unto my sonne, Thomas Hopper, twenty shepe. I give unto Isabell Hopper, my sonne Cuthbert his daughter, foure ewes and lambs, and also one quye. I give unto my daughter Agnes her three children, three ewes and three lambs. I give unto my Brother his son Christopher Hopper, one quye. I give and bequeath the twenty shillings which William Snowball is oweing me unto my Brother his three children, James Hopper, John Hopper, and Isabell Hopper. All my goods, moveable and unmoveable remayning, my funeral dewes and expences being discharged, I leave unto my wife, my sone Nicholas, my sonne Humphrey, my sone Johne, and my sone Thomas. And lastly, I make my wife and my four sonns executors, to duly execute this my last Will and Testament. Witnesses, Robt. Redshaw, William Lawes. Proved, 22 November, 1617.

WILLIAM WATSON.[2]

Aug. 26, 1617. In the name of God, Amen, I William Watson of Whitworth, in the Countye of Durham, Gent. To be buried within the parish Church of Whitworth. I give and bequeath unto

[1] There is a pedigree of this family in the *New County History of Northumberland*, vol. vi., pp. 296-7.

[2] He mar., firstly, Mary, dau. of Henry Brabant, in the parish of Brancepeth; by her he had a dau. Margaret, bapt. at Whitworth, 2 Apl., 1586, mar., 8 Feb., 1607/8, William, son of Cuthbert Baxter of Corbridge, she was bur. at Whitworth, 25 May, 1625, her husband was bur. there, 8 Mch., 1652/3. Their dau., Catherine Baxter, mar., 10 Nov., 1631, Cuthbert Hutchinson. The testator mar., secondly, Mary Salkeld.

my loveing wife, Mary Watson, all my household stuff which she
brought with her to me at our marriage and now remains in my
house at Whitworth. I give moreover to my said wife, Mary, one
stand bedstead in the hall and one short table in the hall, with
all the puffett stooles which she either bought or brought to me
since our marriage, provided alwaies that she doe not claime her
wedowes bedd according to the custom of the country here. I give
to my daughter, Margaret Baxter, her first choice of my three
cubbords, and to my wife Mary, the second choice of another, and
the third cubbord I also give to my said daughter Margarett, which
said two cubbords bequeathed to my daughter Margaret, my will
and meaninge is that after her decease the same shall
remayne, and be to my grandchild, Katherine Baxter. And
the rest of all my household stuff not hereby given or bequeathed.
I give to my said daughter, Margaret Baxter, and to Katherine
Baxter, my grandchild, and to the longer liver of them. I give to
my said wife Mary one kowe and two little old hay rucks in the
Broad Medows. I give and bequeath to my Brother, John Watson,
the sume of 5l. I give and bequeath to John Stowt, my sisters
sonn, 40s. I give and bequeath unto my cozen Margaret
Pemberton, one ringe of 10s. price. I give and bequeathe to my
cosen, Mr. John Pemmerton his wife, another gold ringe of the
same price. I give and bequeath to my Aunt Watson another
gold ring of the same price. I give to my coozen, Wm. Watson of
Staindropp, another gold ring of the same price. I give to
Edward Bigland of Awckland, one twenty shilling piece of gold.
I do remit and forgive to my brother, Charles Watsone, the fouer
pounds he oweth me; and I doe likewise remit and forgive to my
coosen, Thomas Watson, the three pounds he oweth me. I give and
bequeath to my Brother Charles, his three sonns, viz. :—Ralph,
Charles and Anthony Watson, to each of them, 20s., and to my
cosen, Thomas Watson his sonne William, other 20s. I give and
bequeath unto my grandchilde, Katherine Baxter, one stone pott
garnished with silver and guilt and the cover also, my will and
mind is that the lease which I have from Pawl Baning, John Watt,
and Thomas Allabaster of London, of my land in Whitworth shall
be delivered to my coozen, Mr. Michaell Pemmerton of Ayton, to
be kept for the use and behoofe of Mary Watson, my wife, for performance of an annutie of 15l. per annum made to her for her
jointure, and for the use and behoofe of Margaret Baxter, my
dawghter, and Katherine Baxter, my grandchilde. I give and
bequeath unto my sone in law, Mr. William Baxter, the sum of
10l., upon condicon he doe find securtie to the spirituall Chancellor of the Diocise of Durhame to pay yearly for ever the sume of
Twentie shillings of lawfull English money to the poore people
within the towne of Whitworth, viz., the sume of 10s., at Xmas,
and 10s. at Easter. I make my sone in lawe, Mr. William Baxter.

and my godsone, Michaell Richardson, executors of this my last
Will and Testament. Witnesses, George Brabant, Mich. Richardson, Lancelot Iley.

INVENTORY, 149*l*. 6*s*. 4*d*. Proved, 1617.

WILLIAM ANDERSON.[1]

Sept. 27, 1617. In the name of God, Amen, I, William Anderson, of the towne of Newcastle upon Tyne, Milner. To be buried
in the parish church of All Hallowes in Newcastle, aforesaid. I
give to my wife, Isabella Anderson, for a legacy, twenty six
powndes of lawful money of England. I give to Elizabeth Anderson, my eldest daughter, thirtie pounds of lawful money of
England, which money after my decease I will be paid to William
Cooke, Master Mariner, to keep for the use of my said daughter
until it please god that she marie or come to lawful yeares, he
laying in sufficient bond to the ordinary for the repayment of the
same accordingly. I give to my youngest daughter, Barbara
Anderson, thirtye pounds of like lawful money of England, which
money after my decease I will to be paid to Anthony Morpeth of
the said towne, Merchante, to be kept for the use and behoof of
my said daughter, untill such tyme as she marrie or come to lawful
yeares he laying in sufficient bond to the ordinary for the repayment of the same accordingly. I give to my eldest daughter Elizabeth, one silver salt with cover and a ringe of golde of fower
Angells. And I also give to my youngest daughter Barbary, a
dozen of silver spoones with a ringe of gold of the aforesaid value,
the elder daughter haveing her choice of them; and if it shall
happen that either of my said daughters shall dye before she be
married that then the porcon of her who dyeth shall come to the
other sister liveinge. And if it shall please god that both dye before
they be maried then the said porcons to come to my wife, Isabella
Anderson their naturall mother, which said money, plate and
rings givin to my said daughters I gave as legacies. I give to
my wife, Isabella Anderson, my title and right of the lease of my
house wherein I now dwell during her widowhood, and if she shall
marie, then to have the parte thereof which the law will allow her.
I give unto my two daughters, Elizabeth and Barbary, and to their
heires, all my estate, right title, and interest which I have of in
and to one Horse Mill with the appurtenances situate in the
towne of Newcastle aforesaid in a street called the Broade Chaire
now in my own occupation. I give and bequeath unto my said
two daughters, Elizabeth and Barbary, one lease of a house in
Pandon wherein Jane Hall, wydowe, nowe dwelleth with the profitts

[1] The testator was bur. at All Saints, Newcastle, 5 Oct, 1617, his
widow may have been bur. either 21 Jan., 1619/20, or 30 Nov., 1625; his
dau. Elizabeth was bapt. there, 7 Jan., 1600/1, and his dau. Barbara,
also bapt. there, 9 Apl., 1604. (1624, Sept. 12, Christopher Rowell and
Isabel Anderson mar. at All Saints; this may be the second marriage of
his widow.)

thereof which I have for certain yeares yett to come, with all my household stuff and all other moveable goods to me, belonging, my wives part which the lawe alloweth being deducted. I give and bequeath to my kinsman, David Birtley, for a legacy forty shillings. I give and bequeath unto my friend William Matthew ten shillings for a token. And I doe make my two daughters, Elizabeth and Barbary, Executors of this my last Will and Testament. And also I doe nominate and appoint the aforesaid Anthony Morpeth and William Cooke, Supervisors or overseers of this my last Will and Testament and to either of them I give one Angell for a token. Witnesses, Anthony Morpeth, William Cooke, William Matthew, John Shotton, James Scoles. Proved, 1617.

GEORGE ALDER.[1]

Nov. 18, 1617. A true Inventory of the goods and chattles of the late deceased, George Alder of Hobberlaw, in the parish of Alnewick.

Imprimis: one table in the halle, 6s. 8d. One Cubbard, 13s. 4d. Three bedsteds, 15s. Thirteen Ewes and Lambes, 9l. Two wether sheepe, 1l. Eight hogg shepe, 2l.

Nov. 18, 1617. Administration granted to Francis Alder, the son, on behalf of self and other children, not mentioned by name.

WILLM. ANDERSON.[2]

Dec. 12, 1617. In the name of God, Amen, I, Willm. Anderson of Barwick on the hill, in the parish of Pont Iland. To be buried in the parish church of Pont Iland aforesaid, and of my worldly goods I thus dispose: First, I give to my nephew, Ambrose Anderson, a yoke of oxen, and . . . quyes now in the possession of him the said Ambrose, also I give to him, the said Ambrose, my stoned nagg and three poundes in money, which the said Ambrose oweth me. I forgoe to my nephew, Thomas Anderson, all debts and reckenings heretofore due unto me except the sume of five pounds of which [my will is] that he shall pay as he shall be able to my executors four pounds, and twenty shillings he shall give to his two brothers' daughters equally to be divided betwixt them. I give to John Wight, servant to Mr. George Collingwood, a quye stirke of a year old. I give more to my above nephew, Ambrose Anderson, eleven hogg sheepe, now depastureing with Thomas Anderson in the east quarter. I give to the poorer sort of householders in the parish, 20s., willyng my executors notwithstanding to give the accustomed doale at the tyme of my burial. I give to my wife, Jennet Anderson, all that my house and tenement, with

[1] He was the son of George Alder of Hobberlaw, by his wife, Jane, dau. of Sir William Lisle of Felton; he mar. Margaret, dau. of Nicholas Forster of Newham; his son Francis also of Hobberlaw (estate administered, 16 July, 1638), mar. Agnes or Anne Shell.

[2] At Ponteland the testator was bur., 19 Dec., 1617, and his nephew, Ambrose, 15 May, 1624.

the appurtences . . . the terme . . . set and being in the towne
and territories of Morpeth, in the Countie of Northumberland, for
term of her life, and after her decease my will is that the said house
and the appurtenances descend and come to the issue male, of
Ralph Fife, begotten and to be begotten of the body of my
daughter, Jennet, now wife to the said Ralph, and for default of
such issue male, I give and bequeath my said house and tenement
with the appurtenances to my above named nephew, Ambrose
Anderson, and his heires for ever. I give to my sone-in-law,
Raph Fife, my bay colt, and my daughter, Jennet, his wife, two
kyne, the one a brockt, now about my house, and the other a
branded, now in the possession of William Fawcus of Morpeth.
I give to wife, Jennet Anderson, twenty ewes, I give more to my
said wife all the household stuffe that myne is within my house.
I give to my said sonne in law, Rafe Fife, and my said nephew,
Ambrose Anderson, all the timber and other wood which I have at
Brenkbourne, Morpeth, or else where equally to be divided betwixt
them. Also the rest of my goods, moveable and immoveable, I
give and bequeath to my said wife, Jennet Anderson, and Robert
Fife, my grandchild, whom also I make joint executors of this
my last Will, and I appoint Mr. Gilbert Errington and Edward
Wiggham, Clerk, Supervisors of this my last Will, humbly
beseeching them to take care that neither my said wife, in regard
of her simplicitie, nor the said childe, in respect of his infancy,
be wronged in ₎the execution of my said Will or any thing
belonging thereunto. Witnesses, Gilbart Errington, Nicholas Hall
Edw. Wiggam, Robert Jenenson. Proved, 17 August, 1618.

JOHN OVINGTON.

Jan. 16, 1617. In the name of God, Amen, I, John Ovington
of Whorlton, in the County of Durham and pish of Gainford.
To be buried in the Churchyard of Barnard Castle. I give and
bequeath unto my sonne, John Ovington, all my lands of Stub-
house and my whole farme in Whorlton with six oxen, and all
my waine geare with plow and plow geares, and also of half of
Arleny bancks I give unto my sonne, Thomas Ovington, one halfe
tenement which I bought, and one cottage with the other half of
Arleny bancks, and more one Carte. I give unto my sone, Robert
Ovington, fower score pounds. I give unto every of my daughters,
Alice Ovington, Isabell Ovington, Anne Ovington, and Sythe
Ovington, three score pounds apeece. I give unto my brother,
Christopher Ovington, one gray horse. I give unto my brother
Christopher's two daughters, either of them, two gemer hoggs. I
give unto my brother, George Ovington, one black hanked whye.
And all that he oweth me I doe clearlie forgive him. I give unto
my brother, Robert Ovingham, sone Richard Ovington, ten shill-
ings. I give unto my Brother Richard Ovington sonne John
Ovington one gemer hoge, unto his sister Elizabeth, ten shillings.

I give unto my sister Jane, sone John Robinson, three pounds, to be paid unto Ralphe Johnson and Christopher Johnson for the use and benefit of the said John Robinson. I give unto my brother George two children, to either of them, a gemer lamb. I give unto John Applebeyes sone Robert one gemer lamb. I give unto Ralph Johnson daughter, Elsie Johnson, one gemer hogge. I give unto my godsone, Robert Dinsdell, one gemer hogge. I give unto my goddaughter Saulby one gemer hogg. I give the power of Barnard Castle, ten shillings. I give to the power of Whorlton, five shillings. I give to the power of Winston, five shillings. I give unto my cosin Heugh Collinge daughter Jane, one red whye. I doe make my wife and my eldest son John my joynt executors of this my last Will and Testament, and furthers doe appoint and ordeyne my good frends, Ralphe Johnson and Heugh Collinge, and Christopher Ovington and Christopher Heighley, to be supervisors of this my last Will and Testament which I intreat for god's cause to see this pformed according to my trew meaning therein. Witnesses, Robert Allanson, Jo. Saulbye, Raphe Johnson, Hugh Colling, Chris. Ovington.

INVENTORY, 406l. 3s. 0d.

Debts oweing to John Ovington. John Cowlton, 50l., more by him, 7l. 10s., Cuthbert Laten, 5l., George Tailor of Stainton, 6l., Thomas Smailes, 3l.; Christopher Ovington of Winston, 25s. To Mr. Fran. Brackenbury, 3l., Bartholew Taylor, 20s., John Eles, 11s. To Henry Gigleswick, 17s. Robert Allanson of Barnard Castle, 5l., John Smart, 5l. Sir Talbott Bowes, 10l. Mr. Thomas Bowes, 10l. John Soulsby, younger, 2s. 6d. Mr. William Claxton, 10l. Christopher Ovington of Whorlton, 40s. Edward Kyplin of Barnard Castle, 4l. Isabell Appleby of Barnard Castle, 20s. Thomas Blacklock of Barnard Castle, 40s. John Cockfield, younger, 8s. 7d. George Coward of Stranton. 46s. 8d. John Soulby, elder, 5s. Symond Robinson of Barnard Castle, 17s. 6d. Cuthbert Peat of Barnard Castle, 15s. John Appleby of Whorlton, 12l. Richard Heatleye, 9l. 4s. 9d. To Hugh Collin, 10l. John Greevson. 20s. Widow Taylor, 40l., more by her, 10s., more by her, 2s. 6d., more by her, 3s. 4d., more by her, 12s. William Peacock of Barnard Castle, 4s. 4d., Robert Cussoas of Newbiggin, 169l. 6s. more to him, 9l., Christopher Dinsdaile. 15s. Proved, 13 February, 1617.

FRANCIS LIDDALL.[1]

Feb. 7, 1617. In the name of God, Amen, I, Francis Liddall, of the Towne of Newcastle-upon-Tyne, Merchant. To be decently

[1] Bur. 16 Feb., 1617/18 (a). Of his children, Bartram was bapt., 8 Nov., 1592 (b), George, bapt., 8 Sept., 1597 (a), Ephraim, bur., 4 Mch., 1603/4 (a), William, bur., 18 Jan., 1623/4 (b), Jane, mar. Charles Horsley, 5 Dec., 1614 (a), Alice, bapt., 23 Oct., 1575 (a), and mar. Roger Errington, 28 Sept., 1596 (a), Margaret, bapt., 16 Mch., 1591/2 (a), Agnes, bur., 30 Oct., 1597 (b). (a) St. Nich., Newcastle. (b) St. John's, Newcastle

buried at the discretion of my executors, and as touching and
concerning my goods and chattells as well real as psonall, my will
and meaning is that out of them theise legacies hereafter mentioned and expressed shallbe paid, viz. :—To Anne Liddall, my
wyffe, for a token, tenn twentie shillinges peaces. To my daughter,
Rarbara Darlinge, one hundred pound in money, to be paid unto
hir in foure yeares after my death by twenty five pounds a yeare.
To my daughter, Jane Horsley, Ten Tennes of my best coles at
Dunstan, to be delivered uppon fetchinge before Lamas next. To
three children of my daughter Errington, deceased, whereof there
be two daughters and one sonne, forty pounds in money a peece, to
be paid to the two daughters within one yeare after either of them
shallbe maried, and to the sonne when he shall attaine to the age
of one and twenty yeares. And I further bequeath to the eldest
daughter twenty markes more in money to be paid her one the
daie of her mariage to buye her apparell. To William Liddall
and Thomas Liddall, Infantes, being now in the custodie and tuition of me, the said Francis Liddall, the sume of three score
pounds, viz. :—Forty pounds thereof to William, and twenty
pounds to Thomas, when they shall severallie attaine their severall
ages of one and twenty yeares. To my nevew William Sherwood,
five twenty shilling peaces for a token, to Mr. Jeromie, preacher,
a twentie shilling peece, to Mr. Shaw, preacher, one twenty shillinge peece. To my three maides, tenn shillings a peese, to my
sone Bartrame servante, tenn shillings. The residue of all my
goods and chattells as well real and psonal, my detts, and legacies
being paide and funeralles discharged, I will and bequeath
unto my two sonns, Bartram Liddall and George Liddall, to be
equally devyded, whom I make executors of this my last Will and
Testament in the presence of Robert Anderson, Robert Rookesbye,
Charles Horsley, and Theodore Wright.

INVENTORY of the testators estate, 366*l.* 5*s.* 8*d.* Debts oweing
by the testator, 221*l.* 5*s.* 2*d.* Proved, 20 January, 1618.

GEORGE HUTTON.[1]

June 3, 1618. I, George Hutton, of Sunderland, in the County
of Durham, gentleman. My body to be buried in the earth from
whence it came. I give unto my neece, Margaret Forster, 4*l.*, to
be paied her yeerely at the feast of Martymas and Whitsontide by
equall porcons out of all my landes and tenements in Darlington

[1] Richard Hutton of Hunwick had at least two sons. The younger,
Ralph Hutton of Walworth, who made his will, 8 Dec., 1558 (*Surt. Soc.*
112, p. 16), was father of three daughters, one of whom, Mary, dead
by April, 1622, mar. Thomas Biggins, 26 Nov., 1566 (*a*), and of two
sons, viz., George Hutton, the testator, who was bur. at St. Mary-le-
Bow, Durham, 10 Feb., 1620/1 (*inq. p.m.*, at Durham, 27 April, 1622),
and Robert Hutton, a minor at the date of his father's will, aged 60
(*sic*), in April, 1622. See Surtees' Durham III. 333, for the issue of

not yett passed away for and dureing her life naturall. I doe give
and grant unto my nephew, Christopher Biggins of Sunderland,
yeoman, and unto his heires for ever, all my landes, groundes,
tenements, burgages, rents and reversions whatsoever yet unsold,
and not already passed away, situate lyeing and being within the
same feildes and territories of Darneton and Bondgate in Darneton and within the towne of Cockerton or the territoryes thereof
together with all writeings and evidences whatsoever concerneing
the same : To have and to hold unto my said nephew, Christopher
Biggins, and his heires and assigns for evermore and my will
and pleasure is that my said nephew, Christopher Biggins, and

this Robert, who mar., at Witton Gilbert, 16 Oct., 1597, Anne, bapt.
at Haughton-le-Skerne, 14 Nov., 1572, dau. of Francis Parkinson.
 William Hutton of Hunwick, elder son of Richard, mar. Anne,
dau. of Robert Simpson of Henknoll (by Margaret, widow of Thomas
Bellasis, dau. of Sir Lancelot Thirkeld). They had issue, John Hutton
(A), Anthony Hutton (B), Robert Hutton, Henry Hutton, Elizabeth,
who mar., 16 Jan., 1558/9 (a), William Thorp of the Hill, Jane, who
mar., 30 July, 1559 (a), Brian Tunstall of Stockton. (She renounced
administration of her husband's effects, 22 June, 1594.)
 John Hutton (A) of Hunwick (for his will see Surt. Soc. 2, 234),
was bur., 29 Nov., 1566 (a). By his wife, Elizabeth, bur., 15 Oct., 1567
(a) dau. of Ralph Dalton of West Auckland (for her will see Surt. Soc.
138, 23n.), he had issue six daughters, coheirs of their mother's half-
brother, Robert Dalton, viz. (1) Margaret, mar., 27 Nov., 1564 (a),
Christopher Athey of Aldernedge; (2) Jane, wife of Robert Eden of
West Auckland (his will dated 20 June, 1584, Surt. Soc. 38, 105); (3)
Margery, wife of Matthew Craythorne of West Auckland (she was
probably buried at Witton-le-Wear, 8 Nov., 1634, as Margery
Crathorne, " exco." an old gent.); (4) Elizabeth, wife of George Tocketts
of Tocketts; (5) Constance, mar. at St. Mary-le-Bow, 23 Nov., 1574,
John Thomson of Newcastle; (6) Anne, mar. at St. Oswald's, Durham,
14 Nov., 1585, John Craggs.
 Anthony Hutton (B) of Hunwick, bur., 23 March, 1602/3 (a),
by Agnes, bur., 5 Feb., 1660/1 (a), dau. of Christopher Carr of Sherburn
House, had issue,—Christopher Hutton (C), William Hutton (of the
Garth, 1615, and by Dorothy, dau. of Anthony Felton, father of John,
aged 12, 1615, and of Ralph and Henry); John Hutton, bur., 22 May,
1576 (a), Richard Hutton, bapt., 12 Feb., 1580/1 (a), bur., 12 Sept.,
1596 (a); Margaret; Adeline, bapt., 3 Apr., 1575 (a), mar. at Witton-
le-Wear, 26 Nov., 1593, Nicholas Heron; Elizabeth, bapt., 7 May
1578 (a).
 Christopher Hutton (C), aged 12 in 1575, was bur., 28 March,
1601 (a). He mar. Anne, bapt., 21 Dec., 1573 (b), dau. of Henry
Brackenbury of Sellaby (she remar., 26 May, 1606 (a), Henry Birkbeck,
who was bur., 23 Feb., 1637/8 (b)). They had issue—1. Richard
Hutton, bapt., 25 Feb., 1592/3 (a), devisee, 6 Nov., 1601, of his grandfather, Henry Brackenbury (Surt. Soc. 112, p. 180), of Hunwick in
1615, mar. Jemima, dau. of Humphrey Wharton of Gilling, co. York.,
and, by her, father of Humphrey, bapt., 13 May, 1621 (a), Elizabeth,
bapt. 21 March, 1629/30 (a), and Thomas, bapt., 5 May 1633 (a);
2. Timothy Hutton, bapt. 26 Jan., 1594/5 (a), devisee of Henry
Brackenbury, 1601; 3. Francis Hutton, devisee 1601, apprenticed to
Alexander Davison, 19 May, 1616, enrolled, 10 Oct., 1618, Dendy's
Merchant adventurers.
 (a) St. Andrew's, Auckland. (b) Gainford.

his heires for ever shall stand and remaine seised of the said premises and the revercon and revercons the remainder, and remaynders thereof to him and his heires for ever, for the pformance and discharge of this my last Will and testament in manner and forme followinge; first whereas I have already granted unto my sister, Mary Biggins her two sonns, vizt. :—the said Christopher Biggins and Henry Biggins, and to there heires for ever, all my lands in Sunderland, and likewise unto Henry and John Biggins, the other of my said sisters sonnes, and to their heires for ever the moyetye of all my lands and tenements in Darneton, and whereas my brother, Robert Hutton, seemeth discontent with the said grannts and threatneth suites whereby it is likely suites in lawe may hereafter arise concerning the same, and that my bondes for performance of the said grannts may be endangered to the great greife and trouble amongst friendes, for avoiding whereof my will and meaninge is that if my brother, Robert Hutton, and his heires, shall upon reasonable request to him or them to be made after my death confirme and ratifye the said severall grannts to my said nephews respectively. soe that the said partyes may peaceably inioy all the said premises without any suite or trouble of any pson by his or there meanes assent or pcourements accordinge unto my true intent and meaneing, and according to the purport of the grantes which I have formerly made, and that peace may continue amongst them, that then my said nephew, Christopher Biggins, and his heires, shall convey and assure the moyetye of all my saide landes and tenements in Darnton which is not yet disposed of, the remainder and remainders reversion or reversions thereof unto my brother, Robert Hutton, and his heirs for ever, and if he or they shall refuse soe to doe, then my will and meaning is, and I do hereby give grannt and appoint that my said nephew, Christopher Biggins and his heirs shall absolutely hold, possess, and enioye the said landes and tenements to the only use and behoofe of the said Christopher, and his heires and assignes for ever. I give unto my brother, Robert Hutton, and his heirs for ever, all my landes in Woodh[am] upon like conditions, that he and his heires shall confirme all the said grants formerly made and . . . . otherwise my Will and meaneing is that the said premises shall be . . . . I give and devise the same to the said Christopher Biggins, and his heires for ever. All the rest of my goodes and chattels, moveable and unmoveable, not bequeathed, I doe give and bequethe to my said neece, Margaret Foster, my debts and funerall expences being discharged, whom I make full executrix of this my last Will : In witness whereof, I hereunto have putt my hand and seale the day and yeare first above written, in the presence of Jerrard Thompson, Clement Thompson, Rowland Scurfeild, Thomas Arrowsmith. Proved, 1620.

JOHN HEARON.[1]

June 11, 1618. In the name of Gode, Amen, I, John Hearon
of Chipchase, in the Countie of Northumberland, Gent. I give
and bequeath all my land in Kirkheaton to my sonne Cuthbert
Hearon excepting one house called the Blackhall that Randall Todd
dwells in with the barne and the byer belonginge to it which I give
unto my wife, Ellsabeth Hearon. I give all my lands in Heather-
ington to my sonne, Thomas Hearon. I give to my sonne, John
Hearon, one tenement in Barrisford to enter unto it immediately
after the death of Thomas Dodds of Barrisford. I give to my
sonne, Raphe Hearon, all my third part of the Parkend late
in the accupation of one Cuthbert Stang, which he hath an estate
of to my use from Alexander Davison of Newcastle. I give unto
my said sone, Ralph Hearon, one close joining the Parkend and
did belonge to the Parkside March . . . . with the street on the
southside and enterance on the northside. Whereas, John Robson
of the Wardlow hath passed to me an estate of his part of the
Wardlaw being of the yearlie rent of two shillinges for the which
I gave him twenty poundes, and meat, drink, and cloths for
other ten pounds, therefore my will is that the said ground shall
be soled for a sume of money and whatsoever is gotten more for it,
then the twentye poundes that shall be given to my executors. I
give all my goods, moveable and unmoveable, to my sonne, Gray
Hearon, and my daughter, Dorithea Hearon, and my wife to
have her third part out of the same, according as the lawe in that
case hath provided Lastlie I make and ordaine my said sonne,
George Hearon, and my daughter, Dorithiea Hearon, sole executors of this my last Will and testament. I leave my sonne Cuthbert to my brother Cuthbert Hearon. I leave my daughter
Dorithea to my sister in Chipchase, the rest of my children I
leave to my wife. I appoint my Brother Cuthbert Hearon, John
Hearon of Birtley hall, Tristam Fenwick of Kenton, and Henry
Thornton of Gollowhill, to see that my children gett their rights
and susteine noe wronge. Whereas one John Clearke hath made
me an estate of all his goods, I giving him meat, drink, and
clothes during his life naturall, which said estate I give and bequeath to my wife, Ellsabeth Hearon. Witnesses, Cuthbert
Hearon, Henry Liddell, Mark Greenwell, Cleark.

Debts oweing by the testator. To Sir John Fenwick, 20*l*. To
Jane Gray, 11*l*. To Annas Hearon, 11*l*. To Robert Wilson,
4*l*. 13*s*. 9*d*. To Mr. Cuthbert Hearon, 3*l*. To Mr. John Vaux, 5*l*.
Will Proved, 19 January, 1618.

[1] There is a pedigree of the Herons of Chipchase in the *New County
History of Northumberland*, iv., 340-2.

CHRISTOPHER WHARTON.[1]

Aug. 12, 1618. I, Christopher Wharton of Offerton, in the County of Durham, gent. To be buried in the Church or Churchyard of Houghton in the Spring at the descretion of my executors. I give to the poore of the pish of Houghton aforesaid, 10*l.*, to be paid out of that sum of money which Mr. Alexander Davison or his assigns ought to pay to me or myne assigns at Candlemas day next after the date hereof, the said 10*l.* to be putt forth to the use of the poore according to the custom of the pish. I give to Cuthbert Hall an annutie of 5*l.* to be paid yearly at Martinmas and Whitsunday, out of the land in Offerton which I purchased of Richard Redhead. I give to my best beloved wife, Alice Wharton, 40*l.* sterling a year to be paid her at two payments, viz., Martinmas and Whittsunday out of that estate and monies which I do leave unto her. I also give more to my said wife the remainder of my lease and terme of yeares in the land of Offerton, according to the meaning of an Indenture by me formerly made, to hold the same after my decease during her naturall life, and then the remainder thereof to my daughter, Elizabeth Middleton, and after her decease to her sonne, Francis Middleton, if the said lease so long shall last. I give to my daughter, Elizabeth Middleton, all my freehold in Offerton to hold the same after my decease (except the other lease of land lately purchased of Matthew Amcotts deceased), untill Robert Mittford, sonne of Cuthbert Mittford, deceased, be twentie and two yeares olde, and then the said land (except before excepted) to be equally shared and holden indifferently by the said Robt. Mittford and his heires (if the said Robert Mittford shall solong live), and the said Elizabeth Middleton and for lawful heirs for ever. I give more to the said Elizabeth Middleton, my daughter, all the remainder of my lease and terms of yeares in the land att Silksworth to the use of her, and her lawful heirs, after the decease of Margarett Middleton, who now possesseth a moitie of the same. I appoint my said

---

[1] He was the son of George Wharton by his wife, Mary, dau. of Ewen Gilpin, a sister of Bernard Gilpin, " the apostle of the north," to whom he acted as executor. He mar. Alice, dau. of William Shepperdson of Bishopwearmouth, and widow of Percival Gunson of Cockermouth (to whom she was mar., 27 Aug., 1576, at Bishopwearmouth), she was bur. at Houghton-le-Spring, 15 Jan., 1618/19, he was bur. there, 22 Aug., 1618; his dau. Elizabeth, bapt., 31 Aug., 1581, also there, bur., 16 Aug., 1627, as a widow, mar. George Middleton of Silksworth, their son Francis, mar. Joan, dau. of Edward Rowe of South Shields, at St. Giles, Durham, 10 July, 1634; his dau. Mary, mar. Cuthbert Mitford of Mitford (see the wills of Cuthbert and Robert Mitford printed in vol. 38, pp. 242-3, of these publications); George, his only son, died an infant, 1609. His dau. Elizabeth's will is printed in this vol. An *Inq V. off* was taken at Durham, 23 Oct., 1613, and an *Inv. p.m.* was also taken there, 2 Oct., 1619, in the latter it is stated that his dau. *Alice*, aged 38, was widow of George Middleton, this is probably an error for *Elizabeth*.

daughter, Elizabeth Middleton, my sole Executor, to whom I give and bequeath all the rest of my goods and chattels. Witnesses, Anth. Airey, Christopher Hall, James Hall. Proved, 1618.

THOMAS GRAY.[1]

Dec. 10, 1618. Thomas Gray, of the chappelrye of Ulgham in the parishe of Morpeth My body to be buried within the Chappell of Ulgham, aforesaid. I give to my Sonne, Thomas Gray, a black Nagge, together with the waynes plowes, and other furniture their unto belonginge. To my sone, Edward Gray, a foole. To my wife, Magdalin Gray, a black meare, and to be head ruler of my house and tenement during her widowhood. To my brother, Edward Gray, a Quy stirke. To my sisters children, one ewe and a lamb. To Elizabeth Tod, one cowe. Also I give the rest and residue of my goods to my said wyfe and three children, and make them executors. I ordaine George Lawson of Ulgham overseer of this my Will. Witnesses to will, Chris Robinson, Thomas Potts, Willm. Robinson, George Lawson, also Edward Porter, curat. Debts owing by the deceased. To widow Lawson, 26s. To John Gray, 53s. To Elinor Browne, 20s. To Geo. Lawson, 30s. INVENTORY, amounted to 35l. 8s. 0d. Probate, 13 May, 1619.

PETER MOWBRAY.[2]

May 22. 1619. I, Peter Mowbray, of the pish of Stanhope. To be buried within the Churchyard of Stanhope. I gyve to the poore that cometh to my buriall, 3s. 4d. To everye one of the children of my brother, John Mowbray, one sheepe, to be delivered to them presently after they are shorne. My will is that whereas Roger Bradley did gyve to my wyfe one kow when he and I did make a bargaine, of which kow there is now fower more. I give to Esabell Mowbray, my wyfe, the same fower kye in consideration of the benefitt that I have had of the same kow. I give to George Hall, curait of Stanhope, 20s., to se my will executed according to my mynd, and to look that no body do my wiffe any wronge. To my nephew, John Mowbray, the one halfe of the debt that Robert Hedrington owes me. The rest of all my goods, moveable and unmoveable, so that my dettes be paid funerall discharged and I honestlye browght fourthe I give to Esabell Mowbray, my wife, whom I make sole executrix. Witnesses, George Hall, Clarke, George Chapman, John Mowbray and John Feildus.

INVENTORY, 40l. 15s. 4d.

[1] Perhaps this is the Thomas Grey, fifth son of Sir Edward Grey of Howick and Morpeth, from whom the Greys of Angerton descend; if so, his brother, Edward, who had mar. a dau. of Sir Henry Widdrington was bur. at Morpeth, 7 July, 1658.

[2] The testator was bur. at Stanhope, 20 May, 1619, and his widow, Isabel, also there, 19 July, 1622.

MARGARET HEBORNE.[1]

July 4, 1619. Margaret Heborne of Morpith. I give and bequeathe all my rights, arearage, and profitts of lande in Yorkshire dew to me and before the houre of my death, to my daughter Hellenor Midleton. To my said daughter Hellenor the lease and profitts of John Scots farme in Earle, in the County of Northumberland, with arearage and profitts of Ellington, also all bonds and bills dewe unto me by any person. I give unto Thomason Midleton my grandchild all my household stuffe. The rest of all my goods I give to my said daughter and appoint her sole Executrix.

Aug. 10, 1619. Margaret Hebborne. An Inventory of the goods and chattels of Margaret Hebborne of Morpeth, deceased, and also which is in the hands of George Forester of the Stott gate and others at the time of her death. Imprimis. Hir apparell in all 2*l.* A featherbedd and a boulster, 40*s.* Two paire of blankitts, 16*s.* Two coverletts, 13*s.* 4*d.* Six fustyan pillowes, 30*s.* A dossen and a halfe of table napkins, 10*s.* Two longe towells, 5*s.* A damask cubbart clocke, 6*s.* 8*d.* Two lyneing cubbart clothes, 5*s.* A pewther chamber pott and a fishscom, 20*d.* Two carpine clothes of Darnex, 13*s.* 6*d.* Four cubbart clothes of Darnex, 10*s.* A payre of smale lyneing sheets, 10*s.* A paire of Cannobye cushynes, 10*s.* Fower pewther dishes, 4*s.* A bayson and a eure, 5*s.* Two potten dishes, 8*d.* Two pewther candlestickes, 2*s.* A brasse candlesticke, 16*d.* Two sallitt dishes, 16*d.* Two sawcers, 6*d.* One dreeping pan, 12*d.* A spitt and a paire of Rax, 4*s.* A payre of tosting irones, 6*d.* A quarte pott and a pinte potte of pewther, 5*s.* An iron chimney, 6*s.* A paire of gibb crooks and a paire of broyle irons, 18*d.* A wood chest and a box. 3*s.* Two chayres, 2*s.* A judgment versus Arthur Hebborne for the use of the deceased touchinge certayne lands in Yorkshire of 72*l.* or thereabouts. A lease of John Scots farme at Earle at the yearlye rent of 3*l.* 6*s.* 8*d.* p. annum being 12 yeares yet to come, valued to 20*l.* The Arrearage of rents of Ellington being the third part of 6*l.* Rent due to Margret Hebborne for 17 years paste. 34*s.* A legacye or portion given and lefte dewe by the last Will of George Craister to Margrete Craister his daughter then unborne at his death the sume of 60*s.* or thereabouts. Due to the deceased at Midsumer, 1619 for hir quarters rente of Hebborne White house, 5*s.* Probate 1621.

[1] Her burial has not been found in the Morpeth Registers. She was the posthumous dau. of George Craster of Craster, and wife of Michael Hebburn of Hebburn (his will dated, 2 Jan., 1601, proved at York, 24 July, 1613, Raine's Test Ebor.), and mother of Arthur Hebburn, whose will is printed in this vol. Her dau. Eleanor mar. — Middleton.

THOMAS PILKINGTON.[1]

July 28, 1619. In the name of God, Amen, I, Thomas Pilkington of West Rainton, in the County of Durham, gent. I bequeath to my brother in Law, Mr. John Hicks, parson of Whitburn, my gray nagg. I do give unto Alice, his wife, one presse which standeth in his hall at Whitburne, also one Court Cubbord, and standing in the Hall at Rainton with the two cubbord clothes and a glass case, to have these things after the decease of Ursula, my wife, and not before, and I doe also give unto her in forme aforesaid one little beafe . . . . Also I do give unto Elen Hicks, daughter of John Hicks aforesaid, and remayning with me at Rainton, my best black cowe. Also I do give unto Elizabeth Hicks, another of his daughters, my browne cowe. I do also give unto Margarett Pilkington, my sister, late wife unto my brother Isack, one yellow cowe and a little lagged cowe. Also I do will and require my wife that she lett my sister-in-lawe, Margarett Pilkington, my brother Isacks said late wife, have those dozen of silver spoons and little sylver salt which I redeemed of Robt. Suertys for 6*l*. 12*s*. 4*d*., she, my said sister in law, paying for the same unto my said wife the said 6*l*. 12*s*. 4*d*., which I disbursed for them. I do will and require that my cosin Nicholas Walton's wife shall have after my death my signett of golde (which and another ringe my wife hath were both made out of a ringe that I had of my cozin, Nicholas, his wife). Also I do give and bequeath to my Coson, Joseph Pilkington, and his wife, either of them, an angell of gold. I give to Nicholas Verley and his wife betwixt them an angell of gold. I give to the poore of the parish of Houghton, 10*s*. To the poore of St. Maryes, 5*s*., and to the poore of St. Oswalds, 10*s*. I give to the poore of Kely hill (in which parish my freehold lands called Audlee Dalton alias Dalton Norrice do lye), 10*s*. I do give unto my cosin, Isabell Heeth, wife of Mr. John Heethe of Ramsyde, a Jacobus peece of gold being 22*s*. I give to Mr. Doctor Hutton's wife my loveing cosin another Jacobus or 22*s*. piece. I do give unto my brother, Noah Pilkington, halfe of the wood and lime which remayneth at Dalton Norrice. All the rest of my goods, moveable and unmoveable, to my loveing and faithfull wife, Ursula Pilkington, whom I make Executor. Witnesses, John Hethe, Ramsyde, Richard Walton, Geo. Martyn, Wm. Wilkinson.

[1] Although not mentioned in the Pilkington pedigree printed in *Surtees History of Durham*, vol. i., lxxix, he was the son of John Pilkington, archdeacon of Northumberland. The testator mar. Ursula, sister of the Rev. John Hickes, rector of Whitburn, 9 May, 1614, at that church. The testator was bur. at Houghton-le-Spring, 30 July, 1619, his brother, Isaac, mar. at Bishop Middleham, Margaret Woodifield, 1 May, 1604, and his brother, Noah, mar. Meriol, dau. of John Story of Aislaby at Egglescliffe, 28 Oct., 1622.

JANE JOHNSON.[1]

Aug. 10, 1619. ' Jane Johnson of Barwick, widdow of the late Matthew Johnson, Esquire, deceased. I constitute my loveing nephew, Mr. Samuel Sanderson, and my good friend Richard Bartlett, my executors and Trustees; and I give and bequeath unto them my house in Barwick wherein I dwell, together with my writings, deeds, charters, and evidences, touching and concerning the house situate on the North side of Bridge gate street in Barwick aforesaid To have and told to them and their heirs, to be sold to pay my debts, and that they have an especiall care to pay Sir Thomas Smith of London a debt of 20*l.* which I borrowed from him for an other, and the overplus to be imployed for the performance of my last Will and Testament. I bequeath to my nephew, Samuel Sanderson, 40*l.* To my goddaughter Frances Sanderson, 100*l.* To Jane Sanderson her sister, 100*l.* I give to Samuel Balmford, sone of James Balmford, preacher, 10*l.* To Jane Johnson and Margrett Johnson, 5*l.* each. I give to Mr. Henry Killegree and Mr. Robert Killegree in token of my love unto their good mother six pieces to either of them. To Thomas Sanderson sonne of my nephew Mr. Samuel Sanderson all my household stuff and furniture in and about my great capital messuage and dwellinghouse in Newcastle. To my niece, Frances Sanderson, my table dyamond that was my mother's, and to my niece, Jane Sanderson, my little bone coffer trimmed with silver which was my mother's. I give to my loveing brother, Mr. Henry Sanderson, their father one guilte cupp with a cover with two eares weighing seventeene ounces or thereabouts, which guiltt cupp is to be kept by Mrs. Sanderson for Ellinor Sanderson daughter to Samuel, and a silver beare bowle of twelve ounces to be kept by Mrs. Sanderson for Ellinor. I give to the poore of the town of Barwick, 40*s.*, and to the poore of Newcastle other 40*s.* To Mr. Henshawe, the lawyer, dwelling in the Duke's place, London, 40*s.*, for a remembrance. To my counsellor at lawe Edward Turner, Esqr., my spoute pott of silver weighing about ten ounces, praying him to be as helpfull to my executors as he hath been unto me, whereof I have no doubt if they will use his advice. All the rest of my goods and chattels unbequeathed— I give the legacy of 5*l.* to each of my executors. I give to Mrs.

[1] She was bur. at Berwick-on-Tweed, 15 Aug., 1619, being the dau. of Henry Sanderson of Newcastle, Brancepeth and Hedley Hope (his will is printed in these publications, vol. 112, pp. 7 and 8 and dated 23 Jan., 1549/50), by his wife, Eleanor, dau. of Pierce Chaytor of Newcastle; her brother, Henry Sanderson, also of Newcastle, was bur. at St. Nich., Newcastle, 4 Mch., 1650/1, having mar. Mary (also bur. there, 17 Dec., 1623), dau. of Thomas Lawrence of Huntingdon; his son Samuel Sanderson, mar., 18 Dec., 1610, at Brancepeth, Barbara, dau. of Thomas Liddell of Newcastle, bapt., 4 Dec., 1595, at St. Nich., bur., 17 Aug., 1672, at Lanchester; his dau. Frances was bapt., 3 Apl., 1595, at St. Nich., where her sister Jane was also bapt., 18 Mch., 1598/9.

Mary Sanderson wife of my brother, Mr. Henry Sanderson, **and** to my niece Sanderson, my nephew Samuel Sanderson's wife, and to my loving friend Mrs. Lany, and to her good sister, Mrs. Shaftoe, to Allice Wallis and her daughter Jane Smith, to every of them, 20s. a piece to make them hoope rings with my name therein to be written for a remembrance. To my servant, George Parke, 40s., for six years for and in respect of his good service. To Ann Rotheram, wife of George Rotheram, 10s. To Elizabeth Dawson, widow, 10s. I hereby release and discharge my brother, Mr. Henry Sanderson and his sone of all debts whatsoever. The rest and residue of my estate that remaineth over after payment of my debts and performance of my Will shall be equally bestowed among my nephew Mr. Samuel Sanderson and his children to be bestowed for sheep for them. To my niece, Ellinor Sanderson, my bed and furniture of blewe or matchett silke and the quiltt of matchett silke. I give unto my worthy friends, Mr. Hugh Gregson, Alderman of Barwick, and Mr. Michaell Sanderson, Alderman of Barwick, to either of them, one angell of gould for a token, whom I make supervisors of this my will.

INVENTORY, A trunk with olde books, 1l. 13s. 4d. A spout pot of silver, 25 oz. at 4s. 8d. the ounce, 5l. 16s. 8d. Two silver graven boules, 21 oz. at 4s. 8d. the ounce, 4l. 18s. 0d. A maudlin cup of silver, 7½ oz. at 4s. 8d. the ounce, 1l. 15s. 0d. A little trencher salt without cover, 4¾ oz. at 4s. 8d. the ounce, 1l. 2s. 2d. Six silver spoones, 7 oz. at 4s. 8d. the ounce, 9l. 16s. 0d. An old danish chest and an older trunke, a presse and a table upon tresseles, 10s. A little iron chimney, 2s. A candle mould, 4s. A field bedstead, 3s. 4d. An old copper kettle, 3s. 4d. A preserving pott, 5s. Another brass pott, 6s. 8d. A brass frying pann, 3s. 6d. A new fish pann, 2s. 6d. Two brasse ladles, 3s. 4d. A brasse morter and a pestell, 2s. 4d. An iron chimney in the kitchen, 8s. A paire of racks, 6s. 8d. A croke, 6s. 8d. A Jacke, 6s. 8d. Forty two pounds of puter, att 8d. the pound, 1l. 8s. 0d. A bason and a ewer, 5s. Six paire of fine sheetes at 8s. the paire, 2l. 8s. 0d. Twenty three old napkins wrought with greene, at 4d., 7s. 8d. A barrel of Samont taken for the King, 3l. Eight barrells more att 3l. 6s. 8d. the barrell, 26l. 13s. 4d. Two barrells of gillses at 50s. the barrell, 5l., Ready money, 18l. 19s. 0d.

Amount of INVENTORY, 605l. 17s. 11d. Proved, 1619.

THOMAS ADDISON.[1]

Thomas Addison (Will bearing no date) of Eggleston, in the Countie Palentine of Durham, Yeoman. I will that my lease of

[1] There are some particulars of this family given in the *New County History of Northumberland*, vol. xii., p. 56.

my tenement wherein I now dwell be leased and taken in my
Brother John Addison's name, and likewise the cottage to be
taken in his name that I bought of John Cotesworth, the younger :
and that my goodes and lyvinge shall pay for the same, and the
residue of my goods to remayne unto my wiffe and children, and
she to have the education of all my children and the benefit of
my lyvinge to bring them well upp in the feare of God. To my
brother John his liveinge. But in case my wiffe either dye,
marrye againe, or ellse miscarrie or misbehave her selfe with any
man after my decease, that then my said lyvinge to come unto
my brother, John Addisone, and he to dispose of the same, as
he thinks good, during the minortie of my daughters. My will
is that my eldest daughter, Grace Addison, shall have the tenement and fifteene shillings, when she shall come unto the age of
twenty one, giving and paying unto her sister Ann thirteene
pounds six shillings and eight pence, and shall like paye unto
her younger sister, Jane Addisone, the whole sume of twentie
pounds currant English money within a twelvemonth, after that
Grace shall be at her full age, [she] shall discharge both the said
sums unto her sisters. Provided always that my wiffe shall have
the third part of the fifteen shillings during her life naturall if she
doe remayne my wiffe, behaveing her selfe accordinge as before is
mentioned ; and in not performing the same to have no part of
my tenement. I give unto my second daughter, Nann Addison,
the cottage house and garthe that was John Cotesworth's
when she shall accomplish the age of fifteene years. But if it
please god to take to his mercye my eldest daughter before she
accomplish her full age that then my second daughter shall have
the tenement and fifteene shillings and the youngest the cottage
house and Nans portion of thirteene pounds six shillings and
eightpence, and also her owne legacie. The rest remaining after
my debts and funerall expences are discharged be equallie
divided amongst my wiffe and three daughters. I make my wiffe,
Jane Addisone, and my brother, John Addison, executors.
Witnesses, John Leighton, clarke of Ovingham, Rafe Errington. Probate, 25th September, 1619.

CHRISTOPHER ORDE.[1]

Nov. 4, 1619. Christopher Orde of Orde within the liberties of
Norham and Countie Pallatyne of Durham, gentleman. My
bodie to be seamleye buried at the discretion of my
friends. I give unto my eldest sone, Thomas Orde, and

[1] The testator, described as of Orde, gentleman, aged about 44, was
deponent at Newcastle, 10 Sept., 1601 (Chancery Deposns. Eliz.-Car. I. O.
6/2). He was not (as stated in Raine's *North Durham*, p. 250), son of
George Orde, but illegitimate son of George's eldest brother, John
Orde of Newbiggen who died *s. p. m. l.* about the winter of 1578/9.
Chancery Proceedings, James I. O. 1/72, and Chancery Deposns. (before

the heirs male of his bodye, all my messuages, lands
and tenements within the townfields of Orde with there
appurtenances, and one corne mill called Orde mille,
and all my fishing waters I have in Tweede, and failing issue of my
said sone, to my second sone Luke Ord and the heirs male of
his body, and failing issue to my third sone Christopher Orde
and his heirs male and failing issue to my cosin Robert Orde of
Chatton.   I give to my wife Ursula Ord the yearly sume of
6l. 13s. 4d. of my said lands, and I give to her twenty ewes and
thirteene sheapp hogges and also the grass for them and two
kyne in the Westfield of Orde.   I give to my youngest sonns
Luke and Christopher Orde 40l. equally between them.   The
residue of my estate I give to my eldest sone, Thomas Orde, and
appoint him sole Executor.   I make George Orde of Lungridge
and Robert Orde of Chatton supervisors of my Will.   Witnesses,
Robert Orde of Chatton, Robert Orde of Orde, George Short of
Orde.

INVENTORY, amounted to 41l. 16s. 2d.   Probate, 1625.

JOHN HOLBORNE.[1]

Jan. 10, 1619.   In Christen Noble Denmark.   In the name of
God, Amen, I, John Holborne of Newcastle, Mariner.   For my
bodye it lye where it shall please God.   I give unto my wife,
Margaret Holborne, the house wherein I now dwell in with the
tenements thereunto belonging for her widowhood and if she
marrie then to come to my sonne, Roger Holborn, save only her
third pts which I give unto her of all the lands I have for her
lifetime and after her life to come unto my sone, Roger Holborne,
and my daughter, Margaret Holborne, and their heirs.
I give unto my sone, Roger Holborn, the house where
John Carr dwelleth, and the heirs lawfully begotten of his body,
faileing him and his heires to my brother Edward Holborne.   And

1714) 686/59.   He mar. Ursula Collingwood at Berwick-upon-Tweed,
9 Oct., 1592, and with his wife is mentioned in the will of her mother,
Elinor Collingwood, widow, 20 Nov., 1597.   The will of their son Thomas
dated 12 Oct., 1634, was proved in 1635; he, by his wife Mabel, left two
daus. co-heirs.   Luke Orde, mayor of Berwick, 1646, was bur. at
Tweedmouth, 8 Dec., 1659; he mar. at Berwick, 17 Apl., 1632, Isabel
Orde.

[1] His burial has not been found at any of the four ancient Newcastle
parishes; his widow was bur., 28 Dec., 1625, at All Saints, from which
registers the following are taken.   Roger the son, also a Master Mariner,
mar. 17 Dec., 1618, Katherou Smith, who was bur. 19 Aug., 1646; he
had four children, John, bapt., 15 Jan., 1625/6, bur., 1 Sept., 1626;
another John, bapt., 5 Dec., 1627; Margaret, bapt., 18 Dec., 1620, and
Jane, bapt., 28 Sept., 1623; Margaret, bapt., 24 July, 1603, mar. William
Gibson, 27 Sept., 1621.   Edward the brother of the testator had four
daughters, Jane, bur., 7 Mch., 1600/1, Margery, bapt., 6 Sept., 1601,
Elizabeth, bapt., 9 Jan., 1602/3, and Ann, mar. Thomas Bodeley, 24
Oct., 1626.

the lease of the Walke Mill which I have of the towne, he paying unto my brother, , Edward Holborne's four daughters, tenn pounds to everie daughter. I give unto my sonne, Roger Holborne, the lease of my seller and two tenements in the borne Banck, and I give unto my daughter, Margaret Holborne, my horse Mill, also two tenements, where John Robson now dwelleth, and in the other Edward Wilson dwelleth with others. I give unto my daughter Holborne, the house wherein my sone, Roger Holborn, now dwelleth. Also I give unto my daughter, Margaret Holborne, my two houses in the Castle Mote and Balleygat. Also I give unto my daughter, Margaret Holborne, one hundred pounds for a legacy towards her bringing upp which the Trintie house oweth me; failing her and her heires to come to my sone, Roger Holborne, and his heires; failing him and his heires to my brother Edward Holborne four daughters; failing them and their heires male to my brother, Luke Whetstone, and his heirs lawfully begotten for ever. Also I give to my brother, Luke Whetstone, my whistle and best rapper. Also I give unto my sonne, Roger Holborne, my foure tenements standing without the barras at Newcastle, failing him and his heires to my daughter, Margaret Holborne, and her heires; faileing her and her heires to my brother Edward Holborne's children; failing them and their heires male to my brother Luke Whetstone, and his heires for ever. Alsoe for the hundred pounds, which I have given unto my daughter if she die and have no heires, then the use of the hundred pounds to goe unto my wife, Margaret Holborne, for her widowhood and she marrie, then to come to my sone, Roger Holborne, and his heires for ever. For my shipping I will that it be sold to pay my debts all save a sixth part of the Rowbe which I give unto my sonne, Roger Holborne, to goe Mr. of her if the rest of the partners think good; my partners are these Mr. Henry Soame an eight part, my brother Luke Whetstone one eight part, James Stenhouse an sixtene part, a frend of Mrs. Jarrard Reades an eight part, whereof there resteth to me for that part twenty six pounds at the rate of nine hundred and forty poundes, but fortye pound the rest is all my owne of which I have sold to my good friendes in the east countrees merchants one fourth part, to Anthonie Haneland one sixtene, to Ambrose Paine one sixtene, to John Slocom one sixtene, to Thomas Basenfield, one sixtene. All these have bought att the rate of nine hundreth fortie pounds for their partes. I have received noe money as yet but merely a bill of John Slocomes, of William Cowters of Newcastle which sum is to be paid the . . . . I give unto my sonne my silver . . . . to carrye to sea with him. I give unto my daughter Holborne a silver cupp that hath her name on it. The rest of my plate I will it shallbe be equally devided to my wife, my son and my daughter. I give unto my sone all my apparell to me belonging. I charge my wife, son, and daughter, that they doe not wrong my brother, Edward

Holborne's children of the least thing, and not to take anything
of them what I have laid out since their father's death, and I
charge my sonne, Roger Holburne, that he be a father unto them
so long as he liveth as I would have been my selfe, also I charge
him that he be a kind and loving sonne to his mother, and a
kind brother to his sister Also I give unto the poore of the
Trinintie house of Newcastle twenty shillinges to be divided
amongst them, I also give unto the poore of the parish of All
Hallowes, wherein I now dwell, twenty shillings; and I charge my
son, Roger Holborne, to see it done. Also I give unto my daughter,
Margaret Holborne, a small silver cupp which hath her name on it,
and the rest of my plate to be divided to my wife, my sonne, and
daughter Alsoe my minde is that these my good friends shall
be overseers of this my will, that is Mr. William Cockeyn, Merchant
in London and my loveing brother Luke Whetstone at London,
Mariner Also at Newcastle, Mr. Ralph Cole and Henry Johnson,
not doubting but these my good friends will see my debts paid,
and the rest that remaineth to my wife and children. I give unto
these my good friendes before named, every one of them, an
angle for a token : and soe I comit them and my selfe into the
tuicon of the almightie. In Christon Noble, the tenth day of
January, 1619, with my owne hand. Witnesses, Roger Holborne,
Fra. Clarke, Proved, 1622.

HENRIE ORD.[1]

Jan. 19, 1619. Henrie Ord of Norham, gentleman. My
bodie to be buried in decent manner at the discretion of my wife
and other friends. I give unto my eldest sone, Henrie Ord, the
whole of my tithes of Fenwick. I give to my son, Roger Ord, my
waters of Hugh Schield and South Yearrow now or late in the occupation of David Shielde and Alexander Short. I also give to the
said Roger my close in Goswick which now Mr. Henrie Haggerstone holds of me. To my eldest daughter, Ellenor Ord, 20l. per
yeare during eight yeares payable by my brother Thomas Orde,
his sone Thomas Orde out of his lands of Lucker, Warneford,
and Tuggill limited in the lease. I also give to my said daughter,
55l. due by bond at Martinmas last passed 1619 by Mr. William
Reed. Also I give to my second daughter, Isabell Ord, my part

[1] The testator was probably a son of Henry Orde of Horncliffe and,
if so, was younger brother of Thomas Orde of West Orde. It is likely
that his wife (not mentioned by name in the will) was Eleanor, and that
she died before 11 Oct., 1622 (Raine's *Test Dunelm.*, i., 251) having
re-mar. Robert Orde of Chatton (see his will in this Vol.) and borne
to him a dau. Margaret. The testator's son Henry, also of Norham
Castle, made his will 30 Jan., 1637/8, mentioning his brother Roger and
his sisters Eleanor (now wife of Robert Geddes), Isabel (probably wife
of Luke Orde, whom Henry calls " my brother "), and Margery; also
his half-sister Margaret.

of the tythes of Mindrime which I hold of my brother, Thomas
Ord, and are now or late in the occupation of Richard Johnson of
Learmouth and William Johnson of Mindrime. Also I give to my
said daughter, 7*l*. which my sister, Elizabeth Scot of Yearle, and
her sone, Alexander Scot of Yearle, oweth to me. Moreover I give
my said daughter, 8*l*. due by Ralph Muschampe of Liam Hall, due
by his bond. More I give to my said daughter, 4*l*. 10*s*. 0*d*., due
by my cosin Robert Orde of Chattone by bond. More to my
daughter Isabel, 24 bowels of rye and thirteen shillings and fourpence in money due by George Carr of Crookham, and 22*l*. due by
Mr. Thomas Carr, Lord of Ford, as appears by his bond. More to
my said daughter, 10*l*. due by George Carr and Thomas Carr of
Hetherlaw. More to her, 4 markes due by Thomas Carr of Hetherlaw sone to George Carre for two oxen. More the sum of 23*l*. due
by Roger Selbye and his wife. I give to my youngest Daughter,
Margerie Ord, 16*l*. due by James Glendinning and 4*l*. by his
wife. More to the said Margerie, 4*l*. 10*s*. due by William Clerke
of Cornhill. I also give to the said Margerie twenty nobles due
by George Selbie of Milkintone as appeareth by my booke. More
to the said Margerie, 15*l*. due by John Selbie of Grindon, by his
bond. Also to my daughter Margerie, 36*s*. due by Charles Dods
of Tilmouth. More 50*s*. due by William Ramsey of the East
quarter of Swinton. Also to my said daughter Margerie, 9*l*. due
by John Hume and Thomas Hume of Killo. More to my said
daughter Margerie, 14*l*. 6*s*. 0*d*. due by Ralph Gray, Lord of Kilo,
as appears by his father's bond. Also four marks due by Ralph
Willson of Ancroft. More I give to my said Daughter Margerie,
40*s*., due by John Stangwish of Chiswick. To my said daughter,
8*l*., due by Robert Scot and his sone William. I give to my wife
the mortgage of Horkley Mill, which I have of my brother Thomas
Ord. More, I give to my wife my farme of Horkley, which I had
of Thomas Richardson. Also to my wife my interest in the halfe
land I hold of Richard Ferrar for ten years yet to come. Also I
give to my said wife, the land in Norham I bought of John
Lawson with a house and a Malt Kiln and Malt barne. I give
to my wife all the stock I have in Horkley, and also what is
due to me from Thomas Brown the smith in Horkley. I give the
residue of my estate to my said wife, and appoint her sole
Executrix. I forgive my brother, Thomas Ord, 9*l*. which he oweth
me. Also Thomas Ord the younger, my nephew, his sone, twenty
markes. Also I forgive my brother, George Orde of Horkley, 30*l*.,
which he oweth me. I give to my brother, Richard Orde, one
gelding. To the poor of Berwick, 10*s*. I appoint Mr. Marke
Saltenstall, Mr. Nathaniel Orde and Mr. John Orde of Fenwicke
Supervisors. And I leave to Mr. Mark Saltenstall my son Roger
with his portion. My eldest son, Henry Ord, to Mr. Nathaniel
Ord. To my cosin, John Ord, my second daughter Isabell, and to

my wife my daughters Ellinor Orde and Margerie with their portions.

INVENTORY, 9th of February, 1619. A lease taken of the Castle and Manors of Norham of the Earl of Dunbar now ending at Martinmas in 1620. A lease of a farme called the Kent stone a parcel of the Lordship of Kilo in value 6*l*, of which lease yet remaining five years to come. Probate, 1619.

THOMAS BETHOME.[1]

Feb. 14, 1619. In the name of God, Amen, I, Thomas Bethome of Ouseburne in the County of Newcastle on Tyne, Yeoman. To be buried within my pish church of All Saints, near to the quere dore on the right hande within the same dore. And for such goods as it hath pleased god to indew me withall, I do gyve and bequeath them in maner and forme followinge, viz., I give unto my cosin John Thompson, taylor, my best suyte of apparell, wch I weare on the sabboth dayes, viz., a dowlett, a paire of breaches of fustin, and the stockings thereunto belonging. I gyve unto my cosen, Willm. Betham of Morpeth, my next best suyte of apparell, being of kersey and stockings, and the black dowlett, and the workaday cloake wch I usually were together. I do hereby declare that John Harbotle of Ellington and Mary his wife, do owe unto me the some of Thirtene poundes seaventeen shillinges and sixpence Also Richard Turner and Ann his wife do owe unto me twenty shillings which I lent her Also Mr. Henry Dent oweth me twenty shillings in lent money And George Pattison of South Shielpannes doth owe unto me fyve pounds for two Tennes of Coles. John Hunter of the same place oweth me tenne shillinges. Cuthbert Pattison's widow of Shields oweth me fifteene shillings for a remaynder of Coles which he had. The residue of all my goods, leasses, debts and chattels whatsoever, saving that before hereby I have bequeathed to the said John Thompson and William Betham, and all my debts whatsoever (my debtts and funerall charges being paide and discharged) I doe gyve and wholly bequeath unto my loving wyfe Jane, and to our sonne John whom I make nomynate and appoint to be full and sole Executors of this my last Will and Testament. Renouncing and forsakyng all former Wills, legacies and bequests by me in anywise heretofore made or gyven. Witnesses, John Thompson, Andrew Ainsley. Proved, 1620.

[1] The testator was bur. at All Saints, Newcastle, 17 June, 1620, his burial entry reading thus " Thomas Bedome, gent."; his son John was bapt. there, 1 Jan., 1618/19, and bur. there, 28 Oct., 1628; his widow, Jane, may have re-mar., 2 May, 1621, Christopher Ridley at the same church.

GEORGE MUSCHAMP.[1]

March 29, 1620. George Muschamp. Inventory of the goods and chattells of George Muschamp of Lyham in the parish of Chatton, gentleman, deceased, the twentieth day of June, 1619, taken and apprized the 20th day of March, 1620, by Ralph Muschamp of Lyham Hall, gent., and John Peacock and George Younge of Lyham, Yeomen. Imprimis. Five keine and calves, 6*l.* Two quies and one stotte, tow years old, 1*l.* 16*s.* One quie and one stotte a yeare olde, 16*s.* Twenty-six ewes and dinmonds, 5*l.* 4*s.* 0*d.* Eighteen lambes, 1*l.* 10*s.* One sowe, two hoggs and two piggs, 9*s.* Five bedsteads and hurdle bedde, 2*l.* One great cupboarde, tow tables, one courte cupboarde, eight wyned stooles, three chares, three chists, two trunkes, and foure formes, 4*l.* One deft, one little trunk, one paire of tables, and one paire of wooden scales with a woodden balk, 10*s.* Five great tubbs, two little tubbs, tow milch pales, three barrells, one old woodden press, five milch bowles, one hamper, one milch sile, three basketts, and one halbert, 1*l.* 3*s.* One dosen and a halfe of trenchers, 2*s.* Tenne great poulter dishes, eight lesser, six saucers and hande bason, one bason and one ewer, four candlesticks, six litle poulter potts, tow chamber potts, one supporter, tow salts, 2*l.* 14*s.* One brass morter with a pestoll, one chasinge dishe, one candlestick, foure panns, tow potts, one ketle, 1*l.* 16*s.* One frying panne of Iron, one driping panne, tow spitts, one pare of racks, two paire of tongs, one powe, two paire of clippes, one pot lid of Iron, two Iron Chimneys and one fire crooke, 1*l.* Five paire of fine lining sheets, nine paire of courser lining and straking sheets, 4*l.* 17*s.* 8*d.* One holland table clothe, one fine lining table cloath, tow courser lining table cloathes, one diaper plated towell, six diaper napkins, twenty-one fine lining table napkins, two lining hand towells, one strakeing hande towell, five holland pillobers, nine fine linning pillobers, 2*l.* 1*s.* 8*d.* One dornex carpitt, 4*s.* Two tapistrye coveringes, 2*l.* Four coveringes for bedds, 6*s.* Four plads, 4*s.* Five paire of blanketts, 1*l.* 2*s.* 6*d.* Three featherbedds, four bolsters, foure downe pillos, six feather pillos, 3*l.* Five curtains and vallins, three curtains and vallins, 14*s.* 4*d.* Five cushons, 3*s.* 4*d.* Four sacks and one windowing cloath, 4*s.* Corne Sowen, five Kennings of Rye sowen the increase estimated to foure bowles and valued at 1*l.* 4*s.* Five Kennings of beare sowen the increase estimated to four bowels and valued to 1*l.* 1*s.* 4*d.* Debts due out of the Estate : Paid to Hugh Gregson of Berwick, Marchant, for wares due the 11th day of July, 1619, 3*l.* 5*s.* More paid to

---

[1] There is an account of Barmoor and the Muschamps in the transactions of the Berwickshire Naturalists' Club, vol. xxii., pp. 98-117, by the late J. C. Hodgson.

Henry Chapman of Newcastle, Marchant, for flax due the 1st day
of August, 1619, 1*l*. 7*s*. Paid to Sir William Muschamp, Knight,
for the use of Sir William Selby of Kent, Knight, due the 1st
day of August, 1619, 2*l*. More paid to Robert Muschamp of
Midleton for six lambes, due 16th August, 1619, 12*s*.

THOMAS BURRELL.[1]

May 20, 1620. Thomas Burrell of Milfield, in the parish of
Newton, within the County of Northumberland, gentleman. To be
buried within the parish church of Newton aforesaid. I doe give
and bequeath unto my eldest brother, Robert Burrell of Milfield,
gentleman, all that my lande and fermehold with the appurtenances situate and lying within the townefields and territeries of
Homelton within the Countie aforesaid, only to and for the use and
behalf of Ralph Burrell, the sone of the said Robert Burrell, and
to his heirs for ever, and I direct the said Robert to pay all debts
and also legacies by this my Will bequeathed. I give to my sone,
Oswalde Burrell alias Lawes, 15*l*., and comit the tuition of him
and his said portion unto my said Brother, Robert Burrell. To
my daughter, Rachell Burrell alias Muschamp, 15*l*. and I do
comit the government of her to my brother Lancelot Burrell and
Barberie his wife, and if they happen to refuse the tuition of my
said daughter my will is that she be committed unto Phillis Roger,
the wife of Robert Roger of Wooller, and further my will is that
if either of these my children shall depart out of this life before it
come to age or be married that then 5*l*. shall bee added to the
survivor, 40*s*. given to the mother of the deceased child, 40*s*. to
each of those to whom I comit the children, 40*s*. to my brother
John Burrell's children, and 40*s*. to my sisters Barbaries children.
And if it please god that both my children die before they come to
age or bee marryed then my will is that each of their mothers shall
each have four pounds in consideration of the wrong which I have
done unto them. The residue of my estate to be equallie divided
amongst the children of my Brothers, Robert and Lancelot. I
will that Robert Rogers of Wooller and his wife, Phyllis, or the
longer live of them, shall have a ridge of lande lying in the
Netherside of Hommlton now in the tenour of the said Robert
Rogers. I appoint my said brother, Robert Burrell, sole Executor.
Witnesses to will, Em. Trotter clerk, Robert Burrell, Christopher Fletcher, Lancelot Burrell, Ralphe Roger, and Richard
Burrell. Probate, 26th July, 1620.

[1] There is a pedigree of the Burrells of Howtel in the *New County
History of Northumberland*, vol. xi., p. 199, which this will amplifies.

HENRY GRAY.

Aug. 2, 1620. Henry Gray. Inventory of the goods and chattels movable and unmovable of Henry Gray of Ulgham prised by four indefferent men, viz., Henry Browne, Thomas Guning, Ralphe Milburne, Oswald Graye, and John Smith. Imprimis: Eleven oxen, two stirkes, 11*l.* One cowe and a calfe, 26*s.* 8*d.* One mear, one filly, 3*l.* 11*s.* 8*d.* Swine, 10*s.* Coverletts sheetes and other nappry, 4*l.* 8*s.* Pewter, brasse, Iron vessels, 2*l.* 5*s.* 8*d.* His apprill, 26*s.* 8*d.* One amery, a buttery, 40*s.* A presser, fethearbed and bedstead, 4*l.* Chists and other woodden stuffe, 14*s.* Corne, lint, hay, 5*l.* 6*s.* 8*d.* Waine plues and all things belonging to husbandry, 40*s.* Debts owing by the said testator : Edward Runry, 10*l.* Humphrie Greene, 8*l.* John Smith, 10*l.* 6*s.* 8*d.* Thomas Potts, 30*s.* John Selby, 21*s.* 6*d.*. Henry Lawson, 15*s.* Michaell Atkinson, 42*s.* Robert Widdrington, 26*s.* Richard Osmotherley, 52*s.* Henry Widdrington, 40*s.* John Heron, 40*s.* Isabell Taylor, 20*s.* John Smith, 26*s.* Funeral Expences, 40*s.*

HENRY COLLINGWOOD.[1]

Dec. 8, 1620. Henry Collingwood of Berwick-on-Tweed, gentleman. My bodie to bee buried in the earth from whence it came, to be decently interred at the discretion of my executors hereafter named. First, my debts shall be paid which are, to John Floxton of Berwick, 10*l.* 10*s.* To George Smith the elder, 5*l.* To Robert Archibald, 45*s.* To John Derry, 47*s.* To George Simpson, the shepheard, for keeping of my sheepe at Christmas next, 34*s.* or thereabouts. To James Wetherborne, shepheard, for keeping sheepe, 3*s.* Unto Anne, the wife of George Smithe, 15*s.* To Mr. Michaell Sanderson, 5*s.* To Mr. William Morton for the tithe wooll of all the sheepe which I had this last yeare, and payment for tiethe lambes for the same tyme, the sume will appeare by reckoninge with the shepheard. To Thomas Smithe, Scholemaister, 4*s.* 4*d.*, which said several debts I direct shall bee paid fourth of such goodes and chattels as hereafter are particularie mentioned and expressed. To witt there is remayning of my sheepe in the custodie of the said George Smith, fiftie and five sheepe. There is in the custodie of Mr. Henry Collingwoode of Etal, my cosen, nineteen ewes. Mr. Richard Byerley oweth me twenty five bolls and one Kenninge of the last yeare oates, Barwick measure. There is in my lofte at Valentine Fenwicke thirteen bolls of oates and also fourteene stone of wooll. Due unto mee by Mr. Thomas Carr of Ford of lent money, 10*s.*, and also twentye hogge sheepe. My cozen, Henry Collingwood, of

[1] He was bur. at Berwick-on-Tweed, 11 Dec., 1620.

Epleton, oweth mee, 10*s.* Due to mee from Mr. Robert Selby
for lent moneye, 5*s.* 10*d.* After my debts are paide the overplus
of all my goods and chattels I give unto my sonne, John Collingwoode, whom I comitt to the tuition and education of my said
cosen, Mr. Henry Collingwoode of Etal, and my wellbeloved friend,
George Smith, heartelie beseechinge them to see him brought up
in the feare of god, even as my trust and confidence is in them,
and do make and ordeyne them my executors. I will that 20*s.*
be distributed to the present poore people of Berwick. Witnesses,
Law. Steele, Anthony Carr, Michaell Armorer.
INVENTORY, 41*l.* 11*s.* 10*d.* Probate, 6 Nov., 1620.

ANTHONIE MARLEY.[1]

Dec. 21, 1620. In the name of God, Amen, I, Anthonie
Marley of Picktree, within the Countie of Durham. Yeoman.
To be buried in the pish church of Chester in the street as nere
unto the stall where I sitt as possiblie can be. I give and bequeath
the some of fower pounds of lawfull money of England to be
delivered to the churchwardens of Chester pish towards the makeing and encreasinge of a stocke alreadie begune to the use of the
poore in that pish for ever, and the churchwardens yearlie to putt
it to good use for the benefitt of the said poore and most needfull
people as aforesaid for ever. And for the distributione to the
poore and funerall expences at the time of my death, I referr
that to the discretion of my father, frends and executors. I
give and bequeathe unto Margarett Marley, my wife, the some
of 200*l.* of lawful moneye of Englande, and all the howshold stuff
she browght with her, willing and requireinge that she therewith
may be well pleased and be contented to take it in full satisfacon
of her pt of my estate. And for the payment thereof it shall be
assigned and satisffied unto her in such sort as hereafter shalbe
expressed and declared. I give and bequethe unto our maide
servante, Margaret Atkinson, the some of 20*s.* towards the buye-
ing her a coate. And to Thomas Atkinson, our manservant,
other 20*s.* of lawfull money of England. And to Margaret
Harrison, a litle wenche we have, the some of 10*s.* I give and
bequethe unto Thomas Ladley of Chester, aforesaid, the some of
20*s.*, which Thomas Sharpe of Chester aforesaid is endebted unto
me. I give and bequeth unto Anthonie Applebie, the some of
Parcivall Applebie of Chester, aforesaid, to whom I helped to

<hr/>

[1] The testator mar. 24 Aug., 1617, Margaret Turner at Chester-le-
Street, he was bur. there, 9 Dec., 1620, his father. Robert, being also
bur. there, 26 March, 1627; his brother, Ralph, mar. Isabel Wild, 13
July, 1619, at the same church.

give christendome, the sum of 10s. of lawful money of England.
All the residue of my goods and chattles, both moveable and
unmoveable, not formlie bequeathed, my debts paid, legacies discharged, and funerall expences deducted, I give and bequeath
unto Robert Marley, my father, and Ralph Marley, my brother,
who I make and ordeine Joint Executors of this my last Will
and Testament.   In witness whereof I have hereunto sett my
hande the day and yeare first above written.   Witnesses Lancelot Joplin, X his mark, John Catcheside X his mark, William
Marche, John Turner, X his mark, Guy Bainbrigge.

Debts oweing unto the said Anthonie Marley sett downe by
himselfe before the witnesses aforenamed and forth of ascertained
rent and the said debts the two hundred pounds assigned to his
wife to be paid and satisfied unto her in manner and form followinge, viz. : First, the said Anthonie doth assigne unto her the rent
reserved upon a lease and payable unto him by John Catcheside
of Birtleye, during all the tearme of the said Lease together with
20s. the said John Catcheside is endebted unto him, and that all
these shallbe allowed in part of the 200l. aforesaid given unto hir
at the value of onelie of 60l.   Item, The said Anthonie doth
further assign and appoint unto hir all those debts upon
specialtie or otherwise due unto him by John Ditchant which
cometh unto 41l.   Item, The said Anthonie doth further assigne
unto her the debt unto him by Thomas Joplin of Low Stanley
and Robt. Joplin, his sonne, and Lancelott Joplin of Owstone,
which cometh to the some of 22l., and by Lancelot Joplin himself,
4l.   Item, The said Anthonie also assigne unto her the debt due
unto him by John Vasey of Ladlev. for which Guy Bainbrigge
standeth bound, the some of 10l.   Item, The said Anthonie doth
further assigne unto her the debt due unto him by bonde at
Mychaelmas next, 1621, for which Mr. Richarde Hedworth,
Thomas Symth and Guv Bainbrigg standeth bond, the sume of
11l.   Item, The said Anthonie doth also assigne unto her lent unto
Guy Bainbrigge on Friday the 14th of December, 1620, 3l.   Item,
he doth also further assigne unto her which he lent to Charles Robson of Urpeth, payable, 4l.   Item, The said Anthonie doth further
assigne unto her which is in golde and money in the howse, the
some of 24l.   Item, he doth also assigne unto her the half debt
due unto him and Robert Marley, his father, due unto them by
one Mr. Roland Shaftoe and his sonne, his part whereof cometh
to 7l. 6s. 8d.   Item, he doth also assigne unto her his part of a
debt due unto him by Charles Porter which cometh to 8l. 13s.
Item, he doth also assigne unto her a debt due unto him by
Thomas Sanson which was lent money at Mychaelmas gone, 20s.
All these severall soms aforesaid cometh to 195l. 19s. 8d.   The
residue of the 200l. to be paid unto her by his executors as they
shode pay her for the same six pounds.   Proved, 1620.

NICHOLAS COLE.[1]

Feb. 8, 1620. In the name of Gode, Amen, and in the eighteenth yeare of the Reign of our Sovereigne lord James, by the grace of God King of England, France and Ireland, Defender of the faithe, etc., and of Scotland, ... I, Nicholas Cole, of Gateside, in the countie of Durham, yeoman. To be buryed in the parrish church of Gatesheade. I give to the poore of Gateside, 5*l.*, to be given at my buriall amongst them. I give other five pounds to the bringing home of the Water for the good of the poore people of the parrish from the hospitall to Sir Thomas Riddell's gate. I bequeath to my sonne, Railph Cole, and his heires for ever the house wherein I was borne, which was given to my mother, Jane Manwell, by her uncle, Henrie Archbald, whose heire I am. I give to the said Ralph and his heeres for ever the tent close. I give to the said Railph and his heeres for ever nine of my salt panns with the fullers houses and the garners thereunto belonging (except onely the great slait house) wherein Willm. Atkinson dwelleth, which I give to my sonne, John Cole, and to his heires for ever. I give and bequeath to Nicholas Cole, sonne of the said Raiphe Cole, two tents in Hornebie chaire, wherein dwelleth John Hunter and Brian Boumer, and to his heires for ever. I give to my sone, John Cole, and his heires for ever, six salt panns and the great house in the Easter ground. I give to the said John Cole the 4 leases bought of Robt. Thomplinson, one peece of ground joining on the four leases bought of Sir Thomas Riddle. I give to the said John Cole all my houses in Pipewellgate. I give to the said John Cole this house wherein I now dwell and a tenemt next adioying to it on the south, with a Barne adioying to the same house in Pipewellgate and to his heires for ever. I give to the said John Cole and his heires for ever the house bought of William Dunn, wherein Mr. Woodrington did dwell. I give to the said

John Cole and his heirs for ever three tenements, with the garths belonginge to them, which tenemts are right against the Pinfold bought of Craggs. I give to the said John Cole and his heires for ever the close and Barne which was bought of Willm. Pursley. I give to the said John Cole two tenemts and two garths which was bought of Rokesbie and Bliethman and his heires for ever. My will is that my sonne John, shall pay to my daughter, Elizabeth Johnson, 10*l*. per annum, forth out of the howses and garths and lands during her naturall life at two feasts or tearms, viz., Martinmas and Whitsontide, and also that my sonne. Railph, and John Cole shall pay to her 10*l*. likewise during her naturall life at such feast daies and termes as by a covnent made appeareth. I give to the said John Cole the house at the Pant, wherein Richard Grame doth dwell, and to his heires for ever. I give to the said John Cole and his heires for ever three tenemts and two garthes on the west side of Bissie Burn. I give to the said Ralph Cole and John Cole all my Cole leases, that is to say, the lease of the Maudling land, the lease of Robt. Gibson's land, the lease of Willm. Dalton's land, with all other my coal leases ioyintlie betwixt them during the tyme of the leases. I give to Nicholas Hall, sone to Thomas Hall, 13*l*. 6*s*. 8*d*., and to Elizabeth Selbie, daughter to Thomas Hall, ten poundes, and also to Jane Hall, daughter to Thomas Hall, 10*l*. To Bartram Anderson, sone to Henrie Anderson, 20*l*., and to Nicholas Huntley, sonne of George Huntley, 20*l*., and to Nicholas Humphrey, son to Tho. Humphrey, 13*l*. 6*s*. 8*d*., and also to Railph Humphrey, sonne to Thomas Humphrey, 13*l*. 6*s*. 8*d*., and also to Edward Johnson, sonne to Abraham Johnson, 13*l*. 6*s*. 8*d*. I give to Nicholas Parkin, sonne to George Parkin, 6*l*. 13*s*. 8*d*. I give to George Parkin's second sonne, 4*l*., and to his young daughter, 4*l*. To George Parkin, for a token, 20*s*., and to his wife, 20*s*., for a token. I give to Richard Cole's wife, dwelling at London, five pounds. I give to the said John Cole the lease of the stone quarries which I hold of the Bishop of Durham. I give to the said John Cole the lease of two fishings with three score yardes of waist ground which I hold by lease of the Dean and Chapter, which fishing is in the River of Tyne at a place called the Skittermill hole, and the waist ground lieth at or near the sixe salt panns, before menconed, that I have given to my said sonne, John Cole. I give all the rest of my goods and chattells, moveable and unmoveable, to my said sone, John Cole, who I make my full and sole Executor. I give to my daughter-in-law, Jane Cole, late wife of my sone, James Cole, deceased, 5*l*., and I make supervisors of this my last Will and Testament, Anthonie Hebson, Edith Blitheman, Willm. Wall and Abraham Johnson, and I give to everie of them a peece of gold of two and twenty shillings. This my Will and legacies being as my meaning is they shallbe dulie paid by my said Executor, John

Cole, yet I purpose that the somes above said by me bequeathed shall be demanded not for the space of one yeare after the probate of this my Will. Witnesses, Anthonie Selbie, Michael Heworth, Wm. Wall, Peter Marley. Proved, 1626.

CHARLES WREN.[1]

March 9, 1620. I, Charles Wren, of Binchester, in the Countie of Durham, Knight. To be buryed in the quyre of my pish church of St. Andrew's, Auckland. And for my lands and worldlie goods which god haith endewed me withall, my mynd and will is as followeth, first I give and bequeath my capitall messuage and tenet called Binchester, and all my messuages, lands and tenets in Binchester, Billyehall and Billy Rawe, in the said Countie of Durham, with their and evie of their appurtances unto my sonne and heir apparent, Lyndley Wren, and heirs males of his bodie, and for defalt of such issue to remayne to my sonne, Charles Wrene, and the heirs males of his bodie, and for defalt of such issue to remayne to my sonne, Henry Wren, and the heires males of his bodye, and for defalt of such issue to remayne to the right heires of me, the said Sir Charles Wren, for ever. And whereas I have pvyded for the conpetent mainteyance and Pferment of any said sonns, Charles and Henry, by servall grants of anuities unto them for their lives respectivelie furth of my lands at Binchester which I did and do meane and intend to stand in full satisffaction of their child's porcons of my goods, and having a desyre that my said sonne, Charles, should studie the lawe and my sone, Henry, should be a tradesman in London if it shall please god so to dispose of them, therefore for the better encouraging of them to apply themselves accordingly I doe moreover give and bequeath to my said sonne, Charles, if it please god he pceed in the studie of the lawe, 100l., to be paid unto him when he shall be called to the Barre. And I give to my said sone, Henry, 100l., to be paid unto him when he shall be made freeman of London. And I will and appoint that my said sonne, Henry, shall he honestlie and sufficientlie maynteyned at the charge of my executors out of my goodes untill he shall attaine his age of eighteene yeares about which tyme his annuitie is to take place and begyn. Item, I give and bequeathe to my daughter, Gartrude Wren, 40l. yearlye, for her mainteyance untill she shall attayne the age of one and twentie yeares or be maryed, whether shall first happen. I having alredie pryded for securring of a competent porcon for her by a lease of my lands in West Hartburne,

[1] There is a well worked out pedigree of the Wrens of Binchester in vol. 124, pp. 205-8, of this series. The *Inq. p.m.* of Charles Wren was taken at Durham, 15 Aug., 1621; Linleus, aged 20, was his son and heir.

the said 40*l.* per annum to be paid to her quarterlie by my executors during the' tyme aforesaid, and that which can be sparred yearlie out of the said 40*l.* to goe forward towards the amendmt of her porcon. Item, I give unto my said sonne, Lyndley Wren, my wholl terme interest and tytle in my milne of Binchester, and my whole interest tearme and title in my house in Bpp Auckland, now in the possession of Robt. Thompson, clark. Item, I give and bequeath unto my cosin Christopher Lassells of Kirklinton, in the Countie of York, gent, 20*l.* I give unto servante, John Martyndale, 20*l.* Item, I give unto my servant, John Robson, 5*l.* I give to my servant, Peter Dixon, 40*s.* Item, I give to Christopher Wren, 50*s.* Item, I give to my servant, Charles Robinson, 20*s.* To my servant, Nicholas Hunter, 20*s.* To my servant, John Martindale, 20*s.*, and to my servant, John Lamb, 20*s.* The residue of all my goodes and chattells not formerly bequeathed, my debts, and funerall discharged, I give and bequeath to my said sonne, Lyndley Wren, whom togither with my servant, John Martindale, I make executors of this my Will, joining the said John Martindale in executorshipp with my said sonne, Lyndley, only in trust for assisting of my said sonne in the execution of this my Will. Witnesses, Raphe Blaxton, George Trotter, Mathew Bowser, Parcivall Martindell, William Jordan, Anthonye Arundell. Proved, 1621.

SIR CHARLES WREN.

April 4, 1621. A true Inventory of all those goods and chattels, moveable and immoveable, which the Rigt Worpll Sir Charles Wren, late of Binchester, in the Countie of Durham, Knight, dyed possessed of prysed by Henry Bayles, George Trotter, Ouswould Glover, and Anthony Grindon, Imprimis, 18 oxen, 80*l.* 4 fatt stotts, 24*l.* 12 stotts and 2 heffers, 40*l.* 22 younge steares, 33*l.* 12 stirks, 12*l.* 30 kine and one bull, 90*l.* 10 horses and one mare, 48*l.* Eight score and five weathers, 53*l.* 6*s.* 8*d.* 23 fatt weathers, 11*l.* Six score and 17 ewes, 53*l.* 6*s.* 8*d.* 96 sheepe hoggs, 24*l.* 17 swine, 12*l.* Poultry and geese, 1*l.* 10*s* Waynes, plowes, and their appurts, 20*l.* Rye corne in the barne, 5*l.* Oats, 6*l.* Bigg in the barne and one bigg stacke, 14*l.* Oats in the garner, 13*l.* Pees, 3*l.* 6*s.* Malt in the Garner, 85*l.* Corne in the Mille, 1*l.* Bigg in the Garner, 12*l.* In the hall, tables, chaires and stooles, 2*l.* Armour there, 10*l.* In the plour, tables, chayres and stooles, 7*l.* In the green chamber, all furniture, 15*l.* In the Gallery, one table, 3*l.* 6*s.* 8*d.* Sowen woode in the garret over the gallery, 3*l.* In the best Chamber, the bed and furniture, 40*l.* In the bed Chamber, all furniture, 13*l.* 6*s.* 8*d.* Linnen and vyber in the same chamber, 40*l.* Plate there, 80*l.* In the round window, chamber bell, 15*l.* Certaine things in the Clossett, 5*l.* In the nursery chamber, all furniture, 12*l.* In the maide servants' chamber, 2*l*. In the wooll garrett, 2*l*. In the store house, brasse vessell, 13*l*. 6*s*. 8*d*. In the Schoolehouse chamber, 3 beds, 13*l*. 6*s*. 8*d*. In the workman's chamber, beds, 3*l*. In the Garret over the Milkhouse, 1*l*. In the men servants chamber, 3*l*. In the washing house, puter and other things, 10*l*. Vessell in the bakehouse and brewhouse, 30*l*. In the milkehouse, bras vessell and other things, 13*l*. 6*s*. 4*d*. In the Mill, bed and other thinges, 1*l*. 10*s*. In the 2 Larders, puter vessell, 5*l*. In the kitchinge, Salt flesh and fish, 5*l*. In the buttery and seller, 10*l*. In implents in the Mill, 2*l*. 6*s*. 8*d*. The lease of the Mill, 40*l*. The lease of Charwell Crooke, 60*l*. The lease of the house in Auckland, 8*l*. Implements there, 5*l*. The kill hayre winnowing, cloath and sackes, 3*l*. Certain hay in the Staggarth, 3*l*. 6*s*. 8*d*. Books in the studdie, 5*l*. Purse, apparell and furniture, 120*l*. Summa, 1261*l*. 5*s*. 8*d*. Debts owen to the testator, viz., Imprimis, Sir John Claxton, 50*l*., out of which there is due 20*l*. to be paid to Mr. Jo. Claxton, his sonne. Item, John Taylor, 110*l*. William Featherston, 150*l*. William Trotter and Ralph Lockeson, 50*l*. Mr. Robert Allanson, 55*l*. Cuthbert Colling and Richard Maner, 9*l*. John Stevenson, 9*l*. 10*s*. Richard Garry, 1*l*. 5*s*. 8*d*. Mrs. Jeffers, 2*l*. Robert Arthur, 1*l*. An. Rudderford, 12*s*. John Robinson, 18*s*. John Trotter, 7*s*. Georg Whyte, 3*s*. 4*d*. Robert Cowper, 6*s*. 8*d*. Robert Barrey, 1*s*. 9*d*. Robert Hickson, 10*s*. The said 20*l*. deducted remaineth 420*l*. 14*s*. 5*d*. The whole sume cleare is in all 1682*l*. 0*s*. 1*d*.

THOMAS LAWSON.

April 7, 1621. Thomas Lawson, of Lannghurst. My bodie to be buried in the parish church of Bothall. I give to Arthur Thompson, who was my help in my sickness, one chist, a coverlett, a happin and a paire of sheetes. I give to Maude Lawson, my brother's daughter, one cowe in the hands of one Hudson in Lynton. I make Willey Lawson my sole Executor. Probate, 11th July, 1621.

ABRAHAM BARKER.[1]

Sept. 6, 1621. In the name of God, Amen, I, Abraham Barker, of the towne and Countye of Newcastle upon Tyne, Marchant, being at this instant sick in body. My bodye to be buried in the pish church of St. Nicholas in Newcastle upon Tyne aforesaid, and as touching all such worldy goodes as the lord

[1] His father, Robert Barker, who was bur. 4 Aug., 1590 (for his will see 38 *Sur. Soc.*, p. 176), is said to have mar. four wives (Welford's *Newcastle and Gateshead*, iii., 59). Probably by one of the first two he had Eleanor who mar. George Liddell at Ponteland, 29 Sept., 1578. The third wife, Eleanor (bur. 17 Oct., 1577), was probably mother of John,

in this world hath indewed me withall, I give and bequeath the same as followeth. First whereas my house in the Close, now in the occupation of John Marley, Marchant, is mortgaged to Mr. John Claveringe of Newcastle upon Tyne aforesaid, Marchant, for the payment of one hundred and forty poundes of lawful money of England, which the said Mr. Clavering is contented to accept of at any time within the space of two yeares next comying after Martinmas next ensuing as by note under his hand appeareth, my will and mynd is that Henry Barker, my eldest son, shall have the selling and disposing of the said house either to Mr. Claveringe or others, and that the money for which the house shall be sold for over and above the hundred and forty pounds to Mr. Clavering shall redown and be to the use and behoof of the said Henry Barker, which I freely give unto him in full satisfacon of his porcon. I doe give unto my daughter, Jane Barker, all my lynnen and nappery. I doe give unto my children, Jane Barker, Robert Barker, Isaack Barker, George Barker, and William Barker, all my goods and chattells whatsoever. I shall dye possessed of, equally to be devyded amongst them, my debts and funerall being paid for of the same. And I intreat my kind friendes, hereafter named, to take my children and to see them to be educated as they shall think meat and convenient. First I intreat Mr. Christopher Mitford, my loveing Brother-in-law, to see my sonne, George Barker, to be well educated, and to my good Brother-in-law, Mr. Henry Maddison, my sone, Willm. Barker. To my very good friend, Mr. John Clavering, my sonne Isaac Barker, and to my kynd Brother in law Mr. Charles Mitford, my sone Robert Barker, and I doe ordayne my said kind Brother in law Mr. Charles Mitford my sole executor of this my last Will and Testament, renouncing all wills made by me heretofore made. Witnesses, Henry Maddison, Charles Mitford, W. Vincent, Tho. Watson, No. Pub. Proved, 8 July, 1622.

bapt., 5 May, 1573, of Elizabeth, bapt., 17 Oct.. 1574 (mar. 14 May, 1594, Henry Maddison), of Abraham, bapt., 10 Mch., 1575/6, and of Susan, bapt, 21 July, 1577, bur. 13 Feb., 1577/8. By the fourth wife, Margaret, dau. of John Hudson (bapt., 25 June. 1559, mar.. 14 July, 1578, bur., 6 Oct., 1588), he had Susan (mentioned in her father's will, and mar. 15 July, 1595, to Cuthbert Bewick), Jane, bapt.. 14 Apl., 1580, Robert, bapt., 11 Mch., 1581/2, Sarah, bapt., 28 Mch., and bur., 26 Aug., 1584, Isaac, bapt., 25 June, 1585 (devisee, 14 July, 1650, of his sister Elizabeth Maddison), Sarah, bapt., 27 Dec., 1586, Isabel, bur., 2 July, 1587. Abraham Barker was bur., 10 Sept., 1621. By his wife, Agnes, dau. of Henry Mitford (mar., 15 Aug., 1597, bur.. 16 Oct., 1616) he had issue—Jane, bapt., 13 Jan., 1598/9. mar., 21 Feb., 1625/6, William Marley; Henry, bapt., 16 Nov., 1600, apprenticed, 20 June, 1620, with the Drapers Company of London, bur., 26 Jan., 1629/30; Robert, bapt., 26 June, 1605; Isaac, bapt., 16 Oct., 1609 (his wife, Grace, was bur. 8 Nov., 1645); George, bapt., 14 July, 1612; William. bapt., 5 Sept., 1613; Thomas, bur., 1 July, 1609; John, bur., 5 July, 1609.

THOMAS FORCER.[1]

Nov. 16, 1621. In the name of God, Amen, I, Thomas
Forcer, of Harbourhouse, and in the Dioces of Durham, esquire,
sick in body. . . . I give and bequeath to Peter Forcer, my sonne,
two tables, a counter, two longesettles, two chaires, and a pare of
iron barrs standing and being in the Hall. Also two table
boordes, three hoggesheades, three great barrells, and the gantrees whereon they lye and stande togither with a saife for to lye
cold meate in, being in the buttry. Also a great Iron Chimney,
two reckons, a paire of great Iron ropes, two little table ˙boordes,
a caull, a form, a stone morter, and a salt tubb, being in the
kitchen. Also a brewing leade, a maskfatt, a guylefatt, a cooler,
and all other thinges belonging to brewing, being in the brew
house. All which above recited household stuff or heire loomes
my true will entent and meaninge is, that my loving and ˙kynd
wyfe, Margarett Forcer, shall have the use and occupacon of them
during her naturall lyfe, and then to remayne to my aforesaid
sonne, Peter Forcer, and his heires for ever. Also I give and
bequeathe to my servante, Ralph Littlefer, one cottage howse
with the appurtenances in towne of Kellow whensever it shall fall
after the decease of any of my tennantes in towne of Kellowe
aforesaid, during the life natural of the said Raiphe Littlefer,
the said Raiphe Littlefer payeing yearly for the same the annutient
and yearly rent of 6s. 8d. at the dayes and tymes accustomed for
the same. Also I give and bequeath unto my sister, Ellen Forcer,
the sum of 20s. I give to my wyves sister, Dorothy Trollopp,
20s. I give to Francis Forcer, my grandchild, 20s. To Barbery
Hartburne (wyfe of Richard Hartburne), my daughter, 20l. I
give to Mr. Robert Andersone, of Newcastle, 20s. I give to Mr
William Hutton, of the Garth, 20s. To my daughter, Ellen
Forcer, all the residue of my goodes, moveable and unmoveable,
or the value thereof (my debts, legacies, funerall expences, and
my wyves third part payed and deducted), immediately after the
decease of my foresayd loving wyfe, Margarett Forcer, and in
the meantime my true will entent and meaning is, that my aforesaid loveing wyfe, Margarett, shall have the use and occupacon
thereof. And I make the aforesayd Robert Andersonne and
William Hutton, gentlemen, executors of this my last Will and
Testament, and I make Sir John Claxton, of Nettlesworth, Knight,
and John Trollopp, of Thornley, Esquire, supervisors thereof.

[1] He was the son of John Forcer of Kelloe by his wife Mary, dau.
of Christopher Carr of Sherburn House, he mar. Margaret (whose *Inq.
per br. de mand.* was taken at Durham, 9 Nov., 1636), dau. of Francis,
Trollop of Eden; by her he had, perhaps with other issue, John, Francis,
Anthony and Peter (age 25 at the *Inq. p.m.* of his father taken at
Durham, 27 April, 1622), whose will is printed in this vol., Eleanor and
Ursula, wife of Cuthbert Collingwood of Thornton, Northumberland.

Debts which I am indebted and oweing. To John Woodmasse, of towne Kellow, 22*l.* 10*s.* To George Littlefer, 9*l.* 8*s.* To Charles Fletcher, of Chester, 10*l.* To Robert Allen, of Towne Kelloe, 5*l.* To . . . Dand, of towne Kellow, 4*l.* To Robert Colsonne, 40*s.* To Cuthbert Collingwood, 40*s.* To Nicholas Whitfield, 39*s.* Witnesses, Robert Pannell, John Hallyman, George Forcer. Proved, 1636.

WILLIAM TROTTER.[1]

May 10, 1622. I, William Trotter, the elder, of Mydle Merrington, alias Mydlestone, in the Countye of Durham, gentleman, of great age and sickleye of bodye. My bodye to the grounde to be buryed accordinge as allreadye I have appointed in the estate of my lande by me made and passed to my sonne and heire, Anthony Trotter, of Helmden, in the County of Durham, gentleman. And for my worldeley goods being onely sixteene pounds, reserved 10 for my selfe to give by will or otherwise at my death or before, I thus dispose, further I give and bequeath to my loveing frende and neygbour, Mr. Cuthbert Wells, at Kirkmerington, who hath taken much paines to visitt and exhort me, the some of 10*s.* To my daughter, Elizabeth Trotter, 6*l.* I allso give and bequeith to my sonne, Willm. Trotter, the sum of 40*s.* Also I give to my granndchilde, Thomas Pilkinton, 20*s.* To my granndchilde, Leonard Pilkinton, 20*s.* To my granndchilde, Elizabeth Pilkinton, 20*s.*, and to my grandchilde, Ann Pilkanson, 20*s.* Also I give and bequeathe to Henrye Trotter, my grandchilde, son to Anthony Trotter, 10*s.* The reste of the sayd sixteene poundes, not hereinbefore bequeathed, I do give and bequeath unto my sayd daughter, Elizabeth Trotter, as allso the disposeing of such parcell of same as shalbe dewe to the daye of deathe for my table and keepinge of this my last Wil! and Testament. Witnesses, Ra. Greene, clarke, John Richardson, Ralphe Lockson.

[1] He was the son of Christopher Trotter, by his wife Jane, dau. of Thomas Harper of Helmeden; he mar. Catherine, dau. of Robert Sanders (she was bur., 24 Dec., 1620), 2 June, 1573; they had issue, Anthony (aged 46 at the *Inq. p.m.* of his father taken at Durham, 17 June, 1623), bapt., 20 Apl., 1576, bur., 8 Feb., 1639/40, mar. Gertrude (bapt., 26 Mch., 1599), dau. of William Wren, 21 Apl., 1618; William, bur., 2 Feb., 1624/5; Oliver, bapt., 21 July, 1574; Anne, mar. Joseph Pilkington (he was bur. at Durham Cathedral, 12 Feb., 1622/3); Elizabeth, bapt., 18 Dec., 1580, mar. Robert Sickeraham of Whitworth Anthony's son Henry was bapt., 28 Feb., 1618/19, and bur., 17 July, 1645. The testator was bur., 10 Feb., 1622/3. All dates are from St. Andrew's, Auckland, except when otherwise stated, see his brother's will hereafter.

JOHN HEDWORTH.[1]

Memorandum that John Hedworth, of Durham, Esquire, deceased, who dyed in the month of June last, 1622, being then of the age of 80 yeares or thereabouts, sick and weak in bodye but of a very perfect mynde and memory, about eight or tenn dayes before his death with full purpose and intent to make and declare his last will and testament to the effect followinge. After some speeches with Sir John Hedworth, of Harraton, Knight, his kinsmann then present aboute two hundred and odd pounds, wich the said Sir John Hedworth was indebted unto him and of other things by him the said John Hedworth, Esqr, formerly intended to the said Sir John Hedworth, the said Sir John Hedworth then desired the said John Hedworth, now deceased, to declare his last will and testament and mynd concerning the said two hundred and odd pounds after his death, whereupon the said John Hedworth, Esqr., with full mynd and intent to make and declare his last Will and Testament concerning the things followinge, said as follows, Sir John for the money you owe me there shall none trouble you for it after my death for I will give you the same freelye. I also give you freelye this house where in I dwell to you and your heeres for ever, desiring you that you will not sell it. I also give to you and your Ladie the great brass pott which was bought att Horden.

Witnesses hereof, John Lamb, Alice Hedworth and Margaret Neles.

FRANCIS BURRELL.[2]

June 18, 1622. Francis Burrell, of Newcastle on Tyne, Merchant and Alderman. To be buried within the parish church of All Saints, Newcastle upon Tyne, so neare unto my late father, Ralph Burrell, as possible. To the poore of All Saints parish, 20s. I give for the repairing of All Saints Church, 40s. To my sonne, Tymothie Burrell, all my burgage or tenemente wherein I lately dwelt, situate on the Tyne Brigg, with the heirloomes and implements within the said burgage, and in default of issue of the said Tymothie, to my sone Thomas Burrell, and his heirs, and failure of issue to my sone Peter Burrell, and in case of

[1] Son of Anthony Hedworth of Jarrow by his wife Cecily, dau. of Alexander Heron of Meldon, Northumberland; bur., 27 June, 1622, at St. Mary-le-Bow, Durham.

[2] He was apprenticed to Henry Chapman, 26 May, 1577; his first wife, Margaret, was bur. at All Saints, Newcastle, 22 Jan., 1606/7; he mar., secondly, at St. Nich., 2 Feb., 1607/8, Jane, dau. of Christopher Mitford; she was bapt., 10 Sept., 1592, at St. Nich., and re-mar., 22 Aug., 1626, at St. Nich., Ralph Carnaby of Halton. The testator was bur. at All Saints, 15 May, 1624; by his first wife he had issue, Henry, bapt., 29 Sept., 1588, his godparents being, Mr. Henry Anderson, merchant and alderman, Mr. Henry Chapman, merchant and alderman, and Sicila Umphrey being the grandmother, at St. Nich. (where his brothers and sisters were also bapt.), Oswald, bapt., 27 Nov., 1590, Francis, bapt.,

failure of issue to my sone, George Burrell. To my sone, Thomas
Burrell, my burgage·or tenements and shopps situate in Newcastle
aforesaid in the Side (nowe or late in the occupation of Dorothy
Oagle, widow), together with the heirlooms in the said burgage,
and his heirs, and failing issue to my sone Tymothie Burrell,
and failure of issue to my sonns Peter Burrell and George
Burrell. To my sone George Burrell, all that my burgage or
tenement which I lately purchased of William Heeley, situate in
the Broad chaire, now in the occupation of Peter Rand, slaitor.
To my sone Peter Burrell, my house or tenement, situate in the
Castle Moote, for the terme wherein I hold the same. To my now
wife Jane Burrell, my burgage or tenement wherein I now dwell,
situate within the street called the close, in Newcastle on Tyne,
during her natural life, and after her decease to my sone George
Burrell and his heirs. To my sone Henry Burrell, 20*l.* in monie,
which shall be unto him in full satisfaction of his filial portion.
To my said sone Thomas Burrell, 100 marks in money, and
to the said Tymothie Burrell, three score pounds, thirteen shillings and fourpence. To my said sone Tymothie Burrell, my best
signett which weythe eight angles. To my sone Peter Burrell, my
signett which hath a stone fixed therein. To my said sone
George Burrell, one signett which hath the Burrells armes ingraven thereupon. To my daughter Ellinor Burrell, 200 marks.
To my daughter Rebecka Burrell, 200 marks in monie. My
said wife, Jane Burrell, to have the tuition and education of my
said two Daughters with their portions, and to my wife I also
give my great guylte salte, and my will is that she shall sell my
redd skarlett gown to her most advantage. My will and mind
is that my brother in law, Barthram Mitford, shall have the
tuition and education of my son, Peter Burrell, and I bequeath
unto the said Barthram, as a token, one Angell. I give unto my
said sone Tymothie Burrell my best cloake faced with velvett.
All the residue of my apparell I give unto my sone Henry
Burrell. To my two cousins, James Burrell and Thomas Burrell,
two Angells a peece. To Dorothy Wilson, two angells, as a token.
To Francis Coulson, my sister's sone, one angel of gold, as a
token. I nominate Sir Henry Anderson, Knight, Mr. Henrye
Chapman, the elder, merchant and alderman, and John Claveringe,
merchant, Supervisors of this my Will, entreating them to see
everything executed and performed for the benefit of my children,
according to the trust and confidence in them reposed. I do

16 Feb., 1596/7, William, bapt., 25 July, 1598, bur., 11 Nov. 1616, at All
Sts.; Thomas, bapt., 28 Oct, 1599; Timothy, bapt., 23 Jan., 1602/3, mar.
Jane Milburn, 10 May, 1621, and had issue; Francis, bapt., 22 Jan.,
1606/7, bur., 13 Mch., 1606/7 at All Saints, and Peter; the daughters
being Margt., bapt., 3 Oct., 1589, Alice, bapt., 21 Jan., 1592/3, Barbara
bapt., 30 May, 1594; and by his second wife, George, bapt., 16 May, 1613,
Ellinor, bapt., 1 May, 1609, Mary, bapt., 5 Dec., 1611, bur., 19 Sept.,
1614, at All Saints, and Rebecca, bapt., 19 Dec., 1616.

give to each one Angell of gold, as a token of my love towards them. I appoint my sonns Peter Burrell and George Burrell Executors. Witnesses, John Mitford, Mark Orde, Christofer Wallis, Anthonie Errington. INVENTORY amounted to, 532*l*. 16*s*. 2*d*. Probate, 1624.

THOMAS FENWICK.[1]

July 23, 1622. In the name of God, Amen, I, Thomas Fenwick, of the Town and Countie of Newcastle upon Tyne, yeoman, being at this instant sick in body yet whole in mynd, god be praised, and not knowing how long it shall please god I shall live in this mortal life, Doe therefor for the settling of my estate make this my last Will and Testament in maner and form following. First I give and bequeath my soule to almightie god and my bodye to the earth from whence it came, to be buried in the pish church of St. Nicholas, in Newcastle upon Tyne, and as touching my worldly goods, which the Lord in this lifetime has endewed me withall, I give and bequeath as followeth : First I give and bequeath unto my brother Rodger Fenwick his children lawfully begotten of his body my house in Denton Chaire wherein I doe dwell, and failing them to come unto my sister Margarie Merriman's children, Arthur, William, and James Mirryman, and failing them to come unto the neerest of unto me of the Fenwicks. I give and bequeath unto my brother Rodger Fenwick's children amongst them five poundes. I give and bequeath unto my cosene Robert Greenhead six poundes. I give and bequeath unto my cosine William Mirriman forty shillings, and forty shillings more oweing me upon a bill by William Reasley, yeoman. I give and bequeath unto my cossine Arthur Marriman, forty shillings. I give and bequeath to Jane Marriman the sum of fifteen pounds . . . . . . oweing unto me by Robert Jopling. I give and bequeath unto John Fenwicke, servante unto Sir George Selbie, forty shillings, being in the hands of Mr. Matthew Randall. I give and bequeath unto Mrs. Barbara Fenwick, her children, 40*s*. in the hand of Mr. William Jennison, Alderman. I give and bequeath unto my cosine, Garret Fenwicke, twenty shillings. I give and bequeath unto Robert Fenwicke, for a token, twenty shillings. I give and bequeath unto James Hall, foure shillings three pence. I give and bequeath unto Thomas Marley, hatter, twenty shillings, for a token. The rest and residue of all my goods and chattells, moveable and unmoveable whatsoever unbequeathed, my debts, legacies and funeral expences being first paid and discharged, I give and bequeath unto my cosine, James Merriman, whom I make my full and whole executor of this my last Will and Testament renouncing by thes psents all wills by me heretofore made.

[1] The testator was bur. at St. Nich., Newcastle, 25 July, 1622.

156

And I doe hereby pronounce this deed to be my last Will and Testament. Witnesses, Garret Fenwick, Thomas Marley, Robert Selbie, Thomas Stones.

INVENTORY, 83*l.* 5*s.* 0*d.* Proved, 8 Oct., 1622.

REYNOLD CHARLTON.

Dec. 13, 1622. Reynold Charlton, of the Newke, in the parish of Bellingham, and County of Northumberland, yeoman. I give and bequeathe my soule to Allmighie God, my maker and redeemer, and my bodie to be buried within the pish church of Bellingham. I give to my eldest son Gerrard Charlton, all my landes, groundes, houses between Liollscleugh, Studonburne, and Harshay, except six daies worke of meadow in Harshaye, and that I give to my son William Charlton. To my said son William Charlton, All my lande in the Wardelawe, the Mieles and the Buckshawe, the burnehouse rawe; and my lande in Readeswoode, for which Jasper Charlton is bonde, untill such time as the some of 8*l.* is paied for the same land in Readeswoode. To my sone, Thomas Charlton, one tenement or fearmeholde in Wark of the yearlie rent of 20*s.*, and a place called Milburneshaugh of the yearly rent of 12*d.* To my sone, John Charlton, one Tenement or farmehold in Warke of the yearly rent of 5*s.* two daies work of meadow in Warkes fieldhead, two daies work in the Dailes, and two daies worke of meadow without the Dyke. To my sone, Gerrard Charlton, two oxen, and to my sons, Thomas, John and William, each two oxen. To my son, Rowland Charlton, three oxen, six other beasts and tenn sheepe. To Thomison Stokoe, widow, my daughter, three oxen. To my daughter Beall fourteene head of sheepe. To my brother Ambrose Charlton one oxe. To my sister Belle foure yewes and a cowe. To William Robson eight sheepe and a scabd mare. To Alice Browne, one cowe and two ewes. To my sone Thomas Charlton fifteen sheepe hogges, two wheathers and a Ram. I give to my children all my corne to be devided amongst them. I make and ordein my brother Ambrose Charlton, and my sone Gerrard Charlton exors. Witnesses, William Robson, Percivall Dodd, Thomas Charlton. Debts owing to testator : Oswald Milburne, of the leame, 26*s.* John Milburne, of the leame, 18*s.* William Aynsley, of the leame, 2*s.* 8*d.* William Charlton, of the calfclose, 18*s.* Katherine Widdrington, wife of Benjamine Widdrington of Buteland, 6*s.* 4*d.* James Dodd, of Siddwoode, 10*s.* Robert Robson, of Autorhill, 8*s.* 6*d.* Matthew Jameson, for xiiii pecks of oates, 6*s.* Edward Charlton, als Tanner, 9*s.* Thos. Atkinson, of Moatehill, 4*s.* Jane Charlton, wife of John Charlton, of the Dales, 10*s.*, or else a bushell of Newcastle Rye. James Hogg of Readswoode, for oates, 12*s.*

INVENTORY amounted to, 46*l.* 11*s.* 6*d.* Probate, 21st January, 1622.

GEO. COLLINGWOOD.[1]

Dec. 21, 1622. In the name of god, Amen, I, Geo. Collingwood, of Brenkheugh, in the parish of Brenkburne, in the County of Northumberland, being sick in body but in good and pfect remembrance, thanks be to almightie god, do make this my last Will and Testament following. I give to Tho., my eldest sone, two severall bonds, the one from Tho. Robinson of 30*l.*, debt dew by Tho. Robinson, of Ewett, the other of 30*l.* dew by the heirs or executors of Charles Horsley and Robt. Horsley. I give to him more all my hard corne sown upon the ground and the graine dew to me for soweing and to be sown upon the ground and the seed to sow it with out of the corne in the garth and oatts, and the said Tho. my sonne to pay unto Robt. his brother when he comes out of his apprenticshipp, 6*l.* and 10*l.*, for the rent at Whitsuntide next, and he to maintain his mother with meate, drink and clothes, sufficiently during her lief. I give to Tho. my sonne, all my plowe and plowe geare, wane and wane geare, with implements belonging the same. The rest of my goods unbequeathed, my debts paide, funeralls discharged, I give to Mary my wife, whom I make my executrix of this my last Will and Testament. Witnesses hereof, Robt. Wilsone, Jo. Walker, and Gab. Kiplinge.

INVENTORY, 25*l.* 13*s.* 0*d.* Proved, 25th January, 1622.

THOMAS TROTTER.[2]

Dec. 27, 1622. In the name of God, Amen, I, Thomas Trotter, of the Eshes, in the pish of Wolsingham, in the County of Durham, gentle, sick in bodie but in hole in mynde and of good and pfect remembrance, thanks be god, do make, constitute and ordaine this my last Will and testament in mannor and forme followinge. My bodie to be buried in the pish of Wolsingham. I give to my wief, Marie Trotter, and to my sone, Thomas Trotter, one graye nagge. I give to my wief all my household stuff and implements whatsoever. I give to my sonne, Christopher Trotter,

[1] His wife's will is printed in this vol.

[2] He was son of Christopher Trotter of Helmedon by his wife, Jane, dau. of Thomas Harper of the same place; he mar. Mary, dau. of John Shafto of Tanfieldleigh (mentioned in her mother Mary's will, dated 14 Mch., 1594/5, printed in vol. 38, p. 249, of this Society's publications). Their son, Christopher, mar. Elizabeth Fawcett; Emanuel, matric sizar from Trinity College, Cambridge, Michs., 1608, B.A., 1611/12, Vicar of Kirknewton, Northumberland, 1614, father of Thomas adm sizar, aged 15, at St. John's College, Cambridge, 27 Sept., 1656, B.A., 1660/1, M.A., 1664, Curate of Escomb, Durham, 1662, Vicar of Eglingham, Northumberland, 1662 till his death, 26 Sept., 1685, and bur. there two days later. The testator's daus. were bapt. at St. Andrew's, Auckland, Ann, 28 Mch., 1573, Isabel, 27 Oct., 1577, and Alice, 29 June, 1580. In his *Inq. p.m.* taken at Durham, 26 Apl., 1623, Christopher, aged 40, was his son and next heir. See his brother's will above.

my Muskett furnished with sword and girdle. I give also to my sonne, Christopher Trotter, all my wood and tymber that is not sawen about my house or elsewhere. I give to Elizabeth Trotter, wife of my sonne Christopher Trotter, 6s. 8d. To Thomas Trotter, sonne to Christopher Trotter, one ewe and a lamb and my Lute. I give and bequeath to Ralph Trotter, Christopher Trotter, John Trotter and Emanull Trotter, sons of my sonne Christopher Trotter, every one of them a gimorr lambe. To my sonne Emanuel Trotter, one payre of stockings and my velvett capp. I give to the poore of Wolsingham pish, 10s. To my servant, Thomasine Carrocke, a gymor lamb. All the rest of my goodes as well moveable as unmoveable and unbequeathed, my debts, legacies, and funerall expences discharged, I give to my wyfe, Marye Trotter, Emanuel Trotter, and Thomas Trotter, my sonns, whom I make executors of this my last Will and Testament. Witnesses, John Scurfield, Robt. Watson.

INVENTORY, his purse and wearinge apparell, 6l. 6s. 4d. Howshold stuff of all sortes, 13l. 6s. 8d. A draught of oxen, 10l. Five kyne and fower qwhyes, 13l. Fower calves, 1l. 6s. 8d. Thirtie olde sheipe, 5l. 10s. A score of hogges, 2l. 6s. Hay, 1l. 10s. Corne on the earth, 1l. 10s. Tymber wood, 1l. 10s. Plough geare and waine geare, 1l. 10s. 3 bushells of bigg, 13s. A little horse, 1l. 13s. 4d. A musket furnished with Calleiver, 1l. 6s. 8d. Axes, chissells, wimbles and such like, 4s. Pultrie, 10s. Suma 62l. 2s. 8d.

MARY COLLINGWOOD.[1]

Jan. 3, 1622. In the name of god, Amen, I, Mary Collingwood, of Brenkheugh, in the parish of Brenkburne and county of Northumberland, wedowe, sick of bodye. All my goods and chattells, bills, bonds, dewe to my late husband, George Collingwood deceased, or my husband's, or owne whatsoever, I give to Robt. Collingwood my sonne and Lucy my daughter, whom I make Executors jointly of this my last Will and Testament. Witnesses hereof, Thomas Collingwood, Robt. Collingwood, John Whittall and Gab. Kipling, clark.

INVENTORY of goods of George Collingwood of Brenkheugh, gentleman, and Mary, his wife, praised at 25l. 13s. 0d.

ROBERT MILOTT.[2]

March 10, 1622. An Inventory of all such goodes and chattles, both moveable and unmoveable, which latelie did belong to Robert

[1] Her husband's will is printed in this vol.

[2] He was son of Ralph Millot of Whithill (bur., 12 July, 1587, at Chester-le-Street) by his wife, Agnes, dau. of Sir Thomas Tempest; he mar. Dorothy, dau. of Sir William Wray of Beamish, by whom he had issue, Ralph (will dated, 5 Dec, 1692), who mar. Dorothy, dau. of Sir

Milott, of Whithill, within the countie of Durham, Esqr, prised by Guy Bainbridge, Charles Porter, John Watson, and Richarde Hall.

Imprimis : 8 oxen att Whithill, 24*l*. Nyen Kyne there whereof one with a calfe and another elder calfe besides, 18*l*. Six meares and naggs there also, 10*l*. Fiftie weather sheepe and 4 ewe sheepe thereto also, 10*l*. 10*s*. Thre swyne, 13*s*. 4*d*. Five ganders and geese, 5*s*. Foureteene cocks and hens, 5*s*. One litle turkey, 12*d*. Foure ducks, 2*s*. Plowes and plowe geare with waynes and wayne geare with wodd implimts belonging unto husbandrie, 6*l*. Hard corne sowen on the grounde there also, 17*l*. Oates about the house, good and badd, 50*s*. Hay in all at Whithill, 5*l*. At Malande, six oxen, 12*l*. Fower stottrells there, 6*l*. Thre Quyes there, 4*l*. 10*s*. Thirty-eight olde sheepe there also, whereof about 35 ewes with lamb, 8*l*. 4*s*. 8*d*. Fortie hogg sheepe there, 5*l*. 6*s*. 8*d*. Five horses, younger and elder, 8*l*. 6*s*. 8*d*. Hay there also, 20*s*. Item, in the great Chamber at Whithill, Table, cupbords, chairs, stooles, carpett, clothes cupborde, clothes quishions, iron barrs, fire shovell, and tongs, forme, skevene, and picktrowes, 9*l*. Item, in the litle closett nere it, one litle cupbord 2*s*. 6*d*. Item, in the white chamber, stande bedd and truckle bedd with fetherbedds and furniture, chairs, stooles bason and ewer, lyverey cupbord, with carpett cover, quishions, hangings, iron barrs, fire shovell, and tongs, 13*l*. Item, in the Nurserie, one stande bed with two truckle bedd and furniture for servants, one great chist with one borde, litle iron barrs and tongs, 33*s*. 4*d*. Item, in the litle clossett adjoininge to it, candle, chists without candles, bottles, glasses and other necessaries and implemts of household in divers pticulars, 30*s*. Item, in the Parlor next the kitchen, one stande bedd and truckle bedd with there furnitures, cupborde, counter with a coveringe, chists, trunckes, chaire, iron barrs, tongs, with other necessarie implements and furniture of howsehold, 6*l*. 13*s*. 4*d*. Item, in the litle closett adjoininge to it, necessarie pticulars of howshold, 10*s*. Item, in the High Parlor, two stande bedds with furniture, table and coveringe, one wood chare, truncks, litle iron Barrs, fire shovell, tongs, and other necessarie implemts, 7*l*. 10*s*. Item, in the chamber adjoyning to it, one bedsteade with furniture, table and frame, and other howshold necessaries. Item, in the gallerie chamber and litle chamber adjoinying to it, one Cannaybie bedd with furniture, two litle iron chimney and porr chaires, stooles, table and old carpett, with some other necessaries of howshold, 50*s*. Item, in another litle chamber on the north of the gallerie, three truckle bedds with bedd clothes for servantes, 6*s*. 8*d*. Item, in the

William Bellasis of Morton House, born there, 22 Dec., 1623, bur. at Chester-le-Street, 25 Oct., 1708; Wiiliam, bur. at Chester-le-Street, 13 Jan., 1620/1; Elizabeth, who mar. Albert Hodshon of Lintz: Mary, Dorothy, Margaret, Joan and Winifred. The testator was bur. at Chester-le-Street, 26 Feb., 1622/3. In his *Inq. p.m.* taken at Durham, 12 Apl., 1623, Robert, aged 4, is his son and next heir.

Hall, tables and cupbords with coverings, chars, forms, stooles, quishions, iron barrs, porr firè shovell, and tongs, with other howsehold implements, 3*l*. 6*s*. 8*d*. The clocke remaineth to the heir without payment. Item, in the Kitchen, brasse and iron potts, panns, kettles, drippinge panns, iron barrs, iron rackes, speetes, jacke, crookes, galley-bawke, fire shovell, tongs, pot clipps, skimmers, laddles, broyling irons, graters, candlestickes, dishes, trenchers, and all other necessarie implementes of howshold there, 6*l*. 13*s*. 4*d*., the morter being fast, remainethe to the heire without payment. Item, in the Buttrie, hoggheads, barrells, brasse candlesticks, black jacks, breade, ark, forms and other necessarie implements of howshold. Item, in the milkhouse and larder, bowles, skeeles, butter kitts, kirne stands, tubbs. bords, shelves, and other wodd implements. Item, in the brewhouse, tubbs, barrells, bowlting trowe, moldeing bord, great bowl, watersey brewing leade, and other howshold necessarie there, 3*l*. 13*s*. 4*d*. Item, Lynne and harden yarne, 20*s*. Item, Damaske dyper and Lynning of all sorts whatsoever, 18*l*. Item, Silver plate in generall, 16*l*. Item, Pewther of all sorts in general, 5*l*. Item, his apparell and furniture of his bodie, 10*l*. Item, two gimes or bindinge peices, 26*s*. 8*d*. Item, coals wrought at Pitts and Staythe by estimation, 96*l*. 13*s*. 4*d*. Item. firdales about staythe and cole pitts in all, 53*s*. 4*d*. Item, one kele, 20*l*. Soma totalis, 379*l*. 16*s*. 2*d*.

April 12, 1623. Tuition of Elizabeth. Mary, Margaret, Jane, Dorothy, and Winefred, the lawful children of Robert Millot, Esqr., of Whittell parish, Chester, was assigned to Sir William Lambton and Thos. Wrey, Esq., 29 Mar., 1629, Tuition of Ralph son of Robert Millot, Esqr., of Whittell, was assigned to Robert Eden, gentleman.

ROBERT SHAFTO.[1]

Sept. 5, 1623. I, Robert Shafto, of the towne of Newcastle upon Tyne, Marchant and Alderman, being sick in body. My bodye to be buryed in St. Nicholas Church as neare the place where my father was buryed as convently may be. And as touching my lands, tenements, goodes and chattles, wherewith god hath blessed me, I doe give and dispose of them as followeth : To Marke Shafto, my sonne, my tenement in the Cloth markett in

[1] He was the son of Ninian Shafto, merchant of Newcastle (bur., 1 Dec., 1581, at St. Nich., Newcastle, from which registers the other dates are taken, unless otherwise stated), by his wife Anne, dau. of Henry Brandling; he mar. Jane, dau. of Robert Eden of Newcastle, 13 Jan., 1594/5, she was bur., 3 July, 1658. By her he had issue, Robert, bapt., 16 Dec., 1596, bur., 15 Nov., 1670, mar., 6 Apl., 1624, Jane, dau. of Bertram Anderson, bapt., 1 Nov., 1604, and bur., 14 Feb., 1671/2; Mark, bapt., 25 Apl., 1599, bur., 25 May, 1600; Christopher, bapt., 17 Oct., 1611, died about 1613; Mark, bapt., 25 Mch., 1601, matriculated

Newcastle aforesaid, in the occupation of Georg Swane, to him
the said Marke Shafto and his heires males of his bodye lawfully
to be begotton, and for defalt of such issue to my sonne, Nynian
Shaftoe, and the heires males of his bodye lawfully begotton, and
for defalt of such issue to Robert Shafto, my eldest sonne, and the
heires mailles of his bodye lawfully begotton, and for default of
such issue to the right heires of me the said Robert Shafto for
ever. I give unto Nynian Shafto my tenement by the Key side in
Newcastle aforesaid in the occupation of Samuel Rawley and
Isabell Harrison, with all the new buildings built by me their
this year, together with the moitie of a close at Gaitshead, in the
County of Durham, now in the occupation of Ralph Coolle, and the
moitie of a tenement scituate next the new gait in Newcastle
aforesaid, and the moitie of a tenement lyeing on the west sid of
a close ptaining and belonging to Antho. Swinborne, in the
County of Newcastle aforesaid called by some Hopes house and to
the heires mailles of the said Nynian Shafto lawfully to be begotton, and for default of such issue to my sonne, Marke Shafto,
and to heires mailles of his bodye lawfully to be begotton, and for
default of such issue to the said Robert Shafto, my sonne, and to
the heires mailles of his body lawfully begotton, and for default
of such issue to the right heires of me the said Robert Shafto for
ever. I give and bequeath unto my sonne Robert Shafto, the
lease estate and terme of years which I have of a capitall messuage
and tower with all the lands their unto belonging lyeing in
Benwell, in the County of Northumd, nevertheless upon this con-
dison that he said Robert, my sonne, do within Twentie daies
after my death demise and grant by his Indenture under his
hande and seall the said capittal messuage, tower and the lands
their unto belonging to Jane Shafto, my wife, for 28 years if she

pens. at St. John's College, Cambridge, 1616, B.A., 1619/20, admitted
to Gray's Inn, 3 Aug., 1619, Barrister at Law, 1636, Recorder of Newcastle, 1648, M.P. for Newcastle, 1659, died, 25 Feb., 1659/60, mar. at
All Saints', Newcastle, 7 Feb., 1630/1, Mary, dau. of Robert Ledger,
from whom descend the Shaftos of Whitworth; Ninian, bapt., 25 Nov.,
1604, apprenticed to the Drapers' Company, London, 16 Nov., 1622,
bur., 25 Mch., 1647, mar, at All Saints', 1 May, 1627, Jane, dau. of
Leonard Carr, bapt., 31 Dec., 1609, at All Saints', where she was bur.,
5 Mch., 1678/9; Eden, bapt., 7 Dec., 1595, bur., 8 Mch., 1627/8, mar. at
All Saints', 18 Dec., 1613, Anthony Metcalf; Anne, bapt., 8 Jan., 1597/8,
bur., 18 Nov., 1673, mar., firstly, Robert Tempest, and secondly, 8 Sept.,
1618, John Clavering of Axwell, bapt., 2 Dec., 1591, bur., 6 May, 1648;
Dorcas, bapt., 18 July, 1602, bur., 19 Feb., 1626/7, mar., 1 June, 1619,
Henry Cock of Newcastle (bur., 20 Sept., 1642, he mar., secondly,
Isabel, dau. of Ralph Cole of Gateshead, bapt., 7 Apl., 1611, at Gates-
head, mar. there, 17 June, 1628, bur., 2 Aug., 1639); Mary, bapt., 25
Aug., 1608, bur., 28 Feb., 1609/10; Alice, bapt., 8 Oct., 1609, at All
Saints', mar., 13 Apl., 1630, John Emerson; Isabel, bapt., 10 Apl., 1615,
mar., 16 Jan., 1631/2, Abraham Booth. The testator was bur., 12 Sept.,
1623, his sister Margaret bur. at All Saints', 1 July, 1634, mar. Andrew
Gofton, who was also bur. there, 25 Nov., 1631.

the said Jane Shafto so long live, and concerning the residue of
my lands and tenements in Benwell aforesaid, whereof I am seised
of an estate of Inherritance, my will and meaning is that they
shall descend and come to my sonne, Robert Shafto, and his
heirs according as they should have desended and come
according to the course of the common Law and not otherwise.
I give and bequeath my house in Newcastle aforesaid wherein I
now dwell to my sonne, Robert Shafto, and to his heires mailles
of his bodye lawfully begotton, and for default of such issue to
the said Nynian Shafto and his heires mailles of his body
lawfully begotton, and for default of such issue to the right
heirs of me the said Robert Shafto for ever. Provided nevertheless and my will and meaning is that the said Jane, my wife,
shall have the use and occupation of the moietie of my said
dwellinghouse, she dwelling therein. And concerning my lease,
interest and tearme of yeares of a certain part of Coole mynes
in Gaitsid and Whickham, in the County of Durham, called and
known by the name of the grand lease, and my leases and interest
and tearme of yeares in other coalle mynes in the said County
of Durham and Northumbd, I give and bequeath them to my sonne
Robert Shafto, nevertheless upon this condicon that he, the said
Robert Shafto, within twenty days of my death do, by Indenture
under his hand and seale, demise the moitie or half part of my
part in all the said colle mynes saveing in the colle mynes of
Benwell to my wief Jane Shafto, for the term of yeares or so
long as she shall live, and of the moietie of my part of the colle
mynes in Benwell to my said wife for so manie years as I, the
said Robert Shafto, have theirin if the said Jane soe long live.
The residue of all my goods and chattels unbequeathed, my
legacis and debts paid, I give to Jane, my wife, and my said
sonne Robert, equallie betwixt them, saveing that my wife Jane,
shall have over and above her moietie all my lynen and a Dubble
gilt cuppe and a paire of Redd grogren courttens with the furniture. I give unto Mark Shafto, my sonne, one Annuitie of 40l. a
yeare, and to my daughter, Edone Mitcalfe, 10l. a yeare, and if
my said sonne Robert, shall not convey and assure the said severall
annuities as aforesaid that then he shall not take the benefit of
this my Will. My will and meaning is that the said Jane, my
wife, shall have the some of 120l. in money paid her for a
legacye over and over the part of my goods I give, and my
meaning is that my said wife and my sonne Robert, doe paie
unto my sonne Mark Shafto at the end of three yeares, the
some of 100l., and to my sonne Nynian Shaftoe at the end of
his apprenticeshipp, 200l. To my daughter Allis Shafto, when
she attaine the age of 17 years or be married, the some 300l.,
and to my daughter Isabel Shafto, when she attaine the age of
15 yeares, the some of 300l., and if my said sonns and daughter
die before attaining their several yeares, the money remaine to

163

my children surviving equally amongst them. To Jane Metcalfe, daughter to Edone Metcalfe, 50*l.*, and to Ane Mitcalfe, daughter to the said Edon, 50*l.*, when they attain the several yeares of 17 yeares or marrye. I give unto Jane Kirkley, daughter of Mychell Kirkley, Twoe peaces. To my sonne in law, Antho. Metcalfe, and his wife, 100*l.*, and unto my daughter, Dorcas Cocke, 30*l.* I give unto James Clavering, Robt. Clavering, John Clavering, and William Clavering, sonns of my daughter Ann Clavering, 10*l.* each. To William Cocke, son of Henry Cocke, 10*l.* I give unto my sister, Margrett Goften, 3*l.* 6*s.* 8*d.*, and unto Allis Isle, Two peaces. To Isbell Harrison, three peaces. To William Edon, John Edon, Henry Edone, Abraham Edone, and Tobyas Edon, to each of them an angell of gould, as a token. To Martha Patrickson and Sara Edon, an angell of gould, as a token. To Margrett Edon and Barbary Anderson, my servants, 10*s.*, and to every other of my servants, 5*s.* And I doe make my wellbeloved wife, Jane Shafto, and my sonne Robert Shafto my executors of this my last Will and Testament, and my will and desire is That if any question or doubt shallbe maid between my aforesaid children about the meaninge of any part of this my said Will, That they doe stand to and abide the sentence and exposition of Sir Thomas Ryddell, Knight, John Clavering and Henry Cocke, my sonns in lawe, or any two of them. And I give to everie of them a peace for a token. I give 40*s.* to the poore to be distributed att my buriall. In witness whereof I have sett to my hand the daye and yeare above written. Witnesses, John Clavering, Thomas Maddison, William Browne. Proved, 1623.

RALPH GRAY.[1]

Sept. 5, 1623. Ralph Gray, of Chillingham, in the County of Northumberland, Knight. To be buried in the Quire of Chillingham Chancell. I give and bequeath unto my son, John Graye, Bradforth, with all things thereunto belonging, together with Burton, the tithe corne of Sunderland, the house at Barwick, and the fishing of Sanstell and Blayikwell in Twede. To my sonne,

[1] He was the son of Sir Ralph Grey of Chillingham, who died there, 17 Dec., 1565, by his wife, Isabel, dau. of Sir Thomas Grey of Horton. He mar., firstly, Jane, dau. of William Arthington of Arthington, co. York; by her he had issue, William, created a Baronet, 1619, Lord Grey of Warke, 1623, died, 29 July, 1674, bur. at Epping, he mar., firstly, Anne, dau. of Sir John Wentworth of Gosfield, co. Essex, and secondly, Priscilla; Ralph, adm. Fell. Com., at Christ's College, Cambridge, 23 June, 1618, bur. at Great St. Mary, Cambridge, 16 July, the same year; John, matric. Fell. Com., from Christ's College, Cambridge, Lent, 1618/19, resided till 1621, probably admitted at Gray's Inn, 6 Aug., 1621, Coronel in the Parliamentary army, (administration, 10 April, 1647) of Bradforth, after of Bamburgh, slain in Ireland, mar.

Robert Graye, all my lands, tenements and hereditaments at Little Langton upon Swale, within the Countie of York, according as the same is expressed in a certain Deed alreadie written. To my sonne, Edward Graye, all my lands and tenements of Ulgham Grange and Nunakirke, in the Countie of Northumberland, according as the same is expressed in a certain Deed alreadie written and done. To my two daughters, Dorothy Graye and Martha Graye, in satisfaction of their portions, and to raise their portions out of my lands of Ross and Elicke for and duringe the space of twenty one years. To my servante, John Clarke, 7*l*. yearly during his life. To my servante, William Coutte, 5*l*. yearly. To my servant, George Graye, 4*l*. yearly and his farmhold in Fenton during his life. To my wife, Dorothy Graye, her jointure alreadie known and expressed as Harton, East and West Chivington in Northumberland. To my servant, Marie Strother, 7*l*. a year for life. To my servant, Marie Turner, 10*l*. a year for life. To my servant, Arch. Armstrong, 4*l*. yearly for life. I will that Luke Kirklin shall have his wages. I will that my eldest son, Sir William Graye, shall perfect all thees, for I do give and comitt all whatsoever I have to the disposing of my said sonne, Sir William Graye. Witnesses, John Graye, Charles Oxley, Am. Oxley, John Elwicke, William Coutte. Probate, 1623.

THOMAS DANBY.[1]

Sept. 8, 1623. In the name of God, Amen, I,. Thomas Danby, of Great Leak, in the County of York, Esqr.. being sick in body. My body to be buried in my quire of the pishe church of Leake. I doe give unto my grandchilde, Thomas Metcalfe, ten

Mary Orde; Katherine, mar. Matthew Forster of Edderston; Isabel. mar. Anthony Catterick of Stanwick, co. York; Margaret, mar. Edmund Robson of Littlehoughton; Margaret; Dorothy of Berwick; Elizabeth, mar. Sir Francis Brandling of Alnwick Abbey, mar. articles, 18 May, 1618; Margery. By his second wife Dorothy, dau. of Sir Thomas Mallet of Enmore, and wid. of Sir Thomas Palmer he had issue, Robert Grey, adm. Fell. Com. (age 17), at Christ's Coll., Cambridge, 25 May, 1626 B.A., 1627/8, M.A., 1631, B.D., 1638, D.D., 1660, R. of Mashbury, Essex, 1637-43, Preb. of Durham, 1643, Rector of Bishopwearmouth, 1652, ejected, and restored, 1661-1704, bur. there, 13 July, 1704, aged 94; Edward, adm. Fell. Com. (age 15) at Christ's Coll., Cambridge, 25 May, 1626, B.A., 1627/8, adm. at Gray's Inn, 5 Aug., 1629, of Nunnykirk; Martha.

[1] He was the son of James Danby of Braworth; he mar. Ann, dau. of Ralph Anger; by her he had issue, Thomas, aged 23 in 1612, mar. Eliz., dau. of Christopher Carrus of Halghton, co. Lancs.; Miles; John, mar. Dorothy Davile, wid. of Otterington; William, died unmar.; Francis; Edmund of Burroughby, co. York; Elizabeth, wife of Michaell Metcalfe of Little Otterington; Jane, wife of Thomas Middleton of Middleton in Cleveland; Mary, wife of Thomas Appleby of Great Smeaton, co. York.

pounds of currant English money, to be paid unto him when my wife canne conventlie. I give two parts of the copyhold lands and tenemts which I pass unto my cosen, William Graunt, of Pickhall, after my decease unto my sonns, Francis Danby and Edward Danby, and the longer liver of them and their heires, and for want of heires of their bodyes to my son, John Danby, and his right heires, and for the third part of the said lands and tenements I likewise desire my cosen Graunt to surrender it unto my son John Danby and his heeres. I give unto my sone John Danby, after my death, my lease of three parts of Borrowby Milne which I hold of the Reverend Father Richard, bushop of Durham, to him and his heires for ever. I give unto my sonne in law, Michaell Metcalfe, of North Otterington, and his heires All my estate right title and interest of those lands in Thriske, which came unto me by discent from my brother Miles Danby of Braworth. The residue of all my goods and chattells undisposed I give unto Christopher Biarley, of Midridge, in the County of Durham, Esqr., after my debts, legacies, and funerall discharged, whom I make sole Executor of this my last Will and Testament, for whose paines I give three twenty shillings peeces of gold as a remembrance. Witness, Thomas Smith.

SIR HENRY WIDDRINGTON.[1]

Sept. 20, 1623. Widdrington, Henry, Sir, of Widdrington, Knight, In the name of God, Amen, and first, whereas I have maid an estate to my daughter Riddell, before her marriage, of the manor of Ditchburne and the towne of Charlton and of all the lands and tenements and hereditaments thereunto belonging in satisfaction of her portion, but after wards, I agreeing with Sir Thomas Riddalle, to give in marriage with my said

---

[1] He was the son of Edward Widdrington of Great Swinburn, by his wife Ursula, dau. of Sir Reginald Carnaby of Haughton. He mar. Mary, dau. of Sir Nicholas Curwen of Workington Hall, Cumberland, and had issue, William, aged 13 years, 1 month and 24 days at the time of his father's death, created 1st Lord Widdrington, 10 Nov., 1643, mar., 10 Jan., 1629/30, at Blankney, co. Lincoln, Mary, dau. of Sir Anthony Thorold of that place (she was bur., 20 Jan., 1675/6), he was slain at Wigan, 3 Sept., 1651; Katharine, bur. at St. Nich., Newcastle, 21 Aug., 1658, mar. Sir William Riddell of Gateshead, of Univ. Coll., Oxford, matric., 2 Dec., 1614, of Lincoln's Inn, 1623, bur., 21 Jan., 1624/5, at St. Nich., Newcastle; Margaret; Annas (perhaps wife of Sir Nicholas Thornton of Netherwitton); Ursula, will dated 18 July, 1644, wife of Sir Charles Howard, fourth son of Lord William Howard of Naworth, Cumberland; Marv. second wife of Sir Francis Howard of Corby Castle, Cumberland; Elizabeth; others died young.

daughter to his sone the sume of 1,000*l*., my will is that my sone
Riddalle, and my daughter his wife, shall convey and assure the
said manor of Ditchburne and towne of Charlton to my daughter
Elizabeth, in full satisfaction of her portion which I make no
doubt but my sone and daughter will willingly do as was ment and
intended to be done for as much as now the estate they have was
but in trust for my daughter Elizabeth. Item, whereas I have
maid two leases the one of Haughton, Holmeshawe and Haughton
greene, the other of Swinburne, Collwell, Towland, for tenn years
to four of my daughters that is to say:—Margarett, Dorothy,
Annas and Urseley; my daughter Mary, her name being forgot
to be mentioned in the said leases, yett for that it was my full
intent and meaninge that my said daughter Mary shall have her
equall shaire and portion in these leases they being allready sealed
and delivered as my deed, my will and meaning is that my said
daughter Mary her portion shall be maid equall with the other
of her said sisters out my said personal estate of goods and
chattels and creditts, that is to say, that the pfitt of the leases
being divided in four parts my daughter Mary, have as much
out of my goods and psonall estate as will make her as good a
portion as any of my said four daughters have out of the fore
mentioned leases, and if my personal estate of goods and chattels
shall amount to more then to make her portion equal with the
rest, then the overplus thereof to be equally divided in five parts
amongst my said five daughters, Mary, Margarett, Dorothy,
Annas, Ursaly. Whereas the estate of the Manor in Newcastle
is in Sir Nicholas Tempest of Newcastle, Knight, my will is
that the said Sir Nicholas Tempest shall sell the same and the
monies thereof cominge shall be equally divided amongst my
said five daughters, and if he cannot sell it, then my will is that
the same be by him assured and conveyed unto my said five
daughters and their heirs for ever. And I make my said five
daughters, viz., Mary, Margaret. Dorothy, Annas, and Ursaley,
Executors of this my Will and commit the tuition of them to my
brother, Roger, to be brought up and remayne with him and to
see this my will performed and putt in trust my loving friends
Sir Henry Curwen, Sir John Fenwick, and Sir William Lampton,
Knight, and my son-in-law William Riddall, and my brother
Roger Widdrington, and my will is further that if any of my
said five daughters shall die before they marrie or come to yeares
to be able to dispose of their owne portion and do not dispose of the
same, that then the portion of such so dying shall come and inure
to the rest of the said five sisters surviving. Witnesses, Luke
Midford, George Riddell. Debts oweing by Sir Henry Widdrington at the hour of this death : To my Lord Carrie of Leppington
for one halfe yeares rent of Widdrington, 150*l*. The like for
another half yeares rent which did grow due the Christmas after

his death, 150*l.* To the said Lo. Carrie for goods which he entered unto at his takeing of Widdrington, 300*l.* To Sir Thomas Riddaile, Knight, 100*l.* To Sir George Selbie, Knight, 105*l.* To John Rushforde of Acklington, 110*l.* To George Dent of London, 68*l.* To William Hall, son to William Hall of Heppell, 500*l.* To William Hall of Newcastle, Merchant, 5*l.* 11*s.* 0*d.* Sume 1,488*l.* 11*s.* 0*d.* Debts-dew to Sir Henry Widdrington at the hour of his death : From John Ubank of Druridge. 22*l.* 10*s.* Gawin Marshall of Morpith, 8*l.* 17*s.* 4*d.* William Hixon of Fenwicke south shields, 3*l.* John Ogle of Bradford, 6*l.* Henry Johnson of Bothalle, clerk, 12*l.* Medcalfe, woolman, 20*l.* John Fletcher, woolman, 57*l.* James Wilson of Biggins, 27*l.* The sonne James Wilsone, 13*l.* 8*s.* 2*d.* Robert Lawson of Banridge and John Eales of Newton Underwood, 8*l.* 10*s.* Cuthbert Supett, 6*l.* 12*s.* 8*d.* Gawin Rotherford of Rutcherster, 10*l.* William Fenwick of Stainton and Robert Taylor of North Seaton, 9*l.* 10*s.* Gawin Ogle of Kertley and William Wilson of Bedlington, 2*l.* The said Gawin Ogle, 2*l.* 16*s.* 8*d.* John Harbotle, 10*l.* Mr. Robert Widdrington of Plassey, 360*l.* Robert Widdrington of Hauxley, 47*l.* Thomas Carnes of Westhall, in the Countie of Lanchester, Esqr., upon Bond, 10*l.* James Wilson of Biggins, Westmorland, oweing upon bond, 33*l.* 8*s.* 2*d.* Edward Willson and Richard Loansdaile of Kirbie Loandale, upon remainder of bond, 27*l.* Robert Lawson of Benridgg and John Eales of Newton Underwood Park, upon bond, 8*l.* 10*s.* Gawin Ogle of Kirtley and William Watson of Bedlington, upon bond, 2*l.* 16*s.* William Lawson of Soppett and William Pentlum of Phillip, Rowland Robson of Crookden, Robert Lumedon of Yoackhaugh, and George Pott of Harbotle, Andrew Bell of Phillip and Adam Bell, upon bond, for performing of covenants upon articles indented for deliverie of so much and so good stock as they received of great chattell and sheep from Sir Henry Widdrington as in the said indented articles appeareth or otherwise they are to pay in the sume of the value of the said stocke in monies, which is 300*l.* George Thirlwall of Rothbery, Richard Thirlwall of Thirlwall, and Robert Widdrington of Brenkburne, stand bound upon like bond for performance of like covenants for like stock received, valued and prized unto 428*l.* James Smith of Newbiggin, Spittle, and Thomas Railestone of Ellington, upon the remainder of a bond, 2*l.* 2*s.* 6*d.* Christopher Green of Stannington, 1*l.* 13*s.* 0*d.* Robert Readhead of Morpith, 2*l.* 9*s.* Ralph Milburne of Eshatt, 1*l.* 5*s.* Andrew Scott of Widdrington, 2*l.* 2*s.* 6*d.* Roger Willsone, Woleman, for woole sould but not delivered before the death of Sir Henry Widdrington, 225*l.* Sume totale, 1,670*l.* 11*s.* 0*d.* In apperell and linning belonginge to his back, 40*l.* Probate, 28 May, 1624.

JOHN MITTFORTH.[1]

Sept. 29, 1623. John Mittforth of Newcastle-on-Tyne, Marchant, To be buried in Saint George's porch in Saint Nicholas. I give and bequeath unto my sone, Robert Mittforth, this my now dwellinghouse standing upon the Sandhill, and also the lofts and sellers in Elenors chare, formerly in the possession of Cuthbert Bewicke, deceased. To the children of Cuthbert Bewick, late deceased, 150*l*. among them. I give unto my son, Robert Mittforth, a dwellinghouse in the side adjoining a house of Cuthbert Graye on the one side, and a house of Robert Wanlesse on the other, to him and his heirs, and failing heirs, to come to Bartram Mittforth and his sister, Jannie Burrell, and the heirs of their bodies. To my said sone, Robert Mittforth, one eight part of the Collyries of Whitborne now in Lease. I give unto Elizabeth Gray, the wife of Cuthbert Gray, laite deceased, 40*s*., for a token, and to Margaret Graye, 20*l*., for a tockene, and to Agnes Gray, hir daughter, 20*l*., and to the young daughters now livinge. To my cossen, William Graye, sone of Cuthbert Graye, 20*s*. piece, and to John Gray, his Brother, 20*s*., for a tockene. To my uncle, Edward Graye, 10*l*., and to his sone, Thomas, 11*s*. To my uncle, William Graie, 10*l*., upon condition that he do carrie himselfe desenttlie. To my uncle, Oswald Graye, 6*l*. To Jacobe Farnysides, 10*l*., and to his daughter, Margaret Farnyside, 10*l*., and to the other doughter, Marie Farnnyside, 5*l*. To my auntt, Anne Andersone, wife of Cuthbert Andersone, 4*l*., and to his daughter, Bessie Andersone, 6*l*. To Roberte Anderson, hir sonne, 11*s*. To my cossene, Bartrame Mittforth, 20*s*. To Mrs. Janne Burrell, 40*s*., and to hir daughter, Nellie, 11*s*. To my father-in-law, Mr. Robert Bewick, two and twentie shilling peace. To my mother in law, Mrs. Ellinor Bewicke. 20*s*. To my Brother, William, and his wife, to each, 11*s*. To my brother, Thomas Bewicke, 11*s*. To Barberie Bewick. 20*s*., and to his daughter, Sarrie Bewick, 20*s*. To John Bewicke, 20*s*., and to John Buttler and Janie, his wife, and to their children, everie one of them, 10*s*. To Isabell Care, 11*s*. To Bessie Graye, wife of Ralph Graye, 40*s*. To Anne

---

[1] He was the son of Robert Mitford (bur., 31 Aug., 1597, at St. Nich., Newcastle, whence all other dates are taken), by his wife Isabel, dau. of John Grey of Newcastle (mar., 17 Apl., 1592, and bur., 2 Apl., 1615). The testator was bapt., 30 June, 1594, bur., 5 Oct., 1623, mar. Jane, dau. of Robert Bewick, by his wife, Ellinor, dau. of William Huntley (bapt. 27 Jan., 1599/1600, mar., 25 Oct., 1620, bur., 18 Nov., 1621). Their only child, Robert, was bapt., 19 Nov., 1621 (his godparents being Mr. Robert Bewick, grandfather, William Gray, and Jane, wife of John Butler, merchant adventurer), and bur. 18 Apl., 1675; he mar. Elizabeth, dau. of Ralph Maddison of Newcastle, bapt., 7 Nov., 1622, her godparents were the Worshipful Mr. Lionel Maddison, alderman, Mrs. Elizabeth, wife of Mr. Henry Maddison, and Anne, wife of Mr. Alexander Davison; she was bur., 28 July, 1689.

Bowes, his Dowther, 10s. To Elinor Bowes, 10s. To Mr.
Preattcher, 4l., and to Mr. Alline, Preattcher, 20s. To Mr. Francis
Gray, 30s. To Mr. Shawe, Preattcher, 20s. To Mr. Redwell,
Pretcher, 20s. To Robert Graye, his wife and childrene, 10s.
To my servante, Ralphe Bancks, 5l. To Jane Pearsone, 5l. I
give all my worldie goods whatsoever unto Robert Mittforthe
my son, and the heirs of his bodie, and appoint him sole
Executor. For the education and upbringing of my sone, I do
grant him unto my father-in-lawe, Mr. Robt. Bewicke, with such
competent means for his maintence as shall be thought fit. I
constitute and ordaiɳe Supervisors of this my Will, Mr. Robert
Bewicke, Mr. Alexander Davison, Mr. Robert Jennisone, Leonard
Carre, and Edward Gray, hoping that they will se this my will
dewlie executed, as my trust is in them. Witnesses, John
Mallaburn, Henrye Hotun, Ralph Banks, Christopher Nicholson,
John Brasse, Ralph Gray. Probate, 14th October, 1623.

DOROTHY GRAY.[1]

Oct. 18, 1623. Dorothy Gray. To be buried in the Chancell
of Chillingham. I will that my daughter Katherine Palmer
and my daughter Martha Gray shall live together, and for this
I doe give and bequeath my daughter Martha Gray and her
portion to the tuition of the said Katherine, and fayling Mrs.
Katherine, I give her portion to the tuition of my sister Margrett
Hatch. My sone Robert Gray and my sone Edward Gray
with their portions into the tuition of Sir William Gray, and
the right reverend father in God, Richard, Lord Bishop of
Durham, and Sir Francis Brandling, Sir Edward Gray, Sir
Arthur and Sir Roger Gray. To my sone Peregrine Palmer
the land of Dunnington which was belonging unto me, in the
County of Sussex, which was given unto him by his father, Sir
Thomas Palmer. I will that the third of the goods due to me
and my executor be disposed of for the use of my aforesaid
children, Robert, Edward and Martha Gray. I desire and
humbly entreate that if there be any withstanding of my thirds
or other portions due to me, that my Lord of Durham be pleased
to patronage their right and to be a father unto these my poor
fatherless children. I will that my said children, Robert and
Edward, shall be brought up in learneing and discipline by Amor
Oxley, and that he shall continue schoolmaster and tutor unto
them, having the same stipend he had, which he was wont to
have during his life naturall, which was twenty pounds a yeare.
I give unto my sonne, Peregrine Palmer, eight of the best tenements in all my lands during his life, and will and desire that

[1] She was the second wife of Sir Ralph Grey, whose will is printed
in this volume.

Mr. Weekes and Mr. Hatch shall see this performed, and whom
I make Executors for my affayres in the south only. I give unto
Mary Turner, one of the best farms that Mr. Weeks may choose
for her life naturall. To the poor of Chillingham parish, 10*l.*
I appoint Sir Francis Brandling Executor of my Will. Witnesses,
Edward Graye, Arthur Hebborne,. Peregrine Palmer, Charles
Oxley, Arthur Graye, James Birkley. Probate, 18 November,
1635.

ROBERT WILSON.

Feb. 17, 1623. In the name of God, Amen, I, Robert Wilson
of Middleton in Teesdale, within the Countye of Durham,
yeoman, being infirm in bodye. My body to be bured in the
Churchyard of Middleton aforesaid on the south syde of Wall,
as nigh my late wyfe, her grave, as convenentlye may be. Concerning my worldly goods, first, I give and bequethe unto the
poore people of the parish of Middleton the sum of 5*s.*, to be
sett forwards to their uses with the resydue of the stocke. I give
and bequeathe to my nephew, John Wilson of the Town ende of
Middleton aforesaid, his heres and assigns for ever, All my
messuage or tent in Middleton aforesaid, and all my howses,
edifices, buildings, inclosurers, yards and easements, backsydes,
rents, revercons, lands, meadowes, pastures, feedings, commons,
and common of pastures, woods, underwoods, mosses, Turbarie
and lyng, and all other pfitts, commodyties and appurtenances
whatsoever to the said messuages or tenements belonging and
appertaining, except and always reserved out of this gyft all that
rood of meadow ground lying . . . . called Skallards, which for
the accomplishment and pformance of my promise formerly made,
I have otherwise disposed upon . . . . after more at large shall
appeare. To have and to hold all the said messuages or tenements
and all other the premises by these presents mentioned to be
gyven and granted (except before excepted) unto the said John
Wilson, his heirs and assigns for ever, and to the only use and
behoof of the said John Wilson, his heirs and assigns, for ever.
I give and bequethe unto Ralph Bainbridge, sone of Ralph
Bainbridge, late of the towne end of Middleton aforesaid, his
heirs and assigns for ever, all the aforesaid rood of Meadow
ground lying in the Skallards aforesaid, and also the rents,
reservons, meadows, pastures, feedings, commons, pfitts, com-
modities, and appurtenances whatsoever to the said Roode of
meadow ground belonging and appertaining, to have and to
hould all the said roode of medow ground and all other the
premises before by these psents mentyoned to be given and
granted unto the said Ralph Bainbridge, his heires and assignes
for ever, and to the onely use and behoofe of the said Ralph
Bainbridge, his heires and assigns for ever. I give and bequeth

unto the said Ralph Bainbridge that corded bedstead which standeth in the north side of my bed chamber, one pare of harden sheets, one blanket, two happins and one coverlet, and a bolster to furnish the said bed with. I give unto the said Ralph Bainbridge, my little chest standing in my bed chamber, All my schoole books, my great tyn candlesticke, and two ewes and their lambs, to be delivered unto him or his assigns at the feast day of Pentecost next ensewing the day of my death. I will that the said Ralph Bainbridge shall be brought up and maintained at my now dwelling howse with meat, drink, cloth, lodging, fyre and candlelight untill such tyme as he shall accomplish the full age of thirteene yeares, at the costs and charges of the said John Willson, his executors, administrors and assigns. I give unto Anne, now wife of the said John Willson, One hatt band, one gorget, two crosse clothes, a smaller and a rownder, one lyn rayle, one appron, one lyn smocke, and one branched taffetye stomacher, and the deske wherein these orments lye. I give unto Elizabeth, the wyfe of Raphe Bainbrigge, late of the towne of Middleton aforesaid, sett band, two cross clothes, one rayle, one neck clothe, one coyse, one yarde of lin to . . . her an apperan, my late wyfe her purse and her girdle, thereunto annexed one bushell of bygg and one bushell of oates. I give and bequeath unto Leonard and Robt., children of the said John Willson, to either of them, one ewe and a lambe. I give and bequeath to Henry and Christofer, children of the said Raphe Bainbrigg, to either of them, one ewe and a lamb. I give to John Rutter, the elder, my next neighboure, one gymmer shepe to be delivered unto him within ten days next after my decease. I give unto my maide servant, Margarett Turner, fyve shillings over and besides her wages, which she hath deserved. I give unto the said Ralphe Bainbrigge now in my howse, my bow and arrowes. The rest of all my goods and chattells, as well moveable as unmoveable, howsehold stuff and howse implements of what nature, kynd, or qualitye soever they be, or by what names or tytles soever they be called and knowen, and before not disposed upon, my debts payd, legacyes, funerall expences and ordinarie dutyes deducted and discharged, I give and bequeath unto my said nephew, John Willson, whom I make sole and whole executor of this my Will. Witnesses, John Addyson, Henry Bainbrigge, John Colpotts, Henry Bainbrigg.

Debts of the testator : First, to my good Mr. Anthony Maxton, for lent moneye, 20s.; to him for a parcell of the tythe barne, 3l. 7s. 6d. To John Nattress, in lent money, 20s. To the children of the towne, and which is due at Madalenmas, 20s. To Mr. Francis Appleby, dew upon demand as my bill relates. 10s. To Gabriel Wharton, for parchment, 14d. To Robt. Martindale, for the like, 14d. To Phillipp Sanderson, for other wares, 2s. 4d.

ANNE HUTTON.[1]

May 13, 1624. In the name of God, Amen, I, Anne Hutton, of St. Helen, Auckland, in the County of Durham, widow, the unprofitable servant of gode, being weake in body. . . . And as concerning my worldly goodes, first, I give and bequeath unto my sonne, Samuel Hutton, 10*l.* Foreasmuch as my sone, Marmaduke Hutton, hath had the proffitt of my house without making me any account thereof at any time or alloweing me any part of the profitt of it, I doe therefore free and release him of all such reckonings as my executrix might call him in question of about the same. And my further will is that he shall hould himself fully content herewith, without claiming any more of my goodes. But if hereafter in my lyfe tyme he shall reform himselfe of his vaine expence, that I may have any hope that he will use my gift well, I may thereby be moved to alter this will, but otherwise my mind is that it shall stand good in all points, and that he shall not vex nor trouble my executrix. I give and bequeath 40*s.* unto the poore, delt at my death according to the discretion of my executor. And as for the rest of my goods of what kind soever they be, moveable or unmovable (my funeral expences discharged), I give and bequeath unto my daughter, Ann Vaux, whom I make full and sole executrix to this my last Will and Testament. Witnesses, George Dixon, Robert Thompson, Brian Coulson.

Furthermore, I give 20*s.* to the poore of Haughton, because I had my living among them, and I appoint 20*s.* more towards makeing of a Dynner for me to the neighbours there, and the

---

[1] Her husband Robert Hutton, rector of Haughton-le-Skerne, 1590-1610 (will dated 27 Dec., 1610, proved, 9 Jan., 1610/11, desires burial in the quyer at Haughton), was the son of Matthew Hutton of Priest Hutton, parish of Warton, co. Lancs., and brother of Matthew Hutton, Bishop of Durham. They had issue, Thomas of Skerningham; Matthew, bailiff of Bishop Auckland, bur. at St. Andrew's, in that town, 13 Dec., 1623 (his widow Anne's will is printed in this Vol.); Samuel, matric. from Trinity Coll., Camb., c., 1593/4, Scholar, 1596, B.A., 1597/8, M.A., 1601, Fellow, 1599, Preb. of Ulleshelf at York, 1603-29, mar. Elizabeth, dau. of Edward Barnes of Soham, Cambridge (by whom he had Timothy, bapt. at Haughton-le-Skerne, 23 Apl., 1609, matric. pens. from St. John's Coll., Camb., Easter, 1626, B.A., 1629/30, M.A., 1633, Fellow, 1631, tutor, 1637/8, Curate of St. Giles', Cripplegate, London, 1642/72; Thomas, bapt. at Haughton-le-Skerne, 28 Oct., 1610; Toby, bapt. at St. Michael-le-Belfrey, York, 14 May, 1616); Marmaduke; Anne, mar., 5 Sept., 1597, at Haughton-le-Skerne (where her children were bapt.), John Vaux, curate of St. Helen's, Auckland, 1616-33, by whom she had Thomas, bapt., 21 Feb., 1597/8; Timothy, bapt., 26 July, 1601; Marmaduke, bapt., 18 Dec., 1603; Hutton, bapt., 19 May, 1605; John, bapt., 15 June, 1606; Samuel, bapt., 1 Nov., 1607; Richard, bapt., 11 Feb., 1598/9. The husband of the testatrix is not to be confused with his nephew of the same name, who was Rector of Houghton-le-Spring (1589/1623), bur., 19 May, 1623, at that place.

Bells to be rung for a funerall. I give my daughter-in-lawe, Elizabeth Hutton, a double duckett and a golde ringe which lyes in a boxe in my title trunk. I give unto Tymothie Hutton, Thomas Hutton and Toby Hutton, the sonns of my sonne, Samuel Hutton, each of them, a Spurroyall for a remembrance of me. I give unto Mr. George Dixon, a Spurroyall. I give unto my servante, Jane Harrison, my worke daye apparell, three smocks, a paire of straiking sheets, and 10s. in money besides her wages. And this my Will to stand good and effectual in all points without alteration.

A Note of the funeral expences : Given to the poore of the parish of Haughton, 20s. Given to the poore of the St. Helen's, Auckland, 40s. Two Anuell Dynners, one at St. Helen's, Auckland, and her other at Haughton, with other charges about the some of 6l. 12s. 8d. Proved, 1624.

THOMAS COLLINGWOODE.[1]

May 13, 1624. Thomas Collingwoode. Inventory of all such goods and chattells of Thomas Collingwood, late of Reavelie, gentleman, dyed possessed of apprised by Cuthbert Collingwood of Thornton, Robt. Fenwick, Henry Thornton and Cuthbert Collingwood. Att Reavlie : Oxen there, 17 at 30s., price 27l. Twenty-one Kine at 33s. 4d., price 35l. One bull, 30s. Twelve stotts, year old, at 6s. 8d., price 4l. Att Edglie : Oxen there, 13 at 32s., price 21l. 9s. Five Kine att 33s. 4d., price 8l. 6s. 8d. Att St. Margarett's : Three oxen there at 30s., price 4l. 10s. Eighteen younger beasts at 18s., price 16l. 4s. Att Reavlie : Three stoode mares at 40s., price 6l. Two worke mares att 25s., price 50s. Two Rideing horses at 3l., price 6l. Two 2 yeare old colts att 40s., price 4l. One yeare old colt, 20s. Twenty-nine ewes and lambs, 10 scorce weathers and yeald sheep, in total, 9l. Five score and twelve hoggs at 2s. 6d., price 14l. Fourteen goates att 2s. 6d., price 1l. 15s. Corne and insight stuff : Winter corne sowen on the ground att Reavlie and Edglie, in total, 35l. Oates sowen att Reavlie and Edgelie valued at 40l. Oates, sowen att St. Margarett's, valued at 5l. Thirtie bowles of bigge, valued to 15l. Black corne, sowen att Edgelie, valued to 3l. Item, Readie money, 5l. Plate, valued to 9l. Apparrell, valued to 6l. 13s. 4d. Bedds and bedding, valued to 6l. 13s. 4d. Linning, valued to 40s. Tables and stools, 20s. Iron rings, etc., 3l. 6s. 8d. Pewther, valued at 30s. Wooden vessel, 20s. Householdmts and other goods, 3l. 6s. 8d. Due to the deceased for two horses, 5l. 4s. Sume Totall of goods, 394l. 17s. 10d. Debts owing to the deceased att the time of his death amounted to 396l.

[1] He was perhaps the Thomas Collingwood mentioned in the will of Cuthbert, 12 Aug., 1608, printed in this volume.

JOHN KING.[1]

May 19, 1624. Memorandum : John Kinge of the Cittie of Durham, Notarie Public, being sick in bodye but of pefect memorie, did in the presence of the witnesses under named, make declaracon of his last Will and Testament nuncupatively in manner and forme followinge, or words tending to the same effect, viz., he did will that his corne growing on the ground and his horses should be sold towards the payment of his debtes. And the said John King reckoning with Cuthbert Sisson, his sone in lawe, for some moneys that the said Cuthbert was to pay for the said testator's house, situate neare the Pallace Green in Durham, after the said testator's death, the said testator did will That the said Cuthbert, in full satisfacon of such moneys which they then agreed upon to be 60*l.*, should pay unto the now children of his fower daughters the said 60*l.* within fower yeares then next after, viz., the first yeare to his daughter, Ann Hall's children, 15*l.* The second yeare to his the said Cuthbert's, owne children, 15*l.* The third yeare to his daughter, Grace Hilton's children, 15*l.*, and the fourth yeare to his daughter, Elizabeth Benson's children, 15*l.* And willed that the profitt of the 15*l.* given to his said daughter's Hall's children, should yearly go to towards the maintenance of her or them. And his meaning was that that 15*l.* remaine in his executor's hand till the said children could give a lawful discharge for the same. And the said testator having some speeching with his wife about the providing her a house after his death, willed that his sonne, Cuthbert Sisson, should have his interest of his house in King's Street after his death, and out of the same should content his, the testator's wife, for house rent. The said testator did give and bequeath to his sone, John Benson, and his assigns, All his, the said testator's, right, titlle, interest and tenure of yeares in the house in Higate wherein his said sonne, Benson, lately dwelt. And he did nominate and appoint the said John Benson and Cuthbert Sissons Executors of his last Will and Testament, and being askt what should become of the rest of his goods, his debts and legacies paid, he said he would that his daughter, Ānn, should have some helpe forth of the same. Witnesses, Edward Hutten, gent, Edwarde Harrison, clarke.

INVENTORY, 118*l.* 4*s.* 1*d.* Proved, 1624.

[1] The testator was bur. at St. Mary-le-Bow, Durham, from whence other dates are taken, 21 May, 1624. His dau. Isabel, bapt., 9 Nov., 1600, bur., 2 Apl., 1634, mar. Cuthbert Sisson, 12 Dec., 1619, who mar. secondly, 18 Nov., 1634, Merial, dau. of Robert Cooper, bapt., 19 June, 1597; Ann, mar. Charles Hall, 22 June, 1619; Elizabeth, mar. John Benson, Feb., 1608/9; Grace, bur. 18 Feb., 1633/4, mar. as his first wife, James Hilton of Dyons.

JOHN DOWTHWAITE.[1]

July 31, 1624. In the name of God, Amen, I, John Dowthwaite of Westholme, in the pish of Winston, in the Countye of Durham, Gent, being sick in bodie. My bodie (if god permits) to be buried within the Church of Winston under that blewe stone which is at head of my stall there, and the duties accustomed to the said church to be honestlie contented and paid. I give and bequeath unto my mother-in-law, Mrs. Margaret Rawlison, ten kyne for ever dureing her life, to be secured on my pasture belonging to west holme called Roose lease, to be wintered as my other goods be, vizt., Milke kynee amongst milk kyne and drie gueld kyne amongst dry kyne. My will is, that my said mother-in-law, Mrs. Margaret Rawlison, shall receive, she knoweth well where, 9*l.* in old golde, and that she shall either kepe it in her custodie for the use of my sister, Ellinor Scroope, or otherwise give it to her selfe. And forasmuch as I have bene by some defamed and slandered, that I shall have in my handes and power all or the most of my said sister Ellinor her porcon, for the stopping of such slanderous mouthes and for giving satisfacion to the world in that pticular, hereby I doe take it upon my conscience, that I now neither have nor ever had any of what as belonged to my said sister Ellinor, more then the said 9*l.*, and therefore I . . . . . . most unjustlie wronged in and by such reportes. I give to my brother's sonne, John Dowthwaite, a graye fillie, the worse of the two, which I now have on Cleatham pasture. I give to his father, my brother, Barnard Dowthwaite, my lease of Rokebie Moor whereon he now dwelleth, for all the terme that is to come therein, he paying to the lord thereof, Sir Thomas Rokebie, such rents as by the lease I am bound to paye, and observing and pforming what other covenants, containes as by the said lease I am bound to doe. I give to my nephew, Barnard Dowthwaite, son of my said brother, Barnard Dowthwaite, 20*s.*, to buy Bookes withall. I give to my niece, Mary Dowthwaite, daughter of the said Barnard, a whye. I give to Samuel Binson, my servant, 20*s.* I give to Isabell Alder, another of my servants, 40*s.* I give to Franck Clark, 10*s.* I give to my serveant, Anne Frankling, 10*s.* I give and bequeathe to William Alder, a whye. My will is that all the poorer sort of this pish shallbe served with monie at the church

---

[1] His *Inq. p.m.* was taken at Durham, 4 Aug., 1627, in it he is stated to have been the son of *John*, in the pedigree printed in Surtees' *History of Durham,* vol. iv., p. 42, he is stated to have been the son of *William,* who was bur. at Winston, 21 Aug., 1586. The testator was bur. at York, 15 June, 1627, having mar. Mary, dau. of George Scroope (bur., 29 Nov., 1606). His brother, Bernard (aged 66 at his brother's inquisition), was bur., 27 Oct., 1636; the testator's son, John, bapt., 30 Nov., 1606, was bur., 20 Apl., 1628, at Winston.

doore at my buriall. All my goods, chattels, creditts, moveable
and unmoveable, whatsoever herein not bequeathed, I give and
bequeath unto John Dowthwaite, my sone and heire, and doe
make him sole Executor of this my Will and Testt. And I give
and entreat my said Brother, Bernard Dowthwaite, and Thomas
Rayne of Barnard Castle, to be superviseers of this my Will, and
to see the same justlie pformed, and I give unto the said Thomas
Raine my old Angell to buy a Ring withall and that he shall
weare it for my sake. Witnesses, Ambrose Clennett, Thomas
Farrow, Samuell Binson, Richard Darneton, Francis Walker.
INVENTORY, 2,022*l*. 8*s*. 8*d*., including in Bonds, Bills and
other specialtyes, 992*l*. 6*s*. 8*d*. Church books, law books and
other books, 3*l*. In golde and money, 150*l*. Proved, 2 March,
1626.

JOHN GRAY.

Aug. 5, 1624. John Gray, of Alnwick, Glover. My bodye
to be buryed at our parish churchyard of Saint Michaell's the
Archangell, of Alnwick. I bequeath my house in Narrowgate
unto my wife, Dorothy Gray, for her life natural, and if it
please god that my child which she is with prove a male child,
that then the said burgadge shall come to him and to the heirs
of his bodye, and in default of such issue to come to my daughter,
Jane Graye, and the heirs of her bodye, and in default of issue
to my daughter, Margarett Graye, and the heirs of her bodye.
If it please god that my child which my wife is conceived with
be a man or woman child, I give unto him or her all my right
and interest in right of nine riggs or butts of lands which I
hold of Mr. Frances Alder of Hobberlawe upon the redemption
of 5*l*. I give all that my land called the Stokin and waterhaugh
to my child now conceived in my wife's wombe if it be a sone,
if not, unto my daughter, Jane Graye, and her heirs. To
Elizabeth Urwen, daughter of Thomas Urwen of Morpeth, 6*l*.
To my eldest daughter, Jane Graye, 20*l*. To my daughter,
Margaret Gray, 20*l*. To my brother's sone, John Scott, one baye
colte going now at the Snipe house. I appoint my wife sole
Executrix, and make my father-in-law, Robert Fryer, and my
brother, John Scott, and William Hunter and William Widdows,
Supervisors. Probate, 1625.
INVENTORY, 72*l*. 2*s*. 0*d*.
Debtes owing to the testator : Mr. William Bednell of Alnwick,
8*l*., by specially 5*l*. thereof, and the other 3*l*. on account.
Thomas Midforth of Ougham, 7*l*. Robert Midforth of Ougham,
2*l*. 17*s*. 0*d*. Thomas Gray and William Bowman, 18*s*. John
Leichman of Shilbottle, 22*s*.

JANE LEDGAR.[1]

Aug. 7, 1624. In the name of God, Amen, I, Jane Ledgar, being sick in bodie. My boddy to be decentlie buried by my executors, and to be interred by my late husband, Robert Ledgar, deceased. And as to touching the woordlie goods wherewt god hath blessed me, I dispose them in manner and forme following. I give to my sone, Robart Clarkson, Three hundred pounds. To my sone, Thomas Clarkson, Three hundred pounds. I give a peece of Plate to my sone, Robert Clarkson, and a peece of plate to my son, Thomas Clarkson, such as my executors shall make choice of to give them out of my Plate. I give to Rebecca Clarkson, wife of my sone, Thomas Clarkson, two fetherbedds, furnished such as my executors shall make choice of out of my househould stuff. I give to Issabell Selby, tenn poundes she owes me. I forgive unto Barbara Bewick, widow, three poundes shee owes me, and do give her fortie shillings for a token. I give five poundes to her sonn, Samuel Bewick, to be bestowed in placing him with a good master. I give to my niece, Jane Mitford, daughter to my brother, Anderson Mitford, deceased, fiftie poundes. I give to my brother, Henry Mitford, ten pounds for a token. I give to my servant, Edward Wood, Tenn pounds. To my servant, James Walker, five poundes. To Thomas Muschamp, twentie shillings. To my servant, Elizabeth Stubbs, twentye shillings. To Mary Wake, twenty shillings. And of this my last Will and Testament I constitute and appointe Leonard Carr, Marchant, and Richard Bartlett, my executors, renouncing and revoking all former Wills. And whereas they are likewise

[1] In the Society's publications are printed wills of Christopher Mitford, great-grandfather of this testatrix (vol. 116, p. 166), of her grandparents, Christopher and Jane Mitford (vol. 38, p. 30 and 31n), and of her brother, Christopher Mitford (*ibid*, p. 214n). Her father, Robert Mitford, was bur., 4 Dec., 1592, having mar., 12 Sept., 1574, Eleanor Shafto, who was bur., 3 May, 1585. She herself was bapt., 29 June, 1575, and bur., 10 Aug., 1624. Her first husband, mar., 4 Feb., 1593/4, was Thomas Clarkson (bur., 10 Oct., 1605), by whom she had at least nine children; of these the only survivors, it would seem, at the date of her will were Thomas, bapt., 4 Oct., 1601, and Robert, bapt., 21 Jan., 1602/3. Her second husband, mar., 6 May, 1611, was Robert Ledgard, sheriff of Newcastle, 1622-3. He made his will, 16 Apl., and was bur., 21 Apl., 1623; by him she had issue, Elizabeth, bapt., 9 Aug., 1612, bur., 18 Apl., 1613; Thomas Ledgard, bapt., 6 Sept., 1613, Mayor, 1647-8, bur., 8 Jan., 1672/3, mar. (1) at All Saints', 18 May, 1631, Margaret (bapt. there, 2 Mch., 1612/13, bur., 14 June, 1648), dau. of Leonard Carr, (2) Mary (bur., 31 July, 1683), dau. of George Fenwick of Brinkburn; Mary, bapt., 17 Jan., 1614/15, mar. at All Saints', 7 Feb., 1630/1, Mark Shafto (see above under the will of Robert Shafto, his father). The above dates (except three from All Saints') are taken from St. Nich., Newcastle.

by being my executors, mediat executors to Christopher Mitford, my brother, deceased, to whom I am executor, therefore I do entreat them to see the last Will and Testament of the said Christopher Mitford, my brother, faithfullie and trulie executed and performed. And whereas the said Robart Ledgar, my husband, did make Thomas Ledgar, his sonne, an infant, his executor, by reason whereof the tutorshipp of the said Thomas, and of Mary, his sister, an infant, together with the administrator during the minortie of the said Thomas was committed to me by the Right Worshipl Doctor Cradock, Chancellor of Durham, which Admon and tutorship determineth by my death, as I am informed, Therefore I do as much as in me lies give and bequeath the custodie and education of the said Thomas and Mary, my children, with the disposition and government of their legacies and personal estate, to my said executors, because by this means I am fully perswaded they shallbe educated and brought upp virtuouslie and in the true religion and feare of god and their legacies and personal estate trulie and instantlie satisfied and paid unto them. I enerestlie entreat the said Mr. Doctor Cradock to grant the like custodie of my children and administration of the personall estate of my sonne, Thomas, as executor to his father to my executors, and not to graunt it to the next of kin by the father's side or motherside because I do know assuredlie that if they obtein it there personal estate willbe wasted and consumed, and they willbe educated and trained upp in superstition and poperie to the utter hazard and destruction of their soules, wch god for bidd.   Witnesses, Joh Astill, James Carr, Ralph Carr, John Mallabar.

HENRIE WOULDHAVE.[1]

Aug. 26, 1624.   In the name of Gode, Amen, I, Henrie Wouldhave, of the parish of St. John's, within the towne and Countie of Newcastle-upon-Tyne, Sadler, weake in bodie.   My bodee to be buried within the parish Church of Saint John's aforesaid.   I give to Henry Wouldhave, sone to John Wouldhave of Benwell, to be paid by my executrix hereafter to be named, twenty poundes when he shall accomplish the age of eighteen yeares.   I give to Henry Wouldhave, sone to John Wouldhave of Newcastle, five poundes at the age of eighteen yeares.   I give to Henrie Wouldhave, sone to Richard Wouldhave of Benwell,

[1] The testator was bur. at St. John's, Newcastle, 5 Sept., 1624; in that register it is stated that he mar. Barbara, dau. of Thomas Reed, miller, 29 Jan., 1593/4, at Newburn; he was probably son of Christopher Woldhave, whose will, dated 18 Apl., 1584, is printed in Vol. 112, p. 107, of this Society's publications.

deceased, five poundes at the age of eighteen yeares. I give to Robert Wouldhave, son to the said Richard Wouldhave, three pounds six shillings and eightpence, to be paid at the age of eighteen yeares. I give to Thomas Wouldhave, sone to Thomas Wouldhave of Newcastle, 5*l*., to be paid at the age of twenty yeares. I give to Henry Blithman, sone to William Blithman, 40*s*. I give to William Dixon, sone to Henrie Dixon, 40*s*. I give unto Ouswold Delavale, sone to Ouswold Delavale, deceased, 3*l*. 6*s*. 8*d*. I give to John Would-have of Benwell, 10*s*. I give to John Currie of Benwell, 10*s*. I give to John Wouldhave, Saylor, 10*s*. I give to Margaret Dickson, 10*s*. I give to Ann Read, daughter to Henrie Read, Marchant, 6*l*. 13*s*. 4*d*. I give to Thomas Armstrong, and Jane, his wife, each 10*s*. I give to Barbara Armstrong, daughter to the said Thomas Armstrong, 6*l*. 13*s*. 4*d*. I give to Thomas Read, sone to Henrie Read, Marchant, 20*s*. I give to Thomas Read, sone to Bartram Read, deceased, 20*s*. I give to Jane Read, daughter to the said Bartram Read, deceased, 30*s*. I give to Henrie Ourd, 10*s*. I give to Alexander Coulthird, 10*s*. I give to my two maid servantes, to either of them, 10*s*. I give to the Right Worshipfull Sir Peter Riddell, Knight, in token of my due respect unto him, 3*l*. 6*s*. 8*d*. I give to Mr. William Jackson, in token of my love, 20*s*. I give Mr. Lancelot Ogle, gent., 10*s*., and to his wife, Mrs. Ogle, each 10*s*., as tokens of my love. I give to Gerrard Ogle, sone of the said Mr. Lancelot Ogle, 3*l*. 6*s*. 8*d*. I give to Mr. John Shaw, minister of St. John's, halfe a pece, in token of my love. I give to Robert Bartram, Marchant, 10*s*., as a token. I give to Isabell Chater, 10*s*., for a token. I give to Thomas Winn and Elizabeth, his wife, to either of them, 10*s*., for a token. I give to John Matfen, sone to George Matfen, Marchant, deceased, 5*s*. 6*d*., for a token. I give to John Read, chapman, 10*s*., for a token. I give to the poore of the parish of St. John's, 30*s*. All the rest of my goodes, moveable and unmoveable, my funerall discharged, I give to my loveing wife, Barbara Wouldhave, whom I make and ordaine the full and sole Executrix of this my last Will and Testament, hereby renouncing all former Wills or Testaments by me made. Lastly, I doe ordeine and make the Right Worshipfull Sir Peter Riddell, Knight, and Mr. William Jackson, Supervisors of this my last Will and Testament. Memor-andum : That before the either signing or sealing hereof my will, like is that Margaret Dickson, wife of Henrie Dickson, saylor, shall have given her, 20*s*., for a token, and also that Dorothy Sanderlands, wife of Henry Sanderlands, shall have 10*s*., and also Elizabeth Page, wife of Andrew Page, sayler, shall have given her, 20*s*. Witnesses, W. Jackson, Ed. Wiggham, Joh. Shaw, Geo. Nicholson. Proved, 11 Septr., 1624.

GEORGE NICHOLSON.[1]

Sept. 11, 1624. In the name of God, Amen, I, George
Nicholson, of the towne of Newcastle-upon-Tyne, Notary Public,
sick in body. I fullie confirme (so much as in me is) the
Testament and last Will of my late deceased father, George
Nicholson, Cutler, as touching his devise of the house wth the
appurtenances wherein I now dwell in Westgate in Newcastle,
and another little house situate in Iron Markett in the same
Towne, and quit rent of 7s. 4d., issuing forth of Two Tenements
in Westgate aforesaid, willing that the said two houses and quit
rent, descend and passe accordinge to the trew Intendyment of
his said will, without any viola . . . . thereof. And whereas
also, my said late father, George Nicholson, in and by his said
Will and Testament, bequeathed as legacies to my then six
children, namelie, George Nicholson, Richard Nicholson, Thomas
Nicholson, Willm. Nicholsone, Margaret Nicholson and Elizabeth
Nicholson, the some of twenty pounds a peece, being in the whole
one hundred and twenty pounds, which I have alreadie raised
and putt into security, yett seeing it hath pleased almightie
gode to take my eldest sone, George Nicholson, out of this mortall
life and hath sent me another sone, namely, Robert Nicholson,
since the said legacyes bequeathed bye my said father in and by
his said Will, my will is therefore that twenty pounds which was
dew unto my sone, George, shallbe and remane unto my said
sone, Robert, And I will and comand that none of my fyve eldest
children, Doe breake my will or comand in this, And my further
will is that that One hundred and twenty pounds be still continued in good security and moderate intereste for their use
without diminishing any part thereof att the sight of my beloved
wife and supervisors hereunder named, until my said six
children shall respectively in their severall places attayne to the
age of one and twenty yeares or be maryed, and then every of
their said porcons, with the intrest of each porcon, be payd unto
them, then and not before, and in case any of my sixe children
shall dye before their severall parts of the said legacies shallbe
come severallie due unto them as aforesaid, then my will is that
their several parts shallbe equallie divided amongst the survivor
or survivors of them. I give and bequeath unto my eldest sone,

---

[1] The father, George Nicholson, was bur. at St. John's, Newcastle
(from whence the following dates are taken), Sept. 1622, his wife,
Margaret, being also bur. there, 14 Mch., 1608/9. The testator was
bur., 17 Sept., 1624, having mar. at St. Nich., Margaret, dau. of
Richard Swan, 13 Sept., 1608, by her he had issue, George, bapt.,
1 Apl., 1610, bur., 19 Aug., 1624; Richard, bapt., 7 Dec., 1611, bur.,
22 Nov., 1632; Thomas, bapt., 1 Jan., 1613/14; William, bapt., 17 Nov.,
1619; James, bapt., 13 Sept., 1618, bur., 13 July, 1619; Robert, bapt.,
21 Mch., 1623/4, bur., 5 Nov., 1644; Margaret, bapt., 24 Mch., 1615/16
(who may have mar., 26 Nov., 1632, John Strangwish, merchant), and
Elizabeth.

Richard Nicholson, my new house in Sandgate, which I latelie
have erected and builded, with free passage, in, to and from the
same through the yard there bye a back Dore which I will shallbe
built and added to the said house, together also with one house in
Dent's Chaire there, now in the occupacon of Richard Smith,
another house in the occupation of Edward Rotherforde, another
in the occupation of John Storey, another being two lowe rooms
of a new house which I latelie builded in Dent's Chaire aforesaid, now in the severall occupations of Edward Hodgson and
Isabell Robson, together also with severall competent coalholes
to be sett fourth to every of the said houses in the Black beare
yarde, and egress and regress to and from the same att the
discretion of my supervisors hereunder named. And likewise I
give to my said sone, Richard, one third parte of one house
which I latelie purchased of one Christopher Watson, wherein
one George Birtleye, miller now dwelleth in Dent's Chaire aforesaid, he the said Richard paying to Margrett Hunter, widowe,
and her heires for ever, the sume of 13s. 4d. yearlie rent, And
likewise eight shillings to the poore of the pish of All Sts, being
one halfe of sixteene shillings, likewise I give unto my said sonne,
Richard, the house adioning unto my now dwellinghouse in
Westgate which I lately purchased of Isabell Maddison and others.
And my lease of the Sadler's Close, in Freare Chaire, To have
and to hold the same and every part thereof to my said sonne,
Richard, and the heirs of his bodye lawfully begotten for ever,
and in default of such issue the same to come to my sone, Thomas
Nicholson, and the heires of his bodye lawfullie begotten for
ever, and in default of such issue the same to come to my third
sone, William Nicholson, and the heires of his body lawfully
begotten for ever, and in default of such issue the same to come
to my fourthe sone, Robert Nicholson, and the heires of his body
lawfullie begotten for ever, and in default of such issue then
the same to descend and come to my next heire by lawe. I give
and bequeath unto my second sone, Thomas Nicholson, All that
my house or tenement in Sandgate called or knowne by the name
of Blackbeere, nowe in the occupation of Francis Clarke, Merchante, together with so much of the yarde thereof as is not
formerlie hereby disposed, together with free egresse and regresse
to and from the same, in, by and through the said yarde, and
the lint loft in the occupation of Thomas Robinson, and the upp
dwelling adjoining into the said yarde which I lately builtded
in the Milne Steads, and also the Cowe house and two shillings
rent per annum for half of the Keye near unto the river of Tyne,
he, the said Thomas, paying out of the same to the King's Matie,
2s. 8d. p. annum, and 8s. to the poore of the pish of All Sts,
being the other halfe of the sixteene shillings. To have and to
hold the same and everie pte thereof to my said sone, Thomas

Nicholson, and the heires of his bodye lawfully begotten for ever,
And for default of such issue the same to come to my sone,
Willm. Nicholson, and the heires of his bodye lawfullie begotten
for ever, And for default of issue the same to come to my sone,
Robert Nicholson, and the heires of his bodie lawfully begotten
for ever, And for default of such issue then the same to come to
my next heire by the lawe. I give and bequeath to my third
sonne, Willm. Nicholson, Also all those two tenements or farmeholdes with the appurtenances, and a pcell of land called Bells
lying in West Thirston in Northumberland. To have and to
hold one of the said tenements or farmeholdes which I lately
purchased of Robert Carr to my third sone Willm. and the heires
of his bodye lawfully begotten for ever, And to have and to hold
the other tenement or farmeholde and the said Bell land during
my severall tearms of yeares therein. And if it shall happen
my said sone to dye without issue of his body lawfully begotten
then the same to come to my sone, Robert Nicholson, and the
heires of his body lawfully begotten, in manner as above is
demised. And in default of such issue then to come to my next
heire. I give and bequeath unto my fourthe sone, Robt. Nicholson, All those my outrents or quitrents of foure pounds and
eight pence per annum, which I latelie purchased of Mr. William
Jackson, issueing out of severall houses in Sandgate aforesaide,
Also one house or tenemente in Baliegate which I purchased of
John Stocoe, when the same shall fall to me att the expiration
of a lease which wilbe within two yeares; and likewise my lease
or tearme which I holde of one shoppe in the Sandhill granted
from William Boone, Margaret Boone and others. To have and
to hold the said outrents and house in Bayliegate to him, the
said Robert, and the heeres of his bodye lawfullie begotten for
ever, and in default of such issue to the next of my kindred,
And to have and to hold the said Shopp to him, the said Robert,
during the continuance of my terme therein. Yet my will and
pleasure is that there be deducted of the rents of all my lands
in Newcastle above mentioned and hereby devised, thirty poundes
per annum for the space of two yeares next after my decease,
which I give and bequeath to my two daughters, Margarett
Nicholson and Elizabeth Nicholson, to be equallie between them
for the inlarging of their porcons. I give unto the poore of
the pish Church of St. John's in Newcastle, 20s. And I doe
ordaine and make by these psents my faithfull and loving Mr.
William Jackson, Sherife of this towne, and my trustie friend
and father-in-lawe, Richard Swan, supervisors of this my last
Will and Testament, And lastly of all I ordeyne and make my
well beloved wife, Margaret Nicholson, my full and sole executrix
of this my Testament. Witnesses, W. Jackson, Edw. Wiggham,
Francis Newton, John Ainsley. Proved, 1624.

183

RICHARD RAYNE.

Sept. 20, 1624. In the name of God, Amen, I, Richard Rayne of Eggleston, within the Countie of Durham, Yeo., diseased in bodye. My bodie to be buried in the Churchyard of Middleton-in-Teasdale in such a place there as my friends shall think meet and conventlie. I give and bequeath unto Jane Herreson, my eldest daughter, the wife of Christopher Herrison, my son-in-law, All my estate, title and interest of and in all my tenement or farmeholde at Eggleston aforesaid, and to which of her sonns my said daughter, Jane Herrison, shall think most needful thereof to enter presently and immediately on the same after the decease of my selfe and Jenett, now my wife, and the longer liver of us. I give and bequeath unto Jane Herreson, my daughter, and to whatsoever of her sonns she shall think most meet for them all, my carrs, carre geare, ploughes and plough gear, of what kind or qualitie whatsoever they be or by what names or titles soever they be known and called, as axes, woombles and iron geare and all other implements belonging to husbandry. I give and bequeath unto Jane Herreson, my daughter, and whatsoever of her sonns she shall think most meet, One meat table and one Cubbard as heirloomes in the house, one old Ambry and two old bed stocks. I give unto Elizabeth Walker, and daughter of my son in law, John Walker of Cootherston, 20s. of lawful money when she cometh to pfect age, to be paid by the said Jane Herreson or whatsoever of her sonns as she shall have then unmarried for the injoying thereof or their assyns. I give and bequeath to Elizabeth Walker on Reade whye of her first calfe and two Gymmer hoggs. I give and bequeath unto Anthony Herreson, sone of Christopher Herrison, fower lambs, to choose them out of eight lambes where he will. I give and bequeath unto Charles Richardson one cowe and fower wethers. I give unto John Walker, my son-in-law, one cowe and fower weathers. I give and bequeath unto Christopher Herryson, my son-in-law, one Read Stott or a black whye, whether he shall choose. I give and bequeath unto Janet, now my wife, my Kyne, to choose out of all my Kine as Christopher Herryson shall think most necessary or the best, and the whole of all my goods and chattells, as well moveable as unmoveable, before not bequeathed and disposed, upon my debts payd, legacies and funeral expences deducted, I give and bequeathe unto Janett, now my wife, and make her sole Executrix. Witnesses, Rich. Lonsdale, Anthony Addison. Proved, 1624.

SUSANNA LAMBERT.[1]

Oct. 18, 1624. In the name of Gode, Amen, I, Susanna Lambert, alias Colman, of Gateshead, in the Countye of Durham, widow, sick in bodie. My body to be buried within the parish

[1] The testatrix was bur. at Gateshead, 30 Oct., 1624.

Church yarde of Gateside, And for my worldlie goodes which gode
in his mercie hath lent me, I doe dispose thereof as followeth. I
doe give and bequeathe unto the poore of the parish of Gateside
aforesaid, in token of my love towards God's people, 5s. I give
and bequeath the house I now dwell in, with the tenements and
appurtenances belonging to the same, To my naturall daughter,
Elizabeth Lambert (alias Colman), and to the heires of her
bodie lawfully begotten and to be begotton for ever. And faileing
of the heires of her bodie lawfully begotten and to be begotten,
my will is that the same shall descend and come to John Wattue,
my sister's sone, and to the heires of his body lawfully begotten
for ever, and failing of the said John Wattue and his heires my
will is that the same shall descend and come to his Brother,
Richarde Wattue, and the heires of his bodye lawfully begotten
for ever, and failling of such issue to come to his Brother,
Edward Wattue, and his heires for ever. I doe give and bequeath
unto my husband's daughter, Barbara Lambert, alias Colman,
10l., to be deducted out of my goods, that is to say, 5l. to be
paide hir within one yeare next after my decease, other 5ls., that
tyme twelve months. I give and bequeath unto the said Barbara
one Kersay gowne and one day working petticotte. I give and
bequeath the Iron chimney in the fore howse to Ms. Cocks, wyfe
to Samuell Cocke of Newcastle. I doe give to Margaret Goodrie
one brass posnett pott. I give and bequeath to Margaret Schamell,
the daughter of Symonde Schamell, 5s. The rest of my goodes
and chattells, moveable and unmoveable, unbequeathed thereof,
my debts, legacies and funerall expences being paid and discharged, I give and bequeathe unto my daughter, Elizabeth
Lambert, alias Colman, whom I do ordeyne and make sole
Executrix of this my last Will and Testament, and I do appoint
Mr. Nicholas Calverte, gentleman, supervisor to this my last Will
and Testament, to see this my last Will truly executed to the
course of Law, and to him also I commit the education of my
said daughter Elizabeth. Witnesses, Nicho. Calverte, William
Moore, Richard Thompson. Proved, 1624.

JOHN HALL.[1]

Nov. 27, 1624. In the name of God, Amen, I, John Hall, of
Framwellgate, within the Chappelry of St. Margrett's within the sub-
burbs of the City of Durham, Gent . . . I bequeath unto the poore
Ancient househoulders within the said chapelrie of St. Margarett's,

[1] The testator was bur., 9 Dec., 1624, having mar. Jane, dau. of
Christopher Maire of Hardwick, 30 May, 1586; she was bur., 10 Aug.,
1632. By her he had issue, John, bapt., 9 Feb., 1588/9, bur., 7 Mch.,
1626/7; Christopher, bapt., 1 Aug., 1596, bur., 5 Oct., 1600; Thomas,
bapt., 1 Jan., 1602/3, bur., 8 July, 1623; Michael, bapt., 25 Aug., 1605,

the sume of 3*l.* Also I give unto the poere of Chester parish, 20*s.*
Also I give to the poore of Lanchester parish, 20*s.* Also I give to
the poor of Medomsley Chappelry, 10*s.* And whereas I have
estated the most of my lands and tents upon Jane Hall, my wife,
and Michael Hall, my sonne, and the rest of my children, as by
the conveyances thereof formerly made by me will appeare, with
a purpose that my said wife and my sone Michael shall satisfie and
paie all such debts which I am oweing to any mann and do
appoint to be paid by my last Will and Testament, I doe hereby
appoint and require that my said wife and my said sone, Michael
Hall, shall doe, satisfy and discharge [them] out of and by and
with the rents, issues and profitts of the lands and tenements, Also
such debts as contained in a Schedule of parchment hereunto
annexed, signed with my owne hand. Also I will and bequeath
that Jane Hall, my wife, shall have the custodie and tuicon and
keaping of my eldeste sonne, John Hall, who is a single younge
man and without any government or rule of himselfe, and to
receive the annuity granted for his use in trust and maintenance
of meate and drinke and clothes as she shall think most fitt for
him for so long as she shall live, without making any account
to him or any person for him or in his name, without impeachment of him or any other. And if fortune my said wief, Jane
Hall, shall die, leaving my said sone John, then I doe appoint,
will and bequeath that my eldest daughter, Isabell, which is wife
unto John Hopper, or who she shall appoint, shall have the
custodie, government and keeping of my said sone, and the
receipt and ordering and disposing of his said annuity. And
also I will and bequeath and appoint that the said Jane Hall, my
wief, shall have fower silver gobletts, one of them doubled guilded
with a cover for the same, and the other two guilded, and the
fourthe a white silver boule, and one faire silver salt pcell gilt
and fourteene silver spoons with advenis glass, which was great
grandfather's, and one overspe covering and one Tapestree
carpen clothe, and my best stand bedd during her widowhood.
And I doe appoint and bequeath unto Michaell Hall, my sonne,
after my wife's death, three of the said Gobletts, one of them
double gilt, with a coveringe thereunto belonging, and one white

bur., 28 Sept., 1655, mar. Elizabeth (bapt., 16 Nov., 1606, at St. Mary-
the-Less), dau. of John Gill of Barton, 24 Apl., 1625, bur., 2 Mch.,
1676/7; Isabel, bapt., 29 Jan., 1586/7, mar., John Hopper; Jane, bapt.,
22 Aug., 1591, bur., 1 May, 1596; Elizabeth, bapt., 23 June, 1594;
Eleanor, bur., 4 Sept., 1631, mar., Hugh Hutchinson, 22 Jan., 1621/2,
their son, Hugh, bapt., 5 Jan., 1622/3, mar., Elizabeth, dau. of Richard
Rawe of Plawsworth. The above dates are from the registers of St.
Margaret's, Durham. In his *Inq. p.m.* taken at Durham, 5 Mch.,
1624/5, his son, John, aged 35, of "weak mind," is his heir. By
a covenant, 10 Mch., 1612/13, he had settled his lands on his dau.,
Isabella, and his sons, Thomas and Michael, also making provision
for his wife, Jane.

silver Goblett wh . . . . little goblett gilt, and half a dozen of the
appostle silver spoones and my venis glass aforesaid, the overspe
covering and one Tapestree carpett clothe.   And I also will and
bequeath unto Isabell Hopper, my eldest daughter, in full satisfacon of her child's portion with the lands to her formerly
estated, the sum of 40s.   Also I give unto my sone-in-law, Hugh
Hutchinson, and Eleanor, his wife, in full satisfacon of her child
or porcon, with the lands to her formerly estated, the sume of
40s.   And also I give and bequeath unto my daughter, Elizabeth
Hall, with the tenemts to her estated by Coppie of Courte Rowle,
in full satisfacon of her filiall child's part or porcon, the sum
of 40s., and the Tapestree, carpett clothe and the gilt boule,
which two I bought of Mr. Pexall Forster, which are to be
delivered her after her mother's death.   And I also will and
bequeathe unto William Heighington, being a poore youth with
me, the sum of 10l. when he shall accomplish the full aige of
Twenty and foure yeares.   And also I will and bequeath unto
Katheron Noble the sum of 6s. 8d.   And also I will and bequeath
unto my servant, Elizabeth Jobline, 10s.   And also I give and
bequeath unto my servante, Margaret Raw, 20s.   I give to my
servante, Robert Anderson, the sum of 5s., to be bestowed in
clothes.   And I give unto Hugh Hutchinson, the sone of my
daughter Ellinor, the sum of 10s.   And also I give unto my sone,
Michaell Hall, my Armor which I have.   Also I make my wife
sole Executrix of this my Will, and my friend, Mr. Pexall Forster,
Supervisor of this my Will.   Witnesses, Peratt Forster, Rade
Kemp, George Kirkley, Hugh Hutchinson, Lanc. Carnaby.
Proved, 1624.

NUNCUPATIVE WILL OF JOHN GYLL.[1]

July 11, 1625.   Memorandum, John Gyll, of Durham, in the
County of Durham, gentleman, being at Wansford brigges, in
the County of Northampton, visited with sickness yett in very
good and perfect memory, did declare to me, Thomas Gyll, how
he would dispose of his goods and lands, and whished me to
remember the same and maik knowne to his childeren and frendes
(if it should please God to taik him away before he came home).

[1] He was the son of Thomas Gill of Barton, by his wife, Anne,
dau. of Peter Warde of Barton; he mar. Margaret, dau. of John
Harrison of Durham, 27 Feb., 1594/5, at St. Mary-le-Bow, Durham,
bur., 6 Feb., 1619/20 (entered in both the registers of St. Mary-le-
Bow and St. Mary-the-Less).   By her he had issue, John, bur., 15 Sept.,
1662, at Haughton-le-Skerne, mar. Alice, dau. of George Middleton of
Silksworth, 5 Feb., 1625/6, at Houghton-le-Spring, bur., 7 Sept., 1644,
at Haughton-le-Skerne; Thomas, bapt., 20 Sept., 1601, at St. Mary-le-
Bow, will proved, 1662; Clement, bapt., 16 Sept., 1604, at St. Mary-

He did bequeath and give his soule to god and his body to the earth, and did give, legate and bequeathe to his sone, John Gill, all his lands at Haughton and his lease of Halykeld, together with all his goods and howshould stuff at Haughton, and one brass pott and one paire of cobirons and a carpett or table coveringe which was at Durham, which was given to the said John Gyll by his mother. He did give to his sone, Thomas Gyll, 200*l.* in money, which was owing to him by Mr. Warmouth of Newcastle and Mr. Nicholas Whitfeyld of Durham, which was dewe att or before Lamas next, in full satisfaction of his filliall or child's portion of his goods. He did give to his sone, Clement Gyll, 200*l.* in money, and he willed that his said sone John Gyll should let him have the lease of his house att Durham and the close before it for forty marks, which should be rebayted out of his said portion of 200*l.*, which should be in satisfaction of his child's portion. He did give unto his Daughter, Mary Gyll, 200*l.* in money and all the houshould stuff and other implements in his house at Durham except as aforesaid, and the lease of Hallykeld which he did give to his sone John should secure to her her 200*l.*, as in full satisfaction of her child's portion. And lastly, he willed that I, Thomas Gyll, should give all his books and a golde ringe which Mr. Sergeant Davenport gave him. And further, that his aforesaid son, John Gyll, should be whole Executor of his last Will and Testament. Mr. Gill being at London last trinity terme, and being moved by me to make a will, answered vizt., that all his children were provided for saveing Clemt. and Marie, and that to Clemt. he should have 200*l.* and Mary 200*l.* and half his howshold stuff or 50*l.* in lewe thereof or to that effect, and that his sone Tho., though he had not received his portion yet he knew in whose hands 200*l.* was which was meant and provided for him, in words to the effect . . . . plate I hard after he should say his daughter Mary should have, and for the rest of his estate and lands surely he ment them to John and used words to that effect, and never hard him name any executor, but I am purswaded these things being discharged he intended the rest to his sone John. W. Phillipson. Proved, 1625.

the-Less, bur., 23 Mch., 1631/2, at St. Mary-le-Bow; William, bapt., 18 April, bur., 9 Oct., 1609, at St. Mary-the-Less; Margaret, bapt., 27 May, 1599, at St. Mary-le-Bow, bur., 13 Apl., 1623, at St. Nich., mar., 15 Oct., 1616, Nicholas Whitfield, at St. Mary-the-Less, bur. at St. Nich., 3 Apl., 1632; Barbara, bapt., 7 July, bur., 1 Nov., 1600, at St. Mary-le-Bow; Anne, bapt., 3 Oct., 1602, bur., 20 Oct., 1602, at St. Mary-le-Bow; Elizabeth, bapt., 16 Nov., 1606, at St. Mary-the-Less, bur., 2 Mch., 1676/7, at St. Margaret's, wife of Michael Hall (bapt., 25 Aug., 1605, at St. Margaret's, mar. there, 24 Apl., 1625, bur., 22 Sept., 1655, also there); Anne, bapt., 15 Feb., 1607/8, at St. Mary-the-Less, bur., Sept., 1608, at St. Mary-le-Bow.

JOHN TAYLOR.[1]

Aug. 23, 1625. In the name of God, Amen, I, John Taylor, of Whorlton, in the County of Durham, Batchlor, being at the making hereof somwhat infirmed in body. As touching my worldly estate, first, concerning the crop of corne now groweing upon my farme and cottage in Whorlton, I have given it to my mother, in full lewe and satisfacon of 15*l.* which I did owe to her concerning her thirds of the land in Redworth for thre yeares, whereof one of them is almost expired, which said crop of corne and hay I have given her alreadie, so that it is now at the sealing thereof hers and none of mine, and so not to be prized as any part of my goods when as I am dead. Secondly, touching all my lands in Redworth now in the occupacon of Thomas Dobson, I give it freely to Elizabeth, my sister, which is now the wife of Richard Hornsbye, to whom it doth belong after my death to her and her heirs for ever. And further, for the devoiding of strife when as I am dead and gone and clering the truth, Richard Robinson, my halfe Brother, hath used all the meanes that he could for a pfitt [or] sale of my land for himselfe, and to putt it from the right heire, my sister; the said Richard Robinson hath used violence, he hath used . . . . meanes in bringing certain writeings to me which I could not certainly tell what they were, but they did concerne the passing away of my said land, all which I did refuse to seale, so that he and I confesse as I must answer the same before god, that there is non that hath any title or intrest in them but that I may give them freely to my said sister, but Thomas Dobson, which had a lease of the said lands for 3 yeares and the . . . . of my clearing of this matter is because he brought a certain Deed or lease to me with certaine witnesses which were sett, but I . . . none of these persons, and after he was gone I caused my will to be drawen againe and the formore cancelled, because I grew somewhat suspicious of his dealings, and therefor all my lands in Redworth of what title, tenour whatever within the County of Durham, I give them frely to Elizabeth, my sister, to her and her heires of her body for ever. And whereas I am indebted unto Richard Robinson a certaine some of money, I give to him in lieu thereof my farme and cottage in Whorlton, which is well worth the money, and if that he refuse the said farme upon the condition my will is that it goe to Elizabeth, my sister, and if the said Richard Robinson claime any title in my land, my mind and will is that he have nothing to do with any part of other farming nor land nor any part whatsoever is mine, but that it goe, both farme and lande wholy, to my sister abovesaid. I give to the poore of Whorlton, 6s. I give to the use of the church, 10s., and my mynd and will is that my debts be paide out of my goodes. I give to John Hornesby on cowe, All the rest of my goods undisposed I give to Richard Robinson, my halfe brother, whom I make Executor. Witnesses, Hen. Armitage, clericus, John Ovington, William Applebye.

REBECCA WITHERINGTON.[1]

Nov. 1, 1625. In the name of God, Amen, I, Rebecca Witherington, of Stainthropp, in the County of Durham, Spinster, sicke in bodye. To be decently buried where my nephew, Toby Ewbank, shall thinke fitting, whom I make sole Executor of this my last Will and Testament, and whome I appoint to distributte these legacies which I bestow according to this my said last Will. I give and bequeathe unto the said Toby all and singular my goods and chattells, moveable and unmoveable, of what kind, nature or qualitie whatsoever and wheresoever (except such legacies and bequests as I shall hereafter dispose of), first, I give and bequeath to my sister, Martha Samford, fower twentie shillings peeces, and to her daughter, Elizabeth Hilton, one pounde. To Martha Samforde and Margarett Samford, to either of these, one pound, and to Dorithy Samford, tenn shillings. I give to my nephew, Mr. Edward Grey, one pounde, and to John Pemmerton, my godsone, one pound, and to Mary Pemmerton, his sister, five shillings. To Rebecca Witherington, wife of Isaac Witherington, five poundes if she be livinge, otherwise if she be dead then I give the said legacie of five pounds to her brother, Robt. Witherington, to whome I also give other five pounds. I give to my servante, Florence Brasse, 5s. To Widow Robson, 5s. To Elinore Ovington, 5s. To Abraham Herseman, 2s. To John Atkinson, 2s. To John Waterman, 2s. To Isabell Harrison, 2s. To Jane Awde, 2s. To Mary Applebie, 2s., and to Dorithy Watson, 2s. To the poore people of Stainthropp to have 40s. To my formerly named Executor, Toby Ewbanke, and Mary, now his wife, to either of these, two Jacobus peeces, and to Henry

[1] She was a dau. of Sir John Widdrington of Widdrington, by his second wife, Agnes, dau. of Edward Gower. Isaac Widdrington was her brother and Robert his son. Her nephew, Toby Ewbank (son of Henry Ewbank, prebendary of the twelfth stall, Rector of Whickham, bur. at Staindrop, 12 July, 1681), mar., firstly, Elizabeth, dau. of Richard Walton, bapt., 24 Nov., 1584, at St. Nich., Durham, and widow of Richard Stobert (to whom she was mar., 9 June, 1607, at St. Mary-the-Less, he was bur. there, 18 Apl., 1610); she mar., secondly, at the same church, 25 Apl., 1611, and was bur., 25 Aug., in the same year, at Durham Abbey (her burial entry is not entered in the Abbey registers, but is so stated in the registers of St. Mary-le-Less); Toby mar., secondly, Mary, dau. of Sir Henry Grey of Chillingham, 31 Jan., 1613/14, at Grindon; she was bur. at Staindrop, 21 Apl., 1681.

Ewbanke, his sonne, one pound, and to Toby Ewbanke, my god-
sonne, one Jacobus peece, and to his two daughters Anne and
Jane, to either of these, one pound. Witnesses to will, Edward
Gray, Mary Ewbanks, Sissaly Stevenson, Florence Bras.

THOMAS CONYERS.[1]

Jan. 8, 1625. In the name of God, Amen, I, Thomas Conyers,
of Sedgefield, in the County of Durham, Gent., sick of bodye.
I comend my bodye to the earth whereof it is made, hopeing my
executor hereafter named will see it interred in the Church of
Sedgefield as near as convenientlie may be to the place where
my father and other friends lye buryed. I give and bequeath
40s. to be distributed to the poore at the discretion of my
executor. I give to my loveing cosen, Sir George Conyers of
Sockburne, Knight, 5l., which he oweth me, being part of money
due and unpaid upon his bond remayneing in my custodie, and
my desyre is that the same shalbe bestowed in apece of plate
to remain to that house as a remembrance of me. I give to my
nephew, Sir Ralph Conyers of Layton, Knight, one spurrioll,
and to my nece his wife, one triple soveringe. I give to my
nephew Cuthbert Conyers, his eldest sonne, 26l. 13s. 4d., to be
bestowed on a silver basinge and ewre, to be continued to the
heires male of Layton. To my nephew Marmaduke Conyers, his
younger sonne, 3l. 6s. 8d. To my nece Mary, his eldest daughter,
3l. 6s. 8d. I give to my nece Anne Conyers, his second daughter
and my god daughter, 3l. 6s. 8d., and the presse which standeth
in my p'ler. I give to my nece Ellinor Conyers, his youngest
daughter, 3l. 6s. 8d. To my nece Anne Metcalfe, 20s. To my
nece Alice Perrye, 20s. To my nece Katherine Richardson, 20s.,
and to every of hir children, 20s. and to my nece, Averin
Parkinson, 20s. I give to my nephew, Charles Conyers, 50l.
and one trunke with lock and key. To my nece Dorothye Conyers,
his sister, 20l., so as she bestowe hir selfe in marriage or otherwise live in good order to the comfort and likeinge of my said
executor. I give to my nece Ellinor Conyers, his younger sister,
100l. and the stand bed furnished, two chestes, six silver sponnes,
one gold Ringe whereout the stone is lost, one chaire, one cubbert,
one trunke with lock and key, and nine peces of pewther. To my
Servant, John Robinson, 3l., and to my servant, Katherine Orton,
4l. and my kitchin to dwell in dureing the terme if she so long
live. To my nephew, James Lawson of Nesham, one Angell of
golde. To my nece, Anne Jenison, 40s. and my painted Coser.

---

[1] The testator's burial is not recorded in the Sedgefield registers.
He was the seventh son of Cuthbert Conyers of Layton, whose will is
printed in this Society's publications, Vol. 2, pp. 184-6, and dated
28 Sept., 1558. There is a pedigree of this family in Surtees *History of
Durham*, iii., 37.

Whereas my nephew, Robert Wormley, is indebted unto me and
oweth divers somes of money, as his bonds appeareth, I give to
my nece his wife Margaret, 20s., to my godson, Thomas Wormley,
20s., and to my nece, Marye Wormleye, 20s., to be paid by my
executor when the said Robert payeth the said moneys due upon
the said bonds, if the same be paid without delay or charge of
sale, otherwise the said legacies to the said Margaret, Thomas
and Marye to be voyd. I give to my nece, Jaine Hodgson, the
wife of John Hodgson of Mannerhouse, 40s., and to there sone,
John Hodgson, one gold ringe. I give to my cosen, Robert Ward
of Trimdon, 10s. in gold. I give to Anne Haggstone, 5s. To
Sislye Mitcheson, 2s. 6d. Whereas the most of my estate and
meanes is in the hands of other men, to be paid some at days
past, some at dayes to come, my will and meaning is that my
executor shall pay and discharge the severall legacies by me
given and bequeathed as abovesaid within six monthes after he
shall receive the same, and not to be charged to pay them before.
Whereas divers of the legatories above mentioned are young and
unable to dispose and . . . . there said legacies or to give
a lawful discharge upon the receipt thereof, my mind and will
is that my executor shall imploy the legacies given to the said
Charles Conyers, Dorothy Conyers and Ellinor Conyers, his sisters,
for their benefitt till they, and every of them, shallbe of age to
give a sufficient discharge, and in the meantime my will is that
my executor shall from and after the receipt of moneys due unto
me, give the said Charles, Dorothy and Ellinor competent maintenance according to the rate of there severall legacies, and the
rest of all my goods, chattells, debts, or whatsoever else in lawe
or in right, moveable and immoveable, due unto me, my debts
and legacies paid and funerall expences deducted, I give and
bequeath to my loveing nephew, Sir Ralph Conyers of Layton,
Knight, whom I ordeyne to be my sole Executor. Witnesses,
Christopher Burrell, George Heighington, Humfre Mayson,
Charles Conyers.

Jan. 11, 1625. Inventory of the goods of Thomas Conyers,
late of Sedgefield, Gent. Impris, his purse and appell, 27l. One
great gold ringe, 3l. One lesser golde ringe, 10s. Six silver
spoones, 30s. One standbedd, 2 fether bedds, 2 bolsters, 2
pillowes, one paire of blanketts, one green rug, one coverlett, 8l.
Two truckle beds, 3 old fether beds, six old cushiones, one mattris,
5 olde blanketts, one old bolster, 5 coverletts, 2 pillowes, 46s. 8d.
Three pare of lynen sheetes, 2 pare of courser sheetes, 2 towells,
4 pillobeares, 13 napkins, 3 table clothes, 40s. One little counter,
one carpett, 2 chaires, one clostole, one oken chist, one desk, one
forke, one halbert, one gautlett, one broken pistole, one steale
capp, a coate of plate and plate brickes, 2 recon crookes, a parr
of barrs, two parre of tonges, 2 spitts, a parre of rackes, a fyre
shovell, 2 parre of broyle irons, a beefe forke, a dripping pan,

a brasse candlestick and other small emplements, 33s. 4d. One painted coser, 2s. One chaire, three puffett stooles, 3 chestes, one cubbert, one trunke, one deske and box, 40s. One trunke with lock and key, 3s. One press, 30s. One old black nagg, 13s. 4d. One brason morter and pestall, 20s. Twelve puter dishes, 2 brass potts, one kettell, one possnett, one chaising dish, one skimer, 2 pans, 40s. One presser bord, one forme, choppinge knife, one frying pan, 3 shelves, one maskinge tubb, one gilefatt, one tubb stole, one tubb, one coolinge tubb, 2 barrels, and some other small implements, 10s. Hay in the barne, 20s. The lease of the house, with some small things there, 32s.

Dec. 15, 1627. Added to this Inventorie by Mr. Barnabie Hutchinson as followeth, viz., A note of such debts as were due to Thomas Conyers, gent., deceased, and came to the notice of Sir Ralph Conyers, Knight, his executor, since his exhibiting of the Inventeries into the Court. Impris, a bond wherein Anthony Appleby and others stood bound to the said decd in the sume of 400l., for the payment of 200l. One other bond wherein Fra. Welfoote and others were bound in the sume of 200l., for payment of 100l. One other bond wherein Raiph Welfoote and others were bound to the said decd, 80l., for payment of 40l. One other bond wherein Thomas Lucock and others were bound to the said decd in 40l., for payment of 20l. One other bond wherein Geo. Dixon and others in 100l., for payment of 50l. Geo. Heighington and others in 40l., for payment, 20l.

WILLIAM STRINGER.

Feb. 6, 1625. In the name of God, Amen, I, William Stringer, of Borrowby, in the County of York, yeoman, sick in body. To be buried in the Churchyard of Leake. Item, I give to my wife one bedstead which is now at Rounton, one of my best coverlets, one happin, one payre of blanckets, one mattress, one payre of linen shetes, to be taken oute of the best, one payre of curtaynes, and one truncke. I give to my brother, Edmond Stringer, my sword girdell and hingers. I give to my brother, Thomas Stringer, my read clocke, one dublet and one payer of britches. I give to my sister, Agnis Huntrishe, 10s. And I likewise give to my wife, Elesabeth Stringer, all other goods and chattels, moveable and unmoveable, my debts, legasses and funerall expences deducted, and I doe make her sole executrix. I doe give and ad to this my will that sister Margrett Stevenson and hir two sonnes, Thomas and William Stevenson, have 5s. equally between them. And to my frind, Thomas Lumley, who maid this my Will, 2s. 6d. Witnesses, George Taylor, Thomas Smelt, Tho. Lumley.

INVENTORY, 14l. 6s. 0d.

ROBERT CHAMBERS.[1]

Feb. 18, 1625. In the name of Gode, Amen, I, Robert Chambers, of the Towne and Countie of Newcastle upon Tyne, Master Mariner, being sick in bodye. My bodye I comit unto the earthe from whence it came, to be buried within the pish church of All Sts within the towne of Newcastle upon Tyne, so near unto my late wife, Anne Chambers, as possibly I cann or maie. And as for the worldlie goodes which the lord hath endoweth me withall, I give and bequeath as follows, First, I give and bequeath unto the poore of the pish of All Saints aforesaid the sume of tenn shillings, to be distributed unto them at the discretion of my executors hereafter named. I give and bequeath unto my two daughters, Elizabeth and Anery Chambers, All those roomes and howses now in the occupation of me, the said Robt. Chambers, and Robert Anderson, Mariner, situate within the Towne of Newcastle-on-Tyne, in a layne or chaire there called Byker Chaire, To have and to hold all the said roomes and howses, with their appurtenances, untill the said Elizabeth and Anery and their heires, equally to be divided between them for ever. I give and bequeath unto my other three daughters, Anne Ily, wife of George Ily, Jane Houpe, widowe, and Margaret Wardhaughe, wife of William Wardhaughe, Merchant, All those three tenements now in the occupation of Margaret Ord, weadow, Ann Bee, weadow, Margaret Newton, Weadow, situate in Byker chaire aforesaide. To have and to hold All the said three last tenements, with their appurtenances and every pt thereof, unto Ann Ile, Jane Houpe and Margaret Woodhaugh and their heires, equally to be devided amongst them for ever. I give and bequeath unto Jane Mawe, tenn shillings, for a token. I give and bequeath unto Jane Allen, wife of Pheneis Allen, master Mariner, ten shillings, for a token. I give and bequeath unto my daughter, Elizabeth, one oversett bedd, six quishons, six dishes, one beare boule of silver, and two silver spoones. And as for all the rest of my goods and chattells, as well moveable as unmoveable, my debts, legacies and funerall expences being paid and discharged, I give and bequeath unto the said Elizabeth and Anery, my daughters, whom I make and ordeyne my full and sole Executor of this my last Will and Testament. Witnesses, Phineis Allen, William Hayle, Anthony Norman. Proved, 1626.

---

[1] The testator was bur. at All Saints', Newcastle, 5 Mch., 1625/6, where two of his daughters were bapt., Elizabeth, 23 Sept., 1601, and Averell, 13 April, 1604.

WILLIAM HARLE.[1]

April 30, 1626. In the name of God, Amen, I, William Harle of Mouncton, in the County of Durham, Yeoman, being sick of bodie. My bodie to be buryed in Jarrowe Church. As for my temporall goods, I doe give unto my well beloved wife, Ann Harle, the full estate and interest and terme of yeares of my farme in Mouncton aforesaid, within the said County of Durham, during soe long as the said Ann Harle, my wife, contiynieth in my name and my absolute widdow, and after hir decease to come unto my sonn, George Harle, he paying forth unto the rest of my children, as namely, Richard Harle, Alice Harle, Elizabeth Harle and Jane Harle, to every one of them 20*l*. a peece, and failing ane one of them the said 20*l*. to be devided to the surviving as they shall dye without issue, and if it fortune the said George Harle's wyfe shall departe this naturall life, my will is the saide George Harle, my sone, shall then presently enter the half part of the said farme within three dayes next after his said wive's deathe, and faileing the issue of George Harle lawfully begotton of his bodie, then the said farmehold to come unto my successor. It is agreed between the said William Harle and George Harle, his said sonne, at the makeing of this his last Will, that whereas the said William Harle was behind with the said George for certaine reckinings and accompts, they are now agreed that the said William Harle and Ann, his wife, is to content and pay unto the said George Harle the some of 3*l*. of lawful English money for and during the term of tenn yeares next ensueing after the date hereof at two terms in the yeare, that is to say, 30*s*. of lawful English money at, in or upon the feast of St. Martin the Bishop in Winter next ensewing after the date hereof, and the other 30*s*. of like lawful English money at, in and upon the feaste of Penticost, commonly called Whitsunday, next and immediatlie followinge, if the said George Harle doe live soe long. And also two beaste gaits in the oxe pasture for and dureing the terme of tenn yeares next ensewing after the date hereof, if he the said George Harle soe long shall live. And likewise it is agreed between the said William Harle and George Harle that he, the said William Harle, or Ann Harle, his wife, is to content

[1] He was bur. at Jarrow, 4 May, 1626. He mar., firstly, Jane, Atkinson, 24 Nov., 1590, bur., 4 May, 1606; by her he had issue, William, bapt., 10 Sept., 1594; Ralph, bapt., 14 Nov., 1595, bur., 5 Nov., 1596; George, bapt., 12 Feb., 1597/8; Thomas, bapt., 14 June, bur., 25 Aug., 1601; Elinor, bapt., 15 Apl., 1593, bur., 2 June, same year; Elizabeth, bapt., 13 Apl., 1600; Dorothy, bapt., 13 Mch., 1602/3, bur., 22 Aug., 1612; Margery, bapt., 30 May, bur., 30 July, 1606. He mar., secondly, at Boldon, 25 Nov., 1606, Ann, or Agnes Welsh; by her he had James, bapt., 26 Nov., 1609; Richard, bapt., 28 Nov., 1613; Stephen, bur., 25 Sept., 1622; Alice, bapt., 16 Feb., 1607/8; Ellinor, bapt., 15 Mch., 1611/12, bur., 27 Dec., 1612; Elizabeth, bapt., 24 Nov., 1616; Jane, bapt., 22 Aug., 1619, bur., 1 July, 1634; all dates from Jarrow registers.

and pay unto the said George Harle the sume of 6*l.* 13*s.* 4*d.* of lawful English money for his filiall and child's part and porcon of all the said William Harle his goods, and to be paid at such time or times as the said Ann Harle convenientlie shallbe able. And further that the said William Harle is to give unto the said George Harle one browne whye. I doe give my goods that shall remaine of the said farmholde unto my well beloved wife, Ann Harle, and my said children, viz., James Harle, Richarde Harle, Alice Harle, Elizabeth Harle and Jane Harle, equally to be divided amongst them, my debts being paid forth of the said goods. I doe give unto my sonne, James Harle, my three salt panns next adjoining unto William Chapman, and he to pay forthe of the said panns unto my daughter, Alice Harle, 30*l.*, and to Richard Harle, Elizabeth Harle and Jane Harle, my children above saide, to every one of them, 20*l.* a peace, and failing any one of them to come to the survivors to be equally divided amongst them. I doe make my well beloved wife, Ann Harle, and Elizabeth Harle, my daughter, my cheafe executors of all my goods and chattells of the said farme. I doe make Reginald Fawcett of Fullwell and John Welch of Bouldon my cheafe Supervisors of this my will, and doe give to either of them, one two and twenty shilling peaces. I give unto my sister, Margerie Harle, for a remembrance, one two and twenty shilling peaces. Witnesses, Anthonye Young, George Harle, Reginald Fawcett.

INVENTORY, 262*l.* 1*s.* 0*d.* Proved, 1626.

NUNCUPATIVE WILL OF PETER FORSER.[1]

Memorandum, That Mr. Peter Forser, late of Kelloe, decd, who died about the fifteenth day of this instant May, 1626, being of pfect mind and memory, Did divers times during the time of his sickness say, in ye psence of John Trolop and others, that . . . Robinson's debt did the most trooble his mind of any debt he ought, how to discharge the same, and that his desire was that of all others there shold be most special care taken for the due discharge thereof, and verily thinketh his desire was he shold have administration before the rest, knowing that his wife and the rest of his neerest kindred . . . were not capable of it in respect of their recusancyes, Signed, John Trollopp. This appeareth unto me, by the oath of the said John Troulopp, to be the true will of the said Mr. Peter Forser, wch I do admit of, and have accordingly comitt the administration to the said Mr. Roberte Robinson above specified, whom I have sworne. Jo. Craddocke, 24 May, 1626. Proved, 1626.

[1] He was the son of Thomas Forcer, whose will is printed in this volume, by his wife, Margaret, dau. of Francis Trollop of Eden; he mar. Catherine, dau. of Robert Hodshon of Hebburn. By her he had six sons and two daughters, John, bur. at St. Margaret's, Durham, 31 Aug., 1665, mar. Jane, dau. of Sir Thomas Riddell of Gateshead; Francis, Thomas, Peter and Robert, and Anne, and Mary who mar. William Eure of Elvet. His *Inq. p.m.* was taken at Durham, 1 Aug., 1626.

196

NUNCUPATIVE WILL OF ROBERT POTT.[1]

June, 1626. Robert Pott of Hallystone, in the County of
Northumberland, being about to take journey beyond the seas and
to take his fortune in travell, and desiring before he departs to
settle his estate by makeing of his last Will, Did upon or about
the monthe of June, 1626, declare and express his last Will
nuncupative, desireing the same to be set down, containeing
these wordes, or the like in effect. He earnestlie requested his
father-in-law, Michael Potts of the Parkhead, in the parish of
Allanton, to take the care and oversight of his wife and childe,
and to gather up and preserve for them untill his returne those
debts and other things which he had left and trusted forth into
other men's hands. And if it happened that he should never
returne alive again, then he charged his said father-in-lawe very
speciallie, as only he would answer him before the face of God,
that if his wife did afterwards marry againe with another
husbande, he, his said father-in-lawe, should take and bring up
his child, Percivall Potts, during his minortie and receive and
keepe, and for his benefitt putt forwarde the full part of the
said testator's goods, which by lawe should fall due for his said
childe. And lastly, he did appoint his said father-in-law to be
sole Executor. All which words were spoken and declared at
Gateshead about the time aforesaid in presence of Parcivall Pott,
William Pott and Edward Hall.

INVENTORY, 33*l.* 9*s.* 0*d.*   Probate, 1635.

HENRY WIDDRINGTON.

June 14, 1626. Henry Widdrington. Inventory of the goods
and chattells of the said Henry Widdrington of Nether trewhitt,
in the Countie of Northumberland, gentleman, died seized of the
seventh day of December, 1625, viewed, valued and prized by
six in defferent men for that purpose, viz., Thomas Orde of
Thropton spitle, gentleman, John Ripley of Ritton, gentleman,
Gawin Claveringe, Michael Hymers, John Thornton and Thomas
Reiveley, taken the 14th day of June, 1626, as foloweth :—At
Trewhitt : 300 ozen at forty shillings a piece, 60*l.*   8 stotts at
forty shillings, 16*l.*   Foure Kyne at five nobles, 5*l.* 6*s.* 8*d.*   Three
sturdy quies, 1*l.* 10*s.*   Two nagges and a mare, 6*l.*   At Osway
ford : Twenty five kyne and calfes, five nobles each, 41*l.* 13*s.* 4*d.*
Five yeeld kyne, 8*l.* 6*s.* 8*d.*   Five kyne, 8*l.* 6*s.* 8*d.*   Nineteen
two yeare olds at 30*s.* 6*d.*, 34*l.* 4*s.* 0*d.*   Twenty one yeare olds
at twenty shillings, 21*l.*   Two bulls, 3*l.* 6*s.* 8*d.*   Seventy-two
weathers at six shillings a piece, 21*l.* 12*s.* 0*d.*   Six topes,
1*l.* 4*s.* 0*d.*   Ninety lambes, 9*l.*   Ninety four gimmer and dinmonds, 18*l.* 16*s.*   Five score and fifteene ewes, 23*l.*   Three mares

[1] There is a pedigree of the family of Potts of Holystone printed
in *Arch. Ael.*, 3rd ser., iv., 124.

and a folle, 7*l*. 10*s*. 0*d*. Three young colts, 2*l*. 10*s*. Sixteene swine, 2*l*. 13*s*. 4*d*. Att Trewhitt : Five Rye stackes in the yarde, 16*l*. Five oatt stackes, 5*l*. Two peese stackes, 1*l*. 12*s*. One bigge stack, 2*l*. 13*s*. 4*d*. Emplements of husbandry, 4*l*. Ten Kyne and fortie ewes and lambs sold to pay the rent at Whitsontide, 39*l*. 10*s*. Four rye stacks taken in before the value hereof, 20*l*. Five bigg stacks, 19*l*. 10*s*. 0*d*. Seven oatt stacks, 21*l*. Eleven pees stacks, 10*l*. 6*s*. 8*d*. A note of household stuffe at Trewhitt : One longe table, 11*s*. Three kubberts, 30*s*. Three little tables, 6*s*. Three bedsteades, 6*s*. 8*d*. Fower chists, 5*s*. 4*d*. Three chaires, 6*s*. A dozen buffet stooles, 12*s*. Two longe formes, 18*d*. One litle table, 6*d*. Three featherbeds, 20*s*. Sixe paire of blankets, 9*s*. Sixteene paire of sheets, 3*l*. Tenn coverletts, 10*s*. Three bowlsters and fower pillirs, 8*s*. One dozen of linen pillibers, 9*s*. Three linen table clothes, 8*s*. Two dozen of table napkins, 9*s*. Three carpen clothes, 4*s*. Four brasse potts, 13*s*. 4*d*. Three pans, 3*s*. One brewinge cetle, 10*s*. Three litle cetles, 10*s*. Sixteene piece of pewder vessell, 13*s*. 4*d*. Tow pewder pots, 4*s*. Fower pewder candlesticks, 2*s*. 6*d*. Three salt sellers, 18*d*. A bason and a ure, 5*s*. A dozen of pewder spoones, 12*d*. Three chamber potts, 3*s*. 4*d*. Tow dozen of trenchers, 8*d*. Tow speates, tow barrs and tow crookes, 3*s*. Tow pewder bowles, 12*d*. Fower quishiones, 16*d*. One brewing tubb and a gyle fatt, with other implements of wood vessels belonging to them, 6*s*. Debts oweing to the deceased : Agnes Collingwood of Trewicke, 16*s*. From Edward Spraggon of Bickerton, 3*s*. 9*d*. Thomas Davyson of Newton, 40*s*. Young lairde Anderson of Ribsdaile, 2*l*. ·19*s*. 9*d*. George Fletcher of Evystanes, 12*s*. To Matthew Hall of Davysheel, 7*s*. David Henderson of Davysheel, 14*s*. 5*d*. John Brown of Brighouses, 8*s*. George Pott of Tosson, 2*s*. Robert Coxson of Whaton, 17*s*. Total, 160*l*. 6*s*. 3*d*.

Admon. granted 1st July, 1626. Margaret Widdrington, Widow, renounced Admon. Granted to Henry Widdrington, Gentleman, for the use of Oswald Widdrington, Michael, Robert and Roger Widdrington, children.

ROBERT WARCOP.[1]

Oct. 14, 1626. In the name of Gode, I, Robert Warcop, of Streatlam, within the Countie of Durham, Gent., sick in bodie. To be buried in Barnardcastle Church, if it please god I dye or be disolved att this tyme. Whereas I bought Unthank of one Christopher Sigswick and Henry Sigswick to me and myne for

ever, I doe nowe hereby give the said Unthanke unto my nephew,
Mr. Talbott Bowes sonne and heire apparent of my brother, Mr.
Thomas Bowes and unto his heires for ever. In consideracon
whereof my will is that he paye all such debts as I am this daie
oweing, and discharge this my Will. My will is that he pay unto
Alice Gill, 8*l.* To Mr. Thomas Tothall parson of Rombalkirk,
40*s.* To my brother, William Warcop, 40*s.* To John Hartley of
Rippon, three and thirtie shillings and fower pence. To one
Mr. Burnett of Rippon, 6*s.* 8*d.* To Charles Sanderson of Bar-
nardcastle, 10*s.* To Robt. Martindale, 10*s.* To Thomas Raine 5*s.*
To Gregory Applebie, 11*s.* To Philip Sanderson and Michael
Barnes, about twentie and six shillings. I make my said nephew
Talbott Bowes my sole Executore. Thomas Bowes, Ann Bowes,
Myles Gastells, Charles Brass, William Garstill, Leonard Johnson,
Witnesses. Proved, 1626.

ROBERT GREENWELL.[1]

Oct. 19, 1626. Robert Greenwell, of Stobeley, within the parish
of Lanchester in the County of Durham, Batchelor. To be buried
within the parish church of Lanchester. First I freely forgive my
Brother, William Grinwell, 20*l.* that is due to me after my mother's
death. I give to my brother William's children, Thomas Grinwell,
Nicholas Grinwell, Ann Grinwell and Jane Grinwell, 4*l.* equally
amongst them. To my brother, Richard Grinwell, 20*s.* To my
brother Nicholas' sonne, William Grinwell, 20*s.* To my brother
John's children. William Grinwell and Elizabeth, 6*l.* equally
between them. To my sister, Elizabeth Grinwell, 4*l.* The rest of
my goods and chattels I give and bequeath unto my brother, John
Grinwell, whom I make Executor. Inventory, 10*l.* 1*s.* 8*d.*
Debts oweing by the testator : To Peter Grinwell of Butsfeld, 10*l.*
To John Dickson of Durham, tanner, 10*l.* To Anthony Hutchinson, 5*l.* Oweing for three hides, 2*l.* 10*s.* 0*d.* To John Greenwell,
1*l.* Probate, 1626.

[1] The will of the testator's brother, Nicholas Greenwell of Fenhall,
in the parish of Lanchester, yeoman, is dated 12 May, 1640, and is as
follows :—To be buried in Lanchester Church, my will is that the
copyhold at the Ford which was bought of George Hopper shall be
forthwith sold towards the payment of my debts as far as it will go,
and that Anthony Surtees of Medomsley shall receive £25 every year
for 5 years, in full satisfaction of £100 due unto him. My wife to
have the freehold and Fenham and all thereunto belonging during
her life. To my daughter, Agnes, £200, for her child's portion when
21. My brother, William, owes me £10. My wife to have the copyhold which was purchased of Th. Fairbairn, and she to pass the same
back to my son, William. I give to the poor of Lanchester every
year out of my freehold land of the Fenhall, 20s., to be paid at
Christmas and Easter. I give to my brother, John Greenwell's,
children, 10 ewes and lambs. To Elizabeth Greenwell, my brother
John's daughter, a cow and a lamb. To my sister-in-law, Ellinor
Lighton's, children, every of them, one ewe and lamb. To Robert
Greenwell, son of Nicholas Greenwell's son, a whye and stock. Residue
to wife and son William. Pr. 1640.

JOHN SMITHSON.[1]

Nov. 30, 1626. In the name of God, Amen, I, John Smithson, of Church Aycliffe, in the County of Durham, Yeoman, sick in bodye. To be buried in the Churchyarde of Aicliffe. I give and bequeathe all my farme that I have in Aitcliffe aforesaid, which I hold from the Deane and Chapter of the Cathedrall Church of Durham of Christ and the blessed virgin Mary, to Elizabeth my wife, and John my eldest sonne during the whole terme of the lease, if the said Elizabeth kepe her selfe soe long my wief, and whensoever they shall think fit to lease the said terme, that it shall be leased at the cost of them both pportionably and at the end of twenty yeares the said farme to come wholly to my said son John, and if my said sone will not be ruled by my wife, that then she shall pay to him out of the said farme 6l. yearly till the end of the twenty yeares, and if my wife happen to marry, that then my said sone shall enter upon the whole farme and to pay to my wife the sum of 6l. yearly, during the terme of twenty years. I give and bequeath to Mathew Smithson, my sonne, one coat house with the appurtenances thereunto belonginge of the yearly rent of fower shillings and fower pence, which is mentioned in the said lease without paying any thinge except the said rent of 4s. 4d. over and above his child's porcon. I give to my son, Mathew Smithson, 20l., over and above his child's porcon. I give to my daughter, Jane Smithson, 20l., over and above her child's porcon. I give to my daughter, Dorothy Smithson, 20l., over and above her child's porcon. I give unto my daughter Elizabeth, 20l., over and above her child's porcon. Then my will is that if my wief hapen to be with child, that it be made equally with the rest out of my . . . . parte. I give 3l. to be bestowed upon the children of George Crosier of Newbigin and Willm. Taylor of Newbiggin and of Ann Thursbie of Haughton, widow, equally to be divided amongst them, and of this my present Testament I make and ordeine, Elizabeth Smithson my wife, my sole and only Executor. And I make and ordeine, George Crosier of Newbiggin, aforesaid gentleman, Overseer. Witnesses, John Cornforth, George Crosyer. Suma Totalis, 357l. 2s. 4d. Proved, 1626.

[1] The testator was bur. at Aycliffe (whence other dates are taken), 7 Dec., 1626, having mar. at Heighington, 12 July, 1608, Elizabeth Crosyer, who was bur., 9 July, 1629; by her he had issue, Nicholas, bapt., 21 May, 1609, bur., 8 Mch., 1610/11; George, bapt., 2 Sept., 1610, bur., 8 Jan., 1610/11; John, bapt., 1 Apl., 1616; Matthew, bapt., 5 Mch., 1619/20; Anne, bapt., 5 Jan., 1611/12, bur., 7 Mch., 1613/14; Jane, bapt., 3 Feb., 1613/14, mar. at Coniscliffe, 10 May, 1636, George Heighington; Margaret, bapt., 12 July, 1618, bur., 23 Apl., 1619; Dorothy, bapt., 8 July, 1622, bur., 21 May, 1629; Anne, bapt., 12 Dec., 1624; Mary, bapt., 7 June, 1627; Elizabeth, mar. George Heighington, 18 Feb., 1628/9.

RALPH CLAVERING.

Feb. 13, 1626. Ralph Clavering of Tilmouth, within the liberty of Norhame and Countie Pallantyne of Durhame, gentilman. First I bequeath my soulle to god almightie my maker, and to Christ Jesus, his sone, my redeemer. To be buried in the Chancell at Norhame. I give to my daughter, Margarett Selby, one ould angel. To my daughter, Dorothie Burrell, one ould angel. To Margarett Claveringe of Crawhall, my sonn Ralph Clavering's daughter, one ould angel. To my [grand] sone Gilbert Claveringe, son to the said Ralph Clavering, 5*l.* to putt him to one trade. To Henry Armoure one quy going at the licker, and for the true performance of this my Will I institute and make Ralph Clavering and George Clavering my grand-sonns my executors.

INVENTORY : three score and tenne ewes at 4*l.*, the score price, 8*l.* Thirtie hoggs, 3*l.* 15*s.* Tenne Kine, 26*s.* 8*d.* a piece, 13*l.* 6*s.* 8*d.* One mare, 40*s.* Probate, 27th February, 1628.

WILLIAM SCURFIELD.[1]

Feb. 20, 1626. In the name of God, Amen, I, William Scurfield of Elstob, within the parish of Great Stainton, in the County of Durham, Yeoman, now somewhat weake and sick in bodye. To be buried in Stainton Quire. I doe give unto my well beloved wife, Elizabeth Scurfield, my best horse or mare at her choyce. I doe give unto Edward Reye, my sister's sone, twenty shillings. I doe give unto my servante, Henry Archer, twenty shillings yearly during his life nrall, to be paid in money out of fur-lands, as also during the same time that house in Elstob where he now dwelleth, As also a Cowegate in summer in furlands aforesaid, and hay and grass for her in winter in the great shaw close, without any payment for the same during his life, saveing that during his life, shall make and uphold all the out ditches and fences about all my grounds at Elstob at his owne charge, in regard wherof I give him the 20*s.* yearly as is aforesaid, Provided alwayes that he, the said Henry, continue dutifull

---

[1] Matthew, the father of the testator, of Burnigill, in the parish of Brancepeth, was bur. there, 21 Feb., 1600/1, his eldest son, William, the testator, was bur. at Stainton, 13 Apl., 1627, as also was his widow, Elizabeth, 14 Feb., 1644/5, his first wife, Alice, being bur. there, 8 Jan., 1607/8. By his second wife he had William, bapt., 6 May, 1614, bur , 27 Nov., 1694, mar. Elizabeth Cooke of Stockton, 14 June, 1665, at Redmarshall; George, bapt., 18 June, 1615, bur. at Great Stainton, 19 July, 1640, being "slayne," 18 July (Bishop Middleham Regs.), he mar., firstly, Elizabeth Morpeth, 29 May, 1633, bur., 1 Jan., 1634/5, at Redmarshall (her only child, George, bapt., 28 Sept., 1634, bur.; 22 Mch., 1634/5, at the same place); he mar., secondly, Margaret Richardson, who remar. Major Thomas Lilburne of Offerton, 30 July, 1646, at Houghton-le-Spring, she was bur. there, 9 Sept., 1665, he was also bur. there, 25 Mch., 1665; Edward, bapt.,

to my wife and be my servante at my death, otherwise these my
bequests to him given to be utterly voyd. I give and bequeath
unto my sone and heir, William Scurfield, and to the heirs of
his bodye lawfully to be begotten, for ever all and singular my
lands, tents and hereditaments in Elstob, bequeathed with all
the those lands, tenemts and hereditaments in Wowgrave, within
the County of Durham, with all and singular their appurtenances,
and in default of such his issue then I will that all the said
lands shall discend and come to my sone, George Scurfield, and
to the heires of his body lawfully to be begotten for ever, and in
default of such his issue then to descend and come to my sone,
Edward Scurfield, and to the heirs of his body lawfully to be
begotten for ever, And in default of such his issue then the same
to descend and come to my sone, Mathew Scurfield, and to the
heires of his body lawfully to be begotten for ever, And in default
of such issue then the same to discend and come to my daughter
Katharine, now the wife of Robert Johnson, and the heires of her
body lawfully to be begotten for ever, And for default of such
issue then the same to remaine and come to the right heires of
me, the first named William Scurfield, for ever. I give and
bequeath all those my lands, tents and hereditaments in Bradbury,
in the County of Durham, to my youngest sone, Mathew Scurfield,
and to the heers of his body lawfully to be begotten for ever,
and in default of such issue of the body of the said Mathew,
then all my said lands aforesaid at Bradbury to remaine and
come to my sone, Edward Scurfield, and to his heires for ever,
and in default of his heirs to come to the heires of me, the said
William Scurfield, for ever. I give to George Craggs of Durham,
10s. My will is that all my Amor and other like furniture shall
remaine and be kept in my house at Elstob to the use and benefit
of my sone and heire, except my cortelet and that which belongeth
it, which I give to my sonne George. I give to the poore householders of Staineton parish, 20s. in money, to be distributed by
my wife, and to the poore of Stockton, Preston and Hartburne,
20s. To Margaret Maland, wife of Robert Maland, 20s. To

10 Oct., 1619, bur., 17 Mch., 1666/7, mar. Sarah Jackson of Elstob,
10 May, 1649; Matthew, bapt. the same day as his brother, Edward,
mar. Elizabeth Rose, 1 July, 1662, she was bur., 1 Dec., 1696, and
he, 22 Jan., 1701/2; Katharine, bapt., 13 Apl., 1609, mar. Robert
Johnson; Elizabeth, bapt., 5 May, 1611, bur., 19 Apl., 1613; the above
dates are from Stainton, the dates given below from Brancepeth,
unless otherwise stated: Ralph, brother of the testator, was bur.,
7 Mch., 1621/2, being twice mar., his first wife being bur., 20 Aug.,
1611, by her he had John, bapt., 5 May, 1605, mar. Frances Wells,
23 Nov., 1630, at St. Mary-le-Bow, she was bur., 1 June, 1641; by his
second wife, Elizabeth Hoorde, mar., 6 Oct., 1612, at Sedgefield, bur.,
2 Jan., 1636/7, he had William, bapt., 8 Aug., 1613; George, bapt.,
20 Feb., 1619/20, and Elizabeth, bapt., 1 Dec., 1616. His *Inq. p.m.*
was taken at Durham, 1 Sept., 1627. William, aged 12, is his son
and next heir; his son Edward is also mentioned.

my brother John, 10s. for a token, and to John Farriliss of Sedgefield, 10s. Touching my second sonne, George Scurfield, I need not hereby remember him with any other portion or advancement then that which I have already provided and purchased for him jointlye with my selfe, in those landes at Wheatley hill, Shirraton and Shirraton Grange, All which lands I hereby will and intend shall come and discend unto him according to the purchase thereof. And I will that my said sone George shall be educated and brought up with my wife during his minority, and she to have 10l. yearly forth of his rents of his sayd lands towards his mantenance, and more as his charge shall require. And my further will is that my wife shall take and receive the issues and profitts of my said sone George his lands at Wheatley hill, Shirraton, Shirraton Grange during his minority to his use, and put the same forward for his benefit and profitt. Whereas the Reverend Father in God, Richard, now Bpp of Durham, hath by articles under his hand and great seal, granted the wardshipp and custody of my sone or heir or heires, And of such lands as shall after my death descend to my said heire, to such pson or psons as I shall assigne the same in my lifetime, or by my last Will, if the said Wardshipp doe happen to the said Reverend Father as Bpp of Durham, as by the said Articles more at large doth appeare, now my will and meaning is and I hereby give and bequeath the said Wardshipp and grant thereof, together with the marriage of my said sonne with the issues and profitts of his lands, if the same doe fall in the time of the said Rt. Reverend Father to my loveing wife, Elizabeth Scurfield, to the only use and benefit of my said sonne and heir in manner and forme as hereafter shall be expressed (vizt.), my will and meaning is that my wife for her thirds of all my lands at Elstob or elsewhere, for her and my sonne and heires mentioned, shall have and enjoy my house and lands at Elstobb, except the great Shaw Close, the furlands with Sandilands which is now eaten and occupied with the furlands during my sonn's minority, if she so long shall live, and that the yearly rents or value of the said three Closes before named shall yearly be collected and taken by my sayd wife and Robert Johnson, my sonn-in-law, and the same to continue in the keeping of my wife during the minority of my said heire, And to be putt forward for his use by the advice of my friends, to help him to stock his grounds when he comes to age, And my will is that my said heire shall be brought up by my wife or by her direction, and she to have further compact allowance forth of the same lands as his charge shall require. I give unto my daughter Katherine, now the wife of Robert Johnson, that third part of Bowesfield which I have already taken and provided for her by lease from the Lord Bpp of Durham, as also I give unto her 20l. in money, to be payd unto her within six months after

my decease, And these my bequests, together with that I gave
her in marriage, to stand and be to her in full satisfacon of her
filiall porcon, and all other part of my goods, chattells, rights
and creditts whereof I shall be possessed at my death. I give
unto my sonne and heire, William Scurfield, eight draught oxen,
with all my plow geare and wane geare for husbandry remaining
at my death, to be preserved for him, or as good provided for
him when he shall come to age. I also give unto my said sone
William a like third parte of Bowesfield, which I have taken for
him and in his name of the lord Bpp of Durham. I likewise
give to my sone, George Scurfield, the other third part of Bowesfield, taken in his name from the said Lord Bpp of Durham.
And my will is that if the rents yearly of Bowesfield . . . . them
due to my daughter as aforesaid, shall be taken and collected
by my wife and Robert Johnson, my sone-in-law, and remaine
in the custody of my wife during the minority of my said sonns
Wm. and George, and to be put forward to the benefitt and
profitt. I give to my sister, Ellen Harrison, wife of John Harrison
one Cowngate, in Mowgrave, in summer and winter during her life,
if he so long continue and dwell in Stainton parish. I give unto
my well beloved friend and gossip, Mr. George Martyn, 10s., for
a token, being well assured that he will discharge the great trust
that I have reposed in him and that my wife and children doe
receive no wrong, And I beseech him and my gossip, George
Craggs of Durham, to have a care that good bonds be taken of
my wife and others whom I have trusted with my children, for
the performance of this my Will, and that my children be brought
up in the feare of god and other good imployments according
to their opportuytes, that they may be better enabled to govern
themselves and their estates when they shall come of age. My
further will is that if my wife doe depart this life before my
sonne and heire shall come to age, that then my sone-in-law,
Robert Johnson, and my friend, Christopher Morpeth of Stillington, shall jointly have the custody of my said heire and the
receipt of the issues and profitts of his lands and other . . . .
due unto him, to the use and benefitt of my said heire, and the
profitts thereof to be putt forward to his use, and they my said
friend and son-in-law to give an account of the same to my said
sone when he shall come to age, the charge of his education and
the expences about his affairs being to them liberally allowed,
and my will is that noe more or other of my sons groundes be
plowed up during his minority then shall be in tillage at my
death. My further will is that if my wife depart this life before
all or any of my youngest sonns come to age, then I give the gover-
ment of them and their portions and rights to my sone in law,
Robert Johnson, and Katherine, his wife, not doubting but
they will have a special care of their education. All the rest

of my goods, chattells and debts whatsoever formerly not herein
bequeathed, my debts, legacys, funerall expences and my wife's
thirds discharged, I doe give and bequeath to my sone, Edward
Scurfield, And I doe also make and ordaine my said sonne
Edward my full and sole executor of this my last Will and
Testament. And I desire my gossip, Mr. Edward Hutton of
Durham, who is Godfather to my sonne Edward, to have a care
that he may have what is right and due unto him, to whom I
give tenn shillings for a token of my good will. And I make
Supervisors of this my last Will and Testament my Gossips,
Mr. George Martin, and George Craggs, desiring them to
take the same upon them and to have a care that my children
have that which is right and due unto them, and thus for this
time reposing my selfe in life and death in god's mercye and in
the meritts of Christ Jesus in which I hope to be saved, I be take
my selfe to the Almightie. And hereunto I set my hand and
seal. Witnesses, William Rickerbye, Robert Johnson, George
Craggs, Geo. Jackson, Wm. Browne. Proved, 20 August, 1627.

THOMAS DOBBISON.[1]

May 9, 1627. In the name of God, Amen, I, Thomas
Dobbison of Southside in Hamsterley pish in the County
of Durham, yeoman, being at the making hereof sick in bodye.
To be buried in Hamsterley Church as near to my stall where I
used to sitt as convenientlie may be, the duties therefore accustomed and my funerall to be honestlie contented and paide, and
also my mynde and will is that all the poore of the pish shallbe
paid . . . . . peny dale at the said churche doore at my buriall.
Whereas I have this present daye conveyed and granted to Willm.
Dobbison my brother and Christopher Dobbison, his sonne, the
moyetie or half parte of my three closes called Milburne, white
close and Inner Shawe, for the use of Isabell Dobison, my daughter,
during the life of Willm. Duckett and also my tenement rights
thereof, in consideration of a part of her porcon as by the said
Deed appeareth, I give and bequeath to the said Isabell Dobison
my daughter, over and besides that moytie the sume of fortye
pounds of lawful english moneye for her porcon. I give and
bequeath unto my grandchild Thomas Maddison sone of Willm.
Maddison, the sume of thirtye shillings. Also I give to the saide

[1] The testator was bur. at Hamsterley, 28 July, 1627, mar. Grace
Dowson, 29 Sept., 1594, who was bur., 31 Aug., 1614; by her he had
William, bapt., 23 Oct., 1599, bur., 23 June, 1603; Jane, bapt., 6 June,
1595, mar. William Maddison, 29 Sept., 1618; Isabel, bapt., 9 Jan..
1596/7; Alice, bapt., 1 July, 1604; Helen, bapt., 19 Oct., 1606, and
Anne, bapt., 15 Jan., 1608/9.

Thomas Maddison one gymer lambe which when he was christened
I pomised to bestow upon him. I give to my grandchild, Leonard
Maddison, ten shillings. And also I give and bequeath to his
sisters, Anne and Isabella Maddison, each of them a gymer lambe.
Whereas, I have alreadie bestowed upon my daughter, Jane
Maddison, wife of the said William Maddison, such a porcon and
mariage goods as I thought . . . . on her. I give and bequeath
unto the said Jane Maddison, five shillings . . . . in full satisfacon of all her filiall and child's porcon and all other testamentarie
bequests whatsoever, which she can claime of in and to my lands,
goods and psonall estate. Whereas, in like manner I bestowed
upon my daughter, Elizabeth Tewer, wife of Christopher Tewer,
such a porcon as I thought fitting, I will that the same be to her
as my intent was and is a full satisfaction of her filiall and
child's porcon, and I now bequeath to her the sume of twenty
shillings, in full satisfacon of all her claymes and demands
which she can or may ptend or clayme of in my landes, goods,
creditts, and personal estate whatsoever. I give and bequeath
unto Margaret Tewer, their daughter, one gymer lambe. Whereas
at or shortlie after the mariage of my sone in law, John Bancks
with Alice my daughter his now wife, by agreement I gave to
him in mariage goods and porcon with his wief the other moyetie
of the above named three closes as my intent was and now is,
I will that the same be a full satisfacon of his wife's part and
porcon of my goods and chattells. And I now give to the said
Alice, five shillings more in satisfacon of all rights, claims and
demands whatsoever, as she the said Alice and John Bancks her
huband can or may claime. I give and bequeath unto my
daughter, Helayne Dobison, my cupboarde in the fore howse,
wherein I dwell, forthe of part from the residue of my goods.
I give unto my sister Margaret Clerkson a ᴏvmer hogg. I give
unto my nephew, Christoper Dobison, a gymer hogg. I give
to Christopher Dowson, for a token, 12d. All my other goods
and chattells, creditts and debts whatsoever not before bequeathed,
I doe give and bequeath them to my said daughters, Helayne and
Isabella Dobison and doe make and ordeyne them jointe executors
of this my last Will and Testament, I heartlie praye and entreate
Christopher Emmerson of Shotton, Christopher Dobbison and
Christopher Dowson, my neighours to be supervisors of this my
last Will and Testament. to see this my will pformed and to aid
and assist my children with there friendlie counsill and advice
as my trust is in them. I give and bequeath to my grandchilde,
Thomas Bancks, twenty shillings. Witnesses, Christopher
Emerson, Christopher Dowson, Christopher Dobbison, Francis
Walker.

INVENTORY, 77l. 6s. 6d. Proved, 1627.

NICHOLAS HEATH.[1]

June 28, 1627. I, Nicholas Heath, the elder of the Cittye of Durham, Esqr., being aged and sickly in body. To be buryed in most decent manner in St. Giles his church in Durham, desiring to be layed neere unto my Father and Brothers. And I doe give unto the poore of that parish the sum of 40s. I doe give and bequeath unto my sonne, Nicholas Heath, all that my capitall messuage or Mannor house of little Eden, in the County of Durham, being the house wherein my said sonne, Nicholas Heath, now dwelleth in, together with the brewing lead and brewing vessells and all my household stuff there, as bedding, bedsteads, peuther, tables, stools, chayres, cupbords and all other implements there whatsoever. And I further do give unto him all other the howses and buildings as barnes, byers, stables, yards, foulds and stackgarthes thereunto belonginge, with all coate-houses and tenant howses adjoyning to the said capitall messuage, or in anywise belonging, To have and to hold the said capitall messuage and all and singular the premises, with the appur-tenances, unto my said sonne, Nicholas Heath, his heirs · and assigns for ever. I doe give unto my grandchild, Nicholas Heath, eldest son of my sonne, Topp Heath, deceased, the sum of 100l., to be paid unto him when he attains the age of twenty one years for to build him an howse upon his owne land at little Eden aforesaid, which 100l. my sonne, Nicholas Heath, standeth bound to pay at that day, accordingly as appeareth by his Bond. Whereas I have heretofore by my Deed indented, bearing date the 14 October, 1623, given and granted unto my daughter, Margaret Burnell, widdowe, and to my grandchilde, William Heath, second sonne of my sonne, Topp Heath, deceased, two pcells of meadow ground called Beanely meadow and the west calfe close pcell of little Eden aforesaid, To hold the same for their naturall lyves and the longer lyver of them. I doe by this Will ratifye and confirm my said grant to all intents and pur-poses according to the true meaning thereof. I doe also give and bequeath unto my said daughter and grandchild, William Heath, the rent payable forth of the said two closes, To have, hold and receive the same for so longe tyme as the same shallbe due and payable, and if either of them shall depart this lyfe during the contynewance of the said rent, then my will is that the survivor shall receive the same whole and entyre to his or her

[1] He was bur. at St. Giles', Durham, 16 July, 1627, aged 72; mar. Anne, dau. of John Topp of Shillingford, co. Bucks.; by her he had Topp, bur., 5 Apl., 1620, at Bishop Middleham ("Mr. Topp Heath of Eden, gentl., dying upon Mainsforth Moore coming fro a hors race"), mar. Anne, dau. of Sir William Blakiston, she remar. Talbot Lisle of Barmston; Nicholas, bur., 13 Mch., 1659/60, at St. Mary-the-Less, Durham, mar. Elizabeth, dau. of Roger Smyth of Finchley, co. Middlesex, and others. In his *Inq. p.m.* taken at Durham, 1 Aug., 1627, Nicholas, aged 13, his grandson (son of Topp), is his next heir.

owne selfe and benefitt. And if they shall both dye, Then my will is that the Inheritance of the said two pcells of meadow ground called Beanely meadow and west calfe close aforesaid shall come to my sonne, Nicholas Heath, and his heirs for ever. And further I bequeath unto my said daughter, Margaret Burnell, and to my grandchild, William Heath, and to the longer lyver, All that my tenant howse next adjoining to the Seate howse, late in the tenure and occupation of James Forster. To have and to hold, possess and enioy the said Tennant howse for and duringe their naturall lyves and the longer lyver of them. And I hereby charge my sonne, Nicholas Heath, That if my daughter, Margaret Burnell, his sister, and William Heath, his nephew, do permit and suffer him to contynew tenant of the said two closes, That then he doe not faile, but lovingly and peacably pay the said rent. Whereas a lease was made heretofore to me for certain yeares yet endureing by my nephews, Thomas Heath and John Heath of Whitburn, of certayne ground pcell of little Eden aforesaid, amounting to the clear value of 100*l.* by yeare, as by the said lease more particularly appeareth, And whereas I have since assigned the same unto my sonne, Nicholas Heath, and he hath covenanted with me for the true payment of 50*l.* forth of the said 100*l.* during the said terme unto my daughter, Ann Lisle, late wife of my sonne Topp Heath deceased, for and in recompence of her jointure, so that there remaineth due and payable unto me by my said sonne, Nicholas Heath, by virtue of the said lease of assignemt the other 50*l.* I bequeath unto my grandchildren, Nicholas Heath, my heire apparant, William Heath and Ann Heath, and every of them, 10*l.* a peace for and during the contyneance of the said lease, for the necessary relief, education and mayntenance of my said grandchildren. And if it please god that any of my said grandchildren, Nicholas Heath, William Heath and Anne Heath, shall depart this lyfe before the expiration of the said terme, That then the sum of 30*l.* a year so given by 10*l.* a pece shall goe and be to the better educacan and mayntenance and for the raising of a porcon for the survivor, And that the said 30*l.* a yeare be given and paid by my sonne, Nicholas Heath, to my daughter, Ann Lisle, for the education and bringing up of my said grandchildren. And my will is that my said daughter, Anne Lisle, would take the care, educacon and bringing up of her said children and see them well brought up, and instructed in god's true religion now established and cofessed in the church of England, And for the better advancement and raising of porcons for my two grandchildren, William Heath and Ann Heath, I further give them the sum of 20*l.* each, being the residue of the other moitie of 50*l.* during the expiration of the said terme. And my will and mind is that the said 20*l.* shall be payd by my sonne, Nicholas Heath, to such person or persons as my executrix and Supervisors shall think

208

fit for the husbanding of their estates, and for a true . . . . .
and repaying back of all such sums of money as shall be received,
according to the extent and purpose of this my will. And that
my executrix and supervisors shall take good bond and sufficient
security of the aforesaid person or persons. I give unto my
grandchild, John Heath, son of my sonne, John Heath, deceased,
the sum of 50*l*., to be paid forth of the sum of 100*l*. payable
unto me by my said sonne, Nicholas Heath, as by his bond to
me. I doe give the other 50*l*. due by the said bond to Katheryne
and Elizabeth Burnell, daughters of my daughter, Margaret
Burnell, when they shall lawfully marry, and in the meantime
to be employed towards their education. I give to the poor of
Little St. Maryes, 20*s*. I make, nominate and appoint the said
Margaret Burrell sole executrix of this my Will. And I doe give
and bequeath unto her all the residue of my goods and chattels.
And I doe also nominate and constitute my well beloved nephews,
Thomas Heath of Keppere West Grange and John Heath of
Whitburne, Supervisors of this my Will, and doe given to either
of them 40*s*. a peace for their paynes. Witnesses, Mich. Richard-
son, John Heath, Geo. Perk, John Watkins, John Heath, youngest.
Aug. 13, 1627. A true and pfect Inventarie of all the
goodes, chattells and creditts which Nicholas Heath the elder,
Gent, sometimes of Little Eden and late of the pish of St.
Maries in the North Bayley at Duresme, deceased, dyed
possessed of, valued and duely apprized by George Martyn, John
Heath, Cuthbert Sisson and Michael Richardson. Imprimis, In
ready money, 15*l*. His apparell, 22*l*. An artillerie bowe and
a quiver, 20*s*. A pare of garden sheares, 2*s*. 6*d*. Some odd
implements of household stuff in the kitchinge and butterie, as
brasse, some pewter, woodden vessle and barrells, 40*s*. Debts
oweing to the said deceased: One bond of 200*l*., Dated the 24
daie of June, 1626, in and from Nicholas Heath, the younger
(sonne of the said deceased), unto him, the deceased, with condicon for paymt of 104*l*. the 28 daie of December last, of which
4*l*. and consideran for the other 100*l*. are payed untill . . . mas
last past, 1627. Item, one other bond of 200*l*. in and from the
saide Nicholas, the younger, to the said deceased, dated the 27
daie of June, 1627, with condicon for paymt of 100*l*. at Martyn-
mas, 1635, The moneys of wch said two bonds the deceased hath
given in legacies by his last Will and testamt. Item, due to the
said deceased for rent and consideracon, 20*l*. Memorandum:
that whereas Mrs. Margret Burnell, daughter of the said deceased,
hath renounced her executorshipp of the deceased's will and given
waie that her brother, Mr. Nicholas Heath, shall administer
according to the said will, therefore it is agreed between them
that the 15*l*. in readie money first above mentiond disbursed by
her for the deceased funerall shall be allowed her, and he to give
her 20 nobles more in discharge thereof. Proved, 1627.

ELIZABETH MIDDLETON.[1]

July 20, 1627. In the name of God, Amen, I, Elizabeth Middleton of Offerton, in the countye of Durham, widow, being crased and sickly in bodye. To be buried in the parish Church of Houghton-in-the-Spring, as near to my father and mother as convenientlye may be. I give to the poore of Houghton pish, 10*l*., and to the poore of Bishopp Warmouth pish, other 10*l*. I give and bequeath to my eldest sonne, George Middleton, Twelve Apostle silver spoones and two other silver spoones, the one ingraven with Barnard and the other with Gilpin, a little silver bowle, my best bedstead and featherbedd, a paire of my best blanketts and a rugg with two pare of sheets and foure pillowbears and all other furniture, belonging thereunto, and also a damask tablecloth, with two chayres and two stooles all imbroided with silk. I give and bequeath to my younger sonne, Francis Middleton, half a dozen silver spoones a bedstead in the plour, with my next best featherbedd, a rugg, a pare of Blanketts, two pare of sheetes, foure pillowberes, and all the other furniture in the said plour not otherwise disposed of, I give and bequeath unto my daughter, Alice, wife of John Gill, half a dozen silver spoones, with doublewes. And I give to her, the said Alice, one hundred pounds to be paid within a yeare after my death. I give and bequeath to my grandchild, Danyell Gill, 5*l*. to buy him a peece of plate withall. And all the residue of my household stuff not bequeathed as aforesaid I give to my said daughter, Alice Gill. I give to Christopher Hall, 40*s*. I give to Robt. Ayton and Henry Wycliffe, son of William Wycliffe, either of them, 20*s*. I give to Frances Wycliffe, daughter of the said William, 20*s*. and a desk.

[1] She was the dau. of Christopher Wharton of Offerton, bur. at Houghton-le-Spring, 22 Aug., 1618, by his wife, Alice, dau. of William Shepperdson of Bishopwearmouth. Alice had previously mar. at Bishopwearmouth, 27 Aug., 1576, Peter Gunson of Cockermouth, and was bur. at Houghton-le-Spring, 15 Jan,. 1618/19. The testatrix, bapt., 31 Aug., 1581, at Houghton-le-Spring, bur. there, 16 Aug., 1627, mar. George Middleton of Offerton, bapt. at Bishopwearmouth, 14 Jan., 1577/8. Mary (the sister of the testatrix) mar. Cuthbert Mitford of Mitford. The issue of the testatrix were, George, bur., 7 Sept., 1655, at Bishopwearmouth. mar. Elizabeth, dau. of Thomas Heath of Kepyer, bapt., 5 Feb., 1608/9, at St. Giles', mar. there, 30 Dec., 1628, bur. at Bishopwearmouth, 30 Aug., 1651; Francis, bapt., 27 Nov., 1608, at Bishopwearmouth, bur. at Houghton-le-Spring, 10 Sept., 1673, mar. Joan, dau. of Edward Row of South Shields, at St. Giles', 10 July, 1634, bur. at Houghton-le-Spring, 6 May, 1691; Alice, bapt., 10 July, 1603, at Bishopwearmouth, bur. at Houghton-le-Spring, 7 Sept., 1644, mar. there, 5 Feb., 1625/6, John Gill, who was bur. at Haughton-le-Skerne, 15 Sept., 1662; their son, David Gill, bur., 16 Sept., 1680, at the same place, as also was his wife, Rebecca, dau. of William Tillard of Totnes, Devon, 18 Dec., 1673. In the *Inq. per br. de mand* taken at Durham, 30 Aug., 1628, George, aged 63, is her son and next heir, her younger son Francis being also mentioned.

I give to Ruff Younger, 20s. I give to Isabell Nicholson, and
Anne Lambert, either of them, 10s. I give 20s. to be divided
amongst my three plowman and other 20s. amongst my maids.
Whereas, I have by Deed granted to my said sone, Francis
Middleton, all those messuages, lands, tenements, and hereditaments, with the appurtenances in Offerton aforesaid, which I
lately bought and purchased of William Bowes, Esqr., and which
were some tymes parcel of the lands and possessions of John
Swynburne, late of High treason atteynted and all my estate
right, tytle, claime and demand of and in the same. To have and
to hold to the said Francis and his heeres, to the use of myself
during my lief, and after my decease to the use of him, the said
Francis, and his heires and assigns for ever. and to such further
uses, provisors and behoofs as by my last Will and Testament in
wryting, should be expressed and declared, now I doe hereby
express and declare the further use of the said grante to be that
the said Francis Middleton, shall from and after my death, pay
yearly unto Cuthbert Hall, and his assigns during his lief
the small sum of 33s. 4d., out of the issues and pfitts of the
said lands at the feasts of Saint Martin the Bushopp in
Winter and Pentecost, by equal porcons, and shall likewise pay
unto Elizabeth Craggs, 8s. per annum upon the feaste of St.
Martin the bishop in Winter, yearly during her lief or allow
her a pasture gate yearly in the Cowe pasture, during the said
terme in lieu thereof, And moreover, that the said Francis, or
his heirs shall pay unto Robert Mitford, sonne of my sister,
Mitford, deceased, the sum of two hundred pounds within two
years next after the said Robert shall come of full age, provided
that he, the said Robert, upon the atteyning his full age doe make
and seale a general release to my executor of all actions and
demands whatsoever any way due unto him before that tyme
and that the saide Robert, his tutors or guardians, doe not in the
mean tyme molest or trouble my executors for any matter or
thinge due or pretended to be due in right of the said Robert.
And I further declare that if he the said Robert Mitford do make
such release and that my executors be not in the meantime
molested by his tutor or guardians as aforesaid, and that the
said 200l. be not paid unto him as above said that then the said
Robt. Mitforde if he be then livinge, shall from the end of two
yeares next after his atteyning of his full age of 21 yeares, hold,
possess and enjoy the said messuage lands and tenements, granted
to the said Francis as aforesaid, and receive and take the rents,
issues and profitts thereof to his owne use from the tyme forth,
during the terme of tenn yeares then next following in lieu and
consideracon of the said two hundred poundes. And my will
is, the premises notwithstanding. that if either my executors
be troubled or molested by the tutor of the said Robt. Mitford,
during his minortie or that the said Robert upon his atteyning

his full age. Doe refuse to seale such release as aforesaid, then this bequest touching the two hundred pounds to be void. Provided also and I doe hereby declare the further use provided also the said grant to be that if I, the said Elizabeth Middleton, shall at any time hereafter during my lief be enjoynd to revoke the said grant and to that end or purpose pay or lawfully tender to be paid or cause to be paid or lawfully tended the sume of one shillinge of lawfull money of England by the churchwardens within the parish of Houghton-in-the-Spring aforesaid, or any one or more of them to the use of the poore within the same parish in the presence of two or more reliable witnesses that then and from henceforth the said grant or feoffment, made to the said Francis cease and determyne and be utterley void any thinge therein conteyned to the contrary notwithstanding. Whereas I stand interested of certain lands in Silksworth, for the terme of twenty one years next after the death of my mother Margaret Middleton, I doe give and devise the said lands and all my estate and interest therein to my said sonne, George Middleton, he the said George paying and discharging the rent of 36*l.* and 7*l.* per annum to my mother, the said Margaret Middleton during her life naturall. All the residue of my goods and chattells I give and bequeath unto my sonns, George Middleton and Francis Middleton, whom I make joint executors.

Witnesses, Willm. Smythe, Nic. Pemberton, John Gill, Walter Marshall. Proved, 1627, 31st August.

GEORGE EMERSONE.[1]

Oct. 10, 1627. In the name of God, Amen, I, George Emersone of Eastgate, in the pish of Stanhopp in Wardell, in the Countye of Durham, Gentm., being weake in body. . . To be buried in the Churchyard att Stanhopp aforesaid. I give to my brother, Ralph Emerson, twelve pounds, yearly during his life naturall, and to be paid at Whitsontide and Martinmas, by even and equal portions, and the same to be paid out of the Eastgate rent. I give to Edward Burne who married my brother Francis daughter, 40*s*. I doe foregive my sister, Margery Stobbs, 4*l.*, which she owes me and I give unto her more, 20*s.*, to be paid annually on St. Andrew's day, during the terme of fower years. I give and bequeath unto Christopher Herrison, who married my sister, Ann, 10*l.*, yearly during his lease for fower yeares. I give to Margery Emerson, to bynd her an apprentice, 5*l.* I give to John Reade's two children, 6*l.*, to be equally devided between them. To Christopher Herrison's children, 40*s*. apeece. I give to my brother Ralph's children every one of them, 40*s*.

[1] 1627, Oct. 18, George Emmerson of the East Yett, "dyed at Durham and was buried at Stanhop," Stanhope Registers. There is a pedigree of this family in *The English Emersons*, p. 50.

I give to my sister Jane's children, 40s. apeece. To my sister Margerye's children, 40s. apeice, saveing to Ralph Stobbs, to whom I give 20s., only. I give to the poore of Stanhopp pish, 40s., to be paid at Christmas and Easter. To my brother Cuthbert children, 40s. a peice. I also give unto Elizabeth Marshall, 40s. to be paid in fower years, ten shillings every yeare. All the rest of my goods moveable and unmoveable, debts, legacies and funerall expenses discharged, I give unto my nephew, George Emerson and Christopher Herrison, my brother in law, whom I make joint and full executors of this my will. And I make Mr. Ferdinando Moorecroft, one of the Prebends of the Cathedrall Church of Durham and Ralph Emerson of Horseley, Supervisors of this my last Will and Testament, to see all things pformed according to my Will.

Witnesses, Ferd. Morecroft, Wm. Snaith, Richard Emerson, Nicholas Herrison, Ralph Metcalfe.

THOMAS PEACOCK.[1]

Oct. 27, 1627. In the name of God, Amen, I, Thomas Peacock of Stainton, in the Countie of Durham, yeoman, sick in bodye. To be buried in the Churchyard of Barnard Castle. I give and bequeath unto Ellinor my wife the tuition of all my children and the government and the disposing of their severall porcons, until they shall come successively to the full age of one and twenty yeares. I give and bequeath to my daughter, Jane Peacock her heires and assigns for ever all that my messuage at Barnard Castle now in the occupacon of Cuthbert Baynes and garden on the backside thereof, with all appurtenances thereunto belonging, for and in consideration of her filiall and third part and porcon of my goods. The rent thereof being paid to the King's Matie and the services done and performed, my will is that all the revenues of my said burgage after my death be nserved and putt forward for the use of my said daughter, Jane, untill she shall come to the full age of one and twenty yeares and then upon accompt payment thereof to be made unto her and that shee shall in the meen tyme be brought upp of the interest of other my goods and tenements. I give and bequeath unto my daughter, Elizabeth Peacock, if she be liveing thirty pounds in consideration of her filiall and child's porcon, ten pounds thereof to be paid unto her att Magdelen day next after her demand thereof and the other twenty pounds at the Martinmas then next after, but if my said daughter Elizabeth shallbe dead before this

[1] The testator was bur. at Barnard Castle, 9 Dec., 1627, his widow, Ellinor, being also bur. there, 28 Apl., 1648; his son, Simon, bapt., 14 Jan., 1615/16, was bur., 7 Sept., 1638; his dau., Isabel, mar. James Hutchinson, 4 Aug., 1625.

demand and payment, then I give tenn pounds thereof upon certificate of her said death unto my daughter, Ann Bainbrigg. And I give the other twenty pounds thereof unto my children Symond Peacock, Jenet Peacock, Margaret Peacock, and Jane Peacock. I give and bequeath unto my said daughters, Jenett Peacock and Margaret Peacock, either of them thirty poundes in full satisfacon of their filiall and third porcons and to be paid unto them when they shall accomplish the full age of one and twenty yeares. I give and bequeath unto my said sonne, Symond Peacock in consideration of his child's porcon, eighteene pounds which Mr. Thomas Bowes is oweing unto me. I also give and bequeath unto my said sonne, Symond Peacock, his heirs and assigns for ever (my wife's thirds for her life excepted) all other my houses farms and tenements together will all my interest, tenant right, claime and demand thereof, and that he shall enter thereunto, when he comes to the full age of one and twenty yeares. I give unto John Hutchinson, my grandchilde a gimer lamb to be delivered at Mid-Summer next after my death. I give unto Willm. Bainbrigg, son unto my said daughter, Ann Bainbrigg. the keeping of a calfe after it be wayned for three yeares and after that an other for other three yeares if my lease continue so long. All the rest of my goods not formerly bequeathed, my debts being paid and funeral expences discharged I give and bequeath unto Ellinor my wife. in consideration of her thirds whom I make sole Executrix of this my last Will and Testament entreating her to be good to the poore. And I give unto them att my death what shee thinks good. And I intreate my brother, Richard Cowheard, and my sonne. James Hutchinson. to be supervisors of this my Will and to aid and assist my wife with their friendly helpe and counsell as neede shall require.

Witnesses, James Hutchinson, Robt. Cowhearde, George Locke, Charles Foster, Richard Cowheard. Proved, 1627.

EDWARD BLACKET.[1]

Nov. 6, 1627. In the name of God, Amen, I, Edward Blacket, of Bomley Lawe, in the pish of Hamsterley, being sick in bodye. . . . To be buried in the Church of Hamsterley aforesaid. I give to my daughter, Eleanor Blackett, the sume of foure score poundes to be paid unto her out of my goods by mine executors within the space of one whole year next, after my death. I give to William Blacket, my eldest sone, the sum

[1] The testator was bur. at Hamsterley, 1 June, 1628; his son, William, was bapt., 27 Nov., 1593; Henry, bapt., 23 Nov., 1606; Margaret, mar. Peter Maddison, 5 Feb., 1608/9, and Jane, mar. Richard Wood by license, 3 Apl., 1627. all dates from Hamsterley. His *Inq. p.m.* was taken at Durham, 11 Oct., 1628. William, aged 40, is his son and heir, his sons Henry and John are mentioned, as is his wife Agnes.

of twenty pounds and to his wife twenty shillinges, and every one
of his three children the sum of forty shillings, pvided alwayes
that my said sonne William doth reste himself contented with
my sade gifte of twenty poundes without troubling of my wife,
or other childering for any other demand in my goodes or estate,
which if he make any further truble, then my gifte of twenty
poundes to be voyd.   And whereas Petter Maddeson, my sone in
law doeth owe and is indebted unto me the sum of ten pounds,
which ten pounds I gave unto the said Petter, so longe as he
remayneth unmaryed and if he shall happen to marrie, then my
will and pleasure is that he shall devide the same
equally amongst his six childreing, further I give to the
said six childrene of Petter, ... I give unto
George Blacket, my youngest sonne, the sume of one
hundred poundes out of my goodes and chattells, to be payed
by my Executors, when he shall accomplish the agge of twenty
and one years, and if he happen to die before he accomplish his
full agge, my will is that he shall have yearly, for his maintev-
nance, the sume of 3*l*. 6*s*. 8*d*., and if he shall lerne in any trade
as an aprentyce, that then his money goe forward with increase
for his best gayne, and to pav for his aprentyshippe with the
increase thereof.   And further I give to the said George another
100*l*., to be paid by my executors when he shall accomplish the
full agge of twenty and one years, to be made of the wood in the
pasture.   And whereas I have maed a feofdmente in my well
beloved brething Richard Lilburne, George Lilburne of all my
lands in Bomley Rawe to the use of me and my wife, and after
to my two sonns, Henrie Blackett and John Blacket, my harty
desire is that they will joyne with my wife and sonns to
make such good order as with their owne consents may be for
their good and profitts of them all which seemeth good unto
me in these wayes, and as they are all willing unto at this
presente, that is that eyther of mv said sonns shall enter of the
said landes in Bomley Rawe according to the Deed of feftement,
and out of the said lande either of them to paye yearly each the
sum of 5*l*. unto their mother.   Ane during her naturall lief and
for want of payment of the said ten pounds yearly, then it shall
be lawfull for Ane my wife to enter of a close called the lowe
feld and another close called the hollen feld, both in Bomleye
Rawe, in full satisfacon of all thirds or dower which she might
challenge out of my land at Bromley Rawe.   I give and bequeth
unto Annes my wife, a young graye felly, also I give to Ane my
wife and Eleanore, my daughter, all my howsehold stuff to be
equally divided between them saveing one closse presser which I
give unto Henrie, my sonne.   I give to Ane my wife, one bee hyve.
I give unto Jane Wood, my daughter, one younge whye coloured
rede and white.   All my goodes and debts, bills, bonds, covenants,
not given and bequeathed, my debts and funeralls being dis-

charged, I give and bequeath unto Henrie Blacket and John
Blacket, my two sonns, whom I make my sole Executors of this
my last Will and Testament. . And further I doe ordayne and
intreat my well beloved brothers-in-law, Richard Lilburn and
George Lilburne, to be supervisors of this my last Will and
Testament, and I doe give to either of them for their panes therein,
the sum of 20s. of good money of England. Witnesses, Richard
Lilburne, Robert Hodgson. Proved, 1627.

SIR EDWARD GRAY.[1]

Jan. 10, 1627. Sir Edward Gray of Morpeth Castle, in the
County of Northumberland, Knight . . . And my bodie I bequeath
to be buried by myne Executors in the parish Church of . . . .
Whereas I am seised of the Demesne and Manor of Howick, the
one moietie in fee ferme, the other moietie in fee simple to me
and my heirs for ever, after the expiration of one lease formerly
made by me and yet unexpired, my will is, and I hereby give
and bequeath unto Margaret Gray, widow, late wife of my eldest
sonne, Phillip Gray, deceased, one annutie or yearly rent of
thirtie and five pounds by year during her natural life forth of
the said Manor and lands in Howick aforesaid, with clause of
distress. I do give and bequeath the aforesaid Manor and lands
in Howick unto Edward Gray, eldest sone of my sone, Phillip
Gray, deceased, and to the heirs males of his body, and in default
of issue unto John Gray, second sone of my said sone, Phillip
Gray, deceased, and the heirs males of his body, and in default
of issue to Ralph Gray, third sone of the said Philip, deceased,
and the heirs males of his body, and in default of issue to the
heirs males of Philip Gray, the fourth sone of the said Philip,
and in default of male heirs, to my own son, Edward Gray, and
to his heirs for ever. I give unto John Gray, Ralph Gray and
Philip Gray, sons of my said son, Philip Gray, deceased, 500l.
equally among them as they severally attain the age of twenty
one years, such sum to be raised partly out of the stock, going

[1] He was the son of Sir Ralph Grey of Chillingham, by his wife,
Isabel, dau. of Sir Thomas Grey of Horton. The testator was
knighted at Chillingham, 9 May, 1617, mar. Catherine, dau. of Roger-
le-Strange of Hunstanton, co. Norfolk; by her he had Philip, admitted
to Gray's Inn, 26 May, 1598, administration, 10 Feb., 1615/16, mar.
Margaret Weetwood of Weetwood (they had, with other issue, a son,
Edward. bapt., 1 May, 1608, bur., 16 Jan., 1650/1, mar., a dau. of
Martin Fenwick of Kenton; Edward of Morpeth, bur., 7 July, 1658,
mar. Margaret, dau. of Sir Henry Widdrington; William, bapt.,
12 July, 1584, bur., 25 Dec., 1585; Robert, bapt., 2 Apl., 1592, bur.,
22 Nov., 1593; Thomas, bapt., 5 Aug., 1593; Catharine, bapt., 22 Aug.,
1585, mar. Randal Fenwick of Blagdon and Little Harle; Agnes, bapt.,
16 Aug., 1597, bur., 4 Nov., 1602; Elizabeth, bur., 8 Dec., 1657, her
will, dated 11 Dec., 1656, is printed in P.C.C. Wootton, vol. vi., No. 342;
all dates from Morpeth Registers.

and pasturing in Howick and partly out of certain sums of
money remaining in the hands of Randall Fenwick, my son-in-
law. I give to Edward Gray, sone of my said sone Philip Gray,
my household Stuffe in myne house at Howick in the possession
of my son-in-law, Randall Fenwick. I give to my two daughters,
Catherine Fenwick and Elizabeth Gray, 20*l.* each. To my
daughter, Elizabeth Gray, the third part of myne household stuff
remaining in Morpeth Castle. To my grandchild, Elizabeth
Fenwick, daughter of my daughter Catherine Fenwick, 40*l.*
Whereas my sonne, Thomas Gray, hath in his marriage run a
course to his own prejudice and overthrow and to my discontent,
yet nevertheless having formerly intended him the lease of a
tithe called the tithe of Learmouth Demisne for his natural life,
I doe, notwithstanding his miscarriage, by this my last Will
confirm the same unto him according to my former intention,
And I likewise give unto him, the said Thomas Gray, one horse,
to be delivered unto him by my executor, which is and shall be
the filiall and child's portion he may expect from me and no
more. To the poor of Morpeth, 5*l.* To Dorothy Bilton, 20*s.*,
and unto Ann Gray, 20*s.* I leave my men servants unto the
care and consideration of my sone, Edward Gray. The residue
of my estate unto my sonne, Edward Gray, whom I make sole
Executor. Witnesses, Philip Gardner, George Watson, John
Forster. Probate, 1631.

GEORGE RAWLING.[1]

Jan. 14, 1627. The last Will and Testament of George
Rawling. I, George Rawling of Shincliffe, in the County of
Durham, Yeoman, being sick of bodye but of perfect memory
(praised be god) on the fowerteenth day of January, in the year
of our Lord God, 1627, doe make and ordaine this my last Will
and Testament in manner and forme following. My body to be
honestly buryed in Pittington Churchyarde on the west side of
the Church porch in decent forme and manner as is convenient.
I give and bequeath to the poore of Shincliffe towne the sum of
10*s.* of lawful money. I give to the poore of Pittington parish,
2*l.* of lawful money, to be given to the Church stocke and to
continue for the use of the poore to be distributed as it shall
please them with whom it is left. I give and bequeath to Cisley
Wilkinson and Jane Wilkinson, one cowe. I give and bequeath
to Jane Hopper, the daughter of Samson Hopper, five pounds of
lawful money. I give and bequeath to John Hopper, the sone

[1] The testator mar., 2 July, 1581, at St. Oswald's, Durham, Isabel
Greenwell, she was bur. there, 16 Feb., 1617/18, their only son, John,
being also bur. there, 29 June, 1601. The testator was bur. at
Pittington, 27 Jan., 1627/8, his burial entry also being recorded at
St. Oswald's, where he is described as "aiged." His sister, Margaret,
was mar. to Christopher Dixon, 3 July, 1576, at Pittington.

of the said Samson Hopper, one ewe and a lamb and a hogge
which are now in his father's possession, and the first calfe that
the cow hath wich I have given to Cisley Wilkinson. I give and
bequeath unto each of Henry Shadforth sonns, 20s. of lawful
money, And I give and bequeath to Margaret Shadforth, the
daughter of John Shadforth, the sume of 20s. of lawful English
money. I give and bequeath unto Railph Rawling and John
Rawling, my brother William's sonns, 6l. of lawful money to be
equally devided betwixt them. I give and bequeath unto Thomas
Dixon, the eldest sonne of Robert Dixon of Sherburne, the sum
of 20s., and to his younger sone, Robert Dixon, I give and
bequeath 2l. of lawfull money of England, together with a house
in Claypurth, within the suburbes of the City of Durham, to
be and remaine hereafter for ever in his name and for the use
of the said Robert Dixon the younger, Christopher Dixon of
Durham aforesaid having the said house during the terme of
his natural life and paying unto the said Robert Dixon the
younger, the yearly rent of 5s. of lawful English money. I give
and bequeath unto Margaret Dixon, the eldest daughter of the
said Robert Dixon, the sum of 10l., and to each of his daughters
the sum of 2l. I give and bequeath unto Mark Grinwell, the
sum of fower pounds of lawful money. And to Elizabeth Hopper,
the wife of Sampson Hopper, 20s. I give and bequeath unto
John Rawling of Sherburne, the sum of 10l. which the said John
Rawling doth now owe unto me. I give and bequeath unto the
aforesaid Cisley Wilkinson and Jane Wilkinson, daughters to
George Wilkinson, one Cottage in Midlam situte, lieing and being,
together with all and singular profitts and comodities belonging
or appertaining. I doe give and bequeath unto Henry Pearson
and Elizabeth Pearson, the children of William Pearson of Sherburne, the sum of 4l., to be equally divided betwixt them two.
As for the rest of my goods and chattels, together with all my
monies (my debts being payed and funerall honestly discharged),
I doe give and bequeath unto Robert Dixon of Sherburne, my
sister's sonne, whom I doe make and ordaine sole executor of this
my last Will and Testament, revoking all other Wills bearing
date before this in what place soever or to what parties soever
heretofore made and ordained. And if it shall happen at anytime hereafter any ambiguity, doubt or question to grow or arise
by reason of the imperfection or defect of or in any the words,
clauses and sentences in this my psent last Will and Testament,
or in my true intent and meaning therein, That the further and
better explanation, interptation and construction of the said
doubt and ambiguitie, I will that my said executor shall expound
explain and interpret it according to his wisdome and good
discretion. Witnesses, Henry Murray, William Witherington.
Francis Foster, George Wilkinson.

INVENTORY, 105l. 16s. Proved, 1627.

ROBERT COLLINGWOOD.[1]

Jan. 23, 1627. Robert Collingwood. Inventory of the goods and chattels, moveable and unmoveable, which were Mr. Robert Collingwoods of Eslingdon, in the pish of Whittingham, deceased, prized by these foure men, viz. : Clement Hall, Cuthbert Chesemonde, Henry Jackson and John Bell. Imprimis : foure oxen valued at 8*l.*, one graie nagge, 5*l.*, one sorrelde mare, 30*s.* Rie in the yarde, 7*l.* Bigge in the yarde, 9*l.* Oates, 9*l.* Three tables and one courte cupboarde, 40*s.* Twelve covered stooles, 40*s.* Six other stooles, 9*s.* Five chaires, 10*s.* Carpet clothes, 20*s.* One table, one chaire and two courte cupboards, 2*l.* 10*s.* 8*d.* One bedsteade, one trindle bedsteade, one courte cupboard, one great chaire and six cushions, 4*l.* 16*s.* 4*d.* Seaven servants bedsteads, two cupboards, two chaires, two rugges, six cover clothes, six fetherbeds, five paire of blanketts, six paire of sheetes, six pillowebeares, 6*l.* 11*s.* Two linnen table clothes, three dozen table napkins, two short cupboarde clothes, two towells, three paire of courtens and hangers, eight silver spoons, six small spoons, one bearebowle, two wineboules and one silver salt, 13*l.* 6*s.* Twenty one peeces of puder vessell, three basons and nine ewers, one tinne salte, three candlestickes, foure flaggon pots, two brass pots, three speetes, two dripping pans, 4*l.* 7*s.* Corne sowne upon the grounde, 10*l.* Debts oweing by the deceased: His funerall expences with church dueties, 10*l.* Due to the vicar of Whittingham for Easter reckonings, ——. To Sir Matthew Forster, for a sorrelle mare, 22*l.* To the same for a gray stoned nagge, 10*l.* To the same for a grissilde nagg, 8*l.* To William Stealle, 10*l.* To Clement Hall, for oates, 5*l.* 10*s.* To the same, in exchange for a horse, 40*s.* To Rowland Forster, 10*l.* 16*s.* 4*d.* To John Gilpatrigg, for which James Muddie and William Morrison stand bonde, 12*l.* To Edmund Collingwoode, 9*l.* To Alexander Weetewoode, 40*s.* To Mr. William Reede of Titlington, three boules of malt, 54*s.* To Mr. James Lawson of Shawdon, 40*s.* To Gawin Claveringe, 3*l.* 8*s.* To Clement Armorer, 5*l.* 16*s.* To Nicholas Forster, 5*l.* 11*s.* 4*d.* To Janet Millakin, 10*l.* 6*s.* To Elizabeth Oswalde, 10*l.* To Edward Guye, 13*s.* To Elizab. Gray, 36*s.* 6*d.* To Thomas White, 6*s.* To Thomas Pye of Morpith, 4*l.*, whereof he hath received in Rie, 28*s.* To Edward Ogle, a boule of Rie, ——. To Isabell Stainton, 26*s.* To Charles Balmeburgh, 8 boules of malt and a Kenying. To the same, for one nagge, 26*s.* 8*d.* To

[1] He was the son of Sir Thomas Collingwood of Eslington, by his wife, Anne, dau. of Sir Ralph Grey of Chillingham; he mar. Dorothy, dau. of Robert Weetwood of Weetwood, and died without issue. His *Inq. p.m.*, taken at Durham, Aug., 1628; Maria, aged 17, Frances, aged 15, Dorothy, aged 11, and Elizabeth, aged 9, are his kinswomen and next heirs, being the daus. of his sister . . . . Swinburne.

William Thompsone, 26s. 8d. To Ferdinardo Brown, 23s. To
William Browne, 38s. 6d. To John Whitton, 32s. 6d. To George
Roule, 24s. To Thomas Tate, 49s. 6d. To Mark Hall, 5s. 6d.
To Archibalde Elwoode, 44s. To Margaret Hadley, 12s. To
William Cuttie, 10s. To Luke Kirklin, 5s. To Robert Alder,
one bushel of Rie. To Henry Nicholson, 10s. To Richard
Heslewoode, 10s. To Jeffray Prockter, 56s. 8d. To William
Steale, 9s. To Elizabeth Smith, 8s. 6d. To Thom. Strangishe,
10s. To Gilbert Hall, for borrowed money when my Ladie Forster
was buried, 20s. More borrowed of the same, when his Mastr was
at Lilburne, 20s. More paide by the saide Gilbert to Mistr
Prockter, 23s. 4d. More paid by him to Alexander Weetewoode,
13s. 4d. To the same for a stotte, 6s. To Katherin Hall, of
borrowed money, 3s. To William Tate, for one bowle of malt,
11s. More to him, for three bushells of malt, 15s. For the last
court charges to Mr. Hall, 18s. To Agnes Nicholson, 8l. To
Agnes Wilson, 8l.

DOROTHIE COLLINGWOOD.

Dec. 20, 1628. A Declaration of the Accompt of Dorothie
Collingwood of Eslington, widdow, late wife and Administratrix
of Robert Collingwood, Esqr., late of the same, her husband, deceased, made and exhibitted into the Consistorie Court of Durham
as followeth :—Imprimis, the said accomptant chargeth her self to
have had and receiveth of the said deceased goods, creditts and
chattells coming to her hands amounting to the sum of four
score nine pounds ten shillings fower pence, as appeareth by
an Inventorie thereof made and exhibited into the said Consistorie
Court may appear. The said Accomptant hathe paid for the
said deceased's debt, and since his death to Sir Matthew Forster,
Knight, £47. She hath paide or satisfied to William Steele, for
debt as by his bond cancelled appeareth, £10. Hath likewise
paid and satisfied to Clement Hall, the debt of £7 10s. 0d. Hath
paid to Alexander Wetwood, 40s. Hath paide to Mr. James
Lawson of Shawdon, as by his bond appeareth, £6. Hath paid
to Gawen Claveringe, the sum of £3 8s. 0d. Hath paid to
Nicholas Forster, £5 11s. 4d. Hath paid to Jennett Millikin,
the sum of 20s. Hath paid to Elizabeth Oswald, 40s. Hath paid
to Edward Guy, 14s. Hath paid to Thomas White, 6s. Hath
paid to Isabell Stanton, 10s. Hath paid to Charles Bambrough,
£3. To Fardinando Browne, 23s. To William Browne, 36s.
To John Whitton, 16s. To Jennett Rowell, 24s. To Thomas Tate,
49s. She hath also paide to Mark Hall, 5s 6d. To Archbald
Ellet, 48s. To John Vertie, 6s. To Luke Kirklin, 5s., and
Jeffrey Proctor, 56s. To Agnes Nicholson 8l. To Agnes Wilson,
8l. To Gilbert Hall, 4l. 10s. To Rowland Forster, 5l. To John

Harwood, 20s. To Edward Collingwood, 8l. To Clement Stephenson, clarke, 2l. 17s. She craveth to be allowed for the funeral charges of the deceased for the Letters of Administration, with special Commission and other charges thereabouts, 6l. She likewise praieth to be allowed unto her for the drawing and passing this Accompt with testimonialls thereunto annexed and other charges about the same, 23s. 4d. Sum totalis, £152 3s. 2d.

So that it appeareth this accomptant hath fullie administered the said deceased's goods and chattells, and hath paide more then the same Did amount unto by the sume of £62 12s. 10d.

WILL OF HENRY EWBANK.[1]

Jan. 10, 1628. Henry Ewbank, of the towne and County of Newcastle upon Tyne, Cordyner, sicke in bodye. To be buryed within the parish Church of Saint John's, within the towne and County of Newcastle aforesaid, so nigh unto my late mother in law, Jane Tuggell, as conventlye may be. And for the worldly goods which the lord hath indowed me withal, I give and bequeathe as hereafter followeth. Item, I give and bequeathe to my eldest brother, John Ewbank, 22s., and also do forgive him 3s. which he is owing me, and likewise I give him my . . . . coat. To my brother, Thomas Ewbank, my browne cloke which hath buttons, and do forgive him all that he is oweing me. To my brother, James Ewbank, 6l., which my will and mind is shall be given unto my mother Alice Preston's hands to keep until he, the said James, shall be made free if she live so long, And if not, then the same upon her death to be putt into some honest man's hand for the best advantage of the said James, till such time as he shall made free as aforesaid, And also two freze Jerkins and one old clothe rush suite, and one browne suite stitched with silke, and one paire of Carsey breches, together with all my bookes, and all other things which I usually weare, as sherts, bands, stockens and shooes. To my sister, Dorothie Ewbank, 10s. Unto the said Thomas Ewbank, my brother, my sword and my belt. To my father-in-law, Edward Tuggell, 5s. for a token. To Rowland Hedley and Isabell, his wife, 5s. a piece for a token. To John Collingwood and his wife, 5s. a piece. All the rest of my worldly goods to my wife, Alice Ewbank, and I appoint my father in law, Edward Tuggell, to be Supervisor of this my Will, hoping that he will see the same executed as my trust and hope is in him. In witness, John Couplain, Robert Robinson. Proved, 1628.

[1] The testator mar., 5 Feb., 1627/8, at St. John's, Newcastle, Alice, dau. of Edward Tuggell; he was bur. there, 13 Jan., 1628/9, Edward Tuggell being bur. there, 6 Sept., 1636, and his wife Jane, 10 Aug., 1628.

JOHN HOWSON.[1]

Sept. 11, 1629. In the name of Gode, Amen, and in the fifth yeare of the reegne of our Soverigne Lord Charles, by the grace of God of England, Scotland and Ireland, King, defender of the faith, etc., I, John Howson, Doctor in Divinity and Lord Bishop of Durham, being in perfect health both in body and mynd. . . . To be buried, if god shall call me in the Southern partes, in the Chancel of the parish church of Baldwin Brightwell, in the County of Oxford. If in the Northern partes, in the Cathedrall Church of Durham or some other of my chappells as shall best please my executrix. As concerning my personal estate, which is but small, I dispose the same as followeth. First, I give to every one of my children, as well maried as unmarried, 5l. a peece, to be paid them that are of full age or married within one year of my decease, and unto them that are unmarried when they shall attaine respectively their severall ages of one and twenty yeares or be married. Also I give to Charles Farnaby, my daughter Anne's sonne, the sum of 50l., to be paid unto him at the age of seven yeares if he live to attaine that age, And to the first child of my daughter, Mellicent Cleaver, the like some of 50l., to be paid when it shall attain the age of seven yeares, And if either of the said children of my said daughters shall not live unto the age as aforesaid prefixed for receipt of the severall legacies, then my will is that the legacies of such parties so dying shall be void. The residue of my goods, chattells and debts I give and bequeath to my loveing wife, Jane Howson, whom I do constitute of this my last Will sole executrix, not doubting of her care for the education of our children. Witnesses, Henry Mompeson, Robert Parsons.

[1] Born in St. Bride's parish, London, student of Christ Church, Oxford, 1577, B.A., 12 Nov., 1578, M.A., 1581/2 (incorporated at Cambridge, 1583), B.D. and D.D., 1601, Vice-Chancellor, 1602, Preb. of Hereford, 1587, and of Exeter, 1592, V. of Bampton, Oxon., 1598, of Great Milton, Oxon., 1601, R. of Brightwell, Oxon., 1608, an original fellow of Chelsea College, 1610, Bp. of Oxford, 1618, of Durham, 1628-32, died, 6 Feb., 1631/2, bur. at St. Paul's Cathedral. He mar., 10 Aug., 1601, at Blackbourton, co. Oxford, Elizabeth Floyd of Bampton, by her he had, perhaps with other issue, Anne, mar., as second wife, Thomas Farnaby, famous classical scholar, who died at Sevenoaks, 12 June, 1647; Elizabeth, bur. at Durham Cathedral, 18 Oct., 1634, mar. Robert Blakiston, rector of Sedgefield (as his father, Marmaduke was before him), Preb of the seventh stall, bur., 19 Jan., 1634/5, in Durham Cathedral.

WILLIAM GRAY.[1]

March 7, 1629. William Gray of Fenwick, within the Chapellrie of Kiloe, made at Fenwick this date. My bodie to be buried within the chancel of Kiloe. To my sone-in-law, Henry Orde, my twenty oxen and my two plough naggs. I give unto Florence, my wife, my black fillie. To my wife's two daughters, every one of them, ten ewes. To Francis Moore, clerk, a bowle of wheat. To Robert Gray, my nephew, one of the pie kine. To my nephew, Thomas Gray, another of the pie kine. To my cousin, John Gray, one whie. To my cousin, William Louther, one whie stirke. To my brother, Ralph Gray, my sute and cloake being at Berwick, with the points and trimmings I bought for it. To my uncle, Roger Gray, my old sute and cloake. To my son-in-lawe, Henry Ord, my best Sute and cloake. Residue to wife Florence, and appoint her and my son-in-law, Henry Orde, Executors. Probate, 1638.

THOMAS FOLLANSBYE.[2]

April 12, 1630. In the name of God, Amen, I, Thomas Follansbye of Rockwod hill, in the pish of Hamsterley, in the County of Durham, Gent, being sick in body. To be buried within my pish Church. And for my temporall goods and blessings that god hath indued me with, dispose them as followeth, etc. I doe give 6l. 13s. 4d. to help raise and increase the stock of money belonging to the poor people of my parish, and the consideracon arising of the same to be even and equally divided year by yeare and distributed to the poore upon Good Friday and the Friday before the feaste day of the nativity of our Blessed Savior Jesus Christ, and so to continue for ever. I doe give to my loveing wife, Margaret Follansbye, by legacy my graye mare. I doe give unto my eldest sone, Christopher Follansbye, 40s., for a full satisfaction of his child's porcon, further I doe release and acquit my said sone of All former bond or bonds, debts or demands whatsoever between him and me. I doe give unto my son, Robert Follansbye, 3l. 6s. 8d., for a full satisfaction of his child's portion. I give unto my son, Thomas Follansbye, 3l. 6s. 8d., for a full satisfaction of his child's

[1] There is a pedigree of this family in Raine's *North Durham*, p. 337.

[2] There is a hiatus in the Hamsterley registers at the time of the testator's burial; his son, Christopher, mar. Margaret Vasey, 30 Mch., 1619; Thomas, mar. Elizabeth Pinkney, 25 Nov., 1628; Henry, bapt., 18 Mch., 1596/7, mar. Jane Gibbon, 4 Nov., 1623, she was bur., 26 Jan., 1650/1; John, bapt., 10 Feb., 1599/1600; William, bapt., 21 Feb., 1590/1; Grace, mar. Richard Maior, 26 Oct., 1619; Alice, bapt., 19 Feb., 1587/8, bur., 6 Nov., 1661, mar. Stephen Sanderson, 23 May, 1609, bur., 23 Sept., 1659. All dates from Hamsterley.

portion. I give to my sone, Henry Follansbye, 3*l.* 6*s.* 8*d.*, for
a full satisfaction of his child's portion. I doe give unto my
sone, John Follansbye, 3*l.* 6*s.* 8*d.*, for a full satisfaction of his
child's portion. I doe give unto my sone, William Follansbye,
40*l.*, for a full satisfaction of his child's portion, if it do please
god that he be living and come in person to demand the same,
or otherwise if he be dead then my will is that it be equally
divided amongst my other children then living after the knowledge of his deathe. I doe give unto my daughter, Grace Cossin,
3*l.* 6*s.* 8*d.*, for a full satisfacon of her child's portion, and my
will is that the same be equally divided amongst her children
now in livinge, being her former husbandes. I doe give to my
daughter, An. Follansbye, fower score poundes, for a full satisfaction of her child's portion upon this condition, that she shall
and will be directed and advised by her mother and my nephew,
Henry Follansbye, or otherwise my will is that her portion be
but three score pounds by this my Will. I doe give unto my
daughter, Alice Sanderson, 3*l.* 6*s.* 8*d.*, for a full satisfaction of
her portion. I doe give to William Hodgson, Clerke, my writer,
by legacy ten shillings. All the rest of my goods, moveable and
unmoveable, my children's portions, debts, legacies and funerall
expences discharged, I doe bequeathe to my loving wife, Margrett
Follansbye, whom I doe make the executrix of this my last Will
and Testament, And my nephew, Henry Follansbye, to be
Supervisor.

INVENTORY, 290*l.* 15*s.* 7*d.* Proved, 1630.

DAME ELIZABETH FREVILE.[1]

July 1, 1630. In the name of God, Amen, for as much as
to all men living in this transitory worlde it is appoyned once
to dy, but the tyme which is uncertayne, Therefore I, Dame
Elizabeth Frevile of Wallworth, in the Countye Palatine of
Durham, widow, being of sounde and pfect memory, prased be
god, doe make this last Will and Testament. To be buryed in
the parish Church of Sedgefield, in the said County of Durham,
neere to the corps of my deceased husband, Sir George Frevile,
Kt., in such seemly and decent sort as shall seeme best to myne
executor or executors. And for such goods and chattells as it
hath pleased gode to bless me withall, I doe give and bequeth
the same in manner and forme and upon the condicons as shall
appeare by this my will. Imprimis : my funeral and debts being
discharged, I give and allot one hundred marks to be disbursed

[1] She was the dau. of Thomas Jenison of Walworth, by his wife,
Elizabeth, dau. of Edward Birch of Sandon, co. Bucks., she mar. Sir
George Freville of Walworth, bur. at Sedgefield, 25 Nov., 1619, where
she was also bur., 8 Oct., 1630, without issue The *Inq. p.m.* of her
husband was taken at Durham, 12 Apl., 1620.

by my exors (if it be not disbursed in my lyfe tyme) for the
erecting of a tombe or monument over my sayd deceased husband,
George Frevile, within the parish Church of Sedgefield aforesaid
where he lyeth buryed, and to inclose the forepart of the porch
where he lyeth so buryed with iron or wainscott. I give to the
poore of the parish of Sedgefield aforesaid twenty nobles, and to
the poore of the pish of Bp Middleham in the sayd County twenty
nobles, and to the poore of the pish of Heighington in the said
Countye fower pounds, to be distributed amongst them within
one moneth after my death at the discretion of myne exectors.
I will and appoint that myne exor or executors shall within one
yeare after my death (in case I shall not do it in my lifetime)
purchase in fee simple, in the names of such eight persons as he
or they shall noiate, in trust for that purpose, lands, tenements
. . . . of the yearly value of 20l. of lawful English money or a
ppetuity of the same value, the said yearlye sum of 20l. to be
yearly disposed and imployed by the persons trusted, or
some of them, in such manner as is hereunder expressed. That
is to say, Twenty . . . . for the yearly binding of three poor
children apprentice, the same to be equally divided and distributed for the purpose, which said three children shallbe yearlye
chosen by the persons in whose names the sayd lands, tentmts or
heredits or ppetuity shall be purchased . . . . or the survivor.
The choyce to be made for the first two yeares within the pish of
Sedgefield aforesaid, and in the third yeare within the pish of
Bp Middleham aforesaid. And out of the residue of the yearly
fund of 20l. (being 8l.), my will . . . . of the poore of the said
pishes for the tyme being, And if the lands, tents and heredits
purchased as aforesaid or any part thereof after the purchase
thereof shall so fall and abate in the yearly value and rent that
the same shall not be of the yearly value of 20l., then my will
is . . . . of such fall and decay of rent, there shall be a
proporsite defaulcation of the 12l. allowed for binding apprentices, And if the said tenemts and herednts to be purchased as
aforesaid shall happen after purchase to be improved to a greater
rent and yearly value then 20l., then my will is that . . . . and
surplus age during the continuance thereof shall be given,
imployed and bestowed amongst the residue of the poore of the
said parishes pportionally. I do further will and appoint that
when so many of the psons in whose names the said lands, tenemts
and hereditns or ppetuity shallbe purchased as aforesaid shallbe
dead, so that there shallbe butt three of them living, that then
within two months after such death the three surviving psons
shall make and execute a newe assurance of the fee simple of the
said lands, tenemts or hereditns or ppetuity on the like trust,
and for the same purposes as is hereinbefore expressed to eight
other psons to be chosen by the said three surviving persons, and
so to be of new estates from time to time for ever, and the charges

of makeing such new estates to be for that year def . . . . (if
there be not sufficient overplus of rent above the said yearly sum
of 20*l.* out of the money allotted for that year for the binding
of apprentices). The worthy poor children to be bound as apprentices I expressly forbid by this my Will to be putt out to weavers
or . . . . being poor trades. I give to my brother, William
Jenyson, 20*l.* To my brother, Thomas Jenyson, 100*l.* To my
nephew Ralph Jenysone his sone, 20*l.* To Elizabeth, wife of the
sayd Ralph, two dozen of my gold buttons. To my goddaughter,
Elizabeth, daughter of the sayd Ralph, my golde chayne. And
to every other of my brother Thomas Jenyson's grandchildren,
which I xpned as godmother, vz., George Frevile, Mary Frevile
and John Calverley, 5*l.* a piece. To my niece, Margarett
Calverley, my border of goldsmiths work. To my niece, Mary
Frevile, my diamond ring, my second looking glass, my velvet
gowne, my damaske gowne, my satten peticoate, my scarlet
peticoat and my riding suite. To my nephewe, John Jenyson,
20*l.*, and to his brother, William Jenyson, when he shall accomplished his apprenticeshipp (if in my.life tyme I do not otherwise
pvide for him or be att other chardge for him), 40*l.*, and during
the continuance of his apprenticeshipp fower poundes a yeare to
buy him clothes. I give to Michaell Jenyson, my nephew, sonne
to my brother, Michaell Jenyson, 10*l.* And to Mary Jenyson, his
sister, 50*l.* when she shall marry. And from the time of my death
until she be married I desire the said 50*l.* to be putt out and
employed by myne exor to the best advantage for the increase of
the same, And I committ the custody of the said Mary to my
nephew, Nicholas Frevile, and Mary, his wife, and the survivor
of them, and towards the education of the said Mary I doe give
to the said Nicholas and Mary, or the longer liver of them, the
profits of my farme in the township of Bp Middleham which I
lately took on lease of the Bp of Durham, as long as she shall
continue with them or either of them, Provided allwayes that if
the said Mary shall depart from the said Nicholas or Mary before
her said mariage, or shall marry or contract marriage without the
assent and approbation of the said Nicholas and Mary, or of the
survivor of them, or shall become a popish recusant (though not
convicted), thenceforth . . . from the tyme of such departure or
marriage or becoming a Popish recusant as aforesaid contrary to
this my Will, the said legacye so to her bequeathed shall determine
and be merely void, and that after such mariage of the said
Mary or determination of the said legacy the lease and
interest which I have in the said farme shall accrue to
the sayd Nicholas Frevile and Mary, his wife, and the
Survivor of them, and that before she receive the said legacy
she enter into sufficient bond to myne exors, or to him or them
that are to pay the same to her, that if att any tyme during her
life she doe become a Papist that immediately from that tyme of

such her falling to Popery she shall repay the said legacy so
payed to her. I give to my neece, Elizabeth Gray, 20*l.*, and to
her daughter Margarett, 5*l.* I give to my nephew, Sir John
Calverley, Kt., 20*l.* And to my neece, Dame Elizabeth, his wife,
my best cooch and cooch horses and all theyre furniture, and my
best looking glass. And to my nephewe, John Calverley, and to
Timothy Calverley, to Beatrix, Isabell, Anne and Alice, children
of the said Sir John Calverley, 20*s.* a piece. Whereas my
nephew, Nicholas Frevile, is to pay to myne exor for a farm in
Sedgfield within five yeares after my death, my will is and I
do hereby appoint that the said bond for the payment of the said
120*l.* shall be assigned over by myne exors to the aforesaid Sir
John Calverley and Dame Elizabeth, his wife, or the survivor of
them, to and for the use of their three daughters, viz., Barbara,
Elizabeth and Mary, that is to say, to Elizabeth, 60*l.*, to Barbara
and Mary, 30*l.* each, and if any of the three dy before they have
received theyre said portion or legacy, then the survivor or
survivors of them shall have the portion of the pty so dying. I
give to my nephew, Robert Frevile, 5*l* a yeare during his life,
to be chardged and payable out of the demesnes of Bishop-
middleham, if my present lease so long continue. I give to my
cousen, Drusilla Cowlton, 10*l.* To my cosen, Robert Jenyson,
Doctor in Divinity, 5*l.*, and to my cousen, Isabella Carr, his
sister, 5*l.* I give to Sir George Tong, Kt., and to his Lady, to
each of them, a spurroyall. To Gilbert Frevile, 20*l.* To Mr.
Richard Heighington, 40*s.* To Mrs. Isabell Crome, 20*s.* To Mr.
Symon Gifford, 22*s.* To Mr. James Bolland, 22*s.* I give to my
servants, viz., to Nicholas Petifer, 20*l.* To Chrsor Payne, 40*l.*
To Ambrose Payne, fower markes. To Ralph Newby, 20*l.* To
Robert Snayth, 10*l.* To George Parnaby, 10*l.* To Ann Woodmus,
10*l.* And to every other of my household servants a whole yeares
wages over and above that which shallbe due unto them. I give
to Mary Dighton, widow of my servant, two kyne and ten ewes,
and also twenty nobles a year, to be payed thereout of the profitts
of my farme in Nunstaynton, in the Bprick of Durham, during
her life, if my lease thereof shall so long continue. And doe
also assigne the 4*l* a yeare formerly bequeathed to Wm. Jenyson
during his apprenticshipp to be paid out of the vules before my
death. I doe give to him or lend to him any money to imploy
in stock for his owne benefitt, and then the said annuity of 4*l.*
to cease, as also such money as he shall so receive to be accounted
for discharge of so much as pte of the 40*l.* legacy bequeathed to
him by this my will. The said several Annuytes to be beginn
at the first rent dayes next ensuing my death, and to be yearlie
by equall portions at the feasts of Pentecost and Martyn the
Bp in winter. And the whole interest in the farme in Nunstaynton aforesaid I give to my brother, Thomas Jenyson, charged

227

and chargeable as aforesaid. I give to my nephew, George Frevile, from and immediately after my death, one annuitie of ten pounds a yeare, to be issuing out of the demesne of Bp Middleham aforesaid during the continuance of my lease thereof, if he shall so long live, payable by equall porcons at the feaste of St. Martin the Bp in winter and Pentecost, upon proviso and condicon that if the said George Fevile doe assigne or alienate the sayd annuitye to any person or persons (excepting onely to his brother, Nicholas Frevile), or that the same be extended for any of his debts, Or that the sayd George shall impleade or sue his brother, Nicholas Frevile, after my deathe to the impeachment of my deceased husbands will or contrary to the true intent and meantinge thereof, or seek to impeache or hinder the said Nicholas from the quiett enjoying of such lands as were intended to him by him by my said husband's will, notwithstanding any former contract, bargaynes, sales or fines layd and levyed betwixt them since my husband's death, That then the said annuity shall thenceforth cease and determine and this bequest to him to be utterly voide. And my will is that if any of the said annuityes hereby granted out of my leases shallbe behind and unpayed by any of the sayd Wm. Jenyson, Mary Dighton, George or Robert Frevile by the space of forty dayes after any of the said feasts wherein it ought to be payd, that then it shall be lawfull for the party unpayd respectively to enter into such ground wherein his annuity is chargded or any part thereof, and to distreyne for the same and the distresse or distresses to take, lead, drive, carye awaye and impounde so often as need requireth untill the said annuitye or arreages thereof (if there be any) be fully satisfied and payd. And I doe hereby give and bequeath to my brother, Thomas Jenyson, the profitts and emoluments ariseing out of the Parke demesnes and deepewells in Bp Middleham aforesaid charged and chargeable, with all rents, annuityes and chardges heretofore charged upon the same or by this my Will, To have to him and his assigns for the terme of six yeares next ensuing after my death, and after the expircon of the said six yeares I doe give unto my nephew, Nicholas Frevile, and to Mary, his now wife, upon pformance of the condicon and pviso thereafter ensuing, the residue of my terme of yeares in the aforesaid demesnes, Parke and Deepwell, charged and chargeable as aforesaid, And all my interest unto ten beaste gates in a pasture there called Sprewsley, upon condicon and pviso that if the said Nicholas doe not free and dischaidge mine executor or executors of all such bonds, debts. ingagements and chardges forthwith, I stand bound or anywise ingaged for the said Nicholas att all and every such tyme and tymes as they or any of them should be dischardged, that then my executor or executors shall keep in his or there handes the said lease of the said Parke,

Demesnes and Deepewells after the expiracon of the said six yeares, formerly bequeathed to my brother, Thomas Jenyson, untill the said principall debts, with the use and other charges which myne exor or executors shall susteyne or be chargded with or shall discharge, touching or concerning the same, or any of them, be fully satisfyed and payed by myne Exor or executors out of the said Demesnes, Park and Deepewells. I give to George Calverley, sone of the aforesaid Sir John Calverley, at the feast of St. Hellen next ensuing after my death, the whole interest, estate and terme of yeares which I have in the Lady Close in the pish of Brancepeth, in the Bprick of Durham, with condicon that there be payed yearly out of the said lease the sum of 20s to the parson, churchwardens and overseers of the poor of the said pish at the feaste of St. Thomas the Apostle, to be given to the poorest of the said towne of Brancepeth onely. And if he happen to dy, then my will is that the same shall come whollye to his brethern and sisters of the whole blood, and for want of such brother or sister, to my nephew, Ralph Jenyson. Whereas Sir George Frevile, Kt., my late husband, did by his last Will committ the disposing of his household stuff to my discretion after my death, forasmuch as I have made an Inventory . . . . bearing date the 18 of Februarye, 1624, signed with my owne hand and subscribed with my hand att the severall pages thereof, conteyneing all such household stuff as was then remayning in my handes undisposed of, wherein which was my husband's is distinguished from that which . . . . and by the said booke it appeareth what I have disposed of the same, Therefore for so much as was my husband's household stuffe and shall be remayning in my hands undisposed of at the tyme of my death and not given away in my life tyme or shall not by the said book be allowed . . . . others I doe dispose the same in manner and forme followeinge, viz :—To my nephewes, George Frevile, Richard Frevile, and my said nephew, Nicholas Frevile, as heyr-loomes to my house at Hardwyck, my silver basen and ewer, my gilt saltselter and two guilt bowls. I give to my tenants, viz., to John Norton, 3l. 6s. 8d. To John Lynn, 5l. To Willm. Widdefield, 3l. 6s. 8d. To Richard Bell, 40s. I give to my brother, Thomas Jenyson, my lease of the Bishopps Close in the pish of Whitworth, in the Countye of Durham. I will that myne exor or executors shall have two years liberty for the dischargding of this my Will. All the residue of my goodes whatsoever not disposed of and unbequethed by this my will I doe hereby give and bequeath to him or them that att the . . . . death shall stand in state of executor or executors of this my Will. My will is that if my brother, Thomas Jenyson, shall dy before me, that then my nephew, Ralph Jenyson, his sone, shall have whatsoever is hereby bequeathed to my . . . . Revoking all former Wills,

I doe hereby constitute, ordayne and appoynt my Brother, Thomas Jenyson, to be my sole Executor if he be living, and if my said Brother shall dy before me I doe constute and appoint my nephew, Sir John Calverley, Kt., and my nephew, Ralph Jenyson, sone of my brother Thomas Jenyson, to be executors of this my Will. As I have been at charge to keepe my nephew, Richard Frevile, in my house divers yeares, and since ha . . . . at . . . . charges or have about to plesse him in Cambridge and gave hym a yearlie exhibition there of 10*l*. a yeare, therefore I have omitted to give him more then is expressed in thys my Will.

Codicil (2 October, 1630) to the Will of Dame Elizabeth Frevile of Wallworth, Widow. I bequeath of Mr. Ferdinando Morecroft, one of the Prebends of Durham and Vicar of Highington, and to Mr. Raph Richardson, Vicar of Aicliff, unto whom I have ben much beholden in the time of my present visitation of sickness, 3*l*. a peece. To my nephew, John Jenison, as an additional to that which I gave him by will, 30*l*. I give to my servant, Ann Parkinson, twenty nobles, and Ann, the wife of Nicholas Petifer, 5*l*. and two laced aprons and a band of my mourning linen. The residue of my wearing clothes and linen (not disposed of) equally betwixt Mary Dighton, widow, and the said Ann Parkinson, my servant. I give to Elizabeth Gifford and Frances Gifford, daughters of Mr. Symon Gifford, 20*s*. each. I give to Robert Bellarby, my late servant, fower markes. Whereas I have placed of late my nephew, Richard Frevile, at Cambridge, and did give him 10*l*. a year hethtofore for his better maintence out of my desire of his well doing, I do referr the continuance thereof for three yeares longer, to the discretion of my nephew, Sir John Calverley, and my brother, Thomas Jenyson. My further will is (in consideration of the dearth and security that is like to ensue this present year) that my executors shall give every fortnight, 10*s*.; to be distributed unto the poor of Heighington parish by Xpoher Rayne. I give to Mr. Robert Robson of Bishop Auckland, 5*l*.

A.
ENDORSEMENT ON BACK OF THE WILL.

In the High Court of Chancery, Between Sir Dudley Ryder, Knight, his Majesty's Attorney Generale, at the relation of James Leslie, Doctor in Divinity, and James Thompson, Clerk, Informant, and John Burdon, Esquire, Robert Ord, Gentleman, Defts. 20th November, 1753. This parchment writing marked with the letter (A), and was produced and shewen by Ralph Trotter, Gentleman, Sworn and examined as a Witness on the part and behalf of the said Relators at the time of his examination before us, Jno. Hann, David Hilton, Thos. Mascall.

EDWARD LEE.[1]

Dec. 14, 1630. In the name of God, Amen, I, Edward Lee of Sunderland by the Sea, in the County of Durham, Gentleman, being weake in bodye. First I will that all my debts which I may happen to owe be satisfied. I give and bequeathe to my eldest daughter, Mary, 400*l.*, to be paid her bye 100*l.* per annum immediatlie from and after my decease out of the rents and profitts of all my messuages, lands, tenements and hereditaments which I hold of freehold land, as all such by lease, until she shall have the 400*l.* I give to my daughter, Sara, 300*l.*, to be paid likewise by the sum of 100*l.* out of my said messuages and lands. To my daughter, Ellen, 300*l.*, to be paid 100*l.* per annum out of my said lands and messuages. To my daughter Elizabeth, 300*l.*, to be paid yearly by 100*l.* out of my said messuages and landes. I give and bequeathe unto my daughters, Jane and Rebecka, 300*l.* each, to be yearly of 100*l.* each out of my lands and messuages. And I give unto my sonne Thomas, my youngest child, 300*l.*, to be paid to him annually 100*l.* out of my said lands and mesuages. I give and bequeath to my eldest sonne, Edward Lee, to be paid unto him by 100*l.* per annum out of the rents of my said lands and messuages. I give to the poore of Sunderland where I now dwell, 10*l.*, to be distributed amongst them att the discretion of twelve freeman of the said towne of Sunderland. I give and bequeath unto the Wor. my loving friend, Francis James of Hetton, in the County of Durham, Esquire, 5*l.*, and to my loveing friend, Mr. Thomas Shadford of Tunstall, 5*l.* I give to my loveing wief Elizabeth the use and benefitts of all that messuages or tenements in the tenour or occupation of Morrice Prescott, situate and being in Sunderland for the term of her naturall lyfe. I give and bequeath to my said wife and my sonne Edward (my debts, legacies and funeral expences paid), All that my Brewehouse in Sunderland, together with all my stock of money, wine, grain, debts oweing, implements, howsehold stuffe and other things whatsoever to the said Brew house belonging, for there own use and benefit, and for the education and upbringing of

[1] He was the son of Robert Lee, by his wife, Eleanor, dau. of Thomas Watwood of Stafford; he mar., firstly, Mary, dau. of Peter Delaval of Tynemouth, 3 Feb., 1611/12, at Tynemouth; she died, 23 May, 1617, leaving issue, Edward, who mar. Mary, dau. of Toby Tunstall of Cleasby, co. York; Mary, mar. Anthony Shadforth of Tunstall, 26 Nov., 1633, at St. Giles', Durham; Sarah, wife of Thomas Paul of Sunderland, Eleanor, wife of Phineas Allen of Newcastle, she was bur. at All Saints', 21 Aug., 1678. The testator mar., secondly, Elizabeth Ovington, 30 Nov., 1620, at Bishopwearmouth, by whom he had Henry, bapt., 13 Jan., 1621/2; Isabel, bapt., 7 Sept., 1624; Jane, bapt., 21 Sept., 1626; Rebecca, bapt., 30 Dec., 1628; Thomas, bapt., 5 Dec., 1630; all the children of the second family were baptized at Bishopwearmouth.

my family. And after my said children porcons shallbe paid
unto them as aforesaid, I will and bequeth all my lands, leases,
messuages, tenements and hereditaments unto my said sone
Edward and his heirs, he paying unto my said wife the third
of all my rents and profitts that shall arise out of my messuages
and lands. And I do nominate and appoint my said wellbeloved
frends, Francis James and Thomas Shadford, to be executors of
this my last Will and Testament, desireing them and either of
them to see this my last Will and Testament performed in all
things. And I revoke all former Wills by me hertofore made.
Witness, William Backhouse.

Amount of INVENTORY, 584*l.* 4*s.* 0*d.* Proved, 1630.

LIONEL FENWICKE.[1]

1631. Lionel Fenwicke of Blaigdon, in the Countie of
Northumberland, Esqr., deceased. The Declaration of the
Accompt of Edward Lorren, gentleman, Administrator of all and
singular the goods, chattels and creditts of the said Lyonel
Fenwicke. Imprs : This Accomptant and 'Administrator doth
charge himselfe with all and singular the goods, chattels and
creditts of the said Lyonell Fenwick, deceased, conveyed and
specified in an Inventorie therof into this Worshipfull Courte,
and their remayning of record amounting in to the sum of
499*l.* 9*s.* 8*d.*, Out of which this Accomptant and Administrator
doth crave allowances as here after followeth. This accomptant
and Administrator prayeth allowance and deduction of the sum
104*l.* oweing by the deceased in his life time upon Bond to the
Right Wor. Sir John Fenwicke, Kt., and since his death satisfied
and paid by this Accomptant 104*l.* This Accomptant craveth
allowanc of 20*l.* paid to John Fenwick of Butterley, gent., for
debt by bond, 20*l.* Paid more to Mr. Bartiam Liddle of Newcastle, for debt, 28*l.* Craveth likewise deduction of 41*l.* 12*s.* 0*d.*
since paid by this Administrator, from Thomas Crawforth. Paid
in like manner the sume of 120*l.*, due by bond to Ambrose Storie,
and a further Bond for 9*l* 12*s.* 0*d.* Paid to Mr. Robert Cramlington of Newsam, Esqr., 32*l.* Paid to Mr. William Hall,
Merchant of Newcastle, 9*l.* 9*s.* 5*d.* Paid to Mr. Roger Fenwicke

[1] Probably grandson of Lionel Fenwick of Blagdon, and son of
the William Fenwick who before 17 June, 1587 (*New Co. History of
Northd.*, ix., 86), mar. Eleanor, dau. of William Bates, and mortgaged
Blagdon to Sir John Fenwick, 20 June, 1615 (*Surt. Soc.*, cxi., 204).
He died (according to inquisitions taken, 23 Oct., 1630, and 21 Sept.,
1631), 14 Aug., 1630; administration of his goods was granted, 20 Aug.,
1630, to Edward Lorren, for the use of the (younger) children,
John, Henry, Robert and Mary; Julian Fenwick the relict renouncing.
William Fenwick, his son and heir, aged 14 years 4 months on 21 Sept.,
1631, died a delinquent; before 16 Sept., 1650, leaving Margaret, his
widow (*Surt. Soc.*, cxi., 204). Both Margaret and William's younger
brother, Robert, were living in 1670 (*Raine Test., Dunelm.*, ii., 83).

of Shortflatt, Gent, 10*l*. Paid to Mr. Toby Blakiston, or to some of his brother or sister on his behalfe, 50*l*. for rent due from Horton Grange, which the deceased did farme. Paid to Mr. Edward Gray of Morpeth Castle for the rent of Hartford, farmed by the deceased, 18*l*. Paid more to Mr. Bartram Liddle for debt, 5*l*. Paid to Mr. Urwen, rent due out of Horton Grange, 26*s*. 4*d*. Paid to Mr. John Snape, Vicar of Stamfordham, for the tythe rent of Blagdon unpaid at the death of the deceased, 8*l*. This accomptant craveth allowance for the charges of the funerall, 15*l*. The like charges about the Administration, 1*l*. 6*s*. 4*d*. Likewise allowance for the charges in drawinge and passing the accompts under seal and other charges thereabouts, 1*l*. 13*s*. 0*d*. Paid to Bartram Robson of Newcastle for debt, 11*l*. 10*s*. 0*d*. Paid to Mr. Lancelott Fenwick for the use of his child, William, being also a debt, 10*l*. More paid to Mr. Edward Gray for rent of Harforthe, 18*l*. 6*s*. 0*d*. More upon bond to Mr. Edwarde Graye, 6*l*. 14*s*. 0*d*. Paid to Mr. Milner upon bond, 54*l*. Paid for servants' wages, 24*l*. Paid to Mr. Andrew Younge for the rent of Camasse, 26*l*. Paid to Mr. Roger Widdrington, 20*l*. Paid to Gawen Radcliffe, 25*l*.

July (*sic*) 20, 1630. Administration granted to Edward Lorren, gent, for use of John, Henry, Robert, and Mary Fenwicke, children.

ROBERT GRAY.

April 6, 1631. Robert Gray of Aykeld, within the Countie of Northumberland, gentleman. I humblie comende my soule unto the hands of Almightie God, who hath created, redeemed and preserved me, and my bodie to be buryed in the Chancell att Kirknewton in full hope of resurrection unto eternal life through the meritts of Jesus Christ my Saviour. I give unto my sonnes, who were not present alreadie in my lyfetime, vizt., To my sonne, Bryan Gray, 20*l*. To my sonne, Ralphe Gray, 10*l*. And to my sonne, Edward Gray, 10*l*., in full discharge of their filial portions. I constitute my loveing wife, Margarett Gray, and my eldest sone, Arthur Gray, to be Executors. Probate, 1631.

INVENTORY, 88*l*. 14*s*. 0*d*.

WYNIFRIDE MIDLETON.[1]

April 26, 1631. In the name of God, Amen, I, Wynifride Midleton of Barnard castle, within the Bishopricke of Durham, widow and laite wife of George Midleton, of the said Barnard

---

[1] The testatrix was bur. at Barnard Castle, 20 Dec., 1635, where her husband, George, was also bur., 27 July, 1625, he being the son of John Middleton of Carlisle, by his wife, Eleanor, dau. of Thomas Sandford of Askham, Westmoreland; there were two daus. of the

Castle, Esquire, deceased, being of sounde and pfect remembrance, god's holie name be prased, therefore revoking thereby all former wills, testaments and codicills whatsoever, do ordaine and make this this twenty sixth day of April my last Will and Testament. My will and mynd is that my bodye be buryed within the Churche or chapell of Barnard castle as near to my husband's grave as convenientlie may be. And for my temporall estate and goods that I shall leave after my decease, I give and bequeathe them as hereinafter followeth. I give and bequeath unto the poore people of Barnard castle the sum of 40s., to be distributed unto them at my buriall or within one week immediately after. And also 20s. to the poore householders of the towne the week before Christmas next after followinge. I give and bequeath unto my loveing sonne in lawe, Maister Israel Fieldinge, one great silver Bowle, with the cover belonginge unto itt, which is embossed and waved upon the syde and upon the cover and lydd thereof. I give and bequeath unto my servante, Charles Sandersone, whom I have founde ever trustie and faithfull in all my affairs and imployements wherein I have used him, All my tearme of yeares, interest, rights and title that I have in a little parcel of ground commonlie called the Lunnygarth, situate and being within the lordshipp of Barnard Castle, with egress and regress through the little maines unto the same, and to enjoye, hold and occupe it with the accustomed privledges, easements and wayes as nowe it is used or hath been at any time formerlie heretofore, he paying the levies, rent for the same (beinge 6s. 8d. yearlie). I give and bequeath unto the above named, my servante, Charles Sanderson, half of all my whole cropp of corne of what kind or sort soever as shall be growing, reaped, threshed, stacked without or remayning in the barnes or garners, with all my plowe geare and waine geare and whatsoever els belongeth unto husbandrie. And the rather I am induced and moved to bequeathe and give the fore named plough geare and waine geare unto the saide Charles as aforesaid, for that when he came unto my husband's service he furnished us of his owne coste withall necessarie implements belonging to husbandrie. I give and bequeathe unto my said servante, Charles Sanderson, and to his assigns, one Cow gait from Maye daye unto the feaste of St. Michael the Archangell yearlie, and so from year to year, which Cowe gaite is to be in the little maines during the term of yeares I hold the said maines by lease from the Right Worshipful Sir Henry ffaine, Knight. I give unto my godsone, Cliburne Kirkbride, 5s. I give unto my cosen, Lawrence Midleton, a paire of knit stockins of 5s. price.

marriage, Jane, who died unmar., and Elizabeth, wife of John Dent of Barnard Castle, whose only child, Jane, found by *Inq. p.m.*, 19 Aug., 1626, to be aged 8, and heir to her grandfather, George Middleton, mar., 19 May. 1636. at Barningham, Sir Francis Anderson of Bradley, Knt. (Barnard Castle Regs.),

I give and bequeath unto my loveing neighbour and kind frend, Mathewe Stodart, Maister Houring's workes which I nowe have in my custodie and house. I give unto Marie Hutton, my whole ryding suit, viz., Cloake, safegarde and Hoode. I bequeath to my god daughter and servant, Jane Sanderson, 3*l*. 6*s*. 8*d*. towards the buyinge of apparell for her wedding, And I also give unto her my old ryding suite. I give unto Christopher Sanderson, now an apprentice at London, five shillings by yeare during the whole time of his apprenticeshipp. I give unto Charles Sanderson, the son of Charles Sanderson, towards his maintenance at Schole, five poundes. I give unto my cozen Cecill Blenkinsopp's children, 10*s*. I give unto Isabell Sheapheard, my old servant, 5*s*. I give unto all my godchildren for whom I promised in baptism and haith my name, two shillings and six pence each. My will is that my Christian and true frend, Mr. Thomas Glover, now Vicar of Startforth, shall preach at my funerall, and in consideration of his paines I give and bequeath unto him 10*s*. I give and bequeath unto my servant, Charles Sanderson, one bed steade and a little cuppborde standing and remayning in the chamber and rowme wherein he now lyethe in my house, and likewise all the furniture, household stuff and other particular implements which are in the said chambre and in his custodie which is mine. I give and bequeath as aforesaid all the inside particulars for that the most parte of the goods and utensills contained in the said roome, to my knowledge or his owne, and the said Bedstead and the cuppbord were formerly given unto him by my daughter, Jane Midleton, deceased. That whereas Sir Talbot Bowes, Knight, and Maister Thomas Bowes, his brother, Esquire, is indebted unto me a certaine sum of moneye, my will is soe soon as the said money shall be trulie and honestlie be paid unto my executors, upon the receipt thereof they shall give and not before nor out of any of my other goodes or chattells unto my sister, Alice Conyers, in testimony of my christian piťtie and affection towards her, the sume of ten poundes upon this condition and consideration, that is to say, that neither she, the said Alice, nor her husband, Roger Conyers, nor any others, by their meanes, consent or procurements shall suite or serve, contradicte or question my executors, my servants or any other person or persons that haith executed any commission or commissions or did any act or any on my behalf for . . . . and my temporall estate, or shall question the last Will and Testament of my late husband, George Midleton, Esquire, deceased, or by any other waye or means contarie to the true intent and meaning of this my last Will and Testament. It is my will and last testament that my deare and well beloved grandchild, Jane Dente, shall have my lesser peece of guilded plate with the cover, one silver salte with a cover, my Brewing leade racks and spitts withall, All my cubbords, tables and Bedsteades before not bequeathed contained

within my now dwellinghouse. I give and bequeath unto Mary
Glover, the wife of Thomas Glover, vicar of Startforthe, my black
satin kirtle. I give and bequeathe my wrought velvet gowne to
my sister, Dorothie Kirkbride. I give to my sister, Lucie
Warkopp, my blacke stuff gowne. All the rest of my goods and
chattells, moveable and unmovable, unbequeathed, my debts and
funerall expences discharged, I give and bequeath to my dearly
beloved grandchild, Jane Dente, and to my loveing sons in lawe,
Mr. Israell Fieldinge, and Mr. John Dent, with this priviso, that
if any pson or psons after my decease shall molist, question, suit
or trouble my servante, Charles Sanderson, for or concerning any
thing, act or acts, deed or deeds, done by him which did concern
my estate or the estate of my late husband deceased, during all
the time he served us or either of us, upon any pretence or colour
of action whatsoever, my mynd and my last Will and Testament is
that my executor shall defray the charge and costes he shall be
putt to, and from time to time to defend him and to keep him
harmless. I doe ordaine and make the above named my grandchilde, Jane Dente, Maisterr Israell Feildinge and Maister John
Dente my sole executors of this my last Will and Testament.
Witnesses, Amb. Apelby, Lau. Rayne, Thomas Glover. Proved,
1635.

JOHN LUMLEY.[1]

May 6, 1631. In the name of god, Amen, I, John Lumley
of Newton Archdeacon in the County of Durham, Gent. All my
goods I give and bequeth to my cosen, Henry Blaxton of Newton
Archdeacon. Witness, Antho. Harryson.

June 8, 1638. A true Inventory of the goods of John Lumley
of Newton, Archdeacon in the parish of Darnton, Esqr., deceased.
Imprs : his clothes, his bookes, two trunkes and some other small
things in the chamber, 10*l.* One nagg and one mare, 10*l.* In
moneys owing to him, 97*l.* 1*s.* 2*d.*, of which some there is in
disperate debtts fifteen pounds. In presunt moneys, 11*l.* 6*s.* 9*d.*
Somme is 128*l.* 7*s.* 11*d.*

ALEXANDER SELBY.[2]

June 9, 1631. Alexander Selby of Bittlestone, in the parish
of Allanton, Esqr.

A true and perfect Inventorie of the goods and chattels of
the said Alexander Selby. Imprs : Twenty foure oxen, 52*l.* Five
score yewes and lambs, 38*l.* 15*s.* 0*d.* Two Kyne, 4*l.* One cowe,

[1] He was the son of Roger Lumley " that died in the Jayle," and
was bur. in " the queer " of St. Mary-le-Bow, Durham, 30 Mch., 1616.
He was second cousin of Henry Blakiston of Archdeacon Newton, and
was bur. at Darlington, 1638, Longstaffe's *Darlington,* 128.

[2] The testator was the son of Thomas Selby of Biddleston by his
first wife, Agnes, dau. of Gerrard Heron of Meldon. He mar. Joan,

1*l.* 10*s.* 0*d.* Eight Kyne, 13*l.* 6*s.* 0*d.* Three horses, 11*l.* 0*s.* 0*d.* Two stots, 4*l.* Four stears, 2*l.* Two steares, also 2*l.* Twentie yewes, 6*l.* Three score of geald sheepe, 15*l.* The household stuffe, 3*l.* 6*s.* 8*d.* Administration granted to Joan Selbye, the lawful Widow and Relict, Children, Ephraim Selbye, aged 14, Thomas Selbye, aged 11, Alexander Selbye, aged 10, George Selbye, aged 7, Ursula Selbye, aged 6, and John Selbye, 4 years.

ALEXANDER SELBY.

1632. Alexander Selby, late of Bitleston within the parish of Allanton, in the Diocese of Diocese of Durham, Esquire, decd. Declaration of Accompt of Joan Selbie, widow, late wife and Administratrix of the goods and chattels of the said deceased. The said Accompt doth charge herself with all the goods, chattells and creditts which were her said late husband's, at the time of his death being contained in ane Inventarie thereof remaining in this Court of Record, and amounting to the sum of 155*l.* 8*s.* 4*d.* Imprimis : To Thomas Man of Durham, draper, upon bond, 37*l.* To Dorothy Pott of Bitleston, upon bond, 20*l.* To Margaret Jordan of Bitleston, widow, upon bond, 11*l.* To John Harbotle of Alnwick, upon bond, 6*l.* To him more for lent moneye as by his acquittance appeareth, 40*s.* To Roger Huntley of Wooler, upon bond, 6*l.* To Robert Alder of Alneham, upon bond, 5*l.* 2*s.* 6*d.* To George Greine of Scranwood, upon bond, 5*l.* 1*s.* 4*d.* To Mungo Bambrey of Great Ryle upon bill, 40*s.* To Jane Hudson of Alnewick, for burrowed money, 30*s.* To John Collingwood of Newcastle, for boots and other waires, 50*s.* To Roger Widdrington, late sonne of Henry Widdrington of Trewhitt, for his portion remaining in the said intestate's handes, 43*l.* 10*s.* 0*d.* For funerall expences, 8*l.* 13*s.* 4*d.* To Dorothy Pott, a servant, for wages, 5*l.* 9*s.* 6*d.* To Anne Mason, servant, 20*s.* To Margaret Lumbsdon, 16*s.* 10*d.* To Cuthbert Key, servant, 3*l.* 8*s.* 0*d.* To Jane Graie, servant, 27*s.* To John, servant, 10*s.* 6*d.* To Thomas Trumble, servant, 10*s.* 6*d.* To Edward Ellot, a servant, 6*s.* To Ellene Younge, a servant, 10*l.* 2*s.* 0*d.* To Jane Pott, servante, 20*s.* To Margaret Dewers, a servant, 12*s.* To Jane Clarke, servant, 16*s.* For charge in appraizing the goods, making the Inventories, Letters of Administration and other charges about the same, 26*s.* 8*d.* For passing this accompt and letters of testimoniall about the same, 23*s.* 4*d.* To George Pott of Shulmoore, upon bond, 5*l.* Sume, 173*l.* 5*s.* 6*d.* Administration, 4th June, 1631, to Joan Selby, the lawful Widow and Relict.

dau. of Ephraim Widdrington of Trewhit; by her he had issue, Robert, aged 3 in 1615; William, who mar. Hellen, dau. of Sir Thos. Haggerston, Bart.; Mary, who mar . . . . Collingwood of Thornton; Agnes; Ursula, wife of . . . . Pott of Trewit; and Ephraim, Thomas, Alexander, George and John.

SIR WILLIAM MUSCHAMP.[1]

Sept., 1631. Muschamp, Sir William, Knight. A perfect Inventorie of the goods and chattels of the deceased, apprised and valued by Thomas Smart, George Tailor, Adam Cleugh and John Barber. Imprs: Household stuffe in all romes within his dwellinghouse at Barmoore, with bras, pewter and iron, 160*l*. 19*s*. 8*d*. Plate of all sortes, 100*l*. Wearing apparell, 20*l*. Linen of all sortes, 30*l*. Debts due to him for wood, cattell and corne, 508*l*. 16*s*. 4*d*. The tithes of Barmoore, Bowsdon and Getherick held by lease from the Dean and Chapter of Durham, 40*l*. Horses, mares and foales, 55*l*. 6*s*. 8*d*. Oxen for draught, 180*l*. 15*s*. 0*d*. Fatt oxen, 14*l*. 13*s*. 4*d*. Young cattell, 90*l*. 15*s*. 6*d*. Kine calves and bulls, 112*l*. 16*s*. 0*d*. Young stirkes, 15*l*. 10*s*. 0*d*. Corne in all places, 400*l*. 6*s*. 8*d*. Implements of husbandrie in all places, 13*l*. 6*s*. 8*d*. Haye in all places, 27*l*. 0*s*. 0*d*. Sheepe of all sortes, 55*l*. Swine, 6*l*. 0*s*. 0*d*. The lease of the hay of Bowsdon from my lord of Suffolk, 6*l*. 8*s*. 0*d*. The lease of the Colliarie of Etall, houlden of my lord of Suffolk, New Timber, 5*l*. Suma totalis, 2,002*l*. 3*s*. 4*d*. Witnesses, Tho. Haggerston, William Selbye, Robert Stott, Pet. Bolam.

BARTRAM BRADFORTH.

Dec. 19, 1631. In the name of God, Amen, I, Bartram Bradforth of Lamesley, in the Countye Palatine of Durham, Gent, being sicke of bodye. To be buried within the Church or Churchyarde of the parish of Lamesley aforesaid. I give and bequeath the lease of the terme of yeares yet to come and unexpired of the overhouse garth in Ravensworth, in the County aforesaid, made to me from Ralph Sureties, elder, together with the benefitt and advantage of a bond made from the said Raph Sureties to me, the said Bartram Bradforth, bearing date the day of the said lease, with condition endorsed for the performance thereof unto my sone, Hugh Bradforth, to the use of him, his wife and children, their executors, admors and assns, with all the covenants, clauses, sentences and the benefitts and advantages of the pviso in the said lease conteined, he, the said Hugh Bradforth, paying all my debts hereunder named, and my funerall expences discharged, And all other goods, moveable and unmoveable, I give unto my sonne, Hugh Bradforth, and like I doe make him sole Executor of this my Will. Witnesses, John Lowther, Tho. Dowker, Curat. Proved, 1633.

[1] He was the son of George Muschamp of Barmoor by his wife, Elizabeth, dau. of Sir John Selby of Twisell, mar. at Berwick, 11 June, 1583. The testator was knighted at Berwick, 11 May, 1617, sheriff of Northumberland, 1631, mar. Elizabeth, dau. of Sir Nicholas Gilborne of Charing, Kent, she was bur. at St. Andrew's, Holborn, 20 Apl., 1638; by her he had issue, Sir George Muschamp, aged 2 in 1615, mar. Mary, dau. of William Swinhoe of Goswick, and, secondly, Gilbert, dau. of Sir Richard Houghton of Houghton Tower, co. Lancs., and William, Ralph, Margaret and Mary

KATHERIN FORTUNE.[1]

Jan. 2, 1631. In the name of God, Amen, I, Katherin Fortune of Gateside, in the County of Durham, Widow, late wife of George Fortune, Gentleman, deceased, and some time wife of Edward Allen, late of Gateside aforesaid, Master Mariner, also deceased, Being (at this present) diseased and sicklie in bodye. To be buried and layd in or near the Parish Church of Gateside aforesaid, so neare unto my said former husband, Edward Allen, there as may be possible and convenient. And as for the Temporall and decaying estate, which the lord hathe indewed and lent me (in this present lyfe) I give and bequeath as follows. I give and bequeathe unto my sonne, Robert Allen, and to the heires of his bodye lawfully begotten or to be begotten for ever, my now dwellinghouse, with all singular the appurtenances wherein I, the said Katherin, now dwell, and situate and beinge in Gateside aforesaide near unto the head of the Banck there, upon this condition that he or they doe paye forthe of the same the sume of thirty and seven pounds of lawfull money of England to such sevall psons as is herein nominated, to each one of them their severall respective parts and portions according as my will and mynd is, and at such tymes as hereafter in these presents is expressed, that is to say, I give and bequeath unto my Grand-childe, Joseph Bryan, son of Joseph Bryan and Margaret, his wife, my daughter, the sum of twenty pounds, part of the said sum of thirty and seven pounds, to be paid unto him by my said son, Robert Allen, within three years time next after the decease and departure of me, the said Katherin. I give and bequeath unto the said Margaret Bryan, 20s., thereof to be paid unto her by my said sonne, Robert Allen, within the like space of three yeares tyme next after my decease and departure as aforesaid. I give and bequeath unto my Brother, Edmund Swinborne, the sum of twenty shillings, also part thereof to be paid unto him by my said sonne, Robert Allan, also within the same space of three yeares next after the decease also of me, the said Katherin. I give and bequeath unto Mary Anderson, my cosin Henry Anderson's youngest daughter, the sum of 5l., being also part thereof to be paid unto her also by my said sonne, Robert Allen, within the aforesaid tyme of three years next after my decease likewise of me, the said Katherin. I give and bequeath to my grandchild, Katherin Allen, daughter of my said sonne Robert Allen, the sume of tenn poundes residue of the said sume of thirty seven pounds, to be paid unto her by my said sonne, Robert Allen, within the space also of three yeares next after the decease also, of me, the said Katherin. And as

[1] She was bur. at Gateshead, 26 July, 1638.

touching my other goods and chattells either (moveable or unmoveable), of insight geare, of what kind soever, either to be
found within my said two dwellinghouses in Gateside aforesaid
or elsewhere (that shall belong unto me), my mynd and will is,
And hereby I doe appoynt that my executors hereinbefore
nominated with the consent and likeing of my supervisors (also
hereby named), also in convenyient and fitting tyme next after
the decease and departure of me, the said Katherin aforesaid,
cause the same to be pticularlie (in a Catalague) mentioned,
praised and valued by different praisers, and therein to incert
the several sums and values, that every pticular thing shall
amont unto. And what the totall sume shall come to, my further
mynd and pleasure is that the same goods and chattells shall be
sould at and for the best advantage that my executors, with the
likeing, approbation and consent of my supervisors hereafter
appoynted, cann or may. I will and my mynd is, That the
money that such goodes and monies and chattells shall amount
unto shallbe disposed as hereafter is declared. First, my debts,
legacies and funerall expences being first payd and discharged, I
give and bequeath unto my daughter, Margery Prescodd, out
of the same totall sume, that such goods and chattells shallbe
sould for (as aforesaid) the sume of 40*l.* of lawful moneye of
England, To be payed upon the sale of such goods and chattels.
I give and bequeath unto her husband, Marys Prescodd, out of
the same the sume of 20*s.* of like money for a token, in remembrance of my love for him to be payd as aforesaid. The rest
that remaineth of such totall (if any be), be it more or lesse,
I give and bequeath the same to my saide sonne, Robert Allen,
and my said daughter, Margery Prescodd, to be equally divided
between them, which said Robert and Margery I doe hereby
nominate and apoint Executors of this my last Will and Testament, revokeing hereby all former Wills by me heretofore made
in this respect. And lastly, I doe entreat, nominate and appoint
my two good friends, Mr. Railph Cole of Gateside aforesaid,
Esquire, and my said cosin, Henrye Anderson, the Elder, of
Newcastle-upon-Tyne, Merchant, Supervisors of this my last Will
and Testament (as aforesaid) hopeing they will see the same dewly
executed as my mynd is And according to the trust and confidence
I repose in them. And for their paynes and care herein I givé
and bequeath unto each of them 20*s.* a peice, to be payd by my
aforesaid Executors immediately after the decease of me, the said
Katherin (as aforesaid), which I hereby charge them withall.
Witnesses, James Cole, Thomas Durkin and John Ainsley.

The goods appraised and debts owing to the testatrix amounteth
unto 118*l.* 15*s.* 0*d.* The funeral expences of the testatrix
amounteth to 10*l.* 15*s.* 10*d.* Soe theire rests clere, 107*l.* 19*s.* 2*d.*
Proved, 1638.

EDWARD CHARLTON.

March 23, 1631. Edward Charlton of the lee Hall, in the County of Northumberland. To be buried in ye parish Church of Bellingham. Whereas my sone, William Charltonn, is oweing me three poundes, viz., 30s. for a nagg, and 30s. for plough geare and wanes, such sum with twenty nobles be paid within eight years to my children, Cuthbert, Edward, John, Margerie and Barbarie Charlton, by the appointmt and disposing of Cuthbert Hearon of Chipchase, Esqr., and John Hearon of Birkley, Gent. Whereas I owe unto Mrs. Dorothie Thompson of Hexham, 8l., for which Mr. Cuthbert Hearon of Chipchase did pass his word, such sum to be paid by my sonne, William Charlton. I give all the rest and remainder of my goods to my said five children. Witnesses to Will, Cuthbert Loury, Nicholas Rydley. Probate, 1635.

BARTRAM ROTCHESTER.

April 12, 1632. Bartram Rotchester of Ogle, within the parish of Whalton. To be buryed in the Church of Walton. I give unto John Rotchester, all my clothes belonging to my apparell and my sworde. I give unto Bartram Rotchester, the son of the aforesaid John Rotchester, one young whye. To Allison Spraggon, one whye stirke. To Elizabeth Watson, one ewe hoge. To Henry Patterson, one bed stead and a table and two furms, one amyre, a plough and a coulter and one muckle waine, and a pair of speckes; the rest of my goods, both moveable and immoveable, after this manner, I leave unto my wife one half of my goods, and the other half unto John Meggison and Robert Sopwith, my sons-in-law, and make them and my wife Executors.

INVENTORIE, 35l. 6s. 8d. Probate, 1632.

ROLAND ARCHER.

April 22, 1632. Will of Roland Archer of North Seaton, of the pish of Woodhorne. I leave my wife Elsabeth the thirds of all my goods, moveable and unmoveable, wheresoever unto me appertaininge or belonging. I leave to my sonne Rouland's two Boyes, Rouland and John Archer, two stotts or quies to be elected by some indifferent men, viz., Anthonie Brown and John Marshall of Seaton. I leave six stotts, togedder with a long wain, to my grandchild, Rouland Hunter, the youngest of the stotts, to be three (or above) yeares ould. I leave to John Johnson's wife, of Sleikburne, a yellowe cowe. I leave to Barbarie Rea, a whie of 3 yeares old or a stotte, accordinge to her owne pleasure. I leave to Elsabeth Fergison a cowe of 3 yeares ould, and a Bushell of corne at Christmas. To sonne Rouland's two children, viz., Dorothie and Anne, the sum of ten pounds. To James Reas

wife of Stanington, a cowe of 3 years olde. I leave a Cowe to
my Daughter, Dor. Hunter. To Mathew Fergison, a stott. I
give my man, Thomas Shillvington, and my maid, Cathren
Faucus, every of them, a sheepe. I leave my sonne Rouland sole
executor of this my Will, and especiallie of all my lands, goods,
chattels, moveable and unmoveable, whatsoever. I leave to my
sonne Rouland's two Daughters all the insight goods that came
to me by their mother. I leave to my grandchild, John Johnson,
a quie of a yeare olde. Witnesses, Henry Widdrington, John
Erington, Anthonie Browne, Richard Nicholson, Tho. Sootheron.
May 9, 1632. A true and just Inventory of all the goods and
chattels of Rowland Archer of North Seaton, latelie deceased,
praised and valued by these foure men, Willm. Buckles, Willm.
Skipsey, Jacob Patteson, John Johnson. Imprimis: Fower oxen,
18*l.* Eight kyne and 8 calves, 16*l.* Three mares and a horse, 45*l.*
Thirty sixe shepe, 18*l.* Swine praised to 16*s.* Geese, 6*s.* Six
younge beasts, 6*l.* Corne in the garthe and Barne, 9*l.* Furniture
in the house, 40*s.* His appell, 40*s.* In moneye, 17*s.* 1*d.* Corne
upon the ground, 20*l.* Implements of Husbandry, 30*s.* Sum is
114*l.* 9*s.* 1*d.*

Debts oweing bie the testator. Imprimis: to Dorothie Archer,
3*l.* To Ann Archer, 13*l.* To Hellen Harrison of Newcastle,
8*l.* 16*s.* For my rent at Newsom, 7*l.* 10*s.* To Mr. Beniamin
Woodrington, 8*l.* To my man, Thos. Shilvington, 17*s.* To my
maid, 25*s.* 6*d.* To Mathewe Fargesone, 12*d.* His funerall
expences, 3*l.* 15*s.* 8*d.* Sum is 46*l.* 7*s.* 2*d.* Proved, May, 1632.

WILLIAM ROBSON.

May 2, 1632. In the name of God, Amen, I, William Robson
of Norton, in the County of Durham, Yeoman, being sick and
weak in bodye. To be buried in the Churchyard of Norton. My
will is that my sonne, Francis Robson, shall have the lands and
tenements which I have bought after the death of my wife, his
mother, and he to pay when he enters of the same unto his
brother, William Robson, Thirty pounds of good and lawful money
of England. I give to my sonne, William Robsone, one graye
Mayer and a foole, and a filly of the same mayer. I give to my
sonne William, all the grass that I have taken of the town of
Norton in common, in Hardwick field, Owston more and New
Close. I give to my daughter Margrett, thirteen poundes six
shillings and eightpence. My will is that my sonne William,
give unto William, the sonne of William Barwick, the first foole
that his maier hath and to keepe it and let it suck one the maier
till such time as its weaned. I give unto William Barwick's three
children each of them one ewe and one lam. I give unto Alice,
the daughter of Nicholas Jefferson, one ewe, one lam. I give to
my wife one ewe and twenty shillings of golde. I give to my

sonne Francis, Twenty shillings in golde. I give to my sonne, Willm. Robson, twenty shillings in golde. I give to my daughter Margret, twenty shillings in golde. I give to Will. Barwick and his wife, either of them, ten shillings in golde. I give to my sonne, Nicholas Jefferson, and his wife, either of them, ten shillings in golde. I give to my Brother, Robert Robson, one whole suite of clothes from the head to the foote with a cloake. I give unto my sister, the wife of William Savidge, half a stone of woole to make her a coate. I give to my daughter Margarett, one furre cubbart in the hall house with tenn puter dublers on the tope of it, with a pott or salt and a candle sticke and a pann, two payre of lining sheets and a bolster. I give to my sister, the wife of William Fosse, half a stone of woole. The residue of all my goodes and debts and legacees and funerall discharged, I give to Margret, my wife, Francis and William, my sonns, Elizabeth, the wife of William Barwick, and Margaret, my daughter, whom I make joynt executors of this my said Will and Testament. Witnesses, John Wheatlie, Robert Davison, Nicholas Jefferson, William Pallyman, William Chipchaise.

INVENTORY, 190*l.* 9*s.* 6*d.* Proved 1633.

GAWIN CLAVERINGE.

May 7, 1632. Gawin Claveringe of Upper Trewhitt, in the pish of Rothburie, in the Countie of Northumberland, Gentleman. My bodie to be buried in the chancell of the parish church of Whittingham. I give and bequeath to my sone, Robert Claveringe, five Kyne and their caulfes, two quyes, one black ox stirke, one branded ox stirke, two gray mares, one gray filley, two oxen and nineteen gimers and dinmonds. To my daughter, Agnes Claveringe, one rigded oxe, one ox, two kyne, one haulkt quy stirke, one rigded ox stirke, eighteene gimers and dinmons, foure pounds and three shillings in money and ten boules of oates, equally divided betwixt her and my aforesayd sone, Robert Claveringe. I give to my sonne, George Claveringe, and my daughter, Marie Claveringe, equally betwixt them, nine oxen, eight kyne and their caulfes, twentie ewes, eight lambs and ten weathers. I give to Kathran Claveringe, my wife, all the corne on the ground sowen and unsowen, and a brown nagg and eighteen shillings in the Lard of Barrowp's hand, and fiftie five shillings in Francis Red's hand, and fortie two shillings in Francis Collingwood's hand, and twelve shillings in Matthew Hall's hand, and twelve shillings in John Slegg's hand, and twenty eight shillings in Mrs. Katharin Ord's hand, and 11*s.* in Robert Clarke's hand, and 16*s.* 6*d.* in Charles Urpeth's hand, and 5*s.* 6*d.* in Andrew Gaire's hand, and 5*s.* in Thomas Makenlinge's hand, and 4*s.* in Alexander Hall's hand, and 12*s.* in George Selbie's hand, and 20*s.* in James Heslopp's hand, and

30*s.* in Thomas Davison's hand, and 5*s.* 6*d.* in Parst Steavenson's hand, and all these debts I leave to pay my debtes. I give to my wyfe, Katheran Claveringe, my lease of three yeares, of three quarters of the whole towne land att Uppertrewhitt which I now possess and hold of Mr. George Orde, and if he wrong her or trouble her in the said tearme of three yeares which he hath granted unto me, then my will is that my said wife shall sewe the said Mr. George Orde for a coult which I gave to him for a fine for the said three yeares. I leave the tuition of my sonne, Robert Claveringe, and my Daughter, Agnes Claveringe, unto Sir John Claveringe, also I leave my wife, Kathran, my sone George, and my daughter, Mary Claveringe, to the said Sir John Claveringe, whom I humblie intreat to befriend, and see they be not wronged. The residue of my goods, moveable and unmoveable, to my said wife Katheran and my son Robert. I make my said wife and my son Robert, with Bertie Spinks, Executors of this my Will. Witnesses, Martin Danbye, Bertrand Spinks. Probate, 1632.

WILLIAM INGLEBY.[1]

June 25, 1632. In the name of God, Amen, I, William Ingleby of Great Haswell, in the County Pallatine of Durham, Yeoman, being visitted with sickness. To be interred in Easington Churchyard. I give to the stock of the poore of the parish of Easington, 5*l.* I give to my wife, Elizabeth Ingleby, 5*l.* as a legacy. Whereas my wife is now with Child, my will is that if it be a man child he shall have my lease of the Moore-house and halfe of a farme in Rainton when he cometh to the age of eighteen yeares. I give to the said man child 100*l.* when he cometh to the said age. I give to my daughter, Margrett Ingleby, eight score poundes, and shee shall marry with the consent of her mother and my brother-in-law, Richard Thursby, and my brother, John Ingleby. I give her the lease of Flemin field. I give to my second daughter, for her portion, seven score pounds. To my third daughter, Isabell, six score pounds. I give to my fourth daughter, Ann, foure score pounds and the close I bought of John Bell in Rainton. If my wife shall beare me now a and 6*l.* in George Greene's hand, and 5*s.* 6*d.* in Andrew Blithe's daughter, I give and bequeath to the said daughter six score pounds, and then my will is that my eldest daughter Margarett, shall have my lease of the Moore-house, provided alwayes that

---

[1] The testator was bur. at Easington, 12 July, 1632, mar. Elizabeth Thursby at Pittington, 16 June, 1618, by her he had issue, William (with whom she was with child when her husband made his will), bapt., 18 Nov., 1632, at Easington, mar. Anna Mitford, 26 Apl., 1653, at Easington; Margaret, bapt., 25 Apl., 1619, at Pittington; Elizabeth, bapt., 21 May, 1620, at Pittington; Isabel, bapt., 16 July, 1622, also there; Ann., bapt. at Easington, 1 Apl., 1627.

she marry with the consent of her mother and her uncle aforesaid, and if she doe not marrye with their consent I give her
eight score pounds and my lease to goe to her sister, and my will
is that my second daughter Elizabeth shall have my lease in
Rainton if she marry with the consent as aforesaid, and if she
marry without consent, then my will is that she shall have eight
score pounds and the lease to goe to the rest of her sisters, and
my will is that my third daughter Isabell shall have my lease
of Flemin-field if she marry with the consent aforesaid, but if she
marry without consent of her mother and uncle my will is that
she shall have eight score pounds and the lease to be divided
amongst her sisters, and my fourth daughter to have the close I
bought of John Bell and 100l. My will is that none of my
daughters shall have any benefit of my leases until they come
to the age of eighteen yeares. My will is that my daughters shall
live with my wife till they come to age to choose their guardians,
and that each of them shall have 5l. a yeare for their education.
My will is that my fourth daughter Ann, and that daughter
my wife shall beare me shall have their portions made up 300l.
a peece. I give to my nephew, John Ingleby, 20s. I give to
Mangus Burne, 40s. To each of my three men servantes, a noble.
To Christopher Richardson of Shotton, 10s. To George Wanless
of Easington, 10s. To Thomas Sharpe, 10s., whom I make
Overseers of this my Will. I desire my brother-in-law, Richard
Thursby, and my brother, John Ingleby, to see this my Will
performed, and that each shall have 4l. I will that out of my
lands real and goods moveable and unmoveable, my youngest
children that have no lease shall have their portion to be made
equal with those that have the leases, if the goods will amount
to so much. I make my wife, Elizabeth, sole Executor. Witnesses, Christopher Richardson, George Wardell, Ri. Thursbye,
Thomas Sharpe.

INVENTORY, 19 July, 1632, Imprimis: In ready money and
bonds, 210l. His apparell, 6l. 13s. 4d. A beddstead, mattres,
featherbedd, one boulster and two pillows, one paire of blanketts,
2 happins and coverlit, with curtaines and vallance in the fore-
house, 4l. A beddstead, mattres, featherbedd, one bolster and two
pillowes, one paire of blanketts, two happins, a coverlitt, with
curteynes and vallence in the chamber over the house, 3l. 6s. 8d.
A bedstead, featherbedd, one bowlster, two pillowes, one paire of
blancketts, two happins and a coverlett in the chamber over the
parler, 33s. 4d. A trucklebedd, a featherbedd, mattres, a paire
of blanketts, a bowlster, 2 pillowes, 2 happins, one coverlett in
the fore house, 1l. The servantes' bedd, two bowlsters, two paire
of blanketts, fower happins, 1l. The men servants' Bedd, 13s. 4d.
More bedding in a presse, five happins, two coverletts, two
carpitts, a featherbedd ticke, a boulster and curtayne unmayed,
6l. 3s. 4d. A dozen and a half of cushons, 30s. Six paire of

245

linning sheets, sixe paire of pillowbers, 3*l*. A dozen and a half
of gordan sheets and two paire of pillowbers, 3*l*. 12*s*. Two
linnin table clothes, 8*s*. Three dosen of napkins, 36*s*. Two short
course table clothes and six course napkins, 3*s*. 4*d*. Thirtye yards
of lyning cloathe, 30*s*. Fiftye two yards of harden clothe, 25*s*.
Six lynn towells, 6*s*. Fower dosen and fower peice of pewter, a
dosen sawcers, a dosen porindgers, five flagin potts, a pynt pott,
three pewter and seven brass candlestickes. An ewer, fower
double saltsellers, four pewter cupps, thre chamber potts, a cadle
pott, 4*l*. 2*s*. A silver bowle and halfe a dosen spoones, 4*l*. Six
brasse potts att Moorehouse, 20*s*. Three kettles, two fishe panns,
three iron potts, one little brass potte and a skellett, five little
panns, 3*l*. Three Iron Chimneyes, two spitts, one paire of racks,
two dripping panns, two paire of tonges, a fire shovell, two
laddles, a chafin dish, two paire broyling Irons, two shordin
knives, a smoothing Iron and two reckin crookes, two morters
and two pesstells, 20*s*. A presse and linin cupboarde, a chare and
two chists, a glass case, 3*l*. 10*s*. A cuberd and a Cawell, 50*s*.
One table and a forme, three chaires and eight stooles, 40*s*.
Two cubberds and a table att Moore house, 4*l*. All the wood
vessels, 3 dozen of trenchers, 2*l*. 6*s*. 8*d*. A muskett and bandelere
and foweling peece, 30*s*. Plow and plow geare, waine geare,
12*l*. 10*s*. All the poweltry, 6*s*. 8*d*. Two wheate stacks and two
old stacks, 15*l*. Eight loade of Oates in the howse, 3*l*. 4*s*. All
the meadow hay and strawe, with the pfitt of the falloos, 26*l*. 6*s*.
Corne on the grounde, seventeene ackers of wheat, rye and bigg,
and fourteen and one ackers of oates, 60*l*. Butter and cheese,
50*s*. Sixteen Runtes, one Cowe and three stotts in fleming feild,
70*l*. Twentye kyne and two whyes, 7*l*. Foure stotts there, 12*l*.
Twenty oxen in falloefield, 63*l*. 6*s*. 8*d*. Fower stotts there, 12*l*.
Eight stottes there, 30*l*. Twelve oxen there, 57*l*. Seventeen Kyne
and a Bull, 53*l*. Four two yeare ould beasts and a quye,
6*l*. 8*s*. 4*d*. Five calves, 40*s*. Tenn Runts in Deadman dailes,
36*l*. 13*s*. 4*d*. Yewes, two hundred, and twelve tupps, 86*l*.
Weathers and dimmons, 287, 130*l*. Yewes and rigelts, 38,
9*l*. 10*s*. Lammes, 135, 27*l*. Three mares and a foule and a horse,
12*l*. A stonde horse, 4*l*. 10*s*. A black horse, 6*l*. A graye mare,
a bay mare, a sorreld mare and her stagg, 15*l*. Foure swine,
53*s*. 4*d*. One black coulte and a baye filleye, 7*l*. 10*s*. The lease
of Mare house, 400*l*. The lease at Rainton, called Pittfield, 100*l*.
The lease of flemmin field, 100*l*.

ROBERT LAWSON.

Jan. 1, 1632. Robert Lawson of Langhurst. My bodie to be
buried in Bothal church. I give to William, my eldest sone, four
oxen, long waiynes, short waiyes, ploughes and ploughes irons,
yoakes, with all appurtenances husbandry. I give unto my sone

Roger, 20*l.*, to be paid to him when he trades for himself. **To
my daughter, Katherine, 6*l.*,** to be paid when her husband,
Anthony Sotherne, setteth up shopp. To Henry Hancock, a
yewe lambe. To George Hancock, a yewe lambe. To Thomas
Hancock, a yewe lamb, and to Willey Hancock and Isabel Hancock, each a yew lambe. To Ralph Dawson, a yewe lambe, and
to Ann Dawson, a yewe lamb. To Elizabeth Dawson, a yewe
lambe. To Robert Lawson, my grandchilde, a yewe lamb. I give
to my sone Roger more than above, 5*l.* To my sone Thomas, 10*l.*
I give to the poor of Bothall parish, 10*s.* I give to my wife,
Margarett Lawson, my tearme in a Cottage in Langhurst and
what belongeth thereto, with one third of my said tenement for
life, and appoint her sole Executrix.

INVENTORY, 117*l* 18*s.* 8*d.* Probate, 6th February, 1632.

ANN HEATH.[1]

Jan. 22, 1632. In the name of God, Amen, I, Ann Heath of
Barmston, within the parish of Washington, being sick in bodye.
To be buryed in the parish Church of Washington. I give to
my brother, Nicholas Heathe, twenty Nobles. I give to my
Brother, William Heathe, twenty Nobles. To Mr. John Richard-
son of Durham, twenty Nobles. I give to my four brothers,
Talbot, Ralph, James and Robert Liell, each of them five pounds
a piece. I give to my sister, Mary Liell, twenty pounds. I give
to my father-in-law, Mr. Talbot Liell, ten pounds. To Mr.
Gilford Liell, a twenty shilling piece to be bestowed in a ringe.
I give to my uncle, Nicholas Heathe, a twentye shillinge peace to
make him a ringe. To Anne Wilson, daughter of Robert Wilson
of Barmstron, tenn shillings. To Elise Davye, daughter of
William Davye of Barmston, five shillings. To my father's four
servantes, Robert Gray, Marget Anderson, Ann Thomson and
Ann Claxton, each of them two shillings and sixpence a piece. I
give to the poor of the Parish of Washington, ten shillings, to
be disposed on by my father, Mr. Talbot Liell. To my mother,
Mrs. Ann Liell, ten pounds and all the monies due for the interest

---

[1] Nicholas Heath, the grandfather of the testator (whose will is
printed in this volume), mar. Anne, dau. of John Topp of Shilling-
ford, co. Berks.; by her he had Nicholas, bur., 13 Mch., 1659/60, at
St. Mary-the-Less, mar. Elizabeth, dau. of Roger Smyth of Finchley;
William; John; Margaret, wife of . . . . Burnell and Topp, bur.,
5 Apl., 1620, at Bishop Middleham, mar. Anne, dau. of Sir William
Blakiston, their issue being, Nicholas, bapt., 18 Dec., 1614, at St.
Giles', bur., 18 May, 1693, at St. Margaret's, mar. Barbara, bur.,
13 June, 1693, at St. Margaret's; William, bapt., 10 Dec., 1615, at
St. Giles', bur., 13 Jan., 1689/90, at Washington, mar. Jane, bur.,
4 Apl., 1664, at Washington; John, bapt., 25 Apl., 1619, at St. Giles',
and the testatrix, bapt., 30 Nov., 1617, at St. Giles'. Anne, the mother
of the testatrix, mar., secondly, Talbot Lisle of Barmston, and by him
she had Talbot, Ralph, James, Robert and Mary.

of my portion that shallbe overplus more then the legacies amounts unto. I doe constitute and appoint John Richardson of Durham above sayd, Esqr., to be my sole Executor, to receive all such moneys as any way be dewe unto me by vertue of my grand-father's, Mr. Nicholas Heath, his Will, to be disposed as above sayd. Witnesses, John Hylton, Robert Willson. Proved, 1633.

CUTHBERT COLLINGWOOD.[1]

Feb. 7, 1632. Inventory of the goods of Cuthbert Colling-wood of Thronton, in the County of Northumberland, gent., deceased, taken and appraised by Clement Hall, gent., Peter Shankes and John Allison of Whittingham, and John Bartram of Thronton, yeoman. Inventory amounted to 170*l*. 15*s*. 8*d*. Debts oweing unto the deceased. Item, John Forster of Newham, for a rente charge for five years, 60*l*. George Beednell, for a rent charge of 30*l*. per ann. for five yeares, 150*l*. More dew uppon bond by the said George Beadnell and his sone Robert, 46*l*. Mr. Edmond Craster, upon specialty, 86*l*. John Scott of Wark, upon specialty, 20*l*. Henry Haggerston, 10*l*. William Forster, 10*l*. Administration granted, 6 Feb., 1632, to Francis Colling-wood of Thronton, gent., the son.

MATTHEW HORSLEY.

1633. Matthew Horsley of Screnwood, in the parish of Alneham. I leave to my Brother, Robert Horsley, all my goods and chattels, he to pay all my debts, and I appoint him my Executor. I leave to my wife, Jeane Horsley, two kine, one stirke, fowerteen ewes and three hogges. To my daughter, Isabella Horsley, ten pounds of money and a cupboarde. To my daughter, Agnes Horsley, ten pounds. To my daughter, Margaret Horsley, ten pounds.

INVENTORY amounted to 37*l*. 14*s*. 4*d*. Probate, 4th April, 1633, by the said Robert Horsley, for use of self and Agnes, Isabella and Margarett, the children (Minors).

HENRY HORSLEY.

1633. Henry Horsley of Screnwood, in the parish of Alneham, in the Countie of Northumberland. I leave to my wife, Isobell Horsley, all my goods and chattels and appoint her my executrix. To my said wife, foure kine and a foale. To my daughter Jenne, three kine. To my daughter Susanna, five kine. I leave the sheepe equallie between my said wife and two daughters. I

---

[1] Probably the 3rd son of Sir Cuthbert Collingwood of Dalton and Great Eppleton, co. Durham, if so, mar. Ursula, dau. of Thomas Forcer of Harbour house, and by her had Thomas and Francis.

leave to George Howie, my son-in-law, the bay mare. To John
Robson, my son-in-law, the graye foale. To Thomas Reede, two
hoggs, and five to his brother, Percival Reed. Witnesses, Robert
Alder, George Howie. Debts oweing by the deceased : To Robert
Oliver in Screnwood, 46s. Mr. Thomas Lewen of Warkworth,
45s. Mr. Horsley of Screnwoode, 26s. 8d. Debts oweing to the
deceased : By Robert Alder of Alneham, 44s. By Robert Chatter
there, 4l. 3s. 6d. By Thomas Wardell and George Wilson of
Longframlington, 8l. By Robert Gibsone in Alneham, 3l. 13s. 4d.
By Adam Ker of Prendick, 18s. By Robert Lamb of Yetlington,
13s. 4d. By Thomas Smith there, 6s. 8d. By Thomas Anderson
of Little Ryle, 11s. By Samuel Coldwell in Great Ryle, 10s.
More by John Gare there. 10s. Probate, 4th April, 1633.

JOSEPH CRADOCK.[1]

Aug. 1, 1633. In the name of God, Amen, I, Joseph Cradock
of Bp Auckland, in the parish of St. Andrew's, Auckland, in
the Diocese and County of Duresme, Gent., being weak and sickly
of body. . . . My body I desire may be interred in the Chancell
of the church or chappell of St. Hellen, Auckland, as near the
Place as may be where my own Mother was interred. Whereas
on my intermarriage with Margery, now my wife, I did enter
into one bond obligatory in a Penal sum unto Bryan
Walker and William Brasse, with condition that if it should
please god I should depart this life naturall before my said wife,
that she should have and receive out of the profitts of my lands
at Staindropp, in the Bpprick of Duresme, the yearly sume or
annuity of 20l. during so long time as she should continue and
be my widow, and after her intermarriage with any other the
yearly sum or annuity of 10l. during her life, therefore in
pformance of the condition of the said obligation, I do give,
legate and bequeath unto the said Margery, my wife, the sum of
20l. yearly during her said widowhood after my death, and
after her intermarriage with any other the sum of 10l. yearly
during her life naturall, to be paid her at Martinmas and
Penticost yearly by equal porcons forth of the rents, issues
and profitts of my said lands at Staindrop aforesaid, 'the first
payment thereof to comence at the first of the said feasts next
ensueing my death, And I doe by these presents declare that I
am oweing and indebted unto my cousin, Francis Appleby of
Clouelodge, in the County of York, Gent., the annual sume of
rent of 10l. forth of the issues and profitts of my saide lands

[1] The testator, son of Anthony by his first wife, Bridget Dickin-
son, was bapt. at St. Andrew's, Auckland, 26 May, 1594; he mar.
Margery, widow of Henry Maugham, at St. Andrew's, 10 June, 1622;
see the *Inq. per br. de mand* of John Cradock, taken at Durham,
30 Jan., 1629/30.

at Staindropp for the space or time of four yeares or thereabouts
yet to come, which I will that he shall have and receive accordingly, and after the expiration of these yeares and his days of
payment, I do give and bequeath unto the poor of the parish
of Staindropp the sum of Twenty pounds, to be paid by ten
pounds a year unto the Churchwardens, to be of the parish Church
there at the said several feasts, by equal porcons respectively
out of the issues and profitts of my said lands at Staindrop, to
be employed by them as a stocke for the use aforesaid. I give
and bequeath to the poore of the Chappelry of St. Helen, Auckland,
the sum of 5l. forth of my personal estate, and forth of my said
personal estate to the poor of the parish of St. Andrew, Auckland,
the sum of Twenty nobles, to be employed yearly and successively
by the Churchwardens of the said parish and Chappelry respectively as a stock for the purpose aforesaid. I do give, legate
and bequeath unto my full and naturall sister, Mary Curten,
wife of Richard Curten, of the City of Duresme, stationer, during
her life naturall and to the heires male of her bodye begotten or
to be lawfully begotten for ever, all that the Parsonage or Rectory
House in Staindropp aforesaid lately appropriated to the College
of Staindropp, in the said Bishoprick of Duresme, and till the
lands, tenements and hereditaments and appurtenances whatsoever
situate, lying and being in Staindropp aforesaid, whereof I now
stand lawfully seised by virtue of one Deed of Indenture of
bargain and sale made the first day of September, in the fifth
year of the reigne of our Sovereign Lord King James over
England, etc., between Michael Cole and John Rowdon of the
City of Westminster, in the County of Middlesex, Gent., on the
one part and Anthony Cradock, Gent., and me, Joseph Cradock,
son of the said Anthony Cradock, on the other part, and in
default of such issue male, then I give, Legate and bequeath the
said Parsonage House, lands, tenements, hereditaments, appurtenances and premises unto my half Brother, Timothy Cradocke,
son of my said father, Anthony Cradocke, and to his heires male
for ever, and in default of such issue male of the said Timothy
Cradocke, then to William Cradock, his younger brother, and to
the heires male to be lawfully begotten of the body of the said
William, then to John Cradocke, my eldest half Brother, and
to the heires male of his bodye to be lawfully begotten for ever,
and in default of such issue male then to the right heires of me,
the said Joseph Cradock. I do give, legate and bequeath all my
estate, interest, title, claim and demand whatsoever, of, in and
to the lands, tenements and hereditaments with the appurtenances commonly called Woodhouses, in the Chapelry of St. Helen,
Auckland, aforesaid, of, in and to all and every the petty tithes
and appurtenances belonging unto the temporall lands late of the
Deanery of St. Andrew, Auckland, purchased together with the
said lands and tenements of Woodhouses, unto my said half

Brother, John Cradocke, his heires and assigns for ever. I do give and bequeath unto my aforesaide half brother, Timothy Cradocke, and to the heires male of his body to be lawfully begotten, all that my house with the appurtenances situate, lying and being in the Township of Bp Auckland aforesaid, now in the possession of my stepmother, Mrs. Anne Cradocke, and in default of such issue male then to William Cradock aforesaid, my youngest halfe brother, and the heires male of his bodye to be equally begotten for ever, and in default of such issue male of the said William Cradock then to my eldest half brother, John Cradocke, and to heires male of his bodye to be lawfully begotten for ever, and in default of such issues male then to the heires general of me, the said Joseph Cradocke. I do give and bequeath the several legacys following, viz., to my half brother, George Cradocke, 5*l*. To my half sister, Grace Cradocke, 5*l*. To my halfe brother, William Cradocke, 5*l*. To my half sister, Rachell Cradock, 5*l*., and to Mr. Stock, Curate of St. Andrew, Auckland, for my funerall sermon, 20*s*. All the rest of my goodes, creditts and chattells, moveable and immoveable, whatsoever, my debts, legacys and funerall expences first payd and discharged, I give, Legate and bequeathe unto my well beloved wife, Margery Cradocke, whom I do ordaine and make sole executrix of this my last Will and Testament. Witnesses, Cutht. Sisson, Ri. Richardson, Thomas Smurfoot.

Memorandum, that these particulars of household stuff hereafter expressed and appraised were the goods of Henry Maugham, late husband of the said Margaret Cradocke, and the property not being changed in the lifetime of her second husband, Mr. Joseph Cradocke, we are perswaded they ought not to be accounted for as his goods. Proved, 1633.

ROGER WIDDRINGTON.[1]

Aug. 27, 1633. Roger Widdrington, of Colwell, in the Countie of Northumberland, Gentleman. To be buried in the parish church of Chollerton. I will and require my executors carefully and really to perform the will of my Father by the payment of the legacies therein bequeathed in such manner and form as is therein and thereby prescribed, which said legacies remayne all yet unsatisfied or payd, Save onlie 100*l*. thereby given unto my sister Wilson, which said 100*l*. I have already paid. I give to my nurse, Elizabeth Bourne, 10*l*. To the poor of the parish of Chollerton, the sum of 40*s*. I make and ordayne my loveing brother, Ralph Widdrington, sole Executor. And I do hereby require Roger Widdrington of Cartington, Esqr.,

[1] He was the son of Henry Widdrington, whose will is dated 12 July, 1632; his brother, Ralph, was admitted to Gray's Inn, 16 Mch., 1640/1. Thomas Widdrington, mentioned in the will, as son and heir of Lewis of Cheesburn Grange, was admitted to Gray's Inn, 14 Feb., 1618/19.

Thomas Widdrington of Grayes Inn in the Countie of Middlesex,
and George Thirlwell of Rothbury, Gent., to be Supervisors.
Inventory filed amounting to 485*l*. 4*s*. 9*d*. Debts and legacies
paid by the Testator : To his sister Dorothie, 200*l*. To his sister
Anne, 200*l*. To his brother William, 125*l*. To his wyfe, 10*l*.
To the power of the parish, 40*s*. To his servantes at Colwell,
according to particulars, 5*l*. 8*s*. 0*d*. To the servantes at Cartington where he died, according to particulars, 3*l*. 15*s*. 0*d*. His
funeral expences, 13*l*. 6*s*. 8*d*. Probate, 1634.

ROBERT HEARON.

Nov. 6, 1633. In the name of God, Amen, I, Robert Hearon
of East Thriston, in the pish of Felton, wake and sicke of bodye,
but of pfect and good remembrance (the lord be praised for it)
Doe heare make my last Will and Testament in maner and forme
followinge ; I give and bequeath my soule into the hands of
Almighty God, who I hope for my saviour Jesus Christ his sake
will foregive me all my sinns, and I believe that at the generall
resurection at the last day he will raise upp my bodye and joyne
it to my soule and give it life eternall.   I will that my bodye
be buried in the pish church of Felton.   I give unto my eldest
daughter, Ann Hearon, 3*l*. 10*s*., besydes the three oxen and one
old cowe, which she knoweth and hath and long known to be her
owne, also I give unto her all the insight goods which I had in
her mother's time, except one Ambrie standing in the Chamber,
and one brass ketle.   I gyve unto myne eldest sonne, John Hearon,
4*l*. and one great chist standing in the chamber and the bedstead I lye in and the table in the house and the plough with the
irons, when he shall enter to the tenmt of which I dwell.   I
give and bequeath to Thomas Hearon my second sonne, 3*l*. 10*s*.
I give unto Elizabeth Hearon my second daughter, 4*l*., and the
Ambrie in the Chamber and one brass ketle.   I give unto Robt.
my third sonne, 5*l*.   I give unto Barbara my third daughter, 5*l*.
I give unto my sonne, John Hearon, two whole third parts of all
houses, landes, meadowes and all other comidtes and pfits whatsoever belonging to the tent whereon I dwell under the Right
Honourable the Earl of Northd. for and during the terme of yeares
as yet unexpired in my lease and all my full tytle of tenant right
to my said sonne John, he paying yearly his partes of the rent,
and doeing two partes of all such services as are to be done by
the inhabyants of the said farmholde, either to the lord of the
manor, the church or the King his heirs or successors.   I give
unto Mary my wife one whole third part of all the houses, lands,
meadows and all other comdites whatsoever belonging to the said
tent, for and during the terme yet unexpired in my lease for
the better bringing up of my youngest children (if she remaine
a Widow), but if she doe marry againe before the expiration of

the lease then my will is she shall freely give up and leave the said
third parte of the farmhold and every part and parcel thereof,
to my said sonne John, and so forth to enter and have all the
said tent with all the appurtenances whatsoever to the same
belonginge. And my will further is, that my sonne John shall lyve
in howse with my said wife Mary, and that she shall work the
husbandrie, and sow the seedes now at the . . . . I will shall
be taken out of my crop of corne standing in the stackyard, and
my wife to have the remainder to fynd the house, and pay debts,
and rentes withall, so long as they can agree together, and if they
cannot agree to live together Then he to have two parts of the
crop of corne, at the harvest next after such disagreement, and
my wife to have the other third part, And then they both to be
as before is set downe, that is to say, he to have the two partes of
the tent and she to have her third part without molestation
one of the other. The rest of my goodes, moveable and unmoveable (my debts, legacies and funerall expences discharged) I
give unto Mary, my wife, whom I make full executrix of this
my last Will and Testament. And I earnestly intreat Mr. Richard
Hearon of Bokenfield, to be supervisor of this my last Will and
Testament, duly performed and executed. In witness of Nicholas
Bothwell, Cler., John White.

INVENTORY, 45l. 11s. Proved, 1634.

MARGARETT RAWLINSON.[1]

Dec. 20, 1633. In the name of God, Amen, I, Margarett
Rawlinson, nowe of Headlam, in the County of Durham. My
bodie to be buried in the parish church of Winston, if it shall
please god so to permit. I give and bequeth to my grandchilde,
Mary Darcye, for a token of remembrance, two angells of old
golde to make a ringe to weare for my sake, if it please her so
to doe, Also I give and bequeath unto her, the said Mary Darcye,
that great silver Bowle which she hath alreadye in her possession,
And one half dozen of silver spoones which are now at Headlam
marked with these two letters, E D, to make up the half dozen
of spoones of the same mark which I formerly I gave her a whole
dozen. I give and bequeath unto Robert Dowthwaite, Brother
unto my sonne-in-lawe, John Dowthwaite, late of Westholme,
deceased, one angell of gold, as a token as a remembrance to
make a ring with all to weare for my sake. I give and bequeath
to Barnard Dowthwaite the one half of that debt and sume of
100l. which he and his sonne, John Dowthwaite, standeth bound
to paye unto me if I die before it be all paid and discharged
to me. Also I give and bequeath unto him, the said Barnard,
that little silver Bowle which was his brother John Dowthwaite's,
which is now in his own possession. I give and bequeath unto

[1] She was bur. at Winston, 23 Feb., 1634/5.

my friend, Richard Smith, the sume of 40s. I give and bequeath
to every one of Jane Harker's children which she had by her
first husband, 20s. a piece. I give 20s. to be bestowed and delt
amongst the poore people at Winston. I give towards the mending of the churche waie between Headlam and Gainforthe, 20s. I
bequeath and give unto Mrs. Eleanor Merryton, daughter of Mr.
Henry Birckbeck of Headlam aforesaid, All my implements of
househould and household stuff, and all my silver plate (not
formerlie given and bequethed) of what kind, sorte or quantite
soever it be which is now at Headlam or which shall be there at
the tyme of my deathe. And also I give and bequeath unto her,
the said Mrs. Eleanor Merryton, in token of my further remembrance and love towards her, one Spurryall. I give and bequeath
unto Francis Walker of Bernard Castle, 10s. All the rest of my
goods, chattels, debts and creditts, moveable and unmoveable,
whatsoever not before herein by me bequeathed, my debts, legacies
and funerall expences paid and deducted, I give and bequeathe
unto Mr. Henry Darcy, husband of the said Mary Darcye, And
to my honest and loveing friend, the said Mr. Henry Birckbeck
of Headlam aforesaid, whom I make and ordeyne joint executors
of this my Will. Witnesses, Henry Lancaster, Oswald Milburne,
Francis Walker. Proved, 1635.

ROBERT LAWSONE.

Jan. 2, 1633. Robert Lawsone of Bedlington, in the Countie
Palintyne of Durham, Yeoman. My bodie to be buried in the
Church yearde at the Chancel doore. I give to my eldest sone
Robert, my land or farmholde, except the third of the said land
which I give to my wife Ann. To my sonne Cuthbert, 30s., to
be paid out of my land by my sone Robert. I give to my sonne
George, 30s. To my daughter Dorothie, 30s. And the residue
to my said wife and my three youngest children. To my brother
John and his children, a boul of rye. To Elizabeth Pot, my wife's
sister, a peck of wheat. Probate, 1634.

JOHN ADDISON.[1]

March 26, 1634. Will of John Addison of Ovingham. To
be buried in the Chancell if I dye within Ovingham pish. I give
unto my wife, Isabell Addison, fiftie pounds by yeare dureing
her life naturall in full discharge and satisfacon of all my lands

[1] He was son of Sir William Addison (*N.C.H.*, xii., 56, where the
date of his will is incorrectly given). His wife, Isabel, was a dau.
of George Fenwick of East Heddon; she was a deponent, aged about
40, 3 Oct., 1636 (*Chancery Depositions*, Eliz.-Charles I., F. 14/20),
and is said to have died in 1645 (*Chancery Proceedings*, Bridges,
399/111). His brother-in-law, William Fenwick, about May, 1629,
made to him and William Southgate a mortgage of East Heddon,
which led to much litigation. In the visitation pedigree of 1666, John
Addison, the nephew, is incorrectly tabulated as son of the testator.

either that I have by inheritance or Lease, and likewise halfe of all the psonage howsees, halfe of all the howseholde stuff, my great gray mare and her foale, four of my best kyne, and my desire is that shee and my Executor should live togeather and contynue in one house, but if they cannot agree but part howsehold, then I give more unto my wyfe, that is Tenn bowles of Rye, Two bowles of wheate, foure bowles of oates, foure bowles of Malt, yearly during her life naturall to be paid unto her, and likewise to have the feeding and pasturing winter and sumer of foure kyne and a horse or mare in the psonage grounds or where the best grass is, provided and it is my mynd and purpose that if my wyfe will not stand to this my Will and allow what I have heare sett downe for her mayntenance, but by perswasion of frends or out of any further desire of gayne to take what the lawe will gyve or impose upon her, That then my Executors or supervrs shall nott gyve nor bestow any thing upon her what was myne, or heare sett downe, but I hope better. I give and bestow upon my nephew, John Addison, eldest sone of my brother Anthony, all the psonage of Ovengham and all my lands that I have either by inheritance or. leases and all my goodes, moveable and unmoveable, for his life naturall, and after his decease to the heirs maile of his bodie lawfully begotten, and for want of heirs maile to descend unto the heirs maile of William Addison, my brother, and for want of heirs maile to come unto the heirs male of Anthony Addison, my eldest brother, lawfully begotten, and for want of such issue maile then to the next of kin generally of me, the said John Addison, for ever. To my brother, William Addison, and his children, one tenement or farmeholde with the appurtenances lying in Eggleston, in the Countie pallatine of Durham, now in his possession, and heretofore belonging to my neece, Jane Addison, now marryed to John Sanderson. And also I give unto him another tenement lying in Eggleston aforesaid, somtymes belonging to my brother, Thomas Addison, deceased. I give unto my brother William and to his children, to be divided amongst them, £100, to be paid out of the lands of East Heddon now mortgaged to me. To my neece, Anne Addison, £100 out of East Heddon. To my neece, Jane Addison, her sister, £50. I give £50 to be paid out of the said mortgage of East Heddon unto the Churchwardens of Ovingham and their Successors, to be bestowed in land so soone as conveniently maie be by them for and towards the maintenance of a preaching Minister att Ovingham aforesaid, and this to be done, and in the mean tyme imployed by the foure and twentie of the parish and my Executors and Supervisors. And whereas I am indebted to my nephew, John Sanderson, the some of Three score and fifteen pounds remaynder, and in full satisfacon of my neece Jane her porcon, now his wife, my will is that the same be paid att Midsomer next out of my tythe rent money of Ovingham pish then due. To the poore of the pish of Ovingham, £4. To the poor of the Chappelrie of Eggleston, 40s. I give to my cosen, Sara Southgaite, £5. To my cosen, John Prat, £20. To my servant, Isabell Lee, one red heffer now with calfe, and to the rest of my servants, 5s. each. To George Simpson, his two children by Anne his wife, each a white calfe. I give unto William Southgaite his children, 5l. I appoint my nephew, John Addison, sole Executor. My will is that my loveing wife, Isabell Addison, and my nephew, John Sanderson, shall manage the whole of my estate for three years, they paying to my said nephew, John Addison, 30l. per annum for his mayntenance, as it is my desire that he shall remaine during the said three yeares. I make my said wife and nephew, John Sanderson, Supervisors, and I do intreat my loveing friend, Thomas Woodrington of the Grange, Esquire, and my loveing cosin, William Southgate, to assist my Executors. To my cousin, George Simpson, and Anne his wife, either of them a ringe. Witnesses to Will, Anthony Halsall, William Hymers. Proved, 1634.

Codicil to the Will of John Addison. That John Addison, late of Ovingham, in the Diocese of Duresme, gent., in and upon the 26th day of March, Anno Domini 1634, being the same day that he had made his last Will and Testamt In writing, And in the afternoone of the same daye in the presence and heareing of Isabell, wife of the said John Addison, John Sanderson and Jane his wife . . . Thompson clerk and Isabella Lee, he, the said John Addison, contynuing and being in perfette mynd and memory, Did by way of Codicill be annexed to his said last Will and Testament, give, Legate and bequeath in manner and forme following, or in words tending to the like effect, viz., He did give and bequeath to his brother-in-law, Willyam Fenwick of East Heddon, gent., one hundred pounds out of the moneys due by the sayd Willyam Fenwick unto the said John Addison. Item, he did give and bequeathe unto Elizabeth Fenwick, daughter of the sayd Willyam Fenwick, the sum of Fifty pounds, to be likewise payd forth of the moneys to be issueing and payable unto the said John Addison forth of the Lands of East Heddon. Item, he did give and bequeath unto his godsonne, John Sanderson, son of his nephew, John Sanderson, the sume of Fifty pounds, and unto John Fenwick, son of his Brother-in-law, George Fenwick, the sum of Ten pounds, both of which sums to bee likewise payd forth of the moneys to be issueing and payable forth of the Land of East Heddon aforesaid, And earnestly desired his wife and the said John Sanderson to endeavour themselves to see his executor to perform and pay the said severall Legacies so be bequeathed by his said Codicill, saying his Executor was young, and he did not know how he might prove which said John Addison dyed afterwards the same day about six of the clocke in the afternoone. Thomas Thompson, Richard Lee. Proved, 1638.

EDWARD ALDER.[1]

July 4, 1634. Will of Edward Alder of Reevely, in the parish of Ingram, yeoman. To be buried within the Churchyard of Ingram. I give and bequeath to my Daughter, Anne Alder, foure Kyne, tenn sheepe, and five pounds and tenn shillings in money which is in the hands of Ralph Tindale of Olde Bewicke, and I give her seaventeene peckes of beare, to be received from John Skelly of Scranwood which he oweth me, which said beare I will shall be paid to my mother-in-law, Catherine Crispe, for the use of my said Daughter. I give to my Brother, John Oliver, twelve shepe and one cowe, and thre pounds tenn shillings which is in the hands of John Shottonn of Branton. To my said brother, John Oliver, five nobles which is in the hands of George Brown of Ingram, and it is my minde that the saide George Brown shall have the Milk of one Cowe of myne from and after Alnewicke faire next after the daite hereof untill Candlemass followinge, and then it is my mynd that he deliver back againe the said Cowe for the use of my said Daughter, and that he shall keepe the Calfe to himselfe. To my friend, Christopher Alder, fiftie five shillings which is in the hands of John Burne of Ingram, paiable unto me at Alnewick fare last, and I give him more, twentie shillings in the hands of Alexander Pattersonn of Weayden, blacksmith, and more unto the said Christopher Alder, thirtie seaven shillings in the hands of George Howy of Eldam, and also twenty eight shillings in the hands of Robert Chator, and also twenty five shillings in the hands of Robert Alder of Reevely, and further more, two Kyne then beinge in the custodie of Thomas Robson of Saughrigg and the other in the custodie of James Gibsonn of Ingram. I give to John Alder, sonne of Christopher Alder, one Colte stagg. I doe forgive my brother, Thomas Oliver, twentie shillings which he oweth me. I doe likewise forgive my brother, George Oliver, twenty eight shillings. To my two sisters, tenn lambs which are in the custodie of Thomas Robson of Scranwoode equally betwixt them, and I give either of them twenty shillings which is in the hands of John Skellie of Scranwood. To my brother, John Oliver, sixteene shillings which is in the hands of John Hanganshaw of Eldam, payeable to me at Martinmas next. To my owne mother, twentie shillings in the hands of the said John Hanganshaw. To my mother-in-lawe, one bowle of beare which Christopher Alder oweth me, and the soweing of two pecks of beare yearlye soe longe as he continueth at Coate-land. I leave my Daughter's porcon to my mother-in-law, Catherine Crisp, for her upbringing. Witnesses, Thomas Anderson, Christopher Alder, John Oliver.

---

[1] There is a pedigree of the Alders of Prendwick printed in *Arch. Ael.*, 3rd ser., vol., v., p. 24.

HENRY MADDISON.[1]

July 14, 1634. Henry Maddison of Newcastle upon Tyne, Esqr., and alderman deceased. Estimation and Valuation of all the goods and chattells of the deceased by Mr. Ralph Gray, William Marley, Francis Bainbridge and Robert Chrissup. Imprs : Three waggon horses, 6l. Six waggons with all furniture belonging them, 12l. Two Ryding horses, 10l. Five hundred tons of coles at pitt and staythes . . . . A lease of Collerye at Fidgerfield having a part of it, 100l. A part of a lease of Collerye at Linge-field, 100l. A part of a lease of Collerye at Rydingfield, 66l. 13s. 4d. A part of a lease of Collerye at Faddonsfield, 30l. One fourth and sixth part of the Ship called the Henry and John of Colchester, Robert Isles, going Maister of her, 163l. One third and sixteenth part of the ship called the Blessing of Ipswich, Richard Barnes going Maister, 200l. One fourth part of the ship called the Wrym Rose of Newcastle, John Gurling, going Maister of her, 25l. One fourth part of the Isabell of Yorke, John Maisterman going Maister(man) of her 20l. One eight part of the content of Colchester, John Furley, going Maister of her, 80l. One fourth part of the Marygold of Yorke, Seath Archbutt, going Maister of her, 90l. One fourth part of the Neptune of Newcastle, 30l. One eighth and sixteenth part of the Blessing of . . . chester, John Dobsone going Maister of her, 120l. One sixteenth part of the John of London, Thomas Hall, Maister, 40l. One sixteenth part of the Elsabeth of Malding, Edward Lee, Maister, 40l. One sixteenth part of the Mary of Malding, John Dunton, Maister, 40l. One sixteenth part of the Mary Bonaventure of Hull, Robert Story, Maister, 20l. One sixteenth part of the True Love of Albrough, Jeremy Cobb, Maister, 40l. One thirty second part of Dove of Ipswich, Robert Gurling, Maister, 30l. One eighth part of the Elsabeth of Selby. John Hodgson, Maister, 50l. One eigth part of the Gift of Ips-wich, Adam Brown, Maister, 50l. One eighth part of the Indevour of London, John Wrisman, Maister, 30l. One sixteenth part of the Denis of Lyn, James Greeneway, Maister, 25l. One sixteenth part of the Protection of Ipswich, Umphrey Wills, Maister, 25l. In stock with Thomas Cleborne, 300l. In corne that was sown at Marshallands, 14l. Nine Keeles, 200l.

[1] He was the only son of Lionel Maddison, by his wife, Jane Seymour, bapt., 30 Oct., 1574, at St. Nich., Newcastle (from which registers the following dates are taken), bur., 14 July, 1634, mar., 14 May, 1594, Elizabeth, dau. of Robert Barker of Newcastle, who was bapt., 17 Oct., 1574, and bur., 26 Sept., 1653, aged 79.

GEORGE RIPPON.[1]

Aug. 2, 1634. The forme and substance of the layte will and testament nuncupetive of George Rippon of the Chappelry of Witton-upon-weare in the Countye of Durham. To be buryed in the chappell yaird of Wittin upon weare aforesaid. I give unto my two daughters, Margaret Rippon and Marye Rippon, all my household stuffe from the forehouse doore upwards, and Ales my wife to have the use of it during her life. All the rest of my goods and chattells, moveable and unmoveable whatsoever, I give and bequeath unto Ales, my wife, whoe I appoint my whole executor. Witnesses, Robert Fawdon, George Taylor.

INVENTORY, 28*l*. 5*s*.

JEFFREY PROCTOR.[2]

Aug. 13, 1634. Jeffrey Proctor, late of Shawdon, in the parish of Whittingham in the Countie of Northumberland, Esqr., deceased. Declaration of the Accompt of Ephraim Proctor, gentleman, administrator of the goods and chattels of the said Jeffrey Proctor. The said administrator and accomptant doth charge himself with all the deceased his goods and chattells and creditts mentioned in an Inventorie thereof, remaining in this Court and apprized to 164*l*. 9*s*. 0*d*. He chargeth himself with the value of a Lease of three tenants in Glanton, mentioned in the said Inventorie, but not apprized, 22*l*. 17*s*. He chargeth himself with the value of certain goods disposed of by the deceased, sold and valued to 20*l*. Sum totall of the said goods, 207*l*. 6*s*. 0*d*. Imprs: Paid unto Mr. Danyel Gorsuts of the citie of London upon two bonds the sum of 20*l*. Paid to Mr. James Lawson of the Broomehouse upon two bonds, and for charges of suite of the said bonds in the deceased's lifetime and consideration for the said moneys and for some cloths the sum of 60*l*. 8*s*. 8*d*. To Mr. Robert Claveringe of Learchilde, remaining upon bond, 12*l*. Paid to Robert Hadston of Alnwick, upon the deceased's bill, 3*l*. 13*s*. 3*d*. Paid to Edward Reveley of Humbleton, the remainder due on bond, 38*s*. Paid to Richard Parkinson of Abberwicke upon bond, 27*s*. 6*d*. Paid to Patricke Howborne of Alnewicke upon bond, 51*s*. To Thomas Burrell of East Lilburne, upon a bill, 5*l*. 15*s*. To Lancelott Scott of Alnewicke upon bond, 16*l*. To Mrs. Jane Mutis of West Lilburne, widow, upon two bonds, 55*l*. Paid to Sir Arthur Graie, Knight, for ewes and lambs, 11*l*. Paid unto Arthur Graie, bayliffe of Wark, for corne bought

[1] 17 July, 1634, George Rippon, an old man., bur., *Witton-le-Wear Regs.* His widow was bur. there, 10 Dec., 1643.

[2] He was the son of Thomas Proctor of Shawdon, by his wife, Jane, dau. of Robert Eden of West Auckland; he died, 13 Aug., 1633, and was bur. at Whittingham; he mar. Sarah Bunny, "in the house of Anthony Fenwick of Kenton," *circa*, 24 Jan., 1617/18.

of him, 9*l.* Paid to Edmond Reveley of West Lilbourne for an oxe, 36*s.* Paid to Michael Bolam of Neatherton, for long waine, 20*s.* Paid to Thomas Hearon of Crawley, gentleman, for rent of a farme as by two acquittances appeareth, 3*l.* 6*s.* 8*d.* Paid for servants wages, 19*s.* 6*d.* Paid on Probate of the deceased's Will and administration, 31*s.* For drawing and passing this accompt with letters, testimoniall upon the same, 23*s.* 4*d.* Sume totall disbursed, 208*l.* 9*s.* 11*d.*

CUTHBERT COLLINGWOOD.

Jan. 31, 1634. Cuthbert Collingwood of Fawdon in the County of Northumberland, gent. To my eldest sone, Daniel Collingwoode, my two farmes at Reveley and his heirs, and failing issue male, to my second sonne, Thomas Collingwoode, and failing issue male to my youngest sone, Cuthbert Collingwoode. To my mother, Elizabeth Rotchester of Newcastle, 5*l.* I leave my wife, Anne Collingwoode, sole Executrix of all my goods and leave her a house in Berwick in the possession of Ellenor Selby, widow. To my Brother, Robert Collingwood of Branton, and my uncle, John Collingwood of Reveley . . . . witnesses to will, William Selby, Ephraim Collingwoode, John Collingwoode.

URSULA ERRINGTON.

Dec. 22, 1634. Ursula Errington of Wharnley in the parish of Warden, in the County of Northumberland. To be buried in the churchyard of St. John Ley. I give to my sister, Dorothy Errington, 100*l.*, being part of a portion either in my eldest Brother's Henry Errington hands or the hands of Roger Widdrington. To my cozen, John Widdrington of the Hurst, 20*l.* To my cozen, Ursula Widdrington of the Hurst, 20*l.* To my cozen, Catherine Widdrington of the Hurst, 20*l.* To my cozen, Henry Widdrington of the Hurst, 20 nobles. To my cozen, Dorothy Widdrington and my cozen Mary Widdrington (both of Hurst), 20 marks equally between them, all which I direct to be paid out of my portion now in the hands of the said Henry Errington and Roger Widdrington. I make my said sister, Dorothy Errington, sole Executrix. Witnesses, John Widdrington, Ursula Widdrington, Katherine Widdrington and Barbara Shaftoe.

INVENTORY, 369*l.* 18*s.* 7*d.* Probate, 2nd Juiy, 1638, to Dorothy Errington of the Hirst, Spinster, the sole Executrix.

JOHN SHAFTO.[1]

Jan. 13, 1634. John Shafto of Swalwell, Miller, tenant to Mr. Arthur Shafto of Swalwell, within the parish of Whickham, in the County of Durham.

[1] The testator was bur. at Whickham, 14 Jan., 1634/5.

INVENTORY : On tabel frame and one form, 3s. 0d. One long-
setell beed and one caser, 2s. 6d. Four potell chiestes and a
litell tabell, 5s. 6d. For one cupard and one cawell and a little
butterie, 16s. 6d. One littell presse, one bekment and one malt
peck, 3s. 0d. Nineteen peece of puder, 1l. 1s. 0d. One potell
pott and two quart poots of puder, two saltfatts, 6s. 0d. Five
brasse candellstickes and six puder candellstickes, 4s. 6d. Tow
old brasse poots, and one iron poot, and a par of poot scopes,
7s. 0d. One olde Kertell, three old panns, and one new pann,
10s. 6d. One parr of Iron bares, one parr of tonges, one speet,
and on Iron cruke, and one fryen pan, 3s. 6d. Three earthen
dishes and one erthein poot, 4d. Three standes, one washing
tubb, and one skeel, 1s. 6d. One duson of dishes, and one duson
of trenchers and wooden cann and one puder kupe, 1s. 2d. One
duson of course napkines and half a duson of small napkinnes,
6s. 0d. Six paire of curse sheets and three parr of lining sheetes,
and one curse tabell clothe, 18s. 6d. One parr of blanketts, three
happins, one coverlette and one carpin clothe, 16s. 6d. One linen
tabell clothe, 2s. 6d. For his apparell, 4s. 0d. Three piggs,
8s. 0d. One boot, 1l. 10s. 0d. One olde meare, 13s. 0d. One
horse, 2l. 6s. 8d. Two Kye, 3l. 6s. 8d. Signed, Edward
Mallabar, Richard Cocksone, Thomas Courrye.

ANTHONY WILKINSON.[1]

March 1, 1634. In the name of god, Amen, I, Anthony
Wilkinson of Munckhelseden, in the County of Durham, Yeoman,
sick in bodye. To be buried in the Church of Munckheseldon.
I give to the poor of the pish, 20s. I doe ordaine and appoynt
Merioll Wilkinson, my wife, and my eldest son, John Wilkinson,
my sole Executors and Tutors for the Residue of my children.
I give to my sonne, Phillip Wilkinson, the some of 60l., to be
payd by my eldest sonne John when he comethe to the age of 21
yeares. I give to Margret Wilkinson, Raphe Wilkinson, Mary
Wilkinson, Elizabeth and Isabell, the rest of my Children, 60l.
a peece when they come to lawfull yeares. I doe give to my
eldest sonn John all my lands withal my writtings. To my son
John by legacie, two oxen, viz., "pleasure" and "feeting,"
and one graye mayre. And the rest of my children within named
I give all the residue of my goodes to be equally divided among
them. I give all my household stuffe and bedding to my wife
and daughters. I give all plow geare and waine geare to my

[1] The testator was bur. at Monkhesleden, 14 Mch., 1634/5; he
mar. at Easington Merioll Thòmpson, 30 May, 1609, she was bur. at
Monkhesleden (whence all other dates), 11 Mch., 1641/2; by her he
had issue, John; Philip, bapt., 8 Apl., 1616; Ralph., bapt., 19 Aug.,
1621; Anthony, bapt., 1 Feb., 1623/4; Richard, bapt., 10 Feb., 1627/8;
Ann, bapt., 22 Apl., 1613, mar. John Pattison, 18 June, 1633; Margaret,
bapt., 27 June, 1619; Mary, bapt., 9 Apl., 1625; Elizabeth, bapt.,
10 Feb., 1627/8; Isabel, bapt., 8 May, 1631.

sonn John. Witnesses, Mark Hall, John Dodshon, Nicholas Walker, William Thomlingson.

A true Inventorie of all the goods and chattles, moveable and unmoveable, of Anthony Wilkinson of Monkehesleden, Yeoman, deceased, the 13 of March, 1634, prased by these foure honest neighbours, John Dodgson, Mark Hall, John Thomson, Nicholas Walker, as followeth:—Imprimis: his purse and apparell, 3*l.* 6*s.* 8*d.* Twelve Kine and whies with their calves, 28*l.* One whie and foure oxen, 20*l.* 10*s.* Two oxen storkes, 2*l.* Four calves of . . . years old, 2*l.* 13*s.* 4*d.* Two mares, 5*l.* Eighteen ewes and lambes, 10*l.* One and twentye weathers, 9*l.* Nineteene sheepe hogges, 6*l.* 10*s.* Corne sowne on the ground, 20*l.* Plugh and plugh geare, wayne and wayne geare, 5*l.* Other wood about the house, 11*s.* Six peace of puther and potts, panns and kettles, 2*l.* 13*s.* 4*d.* Two cubberts, one Cowwell, tables, forms and stooles, 3*l.* 8*s.* Three bed steeds, 1*l.* Coverletts, hapings, blankets, sheetes, one fetherbed and one mattrasse with bousters, 4*l.* 10*s.* Chist, kirnes, skeeles, bowells, dishes, one spinninge wheale, 1*l.* 2*s.* Yarne tow, 10*s.* Corne in the house, 6*s.* 8*d.* Two payre of bars, one reeking crooke, one payre of tongs and a spete, 13*s.* 4*d.* Bees, ducks and hens, 10*s.* Beafe and bacon, 5*s.*

A. Item, I doe give to my two brothers' daughters, to either of them, a gimmer hogg, and to my sister's daughter a gimmer hogg, and also I give to my brother, John Wilkinson, the bigest black why sturke, and to my sonne, John Pattison, a black hanked why. Proved, 1635.

EDWARD BOULMER.[1]

July 8, 1635. Will of Edward Boulmer, of the parish of All Saints, Newcastle on Tyne, Master and Mariner. My body I committ unto the earth from whence it came, to be buried wheresoever it shall please Almightie God to call me, and as for my

[1] He was probably son of George Bowmer, yeoman, if so, bapt., 28 Oct., 1587, at St. Nich., Newcastle, his godparents being Edward Bowmer, yeoman, Thomas Bowmer, mariner, and Mrs. Isabel, wife of Mr. Robert Eden, apothecary; his first wife, Jane, was bur., 2 Mch., 1626; by her he had Edward, bapt., 16 Mch., 1613/14, bur., 14 Dec., 1614; Charles, bapt., 13 May, 1621 (his first wife, Anne, bur., 6 June, 1647; his second wife, Isabel Wilkinson, whom he mar., 2 Jan., 1648/9, was bur., 19 Oct., 1653); Ruth, bapt., 20 Oct., 1611, bur., 1 Nov., 1614; Isabel, bapt., 5 Nov., 1615, bur., 1 Nov., 1616; Jane, bapt., 10 July, 1618, bur., 18 Mch., 1627/8; Ann, bapt., 29 Oct., 1626, bur., 5 Sept., 1628. His second wife, whom he mar., 24 Apl., 1627, was Anne Peacock (bur., 30 Nov., 1663), widow of William Clavering, son of Robert Clavering of Callaly, by his wife, Mary, dau. of Cuthbert Collingwood, whom she mar., 27 Nov., 1620, he was bur., 26 July, 1624; she mar., thirdly, Robert Babington, 16 Aug., 1640, he was bur., 15 July, 1657; by her the testator had Edward; Alice, bapt., 27 Jan., 1630/1, bur., 30 Sept., 1631, and Margaret, bapt., 3 Aug., 1628. All dates are from the All Saints', Newcastle, registers. The testator's burial has not been found. He was probably "The King's Steersman."

worldie goods I give and bequeath as followeth :—Item, I give and bequeath unto Anne, my now wife, and her heyres for ever, all that Burgage or tenament now in the several occupations of Robert Watson, cooper, and Richard Friend, Marriner, situate and being within the said towne of Newcastle upon Tyne, in a layne or Chaire there called Hornsbye's Chayre, neere unto the Keyside. Item, I give and bequeath All those my two cellars and lofts over the same, situate in a Layne or Chaire there called Pumber Chaire, unto my sonne, Charles Boulmer, for his life, and after his death to their heyres of his body, and in default of issue I give the said cellers and lofts unto my sonne, Edward Boulmer, for his life, and failing issue to the heyres of me, the said Edward Boulmer. I give unto my sonne Charles one large silver beaker which hath the Emdons Arms upon the same. I give unto my said sonne, Edward Boulmer, one other large silver beaker which hath the Marchaunt's Marke upon the same. I give unto my Daughter, Margaret Boulmer, one Silver Cann. Item, I give unto my sister, Alice Fell, a hood and a twenty shillings peece of gold for a token. And as for the residue of my goods, Chattels, moveable and removeable, my debts and legacies paid, unto my said wife Anne, whom I make sole Executor. Witnesses to Will, Roger Peareth, Henry Hawksworth, Anthony Nicholas, Anthony Norman. Proved, 1638.

Account. A Declaration of the Accounts of Anne Bulmer, late wife and sole Executrix of the Will of Edward Bulmer, of the Chappelry of All Saints, Newcastle on Tyne, Master and Marriner, made on her execution of the sd testament and Administration as followeth :—The said Executrix and Accomptant doth charge her selfe with all the goods, chattels and creditts of the said deceased contained in an inventory thereof made and remaining in the Court amounting to the sume of two hundred and fifty pounds foure shillings and ninepence. Whereas she craveth allowance of her disbursements for the deceased's debts and funerall as followeth, viz. :—Impris : by her payd unto the Master of the Trinity house at Newcastle upon Tyne upon the goods deceased's bond, fifty six pounds one shilling. Item, on her payd to his Maties farmers of the custom of Newcastle upon Tyne aforesaid, upon the deceased's bond, thirty eight pounds. Item, by her payd to John Parker of London, habbardasher, upon the said decds bond, fiftie three pound eight shillings. Item, by her payd unto Anthony Proctor, upon the deceased's bond, fifty pounds. Item, by her payd to Mrs. Munt of London, oweing by the deceased at the tyme of his death, tenne pounds four shillings. Item, by her payd to Margtt. Bulmer for a legacie given her by the last Will and Testt of Margtt. Peacock, which was recived by the testator in his lifetime for the use of the said Margtt. Bulmer and was remaining in his hands unpayd at the time of his death, the sum of three score pounds. Item, by her payd upon account

with . . . . Mate to her said late husband in the Shipp where
he was Master upon, for the deceased's funeral expences and debts
in the East lands as by this same account appeareth, the sum of
Fifty seven pounds. Item, by her payd to Robert Browne, Master
and Marriner, upon account made for monies oweing him by the
decd at the time of his death, the sum of sixteen pounds. Item,
the said deceased stands further indebted upon bond to the
Master of the Trinity House in Newcastle aforesaid, which this
Accompt is intended to discharge, the sume of one hundred
pounds. Summe total payd and to be payd, £440 13s. 0d.

EDWARD CLAVERING.[1]

July 31, 1635. Edward Clavering of Tilmouth, within the
libertie of Norham and Countie Pallatine of Durham, Gentleman.
My bodie to be buried in the Chancell at Norham. I give and
bequeathe unto my wife, Isabell Claveringe, all that my farme
called the Kentstone, within the libertie of Elandshire and county
pallatine of Durham during her life natural, so long only as
she shall remaine and continue a widow, and if shee marrie or
take to husband another man, then my will is shee shall have
only tenn pounds out of the tenement of the Kentstone aforesaid,
and the rest of the rent and remainder I give and bequeath to
my younger children, Raph Claveringe, George Claveringe,
Edward Claveringe, Margarett Claveringe and Ellinor Claveringe,
during the life naturall of my wife Isabella aforesaid. I will
that my son and heire, Robert Claveringe, shall confirm and
make good in law this my bequest aforesaid. I bequeath to my
sons, Raph Claveringe and George Claveringe, 100l. each as their
filial portions, and I also give to each of them three score ewes
and six Kine, to be paid out of my stocke as due unto them by
their grandfather's will. To my son, Edward Claveringe, 100l.
for his filial portion, to be paid by my son and heire, Robert
Clavering, when he shall attain seventeen years. To my daughter,
Margrett Claveringe, for her filial child's portion, 100l. when she
comes to seventeen years of age. To my daughter, Ellinor
Claveringe, 100l. when she attains seventeen years of age. I
give unto my wife, Isabell Claveringe, twentie ewes and two kie.
The residue of my estate to my son and heire and appoint him
sole Executor. Probate, 1635.

JOHN BRANDLING.[2]

Oct. 17, 1635. Memorandum that Mr. John Brandling of
Felling, of the pish of Jarroe and Countie of Durham, gent.,

[1] By Inq. v. off., taken at Durham, 25 Oct., 1639, Robert, aged 30,
was found to be his son and heir.

[2] He was the fourth son of Robert Brandling, by his wife, Jane,
dau. of Francis Wortley of Wortley, co. York; he was bapt., 9 June,
1602, at Jarrow, bur. at St. Nich., Newcastle, 19 Oct., 1635; by his
wife, Troth (? Swinburn), who remar. Richard Vincent of Seamer, co.
York, he had sons and daughters.

finding himselfe sick in bodie, yet of sound and pfect mynd and memorie, Did voluntarily make and declare his last Will and Testament nuncupativelie in manner and forme followinge, vizt., I would have my eldest sone to have two hundred pounds, and my younger daughter to have one hundred pounds, and the residue to my wife. Witnesses hereof, Francis Brandling, Knight, Mary Gray, wife of John Gray of Bradforth, Esqr., and Henry Bulmer.

An INVENTORY of all and singular the goods and chattels of John Brandling, late of Fellinge, in the County of Durham, Esquire, deceased, the second day of November, 1635, and prised and valued by Thomas Gascoigne, John Smith, Robert Armstrong and William Wilson. Sum total, 828*l*. 4*s*. 8*d*.

Imprs : hay and oats in the stock yarde, and corne sowen in the field, with a hay ruck in the field, 40*l*. Coales and the interest of a Lease of coliery att Elswick for some yeares yet to come and unexpired, 300*l*. The tithe corne at Longhoughton, 30*l*. A Lease of certaine lands in Hett for three yeres yet to come, 50*l*.

Debts owing to the testator : Upon bond due by Sir Bartram Bulmer, Knight, 138*l*. By bond due by John Smith, payable att severall tymes as by the same will appeare, 43*l*. 10*s*. Owing by one . . . . Dixon of Sherburne, 8*l*.

Debts oweing by the testator : To Sir Francis Brandlinge, Kt., for a whole yeares rent due at Whittnext for Felling, 102*l*. To Sir Nicholas Tempest, Knight, 10*l*. To John Jackson, gent., 14*l*. To John Hilton, gent., 20*l*. To Robert Carr, 30*l*. To Mr. Curtas, the upholster, 8*l*. 9*s*. To William Mickeson, 7*l*. 10*s*. 4*d*. His funerall expences and other extraordinary charges, 60*l*.

Will Proved by Troth Brandling, Widow, the Relict, the Sole Executrix, who was also granted tuition of Isabell and Jane Brandling, the Daughters (Minors). Proved, 11 Nov., 1635.

HUMPHRE WHARTON.[1]

Dec. 14, 1635. I, Humphre Wharton of Gillingwood, in the County of York, Esqr., being sick in body. And concerning my worldly estate, my will is that my debtes be first paid out of my personall estate and the pfitts of such lands, tents, tythes and hereditamtes as I have purchased either in my owne name or in the name of any other, And namely, whereas I did purchase the Rectory of Ravenston Dale and the Mannor of Preston Pattricke, in the County of Westmorland, in the names of Richard Hutton

---

[1] He was the son of Anthony Wharton of Rigwell Grange, co. Westmoreland, by his wife, Mary, dau. of John Beane, lord mayor of York, 1568. He mar. Agnes, dau. of Richard Cleburne of Cleburne, Westmoreland, and died, 1635, leaving issue, Anthony, Thomas of Gillingwood, and Philadelphia, mar. to Robert Mitford of Mitford,

of Hunwick, in the County of Durham, Esqr., and my second son
Anthony Wharton, my will is and I hereby appoint that the said
Richard Hutton and Anthony Wharton shall convey the same
and all the estate therein unto my sonne, Charles Wharton, and
his heirs, or to such other pson or psons and their heires as he
shall noatifi and appoint to be by him disposed of for the paymt
of my said debts. . And whereas I purchased the Mannor of
Gainford, in the County of Durham, by two severall conveyances,
thone thereof being a lease for yeres in the names of the said
Thomas Wharton and of Michaell Waller, and the other being
a grannt of the revercon and inheritance thereof in the names of
the aforesaid Anthony Wharton and of Francis Fawcett, my will
is and I doe hereby declare that the said severall estates shallbe
unto the said Thomas Wharton and his heires, And my will is
that the said Anthony Wharton, Francis Fawcett and Michaell
Waller shall release and convey all the estates and interests unto
the said Thomas Wharton and his heires, or to such other psons
and there heires, executors or admors as he shall noatifi and
appointe to the intent and purpose that the same may be by him,
his heires, executrs or assignes, disposed of for the payment of
my said debts, And whereas heretofore I did grant and convey
all my then personall estate unto the said Richard Hutton and
Anthony Wharton and others for payment of my debtes, I doe
hereby further declare that the same was soe to them conveyed
for the payment of my debtes as I was then oweing or should
hereafter be oweing. And my will is that they shall convey the
same unto my said sonne, Thomas Wharton and his assignes,
And suffer him or them to take, hold, enjoy and dispose of the
same for and towards the payment of my said debts. I will and
bequeth unto my sonne, George Wharton, during his life, one
annuity or yerely rent of 20l., issueing and goeing out of my
tithes in Eppleby and Carlton, within the County of York, to
be yearly paid him att Pentecost and Martinmus by equal porcons.
And my further will is that after my said debts paide, my said
sonne Thomas shall hold all and singular the said Mannors,
lands, tents, goodes and chattells to the sole proper use, behoof
and benefitt of my said sonne, Thomas Wharton, his heirs, exors,
admors and assignees, yet subject to the payment of the said
annuity hereby willed and demised unto my said sonne George
as aforesaid. And I hereby make my said sonne Thomas sole
Executor of this my last Will and Testament. Witnesses, Anthony
Wharton, Mich. Waller, Christofer Philipps, James Fawcett,
Humphrey Hutton, Francis Fawcett.

JOHN ROTCHESTER.

Jan. 1, 1635. John Rotchester of Whalton, in the Countie
of Northumberland, Yeoman. To be buryed in the Churchyard
of Whalton before the quire door of the same church. I give

and bequeathe unto George Rotchester, my eldest sone, all my lands and tenements situate, lying and being in Walton. I give and bequeath unto my sonne, Bertram Rotchester, 15*l.* I likewise give 5*l.* more to the said George Rotchester two years after he shall enter upon the said land. I give unto my now wife, Alice Rotchester, the one whole half part of my goods, and the other half to my said sons, George Rotchester and Bertram Rotchester. I appoint and constitute the aforesaid George Rotchester sole Executor. Thos. Clerk, Thos. Batey. Probate, 1635.

HENRY GRAY.[1]

Feb. 10, 1635. Henry Gray of Kyloe, in the County Pallatine of Durham, Gentleman. I direct to be buried in my parish church of Kyloe as near to my wife's grave as may be. I give and bequeath to Sir Arthur Gray of Spinleston, Sir Roger Gray of Spinleston, Sir William Fenwicke of Meldon and Edward Gray of Morpeth, Esqr., all my lands and tenements in Kyloe, and all houses and appurtenances belonging to them and their heirs, to have and to hold to these fower gentlemen to sell the said lands and goods and distribute the proceeds unto my six daughters, viz., To my daughters, Margaret Gray, Katherine Graye, each 300*l.* To my daughters, Isabel Gray, Ellinor Gray, Frances Gray and Elizabeth Gray, 200*l.* each, and after all my debts are paid I give the residue of such proceeds to my said six daughters. I direct the aforenamed gentlemen shall see my fower youngest daughters brought up and taught to reade, sowe and have other convenient education, and to have such maintenance as the said gentlemen shall seeme fitt. I give to my cosin, Ralph Fayreley, 3*l.* 6*s.* 8*d.* To Margaret Pursell of Kyloe, 5*l.* Unto the poore of the towne of Kyloe, 20*s.* Whereas there is a debt of 35*l.* due to me by my brother, Ralph Graye, as appears by his Will, I doe bequeath the said debt to my brother, Roger Gray of Spinleston. I give unto my sister, Luce Lowther, 5*l.* To my nephew, William Lowther, 40*s.* The residue of my estate to my two Daughters, Margaret and Katherine, and appoint them Executors. I humbly desire the Right Honourable William Lord Gray of Warke to be supervisor of this my Will. I give to Mr. Henry Haggerstone, 20*s.* To Henry Gray of Fenwicke,

[1] The testator was the son of Henry Grey of Kiloe, by his wife, Fortune, dau. of Thomas Manners of Cheswick. He mar. Elizabeth, dau. of . . . . Jenison of Walworth; by her he had Margaret, mar. William Read of Fenham, 15 June, 1636, at Holy Island; Katherine, mar. Bryan Grey of Wark; Isabel, mar. Robert Moore of Hetton; Elinor; Frances, mar. Ralph Reed; Elizabeth, mar. Lionel Bradford of Newham. The testator died, 12 Feb., 1635/6. In his *Inq. p.m.*, taken at Durham, 24 Jan., 1636/7, Margaret, aged 18, Catherine, aged 16, Isabella, aged 13, Eleanor, aged 12, Frances, aged 9, and Elizabeth, aged 7, are his daus. and co-heiresses.

40s. To my nephew, William Gray of Fenwicke, 5l. Whereas there is in my hands 10l., given unto my daughter Margaret by my Lady Frevile, I direct the aforenamed fower gentlemen to pay the same to my daughter. Witnesses, John Gray, Ephraim Gray, Henry Haggerston, Ralph Fairley, Roger Gray, John Oliver, Ralph Haggerston, Edward Mayre. Probate, 1636.

WILLIAM CLAVERINGE.[1]

Feb. 18, 1635. William Claveringe of Gaitside within the County Pallintine of Durham, gentleman. My bodie I comite to the earth from whence it came, to be buryed within the parish church of Gaitside in the place where I now leves. I give to Ester Walker alias Claveringe, 100l., when she comes to the age of fourteen years or at the daye of her marriage, and my will is that my sone, Ralph Claveringe, shall find her meat and drink, and apparell befitting for such a one. And if it please gode that my sone, Ralphe Claveringe, should dye, then my will is that my said grandchild should have the 100l. My will is that William Story, son of William Story, cupper, shall have the house that Lancelot Swinburn doth dwell in, and the house that Richard Nixon doth dwell in. I give to Sir John Claveringe, one 20s. piece, for a token. To John Sudicke, five markes as a token. To my sister, one twentie shilling piece, for a token. To the poor of Gaitside parish, 20s. I make my sone, Ralphe Claveringe, and my wyfe wholl Executors. Witnesses, Ralphe Buntinge, John Snawedon.

INVENTORY amounted to 417l. 13s. 2d. Probate, 1635.

DOROTHY MIDDLETON.[2]

May 16, 1636. Dorothy Middleton of Bellshaw, in the County of Northumberland, widow. To be buried at the discretion of my executor, hereafter named in sure and certain hope of a joyful

[1] The testator was bur. at Gateshead, 5 Mch., 1635/6. By his first wife, whose name is not known, he had a son, Thomas, bapt., 21 Aug., 1608, bur., 28 July, 1634; by his second wife, Elizabeth Wastell, whom he mar., 19 Nov., 1609 (she was bur., 21 Dec., 1643), he had Ralph, bapt., 7 May, 1612 (aged 23 at the Inq. p.m. of his father taken at Durham, 16 Apl., 1636, where he is called his son and heir), bur. at Tanfield, 2 Mch., 1671/2, mar. Isabel Potts, 20 June, 1660; Alice, bapt., 8 July, 1610; Jane, bapt., 28 Nov., 1617.

[2] She was dau. of Sir Robert Bindlosse of Borwick Hall, Lancs., and her sister, Jane, mar. Sir William Carnaby of Bothal. She mar. (settlement, 29 Aug., 1623) Charles Middleton, son and heir of Thomas Middleton of Belsay. He was entered at Gray's Inn, 18 Nov., 1616, and died, v.p, 2 May, 1628. They had issue, a dau., Dorothy, who died before her mother, and Robert Middleton, son and heir, of Christ's College, Cambridge, admitted Fellow Commoner, 3 June, 1642, aged 14; he died unmar., 22 Apl., 1658, and his will, dated 19 Apl., 1658, was proved, 23 June, 1658 (P.C.C., 275, Wootton.)

resurrection at the last day. I give unto my well beloved father in law, Thomas Middleton, Esqr., the trunk that was Charles Middleton's, my late husband's, with all the apparell, and other things contained therein. I give to my christian friend, Priscilla Clerke, widow, of Bellshaw, 6*l.* as a token of my christian affection for her. To William Rathband of Bellshaw, aforesaid clerk, 6*l.* To the poor, 10*l.* To every one of my father-in-law's maid servants, 10*s.* And touching the residue of my estate, I give and bequeath the same to my deare and only sone, Robert Middleton, beseaching the God of Blessing to bless him with a better portion than this fading world can afforde, and if it shall happen that my said sone depart this life before he come to the full age of sixteen yeares, I say then that my goods and chattels as aforesaid shall go to my nephew, William Karnaby, eldest sone and heir apparent of Sir William Karnaby, Knight. I make my kind and loveing father-in-law, Thomas Middleton of Bellshaw, esquire, sole Executor, and commit to him the guardianship of my said sone, trusting that my said sone will perform all offices to his good guardian and grandfather, and I lastly direct that my said sone, shall be brought up in the true fear of God, and as far as possible from the common vices of the times. I do earnestly exhort my said sone to be dutiful, obedient in every way to his said grandfather in all things in the Lord as he ought to remember the Scripture saith, "That to honour father and mother is the first commandment" with promise, and that the promise of long life and much prospertie to them that do observe it . . . the land that God shall give them. Witnesses, Richard Preston, Thomas Rowland.

INVENTORIE amounted to 282*l.* 0*s.* 10*d.* Probate, Sept., 1636.

SIR ARTHUR GRAY.[1]

June 1st, 1636. Arthur Gray, Sir, of Spindleston, in the County, of Northumberland, Knight.

INVENTORY : A Bond of Sir William Fenwick for 500*l.* A bond of Mr. Nichollas Forster of Balmbrough, 26*l.* Five bonds of the said Mr. Nicholas Forster, to be paid in five years at thirty pounds by the yeare, 160*l.* Mr. Gilbart Swinho, his bond for 15*l.* 8*s.* 0*d.* Mr. John Midforth, his bond for 17*l.* 18*s.* 8*d.* George Young, his bond for 4*l.* 13*s.* 4*d.* Thomas Brewhowse, his bond for 5*l.* 8*s.* 8*d.* Mr. Alexander Forster, his bond for 20*l.* Mr. Thos. Claveringe, his bond for 22*l.* Stephen Cramlington, his bond for 11*l.* 11*s.* 0*d.* Gawin Radcliffe's bond for 20*l.* More a bill of the said Gawin Radcliffe for 5*l.* Mr. William Armorer,

[1] He was the son of Sir Ralph Grey of Chillingham, by his wife, Isabel, dau. of Sir Thomas Grey of Horton; he mar. Margaret, dau. of Anthony Bulmer of Tursdale; their only child, Isabel, mar. Sir William Fenwick of Meldon.

his bond for fower years at 24*l*. a yeare. James Cooke, his bond for 15*l*. The rent of Howick, which is due to the said Sir Arthur Gray, deceased, is 195*l*. Sum totalis, 1,116*l*. 19*s*. 8*d*. Moveable goods : Twelve stotts, 64*l*. Three score and fower beasts, 144*l*. Fortie beasts more, 40*l*. Sixteen Kyne, 48*l*. More thirtie fower Kyne, 108*l*. Twentie oxen, 83*l*. Fower studd mares, 32*l*. Five three yeares foalles, 10*l*. More two of the same age, 3*l*. One cowlt, 5*l*. Three horses more, 6*l*. Total, 543*l*.

Wethers, Yowes, Tuppes and Gimers : Foure and thirtie scorce and eight wethers at eight pounds a score, 275*l*. 4*s*. 0*d*. Thirtie fower score and six yewes at eight pounds the score, 273*l*. Eighteen score of hoggs at seven pounds per score, 126*l*. Eight score and fower hoggs at seven pounds the scores comes to 57*l*. 8*s*. 0*d*. Twenty tupps at ten shillings a piece, 10*l*. Of gimmers six score and twelve at seven pounds the score. Total, 788*l*. 8*s*. 0*d*. Plate praised to 100*l*. The furniture in the howse, 140*l*. His owne apperell, 40*l*. And in his purse, 104*l*. Total, 384*l*. Corn in the lofts praised to 57*l*. 7*s*. 0*d*. Corn sowen on the ground praised to 66*l*. 3*s*. 0*d*. Sum totalis, 2,955*l*. 17*s*. 8*d*.

Valued and apprised by Cuthbert Hall of Spindleston and William France of Ulchester, Yeoman.

ARTHUR HEBBORNE.[1]

Aug. 19, 1636. Arthur Hebborne of Hebborne, Esqr., ... weake in bodye. To be buryed at the discretion of my friends. I bequeath to my sone, Arthur Hebborne, and to my sone, Edward Hebborne, and to my sone, John Hebborne for their filial portions, each 100*l*. Unto my eldest daughter, Margaret Hebborne, for her portion, 200*l*., not doubting but my sone, Ralph Hebborne, will agment the sum, 100*l*. more, if God enable him. To my daughter, Dorothy Hebborne, and to my daughter, Frances Hebborne, and to my daughter, Anne Hebborne, and to my

[1] Arthur Hebburn of Hebburn, and the representative of that very ancient house whose tower is still standing within the walls of the enlarged part of Chillingham, mar. Mary, dau. of John Salkeld of Huln, in the parish of Alnwick. He was succeeded by his eldest son, Ralph Hebburn, a colonel in the army of King Charles I., whose estate in 1648 was stated to be worth £500 per annum (*Welford Royalist Compositions*, p. 237), a gross over-estimation, for the Book of Rates of 1663 he was assessed for Hebburn at £120 p.a., and for Earle at £20. He mar. Alice (bur. at Chillingham, 5 Oct., 1688), dau. of Robert Delaval of Cowpen, and had issue; of the testator's younger children, Arthur, Edward, John, nothing is known; Dorothy mar. Henry Pearson of Newton-by-the-Sea, Frances, Anne, Catharine, nothing known except that one of them seems to have mar. Roger Pearson of Titlington; Mary (alias Margaret, died, 24 Feb., 1703/4, aged 105); mar., firstly, Robert Dodsworth of Barton (died, 1651), and secondly, Col. Henry Chaytor, the defender of Bolton Castle against Cromwell (bur., 25 Oct., 1664, at Croft), she was bur. at Barton, 26 Feb., 1703/4; Martha died unmar. and was bur. at Chillingham, 24 Jan., 1705/6.

daughter, Katherine Hebborne, and to my daughter, Mary Hebborne, and to my daughter, Martha Hebborne, for their filiall portions, each 100*l*., which said several portions to be payd out of my lands of Hebborne, Earle and Newton, after the payment of my debts. And for the Execution of this my will, I leave my trusty and welbeloved wife, Mary Hebborne, my sole Executrix, to whose care and custody under God I leave my children, and hopeing she will be carefull of their good education. Witnesses to Will, Robert Urquhart, clerk, Henry Ogle, Ralphe Salkeld. Probate, 1638.

INVENTORY, 700*l*. 12*s*. 2*d*.

ROBERT ORDE.[1]

Sept. 28, 1636. Robert Orde of Chatton, in the County of Northumberland, Gentleman. My bodie to be buried in the parish church of Norham. I give and bequeathe all my lands, tenements, and hereditaments which I hold of the Right Honble. the Earl of Northumberland, in Chatton, and all my other lands whatsoever, to my trustie and well beloved friend and kinsmen, Henry Orde of Norham Castle, Luke Orde of Barwick, Richard Orde of Horkley, and Robert Orde of Ord, Gentlemen to pay my debts and legacies. To my nephew, Robert Orde, son of my brother, John Orde, late of Horkley, 10*l*. And that my said friends shall account for all my lands aforesaid to my daughter, Margaret Ord, and if she die unmarried, then my Will is that all my lands, and tenements, aforesaid, shall descend to Henry Ord, sone of the aforesaid Henry Orde of Norham Castle. I give to my brother-in-law, Thomas Swinhoe, 40*s*. a yeare to be paid out of my lands during his life. I give one acre of land unto Henry Orde, son of the said Henry Orde, now in the possession of George Scott of Norham. To Margery Ord, daughter of my brother, Ralph Orde, deceased, 4*l*. To my daughter-in-law, Margery Ord, 50*l*. due to me on bond from Mr. George Orde. I give towards the repaire of the Church of Chatton, 20*s*. To the poor of the parish of Norham, Barwick and Wilimondswicke, 40*s*. each. My above friends to be Executors. Witnesses, Gilbert Swinhoe, Richard Orde, Daniel Redmond, George Smith. Probate, 1638.

RALPHE FETHERSTONHALGH.[2]

Nov. 24, 1636. Memn. That Ralphe Fetherstonhalgh of Stanhop hall in Weredale in the Countie of Durham, Esquire, sick in bodie, but of good and pfect Memorie

[1] See note on page 137.

[2] The testator was bur. at Stanhope, 27 Nov., 1636. In his *Inq. per br. de mand*, taken at Durham, 22 Sept., 1638, John, aged 37, is his son and heir; this son, John, mar. Alice, dau. of William Mann, at Hamsterley, 11 June, 1618. The testator's dau. Peregrina, mar. Charles Wren, armiger, at St. Giles', Durham, 28 Dec., 1649.

(prased be god) did by worde of mouth nuncupatively declare his last Will and Testament, He did utterly revoke and annull all former wills by him in anie wise before at time made. To be buried within the chanccell of the pish church of Stanhoppe, where his father and other his ancestors have been buried. And his temporall goods and landes he did give and bequeathe, as followes, First his will was that all such debts as were due by him be payd, should be duely and thankfullie paid by his executors, hereafter named out of his personal estate and what shall remaine thereof unpaid out of his personal estate shalbe paid out of the yearlie rents, issues and profitts, as they shall arise of all such lands as he had conveyed unto Ralph Fetherstonhalgh his second son or to anie other pson or psons to or for his use; he did give and bequeath to his daughter Dorothie the sum of 300*l*. for all . . . . To his daughter Marie the like sum of 300*l*. for all her filiall porson. To Peregrine, his daughter the like the sum of 300*l*., also for all her filiall porcon. To his daughter Ann, the wife of Robert Elstobb, 100*l*., for her filiall porcon. To his daughter Elizabeth, wife of Richard Fetherstonhalgh, 100*l*. for her filiall porcon, and these porcons to be paid out of lands at Bruntoft, and that his two daughters, Dorothie and Marie shall receive from the handes of his executors yearlie, each of them six pounds thirteen shillings and fourpence yearly for their maintenance; he did give and bequeath to his sonne, Raphe Fetherstonhalgh, his burgage lands, rents, tenements and hereditaments within Newcastle-upon-Tine or the suburbs or liberties hereof, And all his Burgages, lands, rent, tenements and hereditaments in Hartlepoole, to have and to hold to him, the said Raphe, and his heires for ever, and he did make him, the said Raphe, and his sonne Francis, joint executors, and did make Fardinando Moorecroft of Stanhoppe aforesaid, clarke, and Anthonie Maxton of Wolsingham, in the County of Durham, Clark, Supervisors of his Will, and did appoint Edward Wright of London, in the Countie of Middlesex, Esquire, and the said Anthonie Maxton, to be guardians and tutors of his two sonns, Raphe and Francis, All which the decd did declare in the presence of Jaine Feathstonhalgh, his late wife, and Anth. Maxton, Clerk.

WILLIAM REED.

June 26, 1637. William Reed of Broxfield, in the Countie of Northumberland, Yeoman, Doe make this my last Will and Testament. By reason my wife is dead and the infection of the plague is fare in the country, I thought good to dispose of my goods and chattels in manner following :—I leave unto my son, John Reed, and my daughter, Jane Reed, all my goods and chattels, vizt., seaven kyne, my horse, a yeare old stirke, and all my corne arising and growing of the farme I have of my landlord, Thomas

Gray of Howick. To my father-in-law, John Atchison, one cowe, being one of the two whies at Little Houghton. In the event of the death of my children, I give my cosin, Thomas Reed, all my estate, and I appoint my said cosin, Thomas Reed of Alnwick, executor of this my Will. Witnesses, William Fargy, Bartholomew Fargy. Probate, 1637.

ANN GRAYE.

July 15, 1637. Ann Graye of Morpeth, in the Countie of Northumberland, Spinster. My bodie to be buried at the discretion of my executors. Whereas I am seased of one annutie or rent charge of 26s. 8d. out of certaine lands belonginge to William Fenwick of Nunrydeing, Gent., as appears by conveyance, I bequeath the said annuitie or rent charge unto Mrs. Elizabeth Fenwick of Morpeth and to her heirs for ever. And whereas I have due to me the sum of 58l. out of the lands and profitts of Kiloe, my will and meaning is and I doe desire that my funerall charges and such other remembrances as I have sett down in a note, and delivered unto Mrs. Elizabeth Fenwick, and I give unto the said Elizabeth, twenty markes. I do give the remainder of the 58l. unto my brothers, Edward Gray and Henrye Gray. I likewise give unto my Sister, Fortune Graye, and Margaret Armorer, each 20 nobles. I give to my brother, William Gray, five marks. To my niece, Margaret Gray, five marks. I give unto my cosen, Will. Lowther, five marks. I constitute and appoint my brother, Edward Graye, and my sister, Fortune Gray, Executors. Witnesses, Edward Graye, Thomas Richeson, Chris. Robenson. Probate, 1637.

FRANCIS ALDER.[1]

Aug. 24, 1637. Inventory of all the goods and household stuffe of Francis Alder of Hobberlaw, gentleman, late deceased, valued and appraised by George Alder and William Grene.
Imprimis: One horse, price 50s. Two featherbedds, 20s. Three bolsters, four Codds, 8s. Six coverletts and plade, 13s. 4d. Two paire of blanketts, 6s. 8d. Two paire of Courtings, 5s. Four paire of small shetts and two paire of course sheets, 20s. Two dozen of table napkins, 8s. Two small table clothes and one course table cloath, 4s. Five Code pillowes, 5s. Three towells, 5s. Twelve peace of pewter vessel, 12s. Six Candlesticks, 5s. Two duble salts, 18d. Two chamber potts, 18d. One pottell pot, 18d. Eight Quishions, 4s. Three chaires, 4s. Five buffett

[1] He was the son of George Alder of Hobberlaw, by his wife, Margaret, dau. of Nicholas Forster of Newham; he mar. Agnes Shell.

Stooles, 3s. 4d. Two buffett formes, 2s. One shorte table and a fraime, 3s. Two bedsteads, 3s. Two brass potts, 5s. Three panns, 5s. One friing pan, one paire of yron racks, two speets and one yron chimneye and one yron crook, 6s. Two olde trunks and three chists, 10s. One cupboarde and one butterie, 13s. 4d. Two suits of appell and one cloake, 40s. One carping cloathe, 2s. 6d. Suma totalis, 13l. 7s. 8d.

JOHN GREENWELL.

Sept. 5, 1637. John Greenwell of Steley, in the parish of Lanchester, in the County of Durham, Yeoman. To be buried in the parish church of Lanchester. I make my sonne, Humphrey Grinwell, my soole Executor, to pay all my debts. I give to my Daughter, Annas Grinwell, 40l. and all my household stuffe. To my three servantes, 10s. amongst them. I give to every child that I have witnessed their baptisme, 12d.

INVENTORY : His purse and apparell, 5l. Two oxen and two stotts, 12l. Five kine and in calfe, 10l. Five younge beasts, 7l. One mare, 3l. Five score of wethers, 30l. Forty three ewes and three tupps, 10l. 3s. 4d. Four score of younger sheepe, 14l. 5s. 0d. Fifty lambes, 6l. 13s. 4d. Twenty six stone of wooll, 13l. Wane weare and plough geare with other iron geare, 1l. 0s. 0d. One . . . . cock and two hens, 1s. 4d. The household stuffe, 21l. 13s. 8d. Money owen to me, 5l. A debt of 6l. 2s. 6d., oweing by John Rippon upon a bill. Besides their is 40s. by Robert Grinwell, and 13s. by Mr. Nevill. Probate, 1637.

CHARLES BAINBRIGG.

Sept. 13, 1637. In the name of God, Amen, Charles Bainbrigg of Hardgull, in the pish of Midelton. To be buried in the parish church of Midelton. I give and bequeath to my brother's sone, John Bainbrigg, the best cowe that I have and 40s. Also I give to Gabriell Bainbrigg, 40s. Also I give to Christopher Bainbrigg, 40s. Also I give to Thomas Bainbrigg, 40s. Also I give to Thomas Robinson wife Anne, 40s. Also I give to William Parkin's wife Isabell, 40s. Also I give to my sister's son, Anthony Langstaff, 40s. Also I give to my sister's daughter, Anne Raine, 40s. Also I give to my sister's daughter, Jane Marton, 40s. Also I give unto Christopher Bainbrigg's three children, Charles, Christopher and John, sixe pounds, and to John Bainbrigg and Gabriel Bainbrigg, to set it forward for their use until they come to lawful age that they can guide it themselves. Also I give to John Raine's children, one whye, and to goe forward for their use, and their father to have no title in her, John Bainbrigg or some other fresh frend to set her forward for

their use. Also I give John Raine, my young meare. Also I
give John Bainbrigg's son John, one ewe. I give Christopher
Bainbrigge sone Charles, one ewe. Also I give to Thomas Robinson's son John, one ew. Also I give to William Parkin's son
Robert, one ew. Also I give to Eleanore Martton daughter
Eleanore, one ew and a lamb. Also I give to my maide, Annes
Robinson, 10s. if she staye with me till god call me. And I
ordayne, constitute and make my brother's son, John Bainbrigg
of Crosswhat, my whole executor of this my Will, unto whom I
give and bequeath all the rest of my goods, movable and unmovable whatsoever being unbequeathed. Witnesses, William
Robinson, John Bainbrigg, James Allanson. Proved, 1638.

MARK ERRINGTON.[1]

Nov. 23, 1637. Mark Errington of Pont Iland, in the County
of Northumberland, Esqr. I give and grant unto Sir Thomas
Tempest of Stella, in the Countie of Durham, Baronet, and Sir
John Delavall of South Dissington, in the County of Northumberland, Knight, All my goods, chattels, leases, household stuff,
bills, bonds, plaite, Jewells and readie money whatsoever, and
all my possessions whatsoever within the realm of England for
their absolute uses, And appoint them Executors. Probate, 1637.

ROWLAND ARCHER.[2]

July 25, 1638. I, Rowland Archer of Woodhorne Seaton, in
the County of Northumberland, Yeoman. My will is that there
be payd unto my two Daughters, Dorothy Archer and Ann Archer,
each of them 5l., which was left them by my father, Rowland
Archer, deceased. I give out of my owne estate, 5l. to each of
my said Daughters, which shall be fore their filiall or child's
portions. I give unto my younger sonnes, John Archer and

[1] The testator was the son of Gilbert Errington of Woolsington,
by his wife, Dorothy, dau. of Sir John Delaval of Seaton Delaval; he
mar. Margaret, dau. of Ralph, son and heir of Anthony Mitford of
Ponteland (St. Nich., Newcastle Regs.), bapt., 30 Nov., 1562, at St.
Nich., Newcastle, bur., 23 Mch., 1629/30, at Ponteland. See the
pedigree of Errington of Ponteland (*New Co. Hist. of Northd.*, xii.,
463). This will does not agree with that of a Mark Errington, dated
22 Oct., 1637, printed as a footnote in this Society's publications,
111, pp. 194-5.

[2] The testator was bur. 6 Sept., 1638, at Woodhorn (whence other
dates are taken except where otherwise mentioned), he mar. firstly,
Elizabeth Taylor, 17 Dec., 1619, she was bur. 15 Feb., 1624/5, by her
he had one dau., Alice, bapt. 21 July, 1625; his second wife, Mary
(who perhaps re-mar. Roger Simpson, 22 Jan., 1639/40), bore him three
sons and two daus., Rowland, of whom later, John, bapt. 29 Sept., 1630,
Henry, bapt. 21 Jan., 1634/5, Dorothy and Anne. The testator's son,
Rowland (bapt. 3 Mch., 1628/9, bur. 17 June, 1676, mar., Anne, bur.,
5 Sept., 1698; he had with other issue a son, Rowland, bur. 6 Jan.,
1725/6, who mar., Hannah, dau. of Thomas Metcalf of Stonyhill,

Henry Archer, out of my personal estate, each 6l. 13s 4d., and also to each of them 20l., which shallbe payd by my eldest sonne, Rowland Archer, out of my lands at Woodhorne Seaton, when the sayd John Archer and Henry Archer shall be of the age of 21 years, and in case either of my said sonns, John Archer and Henry Archer, shall dye before they attain 21, then my will is that the one halfe of the portion of either of them so deceased shalbe and remaine to my sayd eldest sonne, Rowland Archer, and the other to the Survivor of my said two yonger Sonns. And for all other goods and chattels unbequeathed, I give the same to my wyfe, Mary Archer, who I make Executrix. Witnesses, John Widdrington, John Preston, Will. Clarke, James Sutton, John Sutton. Proved, 10 Oct., 1638, by Mary Archer, the Executrix, and Guardian of Rowland, John, Henry, Dorothy and Agnes Archer, children (Minors).

An INVENTORY of the goods and chattells of Rolland Archer of Woodhorne Seaton, apprised by Mr. John Widdrington, John Preston, John Sutton and John Johnson, as followeth :—

Imprimis : His apparell, 4l. In linnin, 13s. 4d. In wollen, 1l. 13s. 4d. One fetherbed with its furniture, 1l. 10s. In sacks and wallets, 5s. In bedsteads, 9s. In Cubbords, chists, tables, forms, stooles, together with tubbs, barrells, dishes and bowles, 5l. In peuder dishes, candlesticks, chamber pottes and saltsellers, 1l. 6s. 8d. In Brasse potts, pans and Kettles, 3l. A payre of Iron barres, tonges and crookes, 6s. Two long wanes, two short wanes and other my implemts of husbandry, 5l. 6s. 8d. Two horses, Two mares, one filly and two foles, 14l. Ten oxen, 30l. Four Cowes, 8l. Three young stotts, 3l. 10s. Twentie sheepe, 5l. 6s. 8d. In corne of all graine and Hay, 28l. 13s. 4d. For Bees, 2l. In Fuell, 5s. In poultry, 10s. Three corn chists, 15s. Seves and winnow cloathes, 6s. 8d. In lint yarne, 10s. In swine, 1l. 4s. 119l. 10s. 8d.

Debts owne to ye deceased : Raiph Dridon, 1l. 3s. Hugh Braidforth, 16s.

Debts which the deceased owes : To Mr. Henry Widdrington, 10l. 13s. 4d. To John Sutton, 6l. 14s. 3d. To Will. Lawson, 14s. To Margery Rey, 10s. To his two Daughters, Dorothy and Ann Archer, 20l. To his two sonns, John and Henry Archer, 13l. 6s. 8d. Servants' wages, 5l. 15s. Henry Clark, 5s. Steven Potts, 2s. 4d. Barbry Marshall, 8s. To Margret Watson, 6s. 10d. To Rich. Young, 6s. To Matt. Ruter, 16s. Funerall expenses, 5l. Proved, 10 Oct., 1638.

Alnwick, 25 Aug., 1682, bur. 22 Mch., 1731/2, they had with other issue, William, bapt. 9 Apl., 1696, bur. 14 Feb., 1731/2, mar., Dorothy, dau. of Charles Brandling, bapt. at Morpeth, 12 Oct, 1697, mar. at Horton, 2 Apl., 1727, bur. 26 Aug., 1778, at St. Nich., Newcastle. The testator's parents, Rowland (whose will is printed p. 240 above) and Elizabeth, were buried at Woodhorn, 27 and 29 May, 1632, respectively.

ANTHONY EDEN.[1]

Nov. 5, 1638. In the name of god, Amen, I, Anthony Eden of Carlton, in the County of Durham and Parish of Redmarshall, sicke and infirme. To be buried at the east end of Redmarshall Church. I doe bequeathe and give unto my loveing wife, Grace Eden, 10*l.* which is now in the handes of John Richardson the younger, of Carlton, by him to be paid at Whitsuntyde next. I give to my neece, Mary Wilkinson, 40*s.* which is now in the hands of Thomas Hartburn of Carlton. All the rest of my goods, moveable and unmoveable, together with three pounds which is owinge unto me by John Conyers of Newton Morrell in Richmond-shire, for a Cowe, I do freely give and bequeath unto my loving wife, Grace Eden, whom I doe constitute and make her sole executrix of this my Will. Witnesses, John Rand, Clerke, Marm. Richardson, Robert Willson.

INVENTORY, 22*l.* 13*s.* 4*d.*

GEORGE DOBBISON.[2]

Nov. 9, 1638. Memorandum that George Dobbison of Willington, in the parish of Brancepeth, in the County of Durham, Yeoman, being sick in body but of good and pfect memory, and being advised for to make his will and to dispose of his estate, presently after upon consideration thereof made a declaration of his mynde, which they considered he did with a purpose, to make his Will in manner followinge or to the like effect. My mynd is that my three youngest children shall have twenty poundes a peece portion raised forth of my lands, to be paid them when they come to their full ages, and shall also have their maintenance upon the said landes during their minorities. And my mynd likewise is that Henry, my eldest sonne, shallbe executor of my Will. And I earnestly desire my father-in-law, Mr. William Conyers, to see theis things executed accordinglye. Witnesses, Martin Nicholson, George Iley. Proved, 1639.

[1] The testator was bur. at Redmarshall, 10 Nov., 1638. There was a child of this name bapt. there, 7 Apl., 1580.

[2] He was bur., 11 Nov., 1638, at Brancepeth, whence other dates are taken; he mar. Elizabeth, dau. of William Conyers of Wooley, by his wife, Alice, dau. of Anthony Kendall, of Thorp Thewles (bapt. at Grindon, 6 Jan., 1580/1); she was bapt., 6 Jan., 1602/3, mar., 15 May, 1623, bur., 8 Nov., 1651. By her he had issue, Henry, bapt., 2 May, 1624; Thomas, bapt., 1 Nov., 1627, bur., 4 July, 1628; William, bapt., 6 Dec., 1629, bur., 9 Jan., 1629/30; Ralph, bapt., 3 June, 1632; George, bapt., 7 July, 1633; William, bapt., 24 Sept., 1637, bur., 17 Dec., 1637; Isabel, bapt., 13 Nov., 1625, bur., 4 Apl., 1630; Anne, bapt., 23 Nov., 1635, bur., 5 July, 1643; Elizabeth, bur., 19 Jan., 1638/9.

JOHN HUDSON.[1]

Nov. 22, 1638. In the name of Gode, Amen, I, John Hudson of Greatham, in the County of Durham, sick in body. To be buried in the Parish Church of Greatham according to the discretion of my Executors and other of my friends. And as touching my Temporall estate of lands, goods and chattells wherewith God had endued me, I doe first ratify and confirm one deed with another, assurances made the twentieth day of October, in the fourteenth yeare of the reigne of Our Sovereigne Lord Charles, and in the yeare of our Lorde Gode 1638, whereby I have estated all my freehold lands in Greatham aforesaid to Henry Lowder, Thomasine, his wife, and to their heirs for ever, as by the said Deeds more at large doth appeare. As to all other my lands and tenements which are in lease within the Manor of Greatham, my intent and true meaning is that my loveing wife, Ann Hudson, shall have the full moitie and one halfe of the same, with all and singular the appurtenances whatsoever to the same belonging, with the howse she now dwelleth in with the household stuff in and about the said house and houses, to and for her only use, profitt and benefitt during her naturall life, Also I give and bequeath to my said wife, one mare called the girgell mare and three kyne. The other half of all my aforesaid lands, holden by lease, I doe give and bequeath to Henry Lowder and Thomasine, his wife, with all and singular appurtenances whatsoever belongeth to the same, having those howses about the same tenement and stackgarths and garthes which my wife standeth in need of for necessary uses during her naturall life. And further my will is, that the said Henry Lowder shall have four oxen, four horses and mares, with implements of husbandry as plowes, wanes, wheeles, harrowes, yoakes, bowes, teams, and the rents due to be paid yearly for the aforesaid lands to be payd equally by my wiefe and the said Henry Lowder, and all other requirements whatsoever

---

[1] The testator was bur. at Greatham, 22 May, 1645. He mar. Ann Greenall, 7 Dec., 1597, at Bishop Middleham, she was bur., 20 Sept., 1658. Edward Lowther or Lowder, bur., 3 Jan., 1610/11; mar., firstly, Janet Hudson, 6 July, 1596 (she was bur., 15 July, 1607); he mar., secondly, 17 May, 1609, Katherine Thomson. By his first wife he had issue, the beneficiary (who seems to have been related to the testator through his mother and also, perhaps, through his wife), Henry, bapt., 11 Feb., 1598/9, bur., 21 July, 1664, mar. Thomasine, bapt. at Bishop Middleham, 28 Oct., 1607, dau. of Robert Greenall, where she was mar., 18 Feb., 1627/8, she was bur. at Greatham, 10 Jan., 1670/1. By her he had Francis, bapt., 25 Oct., 1629, mar. Jane Lasenby of Ormsby, Cleveland, co. York, 15 May, 1655; John, bapt., 27 Dec., 1637, bur., 31 Oct., 1655; Edward, bapt., 7 Apl., 1644, bur., 31 Oct., 1655; Jane, bapt., 21 Dec., 1631; Elizabeth, bapt., 25 Jan., 1634/5; Catherine, bapt., 8 Mch., 1639/40; Susanna, bapt., 19 Feb., 1642/3, bur., 1 May, 1643; Susanna, bapt., 21 June, 1650. All dates from Greatham registers unless otherwise stated.

is yearly to be payd. And my will is alsoe that the said Henry Lowder shall yearlie and every yeare during the naturall life of my wief, plowe and manure the said lands withal husbandry that it requireth in due time, and the same to carry home and safely sett the same in the staggarthe of the tenement which my wief doth now dwell upon, and to divide the corne and straw thereof equally by bushels of corne and thraves of straw, so likewise the hay to be divided, and grass in the pasture according to the pporcon in due times. And I doe give and bequeathe unto Francis Lowder, the sone of Henry Lowder, one horse called the girgell colt. I doe give and bequeath unto John Lowder, second sonne of Henry Lowder, two mares and two fooles. My will is that Jane Lowder and Elizabeth, daughter of the said Henry Lowder, shall have either of them a porcon of those goodes which I sett over unto him for the occupation of the said land which I have bequeathed to my wief, for the better enabling of him to doe it, in the best manner of husbandry, and to fetch and bring home unto hir soe many waine loads of cowles every yeare during her naturall life as shall sufficientlie serve her, shee paying for the same att the pitt. I give unto the wiefe of Henry Lowder, one mare called the Dun Mare, And after the decease of my saide wiefe, that land which I have bequeathed unto her, with the appurtenances belonging the same, shall come to the said Henry Lowder, for the better help of him and his children, and specially for the raising of better porcons for his said two daughters, Jane Lowder and Elizabeth Lowder. Provided alwayes, and my will is, that if it please god that my wiefe shall survive the lease of the tenement which now she dwelleth in, That the said Henry Lowder shall renew the lease of the tenement in his own name and for his owne use, yett my wiefe shall have sufficient wherewithall to release her self soe long as she liveth, that she come not to want in old age; this shall be provided of Henry Lowder meanes, and the said Henry Lowder shall have his halfe of the aforesaid tenement sowen with corne of old graine of my corne, now standing in the staggarth for this next year, and the remainder that is left to goe for the use of my said wife to supply her wants, and for this cause and other considerations I give unto the aforesaid Henry Lowder foure oxen and foure horses, with all the aforesaid implements of husbandry which is above mentioned. All the rest of my goods and chattells, moveable and unmoveable, credits, debts and legacies and funerals, with 20s. to be given to the poore the daye of my buriall being first discharged and satisfied, I doe freely give and bequeath unto the aforesaid Henry Lowder, without out . . . . whom I make sole Executor of this my last Will and Testament. Witnesses, William Speeding, Edward Dunn, John Grenell.

INVENTORY, 100*l*. 13*s*. 0*d*. Proved, 1647.

RALPHE HUTTON.[1]

Jan. 19, 1638. I, Ralphe Hutton, doe ordane this my last
Will in manner following :—I bequeath my soule to Almightie
God, my maker, and my bodye to be buried in St. Oswald's
Church in Durham neighe to my dear wife departed, If I dye
where it convenientlie may be pformed. And I give to the poore
of the said pish, to be added to their stocke, the sum of 40s.
Concerning my freehold landes in Mainsforth, within the County
of Durham, purchased by me in my owne and Sir William
Chaytor's names, I give and bequeath them all, together with all
their appurtenances, unto Ralphe Hutton, my sonne, and the
heires of his body lawfully begotten for ever, and in default of
such issue then I give the said lands and their appurtenances to
my sonne, Arthur Hutton, and to the heires of his body lawfully
begotten for ever, and in default of issue then to the right heires
of me, the said Ralph Hutton, for ever. I give and bequeath to
my sonne, Arthur Hutton, All those freehold lands which I have
at Bpp Middleham, purchased by my self in my owne name
and my brother, Christopher Hutton, as also all my interest and
terme of yeares in one tenement or farmhold in Bpp Middleham
which I hold of Lord Bpp of Durham, called Moore's farme, and
also I give him all my right and interest their in a little close
or garth called Butler's garth, as also all my interest and terme
of yeares of a parcel of ground called the paddocks thereto
adjoining, all which I give him in lieu and full satisfaction of
his filial and child's portion. Moreover, I charge my sonne Ralph
by this my Will, that after he come to the age of twenty one
years that he surrender unto his brother Arthur and his sequells,
if he be then living, that copiehold house and garth now in the
possession of Thomas Bell, which if my said son Ralph refuse to
doe, I will and bequeth to my sonne Arthur, in liewe thereof, the
sume of 30l., to be leveyed of lands at Mainsforth immediately
after the portions of my daughters be raised according to a lease
formerly sealed to that purpose. I give unto my beloved wife (over
and besides that 20l. per annum during hir life naturall, which I

---

[1] He was the son of Edward Hutton, matric. sizar from Trinity
College, Cambridge, Michs., 1573, LL.B., 1579, Bailiff of the City of
Durham, by his wife, Anne, dau. of Francis Lascelles of Allerthorpe,
co. York. He mar., firstly, Margaret, dau. of Anthony Chaytor of
Croft, co. York, 4 Apl., 1619, at St Oswald's, Durham (bur. there,
25 July, 1634), secondly, Dorothy, dau. of Thomas Heath of Kepyer;
she mar., firstly, Richard, son of John Cradock, Archdeacon of
Northumberland (bapt. at Gainford, 10 Sept., 1592, bur., 8 Aug.,
1624, at Durham Cathedral), by whom she had three daus., Ann,
Margaret, Dorothy; she mar., secondly, Henry Chapman (*Inq. per br.
de mand.* of John Cradock taken at Durham, 30 Jan., 1629/30), merchant
of Newcastle, 9 June, 1625, at St. Giles', Durham (bur. at St. Nich.,
Newcastle, 18 Feb., 1632/3), by whom she had two sons, viz. :—Thomas,
bapt., 18 Dec., 1627, at St. Nich., Newcastle (his godparents being Thos.

have established to hir by Deed out of my lands at Mainsforth),
all my dwellinghouse in Elvett for hir habitation during her life
naturall in augmentation of hir dower, joynture or maintenance,
she paying all the rents to the King and Dean and Chapter of
Durham and keeping the house in sufficient repaires, but if my
said wife doe not rest contented and satisfied with this provision
intended by me for her, but seek any other redresse or enlarge-
ment, then my will is that this my bequest concerning the house,
and all other legacie or legacies by me hereafter in this my will
to hir given, be utterly voyd and of none effect. I give also unto
my wife all the household stuff which she brought to me in
marriage, or such thereof as remaines with me at the tyme of my
death, and the sume of 50l. in lieu and satisfaction of hir thirds
of my goods and chattells of my personal estate. And whereas
my self and Sir William Chaytor, in whose name I purchased my
lands in trust, have sealed a lease to Nicholas Chaytor, Esqr.,
Arthur Hutton, clarke, Thomas Bullocke, and Robert Joplyn,
gent, dated the 25 day of January, in the 12th year of our
sovereign lord King Charles, for a advancement of my daughter
and my sonne Christopher, now dead, I doe here truely and
fully express my selfe that I have given and payed to my daughter,
Mildred Hutton, the some of 200l., which I express my self to be
soe much of my payment of hir portion, and that she shall reape
noe further benefitt of that lease then an other 150l. in lewe and
full satisfaction of hir filiall and child's portion, or any claime
to that close called the Broomhills which hir grandfather gave hir
by legacye by his last Will. All the rest of my goods, my debts,
funerall and legacies heretofore and after expressed being discharged and payed, I give unto my Three daughters, Mildred,
Garthread and Barbary, whom I doe make executors. Whereas I
have by copie of Court Rolle that cottage or tenemt in Bpp Middleham which belongs to Richard Halliday and his wife, out of which
I doe acknowledge I am but to receive 20s. per annum, I give and
bequeth halfe of that 20s. yearly to the poore of the pish of Bpp
Middleham, The other ten shillings to my Uncle Jo. Hutton and
his wife during the terme, if they live so long, and if they dye

Heath, Yealdart Alvey and Dorothy Chapman), and Henry, bapt.,
11 Nov., 1628, at St. Nich., Newcastle (his godparents being Henry
Maddison, Robert Henderson and Margaret Heath), bur. at St. Giles',
Durham, 12 Oct., 1630, and two daus., Elizabeth, bapt., 9 Jan., 1630/1,
at St. Nich., Newcastle, and Martha, also bapt. there, 27 July, 1633,
bur. at St. Giles', Durham, 15 Feb., 1636/7; she mar., thirdly, the
testator, 26 Nov., 1634, at St. Oswald's, Durham, by whom she had two
sons, Christopher and Arthur, the former bur. before his father. The
burial of the testator at St. Oswald's Durham, is recorded 1638/9,
Feb. 6, "Mr. Ralph Hutton, master of artes (he is not mentioned in
either Foster's Alumni Oxoniensis or Venn's Alumni Cantabrigiensis),
officiall to the Right Worshipfull the Deane and Chapter of Durham
and officiall to the Worshipfull the Archdeacon of Durham, a verie
religious gentleman, bountefull to the poore and needy."

before the expiration then it to come to Richard Halliday. Whereas I have by composition of Richard Bell two bushel of wheat yearly dureing the term of my moytye of the tythe corne in Bpp Middleham which I hould by lease, I give the said two bushells of wheat corne yearly to the poore of Bpp Middleham and Mainsforth, to be distributed, viz., a bushell to either towne at the discretion of the Minister and Churchwardens of the said pish. Witnesses, Henr. Hutton, Tho. Bullocke, Robt. Joplyne, Jo. Simpson.

Codicil. 2nd February, 1638. Whereas by my last Will, in writing under my hand and seal Dated the 19 day of January last past, I have nominated and constituted my three daughters, Mildred, Garthred and Barbary, Co-Executrixes of my last Will, I doe by these presence, as a Codicil to be annexed to my said Will, expressed and declare my selfe that my two younger daughters, Garthred and Barbary, onely shallbe executrixes. And I doe further give unto my said daughter Mildred my best beaver hatt and hir owne mother's best petticoate. And whereas by my said Will I have given unto my wife a legacy of 50*l*., I doe hereby declare and express my selfe that the same shallbe only 30*l*., and I also give unto her my Caskett and all my old gould and whatsoever else is therein, the key whereof I have already delivered unto hir. And I doe appoint my three brethren, Christopher, Arthur and Henry, tutors and guardians over my children to my first wife, and my wife tutor of my sonne by hir. Witnesses, Cuthbert Sisson, Ch. Hildyard, Jo. Simpson.

INVENTORY of the goods at Durham, 112*l*. 13*s*. 3*d*. INVENTORY of the goods at Mainsforth, 97*l*. 4*s*. 6*d*.

THOMAS CHAMBER.[1]

Sept. 5, 1639. Thomas Chamber of Cleadon, in the Countie of Durham, Gent., being in pfect health and memory (thanks be to almightie God). I give and devise unto my sonne, Charles Chamber, of Dagenham, in the Countie of Essex, Gent., my capitall messuage scituate in Pilgrim Streete, in the Towne of Newcastle upon Tyne, as also all cellers, sollers, yards, courts, halls, parlers, chambers, kitchins, lofts, stables, gardens, orchards, casements, with comodities, with all estate, right, interest, use, reversion, remainder, together with all and singular deeds, evidences and

[1] The testator was the son of Gervase Chamber of Kendal. He mar. Barbara, dau. of Thomas Atkinson of Monkwearmouth (bur., 29 Sept., 1637, at Whitburn), by her he had Robert, aged 23 in 1615, mar. Florence (bapt., 8 Jan., 1603/4, at St. Nich., Newcastle, her godparents being Mr. Peter Riddell, Florence Sotherne and Elinor Riddell), dau. of Charles Horsley of Newcastle, 6 Feb., 1620/1, at Whitburn, where she was bur., 4 Mch., 1628/9; Roger, mar. Susan Harrison at Whitburn, 3 Dec., 1616; Charles of Dagenham, Essex,

writings touching the same (now or late in the occupation of John Blaxton, husband of Susan, or their or either of their issues). To have and to hold the said capitall messuage, withal the premises and appurtenances, to the said Charles Chamber and his heirs for ever. Whereas my sonne, Robert Chamber, together with Robert Ferrowe, Edward Blythman and Thomas Atkinson, doe stand bound to me for payment, 430*l*., to be paid unto such persons within six months after my death, as I will nominate and appoint by will or otherwise, as by the said obligation appeareth, I give unto my sonne, Charles Chamber, 230*l*., to be paid unto him as one part of the aforesaid sum of 430*l*., and the remainder being 200*l*., to my daughter, Ann Farrow, for and unto the use of her children. I give unto Thomas Lilborn, George Lilborn, Mary Lilborne and Jane Lilborn, my grandchildren, the 20*l*. which their father is oweing me, and I leave him upon his promise to pay me within one moneth then next after, as by two severall notes under his hand may appear. I give unto William Blythman and Barbary Blythman, my grandchildren, 10*l*. I give to Mary Chamber, daughter of Robert Chamber, 10*l*. To the poore man's stock of the parish of Whiteborne, 3*l*. 6*s*. 8*d*., to be added or put to the twentie Nobles formerly by me given to make up the sume of 10*l*., to be by the Churchwardens and Overseers of the poore of the said parish for the time being, yearly put to the best and most profit they can make thereof, and the same by them to be yearely at Christmas time distributed amongst the said poore for ever. I give to Edward Blythman and Robert Ferrowe, my sonns in law, either of them, one white Ryall for a token. To Robert Chamber, my sonne, one angell of golde in full satisffaction, discharge and conclusion of a child's portion. The rest of my goods, moveable and immoveable, debts, duties, annuities, rents and arrerages whatsoever and whomsoever, due and right ought to be paid unto me (my debts, funerall charges and Churchrights being payd and defraied), I give and bequeathe to my sonne,

adm. to Gray's Inn, 16 May, 1623, matric. pens. from St. John's Coll., Cambridge, Lent, 1623/4, B.A., 1626/7, M.A., 1629, mar. Mary, dau. of . . . . Bird of Bristow, and widow of . . . . Raine and of Robert Adams, both of Dagenham; Anne, bur., 3 Nov., 1660, at Sedgefield, mar. Robert Farrow of Fishburn, 7 Dec., 1624, at Whitburn; Isabel, bur., 8 Nov., 1627, at Whitburn, mar. there as first wife to George, son of John Lilburn (bapt., 16 Jan., 1585/6, at St. Andrew's, Auckland, bur. at Bishopwearmouth, 1 Dec., 1676, aged 99), George Lilburn, mar., secondly, Eleanor, dau of John Hickes, Rector of Whitburn, and widow of Ralph Lambert of Stockton (to whom she was mar. at Whitburn, 28 Nov., 1625), 12 Apl., 1629, at Whitburn; Sarah; Mary, bur., 7 Aug., 1623, at Whitburn, where she mar. Edward Blythman of Westoe, 3 Feb., 1617/18; Alice. The testator, on the death of his wife, probably went to live with his dau., Anne Farrow at Fishburn, as in the Sedgefield registers the following entry occurs, 24 Feb., 1642/3 : " Mr. Chambers of Fishburn " bur.

Charles Chamber, whom I make and appoint my executor. Sealed
and delivered to the uses aforesaid in the presence of us, Francis
Salvin, Ric. Hutchinson. Sealed and delivered to the uses aforesaid this 21 day of October in the presence of us, Geo. Martyn,
Jo. Hull. Codicil. 22 December, 1641. I give and bequeath to my
daughter, **Agnes Farrow**, for and to the use of her children, one
danske chist and the coffer that was her mother's, which I brought
with me to ffishborne forth of my bed chamber at Cleadon, withal
things whatsoever is in them, be it lining, wollen, gold, coyned
silver, silver spoons, plate, of what kind or nature, or by what
name soever it be knowen or called. And I humbly desire that
this legacy or Codicell may be annexed to my will when as my
will shall be presented to the Ordinary to be proved. Witnesses
to same, William Thompson, Francis Salvin, Thomas Jopling.
Proved, 1643.

NICHOLAS GREENWELL.

May 12, 1640. Nicholas Greenwell of Fenhall, in the parish
of Lanchester, in the County of Durham, Yeoman. My body I
give to be buryed in the pish church of Lanchester, near unto my
father. I desire that my copyhold land at the Ford, which was
bought of George Hopper, shall be forthwith sold towards the
payment of my debts as far as it will goe, and that Anthony
Surtis of Medamsley shall receive twenty five pounds every year
during five years from the hands of William Iley, my tennant, in
full satisfaction of 100*l*. dew unto him. And my will is that my
wyfe shall have the freehold Land at Fenhall, with all thereunto
belonging, during hir life naturall, and that my wife and my son
William shall pay unto my daughter Agnes, 200*l*., when she
cometh to yeares; thirty five pounds which Mr. John Hodgson of
Manner House is oweing me, and ten pounds which my brother,
William Greenwell oweth me to be part thereof, and the rest to
be paid out of my lands, goods and chattels. My will is that my
wyfe shall fine the copyhold land which was Mr. Fairheires
according to the custom of the Court, and pass the same back
to my son William for his use. I direct my wife and my son,
William Greenwell, their heirs, executors and assigns, shall pay
yearly and every year for ever to the poor of the parish of
Lanchester, out of the freehold land of the Fenhall, the sum of
20*s*., the sum of 10*s*. at Xmas and 10*s* at Easter. I give to
Bridgett Hopper, 6*l*. 13*s*. 4*d*., to be payd at Whitsuntyde, 1644,
and to pay to George Hopper's children, the sum of twenty
markes at Whitsuntyde, 1648. To my brother John Greenwell's

children ten ewes and lambs. I give to Elizabeth Greenwell, my
brother John's daughter, one ewe and a lambe. I give to William
Greenwell, my brother John's son, one whye stirke. I give unto
my Sister, Elizabeth Bryan, one whye, and hir children, three
ewes and lambs. I give unto my sister-in-lawe Ellynor Lygton's
children, every one a yewe and a lamb. To John Kirkley's
daughter, one whye Stirke. To John Atkinson's son William, one
whye Stirke. To Thomas Hall's son Henry, one whye stirke. To
Elizabeth Atkinson, one whye stirke. To John Hopper, one ewe
and a lambe. To Frances Hopper, one cowe, and hir three
children, every one a hogge. To Robert Pye, one cowe which he
hath in his possession. To every child which I have chrisoned,
one hogge. To Jane Earle, one ewe and a lambe. To William
Hall, 10s. I give unto Robert Greenwell, son of Nicholas Greenwell's son, one whye stirke. Residue of all my goods, moveable
and unmoveable, unto my wife, Mary Greenwell, and William
Greenwell, whom I make Executors, with the assistance of John
Atkinson of Woodsyde and Thomas Hull of Hurbucke which I
make Supervisors. Probate, 1640.

SIR ROGER GRAY.[1]

Jan. 28, 1640. Sir Roger Gray of Ulchester, of the County
of Northumberland, Knight. To be buried within my vault of
Chillingham Church. I give all my houses, lands, tithes and
hereditaments to my nephew, John Gray, and his heirs for ever,
and I direct that 120l. . . . out of Ulchester upon my buriall and
funerall expences. I give to Robert Gray and Mr. Edward Gray,
10l. each. To Mrs. Mary Gray, wife of Mr. John Gray, 40l. To
Mr. Ralph Gray, sone to Mr. John Gray, 50l., and to Mr. Thomas
Gray, his second sone, 20l. To Mrs. Margaret Gray, his daughter,
20l. To Captn Richard Owen, 20l. I give to John Oliver, my
servant, 40l. To John Jobson, 6l. 13s. 4d. I give to William
Wilton, servant to Mr. John Gray, 3l. 6s. 8d. To the poor of
Chillingham, Balmbrough and Doddington, 30l. Twenty pounds
to be at the disposal of Mrs. Mary Gray, wife of my nephew,
Mr. John Gray. I give to Mrs. Ann Collingwood, widow of my
sister, 30l., and to Henry Hardman, 5l., both which legacies are
to be paid out of Stannington. I appoint my nephew, John Gray,
Executor. Probate, 1641.

---

[1] He was the 5th son of Sir Ralph Grey of Chillingham, by his
wife, Isabel, dau. of Sir Thomas Grey of Horton. He was bur. in
the Chancel of Chillingham Church. His sister, Anne, was the widow
of Thomas Collingwood of Eslington.

RAULPHE MARLARY.[1]

March 15, 1640. I, Raulphe Marlary of Pictree, in the
County of Durham, Yeoman, being sick in bodie. To be buryed
in the Church of Chester-in-the-Streete. I give to the poure of
the parish of Chester, 20s. I give to my sonne, Robert Marlery,
a lease of one third part of the lands and grounds and howse
lying and being in a place called Rickellton, in the parish of
Chester in the Street. I also give him a lease of halfe a farm
in Kibblesworthe, which lease is to come for the space of 65 years
or thereabouts. I give unto my sonne, Thomas Marllery, one other
third part of Rickellton, which . . . . Richard Hedworth of
Chester. I give unto my daughter, Katheran Marllery, the eldest
black whye going in my grounds at Pella. I give unto my sonne
in lawe, Thomas Marllary, 3l. of money which he oweth me. I give
unto Thomas Marllery his two children, each one ewe and a lamb.
I give unto my daughter, Jane Surete, wife of William Surete, 20l.
I give unto George Hall, son of Philap Hall of Pelton, one ewe
and one lambe. I doe make my wiffe Isabell sole executor, and
also I doe macke supervisors of this Will Mr. Richard Hedworth
of Chester, Phillap Hall, Ralph Lawson and Thomas Marlery,
whom I doe entreat for god his cause, to se this my Will trully
performed according to the true meaning thereof. In witness
whereof I have to this my last Will and Testament. I give unto
Ralph Lawsone, sone of Ralphe Lawson of Lumley, one ewe and
a lamb. I give unto the poore of the pish of Chester 10s. yearly,
to be payd forth of my land at Pictrye for ever after my death.
Ric. Hedworth, Ra. Surties, Senr., Roberte Colts, Ra. Lowson.
Proved, 1641.

WILLIAM SHAFTOE.[2]

Will bears no date. William Shaftoe of Whickham, in the
County of Durham, Gentleman. I give unto my brother, John
Shaftoe, all my right, title, claime and demande in and to all

[1] The testator was bur. at Chester-le-Street, 30 Apl., 1641 (from
which registers the following dates are taken). He mar., 13 July, 1619,
Isabel Wild, who was bur., 15 Dec., 1653, and by her had Robert,
bapt., 26 Mch., 1622, bur., 8 Apl., 1622; Thomas, bapt., 16 Mch.,
1622/3, bur., 27 Mch., 1623; Robert, bapt., 13 Nov., 1625; Ralph,
bapt., 15 May, 1631; Thomas, bapt., 19 Apl., 1635; Isabel, bapt.,
30 Apl., 1620; Elizabeth, bapt., 29 Aug., 1624, bur., 29 Mch., 1625;
Jane, bapt., 15 May, 1627, and bur. same day; Katherine, mar. Thomas
Morley, 23 Apl., 1639; Jane, mar. William Surrett of Newbottle,
4 June, 1638, at Houghton-le-Spring; Isabel, bapt., 4 Sept., 1636, bur.,
11 Dec., 1637; Ann, bapt., 25 Nov., 1638.

[2] The testator's father, William Shafto, who was bur., 13 Sept.,
1639, at Whickham (whence other dates are taken), by his wife,
Isabel Hedworth (bapt., 2 Dec., 1580, mar., 27 Nov., 1599, bur., 23 Apl.,
1660), had Charles, bapt., 6 Dec., 1601; John, bapt., 23 Dec., 1604,

my lands during the noneage of [the heir] male of Thomas
Shaftoe, deceased, and all my right, title, interest and demand
unto my brethren, John Shaftoe and Clement Shaftoe, in and to
all my copihold land in Whickham after the decease of my mother
and my self. Witnesses, Barthol. Pescod, Ronald Walton, Robt.
Loraine. Probate, 1641.

LANCELOT MIDFORD.

Nov. 1, 1641. Lancelot Midford. Memorandum that about
the first daie of November, 1641, the said Lancelot Midford, of
Mearsen, in the pish of Ponteland, being in perfect minde and
memorie, but sick of bodie, and desirous to make his last Will
and testament, Did by worde of mouthe, in the presence of the
witnesses undernamed, declare the same noncupatively in manner
and forme followinge, or in wordes ending to the like effect, vizt.,
He did give and bequeath unto Jaine Midforth (alias Taylor),
his illegittimate daughter, the sume of tenn poundes, and all the
rest of his goods, chattels and creditts whatsoever, he did give
and bequeathe unto Jaine, his wife, and to Gracie, his daughter,
and did constitute and make his said wife sole executrix of his
said last will. In the presence of John Spunar, William
Haddock, Richard Turner. Probate, 1641.

ROBERT HILTON.[1]

Dec. 23, 1641. In the name of God, Amen, I, Robert Hilton
of Hilton, Esquire, in the County of Durham, being weak in
body. Item, for my worldly goods I bequeath them as follows:
for my annuity of 98 years I bequeath it to my beloved wife,
Margaret Hilton, during her life, and alsoe if shee have another
husband or children to enjoy it soe long as the terme of 98 years
shall continue, and whatsoever shall belong unto me at the time
of my death I freely give unto her, and make her my sole
Executrix, and withall to dispose of the annuity at her death
to whom shee pleases.

Witnesses, Richard Hickes, Thomas Colyer, Thomas Wake.
Will Proved at Durham in the year 1641.

bur., 7 Jan., 1604/5, William (the testator), bapt., 10 Feb., 1606/7,
bur., 20 Nov., 1641; Thomas, bapt., 9 Oct., 1609, bur., 15 Nov., 1641
(he mar. Phillis Ogle, 4 Feb., 1633/4, she remar. Thomas Harrison,
5 June, 1649); Rowland, bapt., 11 Feb., 1611/12; Clement, bapt.,
25 Feb., 1612/13, bur., 29 Dec., 1659; John, bapt., 30 Dec., 1616;
Isabel, bapt., 3 Aug., 1600 (mar. Richard Inman, 17 May, 1636);
Agnes, bapt., 23 Aug., 1601 (mar. Nicholas Todd, 28 May, 1636),
Elizabeth, bapt., 22 Sept., 1602.

[1] He was the son of Thomas Hilton (whose will was dated 2 Mch.,
1597/8) by his wife, Anne, dau. of Sir George Bowes of Barnes; she
was bur. at Whitburn, 3 July, 1605.

ROGER WIDDRINGTON.[1]

March 5, 1641. Roger Widdrington of Harbottle, Esqr. Inventory of all the goods and chattels and creditts of deceased, Apprized by foure men, viz., William Clennell, George Pott, Lancelot Thirlwall and William Dunn. Imprimis : His apparell, Sword, horse, and furniture, with three watches in his pocket, tenn bloodstones, two silver Seales, a greater and a lesse, and one Gold Toothpick, one gold signet on his finger and one hundred and three pounds in his purse, value 200*l*. His books, certain Mathamatical instruments, one table with divers drawers, boxes, one little desk, divers pictures, three chairs with Quishins, one little chist with another iron chist, one silver cupp, three brason candlesticks, with other little implements, value 60*l*. There were likewise certain Webbs and other things conveyed out of the house of the said Roger Widdrington of Harbottle after the death, before Inventory or Administration taken, and the same sent away to Mr. Collingwood at Eslington by Rosamand, late wife of the said Roger Widdrington, deceased, who being thereof questioned, sent for the same againe to Harbottle by William Reevley, son to her first husband, and Barty Spinke, Servant to Mr. Cuthbert Collingwood of Eslington aforesaid, where Inventory and apprizall thereof was made. The webbs were found marked with R W for Roger Widdrington. The parcells and their prices of these things thus sent back—In Sir Ephraim Widdrington's Chamber : One bedstead and Teaster with curtings, vallence, one fetherbed, one mattrass, one bolster, two pillowes and one rugg, one trindle bedstead with one mattrass, one featherbed, one bolster, one pair of blankets, one counterpane and two happings, one little round table with a carpet, and some other implements, valued at 5*l*. 10*s*. 0*d*. The said Roger Widdrington died Seized of a Trunk, which at his death was at the house of Sir George Wentworth at Wooley in Yorkshire, brother to the said Rosamond Widdrington, late wife

[1] He was the son of Sir Edward Widdrington of Great Swinburn, [adm. dated 6 Mch., 1577/8,] by his wife, Ursula (aged 4 in 1545), dau. of Sir Reginald Carnaby of Halton ; she mar., secondly, Thomas Musgrave, Captain of Bewcastle. The testator mar., firstly, Mary, born, 1 June, 1582, dau. of Francis Radcliffe of Dilston, mar. settlement dated 18 Nov., 1601, by whom he had issue, Edward, born, 1614, created a Baronet of Nova Scotia, 26 Sept., 1635, died, 13 June, 1671, aged 57, bur. at the Church of the Capuchin Friars, at Bruges. mar. Christina, dau. of the Hon. John Stuart and granddaughter of Francis, first Earl of Bothwell, [she died before 8 Dec., 1684, bur. at St. Maurice, York;] Mary; Margaret. He mar., secondly, Rosamond, dau. of Michael Wentworth of Woolley, co. York, and widow of Bertram Reveley of Throple, mar. settlement, 22 Dec., 1632; by her he had three daus., Mary, wife of Lancelot Errington of Dunston; Clare, wife of William Orde; Margaret, first wife of Nicholas Errington of Ponteland.

of the deceased. The said Rosamond was desired by the Administrator of the said Roger, before sufficient witnesses, to give her Letter to the said Administrator for delivery of the said trunk, but she absolutely refused. The said Roger Widdrington before his death recorded in his count book the said trunk with the parcells of the goods in it this manner verbatim, signed by his owne hand, and red to the Administrator and appraizors. A Note of things left at Wooley, when I came last from thence, which was in July last, 1641. In the leather Bag: Of gold and silver imbrodered gloves, three paire. Of plaine gloves, six paire. Two wrought purses with gold and silver. One table book of silver. One sett of silver counters, viz., 38, with a silver box. Two silver boxes. Eight red silk and silver points. Two braceletts of Currall and Curralline. One black cheane. Two Black brauceletts. Two gold and thread of pearls. One piece of red plush. One silver bell. One silver hat band. One hot water Celler of plush. One black silk scarfe. Black bone lace. Five paire of silk stockings. Four silk garters. Jewels in one box, one corsaints with diamond, one pearle bracelett, one Co. . . of Gold, two gold crosses, nine gold rings. Fifteen Aggat-beads, silver Bodkins, corrall, one peece. One box with Spirit of Rosemarie. All these things are lapt in two yards and a quarter of new hollon and put in a great leather bagg. This note was left at Wooley, which Humphrey Hedley brought from thence, and which brought from thence a little Silver bell, a little silver taister for hott waters, and two Primmers, which were parcells contained in the note aforesaid. And Richard Clarke did formerly bring from Wooley a Salt silver and gilt, and a dozen plaine silver spoones, parcells of the said note also. The rest remains at Wooley in the custodie of my Neece, Mrs. Mary Olfeild, their till I send for [. . . .]

ROGER WIDDRINGTON,
6th of January, 1641.

Thus farr a true copie of the goods in the trunk aforesaid, taken out of the Countbooke of the said Roger Widdrington, as was examined and found by Mr. Edward Gray of Morpeth and Mr. George Thirlwall of Rothburie, in witness of which they subscribed there names in the Countbook of the said Roger Widdrington after his decease. It is to be noted that in the absence of the said Roger Widdrington, the Trunk above named was sent away as aforesaid by Rosamond, his wife, to avoid the Dainger of the Scotts, as she pretended. Debts: Owing to Mr. Widdrington by George Pott of Shelmore, in remainder of a late purchase due about Lammas next, 350*l*. Debts owing to him by severall persons, as appears by his Countbooks, which though they be old, we are in some hope to receive 165*l*. Owing to him by William Johnson, 26s. 8d. There is likewise divers desperate old debts owing by many severall persons in little sums to the said Mr. Widdrington, deceased, as appears by his said Count-bookes, which debts collected together amount to the Summe of four score pounds, or thereabouts. But these debts we do not adjoine to the Inventorie because it is not fitt that the Administrator be charged with that which he cannot receive. But he will enquire the sufficiency of the parties, and so much as he receives he will be accountable for, and insert it in the Inventorie.

Debts in which the said Mr. Widdrington is principall in the bond: Owing to the Executors and Administrators of the Lord William Howard, late of Naworth, as appears upon bond, 500l. Owing upon bond and other writings of Sir George Whit-moore of the City of London, Knight and Alderman, Mr. William Gibson and William Whitmoore, of the said City Merchant tailers, 1,250l., being principall and interest. More owing upon bond to the aforesaid parties, 500l., principall due ever since December, 1636, and no interest paid, this interest unpaid for five yeares amounts to 200l. Owing more upon bond to the aforesaid parties and interest, 112l. More owing upon bond, and in particular to the above named Mr. William Gibson, and interest, 112l., due the 5th day of January. Owing to Mr. Francis Nevile of Chevit in Yorkshire, the sume of 800l., as appears by bond and a Judgment confest in his Maties Court of King's Bench at Westminster in Easter tearme, in the 17th yeare of the Reign of our Sovereigne Lord King Charles. Owing to Mr. William Butcher of King Street, in Westminster, as appears by Bond and Judgment confest, 200l. Owing upon bond to Mr. Stephen Knight, belonging to Doctors Commons in London, principall and interest, 448l. There was one Mr. Addams, an Attorney in Fawkon's Court in Fleet Street, who procured 150l. of a Merchant and neighbour of his, for which sum the said Roger Widdrington is principall, and the said Mr. Addams and others bound for security, as appears by a Bond: We cannot finde as yet the name of the party to whom it is due, the interest hath run to six pounds, and in all 155l. Owing by the said Roger Widdrington to Rolland Robson of Heeley upon Coquet, 100l. Servants' wages, 8l. 9s. 4d. Other debts due to labourers, 4l. 14s. 10d.

Debts wherein the said Roger Widdrington is not principall but bond for others: One bond dated the 17th of June, 1635, in which his Nephew, Sir William Widdrington, is principall and the said Roger with others bound for security for 540l., taken up in Mr. William Gibson's Shopp above named, due to have been paid the 24th of June, 1636. One bond dated the 19th day of May, 1637, in which Mr. Henry Errington of Befront is principall and the said Roger Widdrington and others are bound for security in 300*l*. principall and 12*l*. interest, due to have been paid the 23rd of November, 1637, this money was likewise taken upp in Mr. Gibson's shopp aforesaid, in all 312*l*. There is likewise some other debts wherein the said Roger Widdrington stands bound, with Sir William Selby of Winlington or his sone William, deceased, as namely a bond wherein the principall is 1,000*l*., besides interest, due to one Mr. Humphrey Shallcross of London, in Fleet Street, Scrivenar. The said Roger Widdrington is likewise bound for the late Earl of Suffolke in divers bonds, which for the present we cannot give satisfaction, but probably we suppose it to be about 300*l*.

INVENTORY of the Leases of the said Roger Widdrington : A Lease from the Earl of Northumberland for some lands in Snitter belonging to Rothburie, which we value to 20*l*. One Lease from the Earl of Suffolke for lands at Norham, valued to 12*l*. One lease from Mark Questhead of London, fishmonger, for tythes in Norham, for which the said Roger Widdrington is bound to pay 50*l*. by yeare. The said Roger Widdrington did afterwards demise the same tythes for 50*l*. by yeare, so this lease is not to be prized. For funeral expences, as appears by several bills and reckonings, 50*l*., for black cloth for his coffin and for torches, 2*l*. 15*s*. 0*d*.

The sume of all : Sume of his goods, 1,446*l*. 14*s*. 7*d*. Sume of his debts, 6,620*l*. 0*s*. 2*d*. The debts surmounts the goods, 5,173*l*. 5*s*. 7*d*. If by mistake we have here reckoned anything to be goods of the said Roger Widdrington, deceased, which afterwards shall appear not to be his, we relinquish it, and if by oversight we have omitted to sett downe any goods of which he died seized, or if we have omitted any debts which either he was owing to others, or others to him, upon search and due finding out we will add to this Inventorie, howsoever for the present we have truly here set down according to our best Judgments, all the goods of which he died seized, of which we can have the sight, other goods there be of his in a trunk in Yorkshire, as appears by what is written above, with the friends of Rosamond, late wife of the said Roger Widdrington, of which we will take Inventorie when we can procure them to be delivered us, But for the present we cannot procure them, nor will she give the Administrator a Letter for their delivery.

Apprizors, William Clennell, George Pott, Lans. Kirkwall, William Dunn.

Administration, 7th March, 1641, to William Johnson of Cartington. The Widow renounced and admitted the said William Johnson as Administrator.

TOBIAS BLAKISTON.[1]

April 24, 1642. In the name of God, Amen, I, Tobias
Blakiston of Newton, near Durham, Gentleman. To be buried
in the parish Church, where is shall please god to call me. I
give to the poore of St. Margarett's parish in Durham, 5*l*. To
my loveing wife, Mrs. Frances Blakiston, one third part of all
my plate and household stuffe and personall estate for her life,
and to dispose of the same at her death to such children as shall
give her best content, And for the lease I have of Malton lands,
which I formerly conveyed by Indenture, bearing date 18th day
of September, 1641, unto Christopher Pearcehay of Ryton, in the
County of Yorke, Esqr., Gerrard Salvin of Croxdaile, in the
County of Durham, Esqr., and Robert Layton of West Layton, in
the Countie of Yorke, Esqr., I bequeath the same to my wife and
younger children in the Deed mentioned. And whereas I bought
of my late father a Lease of certain landes in Newton as appears
by an Indenture bearing date the 4th day of September, 1624,
which Lease I conveyed unto my two sonnes, Francis and Robert
Blakiston, by Indenture bearing date the 14th day of December,
1625, in which there was a promise whereby I might make void
the Lease, I do hereby declare that I have not done any act to
avoid the said Lease. And it is my will that my sonne, Francis
Blakiston, and my sonne, Robert Blakiston, shall have and enjoye
all the grounds in the Lease and Indenture mentioned, viz., Bosse
Meadow, Boss garthe, Pearson's closes or Harrison's closes, and
Cutley Rush, and all houses and buildings thereon. To my
sonne, Francis Blakiston, 100*l*., and to have 8*l*. a year paid to
him until the hundred is paid. Also I give unto my sonne,

[1] He was a son of Marmaduke Blakiston, Prebendary of the 7th stall
of Durham Cathedral, by his wife, Margaret James. He mar.
Frances, second dau. and coheir of Francis Briggs of Old Malton, by
his first wife, Mary, dau. of Sir Marmaduke Wyvill, of Castle Burton,
knt. and bart., at Sedgefield, 3 Oct, 1611. By her he had issue,
Marmaduke, bapt., 27 Oct., 1616 (*a*), bur., 30 Nov., 1621 (*a*); John,
bapt., 1 Feb., 1617/18 (*a*) bur., 25 Apl., 1619 (*b*); Thomas, bapt., 17
Oct., 1619 (*a*); Francis, bapt., 28 Jan., 1620/1 (*a*), adm. pens., aged 16
at Peterhouse, Cambridge, 10 Oct., 1637, Scholar, 1638, B.A., 1641/2,
Fellow, 1642, ejected, 1644, after became a Romanist, entered the
English College at Rome, 27 Oct., 1647, and died a few weeks afterwards ;
Robert, bapt., 10 Apl., 1623 (*a*), bur. at St. Oswald's, Durham, 16 Oct.,
1688 [his wife, Mary, being bur. there, 10 Dec., 1702], adm. pens., aged
16, at Peterhouse, Cambridge, 12 June, 1638; Toby, bapt., 22 Oct.,
1634 (*a*), bur., 2 July, 1680 (*a*), adm. at Gray's Inn, 21 Nov., 1654,
mar. Margaret Foster at St. Nicholas, Durham, 13 July, 1669, who was
bur., 11 May, 1703 (*a*); Elizabeth, bapt., 3 Dec., 1626 (*a*), bur., 1 Aug.,
1627 (*a*); Margaret, bapt., 22 Feb., 1628/9 (*a*), wife of Robert Lawson of
Newcastle; Mary, bapt., 5 Dec., 1631 (*a*), bur., 28 Jan. 1631/2 (*a*);
Dorothy, bapt., 13 Feb., 1638/9 (*a*), bur. 6 Apl., 1716, at Egglescliffe,
mar. Pexall Forster of Durham, who died in Durham gaol, 28 July,
1690 (*Bees diary*), bur. at St. Nicholas, Durham.

(*a*) St. Margaret's, Durham.   (*b*) Sedgefield.

Francis, the Greene cloath bedd with greene silke fringe and
vallance. I give unto my daughter, Margaret Blakiston, 200*l*.,
to be paid sixteen pounds a yeare, provided that if my said
daughter shall marrie in the lifetime of her mother and not with
her consent then she to have no benefitt in the 200*l*., but to be
equally divided amongst my younger children. To my sonne,
Tobias Blakiston, my youngest sone, 200*l*. To my youngest
daughter, Dorothy Blakiston, 200*l*. To my eldest sonne, Thomas
Blakiston (upon condition foregoing and not otherwise), Two
parts of my dwellinghouse at Newton neare Durham, with all
buildings, orchards and gardens thereto belonging, and two parts
of all my lands belonging to the Lopp of Newton to him for life
and the heires male of his body, and for want of heirs male of
his body, to the heirs males of my sone Francis, and so to the
rest of my sonnes, upon condition that all my just debts are
paid. I also give unto my eldest sonne, Thomas Blakiston, all
my goods, plate and all my household stuff, moveable and unmoveable (except what was formerly given), and I appoint my
said eldest son sole Executor. I do freely give and bequeathe
unto my loveing sonne, Francis Blakiston, and his heirs for
ever, Two parts of my lands belonging to the Lopp of Newton
and two parts of my mantion house and buildings thereto, with
all the Orchards and gardens whatsoever, excepting the lands
formerly devised. And my hearty desire is that my wife during
her life will be kind and loveinge to my sone, Thomas Blakiston,
if he amend his course of life and live pleasinge unto her and
my friends. Witnesses, Michaell Hall, William Page, Thos.
Wardell, and Tobias Ingram.

This day being the first of June, I doe race out All that I did
intend my sonne Robert was to have by this my Will, 1646.

These are to Certifye all to whom it doth and may concerne
that on the foure and twentieth day of December, 1646, John
Blakeston, of the towne and County of Newcastle-on-Tyne, Esqr.,
one of the Members of the Honble house of Comons of the Parlia-
ment of England, appeared before the R. Worl Sir Nathaniell
Brent, Knight, Doctor of Lawes, and by ordinance of Parliament
constituted Judge of the Progative Court, and in the presence of
Marke Cottle, Not. Publique and a Deputy Registrar, in the said
Court alledged that Tobie Blakiston, late of Newton, in the
County of Durham, Esqr., his nrall and lawful Brother, whiles
he lived made his last Will and Testament, whereof he nominated
Thomas Blaickeston, his eldest sonn, executor, and then departed
this life, Thomas, his sonne and Executor, then surviving, and
that the said Thomas had by his letters and otherwise shortly
after the deceased's death signified and declared his readines to
take upon him the execution of his said father's will, but dyed
leaveing the same uneffected, and to the end the said Tobye's
estate might be the better pserved and his will effectually

pformed, and being desired by Tobye and Dorothie Blaickeston, children of the said Tobie, to take them into his custody and ptection, they being both in their minoritye, he desired Letters of Administration of the said deceased's estate to be granted unto him; whereupon the said Judge, well weighing the premises and other reasons then suggested, did give an oath unto the said John, well and truly to pforme the deceased's will according to the true meaning thereof, to and for the use of the deceased's children, as also the children of the said Thomas, and ordered tuition should be given for the pformance thereof and then granted him Letters of Administration, with the Will annexed, of the said deceased's estate during the said children's minoritie. And the said John was accordingly Sworne, and entered bond with Suertie in the penall sume of 500*l*., for the due and true Administration of the same estate according to the condition of the said bond remaining in the registry of the said court, dated the 26th day of December, 1646. Proved, 9 Jan., 1646.

ANN   HUTTON.[1]

May 7, 1642. In the name of God, Amen, I, Ann Hutton, of the parish of St. Maries, in the South Bayley, within the City of Durham, in the County of Durham, Widow, being sickly and weak in body. To be buried in the parish church yard of St. Maries aforesaid, soe near to my late deceased mother, Eleanore Bethell, and as convently may be, when it shall please God to call me forth of this transitory life. As for my worldly estate, I dispose of it as follows:—Whereas my late deceased husband, Mr. Matthew Hutton, late of Bishop Auckland, by his last Will in writing and Testament under his hand and seale, bearing date the eleaventh day of December, 1623, gave, legate and bequeathed unto me, the said Ann Hutton, one burgage situate in Auckland aforesaid, wherein Robert Watson then dwelt, during my life naturall, and also a close called Pannyers with the appurtenances, and after my death and decease the said house and close to descend and come to William Stephenson, his grandsone, now

<hr/>

[1] Her mother, Eleanor Bethel, widow " anus " was bur. at St. Mary-the-less, Durham, 23 Jan., 1626/7, where the testatrix was also bur., 20 June, 1643. Her husband, Matthew Hutton, bailiff, of Bishop Auckland, was bur. at St. Andrew's, Auckland, 13 Dec., 1623 (see note, page 172); their only child, Elizabeth, mar. Humphrey Stephenson, mar. bond dated 28 Apl. (*sic*), 1612, mar., 30 Feb., (*sic*), 1611/12, at Houghton-le-Spring; by him she had William, bapt., 1 Apl., 1613, at St. Andrew's, Auckland; Matthew, bapt. there, 10 Apl., 1614; Timothy, bapt., there, 7 July, 1616; Francis, bapt. there, 27 Sept., 1618; Humphrey, bapt. at St. Mary-le-Bow, 18 June, 1622; Elizabeth, bapt. at St. Mary-the-Less, 22 Dec., 1620, and bur. there, 18 Jan., 1620/1; Elizabeth, bapt. there, 10 May, 1626; Anne, bapt. there, 1 Apl., 1629.

also late deceased, and his heirs for ever, and for want of issue of his body the said house and close to accrue and descend to his sone-in-lawe, Humphrid Stephenson, father of the said William Stephenson, and his heires for ever, which said house and close is since sold, and with the consent of the said Humphrey Stephenson, and likewise the said William Stephenson being dead without issue of his body, I therefore by this my Will doe give and bequeath unto the said Humphrey Stephenson the sume of Three score pounds of good and lawful money of England, in consideration and full satisfacon of his house and close aforesaid to him soe bequeathed, and by the death of the said William Stephenson without issue to him of right soe descending as aforesaid, I give unto him Tenne pounds for a legacy, and to his wife Elizabeth, my naturall daughter, other Tenn pounds for a legacy. It is my will and I doe hereby declare that my grandsonne, Mathew Stephenson, shall peaceably enter into possession and enjoy one burgage situate in Newgate, within the Burrowe of Auckland aforesaid, after my death and decease, according to the true intent and meaninge of my late husband's, Mr. Matthewe Hutton, his will aforesaid. Also I give unto the said Mathew Stephenson the sum of Tenn poundes for a legacy. I give unto Tymothie Stephenson the sum of Tenn pounds for a legacy. I give unto Humphrid Stephenson the younger, my grandsonne, the sum of of Tenn poundes for a legacy. And if it please Gode that any of my three grandsonns, Mathew, Tymothie or Humphrid Stephenson the younger aforesaid, shall die without issue of their body lawfull begotten before the legacies to them given hereby be satisfied and paid, Then my will is and I doe hereby that the legacy or legacies of such soe deceased without issue as aforesaid shall descend to the survivor or survivors of them, equally to be divided equally amongst them, And these several legacies I appoint to be paid by my executor soe soone as money can be raised out of my estate after my death. I give and bequeath to Elizabeth Stephenson, my grand daughter, the sume of Thirtie poundes, and to Anne Stephenson, my grandaughter, other Thirty pounds. And I desire my executor hereunder named to employ the same to the best benefitt and advantage for their use till they come to lawful age or be married, and the benefit thereof soe arising by his lawfull endeavours to be for their maintenance in . . . . and good education. I give to my loving friend, Gilbert Marshall, a Twenty shilling peace of gold for a token. All the rest of my goods, chattells and creditts, moveable and unmoveable, whatsoever not hereby given and bequeathed, I give unto my loveing son in lawe, Humphrid Stephenson, whom I constitute and appoint my full and sole Executor of this my last Will and Testament, hereby renouncing and making utterlie void all other and former Wills heretofore by me made, to all intents and purposes in the lawe, and this my present Testament to be in

full force and effect, requiring my said Executor to see my
funerall honestlie performed and duly discharged, and to extend
such charitible almes to the honest, decaid poore people (and
not to the lewd, impudent vagabonds) as he in his discretion
shall think fitt, according to the trust which in him I doe repose.
Witnesses, Richard Foster, John Forster, Elder, Gilbt.
Marshall. Proved, 1647.

WILLIAM KILLINGHALL.[1]

July 8, 1642. In the name of God, Amen, I, William Killinghall of Middleton George, in the County of Durham, Esqr., being
in good and pfect health and rembrance, prased be my Lord
Jesus therefor, but old and therefore fitt for me to prepare
myne selfe for that life which lasteth for ever. To be buried
amongst my ancestors att Middleton aforesaid, but without pomp,
vaine glory or unnecessary affectacon or charges, but if I die
not att or near home then to be buried where it shall
please almightie God to appoint. As for my worldly goods, my
desire is that they be prased to the full worth without favor or
fraud, that soe my wife and children may have there severall
due parts thereof without contencon, being each of them content
peacefully to accept of what I have hereby given them in lieu
and full satisfacon of their severall filiall porcons, in respect
that divers of them have alreadie received some part of their
porcons by me intended them. And first therefore out of that
part which I may by my Will dispose of, I give to my loving
wife all her jewells, my silver cann, six spoones, my lesser silver
salt, two beds furnished, and what maire she will chuse, alsoe
I give to my sonne John. my evidence chist, my painted deske,
my brew leed, and the next mare with foale, and other furniture,
hopeing he will be loveing and kind to my wife and children.
And whereas I have a close or halfe oxgange of land in Midleton, one . . . . by grant from Alice Midleton, widow, and Thomas

[1] The testator was son of Henry Killinghall (bur. at Middleton
St. George, 11 Apl., 1620) by Anne (mar. at Hurworth, 21 Oct., 1572,
bur. at Middleton St. George, 5 Aug., 1617), dau. of Robert Layton of
Sproxton. The testator was bur., 29 May, 1644, at Middleton St. George
having mar., firstly, Susan, dau., of John Moore of York (bapt., 15 Apl.,
1576, at St. Michael-le-Belfrey, York, where she was mar., 6 May, 1600).
By her he had John, bur., 30 Jan., 1651/2, at Hurworth, mar. Margaret,
dau. of William Lambton of Great Stainton, 2 May, 1637, at Haughton-
le-Skerne, bur., 18 Mch., 1691/2, at Middleton St. George; Robert;
Henry; Thomas, bapt., 21 July, 1607, at Sockburn, bur., 24 June, 1663,
at Middleton St. George; George, bapt., 16 Mch., 1608/9, at Sockburn;
William, bapt., 10 Apl., 1617, at Sockburn, adm. pens. (age 17), at St.
John's Coll., Camb., 28 June, 1634; Catharine, bur., 10 Nov., 1670, at
Middleton St. George; Susan, bapt., 31 May, 1610, at Sockburn, mar.
William Nelson of Southwark; Margaret, bapt., 9 May, 1614, at
Sockburn. The testator mar., secondly, Margaret Pepper, 11 July, 1625,
at Middleton St. George.

Wilkinson, her sonne, I doe give and bequeath the same and all my right herein to my son, John Killinghall, to be estated and assured as my other landes formerly to him conveyed, he, the said John, his heirs and assigns, paying 50*l*. for the same to my sonne, Robert Killinghall, his heirs or assigns, within one year next after my death, which if he refuse to pforme, then I doe hereby give and bequeath the same to my sonne, Robert Killinghall, his heires and assigns for ever. Also I give to my daughter, my sonne John's wife, my silke curtains and vallance, as a token of my love and affection, And I give to my said sonne Robert all my schole books and law books, with desire he may make good use of them and follow that profession. And whereas also I have estated all my lands to Sir Thomas Layton and Joseph Conyers, to such uses as in the Indenture are expressed, and have hereby appointed them to receive and take 200*l*. out of the rents, issues and pfitts of the said lands, to be disposed of as I shall appoint, now my desire and will is that as well the said 200*l*., as also all other monies due by any manner or means and waies to my two sonns, Robert and Henry, be imployed and bestowed in the purchase of some land, to be estates to my sonne Robert in such sort as I have alreadie estated my other land, and saveing that next after Robert they shall come to Henrie, and then to John, but in such manner according to the limitacon of the sayd former estate, saving as aforesaid, and of which my will is that my sonne Henrie have an annutie of 14*l*. per annum for his life, in full satisfacon and discharge of all his porcon, in respect the same is wholly to be bestowed in purchasing such lands, And my daughter Katherine, six pounds per annum during her life, in full satisfacon and discharge of her porcon, in regard I have given her a good part alreadie, and both the said annuities to be paid at Pentecost and Martinmas by equal porcons, or within twentye days after the first payment, to begin at Martinmas next after my death. Alsoe I give to Sir Thomas Widdrington and Cuthbert Pepper and their heirs, for the use, benefitt and behoof of my sonne Robt., the next psentacon which shall happen after my death, of that part of my parsonage which Mr. Joseph Cradock hath. And whereas also I have a lease from the said Mr. Cradock of that part of the parsonage which he hath at the yearly rent of 10*l*., during the life of the said Joseph Cradock, granted in my sone John's name in trust, whereof nevertheless I doe receive the benefitt, I doe hereby give the said lease and all the benefitt and pfitt thereof to my sonne Robert for his better maintenance, to be educated in learning. And whereas also Christopher Hall is indebted to me, by his bill taken in the name of Wm. Mantle, in the sum of 50*l*., my will is that the money recovered thereupon may be employed towards the purchase of lands for the use of my sone Robert, in such manner as is before pscribed. And whereas I have an estate of certaine lands in Great Stainton in fee simple, I do hereby give and bequeth all the said lands to my sone, Robt. Killinghall, and his heires for ever, to be estated as aforesaid, saveing if he die without issue male, then the same to come and descend to my grand-child, Wm. Killinghall, to be estated as my other lands, and to his father. And whereas I have alreadie payd my sonne Thomas all his porcon, I doe nevertheless give to his eldest sone, Thomas, 5*l.*, to be paid one yeare after my death, if he be then living, and to my daughter, his wife, 10*s.*, for a remembrance. Also I give to my sone Wm., 50*l.*, in full discharge of his filiall porcon, to be paid one yeare after my death if he be then living. Also I give to my daughter, Susan Nelson, 10*l.*, to be paid within one yeare after my death if she be then living, in full discharge of her porcon. And my further will is that if any of my children refuse to accept peaceably of what I have given them and in such manner, that such opposing the same shallbe absolutely deprived and frustrate of all such benefitt as by this my will may any way accrue or seame due unto them. And my further will is that my sonn John may have my brew vessell and the lead cisterne in the Kilne, and all such other implements of house-hold stuff and husbandry as my Executors can spare (if he require the same), at such reasonable rates as they shallbe praised att by indifferent men. Also I give my brother Francis a mare or fillie, to be appointed by my wife and sonne John, and such suite of my apparell as himselfe will weare for my sake, and to his wife, 5*s.* Also I give to my sister Margery, 10*s.*, and to my sister Katherine, 40*s.*, and to every one of my wives daughters, a noble, to be made in rings to weare in remembrance of me. And I doe lastly give to the poor of Midleton parish, 20*s.*, to be paid yearly by the space of three yeares after my death out of the lands due to my sonne Robert. All the rest of my goods and chattells, moveable and unmoveable, my debts, legacies and funeral expences discharged, I give and bequeath to my wife and sonne Robert Killinghall, whom I make Executors of this my Will, trusting that she will bestowe the greatest part thereof for his use and benefit. And I doe comitt the tuicon and education of my two sonns, Robert and Henry, to my wife, to-gether with the advice, consent and assistance of Sir Tho. Laiton and Sir Thomas Widdrington, Knt., John Wytham and Cuthbert Pepper, Esqr., whom I do require to be supervisors of this my last Will, hoping they will endeavour to see the same truly executed and pformed according to my intencon and trust in them, for which their care and pains during their charge and born by my Executors, I give to each of them a noble to weare in a ringe for remembrance of me. In witness whereof to this my Will being all written with my own handes, I have sett my hand and seale the day and yeare above written. Witnesses, Margaret Pepper, Thomas Rickaby. Proved, 1649.

JOHN PEMBERTON.[1]

Jan. 26, 1642. In the name of God, Amen, I, John Pemberton, of Aisleby, in the County of Durham, Esqr., being sick in body but of good and p̄fect remembrance. To be buryed in the p̄ish church of Egglescliffe. And for the p̄sonall and temporall estate wherewith it hath pleased god to bless me withall I doe hereby give, devise and dispose of the same in man̄r and forme followeinge, first I doe give and bequeath unto Henry Pemberton my youngest sonne in full recompence and satisfaction of all such filiall part or porcon, and other advancement as he should expect for me or outt of my estate, one annutie or annual rent of 40*l.* per year of lawful English money to be yearly issuing outt of all my lands, tents and hereditaments whatsoever situate, lyeing and being in Aisleiby aforesaid, to hold the said annuity or annuall rent of 40*l.* unto the said Henry Pemberton and his assigns immediately from and after my decease, for and during the terme of his naturall life payable, and to be paid yearly unto the said Henry Pemberton or his assigns at the feasts of Pentecost and St. Martins the Bpp in winter by equall porcons or within twenty dayes after either of the said feasts. I doe give and bequeathe in the like man̄r unto my daughter, Anne Pemberton, one other annity of 20*l.* per annum of like mony to hold to her and her assigns for and dureing the terme of her liefe naturall to be issuing outt of all my said lands, tents and hereditaments in Aisleibye aforesaid, and payable in man̄r aforesaid. I doe give and bequethe in like man̄r unto my daughter, Jane Pemberton, one other annutie or annual rente of 20*l.* per annum of like money to hould to her and her assigns for the terme of her lief naturall to be issueing out of my said lands, tents and hereditaments in Aisliebye aforesaid, payable in man̄r and forme aforesaid. I doe give and bequeth unto John Pemberton and Henry Pemberton, my sonns, and to Robert Thorpe of Long Newton in the said County of Durham, Gent., one other annuity or annual rent of 16*l.* of like mony to be yearlye issueing out of all my said lands, tents and hereditaments above mentioned, to hould to them the said John

[1] He was the son of Michael Pemberton of Aislaby (bur., 2 Jan., 1624/5, at Egglescliffe, from which Registers others dates are taken), by his wife, Margaret, dau. of Ralph Watson of Tuddoe (bur., 27 Jan., 1634/5). He mar. Isabel, dau. of Henry Grey of Newminster, 8 June, 1612, at Grindon, she bur., 19 Feb., 1624/5 (her sister, Mary, mar. Toby Ewbank, 31 Jan., 1613/14, at Grindon). By her he had Michael, bapt., 17 Apl., 1615, bur., 6 Mch., 1650/1, mar., Alice, dau. of Christopher Place of Dinsdale (she remar. John Garnett of Egglescliffe, 23 Aug., 1652); John bapt., 22 Nov., 1618; Henry, bapt., 20 Apl., 1620; Mary, bapt., 30 Nov., 1613, mar. Ralph Hurst of Ashe, co. York; Margaret, bapt., 18 Sept., 1617; Anne, bapt., 14 Oct., 1621, mar. Robert Thorp of Yarm, co. York; Jane, bapt., 22 Feb., 1623/4, mar. William Theobalds of Egglescliffe. The testator, aged 34, at the *Inq. p.m.* of his father taken at Durham, 11 June, 1625, was bur., 28 Jan., 1642/3.

Pemberton, Henry Pemberton and Robt. Thorpe and their assigns imediately from and after my decease for and dureing the life naturall of my daughter, Mary Hurste, wife of Railph Hurste, payable in such sorte as is aforesaid, to the intent and purpose that they the said John Pemberton, Henry Pemberton and Robt. Thorpe or their assigns shall satisfie and pay the said annuity or annual rent of 16*l*. as the same is received unto the said Mary Hurste for and towards her maintenance and to noe other. I doe give and bequethe to my grandchilde, Railphe Hurste, one anuity or annuall rent of 6*l*. of like mony to be issuing out of all my said lands, tents and hereditaments aforesaid, to hould to him and his assigns from and after my decease for the terme of tenn yeares payable att the tymes aforesaid. I doe give and bequeth unto my anciente servante, George Dent, for and in respect of his service allredy done one annuity or annual rent of 3*l*. of like mony, to be issuing out of my said lands, tents and hereditaments, together with the house and garth now in his possession for the terme of his lief naturall, the said anutie to be paid as aforesaid. I doe give and bequeath unto my sister, Florence Pemberton, one anuity or annual rent of 10*l*. of like monye to be yearlye issuing forth of my said lands, tents and hereditaments for the terme of her lief naturall, payable as aforesaid, which is the same anuity formerly given her by my deceased father and hitherto paid by me. And my will and mind is that if it fortune that any of the said annities above mentioned or any part thereof shall be behind and unpaid in part or in all by the space of twenty dayes after either of the said feasts or dayes limited for payment thereof, that it shall and may be lawfull to and for every or any of the said parties to whom the said anutie or anuities as granted as aforesaid, or their assignes to enter into all or any of the said lands, tents or hereditaments above mentioned, and distraine, and the goods then and there founde to leade, drive, chase, and carrye away of the same to determine and keepe untill the said severall anuities with the arreages thereof if any be fully satisfied and paid. I doe give and bequeath unto my grandchild, Samuel Hurste, sonne of my daughter, Mary Hurste, the sum of 10*l*. of lawful English monye to be paid unto him within twelve months of my decease. I doe give and bequeth unto my neece, Elizabeth Garnett, 20*s*. for a token. I doe give and bequeth unto my daughters, Anne Pemberton and Jane Pemberton all my household stuff and utensills of household whatsoever within my dwellinghouse at Aisleiby (the lumber stuff within the same and my plowe geere and waine geere only excepted), and except the Beddsteade in the great chamber and the maids furniture and bedding thereto belonginge and my greate quilte . . . . Salt. Whereas I have allready by my writeing under my hand and seale granted, demised, and to farm letten unto my sonne, John Pemberton, for his pferment and advancement all my lands, tents and hereditaments wheresoever

situate, lyeing and being in Tuddo in the said County of Durham
for the terme of one thousand yeares, I doe hereby ratify and
confirm and demise the same and doe hereby give all the rents. I
doe give and bequeath unto my daughter, Ann Pemberton, in
further and full satisfacon of her filiall and child's portion, the
sume of three score pounds of lawful English monye to be paid
within . . . . months after my decease. I doe give and bequeath
unto my daughter, Jane Pemberton, in like manner the like sum
of three score pounds of like money as aforesaid. Whereas I
am indebted in somes of monye by bonds, and therefore to the
intente that the sume may be really paide, and my annityes and
legacies faithfully and truly satisfyed and paid, and for the better
settling of my lands, tents and hereditaments in my name and
bloode, and well hopeing that Michael Pemberton my eldest sonne
and heir to whom I will and bequeathe the same will well and
truly execute and pforme this my last Will and Testament in all
points according to my true intention and meaninge, I doe hereby
in consideration thereof give and bequeath unto my said sonne,
Michael Pemberton, and to his heires and assigns for ever, all that
my Manor of Aislieby, with the appurtenances in the County of
Durham, and all other my landes, tents and hereditaments whatsoever in Aislieby aforesaid with that and every the appurtenances,
provided alwayes nevertheless and my true intent and meaninge
is and if my said sonne, Michael Pemberton, his heires or assigns
shall or doe neglect or refuse to perform this my last Will and
Testament by non-payment of the several annuities and legacies
above mentconed, and not pay my debts in a schedule hereunto
annexed, set down and specified that then this my bequest to him,
the said Michael Pemberton, be utterly frustrute and void to
all intents and purposes whatsoever, and then I give and bequethe
all my said lands, tents and hereditaments whatsoever above
mentioned unto Tobyas Ewbank of Egglestone and Robt. Thorpe
of Long Newton, in the said County of Durham, Gent., their
heires and assigns for ever to the intent and purpose that they
the said Tobyas Ewbank and Robt. Thorpe, their heires and
assigns shall make saile of the said lands, tents and hereditaments,
and outt of the monyes begotten for the same so satisfye, pay
and discharge all the severall debts in the schedule hereto annexed,
and the severall legacies above mentioned, yett my meaninge is
that if the same be sould subject to the said severall annities above
menconed, and after the same soe paid and satisfied to satisfie
and pay the overplus thereof to my said sonne, Michael Pemberton,
his heires or assigns, and in hope that my said sone, Michael
Pemberton, will (as my trust is in him) pforme this my Will and
Testament. All the rest of my goods and chattels, whatsoever
nott hereinbefore bequeathed, my debts, legacies, and funeral
expences discharged, I doe hereby give and bequethe unto my said
sonne, Michael Pemberton, whom I make and ordeane hereby my

0

full and sole Executor of this my last Will and Testament. And
I doe pray and intreat my well beloved brother in law Tobyas
Ewbank and my loveing and kind friend Robt. Thorpe, super-
visors of my Will. Witnesses, John Garnett, Jo. Pemmerton,
Junior, Nic. Lodge.

INVENTORY: Debts oweing by testator, Mr. Harvey, by obligacon and use, 500*l*, Mr. Henry Di . . . by 100*l*., Mr. Chris
Bye . . . y 100*l*. Proved, 1648.

SAMPSON LEVER.[1]

Jan. 14, 1642. In the name of Gode, Amen, I, Sampson
Lever, of Alden Rigg, in the pish of St. Oswalds, in the
County Pallentyne of Durham, Gentleman, the unprofitable
servante of god, weake in body. For as much as noe
learned Councell can be gotten for the making of this my
last Will and Testament in such forme as were fitting, therefor
whatsoever is wanting in points of law may be supplied in equity.
I doe hereby deliver my true intent and meaning, that all may be
disposed accordinge thereunto. And first whereas my lease of
Aldridge is in my sone Robert Lever's name, neither is nor was
estated to him with any intencion frome me that he should have
any proffitt thereby, but upon the pforming of certain covenants
mentionced in Indentures drawne by Mr. Pleasance, which indentures I not having heare, can not particularise and sett downe
the daite; yet this I affirme that he haith already failed in pforming covenantes soe as by the true intente of my passing an estate
to him, and he passing likewise an estate to me. The whole
interest is now wholy myne absolutely to dispose of at my pleasure,
howsoever any defect or clause may be in the indenture to the
contrary. Now, for as much as it is fitting that I should dispose
of all things belonging to me whilst I live as that there may be

[1] The family of Lever of Little Lever, in Lancashire, appear to
have held a number of ecclesiastical appointments in the Counties of
Durham and Northumberland, John Lever, the grandfather of the
testator, had, perhaps with other issue, two sons, Thomas, the father
of the testator (of whom presently), and Ralph, the latter, B.A., 1547/8,
M.A., 1551, B.D., 1578, Fellow, 1549, of St. John's College, Camb., R.
of Washington, 1560, archdeacon of Northumberland, R. of Howick,
1566-74, Preb. of Durham, 1567-85, R. of Stanhope, 1575-7, Master of
Sherburn Hospital, 1577-85, died, 15 Mch., 1584-5, bur. at Durham
Cathedral, mar. Margaret, bur. at Durham Cathedral, June, 1616,
having remar. Thomas Walter of Whitwell. Thomas, the testator's
father, born at Bolton, was Fellow of St. John's Coll., Camb., 1543,
M.A., 1545, B.D., 1552, Master of that college, 1551-3, archdeacon of
Coventry, 1560-77, Master of Sherburn Hospital, 1563, Preb. of Durham,
1564, died, July, 1577, bur., at Sherburn; he had, perhaps with other
children, a dau., Anne (will dated 12 Nov., 1607), who mar. Robert Swift,
Preb. of Durham and R. of Sedgefield, 1562-99, bur. at Durham
Cathedral, and the testator, Sampson. He matriculated pens. from St.
John's Coll., Camb., 1578, and was bur. 7 Mch., 1649/50, at St.

no contrarie amongst my children when I am gone, therefore my whole right and estate which I have in Aldridge aforesaid, I, by this my last Will and Testament doe give unto my sone, Henry Lever, to dispose of according to this my direction hereafter following. Provided alwayes that if my said son Henry shall either refuse to do it, or that his brother Robert, my son, also will not perform all things according to my said direcons, then my Will is and I hereby appoint my eldest sone, Thomas Lever, to enter upon Aldridge and to dispose thereof, as his brother Henry Lever should have done by this my direction following. Now my direction is this that, whereas my son, Robert Lever, within a short tyme . . that he shall enter upon Aldridge by the virtue of the indentures before said, may not enter before he have given good security to perform all covenants agreed upon betwixt him and me, and that I am verely perswayded that he can procure no such security without the sayle of the said Lease of Aldridge, and for that after my death all my children have equall share therein, it being a Lease, a Chattell and now absolutely and wholly in mine own handes, therefore (as before) I give to my aforesaid sone, Henry Lever, to dispose thereof and to pay to my daughter Wikcliffe, one hundreth poundes within half a year after his entering, and to discharge all such debts as are oweing by me. And furthermore I doe hereby make him sole Executor of this my last Will and Testament for his better disposing thereof. Provided allwayes that if he refuse to be my executor for the disposing of this my aforesaid lease of Aldridge then I doe constitute and appoint my eldest sonne, Thomas Lever, my sole executor to enter upon Aldridge and to dispose thereof as his brother Henry Lever failed to do. Now that it may appeare how matters stand betwixt my aforesaid sonne, Robert Lever and me, these are to testify that I upon over much naturall affection to him, he being but my third sone. did first pass my Estate in Aldridge to

Oswald's, Durham. His wife, Margaret, dau. of Philip Hall of Wingate Grange, was bur., 8 July, 1622, at St. Oswald's, Durham. By her he had Thomas; Robert, a merchant in York (who had a son, Robert, bapt. at St. Crux, York, 3 Aug., 1624, adm. pens. (age 17) at Sidney Coll., Camb., 21 June, 1642, migrated as sizar to St. John's, 24 Feb., 1644/5, B.A., 1645/6, V. of Bolam, 1646-60, from which living he was ejected and died, 1 July, 1690, aged 65, having mar. Margaret (bur., 4 Mch., 1715/16, at St. Oswald's, Durham, dau. of Robert Dyneley of Bramhope, Leeds); Ralph; Henry, adm. sizar at Sidney Coll., Camb., 22 Mch., 1623/4, bapt., 18 Jan., 1606/7, at St. Oswald's, Durham, V. of Longhoughton, 3 Feb., 1640/1, R. of Brancepeth, 1644, silenced, 1662, bur. 6 June, 1673, at St. Nich., Newcastle, he mar., firstly, Elizabeth (bur. 13 Jan., 1636/7, at Whitburn), by whom he had a dau., Margaret, bapt., 12 Jan., 1636/7, at Whitburn, where she was bur., 6 Aug., 1638, secondly, 4 Dec., 1637, at Whitburn, Elizabeth dau. of John Hickes, R. of Whitburn and widow of Thomas Dixon of Whitburn, bur., 24 Dec., 1661, at St. Nich., Newcastle; thirdly, Christian Blackett, mar. bond dated 9 June, 1668, bur., 7 Nov., 1696, at St. Nich., Newcastle; a dau. who mar. Robert Thompson and Dorothy, mar. William Wycliffe, 10 Aug., 1624, at Houghton-le-Spring.

him upon covenantes that I should enjoy it during my life, and afterwards also he was soon after his entry to pay certaine sums of money to such as I should nominate and Tenn pounds yearly for seven yeares, moreover he being in great want of money and borrowing one hundred poundes of one Mr. George Martin, for the right was to pay thirty one pounds six shillings and eightpence for ten yeares I engaged some of my ground at Aldridge to Mr. Martin for security, and thereupon had the lease of Aldridge conveyed back to me again their upon (for to prevent the forsetting of my aforesaid ground), I have been forced to pay some of the yearlie rents to Mr. Martin soe as upon accompte he at this instant is indebted to me four score and nyne poundes, there are also two years and a half rent yet to pay to Mr. Martin, which cometh to seaventy eight poundes six shillings and eight pence, both which cometh to 167*l*. 6*s*. 8*d*., besides a bond wherein I am bound for him to my son-in-law, Mr. Robert Thompson, furthermore if I should return Aldridge to him againe, then were he to pay fifty poundes within half a yeare and tenn pounds for seven yeares to such as I shall nominate and for all these were good security to be given, furthermore whereas the estate of my said sonne, Ralphe Lever, deceased, doth wholly belong to me, I doe hereby declare that I have imployed my son, Samuell Lever, to take the Administration of my said sonne Railph Lever's goods in his owne name for my only use, And therefore by this Will I direct, sett downe and appoint that all his estate be equally divided among my children, my sonne, Thomas Lever, having already been allotted one hundred and fifty pounds, and my sonne, Samuell Lever, four score and tenn pounds, and my sonne, Robert Lever, tenn pounds. And I will that my sonne, Samuel Lever, be allowed reasonable charges for his costs and paynes in getting the administration, and all such goods and debts as did belong or were oweing unto my said sonne, Ralph Lever. Moreover, whereas Skuts house is houlden in Soccage tenure, soe that I may dispose thereof at my own pleasure, then upon naturall affection to my sone, Henry Lever, I doe give unto him a yearly annuity of Tenn pounds of good and lawful English money per annum to be paid unto him or his assignes in maner and forme followinge for and during his life naturall of him the said Henry and his now wife, Elizabeth, that is to say five poundes to be payd to him or his assigns, the twenty fifth day of June next after my decease, and five poundes the twenty fifth day of December next after that day, and soe yearlie tenn pounds during their lives or the longest liver of them at the days aforesaid. And if the said rent of five pounds be unpayed upon any date that it is due then for every twenty dayes that is unpayed, he shall have five shillinges for the want thereof, and further he or his assigns shall have liberty and power to enter upon any of the grounds of the said Skutshowse, and to take, lead, drive or carry away and sell what

cattell or goods they shall fynde therein, and pay themselves all
that shall be due and unpayd with their reasonable costs and
charges which they shall be at about the same. Now for my
howse and land at Skutshowse I give it to my sone, Samuel Lever,
to have and to hold soe and during his life naturall. Provided
alwayes that upon any waiste made of howse, lands or woods, his
estate, right and title to be utterlie voyd and the house, landes,
and inheritance therof to come to the heires male of his bodye
lawfully begotten, And for default of such heires male then to come
to my sonne, Henry Lever, for and during his life naturall upon
the like provisoes of forfetting his right and estate upon making
any waiste, and the inheritance thereof to come to the heire male of
his body lawfully begotten, and for default of such heires male to
come to my sonne, Robert Lever, and during his life naturall, upon
the like proviso of forfetting his right, title and estate upon
making any waiste, And the inheritance to come to the heire
male of his body lawfully begotten, and for default of such heire
male, Then the inheritance to come to the heire or heires generall
of me the aforesaid Sampson Lever. And I doe further hereby
authorise my sone, Samuel Lever, to make a jointer of six poundes
thirteen shillings and fourpence to his wife for and during her
life naturall if she shall have . . . . Now for as much as my
desire is that this my Will may be performed without trouble,
therefore I doe give my house, land and inheritance of Skuts-
house to my sone, Henry Lever, for him to dispose thereof according to this my last Will before specified, and for that he should
not fayle in doing thereof. I doe therefore appoint that within
one monthe next after my death before any office thereof be found
he shall enter into sufficient bond to my sonns Samuel Lever and
Robert Lever that neither he or any other in his right shall take,
have to doe or medle with any woods or quarries. And furthermore that he shall see this my said house and ground of Skutshowse rightly disposed thereof according to this my last Will and
Testament, to that end I hereby give him as full power to doe
it as if I myself did it, or were then living and there present to
do it. Witnesses, Robert Carr, Robert Penn, Willm. Hunter.
Proved, 1649.

THOMAS TROLLOPP.[1]

July 9, 1644. In the name of God, Amen, I, Thomas Trollopp
of the City of Durham, Gent., sicke of bodye. To be buried
where my executors shall think fitt. I give to Wm. Trollopp, my

[1] The testator, an attorney-at-law, was bur. at St. Nicholas, Durham,
15 July, 1644, his wife being Dorothy, dau. of Anthony Busby of Cassop;
his son, Francis, bapt., 8 May, 1638, at St. Nicholas, where he was
bur., 11 May, 1646, his dau., Mary, was also bapt. there, 15 May, 1634.
There is a pedigree of this family in vol. 124, p. 172 of this Society's
publications.

eldest sonne, my house wherein I now dwell, to have and to hold
from and after the death of Dorothy, my wife, to him and his
heirs for ever. I give unto my said sonne Willm. my land in
Crossgate called the langt bancks, to him and his heirs for ever,
also I give him the close I hould of the Dean and Chapter by
lease, called the hughes, in Clapworth, and the term of years
therein to him and his executors, admors and assigns. I give
unto Anthony Trollopp, my second son, my tenement in Tuddoe,
bequethed with the revcon of the Collerie there to him and his heirs
for ever. I give unto Anne Trollopp, my eldest daughter, three
score pounds, to be paid her at full age of one and twenty years
or marriage. I give and bequeath unto my loving wife, Dorothy
Trollopp, my waist in Silver Street, and my mind is that she
build a house upon the same, and after her death to Francis
Trollopp, my youngest sonne, and his heires for ever. I give
unto my said wife and my younger children . . . . . All my
plate and household stuff, to be equally divided amongst them.
I give unto my wife all my bills, bonds, debts and creditts, to
raise for my younger children such porcons as she shall think
fitt, more or less as they shall behave themselves and be advised
by her. I give to my said wife all my houses, byers, stables,
garths, stackgarths in Crossgate, and all other lands there, to
hold for the benefit of my younger children and for augmentation
of their porcons as my wife shall think fitt, and after her death,
if any term of yeares of the lease be then to come and unexpired
in the said houses, lands and premises, I give and bequeath the
same to my said two sonnes, Wm. and Anthony Trollopp, equally
betwixt them. And all other my goods and chattels, lands and
tenements hereby unbequeathed, I give and bequeathe the same
for my loving wife, Dorothy Trollopp, and my brother-in-lawe,
Mr. Henry Busbie, and I make them Executors. Witnesses,
Anthony Fawell, Jane Wright, Ric. Hutchinson. Proved, 1646.

JOHN FLETCHER.[1]

Jan. 4, 1644. In the name of God, Amen, I, John Fletcher
of East Brandon, in the parish of Brancepeth, in the County of
Durham, Yeoman, being sick in bodie. To be buried in Brancepeth Church near to my father there, And for my worldly goods
I dispose thereof as followeth :—I give to the poore of the town-

[1] Robert Fletcher, the father of the testator, was bur. at Brancepeth (whence other dates are taken), 22 Nov., 1619. The testator, bapt.,
4 Oct., 1602, bur., 9 Jan., 1644/5, mar. Katherine, dau. of Nicholas
Pearson of Chester (bapt. there, 12 Feb., 1608/9), 1 Oct., 1636, at
Brancepeth; by her he had William, bapt., 18 Feb., 1637/8, bur.,
8 May, 1638; John, bapt., 24 Nov., 1639; Elizabeth, bapt., 22 June, 1642;
Mary, bapt., 5 May, 1644, bur., 14 Mch., 1651/2.

shipp of Brandon, tenn shillings, and to the poore of the township of Brancepeth and Stockley, other tenn shillings. I give to my sonne, John Fletcher, the interest of my farm and tenament in Brandon aforesaid upon the condicions following, saveing and excepting my mother's right and wives herein. I give to either of my daughters, Isabella and Mary Fletcher, the sume of Twenty pounds in liew and satisfaction of their childs parts and porcons, to be paid unto them when they come to their full and lawfull age. I give to my bastard daughter Mary, forty shillings for her maintenance. Now whereas my goods will not extend to the satisfacon of the said porcons to my daughters (my debts and my wives thirds deducted), my mynd therefore is that if my said sonne at any time before he attaine unto the age of one and twenty yeares shall choise an other tutor and leave his mother, that then 20l. of the legacies and porcons given to my said daughters, shall be paid forth of the profitts of my farme and yearly raised to them forth of such part as will fall and be due unto my said sonne, a reasonable maintenance being only allowed to him. And my further will is that my wife have the tuicon and education of my said children. And lastly my mynd and will is that my debts and legacies be payd. The rest of my goods, as well moveable as unmoveable, I give unto my said wife, whom I make executrix of this my last Will and Testament. Witnesses, Gab. Jackson, John Hynde. Proved, 1649.

EPHRAIM PROCTOR.[1]

July 23, 1645. Ephraim Proctor of West Lilburn, in the County of Northumberland, Gentleman. Inventory. Imprs : 11 oxen, 18l. 6s. 8d. 4 kyne, 6l. 13s. 4d. 22 sheepe, 5l. 5s. 0d. 3 horses, 3l. 10s. 0d. 5 Swyne, 1l. 13s. 4d. 12 bolles of corne sowen upon the ground, 4l. 6s. 0d. 15 bolles of Rye, 8l. 18 bolles of oatts, 4l. 10s. 0d. 3 bolles of Pease, 1l. Implements of husbandrie, 1l. 13s. 4d. 3 bedsteads, 1l. 2 cupboards, 2 tables, 3 puffit stooles, 3l. 6s. 8d. 2 featherbeds, 8 paire of sheates, 2 Rugges, 2 plaids, and one paire blankets, 2l. 8s. 0d. For brasse and pewter, 1l. 18s. 0d. A cheste, a cruke, a dripping pann, a pair of rackes, one speate, 10s. 2 chares, 2s. 6d. Two tenements in West Lilburne for a lease of nineteen yeares, worth ten pounds per annum cleare and not above, worth 90l. Two tenements for a lease of 21 yeares, worth 100l. More the eighth part of a tenement for nineteen yeares, worth 3l. 4s. 0d. Debts paid which was dew by the deceased. Paid for funerall expences, 6l. John Alder, upon bond, 5l. George Alder, upon bond, 21l. John Alder of Alnwick upon bond, 8l. Henry Pearson of Hebron,

[1] He was the son of Thomas Proctor of Shawdon, by his wife, Jane, dau. of Robert Eden of West Auckland.

on bond, 7*l.* Arnold Abgin, bill, 5*l.* John Atcheson of West Lilburn, 8*l.* Margaret Carr, 5*l.* Ralph Tuggell, 1*l.* 10*s.* 0*d.* Jane Hardie, 1*l.* 10*s.* 0*d.* John Morrison, 1*l.* 10*s.* 0*d.* Edward Tompson, 2*l.* Andrew Dixon, 2*l.* Margaret Glaster, 11*l.* 10*s.* 0*d.* Adam Oliver, 2*l.* 10*s.* 0*d.* James Younge, 2*l.* Elizabeth Revley, 2*l.* Thomas Browne, 2*l.* Matthew Reveley, 2*l.* Matthew Forster, 1*l.* 10*s.* 0*d.* Edmond Wright, 2*l.* 18*s.* 0*d.* Henry Alder, 6*l.* Margaret Hebron, 1*l.* 5*s.* 0*d.*

JOHN BLAKISTON.[1]

Oct. 7, 1645. I, John Blakiston of Gibside, in the County of Durham, gent., being in good health yett considering the present distractions and the uncertainity of Man's life, which in a moment may be taken away, after which many tymes discords, variances and suites fall amongst their nearest kinsfolks and deerist friends for want of pfect settling of their estates in their lifetime; to prevent which and to avoid all future discords amongst my alliance and friends I have hereby constituted and ordained and made this my last Will and Testament. My body to christian buriall neere such place convenient where itt shall please god to call mee, att the discretion of my executor. My mind and will is concerning my worldly estate, and principally concerning the inheritance of my part of Collery in Galesfield, in the County of Durham, that Margarett, my now wife, shall have the one halfe and a moyety, together with all the issues and profitts thereof, and also the moyety of a keele upon the River of Tyne for carriage of coales during her naturall life, and after her decease all the said collery with appurtenances, and the said Keele, shall be and descend upon William Blaixton, my sone, and his heirs lawfully begotten, soe soon as he shall come to 21 years of age or marry. And that Margarett, my said wife, shall have the occupation thereof, together with all the issues and profitts thereof during her lifetime. My mind and will is and I give and bequeath unto Barbara, my daughter, the sume of 100*l.* out of the said collery equally by the occupiers thereof, within one yeare after my decease, if she be then att lawful yeares or marryed with consent of Margarett my wife, provided alwayes, and it is my true intent and meaning, that if itt fortune that William my sonne dye without issue lawfully begotten, my said Collery and all the issues and pfitts thereof, together with the said keele, shall fall and descend upon Barbara my daughter and her heires lawfull begotten, and for want of

[1] The testator was son of Sir William Blakiston, knt. (bur., 13 Oct., 1641, at Whickham), by his wife, Jane, dau. of Robert Lambton (bur. 11 Nov. 1648, at Whickham), and grand nephew of the William Blakiston whose will dated 5 Feb., 1607/8, is printed in this vol.

such, my mynd and will is, and I doe hereby give and bequeath
the same unto Margarett my wife and her assigns dureing her
life, and then to the right heirs of me, the said John Blaixton.
I give my said wife full power to assign or lett the said Collery,
and charge the same with the payment of 200*l.* sterling, to be
paid to such as she shall appoint and nominate under her hand
within one yeare of my decease. Concerning my personal estate,
after all debts, dues and dutyes paid, which in right and conscience I owe, shall be first paid out of my personal estate, I
give the rest and residue unto Margarett my said wife. Whereas
William Blaixton of Gibside aforesaid, Esq., my great Uncle,
did give unto me, John Blaixton, for a legacy, the sum of 20*l.*
sterling, my will and mynd is and I give the said sum with all
profitts unto my said daughter Barbara. I constitute and make
Margarett, my said wife, my executor.

Witnesses, John Coupland, Isabell Arrowsmith and Thomas
Pierson. Proved, 7 Sept., 1647.

RALPH COLLINGWOOD.[1]

Mar. 31, 1647. Ralph Collingwood of Ditchburne, in the
County of Northumberland, Gent. To be buried in the parish
Church, where it shall please god to take me to his mercy. I
give unto Edward Collingwood, my second sone, all my land in
East Ditchburne. To my eldest daughter Margery, 100*l.* To
Dorothy, my second daughter, 100*l.*, and to Ralph Collingwood,
my youngest sone, 100*l.* I appoint my wife, Dorothy Collingwood, sole executor, and I do appoint my brother-in-law, Edward
Wright, Esqr., with Cuthbert Collingwood, my eldest sone and
heir, supervisors, and I do command my sone Cuthbert to give
that assistance towards the performance of this my Will, that
my debts be discharged (of which I have left a Schedule under
my hand), so that my son Edward may enter on the land at East
Ditchburn when he attains 21 years. Witnesses, John Forster,
Robert Pemberton. Probate, 1647.

[1] The testator, son of Cuthbert Collingwood by his wife, Helen,
dau. of Robert Roddam of Roddam, was bur., at Eglingham, Apl., 1648,
where there is a monumental inscription; he mar at St. Oswald's,
12 Oct., 1591, Dorothy, dau. of Richard Wright, Alderman of Durham,
by his wife, Margery Grey, sister of the Rev. Right Hon. Anthony
Grey, clerk, Rector of Burbage and ninth Earl of Kent (*Regs.*), bapt.,
6 Apl., 1597, at St. Nicholas, Durham, bur., 8 June, 1686, aged 89, at
Eglingham. By her he had Cuthbert, bapt. at Eglingham, 6 Aug., 1628,
bur., 28 Feb., 1687/8, mar Elizabeth; Edward, bapt at Eglingham,
28 July, 1629, admitted to Gray's Inn, 2 Dec., 1654, mar. Anne, widow
of Francis Gray of Newcastle, mercht., and dau. of John Tomkins, at
St. Andrew's, Newcastle, 22 May, 1668, he was bur. at All Saints,
Newcastle, 14 Apl., 1701, she was bur. there, 7 Nov., 1694; Ralph,
perhaps bur. at Eglingham, 19 Nov., 1689; Margery and Dorothy.

HENRY SIMPSON.[1]

April 13, 1647. In the name of God, Amen, I, Henry Simpson of Pittington Hall Garth, in the County of Durham, Gent., weake in body. To be buried att the discretion of my friends, as neare my father and mother in Pittington Quire, with as much convenience as the times will permitt, And as for my lands and goodes and chattells of which I am or ought to be seized and possessed, in possession or reversion, I dispose therefore as followeth. My will and desire is and I doe hereby charge my executor under named, punctually and truly to performe all covenants betwixt myself and other trustees concerning my marriage with my most dear and loveing wife, and that if any question in doubt shall happen about the interpretacon of these covenants, that the same be taken in the most loving and genuine sense, that may be according to the true intent and meaning of all parties. First as to all my said estate, reall and personall, lands, tenements, reversions, leases or in trustees' hands or names, to my use or wife's use or otherwise, goods, chattells, plaite, Jewells, or other psent possessions whatsoever, I doe give and bequeath the same unto my sonne, William Simpson, whom I do hereby make, ordain my sole Executor of this my last Will and Testament, he paying and discharging all jointures, my debts, legacies, ingagements and funerall expences, and likewise to porcons to each of his three sisters, Margaret, Elizabeth and Mary, the sume of three hundred poundes a piece, to be paied to each of them and the survivor of them upon and

[1] The testator was the son of Ralph Simpson of Pittington, bur. there, 11 Sept., 1630, by his wife, Elizabeth Glover, who remar. Ralph Lambton of Tribley (bapt., 24 Jan., 1592/3, at Chester-le-Street), 19 May, 1633, at Pittington, where she was bur., 4 May, 1635. The testator, eldest son of the above, bapt., 31 May, 1615, at Pittington (whence other dates are taken), adm. pens. (age 17), at Christ's Coll., Camb., 17 May, 1631, B.A., 1633/4, adm. at Gray's Inn, 12 Aug., 1631, bur., 28 Apl., 1647, mar., 5 Dec., 1636, at Houghton-le-Spring, Mary, dau. of Sir William Bellasis (bapt. at Morton House, 30 Aug., 1615, bur. 22 Feb., 1663/4, remar. Col. William Blakiston of Old Malton, bur. at St. Oswald's, Durham, 2 Jan. 1684/5); the testator's brothers and sisters were Thomas, bapt., 19 Feb., 1617/18 (his son mentioned as being at Eton and destined for Cambridge, cannot be identified either in the Eton Registers, defective for this period, or in Venn's Alumni Cantabrigiensis); Richard, bapt., 23 May, 1619, bur., 29 Sept, 1646, at Heighington; Oswald, bapt., 14 Sept., 1622, bur., 9 June, 1625; Michael bapt., 10 Oct., 1624, bur., 6 Mch., 1641/2; Mary, bapt., 6 Oct., 1616, bur., 20 May, 1617; Mary, bapt., 15 July, 1621; Mary, bapt., 6 Apl., 1627; Elizabeth, bapt., 27 June, 1628, mar., William Nicholson, 27 Feb., 1646/7. The testator's children were William, bapt., 6 Dec., 1645, adm. pens. (age 17) at Christ's Coll., Camb., 15 May, 1663, died unmar., bur. 19 May, 1675; Margaret, bapt., 2 Dec., 1637, at Houghton-le-Spring, bur., 22 Feb., 1699/1700, mar., 17 Sept., 1671, Edward Shepperdson, who was bur., 15 July, 1707; Elizabeth, bapt., 4 Oct., 1640; Mary, bapt. 4 Aug., 1642, bur., 22 June, 1675.

after their respective marriage, he alloweing in the meantime unto
each of them tenn poundes a piece per annum for her maintenance untill they shall respectively accomplish the age of foure-
teen yeares, and to be brought upp with their mother, and after
they shall accomplish the age of fourteene years my will and
desire is, that my Executor shall allow then unto each of them
twenty poundes a yeare for their maintenance, untill such time
or times as they shallbe respectively married, and after their
marriage respectively that my executor shall pay unto them after
the raite of eight in the hundred, until such time and times as
he or his . . . . shall pay unto them or their assigns their
severall procons of three hundred poundes and the survivor of
them, vizt., Severally, fower and twenty poundes per annum
respectively for their said money unpaid as above. My will and
desire is that presently after my decease all my goodes and household stuff be praised and inventoried, and so much of my goods
sold with as much convenience as the markets will afford, and
the money hereby raised to pay and discharge my debts and
engagements, that my frends that have trusted me with their
monies or them that there are engaged for me be noe way
damnified. And for the remainder of my goods and chattells, and
the rents and profitts of my said landes and leases to be carefully imployed and put forward for the most advantage, and to
be in redines towards the purchase of the inheritance or otherwise of my leases and lands holden of the Dean and chapter of
Durham, provided notwithstanding that my said loveing wife's
thirds of my said personal estate be referred unto her as the
lawe appointeth, and the residue thereof I give to William my
sone, sole Executor, he paying his sister's porcons as above said
and all other engagements whatsoever, they giving him a full
and absolute discharge for the same, in liew and recompense of
all filiall or other demands of my estate whatsoever, but for his
psent maintenance my will is, his estate shall be thus ordered
and appointed, first that my said sone shall have tenn pounds
per annm allowed him for his maintenance until he accomplish
the age of tenn yeares, and after the sum of twenty pounds of
like lawful English money per annm, till he shall be fitt to goe
to the university of Cambridge, and when he is or shallbe there
remaining, to have fifty pounds per annm allowed him for his
maintenance there, and he there to continue soe long as shallbe
thought fitt, and meet with the approbation of those gentlemen
hereafter named, whom I doe hereby appoint to be Tutors and
Guardians of him and supervisors of this my last Will and
Testament, and if it shallbe thought fitt or requisite of his said
Tutors to suite with his health and abilitie of body to goe from
thence to the Innes of Court, that then he have for his maintenance allowed unto him the sume of four score poundes per
annm, so long as he shall there remaine to study the lawes of the

said Kingdome, untill he shall accomplish the age of one and twenty yeares, att which time my will and desire is, he shall enter one all his estate to him bequeathed by these pents, and in the meantime I desire my loving friends, Sir William Darcie of Witton Castle, Knight, Sir Richard Belasis of Durham, Knight, Jerrard Salvin of Croxdaile, and Thomas Delavale of Hetton in the hole, Esqrs., Simond Lackenbie and William Hall of Shadforthe, Gent., to be tutors and guardians of my said sonne William, and to be Supervisors of this my last Will and Testament. And for so much as Simond Lackenby and William Hall are my neare neighbours and the rest are further distant from me, my will and desire is that they, with the approbacon of one, two or three of the other Tutors and Supervisors, shall sell such goods and stock as aforesaid, and to lett to farme my said landes and leases for the best advantage, and the money therefor received by them my will and desire is shall be disposed for and towards the payment of the several sums above mentioned by them, and with the consent of the said tutors and supervisors or one, two or more of them, And when the time shallbe convenient for the purchasing of the inheritance fee farme or renewing of my said leases, I desire and my will is that it be imployed for the purchasing of the same. And that Sir Richard Bellasis, Knight, willbe pleased to take some paines in the effecting thereof, and that his expences and disbursements and of the rest of the said Tutors and Supervisors in and about the premises shallbe raised and paid out of the said estate and allowed unto them respectively. Also my will and desire is that if my said sonne William dye without issue male of his body lawfully begotten, that then my Brother Thomas Simpson's eldest sonne shall have my lands at upper Dinsdale, in Yorkshire, and Helmington Rawe, in and of the County of Durham, to him and his heires males of his bodye lawfully to be begotten and after to his heirs for ever. And if my said sonne shall die without any issue of his body lawfully begotten, then my will and mynd is that my estate be equally divided amongst my three daughters (the estate in land as aforesaid excepted and fore prised by my Brother Thomas his sonne), and if it shall be fortune that my said sonne shall die leaving only daughters of his body lawfully begotten, then my will and mind is that each of his daughters shall have 300l. a piece, like unto my owne, and the remainder of my estate to be equally distributed and divided amongst his and my daughters, his sisters, in augmentation of their filiall porcons formerly bequeathed unto them. And my will and further desire is that if my said sonne William happen to die without issue of his bodye lawfully begotten, that my said loveing wife, being then my widow, shall have during her widowhood Fifty pounds per annum out of my said land and lease, except as afore excepted. or so much sett forth in valew in augmentation of her jointure.

alwaies pvided that the sums be first made upp for purchasing of my leases in the inheritance thereof in Pittington or Pittington Hallgarth as above said, and that for so much she shall pay her approximate rent, sesses and charges, or so much encrease of land out of the same. My will and mind is that my now household stuff shall remaine as heire loomes to my sonne William, or to whom or which of my heires the house or houses of Pittington Hall Garth shall come, descend or remaine, and that my wife shall have all the house and houses att Pittington Hall Garth wherein I now dwell, in as large and ample manner as I now have them during the minority of her said eldest sonne or the minoritie of my next heires, till they accomplish the age of twenty one yeares. Witnesses, George Shaw, John Morland.

Codicil dated 28 January, 1646.[1] This likewise I declare to be my full intent and meaning, that if my wife be with child and if a sone, that then I give and bequeath unto him all my lands at Dinsdale and Helmington Rawe with psent possession and reversion, and if my sone William die without issue male of his body lawfully begotten, then my will is that he shall possess and enjoy all my estate in as full and ample manner as my sone William is to possess and enjoy the same, and that the heires males of my brother, Thomas Simpson, shall not expect any benefitt by this my last Will, unless this sonne likewise dye without issue male (if it soe please God that my wife be with childe and if a sone, and if she be with child and is a daughter, my will is that her portion be equal with the rest in every respect of her sisters). Whereas my Aunt Glover of Awckland hath made me a deed of gift of all her estate, and that I have received forty pounds in silver, for which I am engaged to pay unto her 16 shillings a quarter during her life, my will is that I doe strickly charge my Executor to pay her dewly and honestly. and I desire my wife during the minortie of my executor, and that she will assist her and helpe her in any thing that she stand in need and in her power to helpe her, and that when she dieth she be decently buried. My will and desire is that these six gentlemen, friends and neighbours, whom I have made bold to trouble and nominate Supervisors of this my last Will and Testament may have each of them three half pieces (or 3 Angells, if you will so tearme them), to be bestowed in some rings or other emblems as they shall most fancie, but I desire they may be all alike, and I give unto my much honoured Lady and mother-in-Law, the Lady Bellasis, 2 old pieces to bestow in what she likes, as a tender of my duetifull respects and love. And my last request to her is that her Ladyship willbe pleased to take order that my sonne William be brought upp and educated according

---

[1] This, although the date given on the original document, must be an

to her owne rule and direcon. My will is that my brother, Thomas Simpson, and his wife, Mr. Shawe, my sister Elizabeth Simpson, my Ant Simpson, my Ant Wortley, my Ant Glover, and my Ant Grice, have every one of them a gold ringe with deathes head in it, given them as a token of my love. I give unto Elizabeth Thompson, 40s. a yeare to maintain her during her life, and twenty shillings a yeare to John Laiyne during his life, but my will is that he shall not have power to sell or alienate the same, but is to be bestowed in clothes for him quarterly or half yearly as need shall require. I give unto George Hayword the filly that came with the gray mare and five poundes in silver, the which filly being foaled with her price and the five poundes. I would have him bound to some trade, and the remainder to be putt forwardes to the most advantage for to helpe him to sett upp with. My will is that my brew vessell, nor lead, nor Chimneys, nor wainscott, ceiling or widowes, or any thinge which is fixed to the freehold or by removall will practically deface the house, be not removed, sold or dispersed, but may remaine to the use and benefitt of my sone William, unto whom likewise I give my little silver sworde, with those two bookes that are left, the guilt salte and broad wine bowle, and the best silver Cann, a silver pottinger and spoons. My will is that no more of that land which shall belonge to my sone be plowed before he come to age than what is alreadie. My desire and will is that some prettie sleight monument be erected where my grandfather and grandmothers by both sides, and all or most of us ever since have been buried in the Quire Chancel, but not to exceed twenty poundes. My will and desire is if Barbarie Storie out live her now husband, John Storey, and by age or sickness shallbe driven to necessitie and want, that care be taken that she may have weekly sufficient maintenance allowed her, with one to look to her, and though she should not out live her husband yet be driven to want, let care be had to pvide for her. I give unto my man, John Morland, Jane Haroson and Ann Liddell, each of them twenty shillings for the paines they tooke when I was sicke, to Barbara Story, twenty shillings, and to Jane Burne, ten shillings for paines in watching. If it shall please gode that my owne sonne shall have issue male, or live untill he accomplish the full age of 21 years, and that my brother Thomas, his sonne, shall reape no benefitt out of my estate, then my will is that if my said brother Thomas, his sone, shall prove a Scholler fitt for the universtie, that then my sone and my Executor shall allow him 20 pounds per annm for soe long time as he shall continue at Eaton Collidge, for there are soe many Schollershipps and fellowshipps appriated in King's Collidge in Cambridge for such Scholars as shall come by election from Eaton, and four years after att the universtie, in which time I conceive he may be chosen fellow of King's, and if any of the

twentie poundes per annm can be saved during his time at
Eaton, that the remainder be kept and be bestowed in bookes
when he shall come to the universtie, but if it shall soe happen
that either by idleness or carlessnes he shall neglect his studies
or shall fall into any lude or disorderly course of living, either
at Eaton or King's Collidge, whereby he shallbe put back and
made uncapable and the benefitt of the election, then my will
is that this my legacie shall cease, and that my executor shall not
be compelled to continue any longer the payment either by virtue
of this my Will or any other charges whatsoever. I give unto
the stocke of the poore of the parish of Pittington as much as
shall make the now present stocke upp fiftie pounds. My will
is that my Executor shall give unto Edward Grice a good new
calven cowe worth five pounds att the least upon the day of his
marriage to begin house withall. Proved, 1647.

PETER BRADFORTH.[1]

April 28, 1647. In the name of God, Amen, I, Peter Bradforth of Newham sicke in bodye. To be buried within the porche
of Balmbrough Churche called Braidforth porch. And for my
worldly goods, I leave them as followeth. I bequeath to my sonne,
Peter Bradforth, 40l. I bequeath to my daughter Jane, 40l. I
bequeath to my sone Thomas, 40l. I bequeath to my daughter
Ann, 40l. I bequeath to my daughter Ellenor, 40l.
Debts oweing by this testator. To Allison Brand, 4l. for these
porchons left to pay children; if any of them dye or all before
they accomplish there age, when it should be due, then I give and
freelie there said porchons to my sonne, Lionell Bradforth. To
Ralph Bell of Fenham, 2l. 6s. Memorandum: Whereas I was put
in trust by a kynd frend of myne of a matter of three score pounds
to put out amongst nighbours and friends accordinge to the King's
Statute which although the money was not my owne, yeit my
friends desire was, that the bonds should be taken in my name,
as by the said bond will appeare, now my desire is and by this
my last Will and Testament, I charge my executors to call for
the said moneyes of the parties as they shall fall due and deliver
the same to the parties to whom duely it belongeth. And also I
doe leave my wiffe Ellinore Bradforth and my sonne Lionell
Bradforth my sole executor to se this my will truely pformed.

[1] The inventory of Lionel Bradford, the son of the testator, was
dated 8 June, 1665, and administered by Elizabeth, the lawful widow,
4 Oct., of the same year; she was dau. and heir of Henry Grey of Kyloe
and Morpeth, and was bur. at Bamburgh, 10 Oct., 1672; the testator's
son Peter was bur., 26 June, 1666, at Bamburgh. There is a pedigree
of this family in the *New County History of Northumberland*, vol. i.,
p. 281.

Witnesses, Raph Forster, John Taylor, Tho. Johnson, Raph Thompson.

INVENTORIE : tenne oxen, 30*l.* Fourteene kyne, 35*l.* Two mares, one fillie and a coalt, 12*l.* Fifteene beasts and six stirks, 36*l.* Of old sheepe, nyne score, 72*l.* Of hoggs, fower score and fifteene, 20*l.* Of old swine, seven and two pigs, 2*l.* Of Bee hives, fowre, 1*l.* Proved 1647.

MARKE JACKSONE.[1]

Nov. 21, 1647. In the name of God, Amen, I, Marke Jacksone of Helmedon Rawe, in the parish of Brancepeth sick in bodye. To be buried in the parish church of Brancepeth. I give and bequeath to John Jackson, my sonne, one tenement of the anncient yearly rent of fifteen shillings halpenny, that is one called Hunerfield. Another close called the longfield with another close called the cowe close, and the house thereunto belonging, except the low parler with the loft over the said parlor and two beaste gaites in the aforesaid cow close which I give unto Mary my wife, during her naturall life, if my leas soe long endure, and if Jane Chapman depart this life before my lease expended, I give the same to my sone, John Jacksone. I give to my wief Mary, one piece of another tenement called the East field, during her naturall life. I give to John Jackson, my sonne, six pounds, and to Mary, my wife, fower pounds which Thomas Johnson, my Brother-in-lawe is to pay unto me by covenant of mariage at that day of his mariage. I give to John Jackson, my sonne, the two cupbords. I give unto Mary, my wife, the third of my moveable goods. and if she be with child at this present, my will is that John Jackson, my sonne, shall pay unto it when it shall attain the age of one and twenty years the sum of ten pounds. My will is that Mary Jackson, my wife, and Anthony Jackson and John Maier, shall have the tuicon of my sonne. I give to Grace Jackson, one Ewe and hogge. All the rest of my goods, moveable and unmoveable, debts payed, funeral expences and legacies discharged, I give to John Jackson, my sonne, whom I make full executor. Witnesses, Michael Chapman, John Maier. Proved, 1649.

JOHN GRAY.[2]

Feb. 4, 1647. John Gray. A true inventory of all goods and chattels moveable and unmoveable, which John Gray of Bradforth, Esquire, deceased the fourth of Febry, 1646, died possessed of

[1] The testator was bapt. at Brancepeth, 29 Apl., 1610, being the son of John Jackson of Helmedon Row; he mar. Mary Johnson, 6 July, 1645, was bur., 21 Oct., 1648, in the Church of Brancepeth, and had a son, Thomas, bapt., 18 June, 1648, and bur., 13 Feb. 1648/9.

[2] He was the third son of Sir Ralph Grey of Chillingham. He was a colonel in the army on the side of Parliament and was slain in

viewed and valued by Cuthbert Nicholson. John Forster of Balmbrough, Thomas Child of Belforth and William Walton of Lementon, four indifferent men, viz. : Oxen, ewes, sheep and Implements of husbandry, 125*l.* In the parlor, one paire of hanginge read all furniture belonging to a bed, 4 chaires, 4 lesser stoles, and one litle table with a carpet, a court cupbord in all valued 2*l.* 10*s.* 0*d.* The Greane Chamber, one bedde with greane hangings, a court cobbard and furniture belonging to a bedd in all valued to 1*l.* 0*s.* 0*d.* The outer Chamber, one bed with yellow hangings valued 10*s.* The Read chamber, 2 beds, 2 chares and a stoull with furniture thereunto belonging, valued to 12*s.* The kitching and all things thereunto belonging, valued to 1*l.* 0*s.* 0*d.* The Hall, six chaires and stoules XII, and two tables and two carpits, 1*l.*

The Declaration of the account of John Ourd, administrator of the goods, chattells and creditts of John Gray, Esqr., late of Bradforth of the parish of Balmbrough and Countie of Northumberland, deceased, made upon his administration the said goods as followeth :

Impris : the said administrator by way of account doth charge himself with all the goods and chattels and creditts of the said deceased comprised in an Inventorie thereof remayning on record in this court being duly apprized, amounting to the sume of one hundred and thirtie two pounds twelve shillings and tenpence.—132*l.* 12*s.* 10*d.*

Paid for the funerall charges of the said deceased with other charges, 30*l.* Paid fees for letters of Administration and commission with administratrix of counsell and other charges, 40*s.* Paid to Faith Winell the sume fifteen pounds twelve shilings, being due unto her by the deceased, his bond 15*l.* 12*s.* 0*d.* Paid to Alexander Smyth the sum of forty pounds being due unto him upon the deceased bond, 40*l.* Paid to John Forster the sume of three score and five pounds being due to him upon deceased bill, 65*l.* Paid to William Wilson the sume of ten pounds twelve shillings, being due unto him upon the bill of the deceased, 10*l.* 12*s.* 0*d.* Paid to servants their severall and respective wages, to Adam Anderson and his wife, five pounds, to Matthew Johnson, fiftie five shillings, to Jane Bowdon, twenty shillings, to Elizabeth Stephenson, twentie shillings, to Henry Younger, thirty six shillings, to James Ellott, twenty five shillings, to Richard Winley, thirtie five shillings, to Mary Carver, eighteen shillings, to John Ourd, foure pounds, in all, 19*l.* 9*s.* 0*d.*

Ireland. He mar. Mary Orde and by her had issue, Ralph Grey, who mar. Elizabeth Burrell and was bur. in Chillingham Church, 22 Apl., 1670 (*Bamburgh Regs.*); Thomas, bur. at Bamburgh, 2 June, 1655, and Margaret.

AVERY ROBINSON.[1]

April 14, 1648. In the name of Gode, Amen, I, Avery Robinson of Gateside, within the County Palatine of Durham, Gent., sick of body. To be buried in Gateshead Church, and my goods as followeth : I give and bequeath unto Sir Thomas Riddell the Elder, my Draught and all that belongeth to it, upon condition my servant, John Shanks, still goe with it and be not removed, and to lead every twenty days a load of coles to my servant Mary, att my house. I give all that money that my Maister, Sir Thomas Riddell, senr., oweth me, to be divided amongst his sons, Sir William, his children, upon condition he free me of the Bond wherein I am bound to Mr. Collingwood. I give a dozen of silver spoones to Sir William Riddell, to be at his owne disposing. I give to my Brother Michael all things of mine at Renton, except what my sister Jaine hath, which I will she enjoy for her life without molestation. I give to my Brother Martin that part of my house in Gateshead in the possession of Widow Howe, and the other part in my owne hands, to my maid Mary, with that part of the Garden I reserved to my selfe, and all the furniture as it standeth in the said part which I kept in my owne hands. I give to my maide Mary, 20l. in gold and two stints or gates in St. Eleanor's Close, Also I give her my three Kyne. I give that part of my house wherein I live after my maid's death to George Robinson, my brother Michael Robinson's second son, to him and his heires for ever. I give to Ann Barkas, 5l., whereof one piece to be that which her father gave me att his death. I give to my sister Jaine, 20l. I give to my sister Johnson, 5l. I give to Doctor Willescott, my Phisitian, 5l. in gold, with my watch, upon condition he keep it in remembrance of me. I give unto Christopher Robinson, half of the waggon horse which William Comyn and I have betwixt us, and the reckoning between me and William Comyn I give to my maide Mary. I give 20s. to my maid, Mary Lever. Whatsoever is betwixt Thomas Barkas and me I freely forgive, and for the carriage my Maister, Thomas Riddell, senior, is owen me when the Scotts came first in, I remitt it. I give 5l. to the poore of Gateshead parish, to be distributed as Thomas Potts and John Bulman shall think meet. Concerning moneys due to me for foure oxen which went to Tinmouth Castle, I remitt it until Sir Thomas Riddell, junior, receive money of the King, and then it to be left at the disposal of his father, Sir Thomas, my Maister. I give 20s. a piece to my Brother Michael and Martin's children, except George and Margaret, who have picular legacies. I give Sir William Riddell power to dispose 5l. (out of that moneys which is in hands of Sir Thomas, his father, and above mentioned to be given to Sir William's children) to the

[1] The testator, son of Edward Robinson, was bapt. at Gateshead, 2 Oct., 1625, and bur. there, 20 Apl., 1648.

servants of Gateshead house. I constitute and appoint my
Maister, Sir Thomas aforesaid, my sole and onely Executor of
this my last Will and Testament, and my Brother Ralph Supervisor thereof. In witness whereof I have hereunto subscribed
my name and sett my seale unto this my psent Will and last
Testament the day and year hereinbefore written. I give to my
Brother Ralph, 5*l*. I give to my Brother Michael's sonne, George
Robinson, 5*l*. I give to Martin Robinson's daughter Margaret,
5*l*. I give to my Ladie Katherine and my Ladie Barbara Riddell,
40*s*. (viz.), each of them, 20*s*. I give to Thomas Potts, 10*s*. I
give to Thomas Colt, 10*s*. To John Bulman, 10*s*. I give to
eight God children, 5*s*. a piece. To William Blakey, son of
William Blakey, 5*s*. To Isabell Grame, widow, 5*s*. I give to
Mrs. Avery, 20*s*. I give to Edward Simpson, 10*s*. To Percivall
Potts, 10*s*. To Mr. William Riddell, 5*s*. To Mr. Thomas Riddell,
sone to Sir Thomas Riddell, Junior, 5*s*. To Thomas Riddell, Mrs.
George Riddell's sone, 5*s*. To Mr. Henry Riddell, 5*s*. To Mr.
Robert Riddell, Sir William's sonne, 5*s*. To Mr. Henry Forcer, 5*s*.
To Edward Ellison, one suit of clothes. I give to my maid Mary,
the cropp of corne sowen in the Paddock adjoineing to the Salt
Meadowes, she paying the rent, And also that part of the Lease of
a garth betwixt me and Thomas Compton, she paying my part of
the rent.

Witnesses, Ralph Robinson, Michaell Robinson, Martin
Robinson, Mary Tweddell, Margaret Robinson, Alice Johnson,
and Jane Robinson. Proved, 1648.

JOHN TAYLOR.[1]

May 31, 1649. In the name of God, Amen, I, John Taylor
of Langton in the County of Durham, Yeoman. To be interred
in Gainford Churchyarde. I give to my sonne, Cuthbert Taylor,
my farme in Langton, part of which I bought of James Hilton,
provided he paye to his Ant Eleanor Taylor one hundred poundes
out of this farm, and so long as it is unpayed he shall pay her
the sum of eight pounds per annm. I give to my sonne, John
Taylor, my land in Ingleton, and one close which I bought of
Ralph Singleton, which is in Langton and Betson house and
garth. I give to my daughter, Eleanor Taylor, three score
pounds, to be paid out of my goodes. If my wife be with childe,
I give to it ten poundes, and, if not, it shall redound back to my
daughter, Eleanor Taylor. Residue of all my goods to my wife
Eleanor and appoint her Executor. Witnesses, George Marley,
William Marley, Cuthbert Marley. Proved, 1649.

[1] The testator was buried at Gainford, 5 June, 1649, mar., first,
Elizabeth Iley, 15 June, 1634, at Brancepeth (bur. 8 May, 1639, at
Gainford); by her he had a dau., Eleanor, bapt., 22 Jan., 1636/7, at
Gainford, and secondly, Eleanor Marley of Hilton, 8 Oct., 1639, at
Staindrop, who was bur., 13 Jan., 1664/5, at Gainford, where their two
children were bapt., Cuthbert, 21 Jan., 1640/1, John, 5 July, 1646.

Index of Wills and Inventories

IN

VOLUME IV.

MITFORD, JOHN, 1623, W., 168.
MITFORD, LANCELOT, 1641, W., 286.
MOWBRAY, PETER, 1619, W., 129.
MUSCHAMP, GEORGE, 1620, I., 140.
MUSCHAMP, WILLIAM, SIR, 1631, I., 237.

N

NEWTON, THOMAS, 1612, W., 62.
NICHOLSON, GEORGE, 1624, W., 180.
NOBLE, MATTHEW, 1616, W., 111.

O

ORDE, CHRISTOPHER, 1619, W., 134.
ORDE, HENRY, 1619, W.I., 137.
ORDE, ROBERT, 1636, W., 270.
OTWAY, THOMAS, 1608, W., 38.
OVINGTON, JOHN, 1617, W.I., 122.

P

PEACOCK, THOS., 1627, W., 212.
PEMBERTON, JOHN, 1642, W., 298.
PILKINGTON, THOMAS, 1619, W., 131.
POTT, ROBERT, 1626, W., 196.
PRESTON, RALPH, 1613, W., 73.
PROCTOR, EPHRAIM, 1645, I., 306.
PROCTOR, JEFFREY, 1634, W., 258.

R

RAWLING, GEORGE, 1627, W., 216.
RAWLINSON, MARGARET, 1633, W., 252.
RAYNE, RICHARD, 1624, W., 183.
REED, WILLIAM, SIR, 1604, W., 2.
REED, WILLIAM, SIR, 1615, W., 97.
REED, WILLIAM, 1637, W., 271.
RICHARDSON, JOHN, 1608, W., 37.
RICHARDSON, JOHN, 1616, W., 105.
RICHESON, ANTHONY, 1612, W., 71.
RIPPON, GEORGE, 1634, W., 258.
ROBINSON, ANTHONY, 1616, W., 106.
ROBINSON, AVERY, 1648, W., 317.
ROBSON, ISABELLA, 1607, W., 23.
ROBSON, WILLIAM, 1632, W., 241.
ROTCHESTER, BARTRAM, 1632, W., 240.
ROTCHESTER, JOHN, 1635, W., 265.

S

SADLER, WILLIAM, 1615, W., 94.
SAIRE, FRANCIS, 1605, W., 10.
SALVEN, THOMAS, 1609, W., 41.
SANDERSON, WILLIAM, 1609, W., 39.
SCURFIELD, WILLIAM, 1607, W., 24.
SCURFIELD, WILLIAM, 1626, W., 200.
SELBY, ALEXANDER, 1631, I., 235.
SELBY, ALICE, 1615, W., 95.
SHAFTO, JOHN, 1634, I., 259.
SHAFTO, ROBERT, 1623, W., 160.
SHAFTO. WILLIAM [1641], W., 285.

SHAWDFORTH, GEORGE, 1617, W., 117.
SHERATON, ALISON, 1605, W., 8.
SIMPSON, HENRY, 1647, W., 309.
SMITHSON, JOHN, 1626, W., 199.
SMYTH, ROBERT, 1612, W., 54.
SPENCE, GILBERT, 1607, W., 18.
STEVENSON, CONAND, 1615, W., 92.
STEVENSON, HENRY, 1613, W., 75.
STRINGER, WILLIAM, 1625, W., 192.
STROTHER, LANCELOT, 1611, W., 49.
SUTHACK, WILLIAM, 1606, W., 17
SWAYNSTON, JOHN, 1615, I., 94.

T

TAYLOR, JOHN, 1625, W., 188.
TAYLOR, JOHN, 1649, W., 318.
TEMPEST, ROBERT, 1616, W., 107.
TEMPLE, ISABEL, 1606, W., 14.
THOMPSON, RICHARD, 1616, W., 100.
TONSTALL, JOHN, 1617, W., 114.
TROLLOP, RALPH, 1609, W., 39.
TROLLOP, THOMAS, 1644, W., 304.
TROTTER, THOMAS, 1622, W.I., 157.
TROTTER, WILLIAM, 1622, W., 152.

W

WAILES, ROGER, 1609, W., 45.
WALLIS, JAMES, 1610, W., 48.
WARCOP, ROBERT, 1626, W., 197.
WARDE, STEPHEN, 1616, W., 108.
WATSON, RALPH, 1612, W., 63.
WATSON, WILLIAM, 1617, W., 118.
WAUGH, ROBERT, 1612, W., 56.
WAYLES, THOMAS, 1609, W., 43.
WHARTON, CHRISTOPHER, 1618, W., 128.
WHARTON, HUMPHREY, 1635, W., 264.
WIDDRINGTON, HENRY, SIR, 1623, W., 165.
WIDDRINGTON, HENRY, 1626, I., 196.
WIDDRINGTON, REBECCA, 1625, W., 189.
WIDDRINGTON, ROGER, 1633, W., 250.
WIDDRINGTON, ROGER, 1641, W., 287.
WIDDRINGTON, THOMAS, 1617, W., 112.
WILKINSON, ANTHONY, 1634, W.I., 260.
WILSON, ROBERT, 1623, W., 170.
WOULDHAVE, HENRY, 1624, W., 178.
WREN, CHARLES, 1620, W.I., 147.
WREN, ELIZABETH, 1613, W., 73.

Y

YOUNGE, WILLIAM, 1613, W., 80.

Index of Names.*

[An asterisk (*) signifies that the name occurs more than once on the page.]

A.

(Blank), Dorth., 77; Edw., 9, 64; Grace, 10; Kath., 106*; Mary, 317*, 318; Robt., 33; Sam, 60.

Abgin, Arnold, 307.

Adams, Mary, 282n; Mr., 289*; Robt., 282n.

Adamson, Margt., 61, 95.

Addison, 134*, 254; Anth., 183, 254*; Grace, 134; Isab., 253, 253n, 255*; Jane, 134*, 254*; Jn., 134*, 171, 253, 253n, 254, 255*; Thos., 133, 254; Sir Wm., 253n; Wm., 254*.

Adon, Gawen, 103*.

Ainsley (see Aynsley), And., 116, 139; Jn., 182, 239.

Airdale, Kath., 113.

Aireson, Alice, 65; Chris., 65.

Airey, Anth., 65*, 129.

Alder, Agn., 121n; Anne, 121n, 256; Chris., 256*; Edw., 93, 256; Francis, 93*, 121, 121n, 176, 272; Geo., 93*, 121, 121n, 272, 272n, 306; Hen., 307; Isab., 175; Jane, 93, 121n. Jn., 93*, 256, 306*; Luke, 93; Margt., 121n, 272n; Mary, 113; Rich., 93, 93n, 113; Robt., 93, 219, 236, 248*, 256; Thos., 93; Wm., 113, 175.

Allabaster, Thos, 119.

Allanson, Jas., 274; Robt., 123*, 149; Thos., 13.

Allen, Edw., 238*; Elean., 230n; Jane, 193; Mr., 169; Phineas, 193*, 230n, Robt., 152, 238*, 239*, Thos., 11.

Allison, Jn., 247.

Alvey, Yeldart, 279n.

Amcotts, Math., 128.

Anderson, Adam, 316; Adeline, 51n; Agnes, 90n*; Amb., 121*, 121n, 122; Ann, 90n, 91*, 168; Barbara, 79n, 120*, 120n, 121, 163; Bertram, 76, 79n, 90n, 146, 160n; Bessie, 168; Cuth., 168; Dor. 90n*, 91n*; Elean., 145n; Eliz., 88n, 120*, 120n, 121; Sir Francis, 91n, 233n; Francis, 8*, 79n*, 90n, 91n*, 92*, 145n; Sir Hen., 103; Hen., 7n, 90n*, 91n, 101n, 105, 145n, 146, 153n, 154, 238, 239; Isaac, 90, 91n; Isab., 101n, 120*, 120n; Jane, 91n, 102, 102n, 103*, 160n; Jennet, 121, 122*; Jn., 48; Laird, 197, Margt., 91n*, 246; Marion, 7n; Mary, 238; Robt., 77, 90*, 90n, 91, 91n*, 92, 102n, 124, 151*, 168, 186, 193; Roger, 51n, 91n; Simon, 90n, 91n*; Thos., 121*, 248, 256; Wm., 88n, 120, 121.

Anger, Ann, 164n, Ralph, 164n.

Anthony, Henry, 17, 35.

Appleby, Amb., 235; Anth. 143; Francis, 171, 248, Gregory, 198; Isab., 123; Jane, 65; Jn., 123*; Margery, 64; Mary, 164n, 189; Perc., 143; Robt., 13, 123; Thos., 64, 164n; Wm., 94, 189.

Archbald, Hen., 145; Robt., 16, 142.

Archbutt, Seth, 257.

Archer, Agnes, 275; Alice, 274n*; Ann, 240, 241, 274, 274n*; Doro., 240, 241, 274, 274n, 275; Eliz., 240, 275n; Hen., 200*, 274*, 274n, 275*; Jn., 240, 274*, 274n, 275*; Mary, 274n, 275*; Rowl., 240*, 241*, 274*, 274n*, 275*, 275n; Wm., 275n.

Arkle, Bernard, 64.

* For the purpose of this index the names have been largely modernized, and no distinction has been attempted between the male and female names of Francis and Frances.

Armery, Hen., 105; Robt., 100.
Armitage, Hen., 189.
Armorer, Clem., 218; Hen., 200;
    Mayt., 272; Mich., 143; Wm.,
    268.
Armstrong, Arch., 164; Barb.,
    179, Jn., 114; Robt., 74, 75, 264;
    Thos., 179*.
Arnold, Nich., 31.
Arrowsmith, Isab., 308; Thos., 56,
    116*, 126.
Arthington, Jane, 163n; Wm.,
    163n.
Arthur, Robt., 149.
Arundell, Anth., 148.
Askeham, Geo., 73.
Astill, Jn., 178.
Atchison, Jn., 272.
Athey, Chris., 125n; Margt., 125n.
Atkinson, Barb., 281n; Chas., 62;
    Eliz., 284; Francis, 13; Hen.,
    99*, 100*; Isab., 100; Jas., 64*;
    Jane, 194n; Jn., 76, 100* 189,
    284*, 307; Marg. 99*, 100*, 143;
    Mary, 100*; Mich., 142; Nich.,
    16*, 17; Phillis, 13; Ralph, 64;
    Robt., 64; Thos., 39, 112, 143,
    156, 281n, 282; Wm., 99*, 99n,
    100, 145, 284.
Avery, Mrs., 318.
Awbon, Chris., 95; Cuth., 95*.
Awbot, Randall, 95.
Awde (see Orde), Jane, 189.
Aynsley (see Ainsley), Jas., 70;
    Marion, 107n; Wm., 107n, 156;
Ayre, Jn., 75.
Ayrson, Chris., 70.
Ayton, Robt., 209.

B

Babington, Robt., 261n.
Backhouse, Wm., 231
Badminson, Chris., 50.
Bainbridge, Anne, 213*; Chas.,
    273*, 274; Chris., 36n, 171, 273*,
    274; Eliz., 171; Francis, 257;
    Gabriel, 273*; Guy, 144*, 159;
    Helen, 13; Hen., 171*, Jn., 273*,
    274*; Ralph, 170*, 171*; Roger,
    13*; Thos., 13, 36n, 273; Wm.,
    213.
Baker, Rich., 90.
Balmford, Jas., 132; Sam, 132.
Bambrey, Mungo, 236.
Bamburgh, Chas., 218, 219; Wm.,
    64.
Baning, Paul, 119.

Banks, Alice, 205*; Jn., 205*;
    Ralph, 169*; Thos., 205.
Banne, Margt., 95n.
Barber, Jn., 237.
Barde, Martin, 104.
Barkas, Ann, 317; Perc., 107*
    Thos., 317.
Barker, Abraham, 149, 150n*;
    Agnes, 150n; Elean., 149n*;
    Eliz., 150n, 257n; Geo., 150*,
    150n; Grace, 150n; Hen., 23*,
    150* 150n; Isaac, 150*, 150n*;
    Isab., 150n; Jane, 150*,
    150n*; Jn., 15, 149n, 150n;
    Marg., 150n; Mr., 10, 88; Robt.,
    149n, 150*, 150n*, 257n; Sarah,
    150n*; Susan, 150n*; Thos.,
    150n; Wm., 13, 150*, 150n.
Barnes, Agnes, 80n; Edw., 172n;
    Eliz., 172n; Isab., 13; Mich.,
    198; Rich., 257; Wm., 13.
Barrey, Robt., 149.
Barrowp, Lard of, 242.
Bartlett, Rich., 132, 177.
Barton, Eliz., 111n; Jn., 111n;
    Rich., 3; Roger, 81, 82.
Bartram, Jn., 247; Robt., 179.
Barwick, Eliz., 242; Wm., 241*,
    242*.
Basenfield, Thos., 136.
Bates, Cuth., 95; Elean., 231n;
    Jane, 95; Marg., 82n; Mich., 78;
    Ralph, 82n; Thos., 95*, 96;
    Wm., 231n.
Batey, Adam, 71; Thos., 266.
Baxter, Cath., 118n, 119*; Cuth.,
    118n; Marg., 118n, 119*; Wm.,
    118n, 119*.
Bayles, Hen., 37*, 38, 148; Marg.,
    26n*.
Baynes, Cuth., 212; Wm., 103.
Beadnell, Geo., 247*; Robt., 247;
    Wm., 14, 176.
Beane, Jn., 264n; Mary, 264n.
Bee, Anne, 193.
Bell, Adam, 167; And., 167;
    Charity, 2; Jn., 63*, 71, 218,
    243, 244; Mary, 117; Ralph,
    314, Rich., 228, 280; Robt., 60;
    Steven, 105; Thos., 39, 279.
Bellerby, Robt., 229; Wm., 80.
Bellasis, Bryan, 31; Chas., 31n;
    Doro., 158n; Eliz., 31n; Hen.,
    31n; Isab., 82n; Jas., 31n, 33,
    82n; Joan, 31n, 32; Kath.,
    31n; Lady, 312; Marg., 31n*,
    32, 33*, 125n; Mary, 31n, 32,
    309n; Sir Rich., 311*; Rich.,

31*n*, 32*, 33; Robt., 60; Sir
Thos., 33; Thos., 125*n*; Timothea, 31*n*; Timothy, 31*n*; Sir
Wm., 31*n**, 309*n*; Wm., 32*,
33, 159*n*.
Benson, Eliz., 174, 174*n*; Jn., 174*,
174*n*; Sam., 175, 176.
Best, Geo., 100; Margt., 100.
Bethel, Elean., 293, 293*n*.
Betham, Jane, 139, 139*n*; Jn., 139,
139*n*; Thos. 139, 139*n*; Wm.,
139*.
Bewick, Barb., 168, 177; Chris.,
113*; Cuth., 150*n*, 168*; Elean.,
168, Eliz., 14, 113; Isab., 113*;
Jane, 168*n*; Jn., 168; Robt.,
168, 168*n**, 169*; Sam; 177;
Sar., 168; Sus., 150*n*; Thos.,
168.
Biggins, Chris., 125*, 126*; Hen.,
126*; Jn., 126; Mary, 124*n*,
126; Thos., 124*n*.
Bigland, Edw., 119.
Billingham, Rich., 65; Thos., 65.
Bilton, Dor., 216.
Bindlosse, Sir Robt., 267*n*.
Birch, Dor., 5; Edw., 3*n*, 223*n*.
Bird, Jn., 57; Mary, 282*n*.
Birkbeck, Ann, 125*n*; Hen., 125*n*,
253*.
Birkley, Jas., 170.
Birtley, Dav., 121; Geo. 181.
Blackburn, Margt., 53.
Blackett, Agnes, 213*n*; Ann, 214*;
Christian, 302*n*; Edw., 213;
Elean., 213, 214; Geo., 214*;
Hen., 213*n**, 214*, 215; Jane,
213*n*; Jn., 213*n*, 214, 215;
Margt., 213*n*; Wm., 74, 75, 213,
213*n**, 214.
Blacklock, Thos., 123.
Blakiston, Anne, 206*n*, 246*n*; Barb.,
28, 307*, 308; Dor., 28, 65*n*,
291*n*, 292, 293; Edw., 72*;
Elean., 72*n**; Eliz., 117*n*, 291*n*;
Frances, 27*n*, 291*, 291*n*, 292*;
Geo., 27*n*; Hen., 28*, 235, 235*n*;
Jane, 28*; Joan, 27*n*; Jn., 28,
65*n*, 282, 291*n*, 292, 293*n*, 307,
308*; Lyonel, 28; Margt., 27*n*,
291*n*, 292, 307*, 308*; Marm., 15,
117*n*, 221*n*, 291*n**; Mary, 291*n**;
Nich., 28*; Sir Ralph, 27*n*, 148;
Ralph, 27*, 28*, 29*; Robt.,
221*n*, 291*, 291*n*, 292; Roger,
27*n*, 28; Susan, 282; Toby, 232,
291, 291*n*, 292*, 293; Thos., 66,
67*, 291*n*, 292*, 293; Sir Wm.,

27*n*, 206*n*, 246*n*, 307*n*; Col. Wm.,
309*n*; Wm., 27*, 27*n**, 28*, 29,
43, 307*, 307*n*, 308.
Blakey, Wm., 318*.
Bland, Arth., 98.
Blarton, Jn., 29.
Blenkinsop, Cecil, 234.
Blithe, And., 243.
Blythman (blank), 146; Barb., 282;
Edith, 146; Edw., 282*, 282*n*;
Eliz., 53*n*; Hen., 179; Wm., 53*n*,
179, 282.
Boa . . ., Chris., 23.
Bodeley, Ann, 135*n*; Thos., 135*n*.
Bolam, Mich., 259; Peter, 237.
Bolland, Jas., 226.
Bonner, Agnes, 7; Hen., 7; Mary,
7*, 7*n*, 8; Math., 7; Wm., 7*,
7*n*, 8.
Boone, Margt., 182; Wm., 182.
Booth, Abram., 161*n*; Eliz., 65;
Isab., 161*n*; Jn., 65.
Boothbye, Eliz., 18.
Bothwell, Francis, Earl of, 287*n*;
Nich., 252.
Bourne, Eliz., 250.
Bowden, Jane, 316.
Bowes, Anne, 168, 197*n*, 198,
286*n*; Elin., 169; Sir Geo.,
286*n*; Mrs., 5; Ralph, 69; Robt.,
69, 99*n*; Sir Talbot, 123, 234;
Talbot, 197*n*, 198*; Thos., 123,
197*n*, 198*, 213, 234; Wm., 210;
Bowman, Wm., 176.
Bowmer (*see* Bulmer).
Bowser, Math., 148.
Bowton, Peter, 43.
Brabant, Adaline, 51*n*, 58, 59, 60*;
Anne, 58*n*, 60; Chas., 58*n*, 59*,
60*; Geo., 51*n*, 58*, 58*n**, 59*,
60*, 120; Henry, 118*n*; Hercules,
6, 58, 58*n**; Jane, 58*n*; Jn., 58,
58*n*, 60*; Mary, 58*, 58*n*, 60, 61,
118*n*; Ralph, 58; Robt., 59.
Brackenbury, Anne, 125*n*; Fran.,
123; Hen., 125*n**.
Bradforth, Anne, 314; Bartram,
237*; Elin., 314*; Eliz., 314*n*;
Hugh, 237*, 275; Jane, 314;
Lionel, 266*n*, 314, 314*n*; Peter,
314*, 314*n*; Thos., 314.
Bradley, Roger, 37, 129.
Brameling, Eliz., 95.
Brand, Allison, 314.
Brandling, Anne, 160*n*; Chas.,
275*n*; Doro., 275*n*; Eliz., 164*n*;
Sir Francis, 164*n*, 169, 170, 264;
Francis, 264; Hen., 160*n*; Isab.,

195*, Dor., 194n; Elin., 194n*;
Eliz., 194, 194n*, 195*; Geo.,
194*, 194n, 195*; Jas., 194n,
195*; Jane, 194, 194n*, 195*;
Margery, 194n, 195; Nich., 96;
Ralph, 194n; Rich., 194, 194n,
195*; Steph., 194n; Thos., 194n;
Wm., 194*, 194n, 195*.
Harper, Cath., 152n; Jane, 152n,
157n; Thos., 152n, 157n.
Harrigate, Robt., 34.
Harrison, Ann, 211; Anth., 183,
235; Chris., 183*, 211*, 212;
Cuth., 55*; Edw., 55, 174; Ellen,
203; Geo., 55; Helen, 241; Isab.,
161, 163, 189; Jane, 173, 183*,
313; Jn., 186n, 203; Margt.,
75n, 143, 186n; Nich., 212; Rich.,
55; Robt., 6, 106; Rowl., 17;
Susan 281n; Thos., 286n; Wm.,
16.
Hart, Jn., 62.
Hartburn, Barbery, 151; Rich.,
151; Thos., 276.
Hartley, Cuth., 116; Jn., 198.
Harvey, Mr., 301.
Harwood, Jn., 220.
Haswell, Roger, 107.
Hatch, Margt., 169; Mr., 170.
Hawk, Mark, 107.
Hawksworth, Hen., 262.
Hayle, Wm., 193.
Hayword, Geo., 313.
Heath (blank), 110; Ann, 65n, 206n,
207*, 246, 246n*; Barb., 246n;
Dor., 65*, 65n*, 66, 279n; Eliz.,
65n, 209n, 246n; Isab., 131; Jane,
246n; Jn., 64, 65*, 65n*, 66*, 67,
68*, 69*, 70, 131*, 207, 208*,
246n*; Margt., 65n, 246n, 279n;
Nich., 65, 65n, 70, 206*, 206n*,
207*, 208*, 246*, 246n*, 247;
Thos., 65n, 66*, 67*, 68, 69*, 70,
207, 208, 209n, 279n*; Thomasine,
65n, 110; Topp., 206*, 207, 246n;
Wm., 206*, 207*, 246, 246n*.
Heatley, Rich., 123.
Hebburn (Hebron), Alice, 269n;
Anne, 269, 269n; Arth., 130,
130n, 170, 269*, 269n*; Cath.,
269n; Dor., 269, 269n; Edw., 269,
269n; Elean., 130n; Frances,
269, 269n; Jn., 269, 269n; Kath.,
270; Margt., 130*, 269, 269n,
307; Martha, 269n, 270; Mary,
269n*, 270*; Mich., 130n; Ralph,
269, 269n.
Hebson, Anth., 146.

Heckstetter, Dan., 79n; Jane, 79n.
Hedley, Humph., 288; Isab., 220;
Mr., 25; Rowl., 220.
Hedrington, Robt., 129.
Hedworth, Alice, 153; Ann, 36n*;
Anth., 153n; Chas., 31n, 33;
Chris., 28; Cecily, 153n; Isab.,
285n; Sir Jn., 153*; Jn., 36,
36n*, 153*; Margt., 51n; Rich.,
144, 285*.
Heeley Wm. 154.
Hegg, Steph., 70.
Heighington, Geo., 59, 60, 191, 192,
199n*; Jn., 60; Mary, 60; Rich.,
59, 60, 226; Wm., 186.
Heighley, Chris., 123.
Heiton (blank), 106.
Henderson, Dav., 197; Robt., 279n.
Henshaw, Mr., 132.
Heron, Adeline, 125n; Agnes, 235n;
Alex., 153n; Anne 127, 251;
Barb., 251; Cecily, 153n; Cuth.,
127*, 240*; Dor., 127*; Eliz.,
127*, 251; Geo., 127; Gerard,
235n; Gray, 127; Jn., 127*, 142,
240, 251*, 252*; Margt., 81;
Mary, 251, 252*; Nich., 125n;
Ralph, 127*; Rich., 73, 252;
Robt., 251*; Roger, 81; Thos.,
127, 251, 259.
Heslewood, Rich., 219.
Heslop, Jas., 242.
Hessell, Mary 36n; Sam., 36n.
Heworth, Jane, 145n; Mich., 147.
Hicks, Elean., 131, 282n; Eliz., 131,
302n; Rev. Jn., 131n; Jn., 131*,
282n, 302n; Rich., 286; Ursula,
131n. See Hix.
Hickson, Chris., 80; Robt., 149;
Wm., 167.
Hildyard, Ch., 281.
Hilton, Dav., 229; Eliz., 189;
Grace, 174, 174n; Hen., 52, Jas.,
174n, 318; Jn., 247, 264; Margt.,
286; Mrs., 52; Robt., 286; Thos.,
286n.
Hird, Marm., 56; Robt., 56, 57*.
Hix, Alice, 28. See Hicks.
Hodgson, Albert, 159n, Ann, 116;
Cath., 195n; Chris., 9, 9n, 60;
Edw., 181; Eliz., 159n; Jane,
191; Jn., 116, 117, 191*, 257,
283; Lance., 33; Mary, 33;
Nich., 60; Peter, 9; Phillis, 13;
Rich., 38, 38n, 90n; Robt., 195n,
215; Thos., 9*, 9n, 89; Wm., 9*,
223.
Hogg, Jas., 156.

J

Jackson, Anth., 315; Elean., 101n, Gab., 306; Geo., 204; Grace, 315; Hen., 218; Jas., 64, 65; Jane, 64; Jn., 65, 264, 315*, 315n; Mark, 315; Martin, 74; Mary, 315*; Rich., 23*; Robt., 64; Sar., 201n; Thos., 55, 64*, 65*, 315n; Wm., 179*, 182*.
James, Francis, 74, 230, 231; Margt., 291n; Tim., 74.
Jameson, Math., 156.
Jeffers, Mrs., 149.
Jefferson, Alice, 241; Nich., 241, 242*.
Jenison, Anne, 190; Eliz., 3, 4*, 5, 102n, 225*, 266n; Geo., 4; Jn., 4, 5*, 229; Margt., 4; Martha, 5; Mary, 5; Mich., 5*, 225*; Ralph, 225*, 228*, 229; Rich., 5; Robt., 4, 122, 169, 226; Thos., 3n, 4*, 5, 6*, 60, 61, 223n, 225*, 226, 227, 228*, 229*; Wm., 4*, 5*, 6*, 102n, 103, 155, 225*, 226, 227.
Jeromie, Mr., 124.
Jervice, Alice, 24n.
Jobson, Jn., 284.
Johnson (blank), 317; Abraham, 146*; Alice, 318; Chris., 123; Dav., 2; Edw., 6*, 146; Elsie, 123; Eliz., 145n, 146; Hen., 80, 137, 167; Jane, 58n, 132*; Jn., 29, 80, 240, 241*, 275; Kath., 201, 202, 203; Leo., 198; Margt., 132; Mary, 315n; Math., 132, 316; Ralph, 123*; Rich., 10, 138; Robt., 201, 201n, 202*, 203*, 204; Sam., 80; Thos., 315*; Wm., 138, 289, 290*.
Jones, Hen., 3, 97*.
Jopling (Joblin), Eliz., 186; Jn., 100; Lance., 144*; Robt., 144, 155, 280*; Thos., 144, 283.
Jordan, Margt., 236; Wm., 148.

K

Kellio, Chas., 87; Elean., 87.
Kemp, Ralph, 186.
Kendall, Alice, 276n; Anth., 276n.
Kent, Earl of, 308n.
Ker, Adam, 248.
Key, Cuth., 236.
Killegree, Hen., 132; Robt., 132.
Killinghall, Cath., 295n; Francis, 297; Geo., 295n; Hen., 295n*,

296*, 297; Jn., 295, 295n, 296*, 297*; Kath., 296, 297; Margt., 295n; Margery, 297; Robt., 295n, 296*, 297*; Susan, 295n*; Thos., 295n, 297*; Wm., 295, 295n, 297*.
King, Ann, 174n; Eliz., 174n, Grace, 174n; Isab., 174n; Jn., 65, 70, 117*, 174*; Merial, 174n.
Kinnord, Wm., 97.
Kipling, Edw., 123; Gab., 157, 158.
Kirbie, Kath., 50n.
Kirkbride, Cliburne, 233; Dor., 235.
Kirklawe, Thos., 116.
Kirkley, Eliz., 7*, 7n, 8; Geo., 186; Jane, 163; Jn., 85, 284; Mich., 7n, 8, 163.
Kirklin, Luke, 164, 219*.
Kirton, Hen., 104.
Kirkwall, Lance., 290.
Kitchin, Barb., 111n; Jane, 111*, 111n, 112*; Jn., 111*, 111n, 112.
Knight, Steph., 289.
Knighton, Margt., 19n.
Kuype, Jervaux, 94.

L

Lace, Ursula, 95n.
Lackenbie, Simon, 311*.
Ladley, Thos., 143.
Laing, Jn., 46, 313.
Lamb (blank), 90n; Jn., 83, 148, 153; Margery, 54; Robt., 1n, 248.
Lambert, Anne, 210; Barb., 184; Clem., 74; Elean., 282n; Eliz., 184*; Ralph, 282n; Susan, 183.
Lambton, Ann, 82n; Isab., 82n; Jane, 307n; Joan, 27n*; Jn., 50n, 87; Kath., 50n; Margt., 295n; Ralph, 309n; Robt., 27n*, 307n; Sir Wm., 160, 166; Wm., 82n, 295n.
Lancaster, Hen., 253.
Langstaff, Anth., 273, Jane, 19n.
Lascells, Anne, 278n, Chris., 74, 148; Francis, 278n.
Lawes, Osw., 141; Wm., 118.
Lawrence, Mary, 132n; Thos., 132n.
Lawson, Adeline, 51n; Ann, 253; Cuth., 253; Dor., 51*, 253; Edith, 51n; Eliz., 31n, 51, 51n; Geo., 51, 129*, 253; Hen., 47*, 142; Isab., 47; Jas., 190, 218, 219, 258; Jn., 138, 253; Margt., 246; Mary, 51; Maud, 149; Mich., 51*; Sir Ralph, 51, 102; Ralph,

51, 285*; Robt., 47*, 51*, 167*, 245, 246, 253*, 291n; Roger, 51*, 246*; Thos., 31n, 47*, 51*, 51n*, 149, 246; wid., 129; Wm., 47*, 51, 51n, 149, 167, 245, 275.
Lax, Anth., 10; Jn., 10.
Layburn, Anth., 31; Arth., 25; Grace, 17n; Hen., 31; Jane, 25*; Jn., 25; Margery, 25*; Nich., 17, 25; Peter, 25; Robt., 17n, 60; Wm., 25.
Layton, Anne, 295n; Cuth., 123; Robt., 291, 295n; Sir Thos., 296, 297.
Lazenby, Geo., 75; Jane, 277n; Roger, 74.
Ledgard, Eliz., 177n; Jane, 177; Margt., 177n; Mary, 161n, 177*, 178*; Robt., 161n, 177, 177n, 178; Thos., 177n, 178*.
Lee, Edw., 117n, 230*, 230n, 231, 257; Ellen, 230, 230n; Eliz., 230; Hen., 230n; Isab., 230n, 255*; Jane, 230, 230n; Jn., 72*; Margt., 31n; Mary, 117n, 230n*; Rebec., 230, 230n; Rich., 255; Robt., 230n; Sarah, 230, 230n; Thos., 230, 230n; Wm., 31n.
Leichman, Jn., 176.
Leighton, Elin., 284; Eliz., 198n; Francis, 18, 90, 101; Jn., 134.
Leslie, Jas., 229.
Le Strange, Cath., 215n; Roger, 215n.
Lever, Ann, 301n; Dor., 302n; Eliz., 66, 302n, 303; Heath, 66; Hen., 302*, 302n, 303*, 304*; Jn., 66, 301n; Margt., 301n, 302n*; Mary, 317; Ralph, 301n, 302n, 303*; Robt., 301, 302*, 302n*, 303, 304; Sam., 303*, 304*; Sampson, 301, 301n, 304; Thos., 9n, 65n, 66*, 301n*, 302*, 302n, 303; Thomasine, 65n, 66*, 67*.
Lewen, Hen., 6; Thos., 248.
Lexon, Ralph, 30.
Liddell, Agnes, 101n, 123n; Alice, 102n, 123n; Anne, 124, 313; Anth., 9, 10*; Barb., 2, 102n, 132n; Bartram, 123n, 124*, 231, 232; Chas., 9, 9n, 10*; Dor., 101n; Elean., 101n, 149n; Eliz., 9, 10*, 101n, 102n*; Eph., 123n; Francis, 1, 1n, 2, 9, 10*, 103* 123, 124; Geo., 2, 102n, 123n, 124, 149n; Grace, 102n; Hen., 101, 102, 102n, 103*, 127; Isab.,

57, 101n; Jane, 10, 91n, 102n*, 123n; Jn., 101n; Margt., 1, 101n, 123n; Rich., 9; Robt., 103; Roger, 102*, 102n, 103*; Sir Thos., 57; Thos., 1*, 1n*, 2, 46, 57*, 91n, 101*, 101n, 102, 102n* 103*, 124*, 132n; Wm. 10, 103, 123n, 124*.
Lightfoot, Alice, 72.
Lilburn, Geo., 214, 215, 282, 282n*; Jane, 282, Jn., 282n; Mary, 282; Rich., 214, 215*; Major Thos., 200n; Thos., 282.
Lindley, Sir Hen., 82.
Lisle, Anne, 207*, 246; Gifford, 246; Jas., 246, 246n; Jane, 121n, Mary, 246, 246*; Ralph, 246, 246n; Robt., 246, 246n; Talbot, 206n, 246*, 246n*; Sir Wm., 121n.
Littlefer, Geo., 152; Ralph, 151*.
Litster, Eliz., 72.
Locke, Geo., 213.
Lockson, Jn., 94; Ralph, 149, 152.
Lockwood (blank), 86.
Lodge, Jas., 52; Nich., 301.
Lonsdale, Rich., 167, 183.
Lorrain, Edw., 231, 231n, 232; Robt., 286.
Lowrance, Amb., 104.
Lowry, Cuth., 240.
Lowreyson, Jn., 71.
Lowson, Ralph, 285.
Lowther (Lowder), Cath., 277n, Edw., 276n, 277n; Eliz., 277n, 278*; Francis, 277, 277n; Hen., 277*, 277n, 278*; Jane, 277n, 278*; Jn., 237, 277, 277n; Lucy, 266; Robt., 62; Susan, 277n*; Thomasine, 277, 277n; Wm., 222, 266, 272.
Lucock, Thos., 192.
Lumbsdon, Margt., 236.
Lumedon, Robt., 167.
Lumley, Jn., 235*; Roger, 235n; Thos., 192*.
Lyeley, Wm., 108.
Lynn, Jn., 80, 228; Margt., 100.
Lyons, Jn., 87*.
Lyttle, Jn., 75.

M

Maddison, Anne, 205; Eliz., 46*, 150n*, 168n*, 257n; Hen., 59, 61*, 150*, 150n, 168n, 257, 279n; Isab., 46, 181, 205; Jane, 205, 257n; Jn., 15*; Leo., 205;

Lionel, 168n, 257n; Margt., 46;
Peter, 213n, 214*; Ralph, 59,
168n; Rich., 46*; Thos., 163,
204, 205; Wm., 15*, 46, 204,
204n, 205.
Maire, Chris., 184n; Edw., 267;
Jane, 184n; Jn., 315*; Rich.,
222n.
Makenling, Thos., 242.
Maland, Margt., 201; Robt., 107,
201.
Mallabar, Anne, 115; Edw., 260;
Jn., 77, 178.
Mallaburn, Jn., 169.
Mallet, Dor., 164n; Sir Thos.,
164n.
Maltby, Cuth., 85.
Mann, Alice, 270n; Dav., 95*; Geo.,
42*; Jas., 95; Jn., 95*; Thos.,
42, 43, 236; Wm., 270n.
Manners, Fortune, 266n; Rich., 149;
Thos., 266n.
Mantle, Wm., 296.
Manwell, Jane, 145.
March, Wm., 144.
Mark, Wm., 115.
Markland, Thos., 25.
Marley, Ann, 285n; Anth., 143,
144*; Cuth., 318; Elean., 318n;
Eliz., 285n; Geo., 318, Isab.,
143n, 285, 285n*; Jane, 150n,
285n*; Jn., 150; Kath., 285,
285n; Margt., 143; Peter, 147;
Ralph, 143, 144, 285, 285n;
Robt., 46*, 143n, 144*, 285,
285n*; Thos., 54*, 155, 156,
285*, 285n*; Wm., 31, 150n,
257, 318.
Marshall, Barb., 275; Eliz., 212;
Gawin, 167; Gilb., 294, 295;
Jane, 98; Jn., 115*, 240; Walter,
211.
Martin, Elean., 274*; Geo., 66, 87,
131, 203, 204, 208, 283, 303*;
Jane, 273; Thomasine, 66*.
Martindale, Chas., 74; Chris., 37,
38; Jn., 74, 148*; Perc., 148;
Robt., 171, 198.
Mascall, Thos., 229.
Mason, Anne, 236; Barth., 37, 38;
Humph., 191; Hugh, 100*.
Masterman, Jn., 257.
Matfen, Geo., 179; Jn., 179.
Mathew, Mrs., 2, 5; Thos., 107*;
Wm., 121*.
Maugham, Hen., 248n, 250;
Margery, 248n.
Mawe, Jane, 193.

Maxton, Anth., 171, 271*.
Meaburne, Anth., 29.
Medhope, Hen., 116.
Meggison, Jn., 240.
Merriman, Arth., 155*; Isab., 24n;
Jas., 155*; Jane, 155; Margery,
155; Wm., 155*.
Merrington, Elean., 253*.
Metcalf (blank), 167; Anne, 163,
190; Anth., 90, 161n, 163; Eden,
161n, 162*, 163*, 164n; Hannah,
274n; Jane, 163; Mich., 164n,
165; Ralph, 212; Thos., 164,
274*.
Metham, Sir Thos., 31, 32, 33*, 34.
Middleton, Alice, 128n, 186n, 209n,
295; Barb., 65; Chas., 267n,
268; Dor., 267, 267n; Elean.,
130n; Eliz., 128*, 128n*, 129,
209, 211, 233n; Francis, 128,
128n, 209, 209n*, 210*, 211*;
Geo., 66, 128n*, 186n, 209, 209n*,
211*, 232, 232n, 233n, 234;
Hellen, 130*; Jane, 164n, 233n,
234; Joan, 128n; Jn., 108*,
232n; Margt., 128, 211*; Rich.,
72; Robt., 267n, 268; Thos.,
164n, 267n, 268*; Thomason,
130; Winifred, 232.
Milbanks, Grace, 17n; Jn., 79;
Wm., 17n.
Milburn, Jane, 96*, 154n; Jn., 46,
96, 156; Osw., 156, 253; Pet.,
96; Ralph, 142, 167; Randall,
93.
Miller, Edw., 53*, 54*.
Millikin, Janet, 218; Jennett, 219.
Milliner, Thos. the, 77.
Millott, Agnes, 158n; Dor., 158n*,
159n, 160; Elen., 27n; Eliz.,
159n, 160; Jane, 160; Joan,
159n; Margt., 159n, 160; Mary,
159n, 160; Mr., 13; Ralph,
158n*, 160; Robt., 158, 159n,
160*; Wm., 159n; Winifred,
159n, 160.
Mills, Eliz., 38n; Mary, 90.
Milner, Mr., 232.
Mitcheson, Sislye, 191; Wm., 264.
Mitford, Agnes, 150n; Anderson,
177; Anne, 243n; Anth., 274n;
Bart., 79*, 79n, 154* 168*;
Chas., 150*; Chris., 79, 79n*,
150, 153n, 177n, 178*; Cuth.,
128. 128n*, 209n; Elean., 34n,
79n*; Grace, 286; Hen., 102n,
150n, 177; Isab., 79, 168n;
Jane, 79n*, 102n, 153n, 168n,

337

177, 177n, 286*; Jn., 79n*, 155,
168, 268; Lance., 286; Luke, 166;
Magd., 79n; Mary, 128n; Philadelphia, 264n; Ralph, 274n;
Robt., 34n, 91n, 128*, 128n, 168*,
168n*, 169, 176, 177n, 210*, 264n;
Roger, 79n; Tim., 79n; Thos.,
176; Wm., 168.
Moberlaye, Sam., 60.
Mompeson, Hen., 221.
Moore, Francis, 222; Jane, 15; Jn.,
295n; Mary, 47n; Rich., 73;
Robt., 266n; Susan, 295n; Wm.,
184.
Moorecroft, Ferd., 75, 212*, 229,
271; Mr., 75.
Morland, Dame, 67, 69; Jn., 312,
313; Thos., 53.
Morley, Thos., 285n.
Morpeth, Anth., 120, 121*; Chris.,
203; Eliz., 200n.
Morrell, Johan, 28.
Morrison, Jn., 307; Wm., 115, 218.
Morton, Wm., 142.
Motion, Isab., 15.
Mould, Ann, 44; Jn., 44.
Mowbray, Isab., 129*, 129n; Jn.,
129*; Peter, 129.
Moysere, Alice, 95n.
Moyses, Chris., 95n.
Muddie, Jas., 218.
Munt, Mrs., 262.
Murray, Hen., 217; Wm., 70.
Muschamp, Eliz., 237n; Sir Geo.,
237n; Geo., 35*, 140*, 237n;
Gilb., 237n; Margt., 237n; Mary,
237n*; Rach., 141; Ralph, 138,
140, 237n; Robt., 141; Thos.,
177; Sir Wm., 141, 237; Wm.,
237n.
Musgrave, Thos., 287n.
Mutis, Jane, 258.
Myers, Thos., 78.

N

Nattress, Jn., 171.
Neil, Robt., 113; Thos., 113.
Neles, Margt., 153.
Nelson, Susan, 297; Wm., 295n.
Nevile, Francis, 289; Mr., 273.
Newby, Ann, 6; Eliz., 6; Francis,
6*; Geo., 6; Jn., 6*; Ralph, 60,
226.
Newton, Agnes, 63; Arth., 62, 62n,
63*; Francis, 182; Geo., 100*;
Gilb., 100; Jane, 63*; Margt.,
193; Math., 63; Thos., 62.
Nicholas, Anth., 262.

Nicholson, Agnes, 219*; Chris.,
169; Cuth., 316; Edwin, 53, 53n,
54, 115; Elin., 79n; Eliz., 180,
180n, 182; Geo., 179, 180*, 180n*;
Hen., 219; Isab., 210; Jas.,
180n; Margt., 180, 180n*, 182*;
Martin, 276; Mary, 53n; Ralph,
82; Rich., 180, 180n, 181*, 241;
Robt., 180*, 180n, 181, 182*;
Roger, 79n*; Thos., 180, 180n,
181*; Wm., 180, 180n, 181, 182*,
309n.
Nixon, Edw., 64; Rich., 267.
Noble, Elean., 111n; Eliz., 111n,
112*; Hen., 111*, 111n, 112*;
Isab., 111, 112*; Jas., 111, 111n*;
Jane, 111n; Kath., 186; Margt.,
111, 111n*; Margt., 112*; Math.,
111*.
Norman, Anth., 114, 193, 262.
Norton, Jn., 228.
Northumberland, Earl of, 251, 270,
290.

O

Ogle, Dor., 154; Edw., 218; Gawin,
167*; Gerrard, 179; Hen., 270;
Jn., 167; Lance., 179*; Mark,
72; Phillis, 286n; Thos., 47, 179.
Oldfield, Mary, 288.
Oliver, Adam, 307; Geo., 256; Jn.,
256*, 267, 284; Robt., 248;
Thos., 256.
Ollenex, Thos., 73.
Orde (see Awde), Chris., 134, 135*;
Elean., 137, 137n*, 139; Geo.,
134n*, 135, 138, 243*, 270; Hen.,
137*, 137n*, 138, 179, 222*, 270*;
Isab., 135n, 137, 137n, 138*; Jn.,
134n, 138*, 270, 316*; Kath.,
242; Luke, 135*, 135n, 137n, 270;
Mabel, 135n; Margt., 137n*, 193,
270; Margery, 137n, 138*, 139,
270*; Mark, 155; Mary, 49n,
164n, 316n; Nath., 138*; Ralph,
270; Rich., 138, 270*; Robt.,
135*, 137n, 138, 229, 270*;
Roger, 137*, 137n, 138; Thos.,
49n, 134, 135, 135n, 137*, 137n,
138*, 196; Ursula, 135, 135n;
Wm., 287n.
Orton, Kath., 190.
Osmotherley, Rich., 142.
Oswald, Eliz., 218, 219.
Otway, Jane, 38*, 39; Kath., 38,
38n*; Robt., 38*; Thos., 38*,
38n*, 39.
Ovington, Alice, 122; Anne, 122;
Chris., 122*, 123*; Elin., 189;

22

Eliz., 122, 230*n*; Geo., 122, 123;
Isab., 122; Jn., 122*, 123*, 189;
Rich., 122*; Robt., 122*; Sythe,
122; Thos., 122.
Owen, Capt. Rich., 284.
Oxley, Amor., 164, 169; Chas., 164,
170.

P

Page, And., 45, 179; Eliz., 179;
Wm., 292.
Paine, Amb., 136.
Pallyman, Wm., 242.
Palmer, Dor., 164*n*; Kath., 169*;
Peregrine, 169*, 170; Sir Thos.,
164*n*, 169.
Pannell, Nich., 152.
Park, Geo., 133, 208.
Parker, Eliz., 65*n*; Jn., 65*n*, 262.
Parkin, Geo., 6, 60, '146*; Isab.,
273; Nich., 146; Ralph, 3;
Robt., 274; Wm., 273, 274.
Parkinson, Anne, 125*n*, 229*;
Averin, 190; Francis, 34*n*, 125*n*;
Rich., 258.
Parnaby, Geo., 226.
Parsons, Robt., 221.
Passmore, Anth., 107.
Patterson, Alex., 256; Cuth., 139;
Geo., 139; Hen., 240; Jacob,
241; Jn., 80, 260*n*, 261; Ralph,
90.
Patrickson, Martha, 163.
Paul, Thos., 230*n*.
Payne, Amb., 226; Chris., 226.
Peacock, Ann., 261*n*; Elin., 212,
212*n*, 213; Eliz., 212*; Jane, 212*,
213; Janet, 213*; Jn., 140;
Margt., 213*, 262; Simon, 212*n*,
213*; Thos., 212; Wm., 123.
Pearcehay, Chris., 291.
Peareth, Roger, 262.
Pearson, Chris., 48; Dor., 269*n*;
Eliz., 217; Hen., 217, 269*n*, 306;
Isab., 94; Jane, 169; Jn., 38;
Kath., 305*n*; Nich., 305*n*; Robt.,
39; Roger, 269*n*; Thos., 64, 78,
308; Wm., 18, 217.
Peat, Cuth., 123.
Pemberton, Anne, 298, 298*n*, 299,
300; Florence, 299; Hen., 298*,
298*n*, 299*; Jane, 298, 298*n*, 299,
300; Jn., 119, 189, 298*, 298*n*,
299*; Jn., Junr., 301; Margt.,
119, 298*n*; Mary, 189, 298*n*;
Mich., 74, 119, 298*n**, 300*;
Nich., 211; Robt., 50, 74, 308.
Penn, Robt., 304.
Pension, Rich., 8.

Pentlum, Wm., 167.
Pepper, Cuth., 296, 297; Margt.,
295*n*, 297.
Perkin, Agnes, 13; Jn., 13*.
Perrye, Alice, 190.
Pescod, Barth., 286.
Petifer, Ann, 229; Nich., 6, 60,
226, 229.
Peverell, Ralph, 10; Wm., 60.
Philipps, Chris., 265.
Philipson, W., 187.
Pickering, Rich., 108; Wm., 92.
Pilkington, Ann, 152, 152*n*; Dor.,
92*n*; Eliz., 152, 222*n*; Geo., 93,
111; Helen, 92*, 93; Isaac, 131*n*;
Jn., 78, 111, 131*n*; Jos., 131,
152*n*; Leo., 152; Margt., 131*;
Meriel, 131*n*; Noah, 131, 131*n*;
Thos., 131, 152; Ursula, 131,
131*n*.
Place, Alice, 298*n*; Chris., 298*n*.
Pleasance, Mr., 301.
Porter, Chas., 144, 159; Edw., 129;
Wm., 29.
Potter, Steph., 108; Thos., 108;
Wm., 116*.
Potts, Agnes, 113*; Anth., 95;
Dor., 236*; Eliz., 253; Geo.,
167, 197, 236, 287, 288, 290;
Isab., 267*n*; Jane, 81, 82, 236;
Jenkin, 43; Mark, 113*; Mich.,
196; Perc., 196*, 318; Ralph, 82;
Robt., 39, 196; Roger, 82; Stev.,
275; Thos., 129, 142, 317, 318;
Ursula, 236*n*; Wm., 196.
Powell, Elen., 90.
Powre, Wm., 96.
Prat, Jn., 255.
Preacher, Mr., 169.
Prescodd (Prescott), Margery, 239*;
Marys, 239; Morrice, 230.
Preston, Alice, 220; Gawin, 73;
Gilyan, 73*; Jn., 73*, 275*;
Ralph, 73; Rich., 268; Wm., 73.
Priestly, Francis, 109*n*; Hen.,
109*n*; Jane, 109*n*; Jos., 110*;
Mary, 110.
Proctor, Anth., 262; Eph., 258, 306;
Jane, 258*n*, 306*n*; Jeffrey, 219*,
258*; Mr., 219; Sar., 258*n*;
Thos., 258*n*, 306*n*.
Pryorman, Awdeley, 65; Thos., 65.
Punder, Nich., 103.
Punshon, Edw., 46*, 46*n*; Elspeth,
46; Margt., 46*, 46*n*.
Pursell, Margt., 266.
Pursley, Wm., 146.
Pye, Mally, 72; Robt., 284; Thos.,
218.

Index of Places.

Stanhope, 45*, 129*, 211*, 212, 270, 271, 301n.
Stanley Law, 144.
Stannington, 167, 241, 284.
Stanton, 167.
Stanwick, 164n.
Startforth, 10, 12*, 234, 235; Dobbye Close, 12*; Gillbeck Close, 12.
Stella, 27, 29, 84, 274.
Stillington, 203.
Stobeley, 198.
Stocksfield Hall, 63.
Stockton, 125, 200n, 201, 282n.
Stottgate, 130.
Stranton, 123.
Streatlam, 197.
Studeley, Co. York., 109.
Studon Burn, 156
Sunderland, 73*, 124, 125, 126, 163, 230*, 230n.
Swaffham, Norfolk, 27n.
Swalwell, 259*.
Swinburn, 166; Great 165n, 287n.
Swinton, East Quarter, 138.

T

Tanfield, 27*; Leigh, 157n; Co. York., 197n.
Tempest Leazes, 76.
Thirlwall, 167.
Thirston, Belland, 182; Bells, 182; East, 251; West, 182.
Thornley, 107n, 116.
Thornton, 41*, 64, 82, 151n, 173, 236n, 247*.
Thorpthewles, 63, 276n.
Throckley, 45.
Throple, 287n.
Thropton Spittle, 196.
Tilmouth, 138, 200, 163.
Tittlington, 218, 269n.
Totnes, Devon, 200n.
Towland, 166.
Trewhitt, 197*, 236, 236n; Nether, 196; Upper, 242, 243.
Tribley, 309n.
Trimdon, 105, 106.
Tudhoe, 298n, 300, 305.
Tuggill, 137.
Tunstall, 117*, 230.
Turner Mares, 57*.
Tursdale, 268n.
Twisell, 237n.
Tynemouth, 19*, 19n, 38*, 39, 230n; Back Row, 38; Castle, 49, 317; Preston, 38*; Whitley, 38.
Tyne, River, 307.

U

Ulchester, 269, 284*.
Ulgham, 129*, 142, 164, 176*.
Ulleskelf, Co. York., 172n.
Unthank, 109n, 198.
Uswayforth, 196.
Usworth, 18*, 31n.

W

Walk Mill, 136.
Wallington, 27n.
Wallis Porch, 48.
Walworth, 3, 3n, 4*, 5*, 124*, 223, 229, 266n.
Wansford Bridge, 186.
Wardelawe, 127*, 156.
Warden, 117*, 259.
Wark, 156*, 163n, 247, 258, 266, 266n.
Warksfieldhead, 156.
Warkworth, 62*, 248.
Warneford, 137.
Washington, 65, 246*.
Weaydon, 256.
Weetwood, 215, 218.
Westhall, Co. Lancs., 167.
West Herrington, 64, 106, 107*.
Westholm, 175, 252.
West Merrington, 9*.
Westminster, 97, 249, 289*; King Street, 289.
West Newton, 49.
Westoe, 282n.
Weston, 64; Co. York., 51n.
Whalton, 81, 82, 240*, 265*, 266.
Wharnley, 259.
Wheatley Hill, 202.
Whickham, 27, 29*, 30, 53n, 55, 91*, 162, 189n, 259, 285; Gibside, 27, 27n, 28, 29, 307, 308.
Whitburn, 131*, 131n, 168, 207, 208, 282, 282n, 302n*.
Whitley Mon., 79.
Whitehouse, 31n.
Whitfield, 58n.
Whithill, 158n, 159*, 160*.
Whittingham, 218* 242, 247, 258.
Whitwell, 301n.
Whitworth, 118*, 119*, 152n, 161n, 228.
Whorlton, 122*, 123*, 188*, 188n, 189.
Wicliffe, 42.
Widdrington, 103, 165, 167*, 189n; Park, 104.
Wilimondswicke, 270.
Willington, 276.

354

Wingate, 91*, 91*n*; Grange, 302*n*.
Winlaton, 90*n*, 91*, 290.
Winston, 110, 123*, 175*, 252.
Witton Castle, 311; le Wear, 258*.
Wolsingham, 75, 102, 116*, 157, 158, 271.
Woodespinles, 70.
Woodham, 126.
Woodhorn, 104, 240, 274*, 275.
Woodhouses, 249*.
Woodside, 284.
Wooler, 141.
Wooley, 276*n*; Co. York., 287, 287*n*, 288*.

Woolsington, 274*n*.
Workington Hall, Cumbs., 165*n*.
Worsall, 72.
Wortley, Co. York., 263*n*.
Wowgrave, 201.

Y

Yearle, 137*.
Yetlington, 248.
Yoackhaugh, 167.
York, 36*n*, 175*n*, 257*n*, 264*n*, 295*n*, 302*n*.
Yorkshire, 130*, 290.